Fundamentals of OB: A Core Text for Level 4 Business Studies Students

Fundamentals of OB: A Core Text for Level 4 Business Studies Students

Compiled from:

Management & Organisational Behaviour
Eleventh Edition
Laurie J. Mullins with Gill Christy

Organizational Behavior
seventeenth Global Edition
Stephen P. Robbins and Timothy A. Judge

PEARSON

Harlow, England • London • New York • Boston • San Francisco • Toronto • Sydney • Auckland • Singapore • Hong Kong
Tokyo • Seoul • Taipei • New Delhi • Cape Town • Sao Paulo • Mexico City • Madrid • Amsterdam • Munich • Paris • Milan

Pearson Education Limited
Edinburgh Gate
Harlow
Essex CM20 2JE

And associated companies throughout the world

Visit us on the World Wide Web at:
www.pearson.com/uk

Compiled from:

Management & Organisational Behaviour
Eleventh Edition
Laurie J. Mullins with Gill Christy
ISBN 978-1-292-08848-8
© Pearson Education Limited 2017

Organizational Behavior
seventeenth Global Edition
Stephen P. Robbins and Timothy A. Judge
ISBN 978-1-292-14630-0
© Pearson Education Limited 2017

ISBN 978-1-784-49337-0

Printed and bound in Great Britain by CPI Group.

Contents

CHAPTER 1
Understanding organisational behaviour

In an increasingly global and competitive business environment, particular attention must be given to organisational effectiveness. It is people who are the organisation. It is important to recognise the main influences on behaviour in work organisations, the effective management of the human resource and the nature of the people–organisation relationship.

Learning outcomes

After completing this chapter you should have enhanced your ability to:

- explain the nature and main features of organisational behaviour;
- detail contrasting perspectives on orientations to work and the work ethic;
- evaluate the nature and importance of the psychological contract;
- explain the relevance of the Peter Principle and Parkinson's Law;
- outline the importance of management as an integrating activity;
- assess the impact of globalisation and the international context;
- debate the significance of culture for organisational behaviour.

Critical review and reflection

Although a commonly used term, organisational behaviour is a misnomer. Rarely do all members act collectively in such a way as to represent the behaviour of the organisation as a whole. In practice, we are talking about the attitudes and actions of individuals or small groups within the organisation.

What do YOU see as the significance of this comment? What term would YOU suggest best explains the subject area of organisational behaviour?

The significance of organisational behaviour

A major report from the Chartered Management Institute (CMI) on the state of UK management and leadership points out that the UK lags behind its competitors in terms of productivity and management practice and reminds us that: 'At its heart, the art of management is the art of managing people.'

> *But, worryingly, this is where British managers fall down most. We need a change in attitude in the UK, whereby management is seen as a highly professional role where integrity is seen as a virtue, and where ethics are valued as highly as profitability.*[1]

Increasing recognition is given to the demand not only for technical skills alone, but also for good people skills as a basis of organisational effectiveness. The importance of skills including understanding human behaviour and interpersonal skills is a wide and frequent source of attention, including government agencies such as The UK Commission for Employment and Skills (UKCES), The Department of Business Innovation & Skills, and other bodies such as the Prince's Trust, the Advisory, Conciliation and Arbitration Service (ACAS) and professional institutes. Against this backdrop the study of organisational behaviour can be seen of even greater significance.

> *Organisational Behaviour is one of the most complex and perhaps least understood academic elements of modern general management, but since it concerns the behaviour of people within organisations it is also one of the most central . . . its concern with individual and group patterns of behaviour makes it an essential element in dealing with the complex behavioural issues thrown up in the modern business world.*[2]

Vecchio suggests three reasons for studying organisational behaviour:

- **Important practical applications** that follow from an understanding and knowledge of organisational behaviour and the ability to deal effectively with others in an organisational setting.
- **Personal growth** and the fulfilment gained from understanding our fellow humans. Understanding others may also lead to greater self-knowledge and self-insight.
- **Increased knowledge** about people in work settings, for example the identification of major dimensions of leadership leading to the design leadership training programmes in organisations.[3]

At its most basic level, **organisational behaviour** (OB) is concerned with the study of the behaviour of people within an organisational setting. It involves the understanding, prediction and control of human behaviour. Common definitions of organisational behaviour are generally along the lines of: **the study and understanding of individual and group behaviour and patterns of structure in order to help improve organisational performance and effectiveness.**

However much of a cliché, the inescapable fact is that people are the main resource of any organisation. Without its members, an organisation is nothing; an organisation is only as good as the people who work within it. In today's increasingly dynamic, global and competitive environment, understanding human behaviour at work and effective management of the people resource are even more important for organisational survival and success.

A managerial approach

There is a multiplicity of interrelated factors that influence the decisions and actions of people as members of a work organisation. The scope for the examination of organisational behaviour is therefore very wide. It has always been a feature of this book to acknowledge that while the role, responsibilities and actions of management are, of course, subject to debate, what cannot be denied is the growing importance of effective management, however it is perceived, to the successful performance of work organisations. Clearly, organisational behaviour does not encompass the whole of management. Equally clearly, however, there is a close relationship between organisational behaviour and management theory and practice. Some writers still appear critical of a managerial approach to organisational behaviour. What is also apparent, however, is that in recent years a number of books on organisational behaviour have paid increasing attention to aspects of management and managerial behaviour.

Critical review and reflection

The best way to appreciate the nature and applied skills of organisational behaviour is when study of the subject area is related to an understanding of the importance of management to effective work organisations.

To what extent do YOU support this contention? Do YOU believe a managerial approach is an aid to YOUR future career ambitions?

A multidisciplinary perspective

The bottom line is that sooner or later every organisation has to perform successfully if it is to survive. In order to study the behaviour of people at work it is necessary to understand interrelationships with other variables that together comprise the total organisation. Whatever the approach, the study of organisational behaviour cannot be undertaken entirely in terms of a single discipline. It is necessary to recognise the influences of a multidisciplinary, behavioural science perspective.

Although there are areas of overlap among the various social sciences and related disciplines such as economics and political science, the study of human behaviour can be viewed in terms of three main disciplines – **psychology**, **sociology** and **anthropology**. All three disciplines have made an important contribution to the field of organisational behaviour (*see* Figure 1.1).

A **psychological** approach has its main emphasis on the individuals of which the organisation is comprised. The main focus of attention is on the individual as a whole person, or what can be termed the 'personality system', including, for example, perception, attitudes and motives. Psychological aspects are important but by themselves provide too narrow an approach for the understanding of management and organisational behaviour. Our main concern is not with the complex detail of individual differences and attributes per se, but with the behaviour and management of people within an organisational setting.

A **sociological** approach has a broader emphasis on human behaviour in society. Sociological aspects can be important. The main focus of attention is on the analysis of social structures and positions in those structures – for example, the relationship between the behaviour of leaders and followers. A number of sociology writers seem set on the purpose of criticising traditional views of organisation and management. Many of the criticisms and limitations to which such writers refer are justified and help promote healthy academic debate. However, much of the argument tends to be presented in the abstract and is lacking in constructive ideas on how, in practical terms, action can be taken to improve organisational performance.

Anthropologists are more concerned with the science of humankind and the study of human behaviour as a whole. As far as organisational behaviour is concerned, the main focus of attention is on the cultural system, the beliefs, customs, ideas and values within a group or society, and the comparison of behaviour among different cultures – for example, the importance to Muslim women of wearing trousers to work. People learn to depend on their culture to give them security and stability and they can suffer adverse reactions to unfamiliar environments.

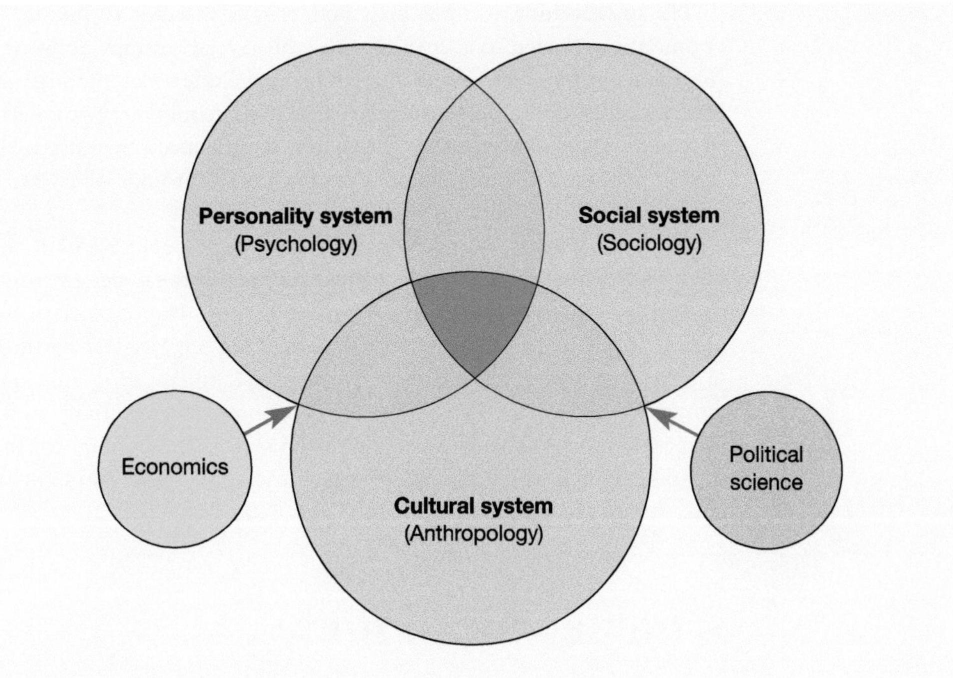

Figure 1.1 Organisational behaviour: a multidisciplinary approach

The contribution of relevant aspects of psychology, sociology and anthropology underpins the field of organisational behaviour. In terms of the applications of behavioural science to the management of people, we need also to consider the relevance and applications of philosophy, ethics and the law.

Interrelated influences on behaviour

This multidisciplinary perspective provides contrasting but related approaches to the understanding of human behaviour in organisations and presents a number of alternative pathways and levels of analysis. For our purposes, the study of organisational behaviour embraces broad parameters within which a number of interrelated dimensions can be identified – the individual, the group, the organisation and the environment – which collectively influence behaviour in work organisations.

The individual – organisations are made up of their individual members. The individual is a central feature of organisational behaviour, whether acting in isolation or as part of a group, in response to expectations of the organisation, or as a result of the influences of the external environment. Where the needs of the individual and the demands of the organisation are incompatible, this can result in frustration and conflict. It is the role of management to integrate the individual and the organisation and to provide a working environment that permits the satisfaction of individual needs as well as the attainment of organisational goals.

The group – groups exist in all organisations and are essential to their working and performance. The organisation comprises groups of people, and almost everyone in an organisation will be a member of one or more groups. Informal groups arise from the social needs of people within the organisation. People in groups influence each other in many ways and groups may develop their own hierarchies and leaders. Group pressures can have a major influence over the behaviour and performance of individual members. An understanding of group structure and behaviour complements knowledge of individual behaviour and adds a further dimension to the study of organisational behaviour.

The organisation – individuals and groups interact within the structure of the formal organisation. Structure is created to establish relationships between individuals and groups, to provide order and systems and to direct the efforts of the organisation into goal-seeking activities. It is through the formal structure that people carry out their organisational activities to achieve aims and objectives. Behaviour is influenced by patterns of structure, technology, styles of leadership and systems of management through which organisational processes are planned, directed and monitored.

The environment – applications of organisational behaviour and the effective management of people at work take place in the context of the wider environmental setting, including the changing patterns of organisations and work. The organisation functions as part of the broader external environment, which affects the organisation through, for example, internationalisation, technological and scientific development, economic activity, social and cultural influences, governmental actions, and corporate responsibility and ethical behaviour. The increasing rate of change in environmental factors has highlighted the need to study the total organisation and the processes by which the organisation attempts to adapt to the external demands placed upon it.

A framework of study

The use of separate topic areas is a recognised academic means of aiding study and explanation of the subject. In practice, however, the activities of an organisation and the role of management cannot be isolated neatly into discrete categories. The majority of actions are likely to involve a number of simultaneous functions that relate to the total processes within an organisation. Consider, for example, a manager briefing departmental staff on a major unexpected, important and urgent task. Such a briefing is likely to include consideration of goals and objectives, organisation and role structures, management systems, known problem areas, forms of communications, delegation and empowerment, teamwork, leadership style, motivation and control systems. The behaviour of the staff will be influenced by a combination of individual, group, organisational and environmental factors.

Topics studied in organisational behaviour should not be regarded, therefore, as entirely free-standing. Any study inevitably covers several aspects and is used to a greater or lesser extent to confirm generalisations made about particular topic areas. Reference to the same studies to illustrate different aspects of management and organisational behaviour serves as useful revision and reinforcement and provides a more integrated approach to your study.

In order to study the behaviour of people at work it is necessary to understand interrelationships with other variables that together comprise the total organisation. As has been said before, the bottom line is that sooner or later every organisation has to perform successfully if it is to survive. (**Organisational performance and effectiveness are discussed in Chapter 16.**)

The study of organisational behaviour embraces, therefore, an understanding of the interactions among:

- the nature and purpose of the organisation, its aims and objectives;
- formal structure and role relationships;
- the tasks to be undertaken and technology employed;
- organisational processes and the execution of work;
- the human element, informal organisation and behaviour of people;
- the process of management as an integrating and co-ordinating activity;
- social responsibilities and business ethics;
- the external environment of which the organisation is part; and
- the need for organisation success and survival.

This provides us with a basic, but convenient, framework of study (*see* Figure 1.2).

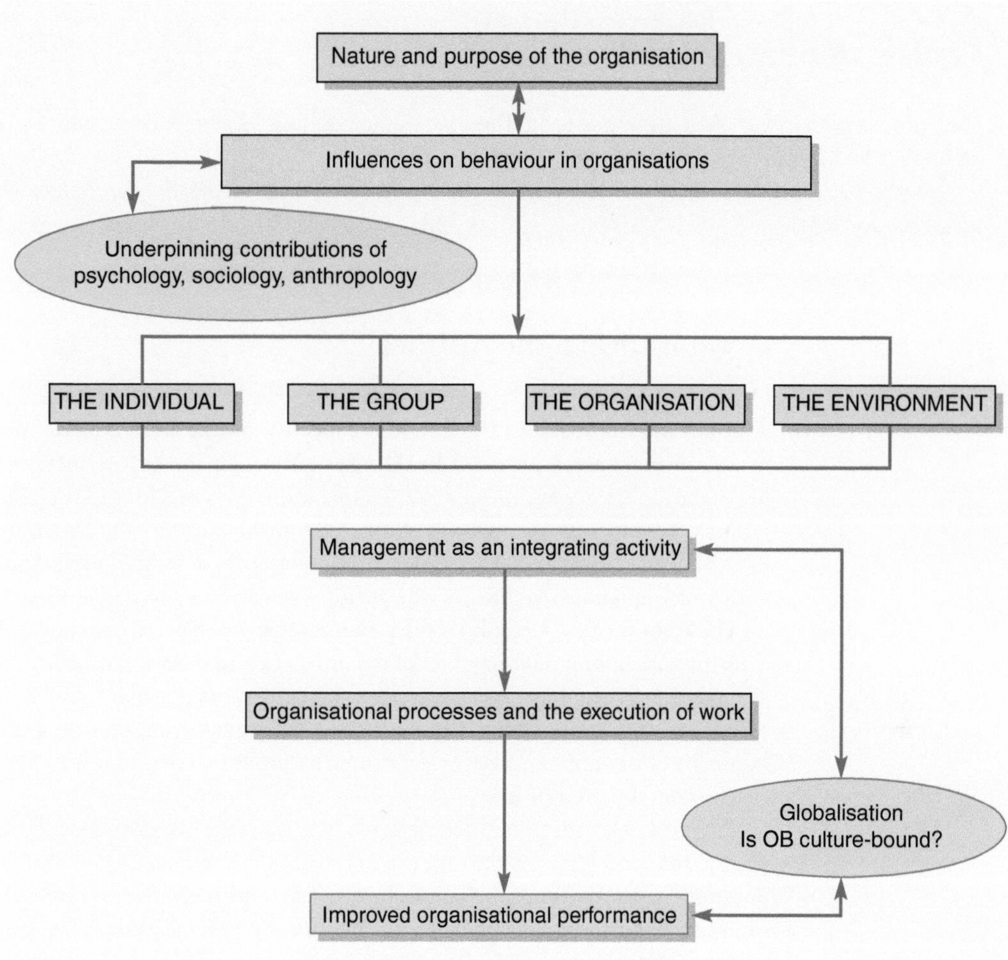

Figure 1.2 Organisational behaviour (OB): a basic framework of study

Relevance of theory

You should not be put off by the use of the word 'theory' in your studies. Most rational decisions are based on some form of theory. Theory provides a sound basis for action and contains a message on how managers might behave. This will influence attitudes towards management practice and lead to changes in actual patterns of behaviour. It further provides a conceptual framework and gives a perspective for the practical study of the subject. Together they lead to a better understanding of factors influencing patterns of behaviour in work organisations and applications of the process of management.[4] As *McGregor* expresses it:

> *Every managerial act rests on assumptions, generalizations, and hypotheses – that is to say, on theory. Our assumptions are frequently implicit, sometimes quite unconscious, often conflicting; nevertheless, they determine our predictions that if we do a, b will occur. Theory and practice are inseparable.*[5]

Patching suggests that all managers who think about what they do are practical students of organisational theory:

> *Theory is not something unique to academics, but something we all work with in arriving at our attitudes, beliefs and decisions as managers. It seems obvious to most of us that some theories are better than others. Many managerial discussions which we undertake in meetings focus upon trying to agree upon which theory will be best for a particular decision.*[6]

Critical review and reflection

The purpose of theory is often misunderstood. Theory helps in building a framework of study and generalised models applicable to a range of different organisations or situations.

What is YOUR view? How does a knowledge of underlying theory help YOUR study of management and organisational behaviour?

Organisational metaphors

Organisations are complex social systems that can be defined and studied in a number of ways. A significant approach to this broad perspective on the nature of organisations and organisational behaviour is provided by *Morgan*. Through the use of metaphors, Morgan identifies eight different ways of viewing organisations – as machines, organisms, brains, cultures, political systems, psychic prisons, flux and transformation, and instruments of domination. According to Morgan, these contrasting metaphors aid the understanding of the complex nature of organisational life and the critical evaluation of organisational phenomena.[7]

These contrasting metaphors offer an interesting perspective on how to view organisations. They provide a broader view of the dynamics of organisational behaviour and how to manage and design organisations. However, Morgan points out that these metaphors are not fixed categories and are not mutually exclusive. An organisation can be a mix of each and predominantly a combination of two or three metaphors. Furthermore, these combinations may change over a period of time.

A number of writers use metaphors to help describe organisations. For example, in discussing the role and logic of viewing the organisation in terms of metaphors, *Drummond* raises questions such as what an organisation is like and the power of metaphors in shaping our thinking, but also points out that all metaphors are partial and no metaphor can explain fully a particular phenomenon.[8]

Realities of organisational behaviour

However one looks at the nature or disciplines of organisational behaviour it is important to remember, as *Morgan* points out, 'the reality of organisational life usually comprises numerous different realities!'[9]

Hellriegel et al. suggest:

> *One way to recognise why people behave as they do at work is to view an organisation as an iceberg. What sinks ships isn't always what sailors can see, but what they can't see.*[10]

The overt, formal aspects focus only on the tip of the iceberg (organisation). It is just as important to focus on what you can't see – the covert, behavioural aspects (*see* Figure 1.3).

Egan refers to the importance of the shadow side of the organisation: that is, those things not found on organisation charts or in company manuals – the covert, and often undiscussed, activities of people, which affect both the productivity and quality of the working life of an organisation.[11] As *Howes* points out, the fiercest battles of the workplace may seem trivial yet they are nothing of the sort. Underlying and unresolved disputes can brew animosity and resentment, and halt production.

> *Forget disagreements over strategies or policy - many of the bitterest workplace battles are fought over the prosaic matters of air conditioning and in-office music.*[12]

Watson reminds us that the biggest challenge we face when trying to analyse or to manage organisations is that they do not actually exist.

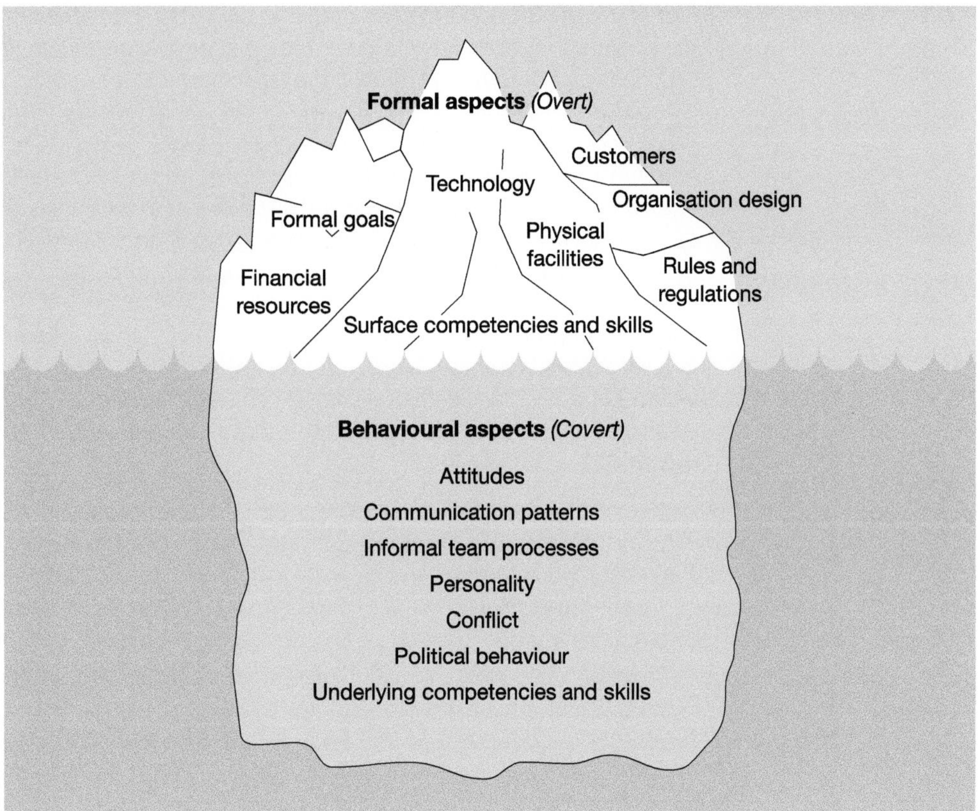

Figure 1.3 The organisational iceberg

Source: From Hellriegel, D., Slocum, J. W., Jr. and Woodman, R. W. *Management*, eighth edition, South-Western Publishing (1998), p. 6. Reproduced by permission.

> *The organisation in which you work or study is not something you can see, hear, touch, smell, kick, kiss or throw up in the air. And this is not just because you might be a relatively junior member of that organisation. The top managers of the organisation are no more capable than you are of relating to the organisation as if it existed in a straightforward way. This, in fact, is one of the most fascinating aspects of organisational and managerial work – and its essential ambiguity.*[13]

Looking outside organisations

Wilson suggests that the meaning of the term 'organisational behaviour' is far from clear. She challenges what constitutes organisational behaviour and questions whether we should be interested only in behaviour that happens within organisations. There is a reciprocal relationship in what happens within and outside organisations. Wilson suggests that we also look outside of what are normally thought of as organisations and how we usually think of work. We can also gain insight into organisational life and behaviour by looking at what happens in rest and play, considering emotion and feeling, considering the context in which work is defined as men's or women's work and looking at less organised work – for example, work on the fiddle and the meaning of work for the unemployed.[14] These suggestions arguably add an extra dimension to the meaning and understanding of organisational behaviour.

What is work?

In a classic 1932 essay 'In Praise of Idleness', *Bertrand Russell* puts forward an interesting view that the road to happiness and prosperity lies in an organised diminution of work.

First of all: what is work? Work is of two kinds: first, altering the position of matter at or near the earth's surface relatively to other such matter; second, telling other people to do so. The first kind is unpleasant and ill paid; the second is pleasant and highly paid. The second kind is capable of indefinite extension: there are not only those who give orders, but those who give advice as to what orders should be given. Usually two opposite kinds of advice are given simultaneously by two organised bodies of men, this is called politics. The skill required for this kind of work is not knowledge of the subjects as to which advice is given, but knowledge of the art of persuasive speaking and writing, i.e. of advertising. Throughout Europe, though not in America, there is a third class of men, more respected than either of the classes of workers, there are men who, through ownership of land, are able to make others pay for the privilege of being allowed to exist and to work. These landowners are idle, and I might therefore be expected to praise them. Unfortunately their idleness is only rendered possible by the industry of others; indeed their desire for comfortable idleness is historically the source of the whole gospel of work. The last thing they have ever wished is that others should follow their example.[15]

Whatever your view of this essay, what is clear is how the nature of work itself has changed over the past eighty years. From work primarily as a wage and means of survival to the growth and power of trade unions, an emphasis on manufacturing and apprenticeship with repetitive mundane work, few professionally qualified managers and the development of business schools, labour disputes, discord and mass industrial relations, broadening work horizons but times of uncertainty, rapid pace of change, working longer and harder, more flexible working, and the impact of information technology.[16]

Donkin, however, maintains that for most citizens everywhere work remains about earning a living and not much else.[17] For most people today, work in one form or another is clearly a major part of their lives, and many people spend a large proportion of their time working.

Orientations to work and the work ethic

People differ in the manner and extent of their involvement with, and concern for, work. From information collected about the work situation, organisational participation and involvement with work colleagues, and life outside the organisation, *Goldthorpe et al.* identified three main types of orientation to work: instrumental, bureaucratic and solidaristic.[18]

- Individuals with an **instrumental orientation** define work not as a central life issue but in terms of a means to an end. There is a calculative or economic involvement with work and a clear distinction between work-related and non-work-related activities.
- Individuals with a **bureaucratic orientation** define work as a central life issue. There is a sense of obligation to the work of the organisation and a positive involvement in terms of a career structure. There is a close link between work-related and non-work-related activities.
- Individuals with a **solidaristic orientation** define the work situation in terms of group activities. There is an ego involvement with work groups rather than with the organisation itself. Work is more than just a means to an end. Non-work activities are linked to work relationships.

Opportunities and choices

According to *Bunting,* although some people in poorly paid jobs requiring long hours do not have other options, for the majority there is a degree of choice in how hard they work. People make their own choices. If they want to work hard, or if they wish to opt out and live the good life, it is up to them.[19] As the number of baby-boomers (born between 1946 and 1963 and typified by a search for security) declines and the proportion of Generation Y (born between 1980 and 1995 and typified by travel first, then a career) increases, this will have a further impact on the future world of work.[20] **(See also a fuller discussion in Chapter 3.)**

Some people may well have a set motivation to work, whatever the nature of the work environment. However, different work situations may also influence the individual's orientation to work. For example, the lack of opportunities for teamwork and the satisfaction of social expectations may result in an instrumental orientation to work and a primary concern for economic interests such as pay and security. In other situations where there are greater opportunities to satisfy social needs, membership of work groups may be very important and individuals may have a more solidaristic orientation to work. This often appears to be the case, for example, with people working in the hospitality industry.

A sense of identity

Work can help fulfil a number of purposes including providing the individual with a sense of identity. Many people see themselves primarily in terms of their career and what they do at work. It defines who they are. *Waller* suggests that work inevitably plays a key role in shaping identity, and at least there you are challenging yourself, developing and learning.

> *In the knowledge economy, where responsibilities morph and working hours are flexible, the boundaries between work and free time blur, and it's hard for many of us to tell when we're off-duty. It follows that if people are getting absorbed by their work-life, they expect their job to help them to discover and develop themselves. Identity can be linked to such basics as the satisfaction of a job well done – yet in a modern economy, work is rarely actually 'finished'.*[21]

For some people who do not necessarily have any financial motivation, work appears to provide a sense of purpose and a structure to their day. It is often even explained as 'a reason to get up in the morning'.

Cultural influences

National culture is also a significant influence on orientations to work. For example, *Reeves* comments on the importance of conversation for effective organisational relationships but how this is resisted in the UK work culture.

> *The Protestant version of the work ethic prevails, implying heads-down work, focused agendas, punctuality, efficiency. In French and Spanish offices, it takes the first hour to kiss everyone, the second to discuss local gossip and the third to pop out for a coffee and croissant. In Britain, these activities would count as sexual harassment, time-wasting and absenteeism. Many firms have built cafés or break out areas and then discovered people are too scared to use them for fear of looking work-shy.*[22]

McCrum refers to a key division in the international world as that between those who live to work and those who work to live.

> *The American appetite for putting work first, even to the extent of giving up weekends, will not be understood in much of mainland Europe or Latin America. Here, regular time off is regarded as essential for family and friends and a go-getting 'familiarisation weekend' would be particularly unwelcome. In the East, of course, the Japanese take their work just as seriously as the Americans.*[23] **(Work/life balance is discussed in Chapter 3.)**

Critical review and reflection

An individual's orientation to work and underlying work ethic is the strongest influence on his or her motivation and organisational performance. The actions of management have only minimal effect.

To what extent do YOU agree with this contention and to what extent is it true for YOU? How would YOU explain YOUR own orientation to work and the work ethic?

Social exchange theory

An important feature that underlies the behaviour and interrelationships of people at work is that of **social exchange theory**. Rooted in cultural anthropology and economics, the central premise of social exchange theory is that a fundamental feature of human interaction is the exchange of social and material resources.[24] Social behaviour is determined by an exchange process. When people enter into a relationship with some other person, there is the expectation of obtaining some kind of reward or benefit in exchange for giving something to the other person in return. Individuals will seek to achieve a positive balance for themselves by maximising the benefits and minimising the costs of such exchanges. Social exchanges are influenced by a complex web of power relationships and as a result are not always equal but have an uneven balance of outcomes.[25]

Exchanges are viewed in terms of a subjective cost–benefit analysis. Benefits and costs can be financial, material, time, social, status, emotional or opportunistic. In different relationships there will be different expectations of the content and balance of the exchange, for example between a senior manager and subordinate or between fellow team members. The level of satisfaction from the exchange will depend not just upon the actual outcomes but on the individual's expectation of likely outcomes. The perceived outcomes of a present relationship may also be viewed in consideration of both past relationships and potential future relationships. The nature of social exchanges impacts upon many other subject areas including the psychological contract, individual differences and diversity, communications, equity theory of motivation, group behaviour, leadership and management, control and power, and organisational culture.

The psychological contract

One significant aspect of organisational behaviour, which has its roots in social exchange theory and the relationship between the individual and the process of management, is the concept of the **psychological contract**. This is not a written document or part of a formal agreement but implies a series of mutual expectations and satisfaction of needs arising from the people–organisation relationship. The psychological contract covers a range of expectations of rights and privileges, duties and obligations that have an important influence on people's behaviour. It is also an important factor in the socialisation of new members of staff to the organisation. Early experiences of the people–organisation relationship have a major effect on an individual's perception of the organisation as a place to work and the quality of management, and can have a major influence on job satisfaction, attitude and levels of performance.

The nature and extent of individuals' expectations vary widely, as do the ability and willingness of the organisation to meet them. It is difficult to list the range of implicit expectations that individuals have; these expectations also change over time. They are separate from any statutory requirements placed upon the organisation; they relate more to the idea of social responsibility of management (**discussed in Chapter 14**). The organisation will also have implicit expectations of its members. The organisational side of the psychological contract places emphasis on expectations, requirements and constraints that may differ from, and may conflict with, an individual's expectations. Some possible examples of the individual's and the organisation's expectations are given in Figure 1.4.

Process of balancing

It is unlikely that all expectations of the individual or of the organisation will be met fully. There is a continual process of balancing, and explicit and implicit bargaining. The nature of these expectations is not defined formally, and although the individual member and the organisation may not be consciously aware of them, they still affect relationships between them and have an influence on behaviour. *Stalker* suggests that successful companies are those that have the ability to balance the unwritten needs of their employees with the needs of the

INDIVIDUALS' EXPECTATIONS OF THE ORGANISATION

- Provide safe and hygienic working conditions.
- Make every reasonable effort to provide job security.
- Attempt to provide challenging and satisfying jobs, and reduce alienating aspects of work.
- Adopt equitable human resource management policies and procedures.
- Respect the role of trade union officials and staff representives.
- Consult fully with staff and allow genuine participation in decisions that affect them.
- Implement best practice in equal opportunity policies and procedures.
- Reward all staff fairly according to their contribution and performance.
- Provide reasonable opportunities for personal development and career progression.
- Treat members of staff with respect.
- Demonstrate an understanding and considerate attitude towards personal problems of staff.

ORGANISATIONAL EXPECTATIONS OF THE INDIVIDUAL

- Uphold the ideology of the organisation and the corporate image.
- Work diligently in pursuit of organisational objectives.
- Adhere to the rules, policies and procedures of the organisation.
- Respect the reasonable authority of senior members of staff.
- Do not take advantage of goodwill shown by management.
- Be responsive to leadership influence.
- Demonstrate loyalty, respect confidentiality and not betray positions of trust.
- Maintain harmonious relationships with work colleagues.
- Do not abuse organisational facilities such as email or Internet access.
- Observe reasonable and acceptable standards of dress and appearance.
- Show respect and consolidation to customers and suppliers.

Figure 1.4 The psychological contract: possible examples of individual and organisational expectations

company. Such companies use a simple formula of Caring, Communicating, Listening, Knowing, Rewarding:

- **Caring** – demonstrating genuine concern for individuals working in the organisation.
- **Communicating** – really talking about what the company is hoping to achieve.
- **Listening** – hearing not only the words but also what lies behind the words.
- **Knowing** – the individuals who work for you, their families, personal wishes, desires and ambitions.
- **Rewarding** – money is not always necessary; a genuine thank-you or public recognition can raise morale.[26]

The changing nature of organisations and individuals at work has placed increasing pressures on the awareness and importance of new psychological contracts. *Ghoshal et al.* suggest the new management philosophy needs to be grounded in a very different moral contract with people. Rather than being seen as a corporate asset from which value can be appropriated, people are seen as a responsibility and a resource to be added to. The new moral contract also demands much from employees, who need to abandon the stability of lifetime employment and embrace the concept of continuous learning and personal development.[27]

Critical review and reflection

Differences in status and power mean that the psychological contract is always balanced in favour of the organisation. Managers will expect individuals to display loyalty and commitment, and put in extra hours, effort and performance. Individuals can only hope for some commensurate fair reward now or later.

To what extent do YOU agree with this contention? How far are the expectations YOU have of the psychological contract met by YOUR university or organisation?

The nature of human behaviour in organisations

It is convenient, here, to consider two sets of observations on the nature of organisational behaviour and what may actually happen, in practice, in organisations: the Peter Principle and Parkinson's Law. Although presented in a satirical manner, these observations nevertheless make a serious and significant point about the management and functioning of organisations and the actual nature and practice of organisational behaviour.

The Peter Principle

This is concerned with the study of occupational incompetence and the study of hierarchies. The analysis of hundreds of cases of occupational incompetence led to the formulation of the **Peter Principle**, which is:

> *In a hierarchy every employee tends to rise to their level of incompetence.*[28]

Employees competent in their position are promoted and competence in each new position qualifies for promotion to the next highest position until a position of incompetence is reached. The principle is based on perceived incompetence at all levels of every hierarchy – political, legal, educational and industrial – and ways in which employees move upwards through a hierarchy and what happens to them after promotion.

Among the many examples quoted by *Peter* are those from the teaching occupation. C, a competent student, teacher and head of department, is promoted to assistant principal and being intellectually competent is further promoted to principal. C is now required to work directly with higher officials. By working so hard at running the school, however, C misses important meetings with superiors and has no energy to become involved with community organisations. C thus becomes regarded as an incompetent principal.

Means of promotion

Peter suggests two main means by which a person can affect their promotion rate, 'Pull' and 'Push':

- Pull is an employee's relationship – by blood, marriage or acquaintance – with a person above the employee in the hierarchy.
- Push is sometimes manifested by an abnormal interest in study, vocational training and self-improvement.

In small hierarchies, Push may have a marginal effect in accelerating promotion; in larger hierarchies the effect is minimal. Pull is, therefore, likely to be more effective than Push.

> *Never stand when you can sit; never walk when you can ride; never Push when you can Pull.*[29]

Parkinson's Law

A major feature of **Parkinson's Law** is that of the 'rising pyramid' – that is, 'work expands so as to fill the time available for its completion.'[30] General recognition of this is illustrated in the proverb, 'It is the busiest person who has time to spare.' There is little, if any, relationship between the quantity of work to be done and the number of staff doing it. Underlying this general tendency are two almost axiomatic statements:

- An official wants to multiply subordinates, not rivals.
- Officials make work for each other.

Parkinson goes on to give the following example. If a civil servant, *A*, believes he is overworked, there are three possible remedies: (i) resignation; (ii) ask to halve the work by having it shared with a colleague, *B;* or (iii) seek the assistance of two subordinates, *C* and *D.* The first two options are unlikely. Resignation would involve loss of pension rights, while sharing work with a colleague on the same level would only bring in a rival for promotion. So *A* would prefer the appointment of two junior members of staff, *C* and *D.* This would increase *A*'s status. There must be at least two subordinates, so that by dividing work between *C* and *D, A* will be the only person to understand the work of them both. Furthermore, each subordinate is kept in order by fear of the other's promotion.

When, in turn, *C* complains of overwork, *A,* with the agreement of *C,* will advise the appointment of two assistants, *E* and *F.* However, as *D*'s position is much the same and, to avoid internal friction, two assistants, *G* and *H,* will also be recommended to help *D.* There are now seven people, *A, C, D, E, F, G* and *H,* doing what one person did before, and *A*'s promotion is almost certain. With the seven people now employed, the second stage comes into operation. The seven people make so much work for each other that they are all fully occupied and *A* is actually working harder than ever.

Among other features of organisational practice that Parkinson discusses are: principles of personnel selection; the nature of committees; personality screen; high finance; the 'Law of Triviality', which means (in a committee) that the time spent on any agenda item will be in inverse proportion to the sum involved; the layout of the organisation's administration block; and 'injelitis' – the disease of induced inferiority.

Relevance of observations

Despite the light vein of Parkinson's writing, the relevance of his observations can be gauged from comments in the Introduction by HRH The Duke of Edinburgh.

> *The most important point about this book for serious students of management and administration is that it illustrates the gulf that exists between the rational/intellectual approach to human organisation and the frequent irrational facts of human nature . . . The law should be compulsory reading at all business schools and for all management consultants. Management structures solve nothing if they do not take the facts of human nature into proper consideration, and one of the most important facts is that no one really likes having to make decisions. Consequently structures may generate a lot of activity but little or no useful work.*[31]

Positive organisational behaviour

A different approach to organisational behaviour is that of positive organisational behaviour (POB), which takes a functionalist or positivist approach. In recent years increasing attention has been given to **positive psychology**, which is defined broadly as 'the scientific study of what makes life most worth living'. Although arguably originated by *Maslow* in his hierarchy of needs theory in 1954 (**see Chapter 7**), positive psychology is associated with the work of *Martin Seligman* in 1998.[32] Rather than focus on finding out what was wrong with people – the 'disease' model – positive psychology complements traditional psychology by focusing on determining how things go right and how to enhance people's satisfaction and well-being. According to *Peterson*, among the major concerns of positive psychology are:

> *positive experiences like happiness and engagement, positive traits like character strengths and talents, positive relationships like friendship and love, and the larger institutions like family and school that enable these.*

Peterson goes on to suggest that the topic of morale can also be placed under the positive psychology umbrella. Morale is used as a cognitive, emotional and motivational stance towards the goals and tasks of a group. In the same way that life satisfaction is an indicator of individual well-being, morale is an indicator of group well-being.[33]

Applications to the work situation

To what extent can positive psychology be applied to the work organisation? *Wong and Davey* maintain that each day, in every organisation, huge amounts of valuable resources are wasted because of human problems, wrong policies or poor training. The focus of leadership needs to be shifted from process and outcome to people and the development of social/emotional/spiritual capital. However, although positive psychology can be introduced into the workplace, they question the ability of managers to apply this to employees in a meaningful way.[34]

Positive organisational behaviour is defined by *Luthans* as:

> *The study and application of positively oriented human resource strengths and psychological capacities that can be measured, developed and effectively managed for performance improvement in today's workplace.*

This definition incorporates many existing concepts from the domains of attitudes, personality, motivation and leadership.[35]

Donaldson and Ko maintain that the primary emphasis of POB is in the workplace and the accomplishment of work-related outcomes and performance improvement. Studies of POB have been conducted at the micro- and meso-levels of analysis using survey research and tend to develop from individual to group to organisational levels of analysis. There appears to be potential to invigorate research and applications in the traditional fields of industrial psychology and organisational behaviour.[36]

POB has been subject to much critique. According to *Wright and Quick*, for example, there still exists some measure of confusion regarding just what constitutes the realm of 'positive' behaviour, and what distinguishes the positive organisational agenda from organisational behaviour in general. However, despite the sceptics and critics, Wright and Quick believe that the role of positive organisational movement will continue to grow and prosper, and gain significant attention in the applied sciences.[37]

The changing world of work organisations

Increasing business competitiveness, globalisation, shifting labour markets, rapid technological progress, the move towards more customer-driven markets, a 24/7 society and demands of work/life balance have led to a period of constant change and the need for greater organisational flexibility. The combination of these influences is transforming the way we live and work. And this clearly has significant implications for management and organisational behaviour. It is important to understand how organisations function and the pervasive influences that they exercise over the behaviour and actions of people.

The power and influence of private and public organisations, the rapid spread of new technology and the impact of various socio-economic and political factors have attracted increasing attention to the concept of 'corporate responsibilities and business ethics (**discussed in Chapter 14**). Increasing attention is also being focused on the ethical behaviour that underlies the decisions and actions of people at work.

A summary of the changing context of work, including topics discussed in subsequent chapters, is set out in the concept map shown in Figure 1.5.

THE CHANGING CONTEXT OF WORK

- TRADITIONAL V. EMERGENT WORK CONTEXTS
- EMPLOYEE SKILLS IN THE NEW ORGANISATION
- WORK/LIFE BALANCE
- FLEXIBLE WORKING RIGHTS

Remember – employees sometimes just need time away from work to pursue their own personal interests!

FLEXIBLE WORKING RIGHTS

Anyone can ask their employer to allow flexible working patterns, but in the UK the government has introduced a statutory right in order to encourage applications. This legal framework allows someone to request flexible working if the person:

- is an employee with 26 or more weeks' service and
- has a child under the age of six (or disabled child under 18) and
- is responsible for that child and is applying to care for that child

or

- is someone caring for an adult living at the same address as the employee

IF THESE CONDITIONS ARE MET, THE EMPLOYER MUST GIVE THE REQUEST "SERIOUS CONSIDERATION". EMPLOYERS CAN REFUSE ON CERTAIN "BUSINESS GROUNDS" DESCRIBED IN THE LEGISLATION

WORK/LIFE BALANCE

FACTORS ASSOCIATED WITH INCREASED EMPHASIS ON THE WORK SITUATION

- Deep interest in the nature of the work itself
- Income a high priority
- Employee unempowered and not confident
- Organisation norms expect attendance
- Organisation pay dictated by time attendance
- Employee has home problems and would rather be at work.

Early trades unions demanded that on working days a worker should have: 'Eight hours work, eight hours leisure, and eight hours sleep'

FACTORS ASSOCIATED WITH INCREASED EMPHASIS ON LIFE OUTSIDE WORK

- Formal recognition by the organisation that employees have commitments other than work (including child/elderly people care)
- Employee outputs based on results, not time attended
- Excellent organisational ICT systems, enabling easy communication with employees
- Organisation climate resulting in confident employees

TRADITIONAL & EMERGENT WORK CONTEXTS COMPARED

NOTE 1 THESE ARE TENDENCIES – EXCEPTIONS CAN OFTEN BE FOUND!

NOTE 2 THE NATURE OF THE ORGANISATION'S WORK MAY DEMAND A TRADITIONAL APPROACH

Some observed differences between traditional & emergent organisations include the following:

CHARACTERISTIC	TRADITIONAL	EMERGENT
Organisation structure (1)	Many management layers	Few management layers
Organisation structure (2)	Hierarchical	Flexible
Career path for employees (1)	Heavily organisation influenced	Principally based on individuals's own plans
Career path for employees (2)	Based in very few organisations	Based in many organisations
Employee development	Largely restricted to current job	Aimed at future as well as current job
Organisation output	Product/service based	Knowledge based
Management style (1)	More formal	More relaxed
Management style (2)	Inward-looking	More broadly based on outside society
Decisionmaking	Often hierarchical	Frequently collective
Workplace	Office location based	Field or home based

EMPLOYEE SKILLS IN THE NEW ORGANISATION

Emergent organisations tend to have fewer management positions. One implication for employees is that in addition to their own technical or professional expertise a working competency is needed in such topics as:

- **Clerical and administrative work** – because support staff are increasingly seen as an unwarranted overhead expense
- **Information & Communications Technology (ICT)** – because emerging organisations are highly dependent on new technologies
- **Advanced personal communication systems** – especially for field or embossed workers
- **'Customer-facing' skills** – because employees increasingly deal with customers/clients
- **Financial skills** – to help in understanding the business as a whole
- **Change-coping and change management capabilities** – because rapid changes in the business are a common feature

Figure 1.5 The changing context of work

Source: Copyright © 2011 The Virtual Learning Materials Workshop. Reproduced with permission.

Management as an integrating activity

Whatever the individual's orientations to work, or the nature of the work organisation or cultural influences, it is through the process of management that the efforts of members of the organisation are co-ordinated, directed and guided towards the achievement of its goals. Management is the cornerstone of organisational effectiveness (*see* Figure 1.6).

It is important always to remember that it is people who are being managed, and people should be considered in human terms. Unlike physical resources, the people resource is not owned by the organisation. People bring their own perceptions, feelings and attitudes towards the organisation, systems and styles of management, their duties and responsibilities, and the conditions under which they are working. Human behaviour is capricious and scientific methods or principles of behaviour cannot be applied with reliability. It is also widely observed that you cannot study the behaviour of people without changing it. At the heart of successful management is the problem of integrating the individual and the organisation, and this requires an understanding of both human personality and work organisations.[38]

Providing the right balance

People and organisations need each other. Management is an integral part of this relationship. It is essentially an integrating activity that permeates every facet of the organisation's operations and should serve to reconcile the needs of people at work with the requirements of the organisation. Management should endeavour to create the right balance between the interrelated elements that make up the total organisation and to weld these into coherent patterns

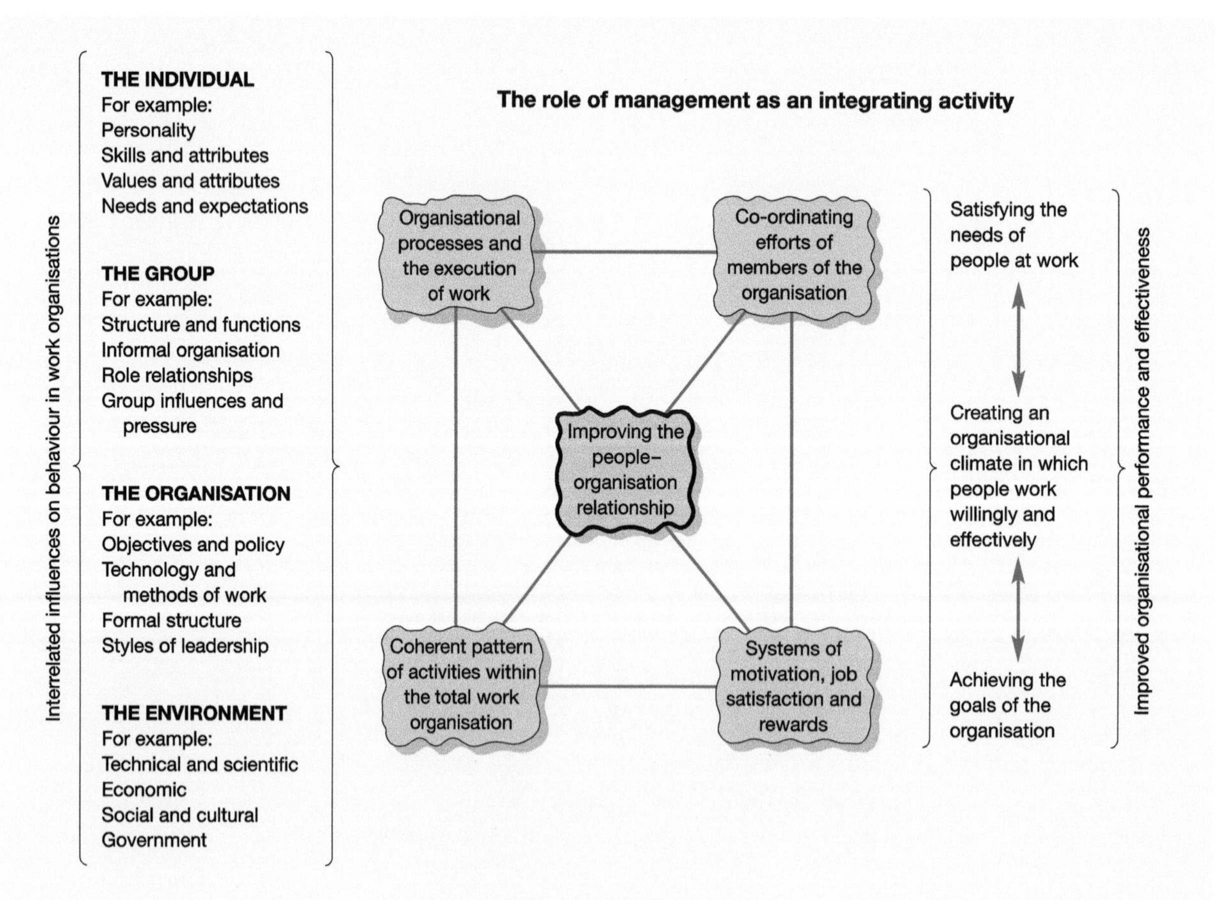

Figure 1.6 Management as the cornerstone of organisational effectiveness

of activity best suited to the external environment in which the organisation is operating. Consideration must be given to developing an organisational climate in which people work willingly and effectively.

According to *Gratton*, for example:

> *When people are engaged and committed they are more likely to behave in the interests of the company and they have less need to be controlled and measured. In essence, engaged people can be trusted to behave in the interests of the company, in part because they perceived their interests to be the same as, or aligned with, the interests of the company.*[39]

The style of management adopted can be seen as a function of the manager's attitudes towards people and assumptions about human nature and behaviour (**discussed in Chapter 10**).

Critical review and reflection

Performance of people at work is determined predominantly by the idiosyncratic behaviour of individuals and a complex combination of social factors and unofficial working methods. In reality, managers have only limited influence.

What is YOUR opinion? How would YOU describe the situation in YOUR own university or organisation?

Management and organisational behaviour in action case study

Fred. Olsen Cruise Lines

An increasingly significant sector of the hospitality and leisure industry is that of cruise ships. The number of holidaymakers choosing a holiday at sea continues to rise, with a record 1.7 million UK holidaymakers taking an ocean cruise in 2014.

In an ever-growing and continually evolving cruise industry, the delivery of a memorable personal service experience is particularly significant as an integral part of organisational effectiveness. Goods and services alone are no longer enough and, in addition to providing a consistently high-quality product, cruise companies need to differentiate themselves by an emotional engagement with customers and the highest levels of customer service.[40]

Fred. Olsen Cruise Lines is one of the only family-run cruise lines in the world, with sailing experience going back over 160 years. Fred. Olsen has stylish, contemporary ships built 'on a human scale', with capacities between 800 and 1,350 guests, departing from ten regional UK ports. The ships are large enough to provide the facilities desired by guests, but small enough to enable a close exploration of a wide range of exciting destinations. Emphasis is on a comfortable, friendly atmosphere, with a 'country house hotel' feel, delivered 'with a smile', by caring and attentive crew. Guests are welcomed as individuals in a relaxed, familiar ambience. Among a number of recent accolades, Fred. Olsen Cruise Lines was awarded the prestigious *Which?* 'Recommended Provider' status in the influential consumer body's first-ever cruise survey and the coveted 'Gold Trusted Merchant Accreditation' by independent review site Feefo for 2014 and 2015.

Successful cruise management is a combination of travel agency, hotel and leisure activities, on-board entertainment and organised tours. It entails a complex and involved series of processes, both at sea and in different ports of call, and is unlike that experienced in hardly any other business organisation. Some particular factors to consider include, for example:

- continual heavy guest occupancy and usage, with rapid turnover, mass entry and exit;
- 'people logistics' – attending to the complex transportation needs of guests pre- and post-cruise, and logistics of a broad variety of shore excursions in different locations;
- wide range of on-board activities and events throughout the day and evening;
- highest standards of safety and maintenance, logistics and tender operations;
- relationships with head office, technical department, port authorities, pilots, etc;

→

- expectations of high-quality cuisine, design and mix of menus, special dietary requirements;
- crew from a diverse range of cultures and backgrounds, with long periods away from home and families;
- health and hygiene, with large numbers of guests and crew in continual close contact;
- crew resource deployment and rotation planning, with unavailability of additional agency or temporary staff, as with land-based organisations, and need for flexible working practices in response to the demands of the business;
- accommodating annual leave requirements, flights for some members of the crew, and managing opportunities for time on shore;
- changeover of crew at the end of contracts - maintaining continuity within the business.

Cruising is associated with a high level of service delivery, and based on preconceived expectations passengers can be very demanding. Passenger satisfaction is dependent to a very large extent on day-to-day contact with - and care and attention from - members of the crew. Crew members work long hours, in often difficult and demanding conditions, and are away from their homes, and in many cases young families, for up to nine months. Management's concern and support for the welfare of its crew are of prime importance. At the same time, the nature of cruising demands attention to a safe and secure environment, for both passengers and crew. This demands a management structure with clear lines of authority, directed leadership and good order. Strong discipline must be maintained at all times.

Fred. Olsen prides itself on providing exceptional service by anticipating, meeting and exceeding its guests' expectations when they are on board its ships. Despite the continually evolving and highly competitive nature of the industry, Fred. Olsen attracts a high level of 'repeat guests' - that is, loyal customers who have cruised with the company at least once before. On a typical Fred. Olsen cruise, more than half of the guests are repeat customers, which is one of the highest return rates of any major cruise line. A particularly noticeable feature of passenger feedback is the extremely favourable and complimentary comments regarding the level of attention from courteous and always smiling crew members.

Gratuities to crew members are an accepted custom throughout the cruise industry. Tips are a recognised feature of the reward system for good performance. It is up to passengers to opt out of payment or vary the amount. The high number of Fred. Olsen crew members returning to complete further contracts (varying between six and nine months), and who have been engaged over many years with the company, is testament to both crew and passenger levels of satisfaction.

Source: Thanks to Rachael Jackson, Fred. Olsen Cruise Lines, **www.fredolsencruises.com**

Tasks

1. Explain particular features of organisational behaviour raised by this case study.
2. What do you think are the most important factors that explain the high level of repeat guests on Fred. Olsen cruise ships?
3. The company has a particular attraction for discerning, traditional guests. What additional considerations do you think this creates for both crew and management?
4. Discuss specific ways in which this case draws attention to the importance of the people–organisation relationship.

Globalisation and the international context

One major challenge facing managers today arises from what many commentators have identified as an increasingly international or **global** business environment. In broad terms, **globalisation** refers to organisations integrating, operating and competing in a worldwide economy. The organisations' activities are more independent across the world, rather than confined nationally. The following factors are frequently cited as potential explanatory factors underlying this trend:

- improvements in international information and communication facilities leading to an increased consciousness of differences in workplace attitudes and behaviour in other societies;

- international competitive pressure – for example, the emergence of newly industrialised and/or free-market nations including, for example, the Far East region and former communist bloc countries;
- increased mobility of labour;
- international business activity, for example: overseas franchising or licensing agreements; outsourcing of business units to other countries (call centres provide a topical example); direct foreign investment and the activities of multinational corporations that, by definition, operate outside national boundaries;
- greater cross-cultural awareness and acceptance of the advantages of diversity.

Globalisation will also impact on the nature of social responsibilities and business ethics. As organisations, and especially large business organisations, adopt a more global perspective this will have a significant effect on the broader context of management and organisational behaviour.

The future of globalisation

Globalisation has been subjected to much criticism, in part at least due to lack of clarity as to its exact meaning and to the confusion about organisations that are very large scale (such as Walmart in the USA) but have only a small proportion of their operations on a global basis. Globalisation has also become the subject of demonstrations and has been blamed for escalating inequalities in the developing world and endangering regional cultures. There appears to be a return to strong nationalistic tendencies in countries such as the USA and France.

Child points out that globalisation is a complex phenomenon and the term is used in so many different ways it is in danger of losing any useful purpose. Globalisation is a trend rather than a condition that necessarily already exists, it is not spreading evenly across the world and many unsubstantiated and sweeping claims have been made: 'The trend towards globalisation is a strong one, but it remains to be seen how far and how fast it will spread. It has powerful opponents.'[41]

By contrast, *McLean* maintains that globalisation is here to stay – it will not go away and if anything will get worse: 'We must face the realism that the world, and indeed organisations and the way they are managed, will never be the same. We must encompass these changes and harness the opportunities they present.'[42]

French, however, reminds us that social trends are, by their very nature, fluctuating. For example, it is quite possible that the trend for global flows of workers may decrease in importance or even be reversed in the future.[43]

Cultural environment

Whatever the extent of globalisation, there are clear implications for organisational behaviour in accommodating international dimensions of management and cultural differences. The importance of people in business understanding cultural differences is illustrated by IBM, which publishes for members of staff a comprehensive guide to the main dimensions of culture and business, and an introduction to concepts, tips, resources and tools for building cross-cultural competencies across national, organisational, team and interpersonal barriers.

Another advantage of adopting a cross-cultural approach to the study of organisational behaviour, and to the management of people more generally, lies in the recognition of variations in workplace attitudes and behaviour between individuals and groups in different cultural contexts.

As an example, in the USA there is a strong commitment to the organisation (the corporation) and work and career are taken very seriously (as the author has experienced for himself). Hard work is accepted as part of the American way of life and good timekeeping is important. It is a long-hours culture and generally there is little concern for the work/life balance. There is a strong emphasis on political correctness and little banter or humour at work (again as the author found out to his cost), especially not in formal meetings. Americans do not like self-deprecation and find it strange that the British are prepared to laugh at themselves.

In China there is an enormous bureaucracy, and hierarchy is an important indication of authority. In the business world you may need to deal with several ascending levels of management before reaching the senior manager. There can be an apparent lack of courtesy – and rather than being taken as given, respect and trust have to be earned. There is a strong superior–subordinate relationship, with staff often undertaking menial tasks for their boss.[44]

In Japan and Korea, where society tends to be male dominated, in the business world men are more likely to be taking the main role in setting agendas, communications and decision-making.

In examining the centrally important topic of motivation, *Francesco and Gold* inform their readers: 'Managers must develop organizational systems that are flexible enough to take into account the meaning of work and the relative value of rewards within the range of cultures where they operate.'[45]

According to *Hare,* we need to embrace the opportunities international management brings. All countries have their issues, but whatever the customs, differences and similarities, most cultures recognise the need to get something done. Successful international management boils down to five simple principles:

1. Listen well so you understand the rationale, motivations and outcomes desired by the other party.
2. Take time to do your research and homework.
3. Be courteous and polite, and mindful of local manners and customs.
4. Develop good working relationships through trust and respect.
5. Embrace the opportunities from international management.[46]

Critical review and reflection

National culture is not only an explanation of human beliefs, values, behaviours and actions, it is arguably the most significant feature underlying the study of management and organisational behaviour.

To what extent do YOU support this contention? What examples can YOU give in support of your view? What effect does national culture have in YOUR university or organisation?

Is organisational behaviour culture-bound?

While it can be valuable to apply organisational behaviour concepts to diverse cultural settings, it should also be borne in mind that some **universal** theories and models may, in reality, contain important culturally derived assumptions. When examining classical frameworks for understanding organisation structure (**discussed in Chapter 2**), *Schneider and Barsoux* point out: 'Theories about how best to organise – Max Weber's (German) bureaucracy, Henri Fayol's (French) administrative model, and Frederick Taylor's (American) scientific management – all reflect societal concerns of the times as well as the cultural background of the individuals.'[47] That writers on work organisations may themselves be influenced by their own cultural backgrounds when compiling their work is unsurprising: however, equally it should not be ignored.

More significant still is the possibility that whole topics within organisational behaviour, per se, may be underpinned by a particular culturally derived frame of reference. *French* examines the extent to which universally applicable pressures or logics effectively rule out significant cultural variations in formal organisational arrangements, such as bureaucracy, as opposed to culture itself viewed as a variable within a range of factors influencing structure.[48]

Culture as understanding

For our most basic common link is that we all inhabit this small planet, we all breathe the same air, we all cherish our children's future, and we are all mortal.

John F. Kennedy, 10 June 1963

There are a number of very good reasons why we could usefully understand cultural difference (and similarity) at work, based on new awareness contributing to our own effectiveness and moreover to the accomplishment of organisational goals. It could also be true to say that an appreciation of culture and its effects may be of intrinsic value. There could therefore be advantages to cross-cultural awareness, which include:

- increased self-awareness;
- sensitivity to difference and diversity;
- questioning our own assumptions and knowledge;
- lessening ignorance, prejudice and hatred.

However, it would be wrong to think that increased cross-cultural awareness or activity will automatically bring about any of these outcomes.

Brooks is one of several commentators who draw our attention to the interlinked nature of culture and commonly held values. Figure 1.7 illustrates the interplay between relevant factors affecting any one national culture.[49] You may wish to consider how these factors have combined to shape your own 'home' culture and that of one other country with which you are familiar.

Above all, those aspects of organisational behaviour that focus on individual differences and diversity, groups and managing people are the most clearly affected by culture and it is essential to take a cross-cultural approach to the subject. (**Organisation culture is discussed in Chapter 15.**)

Critical review and reflection

Despite obvious advantages from an appreciation of culture differences and its effects, it is not easy for everyone to feel comfortable working in a multicultural environment.

To what extent are YOU aware of, and sensitive to, cultural differences? What is YOUR experience of studying in a multicultural environment at your university? What benefits have YOU gained?

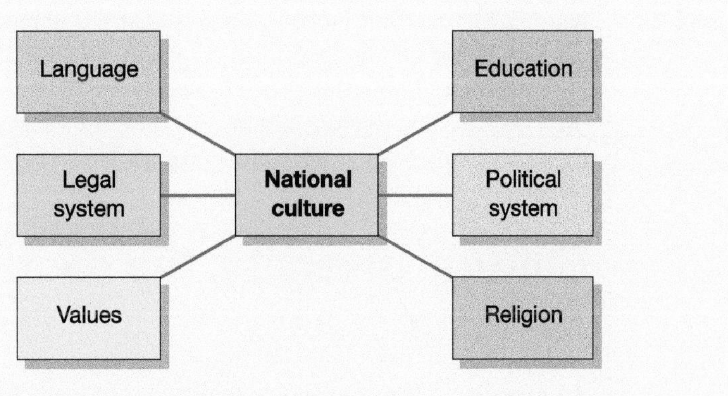

Figure 1.7 Factors affecting national culture

Source: From Brooks, I. *Organisational Behaviour: Individuals, Groups and Organisation*, fourth edition, Financial Times Prentice Hall (2009), p. 272. Reproduced with permission from Pearson Education Ltd.

Five dimensions of culture: the contribution of Hofstede

Geert Hofstede is one of the most significant contributors to the body of knowledge on culture and workplace difference. His work has largely resulted from a large-scale research programme in the late 1960s and early 1970s involving employees from the IBM Corporation, initially in forty countries. In focusing on one organisation Hofstede felt that the results could be more clearly linked to national cultural difference. Arguing that culture is, in a memorable phrase, **collective programming** or **software of the mind,** Hofstede initially identified four dimensions of culture: power distance, uncertainty avoidance, individualism and masculinity.[50]

- **Power distance** relates to the *social distance among people* depending upon management style, hierarchical structure, willingness of subordinates to disagree with superiors, and the educational level and status accruing to particular roles.
- **Uncertainty avoidance** refers to the extent to which members of a society feel threatened by *ambiguity or unusual situations* or accepting of risks and uncertainty.
- **Individualism** describes the relatively *individualistic or collectivist ethic* evident in that particular society, for example the degree of respect for individual freedom or commitment to group membership.
- **Masculinity** refers to a continuum between *'masculine' characteristics,* such as assertiveness and competitiveness, *and 'feminine' traits,* such as caring, a stress upon the quality of life and concern with the environment.

A fifth dimension of culture, **long-term/short-term orientation,** was originally labelled 'Confucian work dynamism'. This dimension developed from the work of *Hofstede and Bond* in an attempt to locate Chinese cultural values as they impacted on the workplace.[51] Countries that scored highly on Confucian work dynamism or long-term orientation exhibited a strong concern with time along a continuum and were therefore both past and future oriented, with a preoccupation with tradition but also a concern with the effect of actions and policies on future generations.

Evaluation of Hofstede's work

Extremely influential, the seminal work of Hofstede has been criticised from certain quarters, for example for its simplicity and limited practical application. In common with other writers in this area, there is a focus on the national rather than the regional level. The variations within certain countries, for example Spain, can be more or less significant. Again in common with other contributors, Hofstede's classifications include medium categories that may be difficult to operationalise, accurate though they may be. Some may also find the masculinity/femininity dimension unconvincing and itself stereotypical. Other writers have questioned whether Hofstede's findings remain current. *Holden* summarises this view: 'How many people have ever thought that many of Hofstede's informants of three decades ago are now dead? Do their children and grandchildren really have the same values?'[52] (**See also discussion on Global Leadership and Organizational Behavior Effectiveness** (GLOBE) **in Chapter 9.**)

Cultural diversity: the contribution of Trompenaars

Another significant contributor to this area of study is *Fons Trompenaars,* whose later work is co-authored with *Charles Hampden-Turner.*[53] Trompenaars' original research spanned fifteen years, resulting in a database of 50,000 participants from fifty countries. It was supported by cases and anecdotes from 900 cross-cultural training programmes. A questionnaire method comprised a significant part of the study, which involved requiring participants to consider their underlying norms, values and attitudes. The resultant framework identifies seven areas in which cultural differences may affect aspects of organisational behaviour:

- Relationships and rules. Here societies may be more or less **universal,** in which case there is relative rigidity in respect of rule-based behaviour, or **particular,** in which case the importance of relationships may lead to flexibility in the interpretation of situations.
- Societies may be more oriented to the **individual** or **collective.** The collective may take different forms: the corporation in Japan, the family in Italy or the Catholic Church in the Republic of Ireland. There may be implications here for such matters as individual responsibility or payment systems.
- It may also be true that societies differ in the extent to which it is thought appropriate for members to show emotion in public. **Neutral** societies favour the 'stiff upper lip', while overt displays of feeling are more likely in **emotional** societies.
- In **diffuse** cultures, the whole person would be involved in a business relationship and it would take time to build such relationships. In a **specific** culture, such as the USA, the basic relationship would be limited to the contractual. This distinction clearly has implications for those seeking to develop new international links.
- **Achievement**-based societies value recent success or an overall record of accomplishment. In contrast, in societies relying more on **ascription,** status could be bestowed through such factors as age, gender or educational record.
- Trompenaars suggests that societies view **time** in different ways, which may in turn influence business activities. The American dream is the French nightmare. Americans generally start from zero and what matters is their present performance and their plan to 'make it' in the future. This is 'nouveau riche' for the French, who prefer the *ancien pauvre;* they have an enormous sense of the past.
- Finally it is suggested that there are differences with regard to attitudes to the **environment.** In Western societies, individuals are typically masters of their fate. In other parts of the world, however, the world is more powerful than individuals.

Trompenaars' work is based on lengthy academic and field research. It is potentially useful in linking the dimensions of culture to aspects of organisational behaviour that are of direct relevance, particularly to people approaching a new culture for the first time.

High- and low-context cultures

A framework for understanding cultural difference has been formulated by *Ed Hall;* his work is in part co-authored with *Mildred Reed Hall.*[54] Hall conceptualises culture as comprising a series of 'languages', in particular:

- language of time;
- language of space;
- language of things;
- language of friendships;
- language of agreements.

In this model of culture Hall suggests that these 'languages', which resemble shared attitudes to the issues in question, are communicated in very different ways according to whether a society is classified as a 'high'- or 'low'-context culture.

The features of **'high'-context societies,** which incorporate Asian, African and Latin American countries, include the following:

- a high proportion of information is 'uncoded' and internalised by the individual;
- indirect communication styles – words are less important;
- shared group understandings;
- importance attached to the past and tradition;
- a 'diffuse' culture stressing the importance of trust and personal relationships in business.

'Low'-context societies, which include the USA, Australia, the UK and the Scandinavian countries, exhibit contrasting features including the following:

- a high proportion of communication is 'coded' and expressed;
- direct communication styles – words are paramount;
- past context is less important;
- a 'specific' culture stressing importance of rules and contracts.

Other countries, for example France, Spain, Greece and several Middle Eastern societies, are classified as 'medium' context.

The importance of organisational behaviour

As part of the *Financial Times Mastering Management* series, *Wood*, in his discussion of the nature of organisational behaviour, suggests that in its concern for the way people behave in an organisational context, organisational behaviour can be regarded as the key to the whole area of management.

> *Is the study of behavior in organizations important? I think it is vital. What the social sciences, humanities and the arts are to university education, OB is to business school education. The more technical a manager's training, the more important organizational behavior becomes. It is arguably the one area that can carry the burden of bringing the collective wisdom of human history into the decision-making calculus of developing managers. And this is no trivial task.*[55]

In the Foreword to Cloke and Goldsmith's thought-provoking book *The End of Management*, *Bennis* claims that a distinct and dramatic change is taking place in the philosophy underlying organisational behaviour, calling forth a new concept of humanising organisations.

> *This new concept is based on an expanded knowledge of our complex and shifting needs, replacing an oversimplified, innocent, push-button idea of humanity. This philosophical shift calls for a new concept of organizational values based on humanistic-democratic ideals, which replace the depersonalized, mechanistic value system of bureaucracy. With it comes a new concept of power, based on collaboration and reason, replacing a model based on coercion and threat . . . The real push for these changes stems from the need not only to humanize organizations but to use them as crucibles for personal growth and self-realization.*[56]

Robbins and Judge remind us that there are few, if any, simple and universal principles that explain organisational behaviour, but that understanding organisational behaviour has never been more important for managers than it is today.

> *For instance, the typical employee in more developed countries is getting older; more and more women and people of color are in the workplace; corporate downsizing and the heavy use of temporary workers are severing the bonds of loyalty that historically tied many employees to their employers; and global competition is requiring employees to become more flexible and to learn to cope with rapid change. The war on terror has brought to the forefront the challenges of working with and managing people during uncertain times. In short, there are a lot of challenges and opportunities today for managers to use OB concepts.*[57]

Critical review and reflection

A noticeable feature of organisational behaviour is the invariable difficulty in identifying a single solution to a particular situation. The absence of one *right answer* not only makes study of the subject complex and frustrating, but also brings into question the value of studying the subject at all.

What are YOUR views? Do YOU feel frustrated by the study of organisational behaviour?

Ten key points to remember

1 At the heart of management is the art of managing people. Increasing attention is focused on good people skills as a basis of organisational effectiveness.

2 Organisational behaviour (OB) is broadly concerned with the study of the behaviour of people within an organisational setting and is of even greater significance.

3 It is necessary to recognise a multidisciplinary approach. Organisational behaviour can be viewed in terms of interrelated aspects of the individual, the group, the organisation and the environment

4 People differ in the manner and extent of their involvement with, and concern for, work. Different situations influence the individual's orientation to work and the work ethic.

5 The psychological contract implies a series of informal mutual expectations and satisfaction of needs arising from the people–organisation relationship.

6 Two important observations on the nature of human behaviour and what may actually happen in organisations are the Peter Principle and Parkinson's Law.

7 A major challenge facing managers today arises from an increasingly international or global business environment that also impacts on social responsibilities and ethics.

8 This highlights the need for a cross-cultural approach to the study of organisational behaviour and understanding the impact of national culture.

9 There are clear implications for organisational behaviour in accommodating dimensions of cultural differences, and the study and understanding of workplace behaviour.

10 There are few absolute principles that explain organisational behaviour, but in its concern for the behaviour of people it has never been more important for managers.

Review and discussion questions

1 Give your own explanation of the meaning, significance and scope of organisational behaviour.

2 Explain reasons for a multidisciplinary approach and suggest main headings under which factors influencing behaviour in work organisations can best be identified.

3 To what extent do you believe people are identified and perceived according to the nature of the work they undertake? Where possible give actual examples in support of your answer.

4 Discuss with supporting examples the nature and significance of (i) social exchange theory *and* (ii) the psychological contract.

5 Explain the extent to which you can identify with examples of organisational practices relating to (i) the Peter Principle *and* (ii) Parkinson's Law.

6 Discuss critically the role of management as an integrating activity. Give your views on the nature and importance of managerial work today.

7 Give your own views on the changing nature of the work organisation and specific changes that you foresee in the next ten years. How do you feel about the possible changes?

→

8 Why is it increasingly important for managers to adopt an international approach? What do you see as the future impact of globalisation?

9 Debate fully the importance and potential difficulties of national culture to the study of management and organisational behaviour. Where possible, give your own examples.

10 Discuss critically what you believe are the main factors to bear in mind with, and particular difficulties presented by, the study of organisational behaviour.

Assignment

It is often said that people are every organisation's most import asset. This is perfectly true but people are not like other assets. As well as being valuable in their own right – in terms of performance, skills and creativity – it is individual employees who bind every other aspect of working life together.

('The People Factor – engage your employees for business success', ACAS, March 2014, p. 4)

Working in small groups, discuss critically:

1 What this statement actually means to you and fellow members of your group.
2 What exactly is meant by 'individual employees binding every other aspect of working life together'?
3 The extent to which members of staff in your own university appear to be valued as an important asset.
4 Shared experiences within your group of any other work situations, with good and/or bad examples.
5 Why is it that, although the importance of people as the most important asset is often preached by organisations, this rarely seems to be the reality.
6 How this assignment relates to your study of organisational behaviour.
7 An agreed written group report on your findings and conclusions.

Personal skills and employability exercise

Objectives

Completing this exercise should help you to enhance the following skills:

- Obtain a clearer picture of your own and other people's attitudes to studying.
- Explore the likely importance of work to you and your orientation to work.
- Relate responses to your personal learning and development.

Exercise

Form into small groups, preferably including any colleagues whom you have not yet got to know very well and/or from a different ethnicity. Discuss openly and honestly how you each feel regarding your attitude, enthusiasm and motivation towards studying. *For example:*

1 What do you find most satisfying about studying?
2 What do you find least satisfying about studying?
3 How well are you able to concentrate on your studies?
4 To what extent do you enjoy studying for its own sake or only as a means to an end?
5 What do you find most distracting or difficult about your studies?
6 Is it possible to learn how to improve the skill of studying?
7 What rewards most encourage you in your studying?
8 At what time of the day and for how long at a time do you usually study best?

9 Do you prefer to fit studies around leisure time or enjoy leisure more if you have studied first?
10 What is the single most important feature of effective studying?

Discussion

- How do your responses compare with those of your colleagues? Do any of the responses surprise you?
- To what extent do you believe the responses are a true indication of work ethic? What do you see as the characteristic traits of a person with a healthy work ethic?
- How far do you agree with the contention that 'we are employed for our skills but valued for our attitudes'?

Case study
Virgin Atlantic and Ryanair

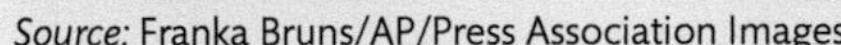
Source: Franka Bruns/AP/Press Association Images

Source: Michael Stephens/PA Archive/Press Association Images

Michael O'Leary (left) and Richard Branson (right) have both created very successful airline companies, but their organisational cultures and values are very different from each other.

This case examines two organisations that have many similarities as well as a number of significant differences. The essential technology and systems behind each organisation may be very similar, but the nature and style of management and its consequent impact on the way people working in these organisations think, feel and behave has created very different organisational cultures. So what are the similarities, and what are the differences?

The most obvious similarity is that both Virgin Atlantic and Ryanair operate in the UK passenger air transport industry. Virgin's air transport business was founded by Richard Branson in 1984[58] and Michael O'Leary took over as chief executive at Ryanair, a small Irish airline, in 1985.[59] Both started life in competition with major national flag-carrier airlines (British Airways and Aer Lingus respectively) and grew to be major challengers to these established companies. As they grew, their scale of operations brought them into competition with a much larger number and range of airlines operating from the UK: Branson's Virgin Atlantic competes with some major intercontinental companies such as American Airlines and Qantas; O'Leary competes with the likes of Flybe and EasyJet in the short-haul market. Both Branson, who was born in 1950, and O'Leary, who is ten years younger, are individuals with strong and distinctive personalities, who have a relentless appetite for media presence and who make extensive use of themselves in their frequent marketing communications. They are readily engaged in advertising stunts, often appear on the news media in relation to stories about the industry, and their faces and personalities are powerfully associated with their companies.

Charting different courses

There are, however, some major differences. Firstly, they differ in their choice of markets. Virgin's air transport business originated in the long-haul, mainly transatlantic market, which might be highly profitable but is also extremely competitive. As the business grew, offshoots were founded as independent companies – for instance, Virgin Australia and the ambitious project for the world's first spaceline, Virgin Galactic,[60] which remains live despite the loss of the first vehicle, Enterprise, in November 2014. Ryanair started as a short-haul carrier

→

and has remained so, focusing on European destinations from a small number of airports in the UK and Eire. Its competitive positioning is also very different. Ryanair is well known as 'The Low Cost Airline'; the first thing that hits you in its publicity material is the price[61] and this is very clearly the core of its business strategy. The 'no frills' approach means just that; even the in-flight food is limited to sandwiches and costs extra. Virgin, by contrast, attracts passengers by offering a superior experience and is firmly positioned at the quality end of the market. Publicity material emphasises style and comfort but with a touch of humour,[62] and there is a range of in-flight extras which, even at the economy end of the price range, includes a full meal and drinks service and a range of entertainment including e-books.

As was noted, both men love publicity stunts and often use humour in their public communications. Branson is usually smiling and in poses that indicate fun and a desire to show close links with his staff and popularity with employees, customers and the public in general. O'Leary is much more likely to be acerbic, critical and uses what might euphemistically be called 'colourful' language in his public statements. He seems to care little about public opinion of him as an individual, and has been in trouble with the Advertising Standards Authorities in the UK and Eire on more than one occasion. The appointment of Kenny Jacobs to head the company's first television advertising campaign in 2013, however, set Ryanair on a slightly different course. While still highlighting its low prices, the new (and cheaply shot) advertising campaign heralded the introduction of allocated seating, an additional carry-on bag and a slicker booking website. These moves, along with the cancellation of its annual 'girlie' calendar, suggested the company was aiming for a family market; and the continued rise in profits during 2014[63] showed that being 'nice' could indeed pay off.[64]

The brand values are also very different. Virgin, as a collection of businesses, does everything from running trains to selling wine via mobile phones and financial services. All these enterprises are linked by the single powerful central image of the founder and the characteristic red livery. Ryanair does one thing and one thing only, but in doing so sets an almost buccaneering tone, readily taking on authorities such as the British Airports Authority over its charging practices (characteristically direct, O'Leary observed that 'people have to pay £10 for the privilege of getting on and off this rain-sodden and weather-beaten island')[65] and European Union bureaucrats, for instance in a spectacularly damning account of EU competition policy in a speech at the EU's own Innovation Convention on 6 December 2011.[66] Branson has certainly had his conflicts with British Airways, notably over the 'dirty tricks' affair of the early 1990s, but is not likely to challenge governments. Virgin tries hard to build customer loyalty and gain repeat business through brand-related service values; Ryanair's repeat business (and for some customers the Ryanair experience is one that inspires the thought 'never again') is on price, not loyalty to the brand. These differences have a significant effect on the nature of employment relations and the psychological contract between the two companies and their employees.

Working for Richard and Michael

The brand image and the treatment of customers by each company have a bearing on the nature of organisational relationship with staff, and vice versa. Aspects of organisational behaviour therefore show through in a variety of interconnected ways to create consistent and very different cultures.

At Virgin Atlantic, cabin crew are there to be helpful and welcoming; they are important projectors of the brand image and their job is partly to encourage the all-important customer loyalty that generates continuing profit. The importance of staff as carriers of company values is clearly reflected in the recruitment material and other statements about the nature of work at Virgin Atlantic.

> *Virgin Atlantic brings together all manner of people in all manner of roles, all playing a crucial role in the smooth running of a very complex operation. But whoever you are and wherever you join us, you'll never stop thinking of our customers and what we can do for them. From frontline cabin crew to IT analysts, everyone here plays a role in delivering the Virgin brand. That means using initiative, taking responsibility for your actions and being ready to support those around you at all times. Similarly, you'll play your part in maintaining the friendly, unconventional professionalism that makes Virgin Atlantic such a unique place of work.*[67]

The recruitment process is lengthy and includes a group interview that acts as a filter for further tests before job offers are made. Training programmes for cabin crew and other staff are run from a dedicated training centre, and there is a wide range of benefits for full-time staff including seven free flights a year, private pensions and medical schemes and discounted goods and services across the Virgin group.

At Ryanair, the cabin crew start by working for a supplier organisation called Crewlink. You can discover if you qualify to apply for a job by answering a series of ten online questions. Successful applicants for cabin crew posts are trained at Crewlink's Hahn centre in Germany, and are expected to pay an upfront charge of €2,349 for the six-week course; or it can be offset against the initial year's salary at a total cost of €2,949. In either case, accommodation during the course is a further €700. Successful graduates get a three-year contract with Crewlink to work on Ryanair flights on a shift work basis and are not expected to have to make overnight stops at its destinations. Post-tax starting salary is said to be 'competitive', with experienced supervisory staff able to earn up to €30,000 pa. Staff must be flexible in terms of their work location across the thirty plus European centres, and Crewlink does not guarantee work if individuals specify a preferred work location.[68]

By comparison with long haul, a short-haul operation involves very tight turnaround times and Ryanair aims for twenty minutes. New aircraft have been commissioned with non-reclining seats that do not have magazine pockets (the required passenger safety instructions are fixed to seat backs), facilitating cleaning and cutting time on the ground. This creates a very different pace and set of pressures on the workforce compared with those at Virgin, which is likely to have higher staffing levels and to give crew longer rest breaks in the destination locations between flights. The nature of customer relations, by contrast, might be more demanding at Virgin than at Ryanair; staff and customers are together for longer and the brand image must be maintained.

Complaints and horror stories can be found about work at both organisations; however, Ryanair is subject to a more systematic and organised campaign of criticism for its employment practices by trade union organisations. In past years the International Transport Workers' Federation ran a major campaign on its website, the purpose of which was to pressurise the management at Ryanair into accepting the role of trade unions in representing the workforce - to no avail.

Both organisations have been successful. Ryanair continues to turn in significant profits in a sector that is prone to disruption and is holding its own during recession.[69] Virgin, unusually, suffered annual losses in 2012 and 2013, partly because of increased fuel costs, but has embarked on a two-year recovery programme and seems on course to return to profitability in 2015.[70] But the cultures and values that get them off the ground could hardly be more different.

Tasks

1 Some writers, such as Morgan, use metaphors to help us understand the nature of organisational behaviour. Identify one of Morgan's metaphors that you think might be applied appropriately to Virgin and one to Ryanair, and then develop two of your own, one for each organisation. How would you explain your choices?

2 Critically evaluate both organisations in terms of either social exchange theory or the notion of the psychological contract given in the chapter.

3 Identify the different demands that might be made of managers to achieve organisational effectiveness in each business (you could use Figure 1.6 as a framework). What are the implications for the role and development of managers in each case?

4 Ryanair has recently considered entering the transatlantic market, and Virgin set up 'Little Red', which operates short-haul domestic flights in the UK. What might be the implication of these changes for the management of cabin staff in each company?

Notes and references

1. 'MANAGEMENT 2020: Leadership to unlock long-term growth', The Commission on the future of management and leadership, CMI, July 2014, p. 14.
2. 'Introduction to Module 6, Organisational Behaviour', *Financial Times Mastering Management*, FT Pitman Publishing (1997), p. 216.
3. Vecchio, R. P. *Organizational Behavior: Core Concepts*, sixth edition, Dryden Press (2005).
4. See, for example, Billsberry, J. 'There's Nothing So Practical as a Good Theory: How Can Theory Help Managers Become More Effective?', in Billsberry, J. (ed.) *The Effective Manager: Perspectives and Illustrations*,

Sage (1996), pp. 1–27; and Naylor, J. *Management,* second edition, Financial Times Prentice Hall (2004), pp. 13–15.

5. McGregor, D. *The Human Side of Enterprise,* Penguin (1987), p. 6.
6. Patching, K. *Management and Organisation Development,* Macmillan Business (1999), p. 11.
7. Morgan, G. *Creative Organisation Theory,* Sage (1989), p. 26.
8. Drummond, H. *Introduction to Organisational Behaviour,* Oxford University Press (2000).
9. Morgan, G. *Creative Organisation Theory,* Sage (1989), p. 26.
10. Hellriegel, D., Slocum, J. W. and Woodman, R. W. *Organizational Behavior,* eighth edition, South-Western Publishing (1998), p. 5.
11. Egan, G. 'The Shadow Side', *Management Today,* September 1993, pp. 33–8.
12. Howes, L. 'The Real Workplace Battle', *Professional Manager,* Winter 2014, pp. 60–3.
13. Watson, T. J. *Organising and Managing Work,* second edition, Financial Times Prentice Hall (2006), p. 55.
14. Wilson, F. M. *Organisational Behaviour and Work: A Critical Introduction,* second edition, Oxford University Press (2004), pp. 1–2.
15. Bertrand Russell 'In Praise of Idleness' by Richard Nordquist, http://grammar.about.com/od/classicessays/a/praiseidleness.htm (accessed 27 June 2012).
16. 'Modern World of Work', BBC 2 Television, March 2011.
17. Donkin, R. *The Future of Work,* Palgrave Macmillan (2010).
18. Goldthorpe, J. H., Lockwood, D., Bechofer, F. and Platt, J. *The Affluent Worker,* Cambridge University Press (1968).
19. Bunting, M. *Willing Slaves,* HarperCollins (2004).
20. Stern, S. 'My Generation', *Management Today,* March 2008, pp. 40–6.
21. Waller, D. 'Are You What You Do?', *Management Today,* October 2008, pp. 42–6.
22. Reeves, R. 'Reality Bites', *Management Today,* March 2003, p. 35.
23. McCrum, M. *Going Dutch in Beijing,* Profile Books (2007), p. 153; see, for example, Robbins, S. P. and Judge, T. A. *Organizational Behavior,* thirteenth edition, Pearson Prentice Hall (2009).
24. Homans, G. C. 'Social Behaviour as Exchange', *American Journal of Sociology,* vol. 63, no. 6, 1958, pp. 597–606; see also Thibaut, J. W. and Kelley, H. H. *The Social Psychology of Groups,* Wiley (1959).
25. Blau, P. *Exchange and Power in Social Life,* Wiley (1964); see also Bacharach, S. B. and Lawler, E. J. *Power and Politics in Organizations,* Jossey-Bass (1980).
26. Stalker, K. 'The Individual, the Organisation and the Psychological Contract', *British Journal of Administrative Management,* July/August 2000, pp. 28–34.
27. Ghoshal, S., Bartlett, C. A. and Moran, P. 'Value Creation: The New Millennium Management Manifesto', in Chowdhury, S. (ed.) *Management21C,* Financial Times Prentice Hall (2000), pp. 121–40.
28. Peter, L. J. and Hull, R. *The Peter Principle,* Pan Books (1970), p. 22.
29. Ibid., p. 56.
30. Parkinson, C. N. *Parkinson's Law,* Penguin Modern Classics (2002), p. 14.
31. HRH The Duke of Edinburgh, 'Introduction' to Parkinson, C. N. *Parkinson's Law,* Penguin Modern Classics (2002), pp. 9–10.
32. Seligman, M. E. P. and Csikszentmihalyi, M. 'Positive Psychology: An introduction', *American Psychologist,* vol. 55, no. 1, 2000, pp. 5–14.
33. Peterson, C., Park, N. and Sweeney, P. J. 'Group Well-Being: Morale from a Positive Psychology Perspective', *Applied Psychology: An International Review,* vol. 57, 2008, p. 20.
34. Wong, T. P. and Davey, M. A. 'Best Practices in Servant Leadership', School of Global Leadership & Entrepreneurship, Regent University, July 2007; Gable, S. H. and Haidt, J. 'What (and Why) is Positive Psychology?', *Review of General Psychology,* vol. 9, no. 2, 2005, pp. 103–10.
35. Luthans, F. 'Positive organizational behaviour: Developing and managing psychological strengths', *Academy of Management Executive,* vol. 16, no. 1, 2002, pp. 57–72.
36. Donaldson, S. I and Ko, L. 'Positive organizational psychology, behaviour and scholarship: A review of emerging literature and evidence base', *Journal of Positive Psychology,* vol. 5, no. 3, 2010, pp. 177–91.
37. Wright, T. A. and Quick, J. C. 'The role of positive-based research in building the science of organizational behaviour', *Journal of Organizational Behavior,* vol. 30, 2009, pp. 329–36.
38. See, for example, Argyris, C. *Integrating the Individual and the Organisation,* Wiley (1964).
39. Gratton, L. *The Democratic Enterprise,* Financial Times Prentice Hall (2004), p. 208.
40. Wong, A. 'The role of emotional satisfaction in service encounters', *Managing Service Quality,* vol. 14, no. 5, 2004, pp. 365–76.
41. Child, J. *Organisation: Contemporary Principles and Practice,* Blackwell (2005), p. 30.
42. McLean, J. 'Globalisation Is Here to Stay', *Manager, The British Journal of Administrative Management,* June/July 2006, p. 16.
43. French, R. *Cross-Cultural Management in Work Organisations,* second edition, Chartered Institute of Personnel and Development (2010), p. 4.
44. See, for example, Slater, D. 'When in China . . . ', *Management Today,* May 2006, pp. 46–50.

45. Francesco, A. M. and Gold, B. A. *International Organizational Behavior,* second edition, Pearson Prentice Hall (2005), p. 140.
46. Hare, C. 'We need to embrace the opportunities international management brings', *Management Today,* May 2012, p. 62.
47. Schneider, S. C. and Barsoux, J, *Managing Across Cultures,* second edition, Financial Times Prentice Hall (2003) p. 167.
48. French, R. *Cross-Cultural Management in Work Organisations,* second edition, Chartered Institute of Personnel and Development (2010).
49. Brooks, I. *Organisational Behaviour: Individuals, Groups and Organisation,* fourth edition, Financial Times Prentice Hall (2009), p. 286.
50. Hofstede, G. *Culture's Consequences: International Differences in Work-Related Values,* Sage (1980).
51. Hofstede, G. and Bond, M. H. 'The Confucius Connection: From Cultural Roots to Economic Growth', *Organisational Dynamics,* Spring 1988, pp. 4–21.
52. Holden, N. J. *Cross-Cultural Management: A Knowledge Management Perspective,* Financial Times Prentice Hall (2002), p. 51.
53. Trompenaars, F. and Hampden-Turner, C. *Riding the Waves of Culture,* second edition, Nicholas Brearley (1999).
54. Hall, E. T. and Hall, M. R. *Understanding Cultural Differences,* Intercultural Press (1990).
55. Wood, J. 'Deep Roots and Far From a "Soft" Option', *Financial Times Mastering Management,* Financial Times Pitman Publishing (1997), p. 217.
56. Bennis, W. 'Foreword', in Cloke, K. and Goldsmith, J. *The End of Management and the Rise of Organisational Democracy,* Jossey-Bass (2002), p. ix.
57. Robbins, S. P. and Judge, T. A. *Organizational Behavior,* thirteenth edition, Pearson Prentice Hall (2009) p. 50.
58. Virgin Atlantic, 'All About Us', http://www.virgin-atlantic.com/en/us/allaboutus/ourstory/history.jsp
59. Creaton, S. *Ryanair – How a Small Irish Airline Conquered Europe*, Aurum (2004).
60. Virgin Galactic, http://www.virgingalactic.com/
61. For instance, at the Ryanair website www.ryanair.com
62. For instance, see its James Bond parody of 2011; or the 'Lion's Den' advert for business travellers, http://www.virgin-atlantic.com/gb/en/the-virgin-experience/let-it-fly.html
63. Ryanair Corporate, http://corporate.ryanair.com/news/news/150202-ryanair-reports-q3-profit-of-49m-guidance-rises-to-840m-850m/?market=en
64. Topham, G. 'Nicely does it', *Guardian,* 23 December 2014, http://www.theguardian.com/business/2014/dec/23/ryanair-richly-rewarded-transformation
65. Allen, K. 'Ryanair reduces Stansted flights by 14%', *Guardian,* 22 July 2009, p. 24.
66. Available on YouTube, http://www.youtube.com/watch?v=p4HYSsrlcq8&list=PL70F799CB0BB756EE&index=2&feature=plpp_video
67. Virgin Atlantic, 'Working for Us', http://www.virgin-atlantic.com/en/gb/careers/workingforus/index.jsp
68. Crewlink, www.crewlink.ie
69. Ryanair website, Investor pages, http://corporate.ryanair.com
70. Virgin Atlantic corporate website press releases, http://www.virgin-atlantic.com/gb/en/footer/media-centre/press-releases/financial-results.html

CHAPTER 2
Approaches to organisation and management

Organisational behaviour is a discursive subject and much has been written about it. The study of organisations, their structure and management has therefore to proceed on a broad front. The comparative analysis of different approaches will yield benefits to the manager. Identification of major trends in management and organisational theory, and the work of leading writers, provide a perspective on concepts and ideas discussed in more detail in other chapters.

Learning outcomes

After completing this chapter you should have enhanced your ability to:

- provide a framework in which to study different approaches to organisation and management;
- identify major trends in the development of organisational behaviour and management thinking;
- evaluate the relevance of different approaches to present-day work organisations;
- debate the significance and value of the idea of postmodernism;
- assess the relevance of study of different approaches to organisation and management;
- debate benefits of management theory and influences on management practice;
- establish a basis for consideration of aspects of management and organisational behaviour discussed in subsequent chapters.

Critical review and reflection

Criticism of the study of theory or history of management is misjudged. More attention to the ideas of leading writers, and to evolutions in management and organisational behaviour, would help improve understanding and performance.

How would YOU attempt to defend this assertion to a group of sceptical managers? What benefits do YOU expect to gain from a study of management theory?

Developments in management and organisational behaviour

A central part of the study of organisational behaviour is the development of management thinking and what might be termed management theory. (**See also Chapter 1.**) Managers reading the work of leading writers on the subject might see in their thoughts, ideas and conclusions a message about how they should behave. This will influence their attitudes towards management practice and bring about change in behaviour.

Writing on organisation and management, in some form or another, can be traced back thousands of years.[1] Also, *Shafritz* makes an interesting observation about the contribution of William Shakespeare (1564–1616):

> *While William Shakespeare's contribution to literature and the development of the English language have long been acknowledged and thoroughly documented, his contribution to the theory of management and administration have been all but ignored. This is a surprising oversight when you consider that many of his plays deal with issues of personnel management and organizational behavior.*[2]

However, the systematic development of management thinking is viewed, generally, as dating from the end of the nineteenth century with the emergence of large industrial organisations and the ensuing problems associated with their structure and management.[3]

Importance of management theory

The study of management theory is important for the following reasons:

- It helps to view the interrelationships between the development of theory, behaviour in organisations and management practice.
- An understanding of the development of management thinking helps in understanding principles underlying the actual process of management and reasons for the attention given to main topic areas.
- Management theories are interpretive and evolve in line with changes in the organisational environment.
- Many of the earlier ideas are of continuing importance to the manager and later ideas on management tend to incorporate earlier ideas and conclusions.

However, if action is to be effective, the theory must be adequate and appropriate to the task and to improved organisational performance. It must be a 'good' theory. To be of any help to the practising manager, theory has to be appropriate. For example, *Lee* refers to:

> *the danger of adopting theories because they are teachable, rather than because they are effective . . . [however,] without appropriate theory, there would be very little communication of the insights of scientific theory to practising managers.*[4]

Crainer points out that although management is active, not theoretical, it is nothing without ideas.

> *Nothing is so practical as a good theory. Ideas drive management as surely as the immediate problems which land on managers' desks or which arrive via their e-mail. Decisions have to be based on ideas as well as instinct. Without ideas managers flit desperately from crisis to crisis. They cannot know where they are going, why they are doing something or what they will achieve, without the vital fuel of ideas.*[5]

Framework of analysis

In order to help identify the main trends in the development of organisational behaviour and management theory, it is helpful to categorise the ideas and work of writers into various 'approaches', based on their views of organisations, their structure and management.

Management theory is a complex area of study in which it is possible to identify a large number of writers and a wide range of comparative and/or conflicting points of view.

There are, therefore, many ways of categorising the various approaches. For example, *Skipton* attempts a classification of eleven main schools of management theory.[6] Whatever form of categorisation is adopted, it is possible to identify a number of other approaches, or at least sub-divisions of approaches, and cross-grouping among the various approaches. The choice of a particular categorisation is therefore largely at the discretion of the observer and the demands of the reader.

For convenience, the following analysis revolves around a framework based on four main approaches, shown in Figure 2.1. Although a simplistic process, it provides a useful framework in which to direct study and focus attention on the progression of ideas concerned with improving organisational performance:

- classical – including scientific management and bureaucracy;
- human relations – including neo-human relations;
- systems;
- contingency.

Attention is also drawn to other 'approaches' or ideas, including technology, decision-making, social action and postmodernism. *See* Figure 2.3 below.

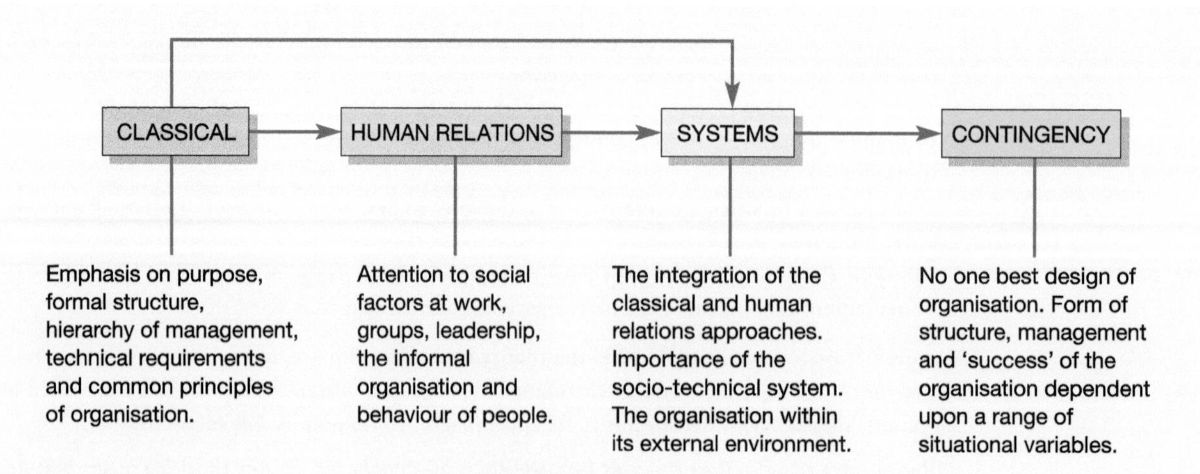

Figure 2.1 Main approaches to organisation, structure and management

Critical review and reflection

It is often claimed that what leading writers say is an important part of the study of management and organisational behaviour. Others say these different ideas are too abstract, are little more than short-term fads and have little practical value.

What do YOU think? To what extent do YOU expect to learn about the realities of management and organisational behaviour from the work of leading writers?

The classical approach

The **classical** writers thought of the organisation in terms of its purpose and formal structure. Emphasis is on planning of work, technical requirements of the organisation, principles of management, and the assumption of rational and logical behaviour. The analysis of organisation in this manner is associated with work carried out initially in the early part of the last century, by such writers as Taylor, Fayol, Urwick and Brech. Such writers were laying the foundation for a comprehensive theory of management.

A clear understanding of the purpose of an organisation is seen as essential to understanding how the organisation works and how its methods of working can be improved. Identification of general objectives would lead to the clarification of purpose and responsibilities at all levels of the organisation and to the most effective structure. Attention is given to division of work, clear definition of duties and responsibilities, and maintaining specialisation and co-ordination. Emphasis is on a hierarchy of management and formal organisational relationships.

Sets of principles

The classical writers (also variously known as the formal or scientific management writers – although scientific management is really only a part of the **classical approach**) were concerned with improving the organisation structure as a means of increasing efficiency. They emphasised the importance of principles for the design of a logical structure of organisation. Their writings were in a normative style and they saw these principles as a set of 'rules' offering general solutions to common problems of organisation and management. Most classical writers had their own set of principles but among the most publicised are those of *Fayol* and *Urwick*.

Fayol identified five managerial activities: planning, organising, command, co-ordination and control, together with a set of principles of management. Fayol recognised that there was no limit to the principles of management but in his writing advocated fourteen[7] (**as discussed in Chapter 10**).

Urwick originally specified eight principles of the requirements of the formal organisation, but these were revised to ten in his later writing.[8]

Brech attempts to provide a practical approach to organisation structure based on tried general principles as opposed to concentration on specific cases or complex generalisations of little value to the practising manager. He sets out the various functions in the organisation and the definition of formal organisational relationships.[9] Although clearly a strong supporter of the formal approach in some of his views such as, for example, on the principle of span of control, Brech is less definite than other classical writers and recognises a degree of flexibility according to the particular situation.

Brech does place great emphasis, however, on the need for the written definition of responsibilities and the value of job descriptions as an aid to effective organisation and delegation. This work builds on the ideas of earlier writers, such as Urwick, and therefore provides a comprehensive view of the classical approach to organisation and management.

Evaluation of the classical approach

The classical writers have been criticised generally for not taking sufficient account of social factors and for creating an organisation structure in which people can exercise only limited control over their work environment. The idea of sets of principles to guide managerial action has also been subject to much criticism. For example, *Simon* writes:

> *Organisational design is not unlike architectural design. It involves creating large, complex systems having multiple goals. It is illusory to suppose that good designs can be created by using the so-called principles of classical organisation theory.*[10]

Research studies have also expressed doubt about the effectiveness of these principles when applied in practice.[11]

However, the classical approach prompted the start of a more systematic view of management and attempted to provide some common principles applicable to all organisations. These principles are still of relevance in that they offer a useful starting point in attempting to analyse the effectiveness of the design of organisation structure. However, the application of these principles must take full account of the particular situational variables of each individual organisation and the psychological and social factors relating to members of the organisation.

Major sub-groupings

Two major 'sub-groupings' of the classical approach are **scientific management** and bureaucracy.

Critical review and reflection

Whatever the nature of modern organisations, attention must still be given to essential principles of effective structure and management. Any criticism should be directed not at the need for such principles but at the manner in which they are implemented by managers.

What is YOUR view? How effectively are the principles of structure and management applied in YOUR university or organisation?

Scientific management

Many of the classical writers were concerned with the improvement of management as a means of increasing productivity. Emphasis was on the problem of obtaining increased productivity from individual workers through the technical structuring of the work organisation and the provision of monetary incentives as the motivator for higher levels of output. A major contributor to this approach was *F. W. Taylor* (1856–1917), the 'father' of scientific management.[12] Taylor believed that in the same way that there is a best machine for each job, so there is a best working method by which people should undertake their jobs. All work processes could be analysed into discrete tasks and that by scientific method it was possible to find the 'one best way' to perform each task. Each job was broken down into component parts, each part timed and the parts rearranged into the most efficient method of working.

Principles to guide management

Taylor was concerned with finding more efficient methods and procedures for co-ordination and control of work, and a believer in the rational–economic needs concept of motivation. If management acted on his ideas, work would become more satisfying and profitable for all concerned. Workers would be motivated by obtaining the highest possible wages through working in the most efficient and productive way. He set out a number of principles to guide management. These principles are usually summarised as:

- the development of a true science for each person's work;
- the scientific selection, training and development of workers;
- co-operation with workers to ensure work is carried out in the prescribed way;
- hierarchical structures of authority and close supervision;
- clear division of tasks and responsibility between management and workers.

In his famous studies at the Bethlehem Steel Corporation, Taylor applied his ideas on scientific management to a group of seventy-five men loading pig iron. Taylor selected a Dutch labourer, Schmidt, whom he reported as a 'high-priced' man with a reputation for placing a high value on money, and of limited mental ability. By following detailed instructions on when to pick up the pig iron and walk, and when to sit and rest, and with no back talk, Schmidt increased his output from 12½ tons to 47½ tons per day. He maintained this level of output throughout the three years of the study. In return Schmidt received a 60 per cent increase in wages compared with what was paid to the other men. One by one other workers were selected and trained to handle pig iron at the rate of 47½ tons per day and in return they received 60 per cent more wages. Taylor drew attention to the need for the scientific selection of the workers. When the other labourers in the group were trained in the same method, only one in eight was physically capable of the effort of loading 47½ tons per day, although there was a noticeable increase in their level of output.

Reactions against scientific management

There were strong criticisms of, and reaction against, scientific management methods from the workers who found the work boring and requiring little skill. Despite these criticisms, Taylor attempted to expand the implementation of his ideas in the Bethlehem Steel Corporation. However, fears of mass redundancies persuaded the management to request Taylor to moderate his activities. Yet Taylor's belief in his methods was so strong that he would not accept management's interference and eventually they dispensed with his services. Continued resentment and hostility against scientific management led to an investigation of Taylor's methods by a House of Representatives Committee, which reported in 1912. The conclusion of the committee was that scientific management did provide some useful techniques and offered valuable organisational suggestions, but gave production managers a dangerously high level of uncontrolled power.

Taylorism as management control

Taylor placed emphasis on the content of a 'fair day's work' and optimising the level of workers' productivity. A major obstacle to this objective was 'systematic soldiering' and what Taylor saw as the deliberate attempt by workers to promote their best interests and to keep employers ignorant of how fast work, especially piece-rate work, could be carried out.

According to *Braverman,* scientific management starts from the capitalist point of view and method of production, and the adaptation of labour to the needs of capital. Taylor's work was more concerned with the organisation of labour than with the development of technology. A distinctive feature of Taylor's thought was the concept of management control.[13] Braverman suggests Taylor's conclusion was that workers should be controlled not only by the giving of orders and maintenance of discipline, but also by removing from them any decisions about the manner in which their work was to be carried out. By division of labour, and by dictating precise stages and methods for every aspect of work performance, management could gain control of the actual process of work. The rationalisation of production processes and division of labour tends to result in the de-skilling of work and this may be a main strategy of the employer.[14]

Cloke and Goldsmith also suggest that Taylor was the leading promoter of the idea that managers should design and control the work process scientifically in order to guarantee maximum efficiency. He believed in multiple layers of management to supervise the work process and in rigid, detailed control of the workforce.

> *Taylor's theories justified managerial control over the production process and removed decision making from employees and from owners as well. The increasingly authoritative operational role of management diminished the direct involvement of owners in day-to-day decision making. Managers saw this as an opportunity to solidify their power and adopted Taylor's ideas wholesale. In the process, they affirmed efficiency over collaboration, quantity over quality, and cost controls over customer service.*[15]

Relevance of scientific management

Taylor's work is often criticised today, but it should be remembered that he was writing at a time of industrial reorganisation and the emergence of large, complex organisations with new forms of technology. He believed his methods would lead to improved management–labour relations and contribute to improved industrial efficiency and prosperity. Workers were regarded as rational–economic, motivated directly by monetary incentives linked to the level of work output.

Among the criticisms are those by *Rose*. Taylor regarded workers from an engineering viewpoint and as machines, but the one best way of performing a task is not always the best method for every worker. The reduction of physical movement to find the one best way is not always beneficial and some 'wasteful' movements are essential to the overall rhythm of work. Rose also argues that the concept of a fair day's pay for a fair day's work is not purely a technical matter. It is also a notion of social equity and not in keeping with a scientific approach.[16]

According to *Drucker*, however, the central theme of Taylor's work was not inefficiency but the need to substitute industrial warfare with industrial harmony. Taylor sought to do this through:

- higher wages from increased output;
- the removal of physical strain from doing work the wrong way;
- development of the workers and the opportunity for them to undertake tasks they were capable of doing; and
- elimination of the 'boss' and the duty of management to help workers.

> *Frederick Winslow Taylor may prove a more useful prophet for our times than we yet recognize . . . Taylor's greatest impact may still be ahead . . . the under-developed and developing countries are now reaching the stage where they need Taylor and 'scientific management' . . . But the need to study Taylor anew and apply him may be the greatest in the developed countries.*[17]

Impetus to management thinking

Whatever the opinions on scientific management, Taylor and his disciples left to modern management the legacy of such practices as work study, organisation and methods, payment by results, management by exception and production control.

Taylor did give a major impetus to the development of management thinking and the later development of organisational behaviour. For example, *Crainer and Dearlove* suggest that although Taylor's theories are now largely outdated, they still had a profound impact throughout the world and his mark can be seen on much of the subsequent management literature.[18]And *Stern* goes a stage further:

> *The 'scientific management' of Frederick Taylor . . . shaped the first coherent school of thought with application to the industrialised world. He was our first professional guru and Taylorism – with its twin goals of productivity and efficiency – still influences management thinking 100 years on.*[19]

Principles of Taylor's scientific approach to management appear still to have relevance today. We can see examples of Taylorism alive and well, and management practices based on the philosophy of his ideas. As an example, large hotel organisations often make use of standard recipes and standard performance manuals, and it is common for housekeeping staff to have a prescribed layout for each room, with training based on detailed procedures and the one best way. Staff may be expected to clean a given number of rooms per shift, with financial incentives for additional rooms.[20]

Modern customer call centres can also be seen to exhibit many features of Taylorism.[21] The strict routine, uniformity, clearly specified tasks, detailed checklists and close control in fast food restaurants such as McDonald's also suggest close links with scientific management.

It is difficult to argue against the general line of Taylor's principles but they are subject to misuse. What is important is the context and manner in which such principles are put into effect. There is arguably one best way *technically* to perform a job – for example, with factory assembly line production in particular. However, account needs to be taken of human behaviour. People tend to have their preferred way of working and the need for variety and more interesting or challenging tasks. Provided work is carried out safely and to a satisfactory standard and completed on time, to what extent should management *insist* on the 'one best way'?

It seems that Taylor did not so much ignore (as is often suggested) but was more *unaware* of the complexity of human behaviour in organisations and the importance of the individual's feelings and sentiments, group working, managerial behaviour and the work environment. However, we now have greater knowledge about social effects within the work organisation and about the value of money, incentives, motivation, and job satisfaction and performance.

Critical review and reflection

Despite strong criticisms of scientific management, in the right circumstances the underlying concepts still have relevance and much to offer work organisations today. It is just that many commentators appear reluctant to admit this openly.

What do YOU think? Where do YOU think scientific management could be applied to the best overall effect in YOUR university or organisation?

Bureaucracy

A form of structure to be found in many large-scale organisations is **bureaucracy**. *Weber*, a German sociologist, showed particular concern for what he called 'bureaucratic structures', although his work in this area came almost as a side issue to his main study on power and authority.[22] He suggested that 'the decisive reason for the advance of bureaucratic organization has always been its purely technical superiority over any other form of organization'. Weber pointed out that the definition of tasks and responsibilities within the structure of management gave rise to a permanent administration and standardisation of work procedures, notwithstanding changes in the actual holders of office.

The term 'bureaucracy' has common connotations with criticism of red tape and rigidity, though in the study of organisations and management it is important that the term is seen not necessarily in a depreciative sense but as applying to certain structural features of formal organisations. Weber analysed bureaucracies not empirically but as an 'ideal type' derived from the most characteristic bureaucratic features of all known organisations. He saw the development of bureaucracies as a means of introducing order and rationality into social life.

Main characteristics of bureaucracies

Weber did not actually define bureaucracy but did attempt to identify the main characteristics of this type of organisation. He emphasised the importance of administration based on expertise (rules of experts) and administration based on discipline (rules of officials).

- The tasks of the organisation are allocated as official duties among the various positions.
- There is an implied clear-cut division of labour and a high level of specialisation.
- A hierarchical authority applies to the organisation of offices and positions.
- Uniformity of decisions and actions is achieved through formally established systems of rules and regulations. Together with a structure of authority, this enables the co-ordination of various activities within the organisation.
- An impersonal orientation is expected from officials in their dealings with clients and other officials. This is designed to result in rational judgements by officials in the performance of their duties.
- Employment by the organisation is based on technical qualifications and constitutes a lifelong career for the officials.[23]

The four main features of bureaucracy are summarised by *Stewart* as **specialisation, hierarchy of authority, system of rules** and **impersonality.** Stewart sees the characteristic of impersonality as the feature of bureaucracy that most distinguishes it from other types of organisations. A bureaucracy should not only be impersonal but be seen to be impersonal.[24]

Robbins and Judge emphasise standardisation as the key concept that underlies all bureaucracies.

> *The bureaucracy is characterized by highly routine operating tasks achieved through specialization, very formalized rules and regulations, tasks that are grouped into functional departments, centralized authority, narrow spans of control, and decision making that follows the chain of command . . . However, it does have its advantages. The primary strength of the bureaucracy lies in its ability to perform standardized activities in a highly efficient manner.*[25]

Criticisms of bureaucracy

Weber's concept of bureaucracy has a number of disadvantages and has been subject to severe criticism:

- The over-emphasis on rules and procedures, record keeping and paperwork may become more important in its own right than as a means to an end.
- Officials may develop a dependence upon bureaucratic status, symbols and rules.
- Initiative may be stifled, and when a situation is not covered by a complete set of rules or procedures there may be a lack of flexibility or adaptation to changing circumstances.
- Position and responsibilities in the organisation can lead to officious bureaucratic behaviour. There may also be a tendency to conceal administrative procedures from outsiders.
- Impersonal relations can lead to stereotyped behaviour and a lack of responsiveness to individual incidents or problems.

Restriction of psychological growth

One of the strongest critics of bureaucratic organisation, and the demands it makes on the worker, is *Argyris.*[26] He claims that bureaucracies restrict the psychological growth of the individual and cause feelings of failure, frustration and conflict. Argyris suggests that the organisational environment should provide a significant degree of individual responsibility and self-control, commitment to the goals of the organisation, productiveness, and work and an opportunity for individuals to apply their full abilities.

A similar criticism is made by *Caulkin*, who refers to the impersonal structure of bureaucracy as constructed round the post rather than the person and the ease with which it can be swung behind unsocial or even pathological ends.

> *The overemphasis on process rather than purpose, fragmented responsibilities and hierarchical control means that it's all too easy for individuals to neglect the larger purposes to which their small effort is being put.*[27]

A number of writers refer to 'adhocracy' as the opposite of bureaucracy. **Adhocracy** is a flexible, loosely structured, adaptable, organic and informal form of organisation. According to *Morgan*, adhocracy is an organic form of organisation, highly suited for the performance of complex and uncertain tasks. It is frequently used for research and development.[28] *Waterman* sees adhocracy as any form of organisation that cuts across normal bureaucratic lines to capture opportunities, solve problems and get results.[29] *Mintzberg* views adhocracy as the project organisations build around project teams of experts, with senior managers linking and dealing to secure the projects.[30]

Critical review and reflection

It is difficult to envisage how large-scale organisations, especially within the public sector, could function effectively without exhibiting at least some of the features of a bureaucracy. Demands for alternative forms of structure are unrealistic.

How would YOU attempt to justify the benefits of bureaucratic structures? To what extent would YOU be comfortable working in a bureaucratic organisation?

Evaluation of bureaucracy

Growth of bureaucracy has come through the increasing size and complexity of organisations and associated demand for effective administration. Effective organisation is based on structure and delegation through different layers of the hierarchy. The work of the classical writers has given emphasis to the careful design and planning of organisation structure and the definition of individual duties and responsibilities. Greater specialisation and the application of expertise and technical knowledge have highlighted the need for laid-down procedures.

Bureaucracy is founded on a formal, clearly defined and hierarchical structure. However, with rapid changes in the external environment, de-layering of organisations, empowerment and greater attention to meeting the needs of customers, there is an increasing need to organise for flexibility. For example, the crisis IBM experienced in the 1980s/1990s over the market for personal computers is explained at least in part by its top-heavy corporate structure, cumbersome organisation and dinosaur-like bureaucracy.[31]

According to *Cloke and Goldsmith*, management and bureaucracy can be thought of as flip sides of the same coin. The elements of bureaucracy generate organisational hierarchy and management, while managers generate a need for bureaucracy.

> *Bureaucracies provide a safe haven where managers can hide from responsibility and avoid being held accountable for errors of judgement or problems they created or failed to solve. In return, managers are able to use bureaucratic rules to stifle self-management and compel employees to follow their direction . . . Yet bureaucratic systems can be broken down and transformed into human-scale interactions. We have seen countless managers recreate themselves as leaders and facilitators, employees reinvent themselves as responsible self-managing*

team members, and bureaucracies transform into responsive, human-scale organizations. Alternatives to organizational hierarchy are both practical and possible.[32]

By their very nature, bureaucracies have always tended to attract criticism. Much of this criticism is valid, but much also appears unfair. For example, according to *Drucker:*

Whenever a big organization gets into trouble – and especially if it has been successful for many years – people blame sluggishness, complacency, arrogance, mammoth bureaucracies. A plausible explanation? Yes. But rarely the relevant or correct one.[33]

Need for alternative structures

As organisations face increasing global competitiveness and complex demands of the information and technological age, the need arises for alternative forms of corporate structure and systems. For example, there appears to be a particular dilemma for management in personal service industries. The underlying characteristics of bureaucracy would seem to restrict personal service delivery, which requires a flexible approach, responsiveness to individual requirements and the need for initiative and inventiveness.[34]

Ridderstråle points out that in the past century the hallmark of a large company was hierarchy, which rests on principles at odds with the new strategic requirements. 'Bureaucracies allowed people with knowledge to control ignorant workers. Now, new structures are needed as knowledge spreads.' Ridderstråle suggests four specific ways in which high-performing organisations have responded to increasingly complex knowledge systems by developing organisational solutions that depart from the traditional bureaucratic model:

- more decentralised and flatter structures in order that quick decisions can be taken near to where the critical knowledge resides;
- the use of more than a single structure in order that knowledge may be assembled across the boundaries of a traditional organisation chart;
- converting companies into learning organisations and giving every employee the same level of familiarity with personnel and capabilities;
- broader sharing of expertise and knowledge, which may be located in the periphery where little formal authority resides.[35]

Stewart suggests that more organisations today contain mainly, or a considerable number of, professionals. Such organisations will still have bureaucratic features, but there is more reliance on professional discretion and self-regulation than on control through rules and regulations.[36]

Public-sector organisations

However, despite new forms of organisation that have emerged, many writers suggest that bureaucracy is still relevant today as a major form of organisation structure.[37] In the case of public-sector organisations, in particular, there is a demand for uniformity of treatment, regularity of procedures and public accountability for their operations. This leads to adherence to specified rules and procedures and to the keeping of detailed records. In their actual dealings with public-sector organisations, people often call for what amounts to increased bureaucracy, even though they may not use that term. The demands for equal treatment, for a standard set of regulations that applies to everyone and that decisions should not be left to the discretion of individual managers are, in effect, demands for bureaucracy.

Green argues that, although bureaucracies are becoming less and less the first-choice format for organisational shape, there is still a place for bureaucracy in parts of most organisations and especially public-sector organisations such as local authorities and universities. The use and implementation of tried and tested rules and procedures helps to ensure essential values and ethics, and that necessary functions are run on a consistent and fair basis.[38] New forms of information technology, such as electronic transactions processed from home or public access terminals, are likely to change processes of government service delivery, administrative workloads and the nature of bureaucracy.[39]

Human relations approach

The main emphasis of the classical writers was on structure and the formal organisation, but during the 1920s greater attention began to be paid to the social factors at work and to the behaviour of employees within an organisation – that is, the **human relations approach.**

The Hawthorne studies

The turning point in the development of the human relations movement ('behavioural' and 'informal' are alternative headings) came with the famous studies at the Hawthorne plant of the Western Electric Company near Chicago (1924–32) and the subsequent publication of the research findings.[40] Among the people who wrote about the Hawthorne studies was Elton Mayo (1880–1949), who is often quoted as having been a leader of the researchers. However, there appears to be some doubt as to the extent of Mayo's actual involvement.[41]

There were four main phases to the Hawthorne studies:

- the illumination experiments;
- the relay assembly test room;
- the interviewing programme;
- the bank wiring observation room.

Illumination experiments

The original investigation was conducted on the lines of the classical approach and was concerned, in typical scientific management style, with the effects of the intensity of lighting upon the workers' productivity. The workers were divided into two groups, an experimental group and a control group. The results of these tests were inconclusive as production in the experimental group varied with no apparent relationship to the level of lighting, but actually increased when conditions were made much worse. Production also increased in the control group although the lighting remained unchanged. The level of production was influenced, clearly, by factors other than changes in physical conditions of work. This prompted a series of other experiments investigating factors of worker productivity.

Relay assembly test room

In the relay assembly test room the work was boring and repetitive. It involved assembling telephone relays by putting together a number of small parts. Six women workers were transferred from their normal departments to a separate area. Researchers selected two assemblers who were friends, then chose three other assemblers and a layout operator. The experiment was divided into thirteen periods during which the workers were subjected to a series of planned and controlled changes to their conditions of work, such as hours of work, rest pauses and provision of refreshments. The general environmental conditions of the test room were similar to those of the normal assembly line.

During the experiment the observer adopted a friendly manner, consulting the workers, listening to their complaints and keeping them informed. Following all but one of the changes (when operators complained that too many breaks made them lose their work rhythm) there was a continuous increase in the level of production. The researchers formed the conclusion that the extra attention given to the workers and the apparent interest in them shown by management were the main reasons for the higher productivity. This has become famous as the 'Hawthorne effect'.

Interviewing programme

Another significant phase of the experiments was the interviewing programme. The lighting experiment and the relay assembly test room drew attention to the form of supervision as a contributory factor to the workers' level of production. In an attempt to find out more about the workers' feelings towards their supervisors and their general conditions of work, a large interviewing programme was introduced. More than 20,000 interviews were conducted before the work was ended because of the Depression.

Initially, interviewers approached their task with a set of prepared questions, relating mainly to how the workers felt about their jobs. However, this produced only limited information. As a result, the style of interviewing was changed to become more non-directive and open ended. There was no set list of questions and the workers were free to talk about any aspect of their work. The interviewers set out to be friendly and sympathetic. They adopted an impartial, non-judgemental approach and concentrated on listening.

Using this approach, interviewers found out far more about workers' true feelings and attitudes. They gained information not just about supervision and working conditions, but also about the company itself, management, work group relations and matters outside of work such as family life and views on society in general. Many workers appeared to welcome the opportunity to have someone to talk to about their feelings and problems and to be able to 'let off steam' in a friendly atmosphere. The interviewing programme was significant in giving an impetus to present-day human resource management and the use of counselling interviews, and highlighting the need for management to listen to workers' feelings and problems. Being a good listener is arguably even more important for managers in today's work organisations and it is a skill that needs to be encouraged and developed.[42]

Bank wiring observation room

Another experiment involved the observation of a group of fourteen men working in the bank wiring room. It was noted that the men formed their own informal organisation with sub-groups or cliques, and natural leaders emerging with the consent of the members. The group developed its own pattern of informal social relations and 'norms' of what constituted 'proper' behaviour. Despite a financial incentive scheme where the workers could receive more money the more work produced, the group decided on a level of output well below the level they were capable of producing. Group pressures on individual workers were stronger than financial incentives offered by management. The workers believed that if they increased their output, management would raise the standard level of piece rates. The importance of group 'norms' and informal social relations are discussed later (**see Chapter 8**).

Evaluation

The Hawthorne studies have received much criticism, for example on methodology and on failure of the investigators to take sufficient account of environmental factors – although much of this criticism is with the value of hindsight. The human relations writers have been criticised generally for the adoption of a management perspective, their 'unitary frame of reference' and their over-simplified theories.[43] Other criticisms of the human relations approach are that it is insufficiently scientific and that it takes too narrow a view. It ignores the role of the organisation itself in how society operates.

Sex power differential

There are a number of interpretations of the results of the Hawthorne studies, including the possible implications of the 'sex power differential' between the two groups. In the bank wiring room, where output was restricted, the group was all male. In the relay assembly room, where output increased, all members were young unmarried women. All except one were living at home with traditional families of immigrant background. In the work environment of the factory, women had been subjected to frequent contact with male supervisors and therefore 'the sex power hierarchies in the home and in the factory were congruent'. It is suggested, therefore, that it was only to be expected that the women agreed readily to participate with management in the relay assembly test room experiment.[44]

Importance of the Hawthorne studies

Whatever the interpretation of the Hawthorne studies, they generated significant new ideas concerning the importance of work groups and leadership, communications, output restrictions, motivation and job design. The studies undoubtedly marked a significant step forward in providing further insight into human behaviour at work and the development of management thinking. They are regarded as one of the most important of social science investigations and the foundation of the human relations approach to management and the development of organisational behaviour.

Supporters of the classical approach adopted a more managerial perspective and sought to increase production by rationalisation of the work organisation. By contrast, the human relations movement has led to ideas on increasing production by humanising the work organisation and strove for a greater understanding of people's psychological and social needs at work as well as improving the process of management.

Recognition of the informal organisation

The human relations approach also recognised the importance of the informal organisation, which will always be present within the formal structure. This informal organisation will influence the motivation of employees who will view the organisation for which they work through the values and attitudes of their colleagues. Their view of the organisation determines their approach to work and the extent of their motivation to work well or otherwise.

In a review of humane approaches to management, *Crainer* asserts: 'The Hawthorne Studies were important because they showed that views of how managers behaved were a vital aspect of motivation and improved performance. Also, the research revealed the importance of informal work groups.'[45]

Human relations writers demonstrated that people go to work to satisfy a complexity of needs and not simply for monetary reward. These writers emphasised the importance of the wider social needs of individuals and gave recognition to the work organisation as a social organisation and the importance of the group, and group values and norms, in influencing individual behaviour at work. It has been commented that the classical school was concerned about 'organisations without people' and the human relations school about 'people without organisations'.

Critical review and reflection

The human relations approach makes all the right noises, with an emphasis on humane behaviour, considerate management and recognition of the informal organisation. However, it is more about what people would like to believe and ignores the realities of the actual working environment.

What is YOUR opinion? To what extent have YOU experienced a genuine human relations approach in a work organisation?

Neo-human relations

Certainly there were shortcomings in the human relations approach, and assumptions that evolved from studies such as the Hawthorne studies were not necessarily supported by empirical evidence. For example, the contention that a satisfied worker is a productive worker was not always found to be valid. However, the results of the studies and subsequent attention given to the social organisation and to theories of individual motivation gave rise to the work of those writers in the 1950s and 1960s who adopted a more psychological orientation. New ideas on management theory arose and a major focus of concern was the personal adjustment of the individual within the work organisation and the effects of group relationships and leadership styles.

This group of writers is often (and more correctly) categorised separately under the heading of **neo-human relations.** The works of these writers are examined later in more detail (**in Chapter 7 and Chapter 10**) but summarised briefly here.

Some leading contributors

A major impetus for the neo-human relations approach was the work of *Maslow* who, in 1943, put forward a theoretical framework of individual personality development and motivation based on a hierarchy of five levels of human needs: physiological, safety, love, esteem and self-actualisation at the highest level.[46] The work of Maslow provides a link with the earlier human relations approach.

Among the best-known contributors to the neo-human relations approach are *Herzberg* and *McGregor.* Herzberg isolated two different sets of factors affecting motivation and satisfaction at work. One set of factors comprises those that, if absent, cause dissatisfaction, and concerned basically the job environment. However, to motivate workers to give of their best, proper attention must be given to a different set of factors, the 'motivators' or 'growth' factors concerned with job content.[47] McGregor argued that the style of management adopted is a function of the manager's attitudes towards human nature and behaviour at work. He put forward two suppositions called Theory X and Theory Y, which are based on popular assumptions about work and people.[48]

Other major contributors to the neo-human relations approach are *Likert,* whose work includes research into different systems of management;[49] *McClelland,* with ideas on achievement motivation;[50] and *Argyris,* who considered the effects of the formal organisation on the individual and psychological growth in the process of self-actualisation.[51] Argyris's major contributions include his work on organisational learning and on effective leadership.[52]

The neo-human relations approach has generated a large amount of writing and research, not only from original proposers but also from others seeking to establish the validity of their ideas. This has led to continuing attention given to such matters as organisation structuring, group dynamics, job satisfaction, communication and participation, leadership styles and motivation. It has also led to greater attention to the importance of interpersonal interactions, the causes of conflict and recognition of employee relations.

The systems approach

Criticisms of earlier approaches to organisation are based in part on the attempt to study the activities and problems of the organisation solely in terms of the internal environment. The classical approach emphasised the technical requirements of the organisation and its needs – 'organisations without people'; the human relations approach emphasised the psychological and social aspects, and the consideration of human needs – 'people without organisations'. The **systems approach** attempts to reconcile these two earlier approaches and the work of the formal and informal writers.

Systems theory is not new and has been used in the natural and physical sciences for a number of years. One of the founders of this approach was the biologist *Ludwig von Bertalanffy*, who used the term 'systems theory' in an article published in 1951 and who is generally credited with having developed the outline of General Systems Theory.[53] The systems approach to organisation has arisen, at least in part, therefore, from the work of biologists, and *Miller and Rice* have likened the commercial and industrial organisation to the biological organism.[54]

From a business perspective, organisations are analysed as 'systems' with a number of interrelated sub-systems. Attention is focused on the total work organisation and the interrelationships of structure and behaviour, and the range of variables within the organisation. The idea is that any part of an organisation's activities affects all other parts. The systems approach encourages managers to view the organisation both as a whole and as part of a larger environment. (**The view of the organisation as an open system is discussed later in Chapter 3.**)

Socio-technical system

The idea of socio-technical systems arose from the work of *Trist* and others, of the Tavistock Institute of Human Relations, in their study of the effects of changing technology in the coal-mining industry in the 1940s.[55] The traditional method of working was small, self-selecting groups of miners working together, as an independent team, on one part of the coal face – the 'single place' or 'shortwall' method. The increasing use of mechanisation and the introduction of coal-cutters and mechanical conveyors enabled coal to be extracted on a 'longwall' method. Shift working was introduced, with each shift specialising in one stage of the operation – preparation, cutting or loading.

However, the new method meant a change in the previous system. Technological change had brought about changes in psychological and sociological properties of the old method of working. There was a lack of co-operation between different shifts and, within each shift, an increase in absenteeism, scapegoating and signs of greater social stress. The 'longwall' method was socially disruptive and did not prove as economically efficient as it could have been with the new technology.

The researchers saw the need for a socio-technical approach in which an appropriate social system could be developed in keeping with the new technical system. The result was the 'composite longwall' method, with more responsibility to the team as a whole and shifts carrying out composite tasks, the reintroduction of multiskilled roles and a reduction in specialisation. The composite method was psychologically and socially more rewarding and economically more efficient than the 'longwall' method.

The **socio-technical system** is concerned with the interactions between the psychological and social factors and the needs and demands of the human part of the organisation, and its structural and technological requirements. The 'socio-technical' system directs attention to the transformation or conversion process itself, to the series of activities through which the organisation attempts to achieve its objectives. Recognition of the socio-technical approach is of particular importance today. People must be considered as at least an equal priority along with investment in technology. For example, *Lane et al.* point out that major technological change has brought about dramatic changes in worker behaviour and requirements. It is people who unlock the benefits and opportunities of information and communications technology.[56]

Technological determinism

The socio-technical system provides a link between the systems approach and a sub-division, sometimes adopted – the **technology approach**. Writers under the technology heading attempt to restrict generalisations about organisations and management and emphasise the effects of varying technologies on organisation structure, work groups and individual performance and job satisfaction. This is in contrast with the socio-technical approach, which did not regard technology, per se, as a determinant of behaviour.

Under the heading of the technology approach could be included the work of such writers as: *Walker and Guest* (effects of the assembly line production method on employee behaviour);[57] *Sayles* (relationship between technology and the nature of work groups);[58] *Blauner* (problems of 'alienation' in relation to different work technologies);[59]and *Turner and Lawrence* (technology and socio-culture)[60]. (**Technology and organisations is examined in Chapter 12.**)

Critical review and reflection

The underlying principles and ideas of the socio-technical systems and technological determinism approaches are of particular relevance and assistance to the practical manager.

To what extent do YOU agree with this assertion? As a manager, how would YOU envisage drawing upon YOUR understanding of these approaches?

Management and organisational behaviour in action case study
'Vanguard Method' for systems thinking

A different, more recent approach to thinking on management applied to service organisations is that of the 'Vanguard Method', which is based on the pioneering work of, among others, W. Edwards Deming, Chris Argyris and Taiichi Ohno. Ohno, the father of the Toyota Production System, drew attention to managers' lack of control on the shop floor and to the importance of continuous revisions, and his ideas gave rise to concepts such as total quality management and just-in-time. Ohno viewed the work organisation as an integrated system, with the focus on flow throughout the system rather than on individual functions. As *Seddon* notes: 'In Ohno's philosophy each person's work is connected to the needs of customers, as opposed to arbitrary and counterproductive measures of activity.'[61]

Vanguard helps organisations change from command and control thinking to a systems thinking on the design and management of work.

Command and control thinking		Systems thinking
Top-down, hierarchy	**Perspective**	Outside-in system
Functional specialisation and procedures	**Design of work**	Demand, value and flow
Contractual	**Attitude to customers**	What matters?
Separated from work	**Decision-making**	Integrated with work
Output, targets, activity, standards: related to budget	**Measurement**	Capability, variation: related to purpose
Contractual	**Attitude to suppliers**	Co-operative
Control budgets, manage people	**Management ethos**	Learn through action on the system
Extrinsic	Assumptions about motivation	Intrinsic

Emphasis is placed on the customer and measurement of success as opposed to targets of expected performance. The consequences are improved service to customers, at lower costs and improved morale. Service is different to manufacturing. In simple terms, there is inherently greater variety in customer demand, hence the need to design to absorb that variety. Vanguard recommends that service organisations avoid the 'tools' developed for 'lean manufacturing' as they do not apply well in service organisations.

Intrinsic to the Vanguard Method is the transfer of expertise to people (managers and staff) in the organisation. Vanguard uses 'sensei', people who are experts in both intervention theory (how you make a change) and systems theory (how to analyse and design work). Vanguard senseis are experts in the 'what' (how a systems design improves performance) and the 'how' (how to make this change).

Steps in the Vanguard Method

Understanding the distinctions - Top management must understand what it means to change from command and control to systems thinking.
Scoping - Assessing the scope for improvement; knowledge about customer demand, revenue and service flows, waste and the causes of waste; the potential scope and value of making this change in practical terms.
Check - People who do the work to be given technical support and check their understanding of the what and why of performance as a system.
Measures and method - In parallel with 'check', managers work on the relationship between measures and method, understanding the need to change and use of measures for managing and improving performance.
Prototyping - The 'check' team and managers work on measures and establish a prototype of the redesign. The purpose is to develop the redesign and determine anticipated economies.
Leader's review - In order to make informed choices about benefits from adopting the new systems design and authorises preparation for implementation.
Proof of concept - Prototype is extended and developed to handle all customer demands; the consequential improvements are tracked with new (system) measures while management develop a new budgeting and management information system.
Constancy of purpose - Leadership of the change with the top management team including, in particular, roles and measures. Clarity about future state and means of implementation.
Implementation - Here a choice can be made: establishing a working pilot (a complete redesign but limited in volume or scope); or making a complete change to the organisation.
Changes to policy and practice - Review matters of policy and practice. Typically they will include budgeting, HR policy and practice, interpretation of regulations and IT.
Finding out what matters to your customers - Having redesigned and improved your service, it is a natural extension to step over the boundary and learn about what matters to your customers. The work leads to new services, designed with customers.

Source: Thanks to David Puttick, Vanguard. Reproduced with permission. **http://vanguard-method.net/**

Tasks

1. What is your view on a systems approach and the Vanguard Method?
2. To what extent do you believe systems thinking can be applied effectively to production organisations?
3. How do you think managers are likely to react to an ethos of learning through action on the system? What potential difficulties do you see?

The contingency approach

The classical approach suggested one best form of structure and placed emphasis on general sets of principles, while the human relations approach gave little attention at all to structure. In contrast, the **contingency approach** shows renewed concern with the importance of structure as a significant influence on organisational performance. The contingency approach, which can be seen as an extension of the systems approach, highlights possible means of differentiating among alternative forms of organisation structures and systems of management. There is no one optimum state. For example, the structure of the organisation and its 'success' are dependent, that is contingent upon, the nature of tasks with which it is designed to deal and the nature of environmental influences.

The most appropriate structure and system of management is therefore dependent upon the contingencies of the situation for each particular organisation. The contingency approach implies that organisational theory should not seek to suggest one best way to structure or manage organisations, but should provide insights into the situational and contextual factors that influence management decisions. Situational variables may be identified in a number of ways and include type of organisation and its purpose, culture, size, technology and environment. Contingency models of organisation and management are discussed later (**see Chapter 11**).

A summary of management theory and some links with other chapters are set out in the concept map in Figure 2.2.

Other approaches to the study of organisations

The fourfold framework of classical, human relations, systems and contingency approaches provides a helpful, although rather simplistic, categorisation. The study of organisations, their structure and management is a broad field of enquiry. Depending on the views and preferences of the writer, other possible main approaches include decision-making and social action.

Decision-making approach

The systems approach involves the isolation of those functions most directly concerned with the achievement of objectives and the identification of main decision areas or sub-systems. Viewing the organisation as a system emphasises the need for good information and channels of communication in order to assist effective decision-making in the organisation. Recognition of the need for decision-making and the attainment of goals draws attention to a sub-division of the systems approach, or a separate category – that of the **decision-making (decision theory) approach.** Here the focus of attention is on managerial decision-making and how organisations process and use information in making decisions.

Successful management lies in responding to internal and external change. This involves the clarification of objectives, the specification of problems and the search for and implementation of solutions. The organisation is seen as an information-processing network with numerous decision points. An understanding of how decisions are made helps in understanding behaviour in the organisation. Decision-making writers seek to explain the mechanisms by which conflict is resolved and choices are made.

Some leading writers

Leading writers on the decision-making approach include *Barnard, Simon* and *Cyert and March*. The scope of the decision-making approach, however, is wide and it is possible to identify contributions from engineers, mathematicians and operational research specialists in addition to the work of economists, psychologists and writers on management and organisation.

Barnard stressed the need for co-operative action in organisations. He believed that people's ability to communicate, and their commitment and contribution to the achievement of a common purpose, were necessary for the existence of a co-operative system.[62] These ideas were developed further by Simon. He sees management as meaning decision-making and his concern is with how decisions are made and how decision-making can be improved. Simon is critical of the implication of 'man' as completely rational and proposes a model of 'administrative man' who, unlike 'economic man', 'satisfices' rather than maximises. Administrative decision-making is the achievement of satisfactory rather than optimal results in solving problems.[63]

Economic models of decision-making, based on the assumption of rational behaviour in choosing from known alternatives in order to maximise objectives, can be contrasted with

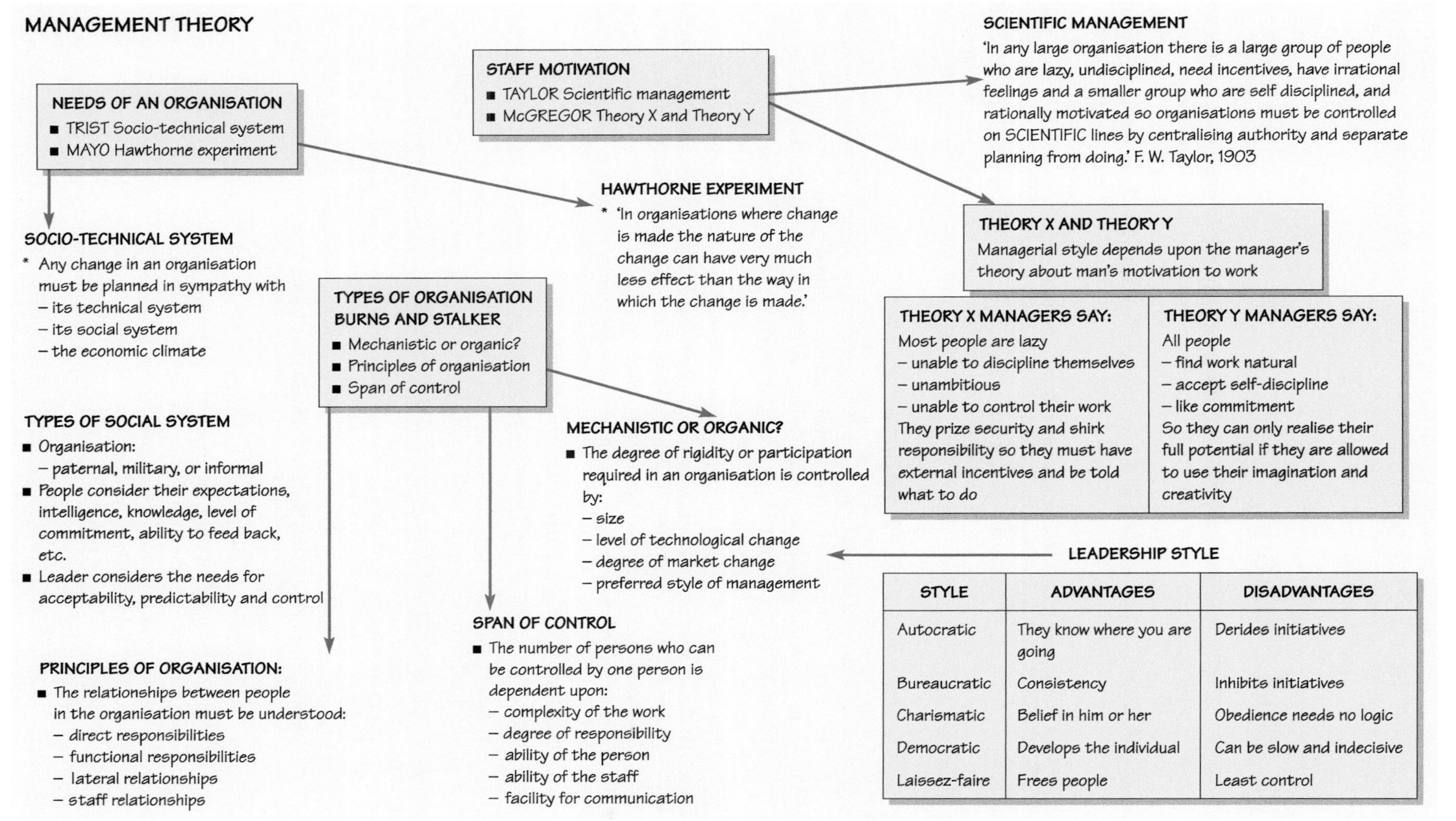

Figure 2.2 Concept map of management theory

Source: Copyright © 2008 The Virtual Learning Materials Workshop. Reproduced with permission.

behavioural models based not so much on maximisation of objectives as on short-term expediency, where a choice is made to avoid conflict and to stay within limiting constraints. Managers are more concerned with avoiding uncertainties than with the prediction of uncertainties.[64] **(See also decision models of leadership in Chapter 9.)**

Social action

Social action represents a contribution from sociologists to the study of organisations. Social-action writers attempt to view the organisation from the standpoint of individual members (actors) who will each have their own goals and interpretation of their work situation in terms of the satisfaction sought and the meaning that work has for them. The goals of the individual, and the means selected and actions taken to achieve these goals, are affected by the individual's perception of the situation. Social action looks to the individual's own definition of the situation as a basis for explaining behaviour. Conflict of interests is seen as normal behaviour and part of organisational life.

According to *Silverman*, 'The action approach . . . does not, in itself, provide a theory of organisations. It is instead best understood as a method of analysing social relations within organisations.'[65]

Criticisms of earlier approaches

A main thrust of social action is criticism of earlier approaches to organisation and management and of what is claimed to be their failure to provide a satisfactory basis for the explanation or prediction of individual behaviour. The human relations approaches have been criticised because of their focus on generalised theories of good management, group psychology and the suggestion of needs common to all individuals at work. The technology approach has been criticised for attributing feelings of alienation to the nature of technology and the status of work groups rather than an analysis that focused on concern for the individual's expectations of, and reactions to, work. The systems approach has been criticised for failure to examine the orientation of individual members to the organisation, the different expectations people have of their work or ways in which the environment influences expectations of work.

Unitarist or pluralist perspectives

Important contributors to a social action approach include *Goldthorpe et al.* (industrial attitudes and behaviour patterns of manual workers)[66] and *Fox*. In a research paper written for the Royal Commission on Trade Unions and Employers' Associations (the Donovan Report), Fox suggests two major ways of perceiving an industrial organisation – a 'unitarist' approach and a 'pluralist' approach.[67] In the search for effective employee relations and a common commitment to the goals of the organisation, consideration should be given to both the unitarist and pluralist perspectives. While neither of the approaches can be seen as 'right' or 'wrong', these contrasting views will influence the nature of employment relations and the management of human resources. **(See the discussion in Chapter 3 on contrasting views of conflict.)**

The unitarist perspective

With the **unitarist perspective** the organisation is viewed as an integrated and harmonious whole, with managers and other staff sharing common interests and objectives. There is an image of the organisation as a team with a common source of loyalty, one focus of effort and one accepted leader. Conflict is perceived as disruptive and unnatural and can be explained by, for example, poor communications, personality clashes or the work of agitators. Trade unions are seen as an unnecessary evil and restrictive practices as outmoded or caused by trouble-makers.

HR policies and managerial development can be seen as reflecting a unitary ideology. *Horwitz* suggests that the unitary perspective views company and trade union loyalty as mutually exclusive. He raises the question of human resource management (HRM) as a reformation of a unitarist managerial ideology. Developments in HRM, in seeking to optimise co-operation and organisational loyalty, can be seen as imposing new forms of control. A managerial approach to facilitating organisational goals and the direct involvement of employees furthers a unitary perspective and can mask an underlying distaste for unionism.[68]

The pluralist perspective

An alternative view suggested by *Fox* is the **pluralist perspective**, which views the organisation as made up of powerful and competing sub-groups with their own legitimate loyalties, objectives and leaders.[69] These competing sub-groups are almost certain to come into conflict. From the pluralist perspective, conflict in organisations is seen as inevitable and induced, in part, by the very structure of the organisation. Conflict is not necessarily a bad thing but can be an agent for evolution, and internal and external change.

Restrictive practices may be seen as a rational response from a group that regards itself as being threatened. The role of the manager would be less commanding and enforcing, and more persuading and co-ordinating. Fox suggests that the pluralist perspective is a more realistic frame of reference. He argues the importance of viewing work situations through the different groups involved rather than attempting a wished-for unitarist approach.

Critical review and reflection

The study of social action may be popular with academics but too much attention is given to the easy option of criticising other approaches. Social action theory offers little that is constructive or of positive value to the practical manager.

What is YOUR view? Can YOU present a counter argument? How much benefit do YOU derive from the study of social action?

Action theory

A theory of human behaviour from an 'action approach' is presented by *Bowey*.[70] She suggests that action theory, systems theory and contingency theory are not necessarily incompatible approaches to the understanding of behaviour in organisations. It would be possible to take the best parts of the different approaches and combine them into a theory that would model empirical behaviour and also facilitate the analysis of large numbers of people in organisations.

The three essential principles of action theory can be summarised as below:

- Sociology is concerned not just with behaviour but with 'meaningful action'.
- Particular meanings persist through reaffirmation in actions.
- Actions can also lead to changes in meanings.

Bowey suggests these three principles apply mainly to explanations of individual, or small-scale, behaviour. She gives four additional concepts, taken from systems theory, on which analysis of large-scale behaviour can be based. These concepts are redefined in accordance with an action approach.

- **Role** – this is needed for the analysis of behaviour in organisations. It explains the similar actions of different people in similar situations within the organisation and the expectations held by other people.
- **Relationships** – this is needed to explain the patterns of interaction among people and the behaviours displayed towards one another.

- **Structure** – the relationships among members of an organisation give rise to patterns of action that can be identified as a 'transitory social structure'. The social factors, and non-social factors such as payment systems, methods of production and physical layout, together form the behavioural structure.
- **Process** – human behaviour can be analysed in terms of processes, defined as 'continuous interdependent sequences of actions'. The concept of process is necessary to account for the manner in which organisations exhibit changes in structure.

The three principles of action theory, together with the four additional concepts from systems theory, provide an action approach to the analysis of behaviour in organisations. Bowey goes on to illustrate her theory with case studies of five different types of organisations, all in the restaurant industry.

Postmodernism

With the development of the information and technological age a more recent view of organisations and management is the idea of **postmodernism**. *Cooper and Burrell* refer to the contrasting postmodern view of 'organisation less the expression of planned thought and calculative action and a more defensive reaction to forces intrinsic to the social body which constantly threaten the stability of organised life'.[71]

In the 1990s, writers such as *Clegg* described the postmodern organisation in terms of the influence of technological determinism and structural flexibility, premised on niches, multi-skilled jobs marked by a lack of demarcation, and more complex employment relationships including subcontracting and networking.[72]

Postmodernism rejects a rational systems approach to our understanding of organisations and management and to accepted explanations of society and behaviour. Postmodern organisations are perceived as highly flexible and responsive, with decentralised decision-making, fluid, less hierarchical structures and with the ability to change quickly to meet present demands.

Generalised sociological concept

The idea of postmodernism is, however, not easy to explain fully in clear and simple terms. It is arguably more of a generalised sociological concept rather than a specific approach to organisation and management. There is even some discussion of two connotations, and theories or philosophies of the concept depending on whether the term is hyphenated or not.[73] Perhaps understandably, therefore, the concept of postmodernism appears to have little interest or appeal to the practical manager. Indeed *Watson*, for example, questions the value of labelling more flexible forms of bureaucratic structure and culture as postmodern or post-bureaucratic and differentiating these from the modernist bureaucratic organisation.

> *The labelling of more flexible forms of bureaucratic structure and culture as 'postmodern' or 'post-bureaucratic' is unhelpful. It is unrealistic to suggest that there is something new occurring to work organisations at the level of the basic organising principle. There is no postmodern or post-bureaucratic organisational form available to us that is* ***essentially*** *different from the modernist bureaucratic organisation. We are indeed seeing different mixes of direct and indirect management control attempts as the world changes. But the world was always changing. Probably from the very beginning of industrialisation there has been a mixing of direct and indirect controls with emphases in one direction and then the other being made at different times.*[74]

Nevertheless, postmodernist organisation can arguably be seen as a healthy challenge to more traditional approaches. It puts forward alternative interpretations of rationality, credibility and ambiguity, and a thoughtful critical perspective on disorders in work organisations, and reminds us of the complexities in our understanding of management and organisational behaviour.

An outline of developments in management theory is set out in Figure 2.3.

Critical review and reflection

The idea of postmodernist organisation can be likened to the 'Emperor's new clothes'. It is easy to champion the idea in the classroom but in reality it is too abstract and vague, and lacks any real adaptive value for the practical manager.

How would YOU attempt to challenge this assertion?

CLASSICAL
(Including scientific management.) Emphasis on formal structure, technical requirements and sets of principles.
Bureaucracy
The organisation in terms of specialisation, hierarchy of authority, system of rules and impersonality.
HUMAN RELATIONS
Attention to the informal organisation, and to psychological and social needs of people at work.
Neo-human relations
Personal adjustment of the individual within the work organisation. Group relationships and styles of leadership.
SYSTEMS
Integration of the formal and informal approaches. A socio-technical approach. The organisation as an open system interacting with the environment.
Social action
Organisations as viewed by the individual members and their interpretation of the work situation.
Technology
Decision-making
CONTINGENCY
Form of structure and management system dependent upon the situational variables.
POSTMODERNISM
Highly flexible and responsive organisations with more complex employment relationships, less hierarchical structures and ability to change quickly and meet present demands.

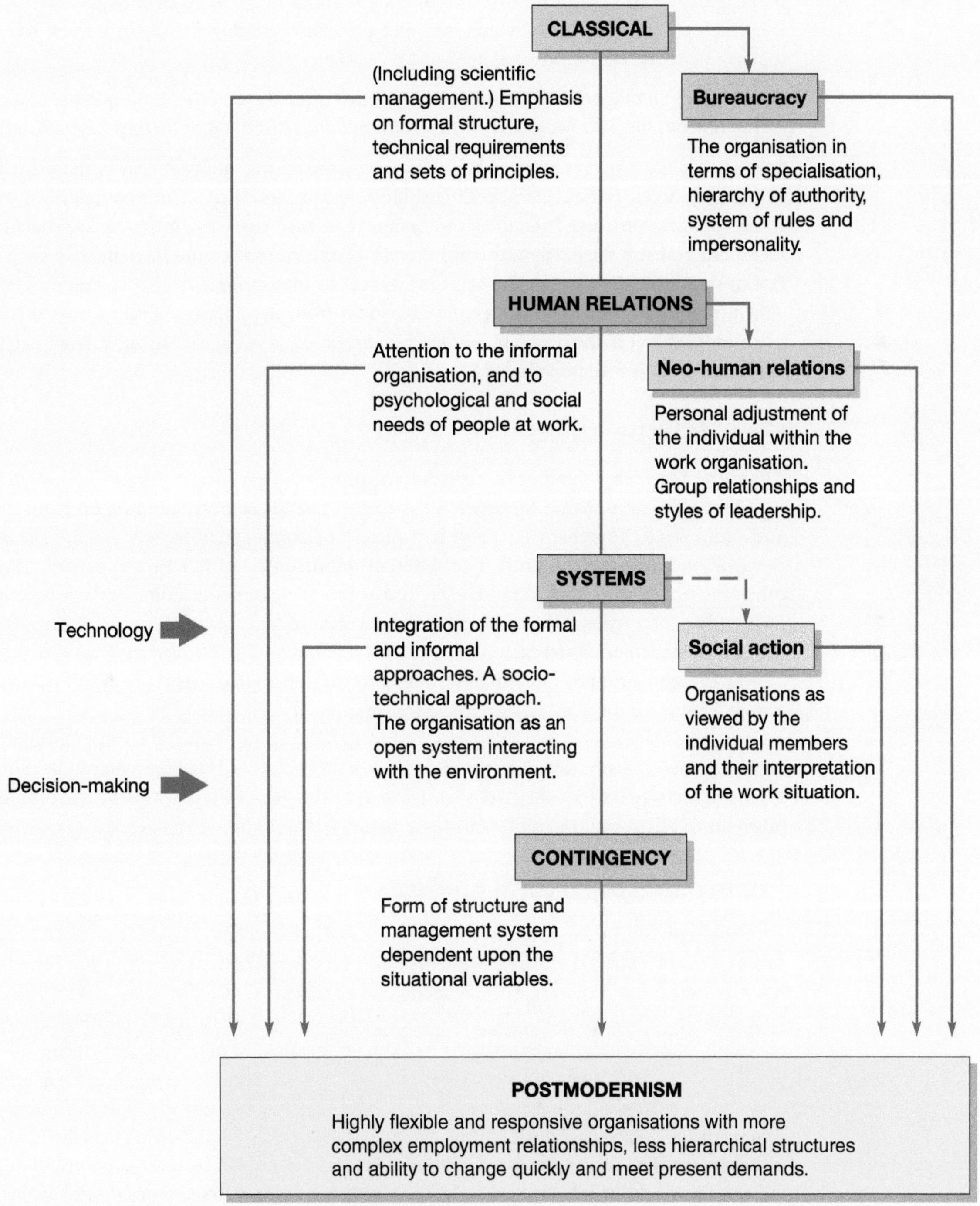

Figure 2.3 Outline of developments in management theory

Relevance to management and organisational behaviour

The different possible categorisations are not necessarily a bad thing; they illustrate the discursive and complex nature of the study and practice of management and organisational behaviour. Discussion on the various categorisations of approaches and the identification of individual writers within a particular approach can provide a useful insight into the subject.

Whatever form of categorisation is adopted, the division of writers on organisation and management into various approaches offers a number of positive advantages. It is helpful in the arrangement and study of material and provides a setting in which to view the field of management and organisational behaviour. As *Miner* points out:

> *Schools of management thought are very much a reality, and the management student who approaches the field without at least a minimal understanding of them does so at some risk.*[75]

A review of the different approaches helps in organisational analysis and in the identification of problem areas. For example, is the problem one of structure, of human relations or of the socio-technical process? It enables the manager to take from the different approaches those ideas that best suit the particular requirements of the job. For example, in dealing with a problem of structure, the ideas of the classical writers or of contingency theory might be adopted. When there is a problem relating to HRM, ideas from the human relations movement might be of most value. If the problem is one of environmental influence, insights from the systems approach might prove most helpful.

Caveats to be noted

There are, however, a number of caveats to be noted.

The various approaches represent a progression of ideas, each building on from the other and adding to it. Together they provide a pattern of complementary studies into the development of management thinking. The different approaches are not in competition with each other and no one approach should be viewed as replacing or superseding earlier contributions. Many ideas of earlier writers are still of relevance today and of continuing importance in modern management practice.

Any categorisation of individual writers into specific approaches is inevitably arbitrary and not all writers can be neatly arranged in this manner. This is only to be expected. Such writers are expounding their current thoughts and ideas in keeping with the continual development of management theory and changes in management practice. The comment made about some management writers that they are saying different things at different times might therefore be taken more as a compliment than as a criticism.

Importance of cultural contexts

A major criticism of the attempt to define generalised models of management theory is the assumption of national culture. *Schneider and Barsoux* draw attention to how the different theories on how to organise all reflect societal concerns of the times, as well as the cultural backgrounds of the individuals. Different approaches reflect different cultural assumptions regarding, for example, human nature and the importance of task and relationships.[76]

Cheng et al. also question the universality of theories of management and organisational behaviour on the grounds that they have not adequately addressed the factor of culture: 'Traditionally, the greatest aspiration of researchers is to discover objective, universalistic principles of behaviour. The tacit assumption behind this is that these principles may be discovered without reference to cultural contexts.' Cheng *et al.* conclude that while there may be some universality to organisation structures, for example the need for some form of hierarchy whatever its shape may be, different national cultures frequently give those structures different meanings.[77]

Value of management theory

Whatever the value of management theory, clearly no single approach to organisation and management provides all the answers. It is the comparative study of different approaches that will yield benefits to the manager. A knowledge and understanding of management theory will help with an awareness and appreciation of the complexities of modern work organisations.

Reporting on a twelve-year study of the knowledge and use of management concepts in technical organisations, *Flores and Utley* suggest that a look back at the theories and principles that have been taught in the past could give an indication of the success of any new approach and help prepare today's and tomorrow's managers for the future.[78] And *Stern* has this to say:

> *Management thinkers still have a lot to tell us. You don't have to believe everything they say, but they may at least offer stimulation; they might provoke senior managers into abandoning complacency and trying to see problems in a new light.*[79]

There is undoubtedly much scepticism about, and criticism of, management gurus. For example, in a cynical and provocative feature in *The Times*, *Billen* suggests that the tide is turning against the gurus and their gobbledegook.

> *In the past two decades, management theory, once rejected in Britain by both management and unions, has been deliberately imposed on almost every aspect of commercial and public life . . . It would be a brave new world without such gobbledegook in it but – to use a management theorist's phrase – an empowered one, too. Managers would be chosen not for their ability to bandy jargon with their superiors but for their empathy, pragmatism, experience and decisiveness with their staff.*[80]

However, according to *McLean:*

> *Of course, management theories have often been the subject of discourse and criticism. Some critics see organisational philosophies as management fads that will be replaced by new ones as other theories are proposed. That may well be the case, but it is good for management theories to evolve, because organisations change, the environment changes, and as a result, management practices and techniques change . . . Theories provide us with valuable insights into how we can be more understanding, influential and ultimately more successful in managing organisations and the turbulent dynamic environments in which they operate . . . you of course, may have a different view!*[81]

There are no definitive or final solutions to the problems of organisations. The nature of work organisations and the environment in which they operate is becoming increasingly complex and subject to continual change. However, at least we do understand more about the dynamics of management and organisational behaviour as a basis for the analysis of human behaviour in organisations.[82] *Stern* suggests that 'Management is both science and art, and the trick of it lies in separating the good ideas from the bad, knowing when to be scientific and when to be artful.'[83]

Conceptual thinking and management theory

In an interesting discussion on learning classic management theories, *Robinson and Francis-Smythe* draw attention to the importance of conceptual thinking for managers and how far knowledge of formal academic theory helps in the discharge of managerial responsibilities. The overwhelming majority of established senior managers will be hard-pressed to identify a single significant occasion of decision-making guided by direct reference to a particular management theory. Even if names of respected theorists can be recalled, managers will be hard-pressed to provide a succinct explanation of their theories. Robinson and Francis-Smythe question what happens to all the theory that managers are exposed to during their training and education.

> *When in the light of their recognition-based decision-making, managers are asked to explain the role that academic theory plays in their approach to managing, they will frequently assert that it 'must' exert a subtle, covert, subconscious, or even subliminal influence over them. Whilst it would be easy to dismiss this as 'wishful thinking', there is good evidence to suggest that these assertions may actually be true . . . The inability to 'name' either a theory or a theoretician should not be taken to imply a failure to understand the theory in a more generalised, more abstract, more conceptual way.*

Robinson and Francis-Smythe suggest that academic knowledge is not, per se, a key professional requirement or an important aspect of managerial competence. Rather it will serve to underpin the process of building a repertoire of concepts that will be held in long-term memories in the way most likely to facilitate subsequent retrieval, good managerial moves and solutions to managerial challenges.[84]

There are, then, many aspects to management. There are no simple solutions, no one best way to manage. However, study of different approaches to organisations, their structure and management is still important for the manager and remains an indispensable part of the job.

Critical review and reflection

The historical study of different approaches to organisations and the development of management theory have little practical relevance. It is no more than a luxury for students and the time could be spent better on the study of more important topic areas.

How would YOU present a counterargument? To what extent has YOUR study of management theory been of personal value to YOU as a potential manager?

Ten key points to remember

1. A central part of the study of organisational behaviour is the development of management thinking and what might be termed 'management theory'
2. The work of leading writers can be categorised into various 'approaches' based on their views of organisations, their structure and management.
3. The classical writers placed emphasis on purpose and structure, technical requirements of the organisation, and assumption of rational and logical behaviour.
4. The human relations writers emphasised the informal organisation, group relationships, and the psychological and social needs of people at work.
5. The systems approach focuses attention on the interactions between technical and social variables and influences of the external environment.
6. Contingency theory highlights possible means of differentiating between alternative forms of structures and systems of management.

7 It is possible to identify a number of other approaches or sub-divisions of approaches including technology decision-making, social action and postmodernism.

8 Whatever form of categorisation is adopted, there are a number of positive advantages but also criticisms and caveats to be noted, including cultural contexts.

9 A knowledge and understanding of management theory will help with an awareness and appreciation of the complexities of modern work organisations.

10 Ideas and instinct are both important to managers. It is necessary to view interrelationships among the development of theory, behaviour in organisations and management practice.

Review and discussion questions

1 Detail fully how you would attempt to identify and analyse developments in management and organisational behaviour.

2 Assess critically the relevance of scientific management to present-day organisations. To what extent does your university exhibit features of scientific management?

3 Argue a positive case for bureaucratic structures. Select a large-scale organisation of your choice and suggest ways in which it displays characteristics of a bureaucracy.

4 What are the main conclusions that can be drawn from the Hawthorne studies? Discuss critically the relevance of these studies for management and organisational behaviour today.

5 Evaluate the application of the systems approach to the analysis of work organisations. Suggest an example of a work situation in which the systems approach might be appropriate.

6 Contrast approaches to improving organisational performance based on attention to technical and structural requirements with those based on concern for psychological and social factors.

7 Explain what is meant by a social action approach. Assess critically the practical relevance of 'action theory'.

8 Discuss critically the practical value and relevance of the postmodernist view of organisations.

9 Present a detailed argument for the potential benefits to managers from a study of management theory.

10 Outline briefly what you believe are the major trends in organisation and management since the beginning of this century. Which *one* writer do you most associate with, and why?

Assignment

1 Specify the *most important key features* associated with the methods of operation, structure and management of each of the following organisations:

- six-star luxury international hotel
- major civil service department
- medical research university
- maternity hospital
- motor-car manufacturer

→

- large comprehensive school
- maximum-security prison
- leisure centre

2 Then, working in small groups:
  (i) Compare and discuss your list of features.
  (ii) How much agreement was there among members of your group?
  (iii) What conclusions do you draw?
  (iv) How does the assignment link with your knowledge of different approaches to organisations and management?

Personal skills and employability exercise

Objectives

Completing this exercise should help you to enhance the following skills:

- Knowledge about the future direction of your work career.
- Recognition of the type of job and work you would enjoy.
- Awareness of the type of organisation structure in which you would feel comfortable working.

Exercise

Answer each question 'mostly agree' or 'mostly disagree'. Assume that you are trying to learn something about yourself. Do not assume that your answer will be shown to a prospective employer.

		Mostly agree	Mostly disagree
1	I value stability in my job.	❑	❑
2	I like a predictable organisation.	❑	❑
3	The best job for me would be one in which the future is uncertain.	❑	❑
4	The army would be a nice place to work.	❑	❑
5	Rules, policies and procedures tend to frustrate me.	❑	❑
6	I would enjoy working for a company that employed 85,000 people worldwide.	❑	❑
7	Being self-employed would involve more risk than I am willing to take.	❑	❑
8	Before accepting a job, I would like to see an exact job description.	❑	❑
9	I would prefer a job as a freelance house painter to one as a clerk for the Department of Motor Vehicles.	❑	❑
10	Seniority should be as important as performance in determining pay increases and promotion.	❑	❑
11	It would give me a feeling of pride to work for the largest and most successful company in its field.	❑	❑

		Mostly agree	Mostly disagree
12	Given a choice, I would prefer to make £40,000 per year as a vice president in a small company to £50,000 as a staff specialist in a large company.	❑	❑
13	I would regard wearing an employee badge with a number on it as a degrading experience.	❑	❑
14	Parking spaces in a company lot should be assigned on the basis of job level.	❑	❑
15	If an accountant works for a large organisation, he or she cannot be a true professional.	❑	❑
16	Before accepting a job (given a choice), I would want to make sure that the company had a very fine programme of employee benefits.	❑	❑
17	A company will probably not be successful unless it establishes a clear set of rules and procedures.	❑	❑
18	Regular working hours and holidays are more important to me than finding thrills on the job.	❑	❑
19	You should respect people according to their rank.	❑	❑
20	Rules are meant to be broken.	❑	❑

Source: Adapted from DuBrin, A. J. *Human Relations: A Job Oriented Approach*, 1st Ed., Reston Publishing/Prentice Hall (1978), pp. 296–7. Copyright © 1978. Reproduced with permission from Pearson Education Inc.

You should then consider the further information supplied to you individually by your tutor.

Discussion

- After receiving feedback from your tutor, share and compare your responses in a small-group situation and attempt to obtain group consensus on the answers.
- How far did members relate the questions to different ideas or studies on the structure and management of work organisations?
- To what extent do you think personal skills and employability are influenced by the type of organisation structure?

Case study

Not being evil: Google

For many people, California-based Google is the most prominent example of a twenty-first-century company. Founded in 1998 by Larry Page and Sergei Brin, it grew very rapidly to become the world's best-known search engine, accompanied by a proliferation of other ventures. The company's name has achieved the rare distinction of becoming a verb in its own right – these days, we google, rather than search (and probably more often than we hoover). The company's 2014 revenue was $66 billion[85] and, in 2015, the two founders were listed by *Fortune* magazine as nineteenth and twentieth in its list of the world's billionaires.[86] This spectacular growth has been achieved by a company whose informal motto is 'Don't Be Evil'. How do the two ideas – commercial success and avoiding evil – work together in practice, and how well will the company be able to respond to the challenges that lie ahead in this turbulent market?

→

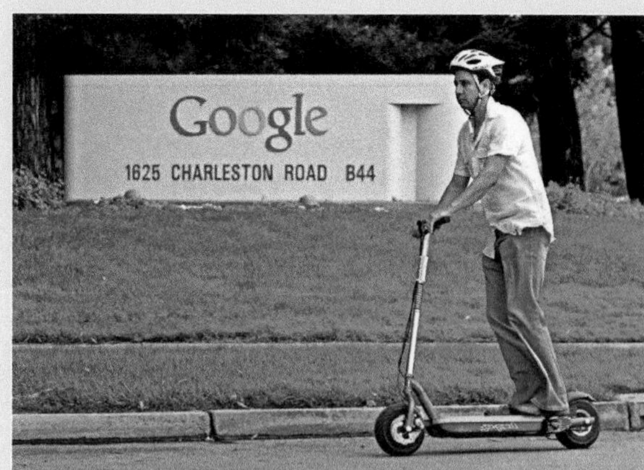

A Street View of Google
Source: Bloomberg via Getty Images

In commercial terms, the predominant contributor has been advertising revenues derived from the Google Internet search operation, which is based upon the highly successful PageRank technology developed by the founders. In common with all of the competitive search engines, the Google Internet search service looks free to users, to the extent that this added value is probably now taken for granted by most. But Google's success in its core business has been accompanied by a steady flow of new and intriguing ideas. For example, it is now completely routine to be able to search images as well as text, to call up detailed maps of anywhere on the planet, to switch to a satellite view or increasingly to photographic images at street level. The YouTube facility, acquired by Google in 2006, allows free access to a vast database of video clips uploaded by organisations and individuals. Google's email service has grown rapidly and its Google+ service is aimed at the social networking market. In what used to be the separate mobile phone market, Google's Android system, as well as Google's range of phones and tablets, are engaged in a fierce battle with Apple's iPhone and iPad.

Google's rapid diversification looks like the very opposite of the 'stick to the knitting' recommendation in a best-selling strategy book twenty-five years earlier.[87] In diversifying, any company is choosing to serve new types of customers in unfamiliar markets and with the opposition of new incumbent competitors, all of which tends to increase the total risk for the company, as well as placing its core resources under strain. However, Google claims in its philosophy statement that this diversity stems from the application of its one core competence: search.[88] From the outset, Google has actively sought out new opportunities and has deliberately fostered a culture to preserve and encourage this restlessness. As Tim Harford observes, Google fully expects most of its new ideas to fail, but its future lies with the ideas that do not fail.[89] In a 2014 interview,[90] Google's two founders commented that a key role of the company was to integrate diversity, in order that the services have a recognisable Google 'feel'.

Growing pains?

How, then, can these cultural values be preserved as a company grows and changes? From its beginnings in a garage, Google had grown by the end of 2014 into a global corporation employing more than 53,000 worldwide and operating out of seventy offices in forty countries around the world.[91,92] It has, however, managed to retain its reputation for an informal and quirky style: for example, the company famously encourages its employees to spend 20 per cent of each working week working on projects that interest them, rather than their main responsibilities. The many accounts of life in its Googleplex headquarters describe the mixture of working hard and playing hard - video games, pool tables, pianos and other leisure facilities are provided and commitment levels are expected to be very high. As can be seen from the examples of Google recruitment questions that can be found in Internet posts, the company is looking for very bright recruits who can think quickly, imaginatively and unconventionally.

In the tough competitive environments in which Google operates, it is hardly surprising that some have questioned how well its 'Don't Be Evil' motto is holding up. Google attracted fierce criticism for its decision to comply with the Internet censorship laws in the People's Republic of China for the search services it provides in that country. As can be seen from the company's transparency statement, the censorship question is a continuing issue for Google (and other similar companies) in many parts of the world.[93] There have also been concerns about privacy and data security, and Google was one of a number of multinational companies criticised for tax avoidance in the UK, a claim it rejects emphatically.[94]

How does Google's strength and culture equip it to deal with the market challenges it now faces? The first part of the answer is to re-examine the assumptions behind the story so far. As Kahneman points out in his book *Thinking Fast and Slow*,[95] we should beware of seeing the story of Google's development as something from which reliable, more general lessons can be learned. Making reference to Nassim Taleb's concept of *narrative fallacy*,[96] he warns against underestimating the role of luck (i.e. alongside hard work, inspiration and talent) in the way it turned out - we should take care to notice the things that did not happen, as well as the well-documented events that make up the story. Above all, we should be cautious about any notion of using our 'understanding' of the story so far to predict the future. This must be doubly so when the future in question is that of the global information industry.

Gentle giant or robber baron?

Google's success has been based upon its mastery of Internet search, which has established it as a powerful global player, both while the Internet was growing around the world and in the later phases of user-generated content and the growth of social networking. But the next challenge is posed by the growing preference of users to access the Internet and its services via mobile smartphones, a change of format that threatens the standard models of revenue generation for a number of players, including Google. The effect of this is that those who want to remain major players have to build up their mobile capabilities.[97] For some years, the smartphone sector has been a fierce (and often litigious) battle between Apple's iPhone and devices based on Google's Android operating system. As the *New York Times* put it in 2012:[98]

> *Last year, for the first time, spending by Apple and Google on patent lawsuits and unusually big-dollar patent purchases exceeded spending on research and development of new products, according to public filings.*

As commentator Bryan Appleyard observes, Android is open - given away free to phone manufacturers - while Apple's is not.[99] Some see this same open/closed contrast in the corporate cultures of the two giants.[100]

From one point of view, consumers around the world have done very well from this competitive melee, with a succession of amazing devices at affordable prices. On the other hand, some (for example *The Economist*),[101] are more critical of the contemporary IT giants, drawing parallels between their plans and the late-career behaviours of the early 20th century US industrialists (Carnegie, Rockefeller, Harriman etc) known as 'robber barons.'

> *'We're charmed by their corporate mantras - for example "Don't be evil" (Google) or "Move fast and break things" (Facebook). In their black turtlenecks and faded jeans they don't seem to have anything in common with Rupert Murdoch or the grim-faced, silk-hatted capitalist bosses of old. . .*
>
> *What gets lost in the reality distortion field that surrounds these technology moguls is that, in the end, they are fanatically ambitious, competitive capitalists. They may look cool and have soothing bedside manners, but in the end these guys are in business not just to make money, but to establish sprawling, quasi-monopolistic commercial empires. And they will do whatever it takes to achieve those ambitions.'*[102]

It is perhaps futile to speculate about how this complex market will look in just a few years. In the twentieth century, much competition took place between well-established large players (say, Ford and General Motors) in market domains characterised by stability and predictability. Twenty-first-century competition is different - technologies and market definitions are endlessly shifting and changing, bringing new players into contention with each other and raising the stakes for all concerned. Google's spectacular success in its relatively short existence so far has given it commercial strength and its culture has given it the flexibility to deal with rapid change.

Tasks

1 Examine the organisational development of Google using two of the four main analytical models in Figure 2.1. Which do you think offers the best explanation of the company's development, and why?

2 What are the main challenges that Google faced in attempting not to 'be evil' as it expanded into new and unfamiliar territories and markets? How might local managers throughout the world create a corporate culture based on this motto?

3 Is Google a 'postmodern' organisation or, in essence, no more than a globalised bureaucracy? Present the arguments on each side of the case.

4 If you were to research the degree to which growth and change has affected the organisational behaviour of Google employees, which theoretical approach would you choose as the basis for your enquiry? Explain and justify your choice.

Notes and references

1. See, for example, George, C. S. *The History of Management Thought,* second edition, Prentice Hall (1972).
2. Shafritz, J. M. *Shakespeare on Management,* Carol Publishing Group (1992), p. xi.
3. For a review of management thinking see, for example, Sheldrake, J. *Management Theory: From Taylorism to Japanization,* International Thomson Business Press (1996); see also Flores, G. N. and Utley, D. R. 'Management Concepts in Use – A 12-Year Perspective', *Engineering Management Journal,* vol. 12, no. 3, 2000, pp. 11–17.
4. Lee, R. A. 'There is Nothing so Useful as an Appropriate Theory', in Wilson, D. C. and Rosenfeld, R. H. *Managing Organisations: Text, Reading and Cases,* McGraw-Hill (1990), p. 31.
5. Crainer, S. *Key Management Ideas,* third edition, Financial Times Prentice Hall (1998).
6. Skipton, M. D. 'Management and the Organisation', *Management Research News,* vol. 5, no. 3, 1983, pp. 9–15.
7. Fayol, H. *General and Industrial Management,* Pitman (1949); see also Gray, I. Henri Fayol's *General and Industrial Management,* Pitman (1988).
8. Urwick, L. *Notes on the Theory of Organization,* American Management Association (1952).
9. Brech, E. F. L. *Organisation: The Framework of Management,* second edition, Longman (1965).
10. Simon, H. A. *Administrative Behaviour,* third edition, Free Press (1976), p. xxii.
11. Woodward, J. *Industrial Organization: Theory and Practice,* second edition, Oxford University Press (1980).
12. Taylor, F. W. *Scientific Management,* Harper & Row (1947). Comprises 'Shop Management' (1903), 'Principles of Scientific Management' (1911) and Taylor's testimony to the House of Representatives' Special Committee (1912).
13. Braverman, H. *Labor and Monopoly Capital,* Monthly Review Press (1974).
14. For a study of employers' labour relations policies, including comments on the work of Braverman, see Gospel, H. F. and Littler, C. R. (eds) *Managerial Strategies and Industrial Relations,* Heinemann Educational Books (1983).
15. Cloke, K. and Goldsmith, J. *The End of Management and the Rise of Organizational Democracy,* Jossey-Bass (2002), p. 27.
16. Rose, M. *Industrial Behaviour,* Penguin (1978), p. 31; see also Rose, M. *Industrial Behaviour,* second edition, Penguin (1988), ch. 2.
17. Drucker, P. F. 'The Coming Rediscovery of Scientific Management', *The Conference Board Record,* vol. 13, June 1976, pp. 23–7; reprinted in Drucker, P. F. *Towards the Next Economics and Other Essays,* Heinemann (1981).
18. Crainer, S. and Dearlove, D. *Financial Times Handbook of Management,* second edition, Financial Times Prentice Hall (2001).
19. Stern, S. 'Guru Guide', *Management Today,* October 2001, pp. 83–4.
20. See also Mullins, L. J and Dossor, O. P. *Hospitality Management and Organisational Behaviour,* fifth edition, Pearson Education (2013).
21. See, for example, Beirne, M., Riach, K. and Wilson, F. 'Controlling business? Agency and constraint in call centre working', *New Technology, Work and Employment,* vol. 19, no. 2, 2004, pp. 96–109.
22. Weber, M. *The Theory of Social and Economic Organization,* Collier Macmillan (1964).
23. Blau, P. M. and Scott, W. R. *Formal Organizations,* Routledge & Kegan Paul (1966).
24. Stewart, R. *The Reality of Management,* third edition, Butterworth–Heinemann (1999).
25. Robbins, S. P. and Judge, T. A. *'Organizational Behavior',* thirteenth edition, Pearson Prentice Hall (2009), p. 561.
26. Argyris, C. *Integrating the Individual and the Organization,* Wiley (1964).
27. Caulkin, S. 'Faceless Corridors of Power', *Management Today,* January 1988, p. 65.
28. Morgan, G. *Images of Organization,* second edition, Sage (1997).
29. Waterman, R. *Adhocracy: The Power to Change,* W.W. Norton (1994).
30. Mintzberg, H. *Managing,* Financial Times Prentice Hall (2009).
31. Tibballs, G. *Business Blunders,* Robinson Publishing (1999).
32. Cloke, K. and Goldsmith, J. *The End of Management and the Rise of Organizational Democracy,* Jossey-Bass (2002), pp. 92–4.
33. Drucker, P. F. *Classic Drucker,* Harvard Business School Press (2006), p. 22.
34. See Mullins, L. J. and Dossor, P. *Hospitality Management and Organisational Behaviour,* fifth edition, Pearson Education (2013).
35. Ridderstråle, J. 'Business Moves Beyond Bureaucracy', in Pickford, J. (ed.) *Financial Times Mastering Management 2.0,* Financial Times Prentice Hall (2001), pp. 217–20.
36. Stewart, R. *The Reality of Management,* third edition, Butterworth–Heinemann (1999).

37. See, for example, Wilson, F. A. *Organizational Behaviour: A Critical Introduction,* Oxford University Press (1999).
38. Green, J. 'Is Bureaucracy Dead? Don't Be So Sure', *Chartered Secretary,* January 1997, pp. 18–19.
39. See, for example, Waller, P. 'Bureaucracy Takes New Form', *Professional Manager,* May 1998, p. 6.
40. There are many versions of the Hawthorne experiments. Among the most thorough accounts is that by Roethlisberger, F. J. and Dickson, W. J. *Management and the Worker,* Harvard University Press (1939); see also Landsberger, H. A. *Hawthorne Revisited,* Cornell University Press (1958).
41. See, for example, Rose, M. *Industrial Behaviour,* second edition, Penguin (1988).
42. See, for example, Buggy, C. 'Are You Really Listening?', *Professional Manager,* July 2000, pp. 20–2.
43. Silverman, D. *The Theory of Organisations,* Heinemann (1970).
44. Stead, B. A. *Women in Management,* Prentice Hall (1978), p. 190.
45. Crainer, S. *Key Management Ideas: Thinkers That Changed the Management World,* third edition, Financial Times Prentice Hall (1998), p. 111.
46. Maslow, A. H. 'A Theory of Human Motivation', *Psychological Review,* vol. 50, no. 4, 1943, pp. 370–96.
47. Herzberg, F. W., Mausner, B. and Snyderman, B. B. *The Motivation to Work,* second edition, Chapman and Hall (1959).
48. McGregor, D. *The Human Side of Enterprise,* Penguin (1987).
49. Likert, R. *New Patterns of Management,* McGraw-Hill (1961); see also Likert, R. *The Human Organization,* McGraw-Hill (1967); Likert, R. and Likert, J. G. *New Ways of Managing Conflict,* McGraw-Hill (1976).
50. McClelland, D. C. *Human Motivation,* Cambridge University Press (1988).
51. Argyris, C. *Understanding Organizational Behavior,* Tavistock (1960); and *Integrating the Individual and the Organization,* Wiley (1964).
52. See, for example, Caulkin, S. 'Chris Argyris', *Management Today,* October 1997, pp. 58–9.
53. Bertalanffy, L. von 'Problems of General Systems Theory: A New Approach to the Unity of Science', *Human Biology,* vol. 23, no. 4, 1951, pp. 302–12.
54. Miller, E. J. and Rice, A. K. *Systems of Organization,* Tavistock (1967).
55. Trist, E. L., Higgin, G. W., Murray, H. and Pollock, A. B. *Organizational Choice,* Tavistock (1963).
56. Lane, T., Snow, D. and Labrow, P. 'Learning to Succeed with ICT', *British Journal of Administrative Management,* May/June 2000, pp. 14–15.
57. Walker, C. R. and Guest, R. H. *The Man on the Assembly Line,* Harvard University Press (1952); see also Walker, C. R., Guest, R. H. and Turner, A. N. *The Foreman on the Assembly Line,* Harvard University Press (1956).
58. Sayles, L. R. *Behaviour of Industrial Work Groups,* Wiley (1958).
59. Blauner, R. *Alienation and Freedom,* University of Chicago Press (1964).
60. Deutsch, S. E. 'Industrial Jobs and the Worker: An Investigation of Response to Task Attributes by Arthur Turner and Paul Lawrence', *Technology and Culture,* vol. 7, no. 3, 1966, pp. 436–8.
61. Seddon, J. *Freedom from Command & Control: A better way to make the work work,* Vanguard Consulting Ltd (2005).
62. Barnard, C. *The Functions of the Executive,* Oxford University Press (1938).
63. Simon, H. A. *The New Science of Management Decision,* revised edition, Prentice Hall (1977).
64. Cyert, R. M. and March, J. G. *A Behavioural Theory of the Firm,* second edition, Blackwell (1992).
65. Silverman, D. *The Theory of Organisations,* Heinemann (1970), p. 147.
66. Goldthorpe, J. H., Lockwood, D., Bechhofer, F. and Platt, J. *The Affluent Worker,* Cambridge University Press (1968).
67. Fox, A. *Industrial Sociology and Industrial Relations,* HMSO (1966).
68. Horwitz, F. M. 'HRM: An Ideological Perspective', *International Journal of Manpower,* vol. 12, no. 6, 1991, pp. 4–9.
69. Fox, A. *Industrial Society and Industrial Relations,* HMSO (1966).
70. Bowey, A. M. *The Sociology of Organisations,* Hodder & Stoughton (1976).
71. Cooper, R. and Burrell, G. 'Modernism, Postmodernism and Organizational Analysis: An Introduction', *Organization Studies,* vol. 9, no. 1, 1988, pp. 91–112.
72. Clegg, S. R. *Modern Organizations: Organization Studies in the Postmodern World,* Sage (1990).
73. See, for example, Legge, K. *Human Resource Management: Rhetorics and Realities,* Macmillan Business (1995).
74. Watson, T. J. *Organising and Managing Work,* second edition, Financial Times Prentice Hall (2006), p. 271.
75. Miner, J. B. *Management Theory,* Macmillan (1971), p. 145; see also Miner, J. B. *Theories of Organizational Behaviour,* Holt, Rinehart and Winston (1980), ch. 1.
76. Schneider, S. C. and Barsoux, J. *Managing Across Cultures,* second edition, Financial Times Prentice Hall (2003).
77. Cheng, T., Sculli, D. and Chan, F. 'Relationship Dominance – Rethinking Management Theories from the Perspective of Methodological Relationalism', *Journal of Managerial Psychology,* vol. 16, no. 2, 2001, pp. 97–105.
78. Flores, G. N. and Utley, D. R. 'Management Concepts in Use – A 12-year Perspective', *Engineering Management Journal,* vol. 12, no. 3, 2000, pp. 11–17.

79. Stern, S. 'Guru Guide', *Management Today,* October 2001, p. 87.
80. Billen, A. 'Goodbye to Glib Gurus and Their Gobbledegook', *The Times,* 9 March 2009.
81. McLean, J. 'Management Techniques and Theories', *Manager, The British Journal of Administrative Management,* August/September 2005, p. 17.
82. See, for example, Klein, S. M. and Ritti, R. R. *Understanding Organizational Behavior,* second edition, Kent Publishing (1984), ch. 1.
83. Stern, S. 'The Next Big Thing', *Management Today,* April 2007, p. 50.
84. Robinson, L and Francis-Smythe, J. 'Managing to abstraction', *Professional Manager,* vol. 19, no. 5, 2010, pp. 36–8[TS5].
85. https://investor.google.com/earnings/2014/Q4_google_earnings.html (accessed 24 February 2015).
86. http://www.forbes.com/billionaires/list/#tab:overall (accessed 24 February 2015).
87. Peters, T. and Waterman, R. H. *In Search of Excellence,* Harper and Row (1982).
88. http://www.google.com/about/company/philosophy/ (accessed 24 February 2015).
89. Harford, T. *Adapt: Why success always starts with failure,* Abacus, Kindle edition (2012), p. 233.
90. http://bgr.com/2014/07/07/google-vs-apple-products-strategy/ (accessed 24 February 2015).
91. http://www.google.com/about/company/facts/locations/ (accessed 24 February 2015).
92. http://en.wikipedia.org/wiki/Google (accessed 24 February 2015).
93. http://www.google.com/transparencyreport/removals/government/ (accessed 24 February 2015).
94. http://www.theguardian.com/technology/2013/apr/22/google-eric-schmidt-tax-avoidance (accessed 24 February 2015).
95. Kahneman, D. *Thinking Fast and Slow,* Penguin (2011), p. 199 *et seq.*
96. Taleb, N. N. *The Black Swan,* Penguin (2008), p. 62 *et seq.*
97. Appleyard, B. 'In the Beginning Was Google', *Sunday Times,* 29 July 2012, http://bryanappleyard.com/in-the-beginning-was-google/ (accessed 24 February 2015).
98. http://www.nytimes.com/2012/10/08/technology/patent-wars-among-tech-giants-can-stifle-competition.html?pagewanted=all&_r=0 (accessed 24 February 2015).
99. Appleyard, B. 'In the Beginning Was Google', op. cit.
100. http://www.think-act.com/blog/2013/google-vs-apple-a-tale-of-two-strategies/ (accessed 24 February 2015).
101. Briefing: 'Robber barons and silicon sultans', *The Economist,* 3 January 2015, p. 49.
102. Naughton, John (2012) 'New-tech moguls: the modern robber barons?', *The Guardian,* 1 July 2015.

CHAPTER 10
Understanding management

Management is fundamental to the effective operation of work organisations. It is by the process of management and execution of work that the activities of the organisation are carried out. Management is essentially an integrating activity that permeates every facet of the operations of an organisation. Attention must be given to the manner in which management is exercised and forms of managerial behaviour.

Learning outcomes

After completing this chapter you should have enhanced your ability to:

- explain the main activities and processes of management;
- analyse the essential nature of managerial work;
- contrast management in private-enterprise and public-sector organisations;
- outline empirical studies on the nature of managerial work;
- examine styles of managerial behaviour;
- debate suggested philosophies for managing with and through people;
- review the importance and future of management.

Critical review and reflection

Managers do not really have much influence. They follow where the organisation appears to be going, and avoid upsetting other people or making serious errors. People regarded as good managers are usually those who are remembered as not being bad managers.

How far do YOU agree with this assertion? What is YOUR experience of a good manager?

The importance of management

Organisations can only achieve their goals and objectives through the co-ordinated efforts of their members. It is by the process of management and execution of work that the activities of the organisation are carried out. Effective management is clearly essential for organisational success.

In certain respects everyone can be regarded as a manager. We all manage our own time and everyone has some choice whether or not to do something, and some control, however slight, over the planning and organisation of their work. However, we are concerned with management as involving people looking beyond themselves and exercising formal authority over the activities and performance of other people.

Even within a work organisation one cannot necessarily identify a manager by what a person is called or by their job title. In some organisations there is a liberal use of the title 'manager' in an apparent attempt to enhance the status and morale of staff. As a result there are a number of people whose job title includes the term 'manager' but who, in reality, are not performing the full activities of a manager. Yet there are many people whose job title does not include the term 'manager' but who, in terms of the activities they undertake and the authority and responsibility they exercise, may be very much a manager.

Management as making things happen

For our purposes, therefore, we can regard **management** as:

- taking place within a structured organisational setting with prescribed roles;
- directed towards the attainment of aims and objectives;
- achieved through the efforts of other people; and
- using systems and procedures.

At its most basic, management may be viewed as 'making things happen'. Recall also the discussion on the nature of leadership (**see Chapter 9**). Whereas leaders are not necessarily managers, it could be argued that all managers should be leaders.

It is the responsibility of management to manage. But organisations can achieve their aims and objectives only through the co-ordinated efforts of their members. This involves good people management.

A heavy responsibility is placed on managers and the activity of management – on the processes, systems and styles of management. Attention must be given to the work environment and appropriate systems of motivation, job satisfaction and rewards. It is important to remember that improvement in organisational performance will come about only through the people who are the organisation. It is also important to bear in mind that the activity of management takes place within the broader context of the organisational setting and subject to the organisational environment and culture. There are also variations in systems and styles of management and in the choice of managerial behaviour. Figure 10.1 shows a basic five-stage framework of study.

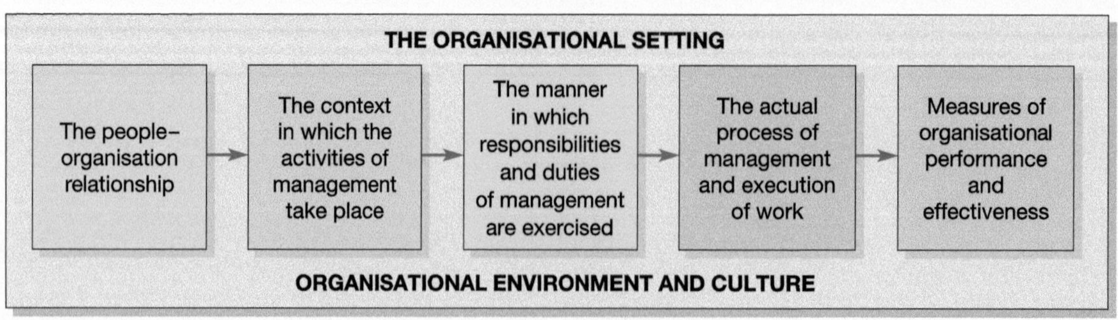

Figure 10.1 A basic framework of study

But what *is* management?

Management is a generic term and subject to many interpretations. A number of contrasting ideas are attributed to the meaning of management and to the work of a manager.[1] There are also different ways of viewing the study and knowledge of management. *Drucker* sees management as denoting a function as well as the people who discharge it, a social position and authority, and also a discipline and field of study: 'Management is tasks. Management is a discipline. But management is also people. Every achievement of management is the achievement of a manager. Every failure is a failure of a manager.'[2]

Significance of cultural influences

Schneider and Barsoux contend that trying to define the meaning of management shows up differences in beliefs and values. Cultural influences are a significant feature of management. Managers in some countries might have more concern for the 'spiritual' aspects of management, while in others there would be greater concern for the business sense. Developing people through work could be seen as an intrusion of privacy, and others may perceive empowerment as another name for manipulation.[3] According to *Francesco and Gold,* if international managers are to perform successfully in the global economy they need to understand the effects of different cultures on organisational behaviour. Reliance on theories developed in one culture is not sufficient.[4]

Managers born or made? Management an art or science?

There is frequent debate about whether managers are born or made or whether management is an art or a science. Briefly, the important point is that neither of these is a mutually exclusive alternative. Even if there are certain innate qualities that make for a potentially good manager, these natural talents must be encouraged and developed through proper guidance, education and training, and planned experience. Clearly, management must always be something of an art, especially in so far as it involves practice, personal judgement and dealing with people. However, it still requires knowledge of the fundamentals of management, and competence in the application of specific skills and techniques – as illustrated, for example, with developments in IT.

> *The trouble is that, for all the techniques at their disposal, managers generally act at a very intuitive level. Managers may have absorbed the latest thinking on core competencies, but are more likely to base a decision on prejudice or personal opinion rather than a neat theory.*[5]

The discussion of management as an art or a science is developed by *Watson,* who suggests that in order to make sense of the complex and highly ambiguous situations in which managers find themselves, management can be viewed not only as both art and science, but also as magic and politics (*see* Figure 10.2).[6]

Two views on management as a science

Dib provides an account of hearing contrasting views on management as a science. One view is *yes* – there is clearly science in management although a purely scientific approach omits human beings as the most important factor. Management is about the application of knowledge: 'The most successful managers are those who use scientific models, theories and concepts, and then apply them using their own style, experience and personality.' The other view is *no* – both management and science apply and extend our knowledge, but management needs more than just observations and experiments and needs to be based on practice, reflection and action. Management is too eclectic to be a science in itself: 'The very nature of management means that without applying and reflecting upon the practice of management we will be more inclined to measure than to take action'.[7]

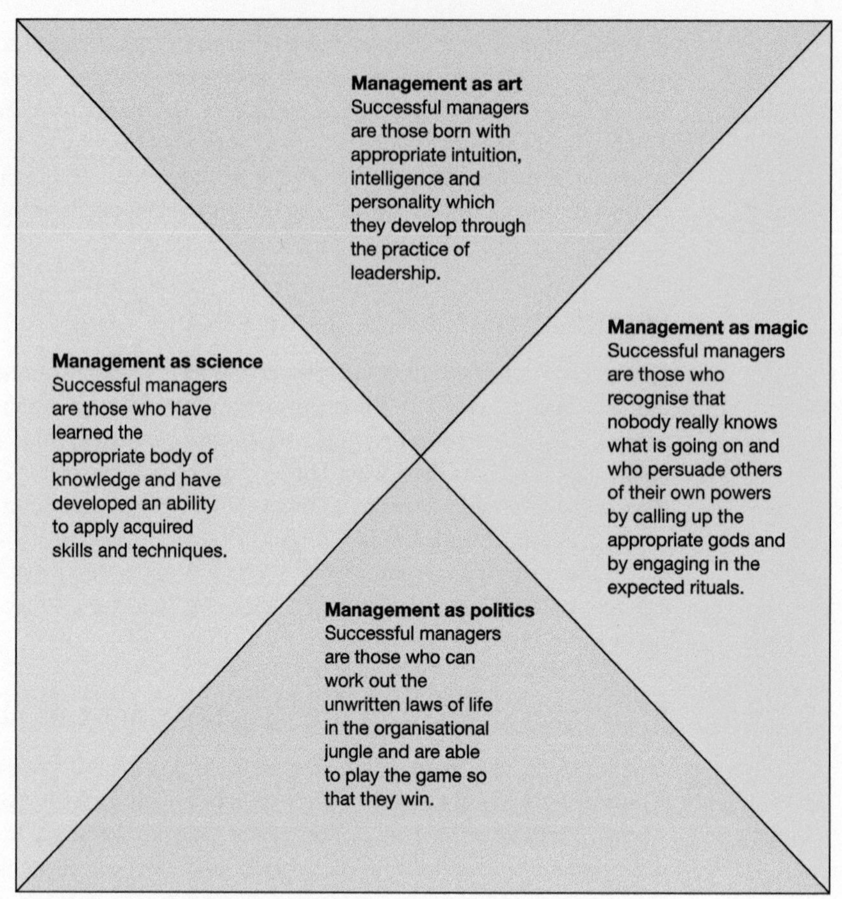

Figure 10.2 Management as art, science, magic and politics

Source: From Watson, T. J. *Management, Organisation and Employment Strategy*, Routledge & Kegan Paul (1986), p. 29. Reproduced by permission of the publishers, Routledge, a division of Taylor & Francis, Ltd.

Thinking about management at university level

Foppen questions the relationship between management practice and education, and whether management has not always been illusory. However, Foppen emphasises the importance of management performance.

> *Management is of pivotal importance for modern society. It is for this reason that, no matter what, thinking about management, certainly at university level, is of great relevance to management practice. So apart from the question of whether management's claim that it is indispensable is really valid or not, the fact that practically everyone believes it is, is what counts.*[8]

Critical review and reflection

According to Foppen, management is of pivotal importance for modern society and thinking about management at university level is of great relevance to management practice.

To what extent is YOUR course of study encouraging YOU to think about management? How do YOU see the relationship between management practice and management education?

The process of management

The nature of management is variable. It is not a separate, discrete function but relates to all activities of the organisation. It cannot be departmentalised or centralised. With the possible exception of the board of directors, or similar, an organisation cannot have a department of management in the same way as it can have a department for other functions, such as research and development, production, marketing or finance. Management is seen best, therefore, as a process common to all other functions carried out within the organisation. Through the execution of work, the central focus of management is on achieving the goals and objectives of the organisation, and satisfying the needs and expectations of its members. **As mentioned earlier** (**Chapter 1**), **management is essentially an integrating activity** (*see* Figure 10.3).

But what does the process of management actually involve and what activities does it encompass? Management is a complex and discursive subject. Moreover, 'management' is not homogeneous. It takes place in different ways and at different levels of the organisation. One approach, especially favoured by classical writers, is to analyse the nature of management and to search for common activities (or functions, or elements) applicable to managers in all organisations.

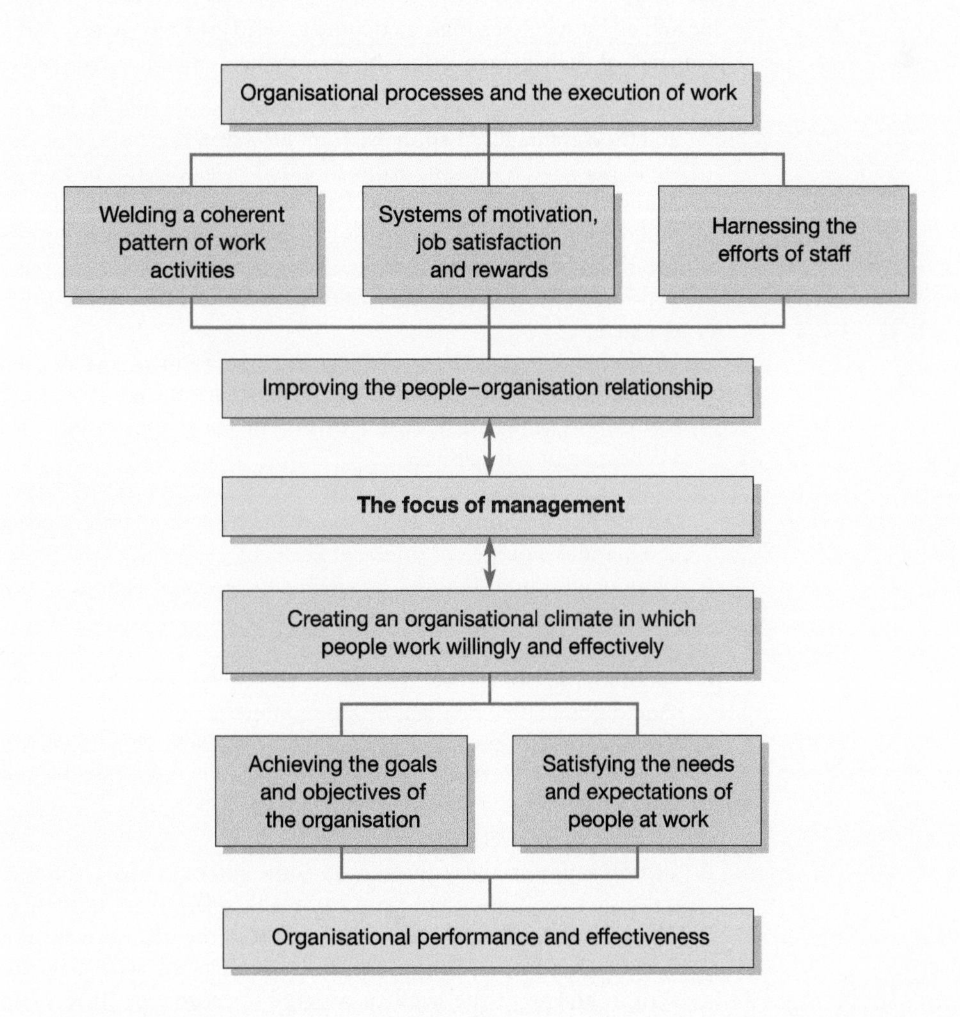

Figure 10.3 The central focus of management

Common activities of management

One of the first, and most widely quoted, analyses is that given by *Henri Fayol* (1841–1925), who divided the managerial activity into five elements of management, defined as: 'to forecast and plan, to organise, to command, to co-ordinate and to control':[9]

- **Forecasting and planning** – examining the future, deciding what needs to be achieved and developing a plan of action.
- **Organising** – providing the material and human resources and building the structure to carry out the activities of the organisation.
- **Commanding** – maintaining activity among personnel, getting the optimum return from all employees in the interests of the whole organisation.
- **Co-ordinating** – unifying and harmonising all activities and efforts of the organisation to facilitate its working and success.
- **Controlling** – verifying that everything occurs in accordance with plans, instructions, established principles and expressed commands.

Principles of management

Fayol also suggests that a set of well-established principles would help concentrate general discussion on management theory. He emphasises, however, that these principles must be flexible and adaptable to changing circumstances. Fayol recognised that there was no limit to the principles of management but in his writing advocated fourteen of them:

1. **Division of work.** The object is to produce more and better work from the same effort, and the advantages of specialisation. However, there are limits to division of work, which experience and a sense of proportion tell us should not be exceeded.
2. **Authority and responsibility.** Responsibility is the corollary of authority. Wherever authority is exercised, responsibility arises. The application of sanctions is essential to good management, and is needed to encourage useful actions and to discourage their opposite. The best safeguard against abuse of authority is the personal integrity of the manager.
3. **Discipline** is essential for the efficient operation of the organisation. Discipline is, in essence, the outward mark of respect for agreements between the organisation and its members. The manager must decide on the most appropriate form of sanction in cases of offences against discipline.
4. **Unity of command.** In any action an employee should receive orders from one superior only; if not, authority is undermined and discipline, order and stability threatened. Dual command is a perpetual source of conflicts.
5. **Unity of direction.** In order to provide for unity of action, co-ordination and focusing of effort, there should be one head and one plan for any group of activities with the same objective.
6. **Subordination of individual interest to general interest.** The interest of the organisation should dominate individual or group interests.
7. **Remuneration of personnel.** Remuneration should as far as possible satisfy both employee and employer. Methods of payment can influence organisational performance and the method should be fair and should encourage keenness by rewarding well-directed effort, but not lead to overpayment.
8. **Centralisation** is always present to some extent in any organisation. The degree of centralisation is a question of proportion and will vary in particular organisations.
9. **Scalar chain** – the chain of superiors from the ultimate authority to the lowest ranks. Respect for line authority must be reconciled with activities that require urgent action, and with the need to provide for some measure of initiative at all levels of authority.

10. **Order.** This includes material order and social order. The object of material order is avoidance of loss. There should be an appointed place for each thing, and each thing in its appointed place. Social order involves an appointed place for each employee, and each employee in their appointed place. Social order requires good organisation and good selection.
11. **Equity.** The desire for equity and for equality of treatment are aspirations to be taken into account in dealing with employees throughout all levels of the scalar chain.
12. **Stability of tenure of personnel.** Generally, prosperous organisations have stable managerial personnel, but changes of personnel are inevitable and stability of tenure is a question of proportion.
13. **Initiative.** This represents a source of strength for the organisation and should be encouraged and developed. Tact and integrity are required to promote initiative and to retain respect for authority and discipline.
14. **Esprit de corps** should be fostered, as harmony and unity among members of the organisation are a great strength in the organisation. The principle of unity of command should be observed. It is necessary to avoid the dangers of divide and rule of one's own team, and the abuse of written communication. Wherever possible, verbal contacts should be used.

A number of these principles relate directly to, or are influenced by, the organisation structure in which the process of management takes place.

Relevance today

Inevitably there are doubts about the relevance of these activities and principles today, but it is hard to argue against their continuing, underlying importance. What is perhaps debatable is the manner of their interpretation and implementation. *McLean* maintains that although proposed almost a hundred years ago, Fayol's definition of management remains one of the most cited of modern times. Fayol has left an indelible mark on management history, and forged an inextricable link between the manager and the organisation.[10]

Hamel suggests that there would be little argument from modern-day executives about Fayol's description of the work of a manager, but puts forward his own synthesis of what the *practice* of management entails:

- Setting and programming *objective*
- Motivating and aligning *effort*
- Co-ordinating and controlling *activities*
- Developing and assigning *talent*
- Accumulating and applying *knowledge*
- Amassing and allocating *resources*
- Building and nurturing *relationships*
- Balancing and meeting *stakeholder demands*.[11]

Critical review and reflection

Despite criticisms of the prescriptive nature of activities and principles of management, they do provide important guidelines for establishing a framework within which the work of an organisation is carried out.

What is YOUR opinion? To what extent do activities and principles of management appear relevant to the execution of work in YOUR university or organisation?

Responsibility for the work of other people

Yet another approach to describing management is given by *Drucker*, who identifies three tasks, equally important but essentially different, that have to be performed:

1. Fulfilling the specific purpose and mission of the institution, whether business enterprise, hospital or university.
2. Making work productive and the worker achieving.
3. Managing social impacts and social responsibilities.[12]

Drucker also argued that the traditional definition of management based on the responsibility for the work of other people is unsatisfactory and too narrow, and emphasises a secondary rather than a primary characteristic. There are people, often in responsible positions, who are clearly 'management' but who do not have responsibility for the work of other people. A person's function and contribution may be unaffected by the number of subordinate staff. A 'manager' is someone who performs the tasks of management whether or not they have power over others.

> *Who is a manager can be defined only by that person's function and by the contribution he or she is expected to make. And the function that distinguishes the manager above all others is the function no one but the manager can perform. The one contribution a manager is uniquely expected to make is to give others vision and ability to perform. It is vision and moral responsibility that, in the last analysis, define the manager.*[13]

Drucker was, according to *Stern*, a visionary predicting future trends ahead of the rest and dealing with big ideas but in a practical and down-to-earth way. His work and insights have lasted. Drucker was arguably the foremost thinker on management and business of the twentieth century and we need him as much as ever.[14]

Essential nature of managerial work

Despite the view expressed by Drucker (in 1977) on the tasks and contribution of a manager, one of the most popular ways of defining management today is that it involves getting work done second-hand – that is, through the efforts of other people. Managers are judged, ultimately, not just on their own performance but on the results achieved by subordinate staff. If we look at how people at work actually spend their time, we should be able to distinguish between those whose main occupation is the carrying out of discrete tasks and the actual doing of work themselves, and those who spend proportionally more of their time in determining the nature of work to be undertaken by other people, the planning and organising of their work, providing directions and advice and guidance, and checking on their performance.

'Managing' and 'doing'

By distinguishing 'managing' from 'doing' in this way, we can see management as clarifying objectives and the planning of work, organising the distribution of activities and tasks to other people, direction of subordinate staff and controlling the performance of other people's work. **This provides us with a convenient description and summary of managerial work as the clarification of objectives, planning, organising, directing and controlling** (*see* Figure 10.4). The degree of emphasis given to these different activities may vary widely, however, from one manager to another. Some managers are likely to spend more time on certain activities than

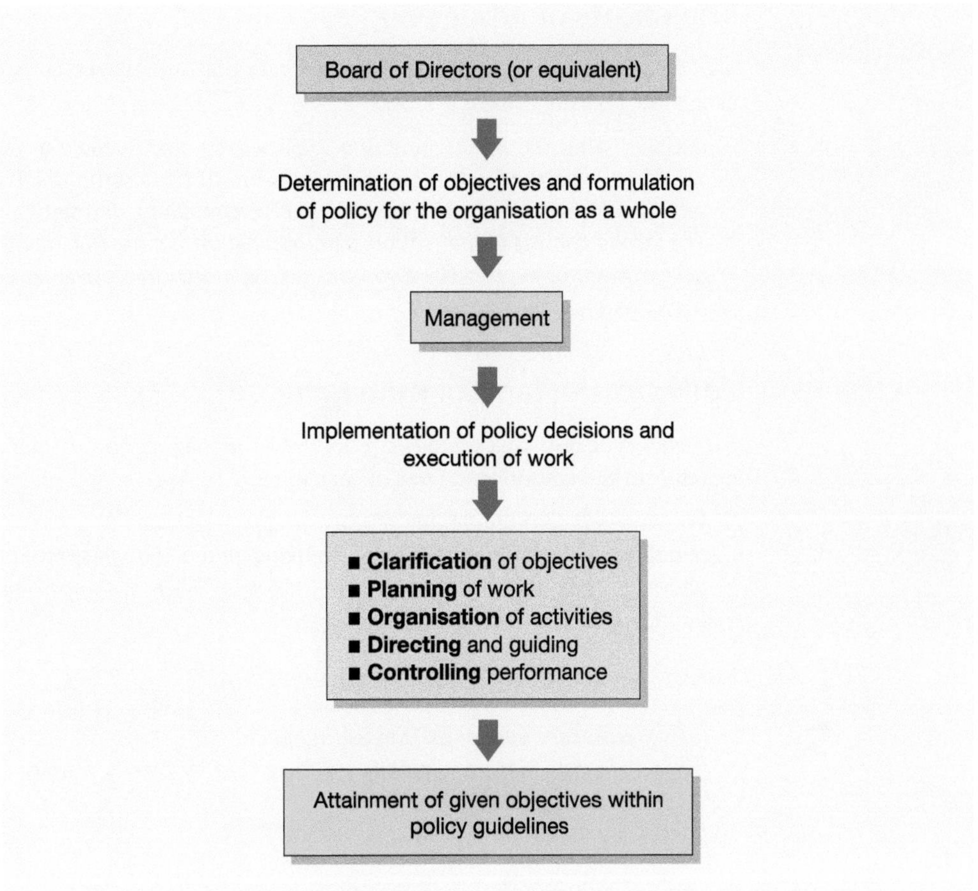

Figure 10.4 Summary of essential nature of managerial work

other managers. The application of these activities reflects a wide range of organisational situations, management practice and managerial style.

Direction, motivation or leadership?

It is tempting to use the term 'motivating' or 'leading', as preferred by some other writers, instead of 'directing' as is shown in our definition of the activities of management above. Motivation and leadership are perhaps less emotive words, but is either an adequate description? It is certainly part of the manager's job to motivate staff, but it also involves development and guidance. Staff need **to perform well in the right areas,** and to be effective as well as efficient. Leadership is clearly important but the efforts of staff need to be **directed** towards the achievement of given objectives in accordance with stated policy. This involves the process of control. It is acknowledged that control is another emotive word and some writers prefer alternatives such as monitoring, inspecting or checking – although, whatever the wording, the functions that it embraces are usually very similar. The real importance is not the particular term itself but what it is intended to achieve and the manner in which 'control' is exercised (**see Chapter 13**). For example, according to *Sir Alex Ferguson:*

> *Management is all about control. Success gives you control and control gives you longevity as a manager. In football very few managers achieve a position of complete control over their teams.*[15]

The efforts of other people

Stewart attempts to integrate the various definitions of management and summarises the manager's job, broadly defined as:

> *deciding what should be done and then getting other people to do it. A longer definition would be concerned with how these tasks are to be accomplished. The first task comprises setting objectives, planning (including decision-making), and setting up formal organization. The second consists of motivation, communication, control (including measurement), and the development of people. The two tasks are separated for convenient analysis, but in practice they may often overlap.*[16]

Folklore and facts of managing

Mintzberg suggests that the basic processes of managing do not change much over time. But he refers to the folklore and facts of managing.

> *We have this common image of the manager, especially in a senior job, as a reflective, systematic planner 'sitting at a desk, thinking grand thoughts, making great decisions, and, above all, systematically planning out the future.' There is a good deal of evidence about this, but not a shred of it supports this image.*
>
> *Facts: Study after study has shown that*
>
> *(a) managers work at an unrelenting pace;*
> *(b) their activities are typically characterized by brevity, variety, fragmentation, and discontinuity; and*
> *(c) they are strongly oriented to action.*[17]

Critical review and reflection

The idea of 'getting work done through the efforts of other people' may not satisfy all possible criteria for the role of the manager. It does, however, have the advantage of simplicity and focuses on what in reality is at the heart of effective management.

What do YOU think? Do YOU agree with Drucker that this definition is unsatisfactory? How would YOU define the true meaning of management?

Management in private-enterprise and public-sector organisations

The general movement of major organisations away from direct governmental control to greater responsibility for managing their own affairs has led to blurring of the traditional distinction between the private and public sectors (**see discussion in Chapter** 3). There are, however, still perceived differences between management in the private and public sectors. These differences arise from particular features of public-sector organisations. For example:

- aims concerned with providing a service for, and for the well-being of, the community rather than just of a commercial nature;
- the scale, variety and complexity of their operations;
- the tendency for them to be subject more to press reports on their activities;

- the political environment in which they operate, and in the case of local government, for example, the relationship between elected members and permanent officers;
- high levels of statutory regulations, legislation and ministerial guidance;
- the generally high level of trade union involvement;
- difficulties in measuring standards of performance of services provided compared with profitability;
- demand for uniformity of treatment and public accountability for their operations;
- tendency towards more rigid HR policies – for example, specific limitations on levels of authority and responsibility, fixed salary grades based on general pay scales, long-term career structures and set promotion procedures.

A number of these features frequently combine to result in increased bureaucracy within public-sector organisations.

Same general problems of management

Both private-enterprise and public-sector organisations, however, face the same general problems of management. Both are concerned with, for example:

- the clarification of aims and objectives;
- the design of a suitable structure;
- carrying out essential administrative functions; and
- the efficiency and effectiveness of their operations.

Basic principles of management apply in any series of activities in any organisation. Although actual methods and procedures will of necessity differ, the common activities and concerns of management apply to a greater or lesser extent in both private-enterprise and public-sector organisations. However, as *Walker* points out:

> *Despite the talent in all three sectors of the economy, cultural differences, alien working practices and even mutual suspicion mean moving between the private, public and voluntary sectors can be a bumpy ride.*

Beyond differences in management styles, a key factor is that in the private sector there is more of a strategic focus, while in the public sector it is much more about here and now. Nine out of ten private-sector employers would be unlikely to take employees offloaded from the public sector.[18]

Richard Vince is the Governor of HMP Manchester, the only UK prison to be run by the prison service under a government contract

I don't have to make a profit. I don't pay dividends. And I don't have shareholders or owners in the strictest sense of the word. I am less exposed to the market and less exposed to financial pressures brought to bear externally. You could argue that this could lead to financial indiscipline. But I would argue that it enables me to spend what I need to spend to deliver the service required. And if there is an excess, I give it back. To say the private sector is always cheaper is a very broad and sweeping statement, particularly if you consider it in the context of PFI (Private Finance Initiative) arrangements. You have to look at the whole life cycle of a contract if you are to evaluate it properly.

I don't doubt that as markets mature, new providers will develop the necessary expertise, but when you are dealing with public safety, public protection and reoffending you need a proven and trusted supplier. That's what the public sector offers.

→

Public service shouldn't be dirty words. Public servants work on behalf of the public and are proud of that. Businesses are there to make a profit - that's an absolute truth. But freed up from those constraints, I'm here to deliver a public service - and there is a clear distinction between those two priorities. They can be conflicting at worst; at a minimum they can create tension.

Any organisation, whether public or private, needs to be showing best value for money against the highest standard of delivery. So my position here has been to deliver public services while applying commercial disciplines in the way that we operate - ensuring we always get the best provider of services, whether internal or external, and that contracts are hard negotiated and hard applied. We view public money not as a right, but something to be managed with great prudence and on which to maximise return. What we mustn't lose sight of is the fact that what we are providing is public services. How that is delivered is really not the issue. It's about the quality of the service and the price.

Source: Management Today, March 2012, p. 53. Reproduced with permission.

Importance of skills and behaviour

A report from the CIPD points out that although public services are not homogeneous and specific issues facing managers will differ between sectors and localities, there is a shared agenda in improving people management in the public-sector workplaces. It is important to recognise that without more effective people management, there is no chance of introducing positive and lasting change. Management need to support and empower front-line staff. The report makes clear that:

> *an improvement in the quality of people management, particularly among line managers and supervisors, is central to more effective delivery of public services and greater local accountability. Inadequate people management skills are also often at the heart of catastrophic service failure.*[19]

Sir Howard Bernstein refers to the challenging economic climate that has focused the public sector on the need for radical reform to tackle the cost pressures on it and the development of the skills to deliver public-sector reform. Significant long-term culture change is required across a range of partners to overcome professional, organisational and technical barriers. All levels of managers and leaders have a vital role in delivering community services in a more integrated way.

> *This type of reform will require different skills and behaviours across all levels of management. Some of the key leadership and management skills necessary for public service reform include the ability to adapt; to lead across organisational boundaries; to exert influence outside traditional hierarchies; to demonstrate political intelligence; and the ability to engage with the community.*[20]

Critical review and reflection

The basis of ownership and finance, public accountability, demand for uniformity of treatment and the political environment in which they work mean the nature of management in the public sector is fundamentally different from that in the private sector.

To what extent are YOU able to challenge this assertion? Do YOU think there are more similarities or differences between management in the two sectors?

Management and organisational behaviour in action case study

Putting the customer first in a service organisation: cultural change at Fareham Borough Council

Faced with continual economic pressure, how does a thriving borough council change the culture of the organisation in a way that results in improved customer service and delivers efficiency savings? Fareham Borough Council is located along the south coast of Hampshire with a growing population, currently 112,800. The biennial Residents' Survey shows existing high levels of customer satisfaction; the 2013 survey identified that over 90 per cent of residents were happy with the way that Fareham Borough Council runs things. With such a high level of satisfaction, the need for further improvement or the possibility of doing so might be questioned; however, the purpose of the work being undertaken is to drive out complacency and ensure that satisfaction does not decline in the future and customers receive the best service possible.

Cultural change is difficult to achieve, but Fareham Borough Council is using a unique approach to achieving cultural transformation by putting the customer at the core of its work. Services are being redesigned to drive out waste and focus on working with an understanding of what matters to the customer. Driven from the top by the Leader of the Council and the Chief Executive, the Council is using the Vanguard Method.

Service is different to manufacturing. In simple terms there is inherently greater variety in customer demand, hence the need to design to absorb that variety. The Vanguard Method transfers expertise to people (managers and staff) in the organisation and helps change from command and control to a systems approach to the design and management of work. Emphasis is placed on the customer and measurement of success as opposed to targets of expected performance. Rather than concern with individual functions or activities, the organisation is viewed as an integrated system. The focus of attention is predominately on the flow of the needs of the customer throughout the system. Vanguard uses guides, people who are experts in both intervention theory (how to make a change) and systems theory (how to analyse and design work). **(See also discussion in Chapter 2.)**

The results

Unlike its traditional application, which is focused on a single service area, Fareham Borough Council has implemented a programme that will see all services reviewed across the whole organisation. Each of the interventions is being led by a Head of Service to provide support to the employees involved and ensure buy-in at all levels of the organisation. Analysing a service from a customer's perspective has revealed dramatic ways to change the way services are delivered. The points below indicate the services being reviewed and key improvements identified so far:

- **Housing repairs** – The average time to complete a day-to-day repair on a council property has fallen from 89 days to less than 8 days. This length of time is from when the customer reports the repair, up to when the repair is complete and stays fixed. Tradespeople are able to access a customer's property on the first visit in over 97 per cent of cases. This demonstrates the success of customers advising the council when it is convenient to them for tradespeople to attend. Changes in the approach to electrical testing are expected to deliver savings of approximately £88,000 per annum (50 per cent of the original cost); savings of approximately £30,000 are also anticipated following changes to the testing of emergency lighting.
- **Planning applications** – Average time taken to process applications has dropped from 56 days to 36.
- **Benefits** – The time taken to process new benefit claims has fallen from approximately 20 days to 6 days. Customers now deal with a single employee as handoffs are virtually non-existent.
- **Parking enforcement** – The number of Informal Challenges to Penalty Charge Notices (PCNs) has dropped from 45 per week to 23. This demonstrates how the Parking Enforcement Officers are making better decisions when issuing a PCN.

Conclusion

By engaging with every employee and understanding what matters to customers, the Council has been able to affect a cultural change at all levels of the organisation. In the first year of the programme, the Council is already seeing significant improvements in customer service and has been able to capture savings of £381,000 per annum.

Source: Thanks to Christopher Cotmore, Corporate Policy Officer, Fareham Borough Council. Reproduced with permission.

→

Tasks

1. What do you think are the main reasons for the key improvements identified by Fareham Borough Council?
2. Discuss critically how you view the idea of culture change with management based on the flow of customer needs rather than individual functions or activities.
3. To what extent do you think managing through putting the customer first could, or should, be applied meaningfully to your university or organisation?

The work of a manager

Despite similarities in the general activities of management, the jobs of individual managers will differ widely. In practice, it will be influenced by such factors as:

- the nature of the organisation, its culture, philosophy, objectives and size;
- the type of structure;
- activities and tasks involved;
- technology and methods of performing work;
- the nature of people employed; and
- the level in the organisation at which the manager is working.

These differences do not just exist between organisations in the private and public sectors; they are often more a matter of degree. For example, many large business organisations may have more in common in their management and operations with public-sector organisations than with small private firms.

The environmental setting

A major determinant of the work of the manager is the nature of the environment, both internal and external, in which the manager is working. Managers have to perform their jobs in the situation in which they find themselves (*see* Figure 10.5).

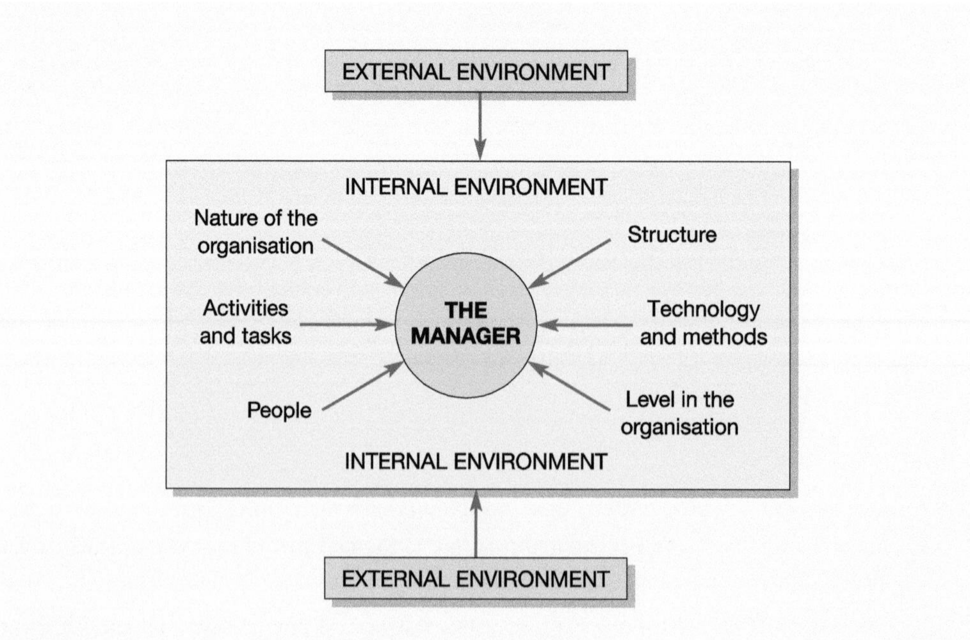

Figure 10.5 The work of a manager: the environmental setting

The **internal environment** relates to the culture and climate of the organisation – 'how things are done around here' – and to the prevailing atmosphere surrounding the organisation. (**Organisational culture and climate are discussed in Chapter 15.**) The **external environment** relates to the organisation as an open system (**discussed in Chapter 3**). Managers must be responsive to the changing opportunities and challenges, and risks and limitations, facing the organisation. External environmental factors are largely outside the control of management.

The diversity of management

Studies on the nature of management have been based on wider observation and research, and have concentrated on the diversity of management and differences in the jobs of managers. Among the best-known empirical studies on the nature of managers' jobs, and how managers actually spend their time, are those by *Henry Mintzberg, John Kotter* and *Rosemary Stewart*.[21]

Managerial roles

Based on the study of the work of five chief executives of medium-sized to large organisations, Mintzberg classifies the activities that constitute the essential functions of a top manager's job.[22] What managers do cannot be related to the classical view of the activities of management. The manager's job can be described more meaningfully in terms of various 'roles' or organised sets of behaviour associated with a position.[23] Mintzberg recognises that people who 'manage' have formal authority over the unit they command and this leads to a special position of status in the organisation.

As a result of this formal authority and status, managerial activities can be seen as a set of ten **managerial roles**, which may be divided into three groups:

- interpersonal roles;
- informational roles; and
- decisional roles.

Interpersonal roles

The **interpersonal roles** are relations with other people arising from the manager's status and authority:

1. **Figurehead role** is the most basic and simple of managerial roles. The manager is a symbol and represents the organisation in matters of formality, participation as a social necessity and being available for people who insist on access to the 'top'.
2. **Leader role** is among the most significant of roles and permeates all activities of a manager. By virtue of the authority vested in the manager, there is a responsibility for staffing, and for the motivation and guidance of subordinates.
3. **Liaison role** involves the manager in horizontal relationships with individuals and groups outside the manager's own unit or the organisation. An important part of the manager's job is the linking between the organisation and the environment.

Informational roles

The **informational roles** relate to the sources and communication of information arising from the manager's interpersonal roles:

1. **Monitor role** identifies the manager in seeking and receiving information to develop an understanding of the working of the organisation and its environment. Information may be received from internal or external sources, and may be formal or informal.

2. **Disseminator role** involves the manager in transmitting external information through the liaison role into the organisation, and internal information through the leader role between the subordinates. The information may be largely factual or may contain value judgements.
3. **Spokesperson role** involves the manager as formal authority in transmitting information to people outside the unit and the general public such as suppliers, customers, government departments and the press.

Decisional roles

The **decisional roles** involve the making of strategic organisational decisions on the basis of the manager's status and authority, and access to information:

1. **Entrepreneurial role** is the manager's function to initiate and plan controlled change through exploiting opportunities or solving problems, and taking action to improve the existing situation.
2. **Disturbance handler role** involves the manager in reacting to involuntary situations and unpredictable events. When an unexpected disturbance occurs the manager must take action to correct the situation.
3. **Resource allocator role** involves the manager in using formal authority to decide where effort will be expended, and making choices on the allocation of resources such as money, time, materials and staff.
4. **Negotiator role** is participation in negotiation activity with other individuals or organisations. Because of the manager's authority, credibility, access to information and responsibility for resource allocation, negotiation is an important part of the job.

Mintzberg emphasises that this set of ten roles is a somewhat arbitrary division of the manager's activities. It presents one of many possible ways of categorising the view of managerial roles. The ten roles are not easily isolated in practice but form an integrated whole. If any role is removed, this affects the effectiveness of the manager's overall performance.

Why organisations need managers

As a result of describing the nature of managerial work in terms of a set of ten roles, Mintzberg suggests six basic purposes of the manager, or reasons why organisations need managers:

- to ensure the organisation serves its basic purpose – the efficient production of goods or services;
- to design and maintain the stability of the operations of the organisation;
- to take charge of strategy-making and adapt the organisation in a controlled way to changes in its environment;
- to ensure the organisation serves the ends of those people who control it;
- to serve as the key informational link between the organisation and the environment; and
- as formal authority to operate the organisation's status system.

Agenda-setting and network-building

From a detailed study of fifteen successful American general managers involved in a broad range of industries, *Kotter* found that although their jobs differed and the managers undertook their jobs in a different manner, they all had two significant activities in common: **agenda-setting** and **network-building.**[24]

- **Agenda-setting** is a constant activity of managers. This is a set of items, or series of agendas, involving aims and objectives, plans, strategies, ideas, decisions to be made and priorities of action in order to bring about desired end results. This requires individual managers responsible for achieving targets to have a continual and changing series of agendas to help bring intentions into reality.

- **Network-building** involves the managers interacting with other people and establishing a network of co-operative relations outside the formal structure. The network often includes a large number of people, many in addition to their boss or direct subordinates, and individuals and groups outside the organisation. Meetings provide exchanges of information over a wide range of topics in a short period of time. A major feature of network-building is to establish and maintain contacts that can assist in the successful achievement of agenda items.

Demands, constraints and choices

Based on earlier studies of managerial jobs, *Stewart* has developed a model for understanding managerial work and behaviour. The model directs attention to the generalisations that can be made about managerial work, and differences that exist among managerial jobs. It acknowledges the wide variety, found from previous studies, among different managers in similar jobs in terms of how they view their jobs and the work they do.[25]

The three main categories of the model are **demands, constraints** and **choices.** These identify the flexibility in a managerial job.

- **Demands** are what anyone in the job has to do. They are not what the manager ought to do, but only what must be done: for example, meeting minimum criteria of performance, work that requires personal involvement, complying with bureaucratic procedures that cannot be avoided, meetings that must be attended.
- **Constraints** are internal or external factors that limit what the manager can do: for example, resource limitations, legal or trade union constraints, the nature of technology, physical location, organisational constraints, attitudes of other people.
- **Choices** are the activities that the manager is free to do, but does not have to do. They are opportunities for one job-holder to undertake different work from another, or to do the work in a different way: for example, what work is done within a defined area, to change the area of work, the sharing of work, participation in organisational or public activities.

Stewart suggests that the model provides a framework for thinking about the nature of managerial jobs, and about the manner in which managers undertake them. To understand what managerial jobs are really like it is necessary to understand the nature of their flexibility. Account should be taken of variations in behaviour and differences in jobs before attempting to generalise about managerial work.

An overview of management is set out in the concept map of Figure 10.6.

Critical review and reflection

The work of a manager is not easy to describe as aspects that are common in many applications escape us in others and all managers have their individual way of working. Understanding the nature of management can therefore be no more than a compromise between the ideas of the more lucid writers on the subject.

To what extent do YOU accept this view of the study of management? How would YOU explain the essential nature of managerial work and the role of the manager?

Importance of managerial style

There appears to be a growing recognition that managers can no longer rely solely on their perceived formal authority as a result of a hierarchical position in the structure of the organisation. More than ever an essential ingredient of any successful manager is the ability to handle people successfully. This changing relationship places a heavy responsibility on managers, and on the systems and styles of management adopted.

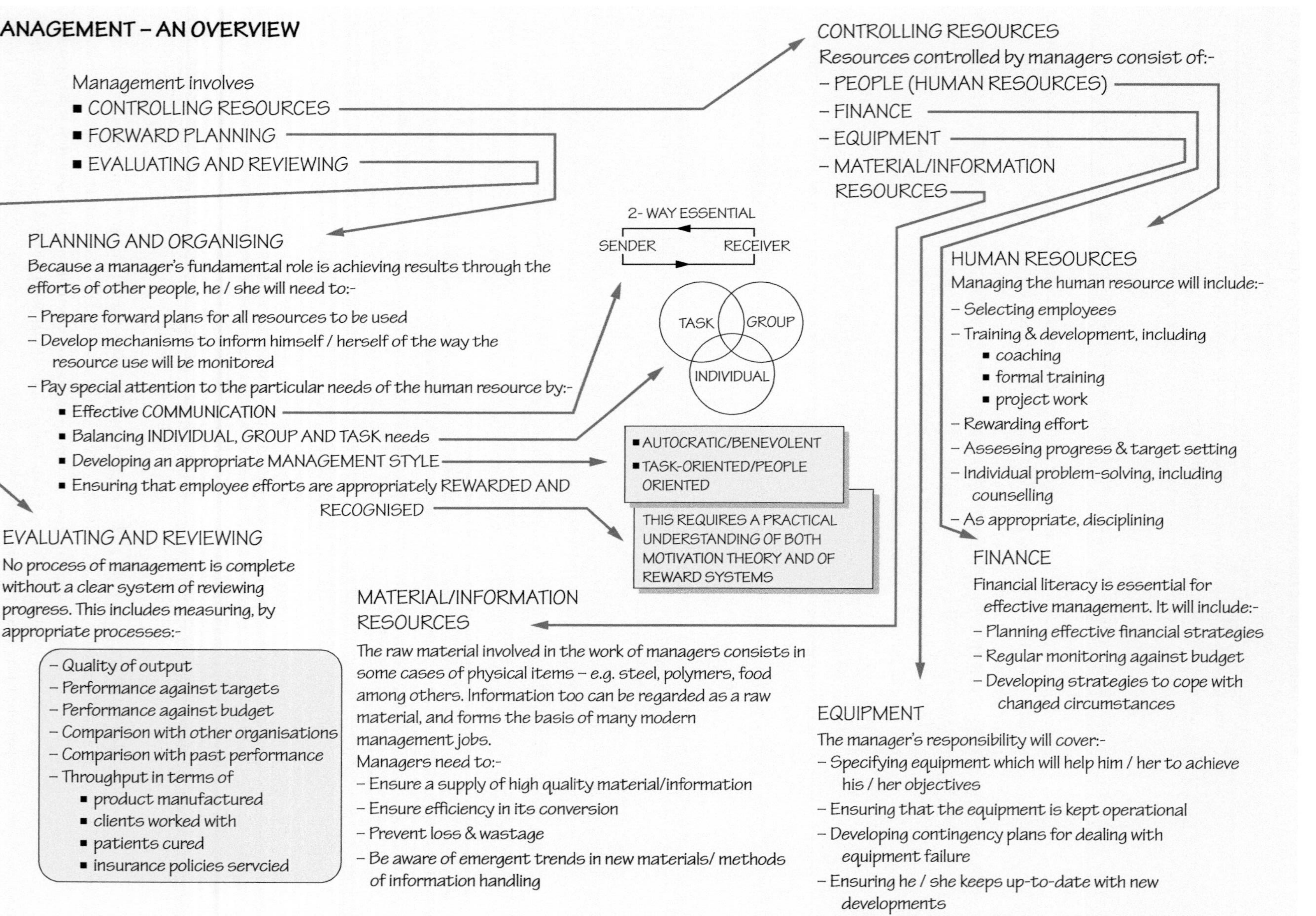

Figure 10.6 Management - an overview

Source: Copyright ©2011 The Virtual Learning Materials Workshop. Reproduced with permission.

It is, however, interesting to note the views of *Watson* who, while acknowledging that to create the goods, services and quality of life that people look for in the modern world, rather complex patterns of co-operative behaviour have to be orchestrated and 'managed', identifies three major problems in thinking about organising and managing work in terms of 'managing people':

- *Firstly,* in a modern democratic society, is it realistic even to contemplate the possibility of managing people and that there are people willing to be managed?
- *Secondly,* can it be argued that a manager has no moral right to direct, manage or boss any individual?
- *Thirdly,* does the focus on people management tend to blur the part played by structures, systems, cultures, processes and the rest?[26]

Good people management

Whatever the veracity of these problems or the importance attached to the management of systems, the organising and management of work depends ultimately on the people who make up the organisation. Without people, systems and procedures and indeed organisations themselves are meaningless. And people need to be managed. But, of course, of increasing importance are:

- how the process of management is actually carried out;
- the style of managerial behaviour; and
- its effectiveness for *both* organisational performance and the satisfaction of its members.

With the general movement towards flatter organisation structures, flexible working and greater employee empowerment, there is more emphasis on an integrating rather than a traditional controlling style of management. Management style and behaviour can be as important as management competence.

Style and context

Mintzberg draws attention to the relationship between managerial style and the importance of context, and questions how much personal style has an influence on what managers do. People do not usually find themselves in managerial jobs by chance to shape as they wish. What you do as a manager is mostly determined by what you face as a manager.

> *Personal style is important, no question. But that seems to be more about how managers do things, including the decisions they make and the strategies they shape, than what they do as managers. In this regard, the literature, practitioner and academic alike, may be vastly overrating the importance of personal style. Style matters and context matters, but mostly they matter together, in a symbiotic relationship.*[27]

Theory X and Theory Y management

The way in which managers approach the performance of their jobs and the behaviour they display towards subordinate staff are likely to be conditioned by underlying predispositions about people, and human nature and work. Drawing on Maslow's hierarchy of needs model (**discussed in Chapter 7**), *McGregor,* in 1960, put forward two suppositions about human nature and behaviour at work. He argued that the style of management adopted is a function of the manager's attitudes towards people and assumptions about human nature and behaviour. The two suppositions are called Theory X and Theory Y and are based on polar assumptions about people and work.[28]

Theory X assumptions

Theory X represents the carrot-and-stick assumptions on which traditional organisations are based. Its assumptions are that:

- the average person is lazy and has an inherent dislike of work;
- most people must be coerced, controlled, directed and threatened with punishment if the organisation is to achieve its objectives;
- the average person avoids responsibility, prefers to be directed, lacks ambition and values security most of all; and
- motivation occurs only at the physiological and security levels.

The central principle of Theory X is direction and control through a centralised system of organisation and the exercise of authority. McGregor questioned whether the Theory X approach to human nature is correct and the relevance of management practices that are based upon it. Assumptions based on a Theory X approach, and the traditional use of rewards and sanctions exercised by the nature of the manager's position and authority, are likely to result in an exploitative or authoritarian style of management.

Theory Y assumptions

At the other extreme to Theory X is **Theory Y**, which represents the assumptions consistent with current research knowledge. **The central principle of Theory Y is the integration of individual and organisational goals.** Its assumptions are:

- for most people, work is as natural as play or rest;
- people will exercise self-direction and self-control in the service of objectives to which they are committed;
- commitment to objectives is a function of rewards associated with their achievement;
- given the right conditions, the average worker can learn to accept and to seek responsibility;
- the capacity for creativity in solving organisational problems is distributed widely in the population;
- the intellectual potential of the average person is only partially utilised; and
- motivation occurs at the affiliation, esteem and self-actualisation levels as well as at the physiological and security levels.

The Theory Y approach is not a 'soft' option. In practice it is often difficult to achieve successfully. It can be frustrating and time consuming, and mistakes will occur. For example, as *Townsend* reports:

> *Since 1952 I've been stumbling around buildings and running primitive Theory Y departments, divisions, and finally one whole Theory Y company: Avis. In 1962, after thirteen years, Avis had never made a profit (except one year when they jiggled their depreciation rates). Three years later the company had grown internationally (not by acquisitions) from $30 million in sales to $75 million in sales, and had made successive annual profits of $1 million, $3 million, and $5 million. If I had anything to do with this, I ascribe it all to my application of Theory Y. And a faltering, stumbling, groping, mistake-ridden application it was.*[29]

Demands of the situation

The two views of Theory X and Theory Y tend to represent extremes of the natural inclination of managers towards a particular style of behaviour. In practice, however, the actual style of management behaviour adopted will be influenced by the demands of the situation.[30] Where the job offers a high degree of intrinsic satisfaction or involves a variety of tasks, an element of problem-solving and the exercise of initiative, or where output is difficult to measure in quantitative terms, then an informal, participative approach would seem to be more effective. In many cases this would apply to work of a scientific, technical or professional nature. Where commitment to the goals of the organisation is almost a prerequisite of membership, such as in certain voluntary or charity organisations, for example, then a Theory Y approach would clearly seem to be most appropriate.

However, even if a manager has a basic belief in Theory Y assumptions, there may be occasions when it is necessary, or more appropriate, to adopt a Theory X approach. This approach may be indicated in emergency situations, or where shortage of time or other overriding factors demand the use of authority in directing actions to the tasks in hand. For example, in the hustle, heat and noise of a busy hotel kitchen preparing fresh meals for a large banquet, with many tasks to be co-ordinated over very short time scales, it seems to be recognised that a Theory X style of management is most appropriate. In such circumstances this style of management appears often to be accepted by the kitchen staff.

Critical review and reflection

Although published in 1960, the underlying concepts of McGregor's Theory X and Theory Y are still some of the most significant and meaningful insights into our understanding of managerial behaviour.

What do YOU think? What experiences have YOU had of Theory X or Y management? What would be YOUR preferred natural style of managerial behaviour, and why?

The Managerial/Leadership Grid®

One means of describing and evaluating different styles of management is the *Blake and Mouton* **Managerial Grid®** (*see* Figure 10.7). First published as the Managerial Grid in 1964, restated in 1978 and 1985[31] and republished in 1991 as the **Leadership Grid®**,[32] the Grid provides a basis for comparison of managerial styles in terms of two principal dimensions: concern for production and concern for people.

- **Concern for production** is the amount of emphasis that the manager places on accomplishing the tasks in hand, achieving a high level of production and getting results or profits. This is represented along the horizontal axis of the Grid.
- **Concern for people** is the amount of emphasis that the manager gives to subordinates and colleagues as individuals and to their needs and expectations. This is represented along the vertical axis of the Grid.

Five basic combinations

The four corners and the centre of the Grid provide five basic combinations of degree of concern for production coupled with degree of concern for people (*see* Figure 10.7a):

1. **Managers with a 1,1 rating,** the impoverished manager, tend to be remote from their subordinates and believe in the minimum movement from their present position.
2. **Managers with a 9,1 rating,** the authority–compliance manager, are autocratic. They tend to rely on a centralised system and the use of authority.
3. **The 1,9 rating managers,** country club managers, believe that a contented staff will undertake what is required of them and achieve a reasonable level of output.
4. **The 5,5 rating,** middle-of-the-road managers, have the approach of 'live and let live' and a tendency to avoid the real issues.
5. **Managers with a 9,9 rating, the team manager,** believe in the integrating of task needs and concern for people.

These five styles of management represent the extremes of the Grid. With a 9-point scale on each axis there is a total of 81 different 'mixtures' of concern for production and concern for people. Most people would come up with a score somewhere in an intermediary position on the Grid.

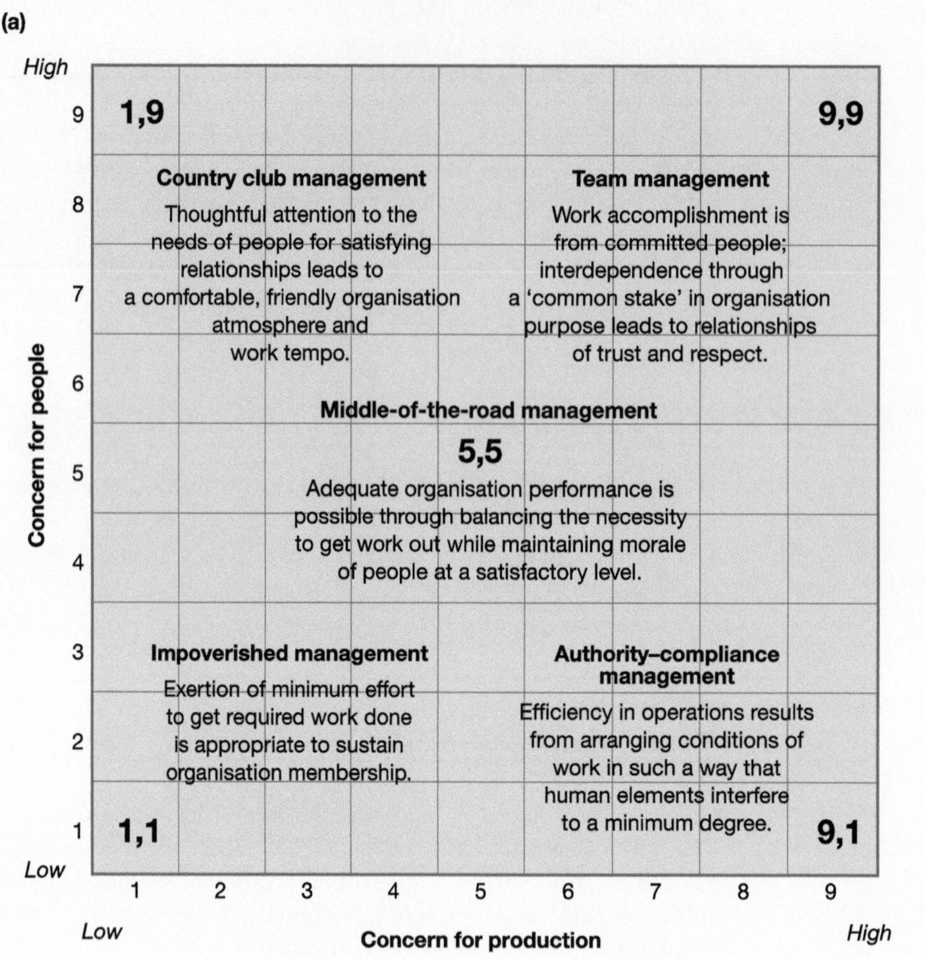

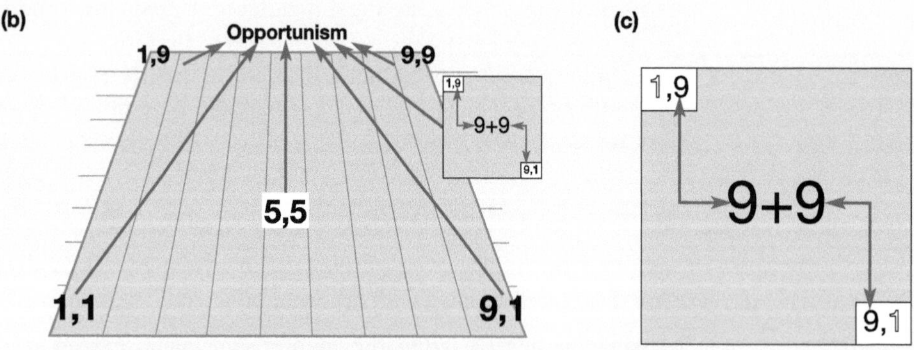

In **Opportunistic management**, people adapt and shift to any Grid style needed to gain the maximum advantage. Performance occurs according to a system of selfish gain. Effort is given only for an advantage or personal gain.

9+9: Paternalism/maternalism Reward and approval are bestowed to people in return for loyalty and obedience; failure to comply leads to punishment.

Figure 10.7 The Leadership Grid®

Source: Blake, R. R. and McCanse, A. A. *Leadership Dilemmas – Grid Solutions*, Gulf Publishing (1991), Grid Figure, p. 29, Paternalism Figure, p. 30, Opportunism Figure, p. 31. Reproduced by permission from Elsevier Ltd.

Two additional grid styles

The 1991 edition of the Grid covers two additional styles, opportunism and 9 + 9 paternalism/maternalism, which take account of the reaction of subordinates. In opportunistic management, organisational performance occurs according to a system of exchanges, whereby effort is given only for an equivalent measure of the same. People adapt to the situation to gain maximum advantage of it (see Figure 10.7b).

In 9 + 9 paternalistic/maternalistic management, reward and approval are granted to people in return for loyalty and obedience, and punishment is threatened for failure to comply (see Figure 10.7c).

A summary of the seven basic combinations of the Grid is given in Table 10.1.

Table 10.1 Leadership Grid style definitions

9,1 Authority-compliance management	Managers in this position have great concern for production and little concern for people. People are seen as 'tools' for production. They demand tight, unilateral control in order to complete tasks efficiently. They consider creativity and human relations to be unnecessary
1,9 Country club management	Managers in this position have great concern for people and little concern for production. They try to avoid conflicts and concentrate on being liked, even at the expense of production. To them the task is less important than good interpersonal relations. Their goal is to keep people happy. (This is a soft Theory X and not a sound human relations approach)
1,1 Impoverished management	This style is often referred to as laissez-faire. Leaders in this position have little concern for people or productivity. They avoid taking sides and stay out of conflicts. They do just enough to maintain group membership
5,5 Middle-of-the-road management	Leaders in this position have medium concern for both people and production. They rely on tried and true techniques and avoid taking untested risks. They attempt to balance their concern for both people and production, but are not committed strongly to either. Conflict is dealt with by avoiding extremes and seeking compromise rather than sound resolution
9 + 9 Paternalistic 'father knows best' management	This leader takes the high 9 level of concern from 9,1 and 1,9 to create a combined style of controlling paternalism. The paternalist strives for high results (high 9 from 9,1) and uses reward and punishment to gain compliance (high 9 from 1,9). The paternalist uses a high level of concern for people to reward for compliance or punish for rejection
Opportunistic 'what's in it for me?' management	The opportunists use whatever Grid style is needed to obtain selfish interest and self-promotion. They adapt to situations to gain the maximum advantage. They may use 9,1 to push their own goals with one person, and 1,9 to gain trust and confidence with another. Performance occurs according to a system of exchanges. Effort is given only for an equivalent measure of the same
9,9 Team management	These managers demonstrate high concern for both people and production. They work to motivate employees to reach their highest levels of accomplishment. They explore alternatives openly and aggressively. They are flexible and responsive to change. This style is considered ideal

Source: Blake, R. R. and McCanse, A. A. *Leadership Dilemmas – Grid Solutions*, Gulf Publishing Company (1991), p. 29. Reproduced with permission from Elsevier Ltd.

Relevance today

According to *Newborough,* 'an organisation's structure, plan and concept are crucial to its effectiveness. Yet beyond these, the most significant single factor is the behaviour of the management team. Its members must act as leaders. They must accomplish their objectives through their ability to guide, motivate and integrate the efforts of others'. The ultimate purpose of studies of managerial style is to aid in the training and development of those who wish to become better leaders. Grid organisation development identifies and applies relevant aspects of behavioural science, and Newborough maintains that the Grid is as relevant today as when it was first launched.[33] And according to *Crainer and Dearlove,* 'Crude as it is, the Grid helps people who are not conversant with psychology to see themselves and those they work with more clearly, to understand their interactions, and identify the sources of resistance and conflicts.'[34]

Critical review and reflection

Whatever the talk about a more consultative style of managerial behaviour, the main complaint from disgruntled members of staff is usually about lack of clear direction and strong decisive management.

To what extent would YOU challenge this contention? What has been YOUR personal experience? How does this relate to YOUR own views on managerial behaviour?

Management systems

Work by McGregor, and by Blake and Mouton, suggests that an organisation is more likely to harness its staffing resources effectively if there is a participative style of management. This view is supported by the work of *Likert,* writing in the 1960s and 1970s. On the basis of a questionnaire to managers in over 200 organisations and research into the performance characteristics of different types of organisations, Likert identifies a fourfold model of management systems.[35] These systems are designated by number:

- System 1 – Exploitive authoritative. Decisions are imposed on subordinates, motivation is based on threats, there is very little teamwork or communication; responsibility is centred at the top of the organisational hierarchy.
- System 2 – Benevolent authoritative. A condescending form of leadership, motivation is based on a system of rewards, there is only limited teamwork or communication; responsibility is at managerial levels but not at lower levels of the organisational hierarchy.
- System 3 – Consultative. Leadership involves some trust in subordinates, motivation is based on rewards but also some involvement, there is a fair degree of teamwork, and communication takes place vertically and horizontally; responsibility for achieving the goals of the organisation is spread more widely throughout the hierarchy.
- System 4 – Participative. Leadership involves trust and confidence in subordinates, motivation is based on rewards for achievement of agreed goals, there is participation and a high degree of teamwork and communication; responsibility for achieving the goals of the organisation is widespread throughout all levels of the hierarchy.

Supportive relationships

The nearer the behavioural characteristics of an organisation approach System 4, the more likely this will lead to long-term improvement in staff turnover and high productivity, low scrap, low costs and high earnings. Likert sets out three fundamental concepts of System 4 management. These are the use of:

- the principle of supportive relationships among members of the organisation and in particular between superior and subordinate;
- group decision-making and group methods of organisation and supervision; and high-performance aspirations for all members of the organisation.

In considering high-performance aspirations, Likert refers to studies that suggest that employees generally want stable employment and job security, opportunities for promotion and satisfactory compensation. They want, also, to feel proud of their organisation and its performance and accomplishments. In System 4 management, superiors should therefore have high-performance aspirations, but so also should every member of the organisation. To be effective, these high-performance goals should not be imposed but set by a participative mechanism involving group decision-making and a multiple overlapping group structure. The mechanism should enable employees to be involved in setting high-performance goals that help to satisfy their needs.

Managing with and through people

Although there are many aspects to management, one essential ingredient of any successful manager is the ability to handle people effectively. Recall, for example, the previous discussion (**Chapter 1**) on people and organisational behaviour. A genuine concern for people and for their welfare goes a long way in encouraging them to perform well. A positive policy of investment in people and an interpersonal relationship approach to management are, in the longer term, worth the effort. For example, the UK government-sponsored initiative Investors in People is based on a commitment to the benefits that organisations can gain through their people and on the vital role of managers.

It is possible to put forward a number of underlying philosophies that arguably are likely to make for the successful management of people, and lead to both improved work performance and more contented staff (*see* Figure 10.8). **These philosophies are not intended to be prescriptive but to encourage discussion on the extent to which you agree with the points of view.**

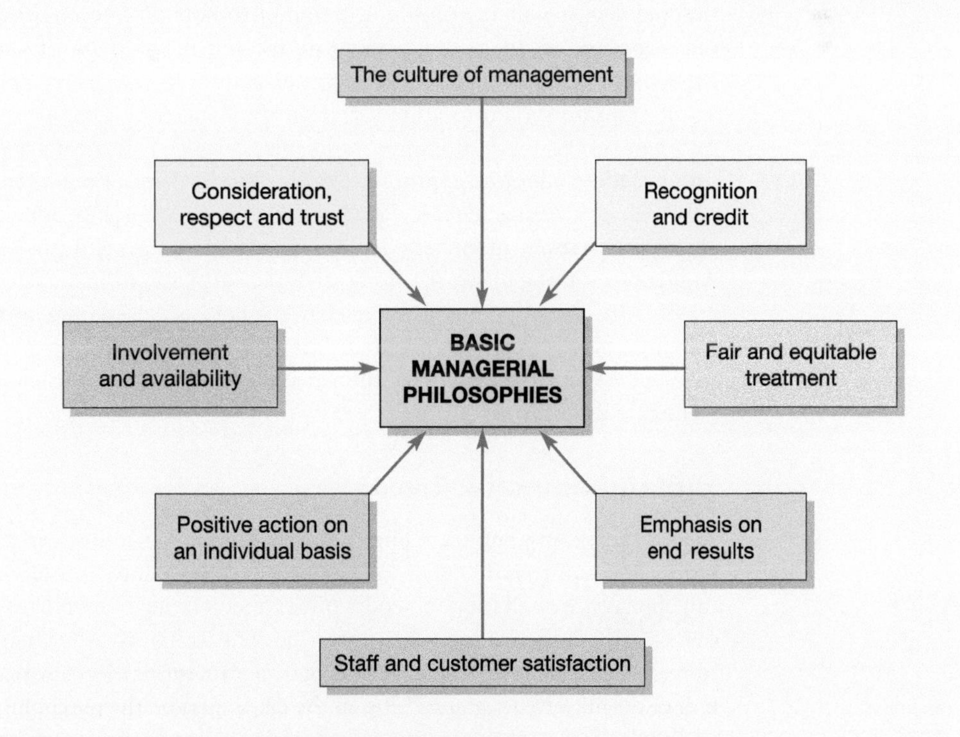

Figure 10.8 The effective management of people

Consideration, respect and trust

People generally respond according to the way they are treated. If you give a little, you will invariably get a lot back. Make people feel important and give them a sense of personal worth. The majority of staff will respond constructively if treated with consideration and respect, and as responsible individuals who wish to serve the organisation well.

However, how can members of staff show that they can be trusted unless trust is first placed in them? **The initiative must come from management:** 'Lack of trust is probably one of the greatest time and resource wasters in the workplace. Managers who do not trust their employees are probably wasting hours every week checking up on them at every turn and failing to utilise the resources at their disposal.'[36]

Research from the CIPD shows that employee attitudes to senior management across the public sector are generally more negative than their private-sector counterparts. Public-sector employees are less likely to feel they are treated with respect by senior managers, and they have less trust and confidence in them.[37]

Recognition and credit

People can be praised to success. Give genuine recognition and credit when it is due and let people know you appreciate them. Too often managers appear unresponsive to good performance, taking this for granted. But they are quick to criticise on the occasions when performance falls below expectations. **It should not be assumed that staff would necessarily take a lack of response as a sign of positive recognition rather than just the absence of criticism.** So often you hear the comment 'Well nobody has complained so I suppose everything is all right.' What a poor indictment of management style! Positive feedback on good performance is a strong motivator and staff are then more likely to accept and respond to constructive criticism.

Involvement and availability

Involve yourself with the work of the staff and make sure you fully understand the difficulties and distastes of their job. Ensure an open flow of communications and encourage participation and feedback. Take an active interest in the work of staff but without excessive supervision or inhibiting their freedom of action. Wherever possible be available to staff as a priority, rather than to administration. Remember the importance of giving time to listen genuinely to the feelings and problems of staff. This means giving staff your full attention including adopting appropriate body language (**recall the discussion in Chapter 6**). The approach of 'Management By Walking About' (MBWA), together with effective communication processes, is often heralded as a positive management practice. However, there is the danger of arousing mistrust among staff, the suspicion of management snooping and doubts about 'what are you doing here?'. MBWA is not just wandering aimlessly. It is unlikely to be effective unless perceived by staff as part of a genuine belief by management in the continuing importance of keeping staff informed and giving time to listen to, and understand, their feelings and problems.

Fair and equitable treatment

Treat people fairly but according to merit. Ensure justice in treatment, equitable systems of motivation and rewards, clear HR policies and procedures, avoidance of discrimination and full observance of all laws and codes of conduct relating to employment. People expect certain outcomes in exchange for certain contributions or inputs. A feeling of inequality causes tension and motivates the person to indulge in certain forms of behaviour in order to remove or to reduce the perceived inequity.[38] **Recall the discussion on the psychological contract (Chapter 1) and equity theory of motivation (Chapter 7).**

Positive action on an individual basis

Deal with individual situations on an individual basis and avoid the 'blanket' approach. For example, it has come to a manager's attention that a couple of members of staff have failed to provide some urgently requested information on time. The manager's reaction is to send a circular email to *all* members of the department reminding them of the need for, and importance of, meeting deadlines. This may appear to be an easy way out to the manager. But what are the likely reactions of staff? The two members concerned might shield behind the generality of the email and persuade themselves that it does not apply particularly to them. They might even choose to believe that the manager must be referring to other members of staff, perhaps in a different section, and take little notice of the circular. In contrast, the majority of staff in the department who do have a good record of providing requested information on time may well be annoyed or upset by the circular.

There could be staff who, despite pressing difficulties, have taken great pride in their work and made a special effort to maintain an excellent record of co-operation – quite possibly without any previous positive recognition from management. **It would be understandable if the reaction of these staff was one of resentment and disillusionment, and with a possible adverse effect on their future attitude to work.**

Emphasis on end results

Place emphasis on end results and levels of actual performance and achievement rather than on compliance with detailed instructions, rules or regulations. Where set attendance times are *clearly* seen as a necessary requirement of the job, it is right that managers should ensure that timekeeping is adhered to and enforced as appropriate. But in many cases rigid times of attendance are not an essential requirement for effective performance. The increasing movement to work/life balance, flexible working patterns and teleworking coupled with demands to boost productivity are placing growing emphasis on what staff actually achieve rather than the time spent at work. The important criteria are the level and quality of performance.

Staff and customer satisfaction

The starting point for customer, or consumer, satisfaction is good manager–subordinate relationships. Supportive and harmonious working relationships are more likely to create a working environment that results in high levels of both staff *and* consumer satisfaction. Managers need to adopt a positive attitude towards staff and to develop a spirit of mutual co-operation. Staff should feel that they are working *with* the manager rather than *for* the manager.

Critical review and reflection

The idea of basic philosophies such as managing by consideration, respect and trust may seem enlightened but is naive and idealistic. Given the natural scepticism of staff, such philosophies are difficult to implement in practice and subject to abuse.

What are YOUR views? To what extent would YOU feel confident in managing by respect and trust?

A looser approach to management

It is not suggested that managers should give up the right to manage: it is a question of *how* they manage and how they use their authority. For example, a Theory X style with emphasis on direction and control, and the use of rewards and sanctions exercised by nature of the manager's position and authority; or a Theory Y style in which individuals may satisfy their motivational needs through integration with meeting the goals of the organisation.

Management may also be based on 'organisational power' derived from status or position within the hierarchical structure, and the use of formal authority; or 'personal power' derived from competence and expertise, identification with subordinates, commanding respect, and urging and encouraging people in the performance of their tasks.[39]

Thomas suggests the need for a loose approach to business, in which tight controls are replaced with a more relaxed management style. As a result of employee and customer expectations, and social and technological change, the modern workforce expects to play a greater role in service delivery and not be hampered by strict rules and inflexible regulations: 'For a business to survive in these changing times, it needs to adopt a far looser approach in which specific rules are replaced with broad business principles . . . You have to build a culture of trust where people want to behave in a way that is best for the organisation.' However, Thomas believes the biggest obstacle is middle managers who fear they do not have authority to make big decisions and rely on management by the rule book, their process, templates and rigid structures.[40]

The importance of emotions and mood

We have mentioned previously that people are not homogeneous and human behaviour is capricious. People bring to work their own perceptions, feelings and attitudes. The importance of human foibles and emotions should not be forgotten. *Robbins,* for example, points out that employees bring an emotional component with them to work every day.

> *Emotions are part of our lives. That is, we not only think, we feel! But the field of management has been guilty for a long time of treating employees as if they're nonemotional. All work behavior is assumed to be fully rational. While this makes for simpler analysis of workplace behavior, it also creates highly unrealistic and inaccurate assessments.*[41]

Bolchover draws attention to the importance of mood as crucial to job performance in areas such as decision-making, creativity, teamwork, negotiation and leadership. Leaders' moods are highly contagious and what makes moods even more potentially beneficial or destructive is their infectiousness. Bolchover suggests that this 'emotional contagion' lies at the root of what we call corporate morale. Managers must appreciate that their own attitudes are contagious, profoundly affecting those who work for them: 'Pretty much everything that determines an employee's fundamental attitude at work is under the control of the manager.'[42]

Guidance on good management

GOV.UK has produced a 'Guidance to Good Management' (published 27 October 2014).

Managers play a central role in any organisation. They connect people to the purpose of their work and help them understand why their work is important. They set tasks and track performance, and they recognise the contribution of each individual in achieving the organisation's goals. They also play a leading role in helping their team to identify the areas they need to develop.

What makes a good manager?

What all inspirational managers have in common is they have taken the time to demonstrate one or more of the following positive behaviours that people look for in a good manager:

- they understand how to model leadership behaviours, inspire a shared vision and enable and support others to act;
- they champion learning and development for themselves and their teams and create an environment where the giving and receiving of feedback is the norm;
- they know and listen to their team and encourage open discussion and constructive challenge.

I am valued and recognised by BIS for the time and effort I put in to people management. BIS provides the tools and training I need and is intolerant of poor practice.

I take my **responsibility** as a line manager seriously.

- I am generous with my time. Supporting my team is a priority.
- I recognise that I am a role model. I lead by example.
- I get the basics right. Appraisals are done well and on time.

I know the people I manage, their abilities, aspirations, frustrations and motivations. I am also self aware, and open about my own strengths and weaknesses.

I create a safe environment for open discussion and construtive challenge by:

- Being **visible** and accessible
- Openly **inviting the views** of others
- **Listening** and acting

I give honest, timely, objective **feedback.**

- I give recognition when people have done well.
- I take prompt action to address under-performance.

I champion **learning and development** including for myself.

I work with my team to **manage workloads,** find **smarter** ways of working and clearly **define our roles.**

I **delegate** responsibilities not tasks. I **coach** more than I direct.

- I understand the fine line between empowerment and abandonment.

I value diversity and promote equality. I show this by being **inclusive** and welcoming the contributions and views of all.

I am supported by staff who live the BIS values, take responsibility for their own development and give me feedback on how I am doing.

Figure 10.9 BIS Manager's Charter

Source: https://www.gov.uk/government/publications/improving-civil-service-skills-good-management, (accessed 19 September 2014)

As part of the Good Management campaign there is a Department of Business, Innovation and Skills (BIS) Manager's Charter (*see* Figure 10.9).

The qualities of a manager and managerial effectiveness are also discussed later (**see Chapter 16**).

The future of management

According to *Owen*, the death of modern management is nigh and the old world of simplistic formulae for strategy, finance and leadership no longer work. After the first wave of management with tradition carefully handed down from master to apprentice, and the second wave of modern management following the Industrial Revolution, we are now embarking on the third wave of management. Organisations are moving from command and control to co-operation and commitment. To manage in an increasingly uncertain world risks must be turned into opportunity and challenges into success.

The job of the manager is changing out of all recognition. Managers are still the glue that holds the organisation together. But it is no longer about connecting the top and bottom of the organisation. It is about connecting a network of power and influence to make things happen through other people. This requires a changed set of skills . . . The job is just not command and control. The job is about orchestrating the skills of the network, helping the organisation discover and deliver the best solution. The job has changed from instructing to enabling. This makes the manager's job harder but more rewarding.[43]

A manager-less workplace?

With the demise of the hierarchy and a future that is flat, *Howes* questions if managers can survive in the workplace. Austerity measures in the UK have resulted in public-sector organisations making several structural changes including a reduction in senior management. However, Howes points out that those making flatter structural changes in the public or private sectors are smaller organisations with fewer employees. In a leadership environment one person dominates naturally. The group must show willingness and consensual agreement to an unofficial manager lurking within the group.

Leadership environments are a good starting point, but ultimately, someone will step up or things won't get done.[44]

But what is actually 'new'?

There is much written today about changes in the workforce and new approaches to management. It is interesting to note, however, the ideas on the nature of managerial behaviour put forward many years ago by eminent writers such as Mary Parker Follett and Peter Drucker.

Over seventy years ago, *Follett's* thinking was based on concern for social, evolutionary progress, and the organisation and management of people for effective performance and a fuller life. Follett envisioned the successful operation of groups, and management responsibility diffused through the organisation and not just concentrated at the top of the hierarchy.[45]

Drucker suggested that one of the essential principles of management is that it is about human beings.

Management is about human beings. Its task is to make people capable of joint performance, to make their strengths effective and their weaknesses irrelevant. This is what organization is all about, and it is the reason that management is the critical, determining factor . . . We depend on management for our livelihoods and our ability to contribute and achieve.[46]

The fact is that management ultimately depends on an understanding of human nature. I suggest it goes much further than that. In the first place, good management depends on the acceptance of certain basic values. It cannot be achieved without honesty and integrity, or without consideration for the interests of others. Secondly, it is the understanding of human foibles that we all share, such as jealousy, envy, status, prejudice, perception, temperament, motivation and talent, which provides the greatest challenge to managers.

HRH The Duke of Edinburgh[47]

Critical review and reflection

A number of writers have drawn attention to the changing nature of management and the work of the manager. Yet reading the ideas of eminent writers such as Mary Parker Follett (1942) and Peter Drucker (1954) it appears little is really new, and the underlying role of management remains unchanged.

What are YOUR views? What specifically do YOU see as the likely role of the manager in ten years' time?

Ten key points to remember

1. Management is fundamental to the effective operation of work organisations. It is essentially an integrating activity that permeates every facet of the organisation.
2. Management is directed towards attainment of aims and objectives, within a structured organisation and achieved through the efforts of other people.
3. One approach to the process of management is attention to common activities and principles of management. These are not prescriptive but guidelines for action.
4. A popular way of describing the essential nature of managerial work is getting work done second-hand and responsibility for the work and efforts of other people.
5. There is debate about the extent to which there are general common features of management in both private-enterprise and public-sector organisations.
6. The jobs of individual managers differ widely and are influenced by a number of factors. There are a number of significant empirical studies into the work of a manager.
7. The way in which managers carry out their responsibilities is important. Increasing attention is given to managerial style and the ability to handle people successfully.
8. Managerial behaviour is likely to be influenced by attitudes towards people and assumptions about human nature and behaviour at work - called Theory X and Theory Y.
9. As a basis for discussion, it is possible to suggest a number of underlying philosophies that arguably make for success in managing with and through people.
10. Much is written today about changes in the workplace and the future of management. However, one can reasonably question how much is actually new.

Review and discussion questions

1. How would you summarise the essential nature of managerial work? In what ways does the job of a manager differ from any other job in a work organisation?
2. Give detailed reasons for whether you believe: (i) managers are born or made; *and* (ii) management is an art or a science.
3. To what extent is it possible to establish rules or principles of good management? Assess critically the practical applications of these rules or principles.
4. Contrast critically the nature of management in private-enterprise and public-sector organisations.
5. Why do organisations need managers? Suggest which *one* writer has in your opinion made the greatest contribution to our understanding of the nature of management. Justify your answer.
6. Give your own views on the importance of managerial style.
7. Contrast sets of attitudes and assumptions about people at work that might be held by managers. Suggest how these attitudes and assumptions might influence actual managerial behaviour.
8. Discuss critically the suggestion that management is a much more human activity than is commonly suggested in management textbooks. Support your discussion with practical examples.
9. Give your own critical views on the practical implementation of basic underlying philosophies for managing with and through people.
10. Explain fully, with supporting reasons, how you see the future of management in work organisations.

Assignment

Complete the 'Your management style questionnaire'. Move quickly and do not think too deeply about each question but give your first immediate response.

Your management style questionnaire

There are ten pairs of statements. Assign a weight from 0 to 10 to each statement to show the relative strength of your belief in the statements in each pair. The points assigned for each pair must total 10 in each case. Be as honest with yourself as you can and resist the natural tendency to respond as you would 'like to think things are'. This instrument is not a test. There are no right or wrong answers. It is designed to be a stimulus for personal reflection and discussion.

1. It's only human nature for people to do as little work as they can get away with. ______(A)

   When people avoid work, it's usually because their work has been deprived of its meaning. ______(B)

   10

2. If employees have access to any information they want, they tend to have better attitudes and behave more responsibly. ______(C)

   If employees have access to more information than they need to do their immediate tasks, they will usually misuse it. ______(D)

   10

3. One problem in asking for employees' ideas is that their perspective is too limited for their suggestions to be of much value. ______(E)

   Asking employees for their ideas broadens their perspective and results in the development of useful suggestions. ______(F)

   10

4. If people don't use much imagination and ingenuity on the job, it's probably because relatively few people have much of either. ______(G)

   Most people are imaginative and creative but may not show it because of limitations imposed by supervision and the job. ______(H)

   10

5. People tend to raise their stakes if they are accountable for their own behaviour and for correcting their own mistakes. ______(I)

   People tend to lower their stakes if they are not punished for their misbehaviour and mistakes. ______(J)

   10

6. It's better to give people both good and bad news because most employees want the whole story, no matter how painful. ______(K)

   It's better to withhold unfavourable news about business because most employees really want to hear only the good news. ______(L)

   10

7. Because a supervisor is entitled to more respect than those below him or her in the organisation, it weakens the supervisor's prestige to admit that a subordinate was right and he or she was wrong. ______(M)

   Because people at all levels are entitled to equal respect, a supervisor's prestige is increased when he or she supports this principle by admitting that a subordinate was right and he or she was wrong. ______(N)

   10

8. If you give people enough money, they are less likely to be concerned with such intangibles as responsibility and recognition. ______ (O)

   If you give people interesting and challenging work, they are less likely to complain about such things as pay and supplemental benefits. ______ (P)

   10

9. If people are to set their own goals and standards of performance, they tend to set them higher than the boss would. ______ (Q)

   If people are allowed to set their own goals and standards of performance, they tend to set them lower than the boss would. ______ (R)

   10

10. The more knowledge and freedom people have regarding their jobs, the more controls are needed to keep them in line. ______ (S)

    The more knowledge and freedom people have regarding their jobs, the fewer controls are needed to ensure satisfactory job performance. ______ (T)

    10

Source: Adapted from Myers, M. S. *Every Employee a Manager*, McGraw-Hill (1970).

Personal skills and employability exercise

Objectives

Completing this exercise should help you to enhance the following skills:

- Act in the role of the manager to handle a number of real-life situations.
- Conduct management-staff interviews and discussions.
- Review critically your ability to deal with emotionally difficult situations.

Exercise

Given below are a number of real-life situations. You are required to:

a. Think through each one and explain how you as the manager might best handle the discussion with your member of staff.
b. Record how you would approach each discussion/interview.
c. Consider what specific questions might you be likely to ask, and why?
d. Share and compare your responses with colleagues in a small-group situation.

Situation 1

One of your employees, who is hard-working and conscientious with tasks, continually arrives late for work. This is the sixth time this has happened. The person's excuse is that they have to take their child to nursery because they are getting divorced and their spouse refuses to do this task.

Situation 2

You receive a complaint from one of your female employees who claims to have accidently found a pornographic image on the PC of another employee and finds this offensive.

Situation 3

One of your permanent employees has been accused of assaulting another member of staff who works in the same organisation but as an independent contractor.

→

Situation 4

You overhear a member of your department comment of you that 'he/she has no idea of the technical complexity of my work . . . I don't know how he/she can manage a department like this!'

Situation 5

A key client calls you to complain about sarcastic and impatient comments made by one of your more experienced technicians. Comments like 'Your people must be really thick if they think that's how it works' have proved less than helpful. You know this person has been working long hours, achieving excellent results and is clearly committed to their job and the department. In fact, you have recently promoted the technician for these very reasons.

Situation 6

In a recent management meeting, a relatively new colleague repeatedly contradicted you and appeared to be 'scoring points' at your expense. Although the colleague had made some valid, even perceptive comments, it is not exactly helping your relationship get off to an encouraging start. Furthermore, this has happened on a previous occasion.

Discussion with colleagues

- How would you summarise the essential nature of the manager–subordinate relationship?
- Using your own examples, explain the importance of using appropriate approaches when dealing with potentially difficult situations.
- What have you learned about your potential skills of effective people management?

Case study
Is everybody happy?

Is happiness an important component of a well-managed organisation? It might seem intuitively correct to believe that people work better when they are relaxed and enjoying their work, and much research has gone into the examination of the links between job satisfaction, work motivation and overall organisational efficiency as demonstrated earlier **(Chapter 7).** But does human happiness per se (as separate from the enjoyment of the work itself) make any difference to performance? Experimental data reported by a team of researchers at Warwick University seem to suggest that it does.[48]

The experiments were similar to those described in the earlier case study on behavioural economics **(Chapter 6).** The 'work' was a simple but uninteresting mathematical task designed to simulate a piece-rate 'white-collar' (non-managerial) type of job. The 'work' could be evaluated for both quantity (how many calculations were performed during a specified time) and quality (how many of them were correct) and participants were paid according to output.

Individuals are asked to add sequences of five 2-digit numbers under timed conditions. This task is simple but is taxing under pressure. We think of it as representing – in a stylized way – an iconic white-collar job: both intellectual ability and effort are rewarded.[49]

Participants' mathematical ability was tested and matched, and payment was offered according to the number of correct results achieved in the timed sessions, which happened over several weeks. The experimental groups were shown a short series of popular comedy sketches before attempting the task. At the end of every session, all groups were asked to complete a questionnaire to gauge both their general levels of happiness and (importantly) any increase in happiness experienced by members of the control group after watching the film. The result? A consistent and significant rise in productivity – up 12 per cent – for the experimental groups compared with the control groups. As the authors conclude:

if well-being boosts human performance, that raises the possibility of self-reinforcing spirals from productivity-to-well-being-to-productivity.[50]

Bad apples

Contrast this with work done back in 2006 that examines an opposing effect: the influence of negativity displayed by a member on group performance.[51] The so-called 'bad apples' who spoil the whole barrel were defined as exhibiting behaviours such as withholding of effort, being affectively negative and violating important interpersonal norms, but not behaving in an illegal way or such as would incur disciplinary sanctions. It was noted that consistent negative behaviour by even one member had a disproportionately severe negative impact on overall group performance. In other words, 'unhappy' members could have a depressing effect on colleagues' output by causing them to withdraw, react against the negativity or to seek distractions.

> *Almost all of us have either had the personal experience of working with someone who displayed bad apple behaviours . . . When this process starts to unfold at work, it consumes inordinate amounts of time, psychological resources, and emotional energy.*[52]

It would seem, therefore, that general workplace happiness - quite distinctly from job satisfaction - is valuable, and unhappiness can be damaging or lead to 'emotional contagion'. So what are the implications for management? One example of a company that seems to take the happiness of its workforce very seriously is media company UKRD.

William Rogers, CEO of UKRD
Source: UKRD Group Limited

Open, honest, fun, fair, professional and unconventional

UKRD owns and operates seventeen commercial radio stations throughout the UK, from Pirate FM in Cornwall to Star Radio in County Durham. It was awarded top place in the *Sunday Times* 100 Best Companies to Work For[53] in 2011 for the first time, and in 2014 it received the same accolade for the fourth year in a row. The award is based on the views of employees - and in 2014 the Chief Executive Officer William Rogers was also named Best Leader in the survey's mid-sized company category - for the third time. In a press release, the Company Chairman explained that:

> *William epitomises the approach to management that we have at all levels in the company and his recognition in the Sunday Times in this way highlights the quality, not only of his leadership, but of the whole UKRD leadership team.*[54]

Rogers, who became CEO of the organisation in 2002, has focused his management team's style around six core values:

- **Open** - Being open-minded to new ways of thinking, being open to criticism constructively delivered from wheresoever it may come and the welcoming of new ideas and opportunities. A requirement not just to hear, but to listen.
- **Honest** - The reflection of views and opinions delivered in a considered but clear and frank way. Expressing your real opinion, upward or downward, and an obligation to deal ethically and with integrity with colleagues and customers.
- **Fair** - A requirement to consider fairness in the broadest sense of the word. Fairness to the business, to colleagues, to customers and, on occasion, to all in balance. What appears to be fair at first sight may be less fair after due consideration.
- **Fun** - Enjoy work. Whether it be spontaneous or organised, delivering an environment in which a smile hits the faces of you and your colleagues on a regular basis is the responsibility of all.
- **Professional** - The highest standards of commitment and delivery across all areas of responsibility for which an individual, at any level, may have.

→

Delivering on commitments, honouring obligations and respecting those things that make a difference to the reputation of the company and those that work for it.

- **Unconventional** – Be different, try different things and challenge the norm. It may be 'done that way', but should it be? Innovate, take risks and be prepared to fail.[55]

He explains that the values are intended to have a direct effect on the way staff behave towards each other, even to change employees' lives for the better; he believes that if people are happy at work then they are generally happy in life too. In the *Sunday Times* survey, 94 per cent of the workforce reported that they loved their jobs, and the company was ranked particularly highly for giving employees a sense of well-being as well as offering opportunities for personal growth. Rogers sees both of these qualities as being vital to unlock the 'discretionary dividend' of individual performance that makes a big difference to the bottom line.

Spread a little happiness

His personal style of management, and that which he insists on for the whole management team, is about approachability and openness. He does not have a personal assistant to gate-keep his diary and allocate his time, and he spends most of his working week out and about visiting the stations. He makes sure he speaks directly to everyone on the team, and takes time to say a proper farewell:

> *If I or any of our senior team are visiting one of the 17 stations that we have around the country – and the meeting is scheduled to go from 10am until 12.30pm, we don't put a 12.30 departure in our diary: it's 12.45 so we build in time to say goodbye to everyone before we leave.*[56]

Rogers also recognises that living the core values, especially for managers, can be a challenge:

> *People have left our business because they didn't get it . . . Two senior managers were removed from our organisation because they couldn't deliver management in a style that reflected those values. Great sales people have been removed or have left because they couldn't operate within those values.*[57]

Nevertheless, management commitment to the values is crucial, and recognised as one of the company's key strengths by the *Sunday Times* adjudicators:

> *'The reason the vision and values work is because they're demonstrated from the top,' says Eagle's managing director Paul Marcus. '[Rogers is] a fabulous person to work for, a joy.' Staff agree: they have a great deal of faith in him (95%, first), and find him inspiring (94%, also first).*[58]

Of course, any organisation could be a nice place to work without actually being efficient. However, if one of the key indicators of organisational performance is return on investment for shareholders, UKRD seems to be on the button. In the summer of 2014 it announced two dividend payments to shareholders based on strong growth and increased revenue across the group. Commenting on the company's performance, Rogers himself made it clear that the true drivers of the business and its profitability, even in difficult times, were the local staff and managers.

> *The local focus is truly paying off and we are seeing the clearest evidence yet that when you deliver truly local radio to an audience that is keen to be served by the kind of committed teams we have in all our stations, the results feed through.*[59]

So maybe real life bears out the findings of the Warwick research team: there is indeed a lot to be said for spreading a little happiness at work.

Tasks

1. What sort of management style does William Rogers exhibit? Base your answer on one of the models in the first part of the chapter. What risks might be associated with this style?
2. Compare and contrast the six core values of UKRD with the eight basic managerial philosophies (*see* Figure 10.8). How far do they overlap, and where do they differ?
3. If, as the evidence suggests, happiness can improve performance, what are the implications for a manager's or team leader's own behaviour towards his or her staff?
4. Consider the concept of 'emotional contagion' described in the chapter and the case. What steps could a manager take to improve a situation where negativity of a member is harming the team's effectiveness?

Notes and references

1. See, for example, Margretta, J. *What Management Is: How it Works and Why it's Everyone's Business*, HarperCollins (2002).
2. Drucker, P. F. *Management*, Pan Books (1979), p. 14.
3. Schneider, S. C. and Barsoux, J. *Managing Across Cultures*, second edition, Financial Times Prentice Hall (2003).
4. Francesco, A. M. and Gold, B. A. *International Organizational Behavior*, second edition, Prentice Hall (2005).
5. Crainer, S. 'The Rise of Guru Scepticism', *Management Today*, March 1996, p. 51.
6. Watson, T. J. *Management, Organisation and Employment Strategy*, Routledge & Kegan Paul (1986).
7. Dib, F. 'Is management a science?', *Professional Manager*, Autumn 2014, pp. 38–9.
8. Foppen, J. W. 'Knowledge Leadership', in Chowdbury, S (ed.) *Management 21C*, Financial Times Prentice Hall (2000), pp. 160–1.
9. Fayol, H. *General and Industrial Management*, Pitman (1949).
10. McLean, J. 'Fayol – standing the test of time', *Manager, The British Institute of Administrative Management*, Spring 2011, pp. 32–3.
11. Hamel, G. with Breen, B. *The Future of Management*, Harvard Business School Press (2007), p. 20.
12. Drucker, P. F. *People and Performance*, Heinemann (1977), p. 28.
13. Ibid., p. 59.
14. Stern, S. 'Peter the Great', *Management Today*, December 2011, pp. 56–7.
15. Ferguson, (Sir) A. in Gwyther, M. and Saunders, A. 'United They Stand?', *Management Today*, April 2005, p. 41.
16. Stewart, R. *The Reality of Management*, third edition, Butterworth–Heinemann (1999), p. 6.
17. Mintzberg, H. *Managing*, Financial Times Prentice Hall (2009), p. 19.
18. Walker, B. 'How to switch sides', *Professional Manager*, Spring 2013, pp. 4–7.
19. 'Building productive public sector workplaces: Part One, Improving People Management', CIPD, January 2010.
20. Bernstein, Sir Howard, 'In My Opinion', *Management Today*, February 2012, p. 62.
21. For a useful summary of the work of the manager, see, for example, Birchall, D. W. 'What Managers Do', in Crainer, S. and Dearlove, D. (eds) *Financial Times Handbook of Management*, second edition, Financial Times Prentice Hall (2001), pp. 110–31.
22. Mintzberg, H. *The Nature of Managerial Work*, Harper and Row (1973).
23. Mintzberg, H. 'The Manager's Job: Folklore and Fact', *Harvard Business Review Classic*, March–April 1990, pp. 163–76.
24. Kotter, J. P. *The General Managers*, Free Press (1982).
25. Stewart, R. *Contrasts in Management*, McGraw-Hill (1976).
26. Watson, T. *Organising and Managing Work*, second edition, Financial Times Prentice Hall (2006).
27. Mintzberg, H. *Managing*, Financial Times Prentice Hall (2009), p. 130.
28. McGregor, D. *The Human Side of Enterprise*, Penguin (1987).
29. Townsend, R. *Further Up the Organisation*, Coronet Books (1985), pp. 168–9.
30. See, for example, Mullins, L. J. 'Management and Managerial Behaviour', *International Journal of Hospitality Management*, vol. 4, no. 1, 1985, pp. 39–41.
31. Blake, R. R. and Mouton, J. S. *The Managerial Grid III*, Gulf Publishing (1985).
32. Blake, R. R. and McCanse, A. A. *Leadership Dilemmas – Grid Solutions*, Gulf Publishing (1991).
33. Newborough, G. 'People vs Production', *British Journal of Administrative Management*, May/June 1999, pp. 13–14.
34. Crainer, S. and Dearlove, D. (eds) *Financial Times Handbook of Management*, second edition, Financial Times Prentice Hall (2001), p. 364.
35. Likert, R. *New Patterns of Management*, McGraw-Hill (1961).
36. Mann, S. 'Give a Little Gain a Lot', *Professional Manager*, March 1999, p. 32.
37. 'Building productive public sector workplaces: Part Three, Developing positive employee relations', CIPD, August 2010, p. 5.
38. Adams, J. S. 'Injustice in Social Exchange', abridged in Steers, R. M. and Porter, L. W. *Motivation and Work Behavior*, second edition, McGraw-Hill (1979), pp. 107–24.
39. See, for example, Beggs, A. 'The Real Meaning of Empowerment', *Financial Times Mastering Management Review*, September 1997, pp. 14–15.
40. Thomas, M. cited in Smith, P. 'Why it's time to break the rules', *Professional Manager*, vol. 20, no. 2, 2011, pp. 33–5; see also Thomas, M. *Loose: The Future of Business is Letting Go*, Headline Publishing (2011).
41. Robbins, S. P. *The Truth About Managing People*, second edition, Pearson Education (2008), p. 202.
42. Bolchover, D. 'Why Mood Matters', *Management Today*, November 2008, pp. 46–50.

43. Owen, J. *The Death of Modern Management: How to lead in the new world disorder*, Wiley (2009), pp. 241–2.
44. Howes, L. 'Life In A Managerless World', *Professional Manager,* Autumn 2013, pp. 42–5.
45. Metcalfe, H. and Urwick, L. (eds) *Dynamic Administration – The Collected Papers of Mary Parker Follett*, Harper (1941).
46. Drucker, P. F. *Classic Drucker,* Harvard Business School Press (2006), p. 194.
47. 'In Celebration of the Feel-Good Factor', *Professional Manager,* March 1998, p. 6.
48. Oswald, A.J., Proto, E. and Sgroi, D., 'Happiness and Productivity', Warwick University (2012), **http://www.andrewoswald.com/docs/6MayOsProtoSgroi2012.pdf** (accessed 20 February 2015).
49. Ibid., p. 9.
50. Ibid., p. 23.
51. Felps, W., Mitchell, T. and Byington, E. 'How, When, and Why Bad Apples Spoil the Barrel: Negative Group Members and Dysfunctional Groups', *Research in Organizational Behavior,* vol. 27, 2006, pp. 175–222. doi:10.1016/S0191-3085(06)27005-9.
52. Ibid., p. 213.
53. The Sunday Times online, **http://features.thesundaytimes.co.uk/public/best100companies/live/template** (accessed 20 February 2015).
54. **http://www.ukrd.com/news/latest-ukrd-news/629214/double-2012-sunday-times-success-for-ukrd-group/**
55. Rogers, W. 'Values: Sound advice', *People Management,* August 2012, pp. 40–3.
56. Ibid.
57. Ibid.
58. The Sunday Times online, **http://features.thesundaytimes.co.uk/public/best100companies/live/template** (accessed 20 February 2015).
59. Radio Today online, **http://radiotoday.co.uk/2015/01/ukrd-celebrating-sixth-sunday-times-award/** (accessed 20 February 2015).

Academic viewpoint

Below you will find the title and abstract of a recent article in an academic journal that explores a topic relevant to the chapters in Part 3.

Marinova, S., Van Dyne, L. and Moon, H. 'Are Good Citizens Good Transformational Leaders as Well? An Employee-Centric Perspective on Transformational Leadership', ***Group & Organization Management*****, vol. 40, no. 1, 2015, pp. 62–87. doi: 10.1177/1059601114561257**

Abstract

Research has demonstrated robust positive relationships between transformational leadership and employee attitudes and behaviors. To date, the preponderance of the literature has been leader-centric and focused on individuals who are already in leader roles. In this article, we adopt an employee-centric perspective and focus on behaviors of professionals who are not in formal leader roles. Specifically, we apply evolutionary theory as a theoretical lens for proposing that those who perform organizational citizenship behaviors (OCBs) will be seen as transformational leaders. We hypothesize linkages between four types of OCBs and four dimensions of transformational leadership. Multi-source field sample results based on more than 1,000 participants provide general support for the predictions. We discuss theoretical and practical implications.

Commentary

The authors have researched their hypothesis that not all people who show leadership are in formal leader or management roles within organisations. In professional organisations where people often put in a lot of 'discretionary effort' (going to great lengths to get jobs done) it seems possible that those who behave in the same way as transformational leaders can affect their colleagues in ways that encourage them to be loyal and put in extra effort on behalf of the organisation (organisational citizenship behaviours or OCBs). Individuals who seem to put the good of the organisation above their own personal interests are often well regarded by their colleagues and become role models. They indicate four ways in which OCB can be demonstrated (being a 'change agent' who tries to improve things, being a 'good Samaritan' who takes care of people, being a 'good soldier' who ensures things go to plan, and being a 'good sportsman' who acts as a stabilizing influence when there is conflict) and the circumstances under which each type of OCB is effective. They conclude that organisations could benefit from this understanding to develop training programmes to encourage transformational leadership and thereby increased organisational effectiveness.

The article might prompt you to consider some of the following questions

- To what extent does your own experience, either at work or in a social or sporting context, bear out the hypothesis that not all those who show leadership are in formal leader roles?
- Do you think it is better for organisations to identify and promote individuals who encourage OCBs or to leave them in non-leadership roles, and why?
- To what extent might managers feel threatened by informal types of transformational leadership in their team?
- Does the nature and structure of an organisation affect the likely emergence of transformational leaders who are *not* formal leaders? Would you expect to find similar results in different types of organisations such as manufacturing plants, large retail businesses or service organisations?

Part 3 Case study
The Eden Project

If a single word can be used to sum up the achievements of Tim Smit, that word might be 'regeneration'. To turn one derelict, neglected corner of southwest England into a successful tourist business attracting millions of visitors is a remarkable achievement, but to do it twice is simply astonishing. Yet this is precisely what Smit has done, and in the Eden Project we can see the nature of this achievement through a blend of visionary and innovative leadership combined with a strong sense of the value of teamwork.

The Eden Project is the realisation of one man's extraordinary vision through powerful teamwork and global co-operation.
Source: Tamsyn Williams/The Eden Project

Before Eden

Cornwall is one of several parts of the UK that suffered economic decline during the later twentieth century. Its industrial heritage has all but disappeared in the wake of globalisation and the shifting nature of the industrial world landscape. The last tin mine closed in 1998, and the ruined mine towers are witness to what was once the largest tin mining industry in the world. The production of china clay remains one of Cornwall's oldest current industries, but that too is in decline and a European Union report of 2014 noted that Cornwall was possibly the poorest region in the UK.[1] The fishing business is contracting, and traditional agricultural and horticultural production, mainly vegetables and flower bulbs, is being challenged by similar, year-round levels of production in developing countries. Cornwall as a county has, for some years, been in receipt of European Union Objective One funding destined to assist with economic regeneration in Europe's poorest regions. This level of relative poverty is probably something that many of the tourists who visit Cornwall's beautiful landscapes, historic properties and wild coastland do not generally see; indeed tourism has become one of the largest single income-generating business sectors in the area. While there are some strong indications that the Cornish economy might be revitalised by the arrival of new, knowledge-based industries that are supported by technological developments, tourism remains at the heart of the county's economy.[2]

In 1990, in a project that would contribute substantially to Cornwall's reputation as a tourist destination, John Willis, Tim Smit and John Nelson began to restore the long-derelict gardens surrounding the stately home and seat of the Tremayne family at Heligan, near Mevagissey. The story of this garden, its dereliction after the start of the Great War of 1914, its rediscovery following

a storm in 1990 and its restoration, in part as a memorial to the gardeners who would have died in the war, is one of enormous poignancy and beauty.[3] For Smit, an archaeology and anthropology graduate who had also developed a love of gardens, it was a project that enabled him to use many of his professional skills, and the garden itself has become one of England's most loved,[4] and a major attraction for Cornwall.

However, while Heligan is horticultural archaeology, and the gardens today are, in essence, a living museum of nineteenth-century estate gardening, the Eden Project was a very different type of restoration, and one that drew upon Smit's additional skills as a rock music producer and showman. What Smit was restoring in his second major project was land, and the vision and purpose behind the Eden Project looks to the future rather than the past.

Ten things to do with a disused clay pit. . .

Photographs of what was to become the Eden Project prior to the arrival of Tim and his team reveal the extent of the transformation. In the mid-1990s the worked-out Bodelva china clay pit near St Austell looked very much like what many believed it to be: a derelict, polluted and worthless piece of land stripped of fertile soil - essentially a 34-acre puddle. The statistics behind its transformation into one of the most spectacular tourist attractions in the country are mind-boggling. The first task, in 1998 when the project began, was to landscape the site and shift 1.8 million tons of earth to reduce the pit-side gradients, a task that took twelve dumper trucks and eight bulldozers six months. During the first few months of work, it rained almost continuously, which resulted in 43 million gallons of water draining into the clay-lined pit.[5] This was both a problem and an opportunity: the problem was to design a drainage system that would prevent the whole site turning into a soggy bog during the average English summer; but the opportunity was to demonstrate one of the founding principles of sustainability, and use the run-off water to service the site. The system designed to meet this purpose collects, on average, 22 litres a second, and about two-thirds of the water needed to run the project (including plant watering, a 22-metre waterfall in the tropical biome and the numerous toilets!) is 'grey' water, in other words that which can be harvested from the site itself. Over 85,000 tonnes of soil, made from waste products and other organic material, were needed to turn the clay-lined puddle into the fertile ground in which over 1,000,000 plants of more than 5,000 species could grow, to create a series of global gardens.

The two original 'biomes', spectacular greenhouses that recreate a humid tropical environment and warm temperate climate respectively, are perhaps what most visitors remember about the project, although more than half the site is actually open air. The Humid Tropics biome is the largest conservatory in the world at 240 metres by 100 metres by 55 metres high, enclosing 15,590 square metres. It houses 'the biggest jungle in captivity' and contains plants native to the tropical areas of the world including Malaysia, West Africa and South America as well as islands like the Seychelles. The Warm Temperate biome covers 6,540 square metres, and replicates a Mediterranean climate housing plants that represent those that grow between 30°–40° north and south of the equator. The 'Core' is the project's education centre, the roof of which is constructed on the same mathematical principle (the Fibonacci sequence of interwoven spirals) that appears in nature in many plant formations, and which is also the way in which some plants pack the maximum number of seeds, spines or leaves into the smallest possible area.[6] And since summer 2012 you can fly over the entire site on a 740-metre-long zipwire - if you have a head for heights!

If you build it, they will come

The Eden Project is a wholly owned subsidiary of the Eden Trust, a registered charity, and initially cost £120 million to build. The money was raised from a variety of sources including grant funding, such as that from the UK government's Millennium Project Fund. Together with commercial loans, the grant money is used for capital investment on the site and educational or conservation projects in other parts of the world. Revenue comes from both the commercial activities of the project and gifts or donations.[7] The money is used to run the operation, maintain the asset base and service the commercial loans; so although as a charity it does not make a profit, it does have to run at commercially successful levels. Visitors provide the major source of revenue, and Eden has regularly attracted over a million a year since it opened in 2001 - although the recession combined with a very wet year saw them drop below that number for the first time during 2012–13. Nevertheless, Eden won the British Travel Awards accolade as Best UK Leisure Attraction for the third year running in November 2013.[8] So what exactly do people come to see?

Tim Smit's vision for Eden is far from being that of just another garden. He is, as we have noted, not a horticulturalist, but an archaeologist, anthropologist and former rock-show organiser. The purpose of Eden is essentially to educate people about the environment and the human relationship with the plant world, but to do so in such a way as to set a conservation and sustainability example that is, above all things, spectacular fun. The 2012–13 Annual Sustainability Report explains how:

> *The Eden Project tells the story of people's dependence on the natural world, of regeneration and what people can achieve when they work together and with nature. It is designed to give our visitors a great day out while demonstrating, in a serious yet playful way, how indispensable plants and people are to each other; how we all can adapt together to this challenging new world; and how even the most barren, worked-out China clay pit can be transformed into a place of beauty. This same message underpins all of our educational and outreach projects which explore new ways of living in the 21st century. Eden is also a social enterprise, demonstrating that doing business while improving the environment and livelihoods and building stronger communities can work hand in hand.*[9]

The Eden Project identifies three essential elements in its approach to this task:

- Educational programmes – This includes the design of the site, and all the events that happen there, many of which are connected with schools and colleges or seek to convey important social messages.[10] Recent activities include an 'Empty Classrooms Day' in July, a national event to encourage schools to make the most of outdoor spaces and use them to animate lessons, and, in collaboration with Anglia Ruskin University, the launch of a masters-level programme, the 'MSc Sustainability: Working for Positive Change', some of which is delivered at the Eden site.
- Operational practice – Eden believes the way it runs the site should be an inspiration and example to both commercial corporations and public bodies; this is part of its aim to develop the notion and currency of social enterprises. As well as its 'waste-neutral' ambitions, the project has partnered with EGS Energy to build a geothermal electricity plant that will not only power the project, but contribute to the national grid.
- Spreading Eden's mission through outreach activities and acting as an agency for change – This aspect involves using the Eden venue to host both major events that facilitate dialogue about significant environmental matters and smaller courses and programmes to teach horticultural techniques. There are business development programmes, team-building workshops and corporate away days, and courses to help teachers integrate outdoor activities into the school curriculum.

The educational purpose that underlies the Eden Project shows that this is, indeed, far more than just another garden. The achievement of these objectives requires both focused and decisive leadership, but also powerful teamwork.

Taking a lead

The television series *Gardeners of Eden*[11], which presented a year in the life of the Eden Project, gives some insight into both the nature of Tim Smit's leadership style and the range of activities undertaken by the different teams required to run the project. It also shows some of the very human problems associated with such an enterprise, including conflicts of interest between the project's main purpose and some of the professional teams whose tasks are to contribute to that objective.

Smit generally dresses casually and has the slightly scruffy air of someone who is not accustomed to spending much of his working day in an office or behind a desk. In a *Guardian* article prior to a major lecture at the Royal Society of Arts (RSA), the interviewer noted some of Smit's key qualities:

> *Smit's secret, if there is one, seems to be that he can bring people of very different disciplines and skills together, get them to brainstorm and collaborate, and come up with the extraordinary. The Eden Project, he says, has attracted locals by the score, but also high-flying artists, businessmen, architects, scientists, engineers, educationalists, horticulturalists and ecologists from all over Britain. 'It feels like a renaissance organisation,' says one woman who left a senior management job to work there as a director and has been amazed both at what gets done and the way it works. 'It's attracted a critical mass of people, and there's this passionate belief, right through the project, that it belongs to everyone who works there, that it's a team thing. I guess it demonstrates that you can have an organisation that is highly effective financially, environmentally and socially. It's a kind of experiment to show that you can work in different ways.' A local woman who has been with Eden since the start is more succinct: 'It's the most equal place I've known,' she says.*
>
> *'This is a stage for change,' says Smit, who admits that Eden can seem like a sect to outsiders. 'Many people have made life choices to come here. Most could earn*

five times as much elsewhere. But I'm aware that if you want to effect real change, and we do, that you must not own it. You have got to make sure that it's owned by more than one person.'[12]

Smit is described as optimistic and positive, with a mission to make people think differently. He is concerned to challenge dogma from all sides and is happy to question the views of committed environmentalists like José Bové, as well as those of traditionalists. Although educational, he is convinced that the Eden Project need not be stuffy or seek to preach; above all, fun, excitement and spectacle are integral to the educational process. This lays him open to the accusation that it is no more than a 'green theme park'; indeed his desire to make the project a centre for spectacle and display brings him into conflict with the horticulturalists on the site. In the year of filming, it is clear that the two managers of the biomes deeply resent the disturbance and damage done to their plants by teams of electricians hired to lay lighting cables in and around the buildings to support some of the spectacles and events that are planned. A third curator-in-waiting is frustrated that the project to build the dry tropics biome, which is planned to house his extensive cactus and succulent collection, has been put back by several years, leapfrogged by the project to build the 'Core' education centre.

Smit is also very 'hands-on' in the sense that he is both integral to many of the special events and equally prepared to help with selling tickets and guiding visitors on the peak season 'tricky days' - peak visitor days on which staff who do not normally work with visitors are encouraged to follow his example and pitch in to help keep the operation moving.[13]

Working in paradise

By 2014, the Eden Project had grown to be a major local employer with almost 500 staff on the payroll, and some 400 or more additional volunteer workers who are drafted in to help with peak seasonal activities such as horticulture and visitor operations. A regular internship programme brings in new graduates, helping them build their CVs and network with professionals in their field while developing practical skills in the workplace. The workforce is focused into a number of 'Eden Teams', the main one being the **Destination Team.** This team includes the **Green Team** of horticultural curators and other experts who manage the biomes and the planting, but in addition the people who run events and exhibitions as well as the retail and catering operations. This team is very much the 'front of house', as the gardeners work in the public eye during the day. However, as the programme shows, they also work outside opening hours, often at night, to carry out certain potentially hazardous activities, such as lopping unstable branches from trees in the rainforest. It is also clear from the series that there can be significant differences of opinion and interest between the Green Team and Smit. This came to the fore when Smit planned the first major winter event, the 'Time of Gifts' festival. This was partly an attempt to increase winter visitor numbers to the site, but required special construction (of an ice rink) and lighting in order to accommodate a variety of story-telling activities in the biomes, as well as 'light-and-magic' processions and shows. The whole event clearly opened something of a rift between members of the Green Team and Smit, since many felt that their values were being compromised and the whole project was becoming a sort of Disneyland. One curator told the BBC crew that the events not only did physical damage, but also damaged the morale of staff. Not only were curators upset, but the catering and housekeeping staff were also very concerned by the heavy demands (not least of which was having to learn to skate!) that would be made, and Smit is seen running a fairly fraught staff meeting with Destination Team personnel in an attempt to encourage them and gain extra commitment. When the event was successful, the staff were thrown a celebratory party, but nevertheless some of the Green Team were absent in protest. Smit explains his view about this conflict of interests:

I'm not into horticulture; my role isn't horticulture. My job is to fizz people into getting excited about horticulture, which is a very very different activity. And actually, the certainties that horticulturalists want are exactly the sort of thing I want to shake up.[14]

While the Destination Team is clearly the face of the Eden Project, other teams include the **Foundation Team**, which works with supporters of the project and also looks outwards to develop education and other scientific and technological projects; the **Marketing Team** and the **Communications Team,** which run an in-house publishing company as well as more traditional communications activities including the website; the **Development Team,** which is involved with major projects such as building and includes people from partner organisations such as architects and construction companies; the **Finance Team,** which ensures the project is economically viable and fully accountable to its various stakeholders; the **Creative Team,** which develops and produces events, including the regular concerts, many of which feature major pop and rock artists (Elton John played to 6,000 people there in June 2015); and the **Organisational Development Team,** which 'looks after our people' and is essentially concerned to link the processes and operations and build the Eden culture. Eden also includes the public as its **Visiting Team,** in other words the paying customers whose interaction with the project is vital to its continuation.

Between them, Tim Smit (who was awarded an honorary knighthood in 2011) and the Eden Project teams have been tremendously successful in both business and educational terms. Not only has a vision been realised in terms of the physical development of the site, but it has created well over 400 jobs, and the majority of staff were recruited locally. But above all, it has provided millions of people with a memorable and exciting experience, which almost all would recommend to others.

Tasks

1. In the television programme, Smit explains part of his management philosophy thus:

   It is essential for me to like everybody I work with, which is not a very professional thing if you were doing an MBA; you employ people on their merits and their CVs. Bugger that for a game of darts! If I'm going to get out of bed in the morning to do something like this, I want to walk through that door really looking forward to seeing everybody that's there. And you know what? I have the tremendous privilege of that being so.

   Using frameworks and concepts from the chapter on work groups and teams, critically review this approach to the creation of work teams and organisations. What are the strengths and the risks of taking such a view about the people who work for you?

2. Analyse Tim Smit's leadership style in the light of appropriate theories. Does it help or hinder his leadership that, as chief executive of a project about plants, he is 'not a horticulturalist'?

3. During 2013, and as a result of a downturn in its business, Eden had to restructure its business and make a number of people redundant (see the Eden Project's Annual Sustainability Report 2012-13, page 16, available on its website for details). How might the organisation's leaders help minimise the effects on staff motivation of this change? Explain whether you think its status as a social enterprise makes the task more or less difficult.

4. Tim Smit now lectures to all sorts of both commercial and non-commercial organisational leaders about management. Analyse the extent to which his approach might be transferable to both profit-making organisations and public-sector ones, whose stakeholder groups are very different from those at Eden.

Notes and references

1 Demianyk, G. 'Cornwall economy slips back in fight with Europe's poorest', *Western Morning News*, 7 May 2014, **http://www.westernmorningnews.co.uk/Cornwall-economy-slips-fight-Europe-s-poorest/story-21063726-detail/story.html** (accessed 16 February 2015).
2 Smale, W. 'How Cornwall's economy is fighting back', BBC News, 2006, **http://news.bbc.co.uk** (accessed 16 February 2015).
3 Smit, T. *The Lost Gardens of Heligan*, Orion Books (2000; first published 1997).
4 Visit the Lost Gardens of Heligan website at **www.heligan.com** to get a feel for this glorious garden.
5 The Eden Project Guide 2004–5.
6 For instance, pine cones, sunflower heads, pineapples and many cacti show this pattern.
7 Eden Project, Annual Sustainability Report 2012–13, **www.edenproject.com** (accessed 16 February 2015).
8 Eden Project Annual Report 2013–14, p. 33.
9 Eden Project, Annual Sustainability Report 2012–13, p. 1.
10 Eden, for instance, ran an 'Africa Calling' concert during the 2005 'Live8' day which featured a host of bands and internationally known artists from many parts of Africa.
11 The BBC DVD, *The Eden Project: The Gardeners of Eden*, BBC (2005), covers part of the years 2004–5.
12 Vidal, J. 'Shaping the Future', *Guardian*, 6 October 2004.
13 BBC DVD 2005, op. cit.
14 BBC DVD 2005, op. cit.

CHAPTER 6
Perception and communication

The process of perception is at the root of our understanding, behaviour and actions. Knowledge and awareness of the perceptual process can help develop insights about ourselves and interactions with others. The words we use and speak, the way we look and the body language we display communicate our view of the world. Managers need to understand the importance of perception and communications in guiding behaviour and for effective personal and work relationships with others.

Learning outcomes

After completing this chapter you should have enhanced your ability to:

- explain the nature and importance of the perceptual process;
- detail internal and external factors that provide meaning to the individual;
- explain the importance of perceptual illusions, and impression management;
- identify difficulties in perceiving other people, including non-verbal communications;
- explain the importance of language and communications in perception;
- evaluate the relevance of neuro-linguistic programming and transactional analysis;
- assess the nature and significance of perceptual distortions and errors.

Critical review and reflection

People differ as individuals. Even confronted with exactly the same situation this will give rise to a variety of responses, behaviours and actions. There is no way managers can cope with such a range of individual perspectives so the study of perception is largely a waste of time.

What are YOUR views? What do YOU expect to gain from a study of perception?

The importance of understanding perception

The significance of individual differences is particularly apparent when focusing on the process of **perception**. Although general theories of perception were first proposed during the last century, the importance of understanding the perceptual process is arguably even more significant today. We all have our own, unique picture or image of how we see the 'reality' of the world around us, and our own way of looking at and understanding our environment and the people within it. This is a complex and dynamic process.

We do not passively receive information, we analyse and judge it, and place significance on certain information and disregard other information as worthless. We may also be influenced by our expectations so that we perceive what we expect to 'see' or 'hear'. A situation may be the same, but the interpretation of that situation by two individuals may be vastly different. Perception is at the root of organisational behaviour; any situation can be analysed in terms of its perceptual connotations. Consider, for instance, the following situation.

A member of senior management has sent an email to departmental managers asking them to provide statistics of overtime worked within their section during the past six months and projections for the next six months. Mixed reactions could result:

- One manager may see it as a reasonable and welcome request to provide information in the hopeful expectation that this will help lead to improved staffing levels.
- Another manager may be extremely upset and suspect the information will be used by senior management to order cutbacks in future overtime in order to reduce staffing costs.
- A third manager may see it as an unreasonable demand, intended only to enable management to exercise closer supervision and control over the activities of the section.
- A fourth manager may have no objection to providing the information but be suspicious that it may lead to possible intrusion into the running of the section.
- Yet another manager may see it as a positive action by management to investigate ways of improving efficiency throughout the organisation.

Each of the departmental managers has their own different perception of the email, which could be influenced, for example, by their working relationship with senior management or previous experiences. Their perceived reality and understanding of the situation provokes individual reactions. In addition, there are likely to be mixed reactions to the use of email as the means of communication in this instance.

The perceptual process

It is not possible to have an understanding of perception without taking into account its sensory basis. We are not able to attend to everything in our environment; our sensory systems have limits. The physical limits therefore insist that we are selective in our attention and perception. Early pioneer work by psychologists has resulted in an understanding of universal laws that underlie the perceptual process. It seems that we cannot help but search for meaning and understanding in our environment. The way in which we categorise and organise this sensory information is based on a range of factors including the present situation, our emotional state and any experiences of the same or a similar event.

Selectivity in attention and perception

Some information may be considered highly important to us and may result in immediate response. In other instances, the information may be simply 'parked' or assimilated in other ideas and thoughts. Some of our 'parked' material may be forgotten or, indeed, changed and reconstructed over time.[1] We should be aware of the assumptions that are made throughout the perceptual process, below our conscious threshold. We have learned to take for granted certain constants in our environment. We assume that features of our world will stay the same and thus we do not need to spend our time and energy seeing things afresh and anew. We make a number of inferences throughout the entire perceptual process. Although these inferences may save time and speed up the process, they may also lead to distortions and inaccuracies.

Perception as information processing

It is common to see the stages of perception described as an information-processing system (*see* Figure 6.1): (top-down) information (stimuli) (Box A) is selected at one end of the process (Box B), then interpreted (Box C) and translated (Box D), resulting in action or thought patterns (Box E). However, it is important to note that such a model simplifies the process and although it makes it easy to understand, it does not do justice to the complexity and dynamics of the process. In certain circumstances, we may select information out of the environment because of the way we categorise the world. The dashed line illustrates this 'bottom-up' process.

For instance, if a manager has been advised by colleagues that a particular trainee has managerial potential, the manager may be specifically looking for confirmation that those views are correct. This process has been known as 'top-down' because the cognitive processes are influencing the perceptual readiness of the individual to select certain information. This emphasises the active nature of the perceptual process. We do not passively digest the information from our senses, but actively attend to and indeed, at times, seek out certain information. (**See also the discussion on self-fulfilling prophecy below.**)

Meaning to the individual

The process of perception explains the manner in which information (stimuli) from the environment around us is selected and organised to provide meaning for the individual. Perception is the mental function of giving significance to stimuli such as shapes, colours, movement, taste, sounds, touch, smells, pain, pressures and feelings. Perception gives rise to individual behavioural responses to particular situations.

Despite the fact that a group of people may 'physically see' the same thing, they each have their own version of what is seen – their perceived view of reality. Consider, for example, the image (published by W. E. Hill in *Puck*, 6 November 1915) shown in Figure 6.2. What do

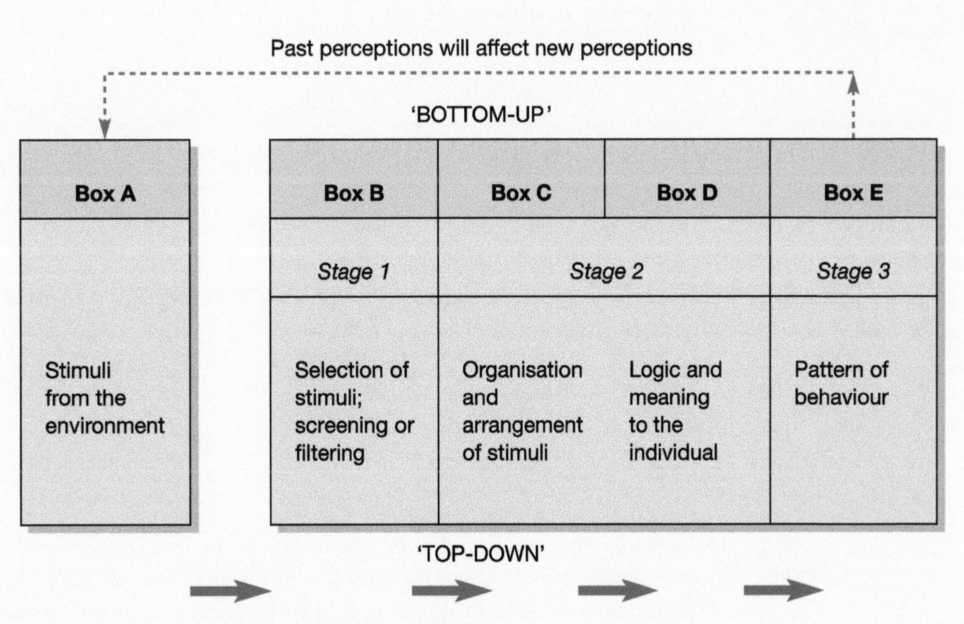

Figure 6.1 Perceptions as information processing

Figure 6.2

you see? Do you see a young, attractive, well-dressed woman? Or do you see an older, poor woman? Or can you now see both? **And who can say with certainty that there is just the one, 'correct' answer?**

Why do we attend to certain stimuli and not to others? There are two important factors to consider in this discussion. The process of perceptual selection is based both on internal characteristics relating to the state of the individual and on the environment and influences external to the individual.

Critical review and reflection

In order to develop our perceptual abilities the first step is recognition and understanding of the process that we determine of our selection and attention of the stimuli around us.

To what extent do YOU identify with this statement? What stimulus factors most catch YOUR attention and selection?

Internal factors

Our sensory systems have limits. For instance, our eyes receive and convert light waves into electrical signals that are transmitted to the visual cortex of the brain and translated into meaning. Our sensory system is geared to respond to changes in the environment. This has particular implications for the way in which we perceive the world and it explains why we are able to ignore the humming of the central heating system but notice instantly a telephone ringing. The term used to describe the way in which we disregard the familiar is 'habituation'.

Sensory limits or thresholds

As individuals we may differ in terms of our sensory limits or thresholds. People differ not only in their absolute thresholds, but also in their ability to discriminate between stimuli. For instance, it may not be possible for the untrained to distinguish between different types of wine but this would be an everyday event for the trained sommelier. We are able to learn to discriminate and are able to train our senses to recognise small differences between stimuli. It is also possible for us to adapt to unnatural environments and learn to cope.[2] We may also differ in terms of the amount of sensory information we need to reach our own comfortable equilibrium. Some individuals would find loud music at a party or gig uncomfortable and unpleasant, whereas for others the intensity of the music is part of the total enjoyment. Likewise, if we are deprived of sensory information for too long this can lead to feelings of discomfort and fatigue.

Psychological factors

Psychological factors will also affect what is perceived. These internal factors, such as personality, learning and motives, will give rise to an inclination to perceive certain stimuli with a readiness to respond in certain ways. This has been called an individual's perceptual set (*see* Figure 6.3).

Differences in the ways individuals acquire information have been used as one of four scales in the Myers–Briggs Type Indicator (**discussed in Chapter 4**). They distinguish individuals who 'tend to accept and work with what is given in the here-and-now, and thus become realistic and practical' (sensing types), from others who go beyond the information from the senses and look at the possible patterns, meanings and relationships. These 'intuitive types' 'grow expert at seeing new possibilities and new ways of doing things'. Myers and Briggs stress the value of both types and emphasise the importance of complementary skills and variety in any successful enterprise or relationship.[3]

Needs of the individual

The needs of each individual will affect their perceptions. For example, a manager deeply engrossed in preparing an urgent report may screen out ringing telephones, the sound of computers, people talking and furniture being moved in the next office, but will respond readily to the smell of coffee brewing. The most desirable and urgent needs will almost certainly affect

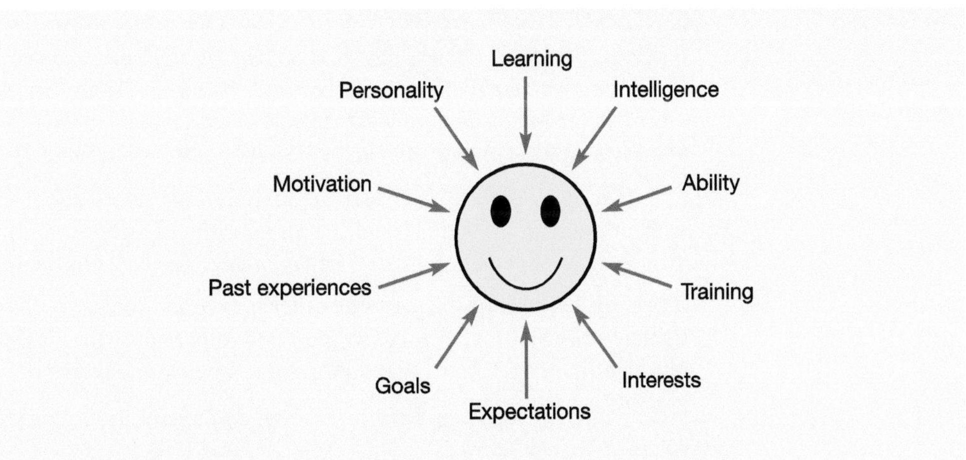

Figure 6.3 Factors affecting an individual's perceptual set

an individual's perceptual process. Members of a church choir might well form a perception of the minister quite different from that of a parishioner seeking comfort after the recent death of a close relative.

The 'Pollyanna Principle' claims that pleasant stimuli will be processed more quickly and remembered more precisely than unpleasant stimuli. However, it must be noted that intense internal drives may lead to perceptual distortions of situations (or people) and unwillingness to absorb certain painful information. (**Perceptual distortions are considered later in the chapter.**)

Learning from experiences has a critical effect throughout all stages of the perceptual process. It will affect the stimuli perceived in the first instance, and then the ways in which those stimuli are understood and processed, and finally the response that is given. For example, it is likely that a maintenance engineer visiting a school for the first time will notice different things about it than will a teacher attending an interview or a child arriving on the first day. The learning gained from experiences colours what is seen and processed.

Cultural differences

The ways in which people interact are also subject to cultural differences and such differences may be misconstrued. There are many ways of describing **culture**, but the following definition from *Schein* helps relate culture to diversity and perception.

> *A pattern of basic assumptions – invented, discovered or developed by a given group as it learns to cope with its problems of external adaptation and internal integration – that has worked well enough to be considered valuable and therefore to be taught to new members as the correct way to perceive, think and feel in relation to these problems.*[4]

Embarrassment and discomfort can occur when emotional lines are broken. This was demonstrated in an American study that researched the experience of Japanese students visiting the USA for the first time. The researchers felt that the Japanese students faced considerable challenges in adapting to the new culture. Some of the surprises that the students reported related to social interaction:

> *Casual visits and frequent phone calls at midnight to the host room-mate were a new experience to them. The sight of opposite-sex partners holding hands or kissing in public places also surprised them . . . That males do cooking and shopping in the household or by themselves, that fathers would play with children, and that there was frequent intimacy displayed between couples were all never-heard-of in their own experiences at home.*[5]

In certain cultures, such as the USA, it is 'normal' to explain all details clearly, explicitly and directly. In other cultures the 'spelling out' of all the details is unnecessary and embarrassing.

> *McCrum refers to a joke circulated on the Web by disaffected UN staff. A worldwide survey was conducted by the UN. The only question asked was: 'Would you please give your honest opinion about solutions to the food shortage in the rest of the world?' The survey was a failure. In Africa they didn't know what 'food' meant; in India they didn't know what 'honest' meant; in Europe they didn't know what 'shortage' meant; in China they didn't know what 'opinion' meant; in the Middle East they didn't know what 'solution' meant; in South America they didn't know what 'please' meant; and in the USA they didn't know what 'the rest of the world' meant.*[6]

Ways in which words are used and the assumptions made about shared understanding are dependent upon an individual's culture and upbringing. Cultural differences often lead to stereotypical views. For example, *Stewart-Allen* discusses a common mindset about Americans:

> *American business people seem to suffer from a long-standing image problem abroad. The stereotypical view is that they are loud and impatient with a 'bigger is better' attitude; they lecture others about how to do business the American way and are insular in outlook.*

However, a more accurate assumption is that Americans lack international exposure.[7] (**Stereotyping is discussed below.**)

Management and organisational behaviour in action case study

Diversity Resource Handbook

Portsmouth Hospitals NHS Trust has produced a comprehensive 'Diversity Resource Handbook' intended to provide members of staff with practical advice and guidelines on delivering a sensitive service to the diverse community it serves. Good communication is fundamental to providing a good quality service. If the correct meaning is not conveyed via effective communication, we risk inducing feelings of confusion, frustration, isolation and perhaps anger. It is important not only to be aware of the appropriate naming systems, but to use them effectively.

Using the right terminology is extremely important, particularly when referring to disability, because the words you use reflect your attitudes and beliefs. The key towards working towards acceptable language is firstly to see the person and not their disability, or background, and choose language that aims to include and value people with a disability. The booklet sets out advice and guidelines on age, disability, race, religious and cultural issues, major world religions, interpreting and translating, sexual orientation and gender, and aids to communication.

The booklet draws attention to the importance and realities of perceptual awareness, including:

Awareness in a multicultural society - some guidelines

Be aware that in some communities it may not be the custom to shake hands, especially amongst women.

Be sensitive to the difficulties that may be caused for ethnic minorities by using jargon and slang.

Be sensitive to using colloquialisms or terms of endearment that may cause offence, e.g. love, dear or darling.

Be aware that in some communities a woman may feel uncomfortable or may not wish to be in a room with a man who is not a relative.

Be aware that an act of comfort, such as putting an arm around a person, may cause embarrassment or offence.

Appreciate cultural differences in body language - for example, looking away instead of maintaining eye contact is not necessarily a sign of dishonesty or disrespect, in some communities it may be the opposite.

Ask for the individual's personal and family name. Don't ask someone what his or her Christian name or surname is.

Just because someone responds to questions in English they may not fully understand what is being said.

Don't underestimate the influence of your own cultural background on your unconscious perceptions and behaviours.

Source: Extracts from Portsmouth Hospitals NHS Trust, *Diversity Resource Handbook*, November 2013. Reproduced with permission.

Tasks

1. What do you think of the idea of an NHS Diversity Resource Handbook? Would you recommend a similar handbook for your own university or organisation?
2. Give your own examples of the importance and realities of perceptual awareness.
3. Discuss how you would attempt to improve awareness of perception and communication in a multicultural society.

Critical review and reflection

The overriding obstacles to effective perception and communication are lack of understanding cultural differences and inappropriate use of language.

From YOUR own experience to what extent do YOU agree with this contention? How much are YOU aware of cultural differences and YOUR own use of language?

External factors

Knowledge, familiarity or expectations about a given situation or previous experiences will influence perception. External factors refer to the nature and characteristics of the stimuli. There is usually a tendency to give more attention to stimuli that are, for example:

- bright
- novel
- repeated
- in strong contrast to their background.

Any number of these factors may be present at a given time or in a given situation. The use of these stimuli is a key feature in the design of advertising. (Think of your own examples.) It is the **total pattern** of the stimuli together with the **context** in which they occur that influence perception. For example, it is usually a novel or unfamiliar stimulus that is more noticeable, but a person is more likely to perceive the familiar face of a friend among a group of people all dressed in the same-style uniform (*see* Figure 6.4).[8]

We are all familiar with the expression 'what on earth is that doing here?'. The sight of a fork-lift truck on the factory floor in a manufacturing organisation is likely to be perceived quite differently from one in the corridor of a university. Consider another example: the sight of a jet ski (left temporarily by a neighbour moving house) in the garage of a person known

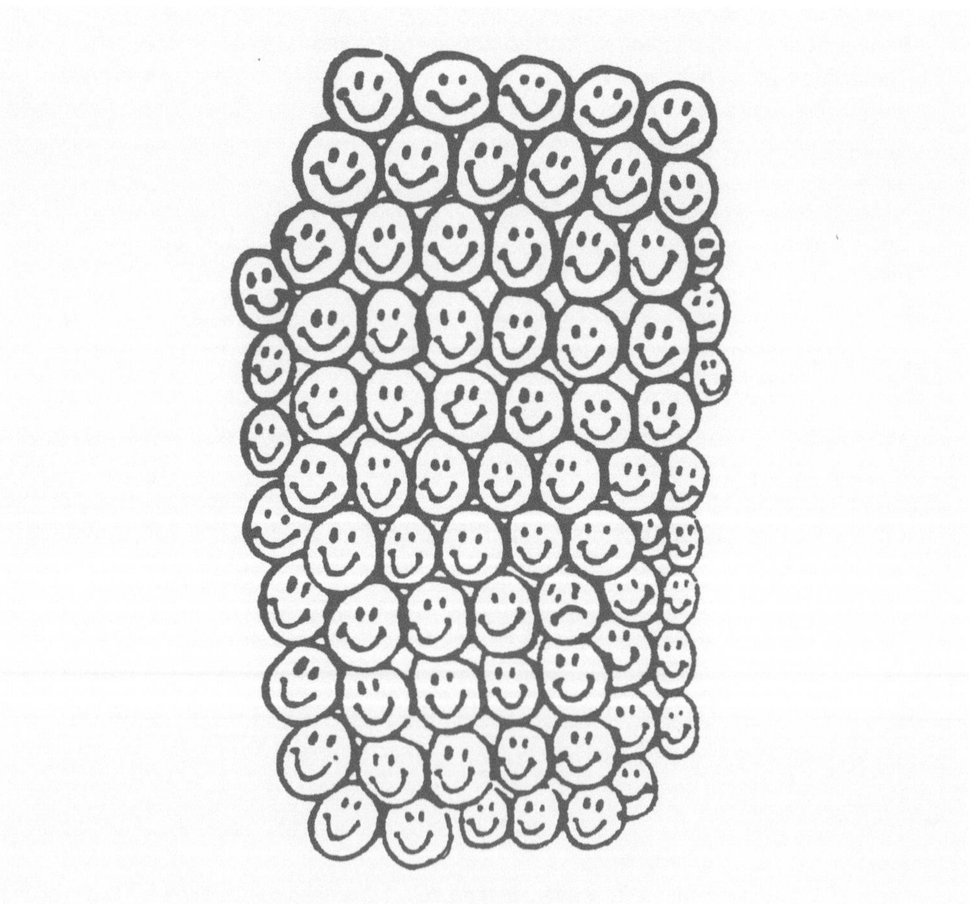

Figure 6.4 Is everybody happy?
Source: Block, J. R. and Yuker, H. E. *Can You Believe Your Eyes?*, Robson Books (2002), p. 163.

to be scared of water is likely to elicit such a remark. Yet the sight of numerous jet skis on the beach is likely to pass without comment. The word 'terminal' is likely to be perceived differently in the context of: (i) a hospital, (ii) an airport, or (iii) a computer firm. Consumer psychologists and marketing experts apply these perceptual principles with extraordinary success for some of their products.

Organisation and arrangement of stimuli

The Gestalt School of Psychology led by Max Wertheimer claimed that the process of perception is innately organised and patterned. It described the process as one that has built-in field effects. In other words, the brain can act like a dynamic, physical field in which interaction among elements is an intrinsic part. The Gestalt School produced a series of principles, which are still readily applicable today. Some of the most significant include the following:

- figure and ground
- grouping
- closure.

Figure and ground

The figure and ground principle states that figures are seen against a background. The figure does not have to be an object; it could be merely a geometrical pattern. Figure and ground relationships are often reversible, as in the popular example shown in Figure 6.5. What do you see first? Do you see a white chalice (or small stand shape) in the centre of the frame? Or do you see the dark profiles of twins facing each other on the edge of the frame? Now look again. Can you see the other shape?

The figure and ground principle has applications in occupational situations. It is important that employees know and are able to attend to the significant aspects (the figure) and treat other elements of the job as context (background). Early training sessions aim to identify and focus on the significant aspects of a task. Managerial effectiveness can also be judged in terms of chosen priorities (the figure). Stress could certainly occur for those employees who are uncertain about their priorities and are unable to distinguish between the significant and less significant tasks. They feel overwhelmed by the 'whole' picture.

Figure 6.5

Grouping

The grouping principle refers to the tendency to organise shapes and patterns instantly into meaningful groupings or patterns on the basis of their proximity or similarity. Parts that are close in time or space tend to be perceived together. For example, in Figure 6.6a, the workers are more likely to be perceived as nine independent people, but in Figure 6.6b, because of the proximity principle, the workers may be perceived as three distinct groups of people. Consider the importance of the layout of the room and tables for a large wedding reception and the perception of people in terms of both the table where they are sat and with whom they are grouped!

Taxi firms often use the idea of grouping to display their telephone number. In the example below, which of the following numbers – (a), (b) or (c) – is most likely to be remembered easily?

(a) 347 474 (b) 347474 (c) 34 74 74

Similar parts tend to be seen together as forming a familiar group.

In the following example there is a tendency to see alternate lines of characters – crosses and noughts (or circles). This is because the horizontal similarity is usually greater than the vertical similarity. However, if the page is turned sideways the figure may be perceived as alternate noughts and crosses in each line.

× × × × × × × ×
○ ○ ○ ○ ○ ○ ○ ○
× × × × × × × ×
○ ○ ○ ○ ○ ○ ○ ○

It is also interesting to note that, when asked to describe this pattern, many people refer to alternate lines of noughts and crosses – rather than crosses and noughts.

There is also an example here of the impact of cultural differences, mentioned earlier. The author undertook a teaching exchange in the USA and gave this exercise to a class of American students. Almost without exception the students described the horizontal pattern correctly as alternate rows of crosses and noughts (or zeros). The explanation appears to be that Americans do not know the game as 'noughts and crosses' but refer to it as 'tic-tac-toe'.

Closure

There is also a tendency to complete an incomplete figure – to fill in the gaps (mentally) and to perceive the figure as a whole. This creates an overall and meaningful image for the individual rather than an unconnected series of lines or blobs.

In the example in Figure 6.7[9] most people are likely to see the blobs as either the letter B or the number 13, possibly depending on whether at the time they had been more concerned with written material or dealing in numbers. However, for some people the figure may be described in terms of just a series of eleven discrete blobs, or perceived as some other (to them) meaningful pattern/object. According to Gestalt theory, perceptual organisation is instant and spontaneous. We cannot stop ourselves making meaningful assumptions about our environment.

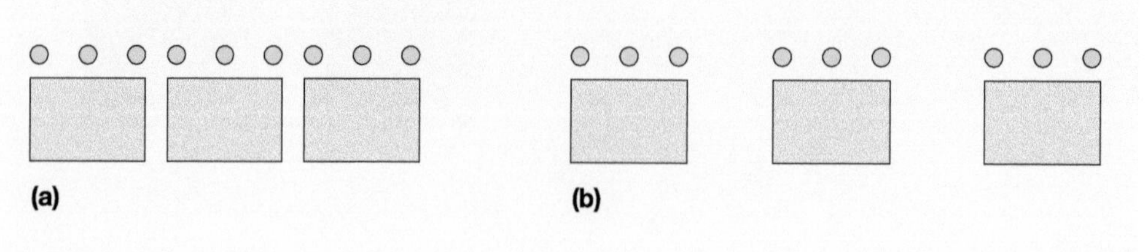

Figure 6.6

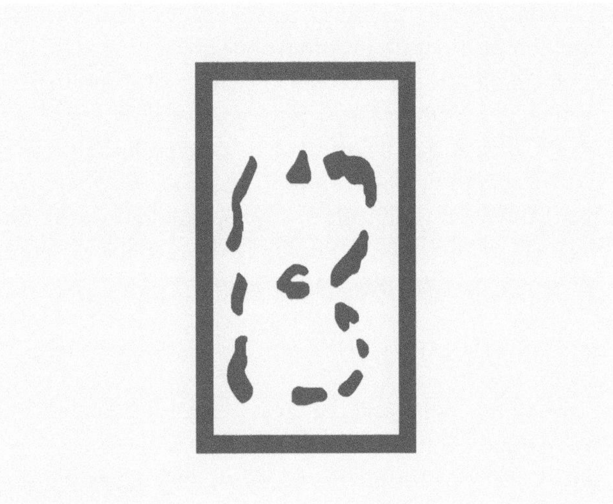

Figure 6.7
Source: King, R. A. *Introduction to Psychology*, 6th edition, McGraw-Hill (1966). Figure 10.22, p.339. Reproduced with permission from the author, Professor Richard King.

The Gestaltists emphasised the ways in which the elements interact and claimed that the new pattern or structure perceived had a character of its own, hence the famous phrase 'the whole is more than the sum of its parts'.

Perceptual illusions

Here are some examples to help you judge your perceptive skills. In Figure 6.8 try reading aloud the four words. It is possible that you find yourself 'caught' in a perceptual set that means that you tend to pronounce 'machinery' as 'MacHinery', as if it too were a Scottish surname.

In Figure 6.9, which of the centre blue circles is the larger – A or B?

M-A-C-D-O-N-A-L-D
M-A-C-P-H-E-R-S-O-N
M-A-C-D-O-U-G-A-L-L
M-A-C-H-I-N-E-R-Y

Figure 6.8

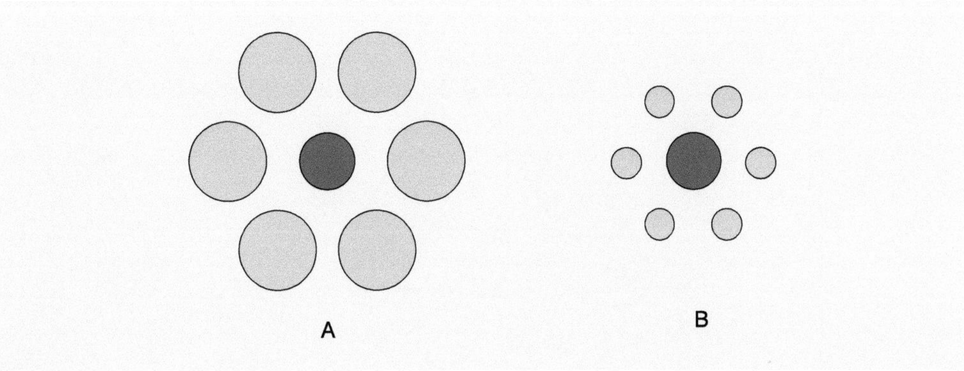

Figure 6.9

Although you may have guessed that the two centre circles are in fact the same size, the circle on the right (B) may well **appear** larger because it is framed by smaller circles. The centre circle on the left (A) may well **appear** smaller because it is framed by larger circles.

In Figure 6.10 try saying the *colour* of the word, *not* the word itself.

The physiological nature of perception has already been discussed briefly, but it is of relevance here in the discussion of illusions. Why does the circle on the right in Figure 6.9 look bigger? Why is it difficult to say the colour, not the word? These examples demonstrate the way our brain can be fooled. Indeed, we make assumptions about our world that go beyond the pure sensations our brain receives.

Beyond reality

Perception goes beyond the sensory information and converts patterns to a three-dimensional reality that we understand. This conversion process, as we can see, is easily tricked. We may not be aware of the inferences we are making as they are part of our conditioning and learning. The Stroop experiment shown in Figure 6.10 illustrates this perfectly.[10]

An illustration of the way in which we react automatically to stimuli is the illusion of the impossible triangle (*see* Figure 6.11).

Even when we know the triangle is impossible we still cannot stop ourselves from completing the triangle and attempting to make it meaningful. We thus go beyond what is given and make assumptions about the world, which in certain instances are wildly incorrect. Psychologists and designers may make positive use of these assumptions to project positive images of a product or the environment. For instance: colours may be used to induce certain atmospheres in buildings; designs of wallpaper or texture of curtains may be used to create feelings of spaciousness or cosiness; and packaging of products may tempt us to see something as bigger or perhaps more precious.

BLUE	GREY	YELLOW	MAUVE
BLACK	ORANGE	GREEN	RED
WHITE	PURPLE	BLUE	BROWN

Figure 6.10

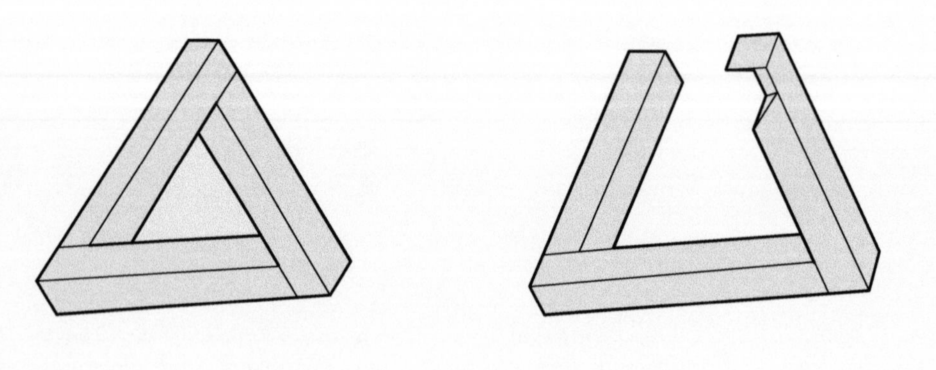

Figure 6.11

Source: Gregory, R. L. *Odd Perceptions*, Methuen (1986), p. 71. Reprinted by permission of the publishers, Routledge, a division of Taylor & Francis Ltd.

Impression management

In some situations we all attempt to project our attitudes, personality and competence by paying particular attention to our appearance and the impact this may have on others. This has been labelled 'impression management'.[11] The selection interview is an obvious illustration. Some information is given more weight than other information when an impression is formed. It would seem that there are central traits that are more important than others in determining our perceptions.

What information do we select and why? The social situation consists of both verbal and non-verbal signals. Non-verbal signals include:

- bodily contact
- proximity
- orientation
- head movements
- facial expressions
- gestures
- posture
- direction of gaze
- dress and appearance
- non-verbal aspects of speech.

Verbal and non-verbal signals are co-ordinated into regular sequences, often without the awareness of the parties. The mirroring of actions has been researched and is called 'postural echoing'.[12] There is considerable evidence to indicate that each person is constantly influencing the other and being influenced.[13]

Lucas refers to the importance of the 'personal brand' that we all have.

> *You may not be aware of it and you probably haven't consciously developed it, but it's what drives how you are perceived at work and how successful you are in your daily dealings with colleagues and clients. Your personal brand is about the way you come across to others. It's about the messages you send with the way you dress, the tone of your voice and your body language.*[14]

Rigby points out that although it would be good to think all managers view staff as equal and judged only on results, there are still plenty of ways in which people discriminate. Eleven factors that can hold back your career are:

- dress sense
- appearance
- body modification
- accent
- education
- parentage
- height
- hair
- weight
- politics
- religion.[15]

Despite becoming somewhat clichéd, *Everett* reminds us of the truth of the expression that 'you never get a second chance to make a first impression'. It takes five to seven seconds to make a first impression.

> *To begin with, the person we are meeting will take in our non-verbal impact, beginning with our body language and then our dress and appearance. That will be followed by the quality or clarity of our voice, and thirdly what we say. This does not mean that image is more important than content – far from it, we need real substance too . . . Making a positive first impression sounds like common sense, but it is not common practice. Bring it into your conscious thoughts every day and manage that instant portrayal of your person brand more effectively.*[16]

Research by *Willis and Todorov* demonstrated that an exposure time of no more than a tenth of a second is sufficient to form an impression of a stranger from their facial appearance. Longer exposure time increases confidence in judgements but does not alter significantly the first impression.[17]

Dress code and culture

The meanings we ascribe to these non-verbal signals are rooted in our culture and early socialisation. Thus it is no surprise that there are significant differences in the way we perceive such signals. For instance, dress codes differ in degrees of formality. *Schneider and Barsoux* summarise some interesting cultural differences:

> *Northern European managers tend to dress more informally than their Latin counterparts. At conferences, it is not unlikely for the Scandinavian managers to be wearing casual clothing, while their French counterparts are reluctant to remove their ties and jackets. For the Latin managers, personal style is important, while Anglo and Asian managers do not want to stand out or attract attention in their dress. French women managers are more likely to be dressed in ways that Anglo women managers might think inappropriate for the office. The French, in turn, think it strange that American businesswomen dress in 'man-like' business suits (sometimes with running shoes).*[18]

Ziolo discusses how the collective set of each generation differs due to different life experiences, work ethic and culture. Even if we have to make large generalisations, an understanding of sartorial trends of each generation can lead to a better understanding of the culture that guides them.

> *Even if you are not a dedicated follower of fashion what you wear is defined not just by your individual tastes but also by the societal and cultural experiences of your era. With most senior managers and executives hailing from the old school, clothing is not an expression of self, but a business uniform identifying the divide between the professional self and the self at leisure – therefore, a suit is the norm. Younger employees are less likely to make this distinction, seeing work much more part of what defines them, where expression of personality matters.*[19]

Critical review and reflection

Popular sports, film or television celebrities often appear to have a far greater impact on perception, communications and behaviour of people at work than any textbook, manager or training course.

Why do YOU think this is the case and is it necessarily a bad thing? To what extent does this apply to YOU?

Organisation and judgement

The way in which we organise and make judgements about what we have perceived is, to a large extent, based on experiences and learning. It is important to be aware of the inferences and assumptions we make that go beyond the information given. We may not always be aware of our pre-set assumptions but they will guide the way in which we interpret the behaviour of others. In the same way that we make assumptions, about the world of objects and go beyond the information provided, we also make critical inferences about people's characteristics and possible likely behaviours.

A manager might well know more about person A, a member of staff who has become or was already a good friend, who is seen in a variety of social situations and with whom there is a close relationship, than about person B, another member of staff in the same section as A and undertaking similar duties, but with whom there is only a formal work relationship and a limited social acquaintance. These differences in relationship, information and interaction might well influence the manager's perception if asked, for example, to evaluate the work performance of A and B.

Judgement of other people can also be influenced by perceptions of such stimuli as:

- role or status
- occupation

- ethnicity, gender and age
- physical factors and appearance
- non-verbal communication and body language (**discussed below**).

Physical characteristics and appearance

There are frequent popular surveys and articles that refer to the suggestion that tall people, both men and women, are more likely to be successful both socially and professionally. For example, *Cohen* comments that taller people who look down on shorter colleagues are perceived to have confidence and respect. In an interesting account celebrating the lives of tall people, Cohen maintains that height is a pivotal piece of identity and the most defining force in our lives. Height determined her choice of sports (swimming), boyfriends (tall), social circle (tall), my college (tall), and my personality (big enough to fill the tall).[20]

An example is the appointment (June 2009) of the Speaker of the House of Commons, John Bercow, who is 5 ft 6 in tall (1.68 m). This appointment prompted newspaper articles about 'heightism' and perceptions about the 'shorter man'.[21]

In the work situation there are similar comments that taller people have better promotion prospects and earn higher salaries than short people. (We leave you to make your own judgement about this claim!)

In a discussion of physical attributes and good leadership, *Dib* suggests that 'we seem to associate the effectiveness of leaders with certain personality traits, which are in turn assumed as a consequence of their looks'. Examples are gender, hair colour, face, height, ethnicity and weight.

> *Of course there is no scientific evidence of correlation between height and intelligence, or height and the ability to lead people. Yet tall people are massively overrepresented in leadership roles. Similarly, other illogical preferences on hair colour, weight and facial features have nestled into our subconscious through societal, cultural and historical channels, and continue to affect the decisions we make and the leaders we turn to.*

Dib reports that there are convincing arguments for why we need to confront and overhaul ingrained preconceptions and stereotypes.[22] (**Stereotyping is discussed below.**)

Note also that *Mintzberg* includes 'tall' in a composite list of basic managerial qualities.[23] (**See Figure 16.3 in Chapter 16.**)

Framing

The term 'framing' is used to explain how we interpret particular circumstances. Rather like a picture frame, we place into the frame our particular perspective, focus and colour on things. So if we are feeling happy our experience is being 'framed' in a positive way. What is in the 'frame' will depend on what is filtered in or out. Whether we look at a difficult situation as a 'problem' or as an opportunity, or whether we see a mistake as a terrible failure or as a learning moment, will depend on how we have 'framed' the experience. If we are in a good mood we may only filter in messages from our environment that confirm our happy state; we may create an inner dialogue in which our inner voice is reaffirming why we are feeling so content. We may also be visualising a situation in which we are successful and these thoughts are establishing neural pathways. Helping people to reframe situations can be part of the mentoring and coaching process (**see Chapter 5**).

Critical review and reflection

We often mask what we really feel, act in ways that cover our true emotions and speak words that we do not really mean. In our dealings with other people we need to look beyond what is seen and heard and delve beneath the surface.

To what extent do YOU mask YOUR feelings and emotions? How do YOU think we can best judge the true beliefs and intentions of other people?

Perceiving other people

There are a number of well-documented difficulties that arise when perceiving other people. Many of these problems occur because of our limitations in selecting and attending information. This selectivity may occur because:

- we already know what we are looking for and are therefore 'set' to receive only the information that confirms our initial thoughts;
- previous training and experience have led us to shortcut and see only a certain range of behaviours;
- we may group features together and make assumptions about their similarities.

The Gestalt principles apply equally well to the perception of people as to the perception of objects. Thus we can see, for example, that if people live in the same geographical area, assumptions may be made about not only their wealth and type of accommodation, but also their attitudes, their political views and even their type of personality.

> *To interact effectively (present ourselves and communicate appropriately, influence others, work with them in relationships and groups or lead them) we must have a grasp of what others are thinking and feeling, including their motives, beliefs, attitudes and intentions. In social perception, accuracy and differentiation are essential but difficult. Achieving them may be linked to the complexity of a person's system of cognitive constructs.*[24]

The way we see others, the habits we have formed, the associations we have made and the assumptions we make lead us to make errors and distortions when perceiving others. The focus of the following section is to examine the perception of people and to consider the impact this has on the management and development of people at work. The principles of perceptual differences explained earlier apply to the way we perceive others. Some examples might be as follows:

- **Grouping** – The way in which a manager may think of a number of staff, for example either working in close proximity, or with some common feature such as all IT staff, all graduate trainees or all older workers; as a homogeneous group rather than a collection of individuals, each with their own separate identity and characteristics.
- **Figure and ground** – A manager may notice a new recruit and set the recruit apart from the group because of particular characteristics such as age, appearance or physical features.
- **Closure** – The degree to which unanimity is perceived and decisions made or action taken in the belief that there is full agreement with staff when, in fact, a number of staff may be opposed to the decision or action.

A manager's perception of the workforce will influence attitudes in dealing with people and the style of managerial behaviour adopted. The way in which managers approach the performance of their jobs and the behaviour they display towards subordinate staff are likely to be conditioned by predispositions about people, human nature and work. An example of this is the style of management adopted on the basis of McGregor's Theory X and Theory Y suppositions (**discussed in Chapter 10**). In making judgements about other people it is important to try to perceive their underlying intent and motivation, not *just* the resultant behaviour or actions.

The perception of people's performance can be affected by the organisation of stimuli. In employment interviews, for example, interviewers are susceptible to contrast effects and the perception of a candidate may be influenced by the rating given to immediately preceding candidates. Average candidates may be rated highly if they follow people with low qualifications, but rated lower when following people with higher qualifications.[25]

Recognising assumptions held and testing these out requires a heightened level of critical reflection. Many leadership and management development courses start with a 'self-awareness and diagnostic' module intended to help participants understand and recognise their style and preferences and the impact on others. Courses that take a more challenging stance will encourage managers to question their existing frames of mind and challenge them constantly to re-evaluate their purpose, strategies and action.

Dynamics of interpersonal perception

Unlike the perception of an object that just exists, when you perceive another individual they will react to you and be affected by your behaviour – the dynamics are all-important. This interaction is illustrated in the following quotation:

> *You are a pain in the neck and to stop you giving me a pain in the neck I protect my neck by tightening my neck muscles, which gives me the pain in the neck you are.*[26]

The interaction of individuals thus provides an additional layer of interpretation and complexity. The cue that we may attend to, the expectation we may have, the assumptions we may make, the response pattern that occurs, leave more scope for errors and distortions. We are not only perceiving the stimulus (i.e. the other person), but also processing their reactions to us at the same time that they are processing our reactions to them. Thus interpersonal perception differs from the perception of objects because it is a continually dynamic and changing process, and the perceiver is a part of this process who will influence and be influenced by the other people in the situation (*see* Figure 6.12).[27]

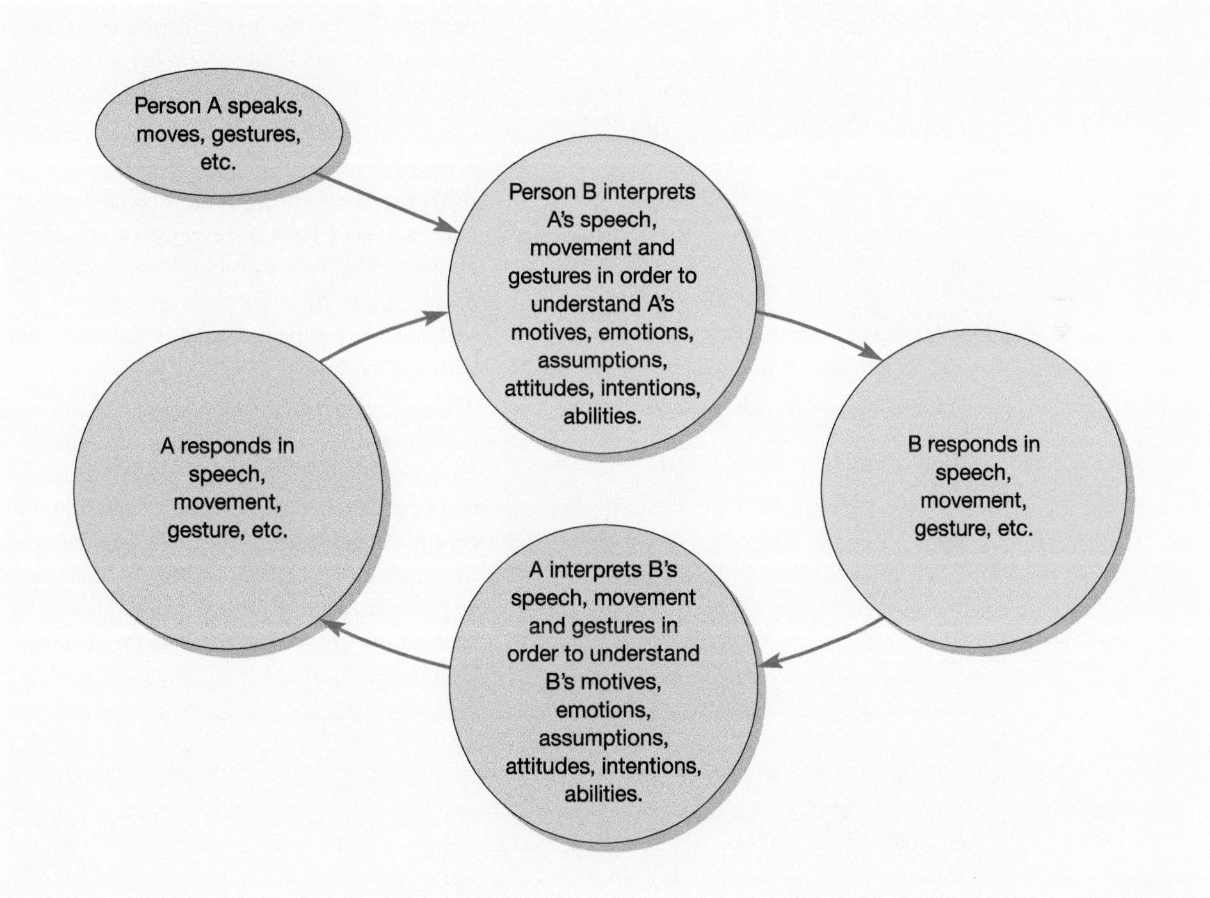

Figure 6.12 Cycle of perception and behaviour

Source: From Guirdham, M. *Interactive Behaviour at Work*, third edition, Financial Times Prentice Hall (2002), p. 162. Reproduced with permission from Pearson Education Ltd.

Setting and environment

Interpersonal perception will also be affected by the setting, and the environment may play a critical part in establishing rapport. For example, next time you are involved in a formal meeting such as attending an in-house development centre, consider the following factors that will all influence the perceptual process:

Why?	Purpose of and motives for meeting	Likely to be an important event for the participant, may be a catalyst for promotion and may signal new and relevant development opportunities. Chance to be visible and demonstrate skills and abilities. Opportunity to network with other managers. Thus high emotional cost to participant
Who?	Status/role/age/gender/ethnic group/appearance/personality/ interests/attitudes	How participant prepares for the event will be influenced by factors listed opposite and previous history and encounters of all parties
When?	Time, date of meeting	The timing of the event might be particularly affected by events outside of the workplace. So if the participant has dependants or responsibilities, the timing of this event may become significant. If the participant is asked to attend in the middle of a religious festival, then again the relevance of time is critical
Where?	Environment/culture	Organisations will often stage development events away from the 'normal' workplace in an attempt to bring about objectivity and neutrality. How the event is staged, the amount of structure and formality, how feedback is given, the demonstration of power and control will be evidence of the culture of the organisation
How?	Past experience/rapport	The experience of the development event will in part be influenced by the expectations of the participant. If this is the second development centre, then experiences of the first will colour the perceptions; if this is the first centre, then the participant may be influenced by previous experiences of similar events (selection event) or by stories from previous attendees

Critical review and reflection

Most people do not consciously think about the person with whom they are interacting. They translate their view of the world around them from their own perceptions and assume that others are working from the same view.

To what extent are YOU able to challenge this assertion? How well do you think YOU relate to, and interact with, other people?

The importance of language and communication

Our language plays an important role in the way we perceive and communicate with the world. Language not only labels and distinguishes the environment for us, but also structures and guides our thinking patterns.

Marrs points out that every profession has its own language. For example, accountants and marketing executives are experts at bamboozlement and mysterious acronyms but perhaps the IT profession has the worst reputation.

> *Managers need to get straight answers from their IT professionals at several key points in the business cycle . . . If the IT department can't communicate without using jargon or acronyms . . . then you have got a solution looking for a problem rather than the other way round . . . Senior managers have to pick the people to run their IT departments. They need those who have technical skills – but who are also able to communicate IT considerations simply to the rest of the business.*[28]

Language as part of culture

Our language is part of the culture we experience and learn to take for granted. Culture differences are relevant because they emphasise the impact of social learning on the perception of people and their surroundings. Language not only reflects our experiences, but also shapes whether and what we experience. It influences our relationships with others and with the environment.

Consider a situation where a student is using a library in a UK university for the first time. The student is from South Asia, where the word 'please' is incorporated in the verb and in intonation; a separate word is not used. When the student requests help, the assistant may consider the student rude because they did not use the word 'please'. By causing offence the student has quite innocently affected the library assistant's perceptions.

Much is also communicated in how words are said and in the silences between words. In the UK, speech is suggestive and idiomatic speech is common: 'Make no bones about it' (means get straight to the point), 'Sent to Coventry' (means to be socially isolated). And action is implied rather than always stated: 'I hope you won't mind if I' (means 'I am going to'), 'I'm afraid I really can't see my way to . . . ' (means 'no').

Conversational pitfalls

A well-known quotation, attributed to George Bernard Shaw, is:

> *England and America are two countries divided by a common language.*

From frequent visits to America, the author can give numerous personal testimonies to this, including these actual words: 'I am just going to the trunk (boot of the car) to get my purse (handbag), fanny bag (bum bag) and money wallet (purse).'

McCrum gives some examples of conversational pitfalls[29](many of which the present author can attest to from personal experience).

Australia	Talking disparagingly about Aboriginal people
China	Human rights; Tibet, Taiwan; sex; religion; bureaucracy
Far East	Confusing Japanese, Chinese or Korean
Greece/S. Cyprus	Asking for Turkish coffee
India	Poverty; sex; dowry deaths
Ireland	Referring to Great Britain as the 'mainland'; talking about 'the British Isles' to include Ireland; asking why they use euros rather than pounds sterling

Latin America	Talking about 'Americans' to mean just North America
Mexico	Nepotism
The Netherlands	Calling the country 'Holland' (inaccurate and offensive to people not from the Holland provinces)
New Zealand	Using the term 'mainland' for either North or South Island; mispronouncing Maori place-names
Northern Ireland	Asking people whether they are Catholic or Protestant
Russia	Corruption, contract killings, etc.
South Africa	Banging on about apartheid (it ended some time ago)
Spain	Criticism of bullfighting
US South	The Confederate flag

Source: McCrum, M. *Going Dutch in Beijing*, Profile Books (2007), pp. 44–5. Reproduced with permission from Profile Books Ltd.

Non-verbal communication and body language

We have referred previously to the significance of non-verbal communication and body language. This includes inferences drawn from posture, gestures, touch, the use of personal space (proxemics), extent of eye contact, tone of voice or facial expressions. People are the only animals that speak, laugh and weep. Actions are more cogent than speech and humans rely heavily on body language to convey their true feelings and meanings.[30]

As *'Pease and Pease'* point out:

> *All things are not what they seem. The ability to work out what is really happening with a person is simple – not easy, but simple. It's about matching what you see and hear to the environment in which it all happens and drawing possible conclusions. Most people, however, only see the things they think they are seeing.*[31]

According to *Mehrabian,* in our face-to-face communication with other people as much as 93 per cent of the messages about our feelings and attitudes come from non-verbal channels:

> 7 per cent from the words we use;
> 38 per cent from our voice; and
> 55 per cent from body language, including facial expressions.

Significantly, when body language such as gestures and tone of voice conflicts with the words, greater emphasis is likely to be placed on the non-verbal message.[32]

Although actual percentages may vary, there appears to be general support for this contention. According to *Pivcevic,* 'It is commonly agreed that 80 per cent of communication is non-verbal; it is carried in your posture and gestures, and in the tone, pace and energy behind what you say.'[33]

McGuire suggests that when verbal and non-verbal messages are in conflict, 'Accepted wisdom from the experts is that the non-verbal signals should be the ones to rely on, and that what is not said is frequently louder than what is said, revealing attitudes and feelings in a way words can't express.'[34]

According to *James,* in a sense we are all experts on body language already and this is part of the survival instinct:

> *Even in a 'safe' environment like an office or meeting room you will feel a pull on your gaze each time someone new enters the room. And whether you want to or not, you will start to form opinions about a person in as little as three seconds. You can try to be fair and objective in your evaluation, but you will have little choice. This is an area where the subconscious*

mind bullies the conscious into submission. Like, dislike, trust, love or lust can all be promoted in as long as it takes to clear your throat. In fact most of these responses will be based on your perception of how the person looks.[35]

In our perceptions and judgement of others it is important therefore to observe and take careful note of their non-verbal communication. Managers should also be aware of the sub-conscious message that their own body language conveys to members of staff. For example, *Kennett* points out that we take signals from our leaders, and if managers are exhibiting signs of anxiety their body language and critical talk will amplify employees' susceptibility to stress.[36] However, although body language may be a guide to personality, errors can easily arise if too much is inferred from a single message rather than a related cluster of actions.

Consider the simple action of a handshake and the extent to which this can provide a meaningful insight into personality. Does a firm handshake by itself necessarily indicate friendship and confidence? And is a limp handshake a sign of shyness or lack of engagement with the other person? The reality is that body language is not a precise science. One gesture can be interpreted in several ways. It may give a possible indication of a particular meaning but by itself cannot be interpreted with any certainty. Crossing the arms is often taken as a sign of defensiveness but could equally mean that the person is feeling cold or finds this a comfortable position.[37] Despite these limitations, it is essential that managers have an understanding of non-verbal communication and body language and are fully cognisant of the possible messages they are giving out.

Cultural differences

There are many cultural variations in non-verbal communications, the extent of physical contact and differences in the way body language is perceived and interpreted. Italians and South Americans tend to show their feelings through intense body language, while the Japanese tend to hide their feelings and have largely eliminated overt body language from interpersonal communication. When talking to another person, the British tend to look away spasmodically, but Norwegians typically look people steadily in the eye without altering their gaze. In South Korea, women refrain from shaking hands. The Japanese often have a weak handshake, whereas in the UK a firm handshake is encouraged. When the Dutch point a forefinger at their temples this is likely to be a sign of congratulations for a good idea, but with other cultures the gesture has a less complimentary implication. In many European countries it is customary to greet people with three or four kisses on the cheek and pulling the head away may be taken as a sign of impoliteness.

All cultures have specific values related to proxemics, that is the use of personal space and 'comfort zone'. Arabs tend to stand very close when speaking to another person, but most Americans when introduced to a new person will, after shaking hands, move backwards a couple of steps to place a comfortable space between themselves and the person they have just met. One reason why Americans tend to speak loudly is that their sense of personal space is twice that of the British.[38] (**See also discussion on violation of territory in Chapter 3.**) A concept map of interacting and networking with other people is set out in Figure 6.13.

Critical review and reflection

There are so many forms of non-verbal communication cues, either intentional or unintentional, that can be interpreted in different ways. There are also wide cultural variations in the context and essential meaning of the cues. Attempting to make valid inferences from body language is of little real value and its use should be discouraged.

How would YOU argue against this assertion? How well can YOU read body language and non-verbal communication?

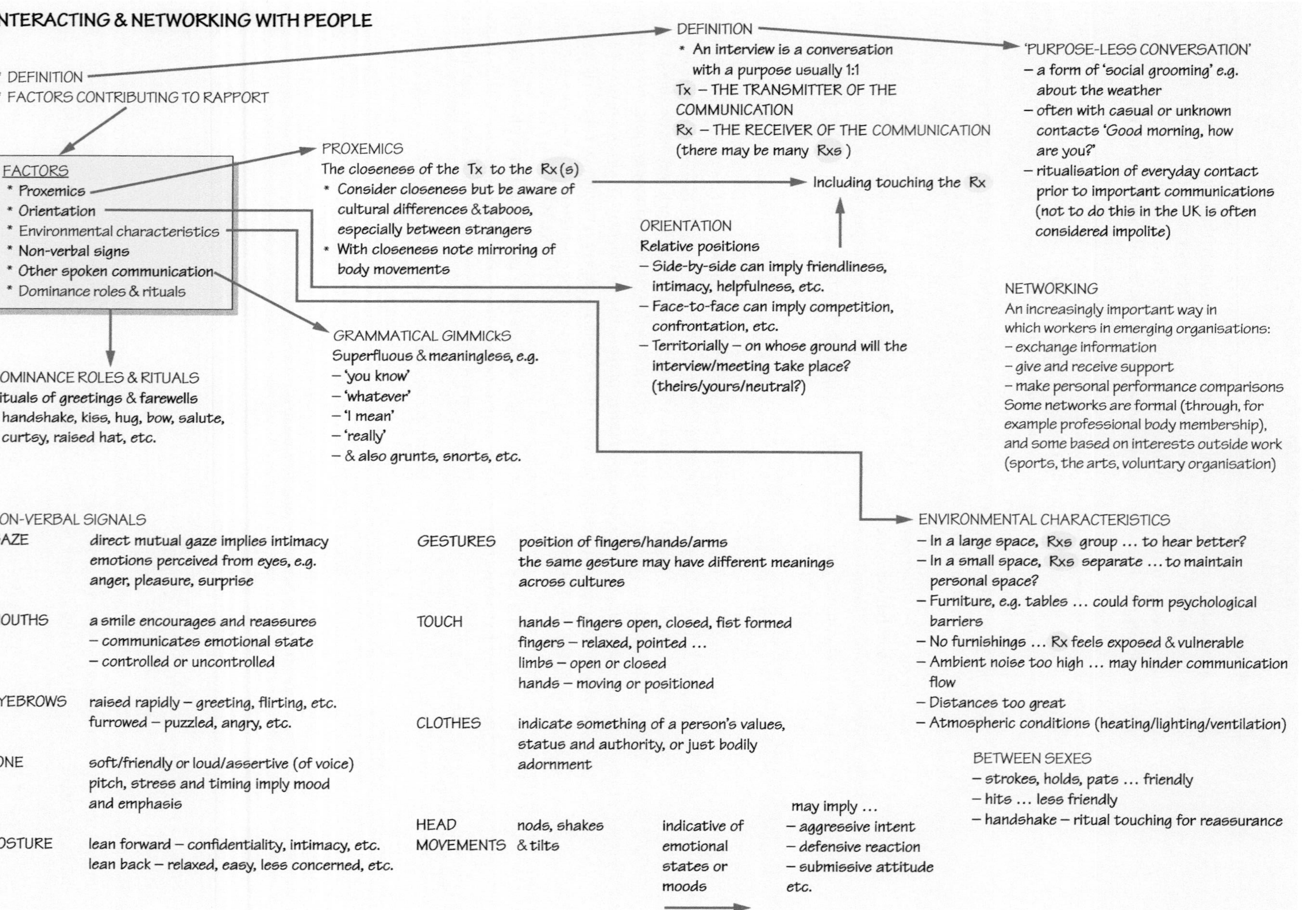

Figure 6.13 Interacting and networking with people

Source: Copyright © 2009 The Virtual Learning Materials Workshop. Reproduced with permission.

Interpersonal communications

It is difficult to consider the process of interpersonal perception without commenting on how people communicate. Communication and perception are inextricably bound. How we communicate to our colleagues, boss, subordinates, friends and partners will depend on our perception of them, on our 'history' with them, on their emotional state.

Fitzherbert draws an interesting comparison between magic, perception and communication.

> *Magicians are acutely aware that the moment people see, hear, feel, taste or smell anything it automatically triggers a range of expectations and perceptions in their minds. In effect, it opens up a 'file' in their brain that tells them what they already know about the subject and rejects anything that doesn't fit. Magicians build their communication and effects around the expectations and perceptions they trigger.*

Clarity and impact aside, communication will be effective only if you can convince the audience about what you are telling them or showing them. Fitzherbert sets out twenty rules of perception and communication, shown in Figure 6.14.[39]

ENGAGEMENT	ATTENTION	IMPACT	CONVICTION
1 The framework for any communication is determined by the **expectations and perceptions** that you **trigger** **2** Expectations and perceptions can be reinforced or diminished by **prestige, atmosphere and environment** and **desire** **3** Communication can only register effectively when it builds on **what the audience already knows** **4 The brain filters** out most information it receives, leaving only what it considers important	**5** Concentrated attention requires a **single point of focus** **6** Attention **tracks from left to right**, then settles at the left **7** The audience will look where you **look**, where you **point**, where you **tell them** to look **8 Curiosity, movement, sound, contrast** and **anything that is new or different** are friends *and* foes. Each has the potential to seize attention **9** The **wider environment** can often add to or detract from your message **10** Every element of your **content** will either **add to or detract** from your message **11** Attention is sustained by variation, which **shortens mental time**	**12** The senses offer **five different ways** into the brain **13 Firsts and lasts** are remembered **14 Negatives impede** communication as they need unscrambling before the meaning can be interpreted **15 Over-familiarity** leads to 'invisibility' **16** Sustained impact depends on transferring information **to long-term memory**	**17** To be convincing you, yourself, must **be convinced** **18** Doubts are reduced by **openness**, but may be increased by **over-stressing** **19** People put more reliance on something they have **worked out for themselves** **20** People's reactions are influenced by those of their **peers**

Figure 6.14 Twenty rules of perception and communication

Source: Nick Fitzherbert, www.fitzherbert.co.uk. Reproduced with permission.

Getting your message across

Baguley points out that workplace communication can have a variety of aims and objectives, and if it is going to be successful there must be a two-way process. Channels of communication are proliferating but many people still struggle to get their message across effectively. It is important to use the right medium for your message: 'I'm appalled by incidents like, for example, sacking employees by text message'. To be a good communicator, Baguley suggests you need the following skills and understanding:

- Listen actively, rather than passively.
- 'Wear the other person's shoes' and understand the why and how of where that other person is coming from.
- Empathise with what is being said and felt by the other person.
- Be aware of and carefully observe body language.
- Plan your communication to take into account your objectives, the needs and abilities of the other person, the social and physical environment of the communication and the nature of the message.[40]

Importance of feedback

Feedback is a vital ingredient of the communication process. We may misjudge the receiver and regard our communication as unsuccessful, but unless we have some feedback from the other party we may never know whether what we have said or done was received in the way it was intended. The feedback may reaffirm our perceptions of the person or it may force us to review our perceptions. In our dealings with more senior staff the process of communication can be of special significance, including non-verbal communication, posture and tone.[41]

Two major approaches to, and ways of explaining, interpersonal communications are neuro-linguistic programming and transactional analysis.

Neuro-linguistic programming

Neuro-linguistic programming (NLP) emerged in the early 1970s as an offshoot of psychotherapy, psychology and hypnotherapy. It represents a collection of ideas and appears to offer lots of different things to different people. A popular definition of NLP is in terms of a model of interpersonal communication concerned with the relationship between successful patterns of behaviour and subjective experiences that underlie them. *John Grinder* and *Richard Bandler*, the co-founders of NLP, saw it as a means of helping to provide people with better, fuller and richer lives.[42] It is an approach that aims to enhance the effectiveness of interpersonal communications and facilitate learning and personal development. The name originates from the three disciplines that all have a part to play when people are communicating with others: neurology, linguistics and programming.

- **Neurology** – the nervous system, and processes linking body and mind.
- **Linguistics** – the study of words and how these are understood and communicated.
- **Programming** – refers to behaviours and strategies used by individuals.

The application of NLP shifted from therapy situations to work organisations, with clear messages for communicating and managing others. NLP emphasises the significance of the perceptual process and the way in which information is subjectively filtered and interpreted.

These interpretations are influenced by others and the world in which we live. Gradually, individuals learn to respond and their reactions and strategies become programmed, locked in, automatic.

Awareness and change

At its heart, NLP concerns awareness and change. Initially knowing and monitoring one's own behaviour and being able consciously to choose different reactions are fundamental to the process. Selecting from a range of verbal and non-verbal behaviours ensures control happens and changes 'automatic' reactions into consciously chosen programmes. Many different approaches and techniques are incorporated into NLP. Some concern mirroring and matching the micro-skills of communication in terms of body movements, breathing patterns or voice tempo. Others concern the positive thinking required in goal-setting 'outcome thinking' and the personal resources required in its achievement.

Another feature of NLP is 'anchors' that we all have. Anchors are 'triggers' that help keep habits in place and put us in a certain state of mind.[43]

> *Anchors can be visual, like people, clothes and cars. They can be auditory, like a particular piece of music, an advertising jingle or the voice of a dear friend. They can be kinaesthetic, like the feel of your favourite clothes, sitting in your armchair or the warmth of a hot bath. They can be olfactory or gustatory, like the smell of a hospital (why do they all smell the same?) or the taste of coffee or chocolate (Lindt!). Words can be anchors because they evoke ideas; your name is a powerful anchor for your identity. Anchors evoke emotional states and most of the time we do not notice the anchors, only the states. Some anchors are neutral. Some put us into good states. Others put us into bad states.*[44]

Agness suggests that in a tough market NLP can be applied to the main challenges faced by today's leaders, and identifies three main skills of NLP that help to get on customers' wavelength:

- **Sensory acuity** – developing an acute sense of awareness of what is going on around you moment to moment, and changes in your customer's physiology.
- **Rapport building** – developing fast a strong connection with your customers.
- **Improving sensory awareness** – intuitively picking up non-verbal signals in others. Increasing sensory acuity will improve communication with others.[45]

NLP and coaching

NLP has attracted considerable interest in recent years and there are a number of passionate devotees. There are numerous courses and seminars intended to demonstrate to participants how they can learn the skills to change themselves for improved personal or professional effectiveness and a greater enjoyment from life. It is also a popular approach to coaching (**discussed in Chapter 5**). Paul McKenna, the well-known television hypnotist, is a registered NLP practitioner and makes use of NLP principles in his courses on life training, including for example helping people to lose weight.

Paxton-Doggett reports on the use of NLP as part of executive coaching in business to aid freer and more open thinking in employees, and to achieve better results professionally and personally.

> *Underlying much modern coaching practice is 'Neuro-linguistic programming' or NLP. Rather than simply moving a person towards new goals, NLP works on a more fundamental level by exploring the interaction of thoughts (Neuro), verbal and non-verbal communication (Linguistic) and patterns of behaviour and emotional responses (Programming). By using the methodology and techniques of NLP in coaching, thinking and behaviour are changed and different results produced.*[46]

Critical review and reflection

Although much is written about the value of neuro-linguistic programming (NLP) it is really no more than an assembly of different ideas. It is a difficult concept to grasp and too abstract and theoretic to have meaningful applications for the practical manager.

What do YOU think? If YOU were a manager how might YOU apply NLP in a meaningful manner?

Transactional analysis

Transactional analysis (TA) is one of the most popular ways of explaining the dynamics of interpersonal communication. Originally developed by *Eric Berne,* it is a model of people and relationships that encompasses personality, perception and communication.[47] Although Berne used it initially as a method of psychotherapy, it has been convincingly used by organisations as a training and development programme.

TA has two basic underlying assumptions:

- All the events and feelings that we have ever experienced are stored within us and can be replayed, so we can re-experience the events and the feelings of all our past years.
- Personality is made up of three ego states that are revealed in distinct ways of behaving. The ego states manifest themselves in gesture, tone of voice and action, almost as if they are different people within us, and they converse with each other in 'transactions', either overtly or covertly.

Berne identified and labelled the ego states as follows, each with their own system of communication and language:

- **Adult ego state** – behaviour that concerns our thought processes and the processing of facts and information. In this state we may be objective, rational, reasonable – seeking information and receiving facts.
- **Parent ego state** – behaviour that concerns the attitudes, feelings and behaviour incorporated from external sources, primarily our parents. This state refers to feelings about right and wrong and how to care for other people.
- **Child ego state** – behaviour that demonstrates the feelings we remember as a child. This state may be associated with having fun, playing, impulsiveness, rebelliousness, spontaneous behaviour and emotional responses.

Berne believed that these transactions, which take place in face-to-face exchanges and verbal communication, form the core of human relationships. He claimed that the three ego states exist simultaneously within each individual, although at any particular time any one state may dominate the other two. All people are said to behave in each of these states at different times. We may be unaware which ego state we are operating in and may shift from one to another.

Preferred ego state

We all have a preferred ego state which we may revert to: some individuals may continually advise and criticise others (the constant Parents); some may analyse, live only with facts and distrust feelings (the constant Adult); some operate with strong feelings all the time, consumed with anger or constantly clowning (the constant Child). Berne emphasised that the states should not be judged as superior or inferior but as different. Analysis of ego states may reveal why communication breaks down or why individuals may feel manipulated or used.

Berne insists that it is possible to identify the ego state from the words, voice, gestures and attitude of the person communicating. For example, it would be possible to discern the ego state of a manager if they said the following:

'Pass me the file on the latest sales figures.'
'How do you think we could improve our safety record?'
(Adult ego state)
'Let me help you with that - I can see you are struggling.'
'Look, this is the way it should be done; how many more times do I have to tell you?'
(Parent ego state)
'Great, it's Friday. Who's coming to the pub for a quick half?'
'That's a terrific idea - let's go for it!'
(Child ego state)

Understanding human behaviour

Knowledge of TA can be of benefit to employees who are dealing with potentially difficult situations. In the majority of work situations the Adult–Adult transactions are likely to be the norm. Where work colleagues perceive and respond by adopting the Adult ego state, such a transaction is more likely to encourage a rational, problem-solving approach and reduce the possibility of emotional conflict.

Given the incidence of stress in the workplace, analysis of communication may be one way of understanding such conflict. By focusing on the interactions occurring within the workplace, TA can aid the understanding of human behaviour. It can help to improve communication skills by assisting in interpreting a person's ego state and which form of state is likely to produce the most appropriate response. This should lead to an improvement in both customer relations and management–subordinate relations. Therefore TA can be seen as a valuable tool to aid our understanding of social situations and the games that people play, both in and outside work organisations.[48]

Attribution theory

Part of the process of perceiving other people is to attribute characteristics to them. We judge their behaviour and intentions on past knowledge and in comparison with other people we know. It is our way of making sense of their behaviour. This is known as **attribution theory**. Attribution is the process by which people interpret the perceived causes of behaviour. The initiator of attribution theory is generally recognised as *Heider*, who suggests that behaviour is determined by a combination of **perceived** internal forces and external forces.[49] **Internal forces** relate to personal attributes such as ability, skill, amount of effort or fatigue. **External forces** relate to environmental factors such as organisational rules and policies, the manner of superiors, or the weather. Behaviour at work may be explained by the locus of control, that is whether each individual perceives outcomes as controlled by themselves or by external factors. Judgements made about other people will also be influenced strongly by whether the cause is seen as internal or external.

Basic criteria in making attributions

In making attributions and determining whether an internal or external attribution is chosen, *Kelley* suggests three basic criteria: distinctiveness, consensus and consistency.

- **Distinctiveness** – How distinctive or different was the behaviour or action in this particular task or situation compared with behaviour or action in other tasks or situations?
- **Consensus** – Is the behaviour or action different from, or in keeping with, that displayed by most other people in the same situation?

- **Consistency** – Is the behaviour or action associated with an enduring personality or motivational characteristic over time, or an unusual one-off situation caused by external factors?

Kelley hypothesised that people attribute behaviour to internal forces or personal factors when they perceive **low distinctiveness, low consensus** and **high consistency.** Behaviour is attributed to external forces or environmental factors when people perceive **high distinctiveness, high consensus** and **low consistency.**[50]

Implications of attribution theory

Employees with an internal control orientation are more likely to believe that they can influence their level of performance through their own abilities, skills or efforts. Employees with an external control orientation are more likely to believe that their level of performance is determined by external factors beyond their influence.

People with a high-achievement motivation may perceive that successful performance is caused by their own internal forces and their ability and effort rather than by the nature of the task or by luck. If members of staff fail to perform well on their tasks they may believe that external factors are the cause and as a result may reduce the level of future effort. However, if staff perform well but the manager perceives this as due to an easy task or to luck, the appropriate recognition and reward may not be given. If staff perceive that good performance was due to ability and/or effort, the lack of recognition and reward may well have a demotivating effect. (**Achievement motivation is discussed in Chapter 7.**)

Perceptual distortions and errors

We have seen that our perception results in different people seeing different things and attaching different meanings to the same stimuli. Every person sees things in their own way and as perceptions become a person's reality this can lead to misunderstandings. The accuracy of interpersonal perception and the judgements made about other people are influenced by:

- the nature of the relationship between the perceiver and the other person;
- the amount of information available to the perceiver and the order in which information is received;
- the nature and extent of interaction between the two people.

There are five main features that can create particular difficulties and give rise to perceptual problems, bias or distortions in our dealings with other people. These are:

- stereotyping
- the halo effect
- perceptual defence
- projection
- self-fulfilling prophecy.

To which could be added a sixth:

- unconscious bias.

See Figure 6.15.

These difficulties with people perception arise because of selectivity that exists in the perceptual process. We do not enjoy living in a world where uncertainty abounds and our perceptual system works to minimise energy consumption. We do not have to start every day afresh – we have our store of memories and experiences to guide us. The paradox is that this process is also our downfall.

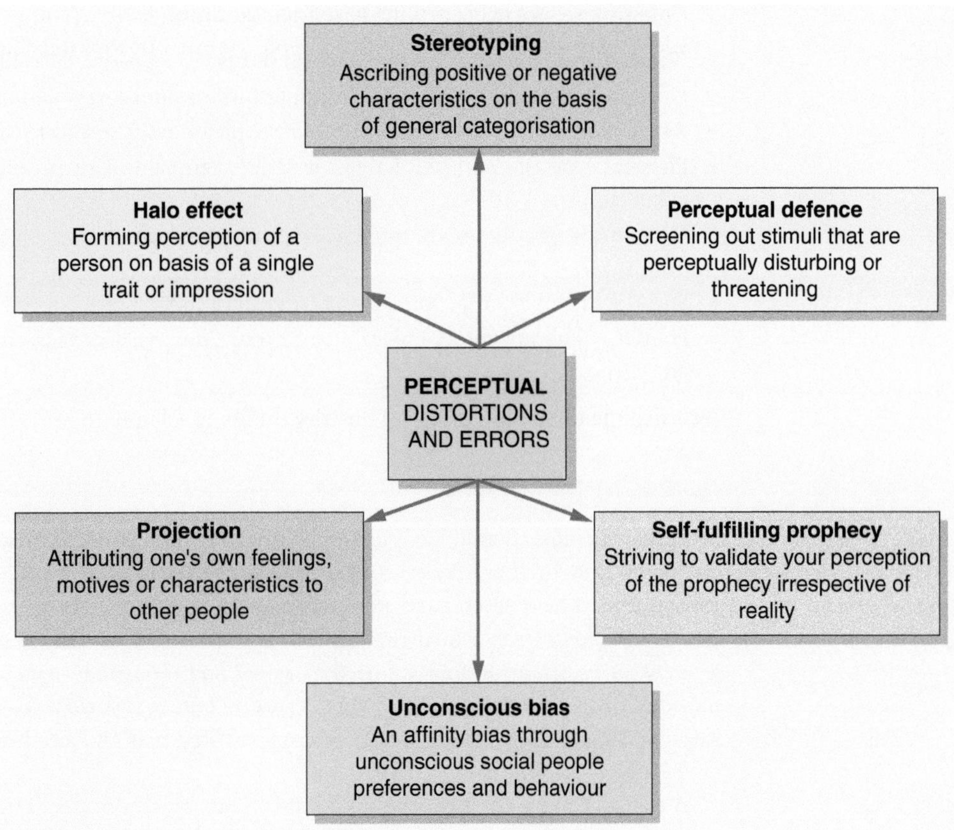

Figure 6.15 Causes of perceptual distortions and errors

Critical review and reflection

Bias and prejudice are inherent features of interpersonal perception and communication. Although exhortations can be made for us to become more aware of our own biases and to take more time in making judgements, we are working against our normal quick-fire perceptual system.

Do YOU believe this is fair comment? To what extent are YOU aware of YOUR own bias and prejudice?

Stereotyping

This is the tendency to ascribe positive or negative characteristics to a person on the basis of a general categorisation and perceived similarities. The perception of that person may be based more on certain expected characteristics than on the recognition of that person as an individual. It is a form of typecasting. **Stereotyping** is a means of simplifying the process of perception, making sense of the world and making judgements of other people instead of dealing with a range of complex and alternative stimuli. When a person is judged on the basis of the group to which it is perceived that the person belongs and as having the same characteristics, we are stereotyping. Pre-judgements are therefore made about an individual without ever really knowing whether such judgements are accurate; they may be wildly wrong.

Common stereotyping may be based on, for example:

- **Nationality** – Germans are orderly and industrious; Australians like cricket.
- **Occupation** – accountants are boring; librarians are serious and undemonstrative.
- **Age** – young people are unreliable; old people do not want to learn new ideas.
- **Physical** – people with red hair have a fiery temperament; people with visible tattoos are exhibitionists.
- **Education** – graduates are intelligent; graduates from Oxford or Cambridge are especially bright.
- **Social** – unemployed people are lazy; immigrants do not want to learn English.
- **Politics** – Labour voters favour strong trade unions; Conservative voters support private enterprise.

(**See also the discussion of social identity theory in Chapter 8.**)

Social implications

Stereotyping infers that all people within a particular perceived category are assumed to share the same traits or characteristics. A significant social implication of stereotyping is therefore the perception held about particular groups of people based on, for example, ethnicity, gender, disability, appearance, sexual orientation, age or religious belief. Stereotyping condenses the amount of information that we need to know and thus enables us to cope with a vast information flow. However, the consequences of attributing incorrect characteristics are extremely negative. Stereotyping can lead to misinterpretation, bias and a failure to try and really understand other people.[51]

A major danger of stereotyping is that it can block out accurate perception of the individual or individual situation. Stereotyping may lead to potential situations of prejudice or discrimination. An example might be the perception of people with HIV or AIDS.[52] Stereotyping may work either negatively or favourably for a particular group of people. For example, a sizeable number of employers still appear to maintain negative and inaccurate stereotypes about the capabilities and training of older workers. However, some firms, such as B&Q, the home improvement chain, have a policy of staffing certain stores with people over 50 years of age. (**See the case study at the end of Chapter 4.**)

The halo effect

The **halo effect** is the process by which the perception of a person is formulated on the basis of a single (or single series of) favourable or unfavourable trait or impression. The halo effect tends to shut out other relevant characteristics of that person. Some examples might be as follows:

- A candidate for employment who arrives punctually, is smart in appearance and friendly may well influence the perception of the selectors, who then place less emphasis on the candidate's technical ability, qualifications or experience for the job.
- A new member of staff who performs well in a first major assignment may be perceived as a likely person for promotion, even though that assignment is not typical of the usual duties the member of staff is expected to undertake.
- A single trait, such as good attendance and timekeeping, may become the main emphasis for judgement of overall competence and performance rather than other considerations such as the quantity, quality and accuracy of work.

A particular danger with the halo effect is that where quick judgements are made on the basis of readily available stimuli, the perceiver may become 'perceptually blind' to subsequent stimuli at variance with the original perception and (often subconsciously) notice only those characteristics that support the original judgement. (**See also the self-fulfilling prophecy, discussed below.**)

The rusty halo effect

The process may also work in reverse: the **rusty halo effect**. This is where general judgements about a person are formulated from the perception of a negative characteristic. For example, a candidate is seen arriving late for an interview. There may be a very good reason for this and it may be completely out of character. But on the basis of that one particular event the person may be perceived as a poor timekeeper and unreliable. Another example may be a new member of staff who performs poorly in a first major assignment. This may have been due to an unusual set of circumstances and not typical behaviour, but the person may still be perceived as a bad appointment.

Perceptual defence

Perceptual defence is the tendency to avoid or screen out certain stimuli that conflict with strongly held values and are perceptually disturbing or threatening. People may tend to select information that is supportive of their point of view and choose not to acknowledge contrary information. For example, a manager who has refused steadfastly to support promotion for a member of staff against the advice of other colleagues may select only unfavourable information which supports that decision and ignore favourable information which questions that decision.

Projection

Attributing, or projecting, one's own feelings, motives or characteristics to other people is a further distortion that can occur in the perception of other people. Judgements of other people may be more favourable when they have characteristics largely in common with, and easily recognised by, the perceiver. **Projection** may also result in people exaggerating undesirable traits in others that they fail to recognise in themselves.

Perception is distorted by feelings and emotions. Projection may be used as a means of attempting to externalise difficult or uncomfortable feelings. For example, a manager who is concerned about possible redundancy may perceive other managers to be even more concerned. People have a tendency to perceive others less favourably by projecting certain of their own feelings or characteristics onto them. As another example, supervisors may complain that their manager did not work hard enough to secure additional resources for the department when in fact the supervisors failed to provide the manager with all the relevant information and statistics. However, projection may also be used to externalise positive feelings onto other members of staff by attempting to create an overstated and unrealistic level of expectations and performance. (**Perception of 'self' and how people see and think of themselves, and evaluate themselves, are discussed in Chapter 8.**)

Self-fulfilling prophecy

A common feature of social interaction is the concept of the **self-fulfilling prophecy** (sometimes known as the Pygmalion effect), a term that is usually attributed to *Merton*.[53]The essence of the prophecy is that simply because it has been made, this will cause it to happen. People strive to validate their perceptions irrespective of the actual reality. People's beliefs or expectations influence their actions and behaviour in such a way as to make the beliefs or expectations more likely to come true. If staff believe a rumour (prophecy) that there will be no promotions or bonuses for the foreseeable future, they are likely to behave in such a way that their performance would not justify promotion or bonuses (even if the rumour was not true).

The expectation of managers has a powerful influence on the behaviour and performance of staff. (**See McGregor's Theory X and Theory Y assumptions in Chapter 10.**) If a manager expects only minimal performance from staff, they are not likely to perform to the best of their abilities. Therefore, managers need to establish an organisational framework and supportive culture that reinforces positive performance expectations at all levels of the organisation. Staff should also be encouraged to have high self-expectations of performance through working towards common goals.

Unconscious bias

Dan Robertson, Diversity and Inclusion Director of Employers Network for Equality and Inclusion, in conversation with *Davies*, draws attention to our 'preferred people preferences' that affect our unconscious social preferences. This type of **unconscious bias** may be demonstrated in 'micro-behaviours'.

> *For example, we may exhibit an affinity bias, where we respond positively to people who are similar to us or with whom we have something in common. We might give that person more airtime in a meeting, or agree more often with what they say. In contrast, we might cut short those with whom we do not have an affinity or disregard their viewpoints.*

These are subtle, unconscious behaviours and different from overt and discriminatory behaviour. Robertson maintains that such unconscious biases are hard-wired into us. We cannot eliminate them altogether so it is important to be aware of them and to change the way we work.[54]

Understanding the organisational process

The process of perception has been outlined as selective and subjective: we perceive the world in our own terms and expect the world to 'fit' into our constructs. Throughout our development we learn to distinguish what is important and significant (figure) from information that is additional and contextual (ground). This process is repeated when we join new organisations or take a new job within the same organisation. Fitting into the organisation involves selecting information that is necessary from that which is less significant. At times, the process can be distorted and we can also be 'tricked' into seeing the world in particular ways.

Although some organisations may discriminate, stereotyped perceptions are not always calculated: they are often made automatically and without conscious thought – in much the same way as we may be tricked by visual illusions. In fact, perceptual illusions are a very appropriate way of understanding the organisational setting.

For any organisation to be effective it is imperative that the staff are competent to undertake their work and satisfy the 'psychological contract' (**discussed in Chapter 1**). Part of the role of managers is to select and train individuals whom they predict will perform successfully on the job, and then to monitor and assess their competence for promotion. Accordingly, it is clearly important for managers to be aware of their own prejudices and assumptions. By opening channels and encouraging and developing all staff, trust might be fed back into the system from which equality and inclusion could flourish.

Critical review and reflection

It is not unreasonable to argue that there is no such thing as reality - only the individual's perception or interpretation of reality. Yet, managers require an understanding of perception in order to help interpret the behaviour and intentions of other people.

How can this conundrum be overcome? If YOU were a manager how would YOU hope to avoid organisational problems that result from perceptual differences?

Ten key points to remember

1. Perception is the root of all management and organisational behaviour and any situation can be analysed in terms of its perceptual connotations.
2. We all have our unique image of how we interpret the 'reality' of the world around us. A situation may be the same but individual interpretations may differ vastly.
3. The process of perception is based on both internal factors related to the individual's sensory limits or thresholds and external factors related to the nature and characteristics of the stimuli.
4. Perception gives rise to individual behavioural responses in given situations. It is important to be aware of potential perceptual illusions and impression management.
5. Managers must take care with how they organise and make judgements about their perceptions of other people, including both positive and negative messages.
6. There are many potential difficulties when perceiving other people. The manager's perception will influence the style of behaviour and relationship with other staff.
7. It is important to recognise the importance of the use of language and communication including cultural differences, and non-verbal communication and body language.
8. Perception and interpersonal communication are inextricably bound. Two major approaches to interpersonal communications are neuro-linguistic programming (NLP) and transactional analysis (TA).
9. Part of the process of perception is to attribute characteristics to other people. Attribution is the process by which people interpret the perceived causes of behaviour.
10. Perception results in different people attaching different meanings to the same stimulus. This gives rise to a number of potential perceptual distortions and errors.

Review and discussion questions

1. Explain fully why an understanding of perception is important in the study of management and organisational behaviour.
2. Discuss, with your own examples, both internal and external factors that affect selection and attention in the process of perception.
3. Debate the significance of impression management, including your own views on the importance of dress codes.
4. Identify clearly the most significant factors that you believe influence the judgement of other people. Provide your own example of each of these factors.
5. Discuss fully the importance of language and communication in the process of perception. Give your own examples of conversational pitfalls.
6. Discuss critically the amount of attention that you believe should be given to non-verbal communications and body language.
7. Justify what you see as the practical benefits of (i) neuro-linguistic programming (NLP) and (ii) transactional analysis (TA) as approaches to interpersonal communications.

→

8 Explain the principles of attribution theory and its importance to, and implications for, management. Apply the principles to your own working life.

9 Give your own examples of what you believe are the main causes and implications of perceptual distortions and errors.

10 Explain fully, with supporting examples, the importance of understanding cultural differences as an integral part of the perceptual process.

Assignment

Work in small groups, and share and discuss your responses with colleagues.

1. Think back to Figures 6.2, 6.5 and 6.7 in the text. For each of these figures:
   a. What image did you see first and how quickly?
   b. How difficult was it to see alternative images, including those suggested by your colleagues?
2. The text refers to the influence on perception from external stimuli such as:
   a. bright
   b. strong contrast to their background.

   Give your own example of how these stimuli feature in any two different advertisements, in any format, that have particularly caught your attention - in either a positive or negative manner. Can you think of any additional external stimuli that influence perception?
3. What did you learn from this assignment about the nature of perception?

Personal skills and employability exercise

Objectives

Completing this exercise should help you to enhance the following skills:

- Reflect on your understanding of, and behaviour towards, other people.
- Review your personal experiences of the process of perception.
- Learn and understand more about your inner self.

Part 1

Look back at the different reactions from five managers to the situation referred to at the start of this chapter. What do you think might be the underlying reasons for the individual responses and how might these responses relate to the perceptual process?

Part 2 - Exercise

You are required to work in small self-selecting groups with colleagues you trust and feel comfortable with, and with whom confidences are assured.

Relate honestly and fully:

a. your bias and prejudices about other people; and
b. bias and prejudices you perceive in other people.

Examples when you have been guilty of:

c. making a pre-judgment about an individual without really knowing the true circumstances. To what extent did you then filter stimuli to receive only that which supported your initial reactions? How did you eventually resolve or reconcile this pre-judgment?
d. impression management.
e. perceptual errors or misjudgements arising from cultural differences. What action did you take subsequently and to what extent was the 'error' resolved?

Discussion

- What were your colleagues' reactions to your revelations? Did anything surprise you? Or them?
- To what extent has undertaking this exercise made you more aware of yourself?
- What have you learnt from this exercise and what conclusions do you draw?

Case study
Behavioural economics

So, you have an assignment due tomorrow, 2,500 words, deadline 16:00. Have you written it yet? Maybe a paragraph or two? But you have got lots of notes, a heap of books from the library, a few articles downloaded from Google Scholar and some ideas, but you just have not quite got them down on paper yet. And you have known about this deadline for, what, two weeks? A month? More . . . ? Still, no worries; twenty-four hours to go. But first you need some more coffee - and, drat! The milk has run out so a quick trip to the corner store. And perhaps you can just have a quick glance at Facebook. And then you can get on with it. Honestly.

If you are 'human', the chances are you may recognise at least part of this scenario. The good news is that almost everybody else does. The less good news is that you will probably do it again. It is painful, it is frustrating, but it is true. Luckily, a few recent and highly readable studies by behavioural economists can give you an insight into why, and how it can be avoided.

Behavioural economics explores the links between perception, thought and behaviour, particularly in terms of the economic choices people make in their everyday lives.
Source: David Samuel Robbins/Getty Images

Reason and irrationality

The basis for these ideas is the link between perception, thought and behaviour, and particularly our behaviour in terms of the economic decisions and choices people make in their everyday life. Many of these choices are personal: how much to pay for a coffee at Waterloo train station, where to rent or buy a house, how much to put into a pension plan or why you should be the first to order your food when you go out to dinner with a group of friends.[55] However, the principles shed light on the perception - thought - behaviour process, which is equally important in organisational contexts. Some choices and decisions are specifically related to management and organisational behaviour: matters of pay, reward, performance, honesty and discrimination. In the cases discussed, the decisions people make appear to be both irrational and entirely understandable. This was the starting point for Dan Ariely, who explains that behavioural economics is a relatively new field that links economics and psychology; it focuses on judgement and decision-making and seeks to identify the causes of 'irrational' behaviour. Moreover, he considers that:

> *we are not only irrational, but predictably irrational - that our irrationality happens in the same way, again and again. Whether we are acting as consumers, businesspeople or policy makers . . . Moreover, these irrational behaviors of ours are neither random nor*

→

senseless. They are systematic, and since we repeat them again and again, predictable.[56]

Social and market norms

Much of Ariely's research has been experimental, and one set of experiments offers an insight into the nature of the effort-reward bargain. Do we work harder when we are paid? Not necessarily. The experiment that revealed this involved three groups of participants who were asked to carry out a simple repetitive task of clicking and dragging circles across a computer screen using a mouse. The system counted how many circles were moved in the five minutes given for the task. Some groups were paid well for participating, others paid less well and yet others asked to take part as a favour. As anticipated, the well-paid worked harder than the poorly paid (by about 50 per cent), but the unpaid outperformed both. Why? Ariely's conclusion was that different norms had been applied - social ones rather than market ones - and that in many circumstances social norms are more effective motivators.

Does this mean organisations can use social norms as well as market norms to encourage effort? A group of lawyers was shown to be content to offer *free* legal advice to needy retired clients, but not at all likely to offer the same service for a reduced fee. Here social norms were powerful whereas market norms actually had a deterrent effect. Indeed, further experiments showed that even the mention of money could drive out social norms and change behaviour. The psychological technique of 'priming' (the creation of a certain set of expectations, indirectly, prior to some kind of activity) was used to introduce the *idea* of market norms to some people but not others, although nobody was actually going to be paid for taking part this time. Some participants were primed to think about money via a sentence unscrambling task before attempting a difficult visual puzzle (the sentences they were given used words like salary), and others were given neutral sentences. The behaviour of the primed participants during the puzzle element was notably different:

> *They were more selfish and self-reliant; they wanted to spend more time alone; they were more likely to select tasks that required individual input rather than teamwork; . . . Indeed, just thinking about money makes us behave as most economists believe we behave - and less like the social animals we are in our daily lives.*[57]

Moreover, it seems that once we have switched over from social to market norms in our thinking, it is very difficult for us to switch back. The social relationship may have been irretrievably ruined.[58]

Obviously, the vast majority of work organisations rely on market norms to a significant extent, and rarely more so than when people are paid for performance. The link between pay and performance seems logical, and much managerial work involves performance measurement and judgement with the aim of improving performance. For instance, when salaries were replaced by piecework in a car windscreen repair business (workers were paid per windscreen refit, and required to correct any mistakes they made without extra pay), productivity improved and errors were reduced.[59] However, the problem for advocates of this type of incentive scheme is that performance in most jobs is not as easily measured as it is in the windscreen repair business, and workers will generally adjust their behaviour to achieve the measured targets, regardless of the overall result.

> *It's simply too difficult for managers to work out the details of what should be done, and to judge whether what should be done is being done. The frustrations of working life are a direct result of that struggle.*[60]

All you need is nudge

An example of the application of behavioural economics shows how people can be encouraged, rather than forced, to behave in ways that are seen to be beneficial (to themselves, to their communities, the environment, etc.) and deals with the age-old problem of why we cannot seem to do things that we know are good for us or 'right'. We lack self-control, especially when costs are felt immediately but the pay-off does not arrive for some time. This is why dieting is hard but chatting on Facebook is easy. We tend to defer changes to our behaviour and are over-optimistic about our future behaviour; our diets always start tomorrow and will be spectacularly effective. But it seems that we can be 'nudged' to change our *future* behaviour in a way that makes it stick. For instance, *Thaler and Sunstein* report on the success of the 'Save More Tomorrow' plan as a means of encouraging people to contribute more sensibly to pension schemes. Instead of requiring people to contribute more of their pay today, they were asked to commit to increasing their savings in the future. The savings plan deducted the money from their salaries, and the increased deductions were timed to coincide with pay raises.

> *By synchronising pay raises and savings increases, participants never see their take-home amounts go down, and they don't view their increased retirement contributions as losses.*[61]

The scheme enlisted the power of four key behavioural responses to perceived factors. The 'painful' part was deferred; there was never a perception of 'loss', in this case of spending power; the system was easy and the default contributions were the increasing ones; and the power of inertia meant that opting out of the increases was more effort than staying in. The combined effects meant that the 'nudge' was effective, even though there was no obligation to continue with the increases.

Now, about that essay

A further practical example of this is the website created by Yale Economics Professor Dean Karlan called **'StickK.com'** which is described as a 'commitment store', and which is based on two key principles of behavioural economics:

1. People do not always do what they claim they want to do.
2. Incentives get people to do things.

The process is described by Thaler and Sunstein:

> *An individual puts up money and agrees to accomplish a goal by a certain date. He also specifies how to verify that he has met his goal. For example he might agree to a weigh-in at a doctor's office . . . (if the goal is to lose weight). If the person reaches his goal, he gets his money back. If he fails, the money goes to charity.*[62]

A review in 2014 suggests that the most effective 'stick-Kers' are those who publish their goals via the site to a group of friends, family or colleagues who can monitor their progress and cheer them on - effectively using social norms to reinforce behaviour.[63]

So, back to that essay. Only twenty hours to go and still only 426 words. If only you had written 250 words a day for the last ten days, you would be polishing off the references and making it look nice by now! So, next time you get an assignment, how about you and your mates visit **StickK.com?**

Tasks

1 Discuss and plan an experiment like the 'circle dragging' one carried out by Ariely, which you could use to see if you find the same differences in motivation resulting from the use of 'social' and 'market' norms.

2 To what extent should managers appeal to 'social' norms when planning the work of their staff? What are the benefits and what are the dangers?

3 Consider the idea of 'priming'. Explain how this might fit into the cycle of perception and behaviour illustrated in Figure 6.12. How might a manager, either consciously or unconsciously, 'prime' others to receive their communications in different ways?

4 What can we learn from the ideas behind the 'Save More Tomorrow' scheme or **'StickK.com'** about how to help people to change both their perceptions and behaviour at work in such a way as to improve personal effectiveness?

Notes and references

1. Bartlett, F. C. *Remembering Cambridge,* Cambridge University Press (1932).
2. Kohler, I. 'The Formation and Transformation of the Visual World', *Psychological Issues,* vol. 3, 1964, pp. 28–46, 116–33.
3. Myers, I. B. *Introduction to Type,* Oxford Psychologists Press (1987).
4. Schein, E. H. *Organizational Culture and Leadership,* Jossey-Bass (1992), p. 9.
5. Ling, C. and Masako, I. 'Intercultural Communication and Cultural Learning: The Experience of Visiting Japanese Students in the US', *The Howard Journal of Communications,* vol. 14, 2003, pp. 75–96.
6. McCrum, M. *Going Dutch in Beijing,* Profile Books (2007), p. vii.
7. Stewart-Allen, A. L. 'Changing the Mindset about Americans', *Professional Manager,* vol. 15, no. 5, 2006, p. 37.
8. Block, J. R. and Yuker, H. E. *Can You Believe Your Eyes?,* Robson Books (2002).
9. Morgan, C. T. and King, R. A. *Introduction to Psychology,* third edition, McGraw-Hill (1966), p. 343.

10. Stroop, J. R. 'Studies of Interference in Serial Verbal Reactions', *Journal of Experimental Psychology,* vol. 4, no. 18, 1935, pp. 643–62; and Penrose, L. S. and Penrose, R. 'Impossible Objects: A Special Type of Illusion', *British Journal of Psychology,* part 1, February 1958.
11. Goffman, E. *The Presentation of Self in Everyday Life,* Penguin (1971).
12. Kendon, A. 'Some Functions of Gaze Direction in Social Interaction', *Acta Psychologica,* vol. 26, 1967, pp. 22–63.
13. Mehrabian, A. *Nonverbal Communication,* Aldine Atherton (1972).
14. Lucas, E. 'Check the label', *Professional Manager,* November 2009, pp. 22–5.
15. Rigby, R. 'What's Holding Him Back?', *Management Today,* December 2009, pp. 54–6.
16. Everett, L. 'First impressions', *Governance + Compliance,* November 2012, p. 54.
17. Willis, J. and Todorov, A. 'First Impressions: Making Up Your Mind After a 100-Ms Exposure to a Face', *Psychological Science,* vol. 17, no. 7, 2006, pp. 592–8.
18. Schneider, S. C. and Barsoux, J. *Managing Across Cultures,* second edition, Financial Times Prentice Hall (2003), p. 29.
19. Ziolo, K. 'A stitch in time', *Professional Manager,* July/August 2011, pp. 31–3.
20. Cohen, A. *The Tall Book: A Celebration of Life from on High,* Bloomsbury (2009).
21. See, for example, Leitch, L. 'The Big Problem that Short Men Face', *The Times,* 24 June 2009.
22. Dib, F. 'The Anatomy of a Leader', *Professional Manager,* September/October 2012, pp. 34–8.
23. Mintzberg, H. *Managing,* Financial Times Prentice Hall (2009).
24. Guirdham, M. *Interactive Behaviour at Work,* third edition, Financial Times Prentice Hall (2002), p. 161.
25. Wexley, K. N., Yukl, G. A., Kovacs, S. Z. and Sanders, R. E. 'Importance of Contrast Effects in Employment Interviews', *Journal of Applied Psychology,* vol. 56, 1972, pp. 45–8.
26. Laing, R. D. *Knots,* Penguin (1971), p. 30.
27. Guirdham, M. *Interactive Behaviour at Work,* third edition, Financial Times Prentice Hall (2002).
28. Marrs, C. ' It's all geek to me', *Professional Manager,* Winter 2012, pp. 32–5.
29. McCrum, M. *Going Dutch in Beijing,* Profile Books (2007), pp. 44–5.
30. See, for example, Torrington, D. *Face-to-Face in Management,* Prentice Hall (1982).
31. Pease, A. and Pease, B. *The Definitive Book of Body Language,* Orion (2005), p. 2.
32. Mehrabian, A. *Tactics of Social Influence,* Prentice Hall (1970).
33. Pivcevic, P. 'Taming the Boss', *Management Today,* March 1999, p. 70.
34. McGuire, T. 'Don't Just Listen', *Chartered Secretary,* September 1998, p. 24.
35. James, J. *Body Talk at Work,* Piatkus (2001), p. 3.
36. Kennett, M. 'First-Class Coach', *Management Today,* May 2008, p. 68.
37. See, for example, James, J. *The Body Language Bible,* Vermilion (2008).
38. For other examples of cultural differences, see French, R. *Cross-Cultural Management in Work Organisations,* second edition, Chartered Institute of Personnel and Development (2010).
39. 'Nick Fitzherbert Applies the Rules of Magic to Coaching People in Communication Skills', **www.fitzherbert.co.uk**; see also Fitzherbert, N. 'Magic Tricks in Communication', *Professional Manager,* vol. 14, no. 5, 2005, pp. 32–3.
40. Baguley, P. 'Putting Your Message Across', *Professional Manager,* September 2009, pp. 33–5.
41. See, for example, Pivcevic, P. 'Taming the Boss', *Management Today,* March 1999, pp. 68–72.
42. Bandler, R., Grinder, J., Dilts, R. and Delozier, J. Neuro *Linguistic Programming Volume I: The Study of the Structure of Subject Experience,* Meta Publications (1980).
43. Shapiro, M. 'Getting Your Brain in Gear', *Professional Manager,* vol. 16, no. 5, 2007, pp. 26–9.
44. O'Connor, J. and Lages, A. *Coaching with NLP,* Element (2004), pp 114–15.
45. Agness, L. 'Using NLP to get on your customers' wavelength', *Manager, The British Journal of Administrative Management,* Summer 2011, pp. 22–3.
46. Paxton-Doggett, K. 'Unlocking the Inner Genius', *Governance + Compliance,* September 2013, pp. 52–3.
47. Berne, E. *Games People Play,* Penguin (1966).
48. For a summary of NLP, TA and other thoughts on business psychology, see Butcher, D. 'Buyer's Guide to Business Psychology', *Management Today,* May 2005, pp. 54–7.
49. Heider, F. *The Psychology of Interpersonal Relations,* Wiley (1958).
50. Kelley, H. H. 'The Process of Causal Attribution', *American Psychologist,* February 1973, pp. 107–28.
51. See, for example, Stewart-Allen, A. L. 'Changing the Mindset about Americans', *Professional Manager,* vol. 15, no. 5, 2006, p. 37.
52. Goss, D. and Adam-Smith, D. *Organizing AIDS,* Taylor & Francis (1995).
53. Merton, R. K. *Social Theory and Social Structure,* Free Press (1957).
54. Davies, C. M. 'You are blind to your bias', *Professional Manager,* September/October 2012, pp. 53.

55. Ariely, D. *Predictably Irrational: The Hidden Forces that Shape our Decisions,* Harper Collins (2008), see ch. 13.
56. Ibid., p. xx.
57. Ibid., p. 75
58. The first of the 2009 Reith Lectures by Professor Michael Sandel 'Markets and Morals' makes similar points; available as a podcast and transcript from the BBC website **http://www.bbc.co.uk/programmes/b00729d9**
59. Harford, T. *The Logic of Life,* Little, Brown (2008).
60. Ibid., p. 102.
61. Thaler, R. and Sunstein, C. *Nudge; Improving Decisions about Health, Wealth and Happiness,* Yale University Press (2008), p. 11.3
62. Ibid., p. 231.
63. Blanding, M. 'The Business of Behavioural Economics', Harvard Business School Working Knowledge, 11 August 2014, **http://hbswk.hbs.edu/item/7588.html** (accessed 16 February 2015).

CHAPTER 7

Work motivation and job satisfaction

Effective organisational performance is dependent upon human activity and the efforts of members of staff. The structure of the work organisation, styles of leadership and the design and content of jobs can have a significant effect on the attitude, motivation and satisfaction of staff. The manager needs to know how best to elicit the co-operation and motivation of staff, and direct their efforts to achieving the goals and objectives of the organisation.

Learning outcomes

After completing this chapter you should have enhanced your ability to:

- explain the significance and underlying concept of motivation;
- detail the various needs and expectations of people at work;
- examine content theories of motivations and the work of leading writers;
- review process theories of motivation and relevance to particular work situations;
- assess broader approaches to work motivation and satisfaction;
- explore the nature and dimensions of job satisfaction, frustration-induced behaviour and alienation;
- evaluate the relationships between work motivation, satisfaction and performance.

Critical review and reflection

Some writers argue that people do not lack inherent motivation, only the right triggers to evoke their efforts. Some claim that motivation can only come from within and attempts from other people to motivate you have little lasting influence.

What are YOUR views? In YOUR own words, what motivates YOU most and to what extent are YOU influenced by other people?

The significance of motivation

The relationship between the organisation and its members is influenced by what motivates them to work and the rewards and fulfilment they derive from it. The more highly engaged and motivated the workforce, the more likely the success of the organisation in achieving its goals and objectives. Motivation is at the basis of all organisational activity.

The study of **motivation** is concerned, basically, with why people behave in a certain way. The basic underlying question is 'Why do people do what they do?' In general terms, motivation can be described as the direction and persistence of action. It is concerned with why people choose a particular course of action in preference to others, and why they continue with a chosen action, often over a long period and in the face of difficulties and problems.[1]

From a review of motivation theory, *Mitchell* identifies four common characteristics that underlie the definition of motivation:

- Motivation is typified as an individual phenomenon. Every person is unique, and major theories of motivation allow for this uniqueness to be demonstrated in one way or another.
- Motivation is described, usually, as intentional. Motivation is assumed to be under the worker's control, and behaviours that are influenced by motivation, such as effort expended, are seen as choices of action.
- Motivation is multifaceted. The two factors of greatest importance are: (i) what gets people activated (arousal); and (ii) the force of an individual to engage in desired behaviour (direction or choice of behaviour).
- The purpose of motivational theories is to predict behaviour. Motivation is not the behaviour itself and it is not performance. Motivation concerns action and the internal and external forces that influence a person's choice of action.

On the basis of these characteristics, Mitchell defines motivation as 'the degree to which an individual wants and chooses to engage in certain specified behaviours'.[2]

A fuller definition from the Chartered Management Institute is:

> *Motivation is the creation of incentives and working environments that enable people to perform to the best of their ability. The aim of motivation is to engage people with the work they are doing in order to achieve the best possible outcomes for individuals and the organisation as a whole.*[3]

Underlying concept of motivation

The underlying concept of motivation is some driving force within individuals by which they attempt to achieve some goal in order to fulfil some need or expectation. This concept gives rise to the basic motivational model, illustrated in Figure 7.1.

People's behaviour is determined by what motivates them. Their performance is a product of both ability level and motivation:

Performance = function (ability × motivation)

Kreitner et al. suggest that although motivation is a necessary contributor for job performance, it is not the only one. Along with ability, motivation is also a combination of level of skill, knowledge about how to complete the task, feelings and emotions, and facilitating and inhibiting conditions not under the individual's control.[4] However, what is clearly evident is that if the manager is to improve the work of the organisation, attention must be given to the level of motivation of its members. The manager must also encourage staff to direct their efforts (their driving force) towards the successful attainment of the goals and objectives of the organisation.

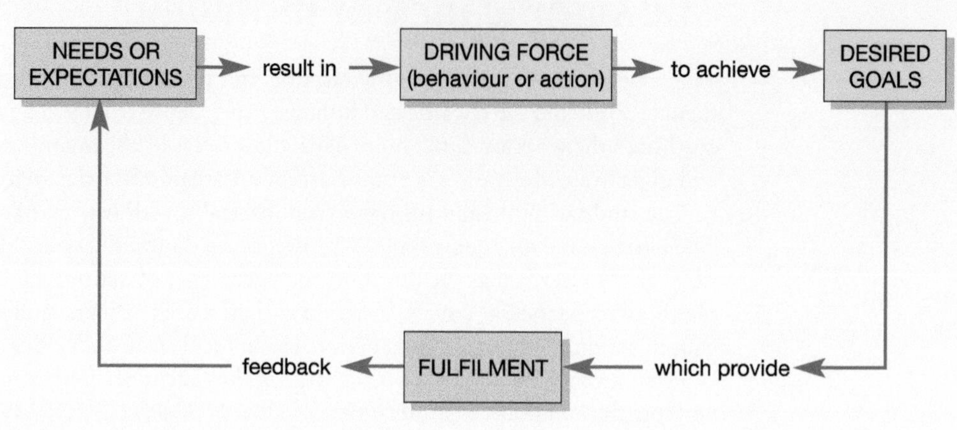

Figure 7.1 A simplified illustration of the basic motivational model

Needs and expectations at work

But what is this driving force and what do people really want from work? What are people's needs and expectations and how do they influence behaviour and performance at work? Motivation is a complex subject, it is a very personal thing and it is influenced by many variables. For example, *Farren* reminds us of the twelve human needs that have been around since the beginning of recorded history: family, health and well-being, work/career, economic, learning, home/shelter, social relationships, spirituality, community, leisure, mobility and environment/safety: 'Work and private life in the new millennium will continue to revolve around the 12 human needs.'[5]

Early writers, such as F. W. Taylor, believed in economic needs motivation. Workers would be motivated by obtaining the highest possible wages through working in the most efficient and productive way. Performance was limited by physiological fatigue. For Taylor, motivation was a comparatively simple issue – what the workers wanted from their employers more than anything else was high wages. The ideas of F. W. Taylor and his **rational-economic concept of motivation** (**discussed in Chapter** 3) and subsequent approaches to motivation at work have fuelled the continuing debate about financial rewards as a motivator and their influence on productivity.

Money as a motivator

Where there is little pleasure in the work itself or the job offers little opportunity for career advancement, personal challenge or growth, many people may appear to be motivated primarily, if not exclusively, by money. *Weaver* suggests that for many hourly workers in the hospitality industry, such as dishwashing, waiting or housekeeping staff, the work does not change much among different companies and there is little attachment to a particular company. For such staff, Weaver proposes a 'Theory M' programme of motivation based on direct cash rewards for above-average performance. A percentage base is calculated from the average performance of workers on the staff.[6]

Different generations in the workforce (**discussed in Chapter** 3) are also likely to have contrasting sets of motivations. For example, baby-boomers may well be concerned primarily about security, paying their large mortgages or funding their retirement. Generation X may be concerned about the changing nature of the work organisation, their financial future and continuing job security for the rest of their working life. On the other hand, Generation Y may be more footloose, have less interest in or doubts about affording to buy their own home and be less concerned about security or a long-term career.

For the vast majority of people, money is clearly important and a motivator at work *but* to what extent and *how* important depends upon personal circumstances and other satisfactions they derive from work. Although pay may still make people tick, there are now a number of other important influences on motivation. For many people, the feeling of being recognised and valued appears more important than money in motivating them to stay in a particular job. Note also that money may seem important as symbolising successful task performance and goal achievement. (**See achievement motivation below; see also the ultimatum game below.**)

As *Chamorro-Premuzic and Fagan* point out, few management topics have attracted as much discussion as the relationship between money and motivation. It seems that money is not a great motivator at work, and under certain circumstances may even demotivate. Extrinsic incentives such as financial rewards may extinguish or crowd out intrinsic rewards such as engagement and job satisfaction. This finding has important implications for managers.

> *It suggests that before incentivising their employees with external rewards – money, promotions or titles – they must first work out to what degree the job or task is meaningful or interesting for employees. And just as money can compensate for drearier jobs, it may also dilute employees' passion and joy in doing something that they love – like the artist whom is offended by questions about the price of his work.*

The authors also report on evidence that suggests that people are far more sensitive to the loss of money than the gaining of money. A pay rise may not necessarily make people happy, but a pay cut will be sure to make them miserable.[7]

Critical review and reflection

It is all very well talking about a contented workforce, praise and recognition, but at times of recession, rapid change or uncertainty, a secure job and high income are the true motivators. In the real world, money is the most potent need and strongest motivator.

Can YOU argue convincingly against this contention? To what extent are YOU motivated by money?

Extrinsic and intrinsic motivation

The various needs and expectations at work can be categorised in a number of ways – for example, the simple divisions into physiological and social motives or into extrinsic and intrinsic motivation.

- **Extrinsic motivation** is related to 'tangible' rewards such as salary and fringe benefits, security, promotion, contract of service, the work environment and conditions of work. Such tangible rewards are often determined at the organisation level and may be largely outside the control of individual managers.
- **Intrinsic motivation** is related to 'psychological' rewards such as the opportunity to use one's ability, a sense of challenge and achievement, receiving appreciation, positive recognition and being treated in a caring and considerate manner. The psychological rewards are those that can usually be determined by the actions and behaviour of individual managers.[8]

According to *Sauermann and Cohen,* overall intrinsic motives, particularly the desire for intellectual challenge, appear to benefit innovation more than extrinsic motives such as pay: 'However, management also need to recognise that appealing to individuals' motives can occasionally detract from organizational goals. For example, there are cases where individuals pursued research projects out of their own interest, against explicit policies of management.'[9]

Broader intrinsic motivation

Popular press reports appear to indicate that many people are increasingly motivated by broader concerns such as their work/life balance (**discussed in Chapter 3**), opportunities for flexible working, career advancement and personal development and growth and a feeling of identification with the values of the organisation. The motivation to work is also influenced by the changing nature of the work environment and the concept of the 'psychological contract' (**discussed in Chapter 1**).

However, according to *Gratton,* finding intrinsically motivating tasks is not easy.

> *Finding tasks and experiences that are intrinsically motivating sounds relatively straight forward but in fact it requires a heightened awareness of who we are. Without this emotional self-awareness we have no capacity to judge whether the tasks available to us could be intrinsically motivating . . . Finding intrinsically motivating tasks also requires the companies of which we are members to communicate the tasks available and to encourage volunteering.*[10]

Waller refers to the importance today of identity, and that work inevitably plays a key role in shaping identity. Waller questions how much of ourselves we put into our job. He points out that, not long ago, a job was something you did to put bread on the table, but nowadays (global financial situation apart) people in a cushy job with a decent salary, paid holiday, pension, healthcare and a well-stocked sandwich trolley will jack it all in, saying 'It's not really me.' If people are getting absorbed by their work-life, they expect their job to help them to discover and develop themselves.[11]

According to *Kets de Vries,* the best-performing companies possess a set of values that creates the right conditions for high performance. In addition to the motivational needs system for physiological needs, sensual and enjoyment needs and the need to respond to threatening situations, companies that get the best out of their people are characterised by a system based on a higher set of motivational needs:

- **attachment/affiliation** – concerning the need for engagement and sharing, a feeling of community and a sense of belonging to the company; and
- **exploration/assertion** – concerning the ability to play and work, a sense of fun and enjoyment, the need for self-assertion and the ability to choose.[12]

Developing a passion for work

Blanchard has identified eight critical employee needs that should be in place if organisations are to develop a passion for work and get the best out of their people and have them thrive:

- **Meaningful work** – People need to know that their work is worthwhile at both the individual and organisation levels and this is arguably the most important need.
- **Collaboration** – Working in a culture and environment that is encouraging, collaborative and co-operative.
- **Fairness** – People expect to be treated with respect, ethically, fairly and justly.
- **Autonomy** – To have influence and input over how tasks are performed, and freedom to make personal decisions about their work.
- **Recognition** – The feeling they are making a positive contribution through praise and appreciation or other recognition for their achievements.
- **Growth** – The opportunities to learn, grow and develop skills that lead to advancement in a chosen career.

- **Connectedness with leaders** – People need leaders they can trust and who share information and build rapport with them.
- **Connectedness with colleagues** – Solid relationships with colleagues and co-workers in order to provide willingness to apply discretionary effort.[13]

Threefold classification

Given the complex and variable nature of needs and expectations, the following is a simplistic but useful, broad, threefold classification as a starting point for reviewing the motivation to work (*see* Figure 7.2):

- **Economic rewards** – such as pay, fringe benefits, pension rights, material goods and security. This is an instrumental orientation to work and concerned with 'other things'.
- **Intrinsic satisfaction** – derived from the nature of the work itself, interest in the job and personal growth and development. This is a personal orientation to work and concerned with 'oneself'.
- **Social relationships** – such as friendships, group working and the desire for affiliation, status and dependency. This is a relational orientation to work and concerned with 'other people'.

A person's motivation, job satisfaction and work performance will be determined by the comparative strength of these sets of needs and expectations and the extent to which they are fulfilled. For example, some people may make a deliberate choice to forgo intrinsic satisfaction and social relationships in return for high economic rewards and/or job security. For other people, psychological well-being or social relationships would appear to be an important feature. For people working in caring organisations or the hospitality industry, where pay is often not very high, the interactions with other people and importance of supportive working relationships and good teamwork can be strong motivators at work.[14]

However the needs and expectations at work are categorised, a central motivational issue is the underlying importance for management to foster a genuine sense of engagement so that employees have a feeling of connection with the organisation and their jobs. (**Employee engagement is discussed in Chapter 16.**)

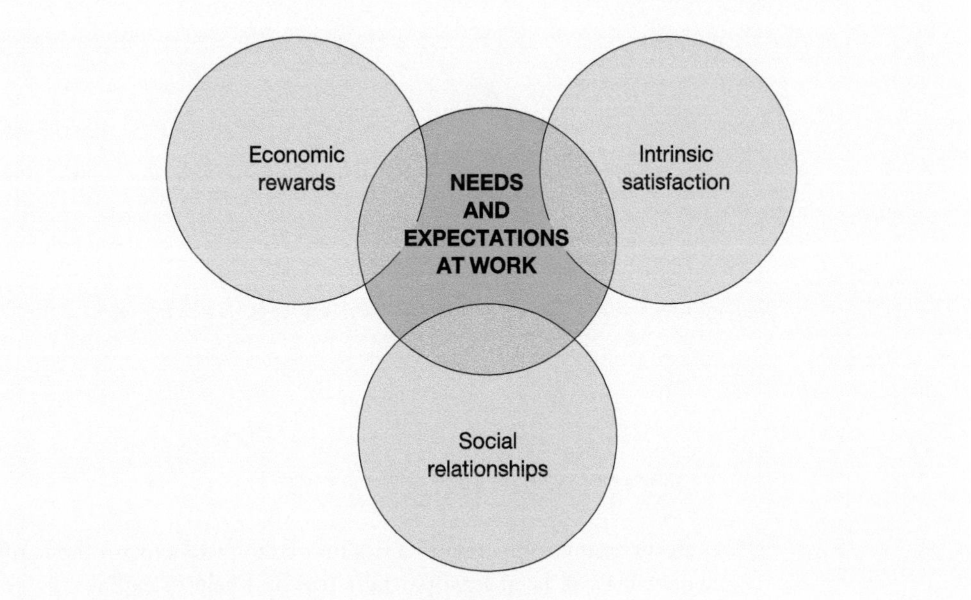

Figure 7.2 Needs and expectations of people at work

Critical review and reflection

Given the large number of identified critical employee needs and expectations at work, the threefold classification of economic rewards, intrinsic satisfaction and social relationships is far too simplistic as a meaningful focus of analysis.

What is YOUR view? What manageable and useful framework of analysis would YOU propose?

Management and organisational behaviour in action case study

Happy and productive workplace

Henry Stewart of the training company Happy draws attention to the positive correlation between staff engagement and profitability. Employee contentment is an underlying key to maximising growth and performance. Key factors to a happy workplace include a no-blame culture, a good work/life balance, transparency and a genuine commitment to the wider community. Applying the ten guiding principles of the Happy Manifesto across many organisations has created happier and more productive workplaces.[15]

Ten steps to a happy workplace

1. Trust your team. Step out of approval. Instead, pre-approve and focus on supporting your people.
2. Make your people feel good. Make this the focus of management.
3. Give freedom within clear guidelines. People want to know what is expected of them. But they want freedom to find the best way to achieve their goals.
4. Be open and transparent. More information means more people can take responsibility.
5. Recruit for attitude, train for skill. Instead of qualifications and experience, recruit on attitude and potential ability.
6. Celebrate mistakes. Create a truly no-blame culture.
7. Community: create mutual benefit. Have a positive impact on the world and build your organisation too.
8. Love work, get a life. The world, and your job, needs you well rested, well nourished and well supported.
9. Select managers who are good at managing. Make sure your people are supported by somebody who is good at doing that, and find other routes for those whose strengths lie elsewhere. Even better, allow people to choose their own managers.
10. Play to your strengths – make sure your people spend most of their time doing what they are best at.

Source: Stewart, H. *The Happy Manifesto: Make Your Organisation a Great Workplace – Now!* Happy (2012), p. 121. Reproduced with permission.

Tasks

1. To what extent do you accept the contention that employee commitment is an underlying key to maximising growth and performance?
2. Discuss how you view the relationship between a genuine commitment to the wider community and a happy workplace.
3. Explain how *you* would place in order of importance the ten steps to a happy workplace.

Theories of motivation

There are many competing theories that attempt to explain the nature of motivation. These theories may all be at least partially true and help to explain the behaviour of certain people at certain times. The complexity of motivation and the lack of a ready-made solution or single answer for motivating people at work is what makes the different theories important to the manager. They show there are many motives that influence people's behaviour and

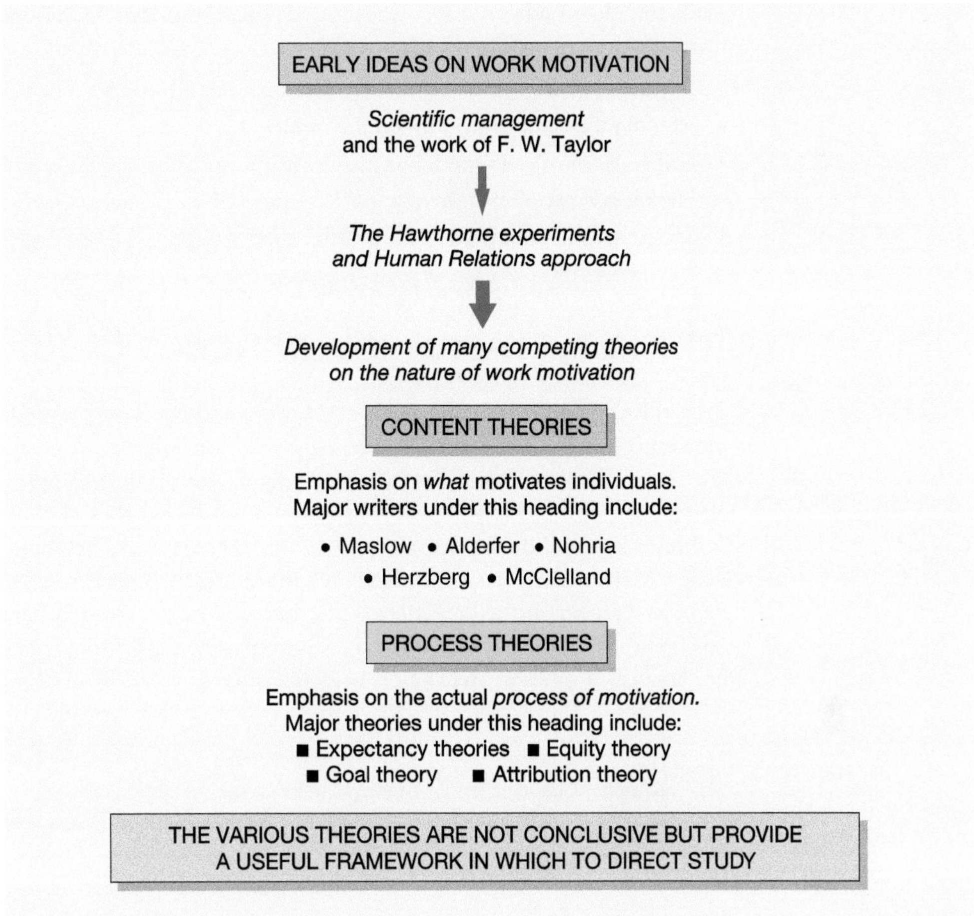

Figure 7.3 An overview of the main theories of work motivation

performance. Collectively, the different theories provide a framework within which to direct attention to the problem of how best to motivate staff to work willingly and effectively.

The usual approach to the study of motivation is through an understanding of internal cognitive processes – that is, what people feel and how they think. This understanding should help the manager to predict likely behaviour of staff in given situations. These different cognitive theories of motivation are usually divided into two contrasting approaches: content theories and process theories.

It is important to emphasise, however, that these various theories are not conclusive. They all have their critics (this is particularly true of the content theories of motivation) or have been subject to alternative findings. Many of these theories were not intended initially to have the significance that some writers have subsequently placed upon them. It is always easy to quote an example that appears to contradict any generalised observation on what motivates people to work. Despite these reservations, the different theories provide a basis for study and discussion, and for review of the most effective motivational style (*see* Figure 7.3). The manager must judge the relevance of these different theories, how best to draw upon them and how they might effectively be applied in particular work situations.

Content theories of motivation

Content theories of motivation attempt to explain those specific things that actually motivate the individual at work. These theories are concerned with identifying people's needs and their relative strengths, and the goals they pursue in order to satisfy these needs. Content theories place emphasis on the nature of needs and what motivates. Major content theories of motivation include:

- Maslow's hierarchy of needs theory;
- Alderfer's modified need hierarchy model;
- Nohria's four-drives model of motivation;
- Herzberg's two-factor theory;
- McClelland's achievement motivation theory.

Maslow's hierarchy of needs theory

A useful starting point is the work of *Maslow* and his theory of individual development and motivation, published originally in 1943.[16] Maslow's basic proposition is that human needs are arranged in a series of levels, a hierarchy of importance. People are wanting beings, they always want more, and what they want depends on what they already have.

Huczynski and Buchanan refer to the nine innate needs, including drives and goals, identified by Maslow (*see* Figure 7.4). However, the hierarchy is usually shown as ranging through five main levels from, at the lowest level, physiological needs, through safety needs, love needs and esteem needs, to the need for self-actualisation at the highest level. The **hierarchy of needs** may be shown as a series of steps but is usually displayed in the form of a pyramid (*see* Figure 7.5).

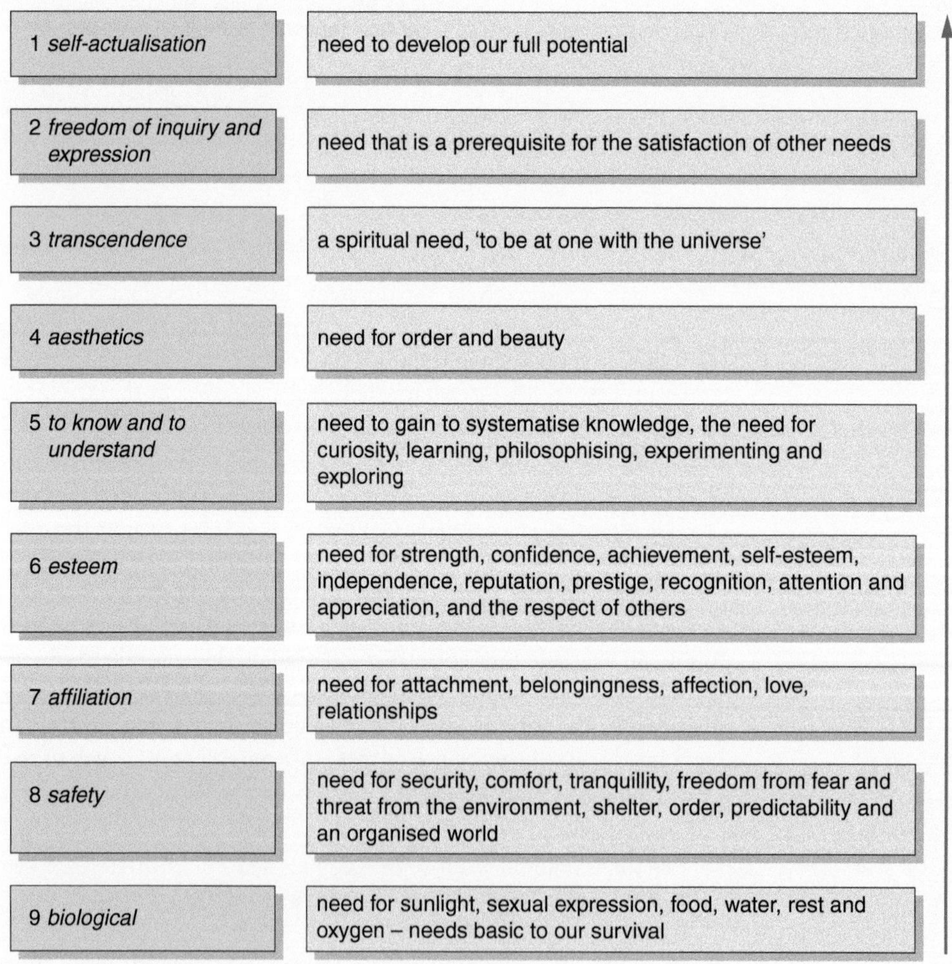

Figure 7.4 Abraham Maslow's needs hierarchy

Source: reproduced with permission from Andrzej A. Huczynski and David A. Buchanan, Organizational Behaviour, Pearson Education, 8th ed., p.293

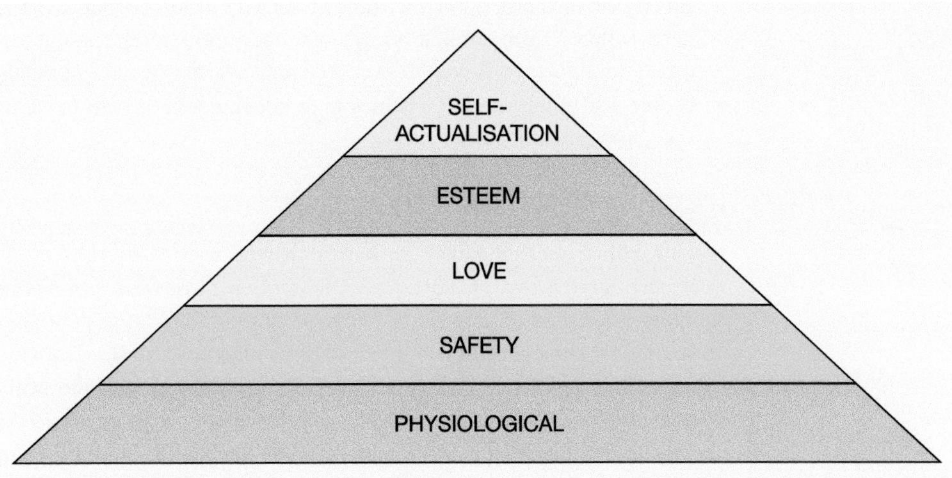

Figure 7.5 Maslow's hierarchy of needs model

This is an appropriate form of illustration as it implies a thinning out of needs as people progress up the hierarchy:

- **Physiological needs** – include homeostasis (the body's automatic efforts to retain normal functioning), such as satisfaction of hunger and thirst, the need for oxygen and to maintain temperature regulation, and also sleep, sensory pleasures, activity, maternal behaviour and, arguably, sexual desire.
- **Safety needs** – include safety and security, freedom from pain or threat of physical attack, protection from danger or deprivation, and the need for predictability and orderliness.
- **Love needs** (often referred to as social needs) – include affection, sense of belonging, social activities, friendships and both the giving and receiving of love.
- **Esteem needs** (sometimes referred to as ego needs) – include both self-respect and the esteem of others. Self-respect involves the desire for confidence, strength, independence and freedom, and achievement. Esteem of others involves reputation or prestige, status, recognition, attention and appreciation.
- **Self-actualisation needs** – once a lower need has been satisfied, it no longer acts as a strong motivator. The needs of the next higher level in the hierarchy demand satisfaction and become the motivating influence. Only unsatisfied needs motivate a person. Thus Maslow asserts that '*a satisfied need is no longer a motivator*'. Maslow claims the hierarchy is relatively universal among different cultures, but recognises there are differences in an individual's motivational content in a particular culture.

Not necessarily a fixed order

Although Maslow suggests that most people have these basic needs in about the order indicated, he makes clear that the hierarchy is not necessarily a fixed order. For some people there will be a reversal of the hierarchy, for example:

- Self-esteem may seem to be more important than love to some people. This is the most common reversal of the hierarchy. People who seek love may try to put on a show of aggressive, confident behaviour. They are not really seeking self-esteem as an end in itself but for the sake of love needs.
- For some innately creative people the drive for creativity and self-actualisation may arise despite lack of satisfaction of more basic needs.
- Higher-level needs may be lost in some people who will continue to be satisfied at lower levels only, for example a person who has experienced chronic unemployment.
- Some people who have been deprived of love in early childhood may experience the permanent loss of love needs.

- A need satisfied over a long period of time may be undervalued. For example, people who have never suffered from chronic hunger may tend to underestimate its effects, and regard food as rather unimportant. A higher-level need may assume greater importance than more basic needs.
- People with high ideals or values may become martyrs and give up everything else for the sake of their beliefs.

Degrees of satisfaction

Maslow points out that a false impression may be given that a need must be satisfied fully before a subsequent need arises. He suggests that a more realistic description is in terms of decreasing percentages of satisfaction along levels of the hierarchy. The relative importance of these needs changes during the psychological development of the individual. Maslow subsequently modified his views by noting that satisfaction of self-actualisation needs by growth-motivated individuals can actually enhance these needs rather than reduce them. Furthermore, he accepted that some higher-level needs may still emerge after long deprivation of lower-level needs, rather than only after their satisfaction.

Applications to the work situation

Based on Maslow's theory, once lower-level needs have been satisfied, giving more of the same does not provide motivation. Individuals advance up the hierarchy as each lower-level need becomes satisfied. Therefore, to provide motivation for a change in behaviour, the manager must direct attention to the next higher level of needs that seek satisfaction. However, there are a number of difficulties in relating Maslow's theory to the work situation. These include the following:

- People do not necessarily satisfy their needs, especially higher-level needs, just through the work situation but through other areas of their life as well. The manager would need a complete understanding of people's private and social lives, not just their behaviour at work.
- Individual differences mean that people place different values on the same need. For example, some people prefer what they see as the comparative safety of working in a bureaucratic organisation to a more highly paid and higher-status position, but with less job security, in a different organisation.
- Some rewards or outcomes at work satisfy more than one need. Higher salary or promotion, for example, can be applied to all levels of the hierarchy. Even for people within the same level of the hierarchy, the motivating factors will not be the same. There are many different ways in which people may seek satisfaction of, for example, their esteem needs.
- Maslow viewed satisfaction as the main motivational outcome of behaviour. But job satisfaction does not necessarily lead to improved work performance.

Useful basis for evaluation

Although Maslow did not originally intend that the need hierarchy should be applied to the work situation, it remains popular as a theory of motivation. Despite criticisms and doubts about its limitations, the theory has had a significant impact on management approaches to motivation and the design of organisations to meet individual needs. It is a convenient framework for viewing the different needs and expectations that people have, where they are in the hierarchy and the different motivators that might be applied to people at different levels. The need hierarchy model provides a useful base for the evaluation of motivation at work. For example, *Steers and Porter* suggest a list of general rewards and organisational factors used to satisfy different needs.[17]

Saunders contends that, despite the time that has elapsed, Maslow's theory remains watertight.

> *When prehistoric man first took shelter in a cave and lit a fire, he was satisfying his lowest – physiological and safety – needs. When a Buddhist achieves a state of nirvana, she is satisfying the fifth and highest – self-actualisation . . . The cave these days might be a three-bedroom semi with garden and off-street parking, but the fact remains that once we've got enough to feed, clothe and house our families money is a low-level motivator for most people. The dash for cash is soon replaced by the desire for recognition, status and ultimately (although Maslow reckoned that a lot of us never get this far) the need to express yourself through your work.*[18]

Critical review and reflection

Adair points out that presenting Maslow's hierarchy as a pyramid model gives the impression that the greatest needs are in the lower levels. Adair suggests that the pyramid should be inverted as physiological needs, for example, are limited but there are fewer limitations the further up you go.[19]

How would YOU best explain and present Maslow's hierarchy of human needs?

Alderfer's modified need hierarchy model

A modified need hierarchy model has been presented by *Alderfer*.[20] This model condenses Maslow's five levels of need into only three levels, based on the core needs of existence, relatedness and growth (ERG theory):

- **Existence needs** are concerned with sustaining human existence and survival and cover physiological and safety needs of a material nature.
- **Relatedness needs** are concerned with relationships to the social environment and cover love or belonging, affiliation and meaningful interpersonal relationships of a safety or esteem nature.
- **Growth needs** are concerned with the development of potential and cover self-esteem and self-actualisation.

A continuum of needs

Alderfer suggests that individuals progress through existence needs to relatedness needs to growth needs as the lower-level needs become satisfied. However, these needs are more a continuum than hierarchical levels. More than one need may be activated at the same time. Individuals may also progress down the hierarchy. There is a frustration–regression process. For example, if an individual is continually frustrated in attempting to satisfy growth needs, relatedness needs may reassume most importance. The lower-level needs become the main focus of the individual's efforts.

Unlike Maslow's theory, the results of Alderfer's work suggest that lower-level needs do not have to be satisfied before a higher-level need emerges as a motivating influence. The results, however, do support the idea that lower-level needs decrease in strength as they become satisfied. ERG theory states that an individual is motivated to satisfy one or more basic sets of needs. Therefore, if a person's needs at a particular level are blocked, attention should be focused on the satisfaction of needs at the other levels. For example, if a subordinate's growth needs are blocked because the job does not allow sufficient opportunity for personal development, the manager should attempt to provide greater opportunities for the subordinate to satisfy existence and relatedness needs.

Nohria's four-drives model of motivation

Another theory similar to Maslow's is that by *Nohria et al.* Based on a survey of a wide range of Fortune 500 and other companies, they formulated a model to increase work motivation based on four basic innate drives:

- The drive to **acquire** – scarce goods and intangibles such as social status.
- The drive to **bond** – connections with individuals and groups.
- The drive to **comprehend** – satisfy curiosity and master the world around us.
- The drive to **defend** – against external threats and to promote justice.

For each of these drives there is a primary organisational lever that front-line managers can use in order to best meet these deep needs and drives. Reward systems that value good performance fulfil the drive to acquire. A collaborative and open culture fulfils the drive to bond. Meaningful and challenging jobs fulfil the need to comprehend. Transparent performance management systems fulfil the drive to defend. All four levers are important, and failure to fulfil any one drive adequately will impact on the satisfaction of other drives. However, using all four levers simultaneously can lead to a noticeable increase in motivation.[21]

Herzberg's two-factor theory

The link between motivation, job design and satisfaction was established by *Herzberg et al.,* who used a critical incident method in interviews with 203 accountants and engineers from different industries in the Pittsburgh area of the USA. Subjects were asked to describe times when they felt exceptionally good or exceptionally bad about their present job or any previous job. Responses to the interviews were generally consistent and revealed that there were two different sets of factors affecting motivation and work. **This led to the two-factor theory of motivation and job satisfaction.**[22]

Hygiene and motivating factors

One set of factors is those that, if absent, cause dissatisfaction. These factors are related to job context; they are concerned with job environment and are extrinsic to the job itself. They are the **hygiene or maintenance factors** ('hygiene' being used as analogous to the medical term meaning preventive and environmental). The other set of factors is those that serve to motivate the individual to superior effort and performance. These factors are related to job content of the work itself. They are the **motivators or growth factors**. The strength of these factors will affect feelings of satisfaction or no satisfaction, but not dissatisfaction. **The opposite of dissatisfaction is not satisfaction but, simply, no dissatisfaction** (*see* Figure 7.6).

Herzberg emphasises that hygiene factors are not a 'second-class citizen system'. They are as important as the motivators, but for different reasons. Hygiene factors are necessary to avoid unpleasantness at work and to deny unfair treatment: 'Management should never deny people proper treatment at work.' To motivate workers to give of their best, the manager must give proper attention to the motivators or growth factors. The motivators relate to what people are allowed to do and the quality of human experience at work. They are the variables that actually motivate people.

Evaluation of Herzberg's work

Herzberg's theory is a source of frequent debate. There are two common general criticisms of his theory. One is that the theory has only limited application to people in largely unskilled jobs or whose work is uninteresting, repetitive and monotonous, and limited in scope. Yet these are the people who often present management with the biggest problem of motivation. Some workers do not seem greatly interested in the job content of their work or with the motivators or growth factors. A second, general criticism concerns the critical incident methodology. People are more likely to attribute satisfying incidents at work, that is, the motivators, as a favourable reflection on their own performance. The dissatisfying incidents, the hygiene factors, are more likely to be attributed to external influences and the efforts of other people.

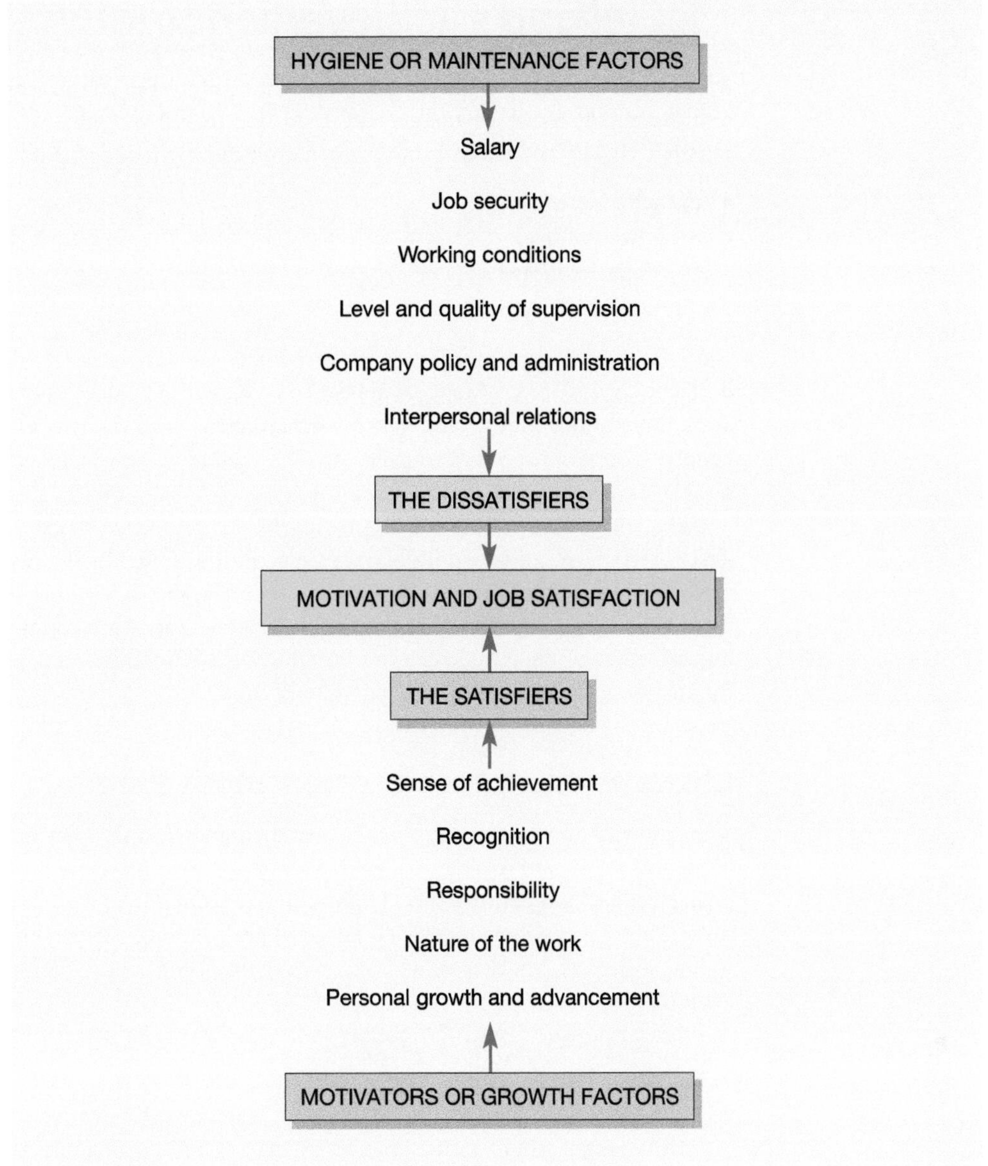

Figure 7.6 Representation of Herzberg's two-factor theory

Despite such criticisms, there is still evidence of support for the continuing relevance of the theory. For example, according to *Crainer and Dearlove:*

> *Herzberg's work has had a considerable effect on the rewards and remuneration packages offered by corporations. Increasingly, there is a trend towards 'cafeteria' benefits in which people can choose from a range of options. In effect, they can select the elements they recognise as providing their own motivation to work. Similarly, the current emphasis on self-development, career management and self-managed learning can be seen as having evolved from Herzberg's insights.*[23]

Whatever the validity of the two-factor theory, much of the criticism is with the benefit of hindsight, and Herzberg did at least attempt an empirical approach to the study of motivation at work and job satisfaction. Furthermore, his work has drawn attention to the importance of job design in the 'quality of work-life'. The work of Herzberg indicates it is more likely that good performance leads to job satisfaction rather than the reverse.

McClelland's achievement motivation theory

McClelland's work originated from investigations into the relationship between hunger needs and the extent to which imagery of food dominated thought processes. From subsequent research McClelland identified four main arousal-based, and socially developed, motives:

- the **achievement** motive;
- the **power** motive;
- the **affiliative** motive;
- the **avoidance** motive.[24]

The relative intensity of these motives varies between individuals. It also tends to vary between different occupations. Managers appear to be higher in achievement motivation than in affiliation motivation. McClelland saw the achievement need (n-Ach) as the most critical for the country's economic growth and success. The need to achieve is linked to entrepreneurial spirit and the development of available resources.

Research studies by McClelland use a series of projective 'tests' – Thematic Apperception Tests (TATs) – to gauge an individual's motivation. Individuals are shown a number of pictures in which some activity is depicted. They are asked to look briefly (10–15 seconds) at the pictures and then describe what they think is happening, what people in the picture are thinking and what events have led to the situation depicted.[25] The descriptions are used as a basis for analysing the strength of the individual's motives.

Characteristics of achievement motivation

Some individuals rate very highly in achievement motivation. They are challenged by opportunities and work hard to achieve a goal. Money is not an incentive but may serve as a means of giving feedback on performance. High achievers seem unlikely to remain long with an organisation that does not pay them well for good performance. Money may seem to be important to high achievers, but they value it more as symbolising successful task performance and goal achievement.

From empirical research McClelland identified four characteristics of people with a strong achievement need (n-Ach):

- **Moderate task difficulty and goals as an achievement incentive.** If the task is too difficult or too risky, it would reduce chances of success and gaining need satisfaction. If the course of action is too easy or too safe, there is little challenge in accomplishing the task and little satisfaction from success.
- **Personal responsibility for performance.** They like to attain success through the focus of their own abilities and efforts rather than by teamwork or chance factors outside their control. Personal satisfaction is derived from the accomplishment of the task and recognition need not come from other people.
- **Need for clear and unambiguous feedback on how well they are performing.** A knowledge of results within a reasonable time is necessary for self-evaluation. Feedback enables them to determine success or failure in the accomplishment of their goals and to derive satisfaction from their activities.
- **More innovative.** As they always seek moderately challenging tasks, they tend always to be moving on to something a little more challenging. In seeking shortcuts they are more likely to cheat. There is a constant search for variety and for information to find new ways of doing things. They are more restless, avoid routine and also tend to travel more.

McClelland and Burnham have also suggested that as effective managers need to be successful leaders and to influence other people, they should possess a high need for power.[26]

However, the effective manager also scores high on inhibition. Power is directed more towards the organisation and concern for group goals and is exercised on behalf of other people. This is 'socialised' power. It is distinguished from 'personalised' power, which is characterised by satisfaction from exercising dominance over other people, and personal aggrandisement.

Critical review and reflection

The difficulty with the theory of achievement motivation is that far too few organisations provide the culture or opportunities for individuals to satisfy the characteristics of high achievement needs.

To what extent do YOU believe this is fair comment? How would YOU describe the extent of YOUR own need for achievement?

Process theories of motivation

Process theories of motivation, or extrinsic theories, attempt to identify the relationships among the dynamic variables that make up motivation and the actions required to influence behaviour and actions. These theories are concerned more with the actual process of motivation and how behaviour is initiated, directed and sustained. Many of the theories cannot be linked to a single writer, but major approaches and leading writers under this heading include:

- expectancy-based models – Vroom, and Porter and Lawler;
- equity theory – Adams;
- goal theory – Locke;
- attribution theory – Heider and Kelley (**discussed in Chapter 6**).

Expectancy theories of motivation

The underlying basis of **expectancy theory** is that people are influenced by the expected results of their actions. Motivation is a function of the relationship between:

1. effort expended and perceived level of performance; and
2. the expectation that rewards (desired outcomes) will be related to performance.

   There must also be:

3. the expectation that rewards (desired outcomes) are available.

These relationships determine the strength of the 'motivational link' (*see* Figure 7.7). Performance depends upon the perceived expectation regarding effort expended and achieving the desired outcome. For example, the desire for promotion will result in high performance only if the person believes there is a strong possibility this will lead to promotion. If, however, the person believes promotion to be based solely on age and length of service, there is no motivation to achieve high performance. A person's behaviour reflects a conscious choice between the comparative evaluation of alternative behaviours. **The choice of behaviour is based on the expectancy of the most favourable consequences.**

More recent approaches to expectancy theory have been associated with the work of Vroom and of Porter and Lawler.

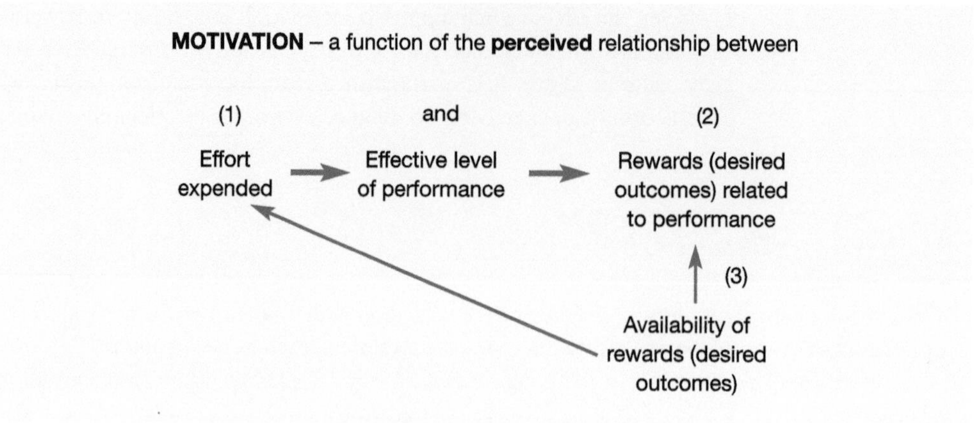

Figure 7.7 Expectancy theory: the motivational link

Vroom's expectancy theory

Vroom was the first person to propose an expectancy theory aimed specifically at work motivation.[27] His model is based on three key variables: **valence, instrumentality** and **expectancy** (VIE theory or expectancy/valence theory). The theory is founded on the idea that people prefer certain outcomes from their behaviour over others. They anticipate feelings of satisfaction should the preferred outcome be achieved.

- **Valence** – the term used for the feeling about specific outcomes. **This is the attractiveness of, or preference for, a particular outcome to the individual.** It is the anticipated satisfaction from an outcome. The valences of certain outcomes may be derived in their own right, but more usually are derived from other outcomes to which they are expected to lead. An obvious example is money. Some people may see money as having an intrinsic worth and derive satisfaction from the actual accumulation of wealth. Most people, however, see money in terms of the many satisfying outcomes to which it can lead.
- **Instrumentality** – from which the valences of outcomes are derived. This leads to a distinction between first-level outcomes and second-level outcomes. **The first-level outcomes are performance related.** Some people may seek to perform well as part of their work ethic and without thinking about the expected consequences of their actions. Usually, however, performance outcomes acquire valence because of the expectation that they will lead to other outcomes as an anticipated source of satisfaction – second-level outcomes. **The second-level outcomes are need related.** Many need-related outcomes are dependent upon actual performance rather than effort expended. People generally receive rewards for what they have achieved rather than for effort alone or through trying hard. On the basis of Vroom's expectancy theory it is possible to depict a general model of behaviour (*see* Figure 7.8).
- **Expectancy** – when a person chooses between alternative behaviours that have uncertain outcomes, the choice is affected not only by the preference for a particular outcome but also by the probability that the outcome will be achieved. This is expectancy. People develop a perception of the degree of probability that the choice of a particular action will actually lead to the desired outcome. Expectancy relates effort expended to the achievement of first-level outcomes. Its value ranges between 0, indicating zero probability, and 1, indicating certainty that an action will result in the outcome.

Motivational force

The combination of valence and expectancy determines the person's motivation for a given form of behaviour. This is the **motivational force.** Expressed as an equation, motivation (M) is the sum of the products of the valences of all outcomes (V) times the strength of expectancies

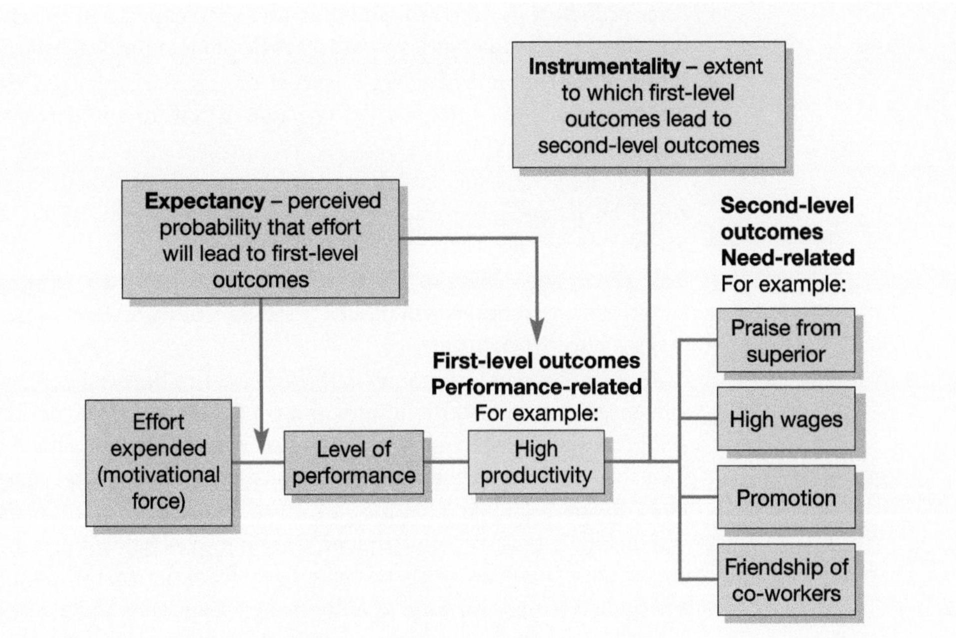

Figure 7.8 Basic model of expectancy theory

that action will result in achieving these outcomes (*E*). Therefore, if either, or both, valence or expectancy is zero, then motivation is zero. The choice between alternative behaviours is indicated by the highest attractiveness score.

$$M = \sum_{n} E \cdot V$$

There are likely to be a number of outcomes expected for a given action. Therefore, the measure of *E•V* is summed across the total number of possible outcomes to arrive at a single figure indicating the attractiveness for the contemplated choice of behaviour.

The Porter and Lawler expectancy model

Vroom's expectancy/valence theory has been developed and expanded by *Porter and Lawler*.[28] Their model goes beyond motivational force and considers performance as a whole. They point out that effort expended (motivational force) does not lead directly to performance. It is mediated by individual abilities and traits, and by the person's role perceptions. Porter and Lawler also introduce both intrinsic rewards and extrinsic rewards as intervening influences with feedback to perceived effort–reward probability. Perceived equitable rewards is also an influence on the level of satisfaction.

Explanation of relationships

Porter and Lawler see motivation, satisfaction and performance as separate variables and attempt to explain the complex relationships among them. In contrast to the human relations approach, which tended to assume that job satisfaction leads to improved performance, Porter and Lawler suggest that satisfaction is an effect rather than a cause of performance. It is performance that leads to job satisfaction.

- **Value of reward** is similar to valence in Vroom's model. People desire various outcomes (rewards), which they hope to achieve from work. The value placed on a reward depends on the strength of its desirability.

- **Perceived effort–reward probability** is similar to expectancy. It refers to a person's expectation that certain outcomes (rewards) are dependent upon a given amount of effort.
- **Effort** is the amount of energy exerted on a given activity. This is dependent upon the interaction of the input variables of value of reward and perception of the effort–reward relationship.
- **Abilities and traits** suggests that effort does not lead directly to performance but is influenced by individual characteristics such as intelligence, skills, knowledge, training and personality.
- **Role perceptions** refers to the way individuals view their work and the role they should adopt. Role perceptions will influence the direction and level of action believed to be necessary for effective performance.
- **Performance** depends not only on the amount of effort exerted, but also on the intervening influences of the person's abilities and traits, and their role perceptions. Lack of the right ability or an inaccurate role perception of what is required may result in a low level of performance or task accomplishment, despite exertion of a large amount of energy.
- **Rewards** are desirable outcomes. Intrinsic rewards derive from the individuals themselves and include a sense of achievement, a feeling of responsibility and recognition (e.g. Herzberg's motivators). Extrinsic rewards derive from the organisation and the actions of others and include salary, working conditions and supervision (e.g. Herzberg's hygiene factors). The extent of the relationship depends upon the nature of the job and the extent to which it permits variety and challenge, so that people feel able to reward themselves for good performance.
- **Perceived equitable rewards** – most people have an implicit perception about the level of rewards they should receive commensurate with the requirements and demands of the job. Self-rating of performance links directly with the perceived equitable reward variable.
- **Satisfaction** is not the same as motivation. It is an attitude, an individual's internal state. Satisfaction is determined by both actual rewards received and perceived level of rewards from the organisation for a given standard of performance. The experience of satisfaction derives from actual rewards that meet or exceed the perceived equitable rewards.

Lawler's revised expectancy model

Following the original Porter and Lawler model, further work was undertaken by *Lawler* (*see* Figure 7.9).[29] He suggests that in deciding the attractiveness of alternative behaviours, there are two types of expectancies to be considered: effort–performance expectancies (E → P) and performance–outcome expectancies (P → O).

The **first expectancy (E → P)** is the person's perception of the probability that a given amount of effort will result in achieving an intended level of performance. It is measured on a scale between 0 and 1. The closer the perceived relationship between effort and performance, the higher the E → P expectancy score.

The **second expectancy (P → O)** is the person's perception of the probability that a given level of performance will actually lead to particular need-related outcomes. This is measured also on a scale between 0 and 1. The closer the perceived relationship between performance and outcome, the higher the P → O expectancy score.

Motivational force to perform

The multiplicative combination of the two types of expectancies, E → P and the sum of the products P → O, determines expectancy. The motivational force to perform (effort expended) is determined by multiplying E → P and P → O by the strength of outcome valence (V):

$$E(\text{Effort}) = (E \rightarrow P) \times \sum[(P \rightarrow O)V]$$

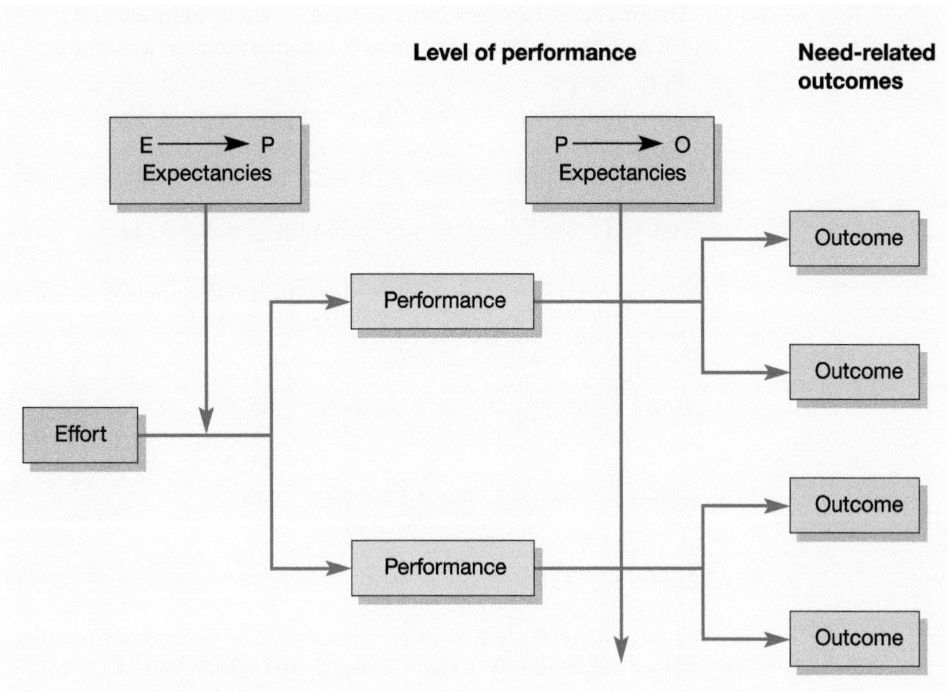

Figure 7.9 An illustration of the Lawler expectancy model

The distinction between the two types of expectancies arises because they are determined by different conditions. E → P expectancy is determined in part by the person's ability and self-confidence, past experience and the difficulty of the task. P → O expectancy is determined by the attractiveness of the outcomes and the belief about who controls the outcomes – the actual person or other people.

Implications of expectancy theories

There are a number of versions of expectancy theory. The main elements tend to be very similar, however, and this suggests the development of a generally accepted approach. Expectancy models are not always easy to understand, or to apply. There are many variables that affect behaviour at work. A problem can arise in attempting to include a large number of variables or in identifying those variables that are most appropriate in particular situations.

Expectancy theory does, however, draw attention to the complexities of work motivation. It provides further information in helping to explain the nature of behaviour and motivation in the work situation, and helps to identify problems in performance. Expectancy theory indicates that managers should give attention to a number of factors, including the following:

- Use rewards appropriate in terms of individual performance. Outcomes with high valence should be used as an incentive for improved performance.
- Attempt to establish clear relationships between effort–performance and rewards, as perceived by the individual.
- Establish clear procedures for the evaluation of individual levels of performance.

- Pay attention to intervening variables such as abilities and traits, role perceptions, organisational procedures and support facilities, which, although not necessarily direct motivational factors, may still affect performance.
- Minimise undesirable outcomes that may be perceived to result from a high level of performance, such as industrial accidents or sanctions from co-workers, or to result despite a high level of performance, such as short-time working or layoffs.

Porter and Lawler also emphasise that the expectancy model is just a model and that expectancy theory applies only to behaviours that are under the voluntary control of the individual. The two general types of choices over which individuals have voluntary control of work performance in organisations are the amount of effort and energy expended, and the manner in which they go about performing their work.

> *There is always a choice about the way you do your work, even if there is not a choice about the work itself. You always have a choice about the attitude you bring to the job.*
>
> *World famous Pike Place Fish Market, Seattle*[30]

Strategic and total rewards

The value of rewards is an important aspect of expectancy theories of motivation. The CIPD distinguishes between **strategic rewards** and **total rewards.**

> *Strategic reward is based on the design and implementation of long-term policies and practices to closely support and advance business or organisational objectives as well as employee aspirations. The concept of **total reward** encompasses all aspects of work that are valued by employees, including elements such as learning and development opportunities and/or an attractive working environment, in addition to the wider pay and benefits package.*[31]

The need to maintain the motivation, development and performance of employees has resulted in many organisations giving greater attention to a more comprehensive approach of total rewards, including attention to both extrinsic and intrinsic rewards (**discussed above**).

Critical review and reflection

Expectancy theories of motivation may make for interesting discussion in the classroom but are unlikely to have much appeal to the practical manager in modern work organisations.

What do YOU think? How would YOU justify the potential benefits of expectancy theory to a sceptical manager?

Equity theory of motivation

One of the major variables of satisfaction in the Porter and Lawler expectancy model is perceived equitable rewards. This leads to consideration of another process theory of motivation – **equity theory**. Applied to the work situation, equity theory is usually associated with the work of *Adams.*[32]

Equity theory focuses on people's feelings of how fairly they have been treated in comparison with the treatment received by others. It is based on social exchange theory (**discussed in Chapter 1**). Social relationships involve an exchange process. For example, a person may expect promotion as an outcome of a high level of contribution (input) in helping to achieve an important organisational objective. People also compare their own position with that of others. They determine the perceived equity of their own position. Most exchanges involve a number of inputs and outcomes. According to equity theory, people place a weighting on these various inputs and outcomes according to how they perceive their importance. When there is an unequal comparison of ratios the person experiences a sense of inequity.

Behaviour as a consequence of inequity

A feeling of inequity causes tension, which is an unpleasant experience. The presence of inequity therefore motivates the person to remove or to reduce the level of tension and the perceived inequity. The magnitude of perceived inequity determines the level of tension and strength of motivation. Adams identifies six broad types of possible behaviour as consequences of inequity (*see* Figure 7.10):

- **Changes to inputs** – Increasing or decreasing level of inputs, for example through the amount or quality of work, absenteeism, or working additional hours without pay.
- **Changes to outcomes** – Attempting to change outcomes such as pay, working conditions, status and recognition, without changes to inputs.
- **Cognitive distortion** – Distorting, cognitively, inputs or outcomes to achieve the same results. Attempting to distort the utility of facts, for example the belief about how hard they are really working, the relevance of a particular qualification, or what they can or cannot obtain with a given level of pay.
- **Leaving the field** – Trying to find a new situation with a more favourable balance, for example by absenteeism, request for a transfer, resigning from a job or from the organisation altogether.

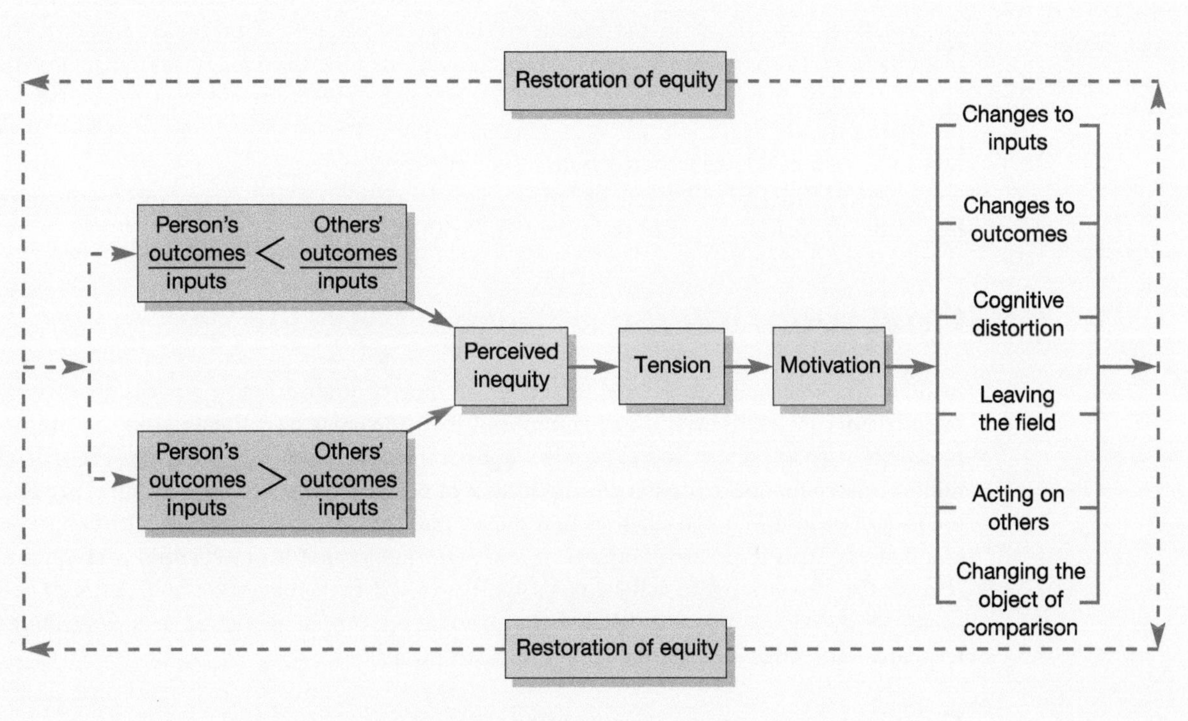

Figure 7.10 An illustration of Adams' equity theory of motivation

- **Acting on others** – Attempting to bring about changes in others, for example to lower their inputs or accept greater outcomes. The person may cognitively distort the inputs and outcomes of others, or alternatively try to force others to leave the field.
- **Changing the object of comparison** – Changing the reference group with whom comparison is made. For example, where another person with a previously similar ratio of outcomes–inputs receives greater outcomes without any apparent increase in contribution, that other person may be perceived as now belonging to a different level in the organisation structure.

Under the control of the manager

The manager may seek to remove or reduce tension and perceived inequity among staff by influencing these types of behaviour – for example, by attempting to change a person's inputs or encouraging a different object of comparison. People measure and compare their total inputs and outcomes, so, for example, a working parent may prefer greater flexibility in working hours in return for lower monetary rewards. However, there are likely to be only two courses of action under the direct control of the manager. Outcomes can be changed by, for example, increased pay, additional perks or improved working conditions; or by instigating a person leaving the field through transfer, resignation or, as an extreme measure, dismissal. It is important to remember that equity theory is about the **perceived** ratio of inputs to outcomes and these perceptions may not reflect the reality of the situation.

The ultimatum game

The **ultimatum game** is an economic behavioural game that can arguably be related to the concept of equity theory.[33] Two participants, A and B, are given the opportunity to split a given sum of money between them. The game is played anonymously and once only. One person (A) has to decide to make a one-time, take-it-or-leave-it offer (ultimatum) to the other person (B). If person B agrees to the division, both A and B keep their share of the money. However, if the offer is rejected then neither person receives anything. Experiments indicate that if A offers around 50 per cent of the money then B will accept the offer. But if A offers a noticeably lesser amount than 50 per cent, B will typically refuse the offer in which case neither participant receives anything. One might expect B to accept because even a lesser amount, whatever the offer, is better than nothing.

The conclusion appears to be that people do not like to be taken advantage of, and in certain circumstances at work, fairness in treatment is more important than money. Can you see how this might be related to perceptions of equity theory?

Viewers of the ITV1 television quiz programme *Divided*, in which contestants have to agree how to divide a cash prize, may see a similarity with the ultimatum game.

Goal theory

Another theory usually considered under the heading of motivation to work is **goal theory**, or the theory of goal-setting (*see* Figure 7.11). This theory is based mainly on the work of *Locke*.[34] The basic premise is that people's goals or intentions play an important part in determining behaviour. Locke accepts the importance of perceived value, as indicated in expectancy theories of motivation, and suggests that these values give rise to the experience of emotions and desires. Goals direct work behaviour and performance and lead to certain consequences or feedback. People strive to achieve goals in order to satisfy their emotions and desires. *Locke* subsequently pointed out that 'goal-setting is more appropriately viewed as a motivational technique rather than as a formal theory of motivation'.[35]

Goal-setting and performance

The combination of **goal difficulty** – the extent to which it is challenging and demanding – and the **extent of the person's commitment** regulates the level of effort expended. People with specific quantitative goals, such as a defined level of performance or a given deadline for

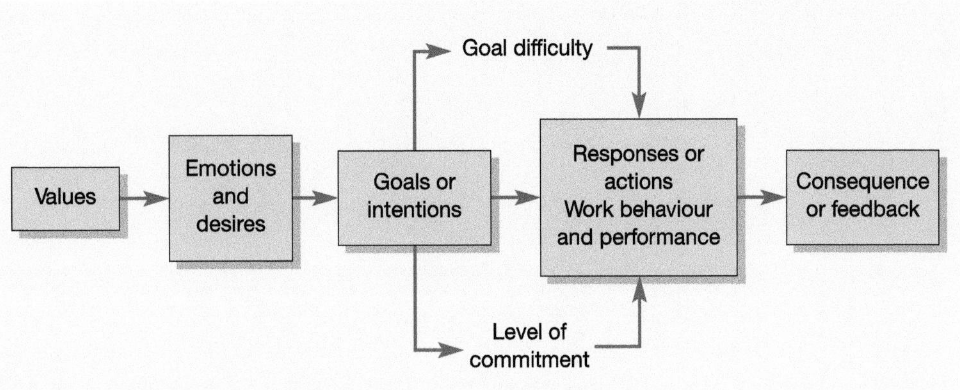

Figure 7.11 An illustration of Locke's theory of goal-setting

completion of a task, will perform better than people with no set goal or only a vague goal such as 'do the best you can'. People who have difficult goals will perform better than people with easier goals.

Gratton refers to 'stretch goals', which are ambitious, highly targeted opportunities for breakthrough improvements in performance. These goals should stem from critical success indicators and come from deep discussions within the company, and from collaboration within and across task forces, and lead to the development of activities and tactics to achieve the goals.[36] People lacking positive motivation at work may also help gain improved results and a better sense of achievement by setting themselves specific goals and identifying tasks directly related to their work and measurable targets of time and performance.

Practical implications for the manager

Goal theory has a number of practical implications for the manager:

- Individuals lacking in motivation often do not have clear goals. Specific performance goals should systematically be identified and set in order to direct behaviour and maintain motivation.
- Goals should be set at a challenging but realistic level. Difficult goals lead to higher performance. However, if goals are set at too high a level or are regarded as impossible to achieve, this can lead to stress and performance will suffer, especially over a longer period.
- Complete, accurate and timely feedback and knowledge of results is usually associated with high performance. Feedback provides a means of checking progress on goal attainment and forms the basis for any revision of goals.
- Goals can be determined either by a superior or by individuals themselves. Goals set by other people are more likely to be accepted when there is participation. Employee participation in the setting of goals may lead to higher performance.

However it is viewed, the theory of goal-setting provides a useful approach to work motivation and performance. And *Hannagan* goes so far as to suggest: 'At present goal-setting is one of the most influential theories of work motivation applicable to all cultures.'[37]

A concept map of motivation and work is set out in Figure 7.12.

Critical review and reflection

The underlying essence of motivating employees to improved performance is easy. An emphasis on clear, stretching but attainable targets; constructive feedback; and an equitable system of extrinsic and intrinsic rewards.

What is YOUR critical view of this assertion? How would YOU explain the underlying essence of work motivation?

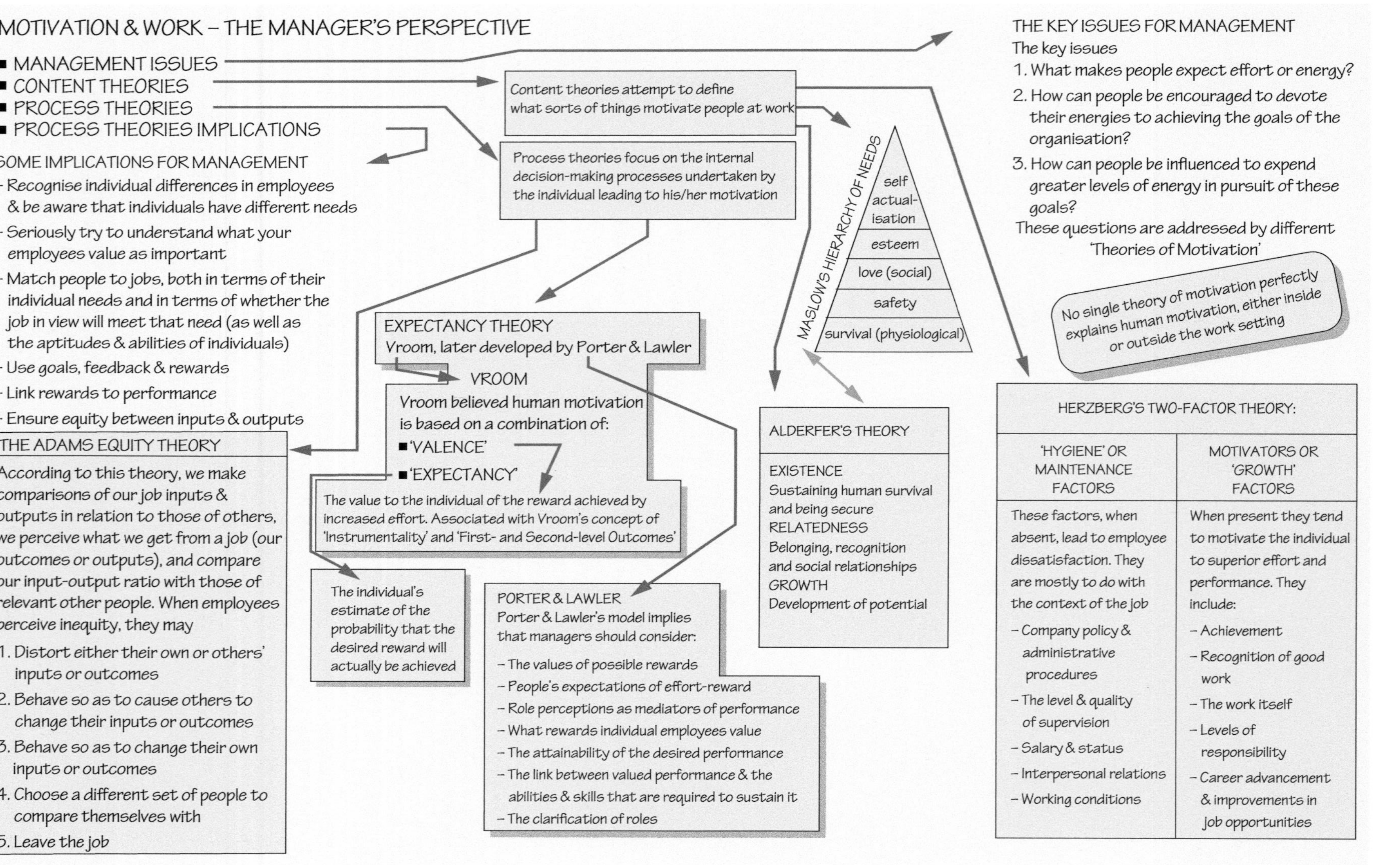

Figure 7.12 Motivation and work – the manager's perspective

Source: Copyright © 2011 The Virtual Learning Materials Workshop. Reproduced with permission.

Attribution theory

A more recent approach to the study of motivation is attribution theory. Attribution is the process by which people interpret the perceived causes of behaviour. **Attribution theory was discussed in detail in Chapter 6.**

Relevance today

Given that most major theories of motivation date back many years, it is inevitable that questions are raised about their relevance today. The Chartered Management Institute suggests that looking at both theories and real-life examples of motivation should stimulate your thoughts, and give you some 'starter' ideas on how to motivate your own people.[38]

Whatever the relevance of the different theories of motivation, to what extent do individuals have control over their own level of motivation or how much is dependent upon the leadership they encounter? *Adair* reassesses the theories of Maslow and Herzberg in terms of action-centred leadership (**discussed in Chapter 9**). Adair also argues that the extent to which you can motivate anyone else is limited and refers to the fifty–fifty rule of motivation, that is:

> *Fifty percent of motivation comes from within a person and 50% from his or her environment, especially from the leadership encountered there. The fifty-fifty rule in motivation does not claim to identify the different proportions in the equation exactly. It is more like a rough and ready rule of thumb. In effect it says no more than a substantial part of motivation lies with a person while a substantial part lies, so to speak, outside and beyond control.*[39]

Cross-cultural dimensions of motivation

Whatever the popularity of different theories of motivation, doubts are raised about their universality on the ground that they have not adequately addressed the factor of culture.[40] Are theories of motivation universally applicable or are there meaningful differences in motivation at work, or in life more generally, in different societies? A number of writers have questioned whether motivational theories and models originating in one culture are amenable to transference to other parts of the world. For example, *Francesco and Gold* devote a substantial proportion of a discussion of motivation to examining the extent to which American motivation theories are applicable outside the USA.[41]

One criticism of content theories of motivation centres on its relative applicability in different circumstances, and the suggestion that there may be variations across cultures falls within this line of reasoning. However, perhaps less obviously, process theories of motivation have also been criticised for being culture-bound. As they focus on process rather than content, such theories may appear to be more applicable in diverse cultural contexts. Nonetheless it has been suggested that process theories of motivation contain certain inbuilt assumptions that are themselves culturally derived.

Adler reminds us that expectancy models of motivation assume that individuals believe that they can, to some extent, control their environment and influence their fate. If, as in the cases of more fatalistic cultures such as China, people do not have the same sense of internal attribution, the expectancy model may have less force and therefore less applicability. When Adams' equity theory is applied across the world, differences in interpretation have been recorded.[42]

Organisational behaviour modification

Another possible approach to motivation is that of **organisational behaviour modification (OBMod)**. This is the application of learning principles to influence organisational behaviour. In particular it can be seen as a form of Skinner's operant conditioning, or reinforcement theory (**discussed in Chapter 5**). Reinforcement is a feature of the behaviourism approach and is shaped by environmental influences. The reward for a particular form of behaviour is likely to result in the reinforcement of that behaviour. A negative outcome or lack of acknowledgement for the behaviour is likely to mean that the behaviour will stop. *Luthans and Kreitner* suggest that OBMod 'represents a merging of behavioral learning theory on the one hand and organizational behavior theory on the other'.[43]

According to Luthans and Kreitner, a major premise of OBMod is that positive consequence management is much more effective than negative consequence management. Organisations that encourage the members to learn and undertake desired behaviours and not to undertake undesired behaviours follow five main steps:

1. **Identify** the observable, objective and measurable behaviours relevant to the desired organisational performance.
2. **Measure** the frequency with which those behaviours actually occur under normal conditions. Provide baseline performance data as a point of reference to compare with changes in step 5.
3. **Determine** the antecedents of the behaviours, the reinforcements to encourage patterns of behaviour and the consequences that follow from those behaviours.
4. **Develop** an intervention strategy for change in order to strengthen desirable behaviours and weaken undesirable behaviours, through the use of operant conditioning and reinforcement theory including punishment if necessary.
5. **Measure and evaluate** systematically (using the same measure as in step 2) the extent to which the frequencies of desired behaviours and undesired behaviours have changed, and improvements in organisational performance.

Applications of OBMod

To what extent can OBMod be applied effectively to improve motivation and performance in work organisations? OBMod works best for behaviours that are specific, objective and countable. There have been a number of studies in the USA that indicate positive results in behaviours that improved performance in reducing errors, attendance and punctuality, health and safety and customer service.[44]

In a study of a Russian textile factory, following the OBMod approach, workers were subjected to two forms of intervention – extrinsic rewards and social rewards. The extrinsic rewards provided valued American products, such as clothing, music tapes and hard-to-get foods, for improved performance. Social rewards such as attention, recognition and praise from supervisors were for performing specified actions such as checking looms, undertaking repairs and helping others.

Both the extrinsic and social interventions led to highly significant increases in performance. This contrasted with a previous participative job design approach that involved asking workers for ideas for improving performance and enriching their jobs that did not work. The researchers suggest cultural issues and the workers' past experiences may explain the failure of the participative intervention strategy, and that the OBMod approach has wider application.[45]

Although there appear to be a number of supporters in the USA, in the UK it is a controversial concept. Critics claim that OBMod is not an accepted theory of motivation and that there are too many individual differences for people to be treated as subjects of operant conditioning. OBMod is concerned only with shaping. There is the added criticism of a 'Big Brother' approach with excessive management manipulation and control over employees, more in line with scientific management (**recall the discussion in Chapter 2**). This in turn could also have the added disadvantage of discouraging individual initiative and adaptability to change circumstances. Workers subject to OBMod programmes may tend to ignore those aspects of voluntary behaviours, such as social support or assistance to colleagues, that are not subject to direct reward and reinforcement.

Motivation of knowledge workers

Recent advantages in telecommunications and in scientific and technological knowledge have led to greater emphasis on the knowledge and expertise of staff and the importance of creativity. *Tampoe* suggests that at the core of the new industrial trend are the 'knowledge workers' – those employees who apply their theoretical and practical understanding of a specific area of knowledge to produce outcomes of a commercial, social or personal value. The performance of knowledge workers should be judged on both the cleverness of ideas and the utility and commercial value of their applied knowledge. Creativity is necessary and needs to be encouraged, but should be bounded by commercial realism. This presents management with a new challenge of how to motivate the knowledge workers.[46]

Tampoe suggests that the personal motivation of knowledge workers is based on the value they place on the rewards they expect to earn at work. In addition to the individual's own motivation, the performance of knowledge workers is dependent upon four key characteristics (*see* Figure 7.13):

- task competence;
- peer and management support;
- task and role clarity; and
- corporate awareness.

The challenge to management is to ensure the effectiveness of the four key variables and to recognise the need for staff to supervise and manage themselves and the wider rewards expected by knowledge workers.

Climate of creativity

Whitmore suggests that in order to create a climate for creativity among employees, recognition must be given to the importance of two human needs that rise above all others and exist independent of race, creed and culture: the need for self-belief and the development of emotional intelligence; and the ever-present need that every human being has for a sense of meaning and purpose in their lives.

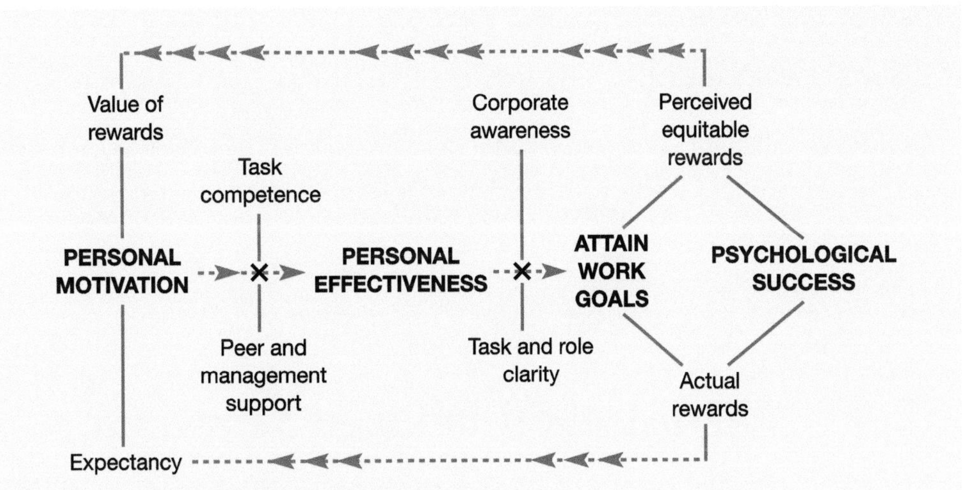

Figure 7.13 Motivating knowledge workers

Source: Tampoe, M. 'Knowledge Workers: The New Management Challenge', *Professional Manager*, Institute of Management, November 1994, p. 13. Reproduced with permission from Chartered Management Institute.

> *Self-belief and meaningful work are the fundamental bedrocks that underlie business performance. Of course, pay and conditions are important too, but we know that. It is these two others that are barely recognised . . . but business leaders ignore them at their peril.*[47]

Matson and Prusak of management consultants McKinsey & Company report that despite the high stakes in knowledge workers, there is a lack of understanding of what it takes to bolster their productivity. This lack of clarity is partly because knowledge work involves more diverse and amorphous tasks than do production or clerical positions, and partly because performance metrics are hard to come by in knowledge work. Knowledge workers spend half their time on interactions and, in order to improve their productivity, companies should explore the barriers that impede these interactions:

- **Physical and technical** – including geographical distance, different time zones or lack of effective tools.
- **Social or cultural** – including rigid hierarchies or ineffective incentives.
- **Contextual** – the sharing of and translating knowledge from colleagues in different fields.
- **Time** – or rather the perceived lack of time.[48]

Goffee and Jones suggest that future prosperity rests with organisations that make their living from the knowledge they themselves are able to develop. Clever people are highly talented individuals with the potential to create disproportionate amounts of value from the resources that the organisation makes available to them. Keeping and leading the clever people who inhabit these organisations becomes a critical challenge.

> *Exceptionally sharp and creative executives often come with characteristics that make them hard to handle. They can be egotistical, disdainful of hierarchies and prone to asking awkward questions . . . Yet research has repeatedly demonstrated that creativity and innovation are inextricably linked to energy, edge and fun, which organisational attrition is in danger of crushing.*

Clever people do not like to be led or told what to do and are at their most productive when faced with really hard questions. Tell them something is not possible and they will be highly motivated to prove you wrong. They must be given enough space to try out new things and given recognition for their work. Goffee and Jones suggest that clever people can be difficult to lead and have developed new rules to help guide their leaders.[49]

Critical review and reflection

The motivation of so-called knowledge workers is no different from motivating any other worker - that is, recognition of their individual value to achieving the objectives of the organisation.

What do YOU think? How far do YOU agree with the characteristics of clever people? Do you see YOURSELF as a potential knowledge worker?

Frustration-induced behaviour

What happens if a person's motivational driving force is blocked and they are unable to satisfy their needs and expectations, and what is the likely effect on their work performance? There are two possible sets of outcomes: constructive behaviour or frustration (*see* Figure 7.14). **Constructive behaviour** is a positive reaction to the blockage of a desired goal and can take two main forms: problem-solving or restructuring.

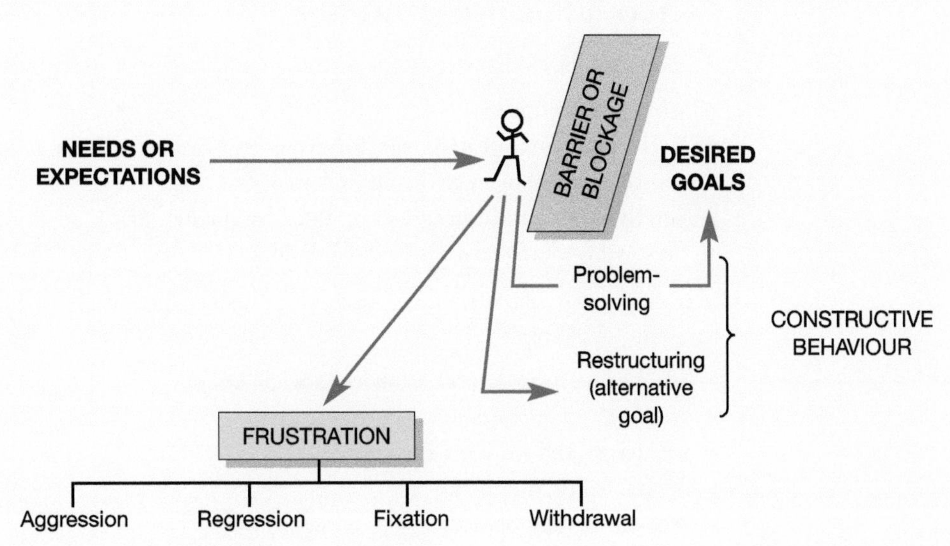

Figure 7.14 A basic model of frustration

- **Problem-solving** is the removal of the barrier – for example, finding an alternative means of undertaking a task, repairing a damaged machine or bypassing a non co-operative superior.
- **Restructuring,** or compromise, is the substitution of an alternative goal, although such a goal may be of a lower or different order – for example, taking an additional part-time job because of failure to be promoted to a higher grade, or reassessing the work/life balance.

Frustration (negative responses)

Frustration is a negative response to the blockage of a desired goal and results in a defensive form of behaviour. There are many possible reactions to frustration caused by the failure to achieve a desired goal. These can be summarised under four broad headings: aggression, regression, fixation and withdrawal.[50] However, these categories are not mutually exclusive. Most forms of frustration-induced behaviour at work are a combination of aggression, regression and fixation.

Aggression is a physical or verbal attack on some person or object, for example striking a supervisor, rage or abusive language, destruction of equipment or documents, or malicious gossip about a superior. Where a direct attack cannot be made against the actual barrier or blocking agent, because for example the source of frustration is not clear or specific, or where the source is feared, as with a powerful superior, aggression may be displaced towards some other person or object. With **displaced aggression** the person may find a scapegoat for the outlet of frustration – for example, picking arguments or being short-tempered with colleagues or slamming the filing cabinet. A more constructive form of displaced aggression is working off frustrated feelings through demanding physical work or sport, or perhaps by shouting/cursing when alone or in the company of an understanding colleague.

Regression is reverting to a childish or more primitive form of behaviour – for example, sulking, crying, tantrums or kicking a broken machine or piece of equipment.

Fixation is persisting in a form of behaviour that has no adaptive value and continuing to repeat actions that have no positive results – for example, the inability to accept change or new ideas, repeatedly trying a door that is clearly locked or a machine that clearly will not work, or insisting on applying for promotion even though not qualified for the job.

Withdrawal is apathy, giving up or resignation – for example, arriving at work late and leaving early, sickness and absenteeism, refusal to accept responsibility, avoiding decision-making, passing work over to colleagues or leaving the job altogether.

Factors influencing frustration

Among the factors that determine an individual's reaction to frustration are the:

- strength of motivation;
- level and potency of need (see, for example, Maslow's theory of motivation);
- degree of attachment to the desired goal;
- perceived nature of the barrier or blocking agent; and
- personality characteristics of the individual.

It is important that managers attempt to reduce potential frustration-induced behaviour through, for example:

- effective recruitment, selection and socialisation;
- training and development;
- job design and work organisation;
- equitable HRM policies;
- recognition and rewards;
- effective communications;
- participative styles of management; and
- attempting to understand the individual's perception of the situation.

Critical review and reflection

Motivation at work is very subjective and affected by many variables including personality, cultural influences, unknown circumstances and relationships outside of work. Generalised theories cannot meet all individual circumstances and are therefore a complete waste of your study time.

To what extent do YOU agree? What practical value do YOU place on the various theories of motivation?

Job satisfaction

Attempting to understand the nature of job satisfaction, its relationship with motivation and its effects on work performance is not easy. Job satisfaction is a complex and multifaceted concept, which can mean different things to different people. Although the level of job satisfaction may well affect strength of work motivation, this is not always the case. Satisfaction is not the same as motivation. **Job satisfaction** is more of an attitude, an internal state. It could, for example, be associated with a personal feeling of achievement, either quantitative or qualitative.

The relationship between job satisfaction and work performance is an issue of continuing debate and controversy. One view, associated with the early human relations approach, is that satisfaction leads to performance. An alternative view is that performance leads to satisfaction. Recall, for example, the Porter and Lawler expectancy model (**discussed above**).

Reeves draws attention to the relationship between accomplishment at work and the need to 'work harder':

> *All this busy-ness and stress is creating more heat than light. It is a sign not of work being too hard but too shallow. Human nature is driven by a desire to accomplish things, and so the fewer opportunities for accomplishment a job contains, the more likely we are to fill the void by tearing around in a frenzy in an effort to persuade ourselves and others that our work has a purpose, that it is important.*[51]

Dimensions of job satisfaction

There is doubt whether job satisfaction consists of a single dimension or a number of separate dimensions. Some workers may be satisfied with certain aspects of their work and dissatisfied with other aspects. The level of job satisfaction is affected by a wide range of variables relating to individual, social, cultural, organisational and environmental factors:

- **Individual factors** include personality, education and qualifications, intelligence and abilities, age, marital status, orientation to work.
- **Social factors** include relationships with co-workers, group working and norms, opportunities for interaction, informal organisation.
- **Cultural factors** include ethnicity, underlying attitudes, beliefs and values.
- **Organisational factors** include nature and size, formal structure, HR policies and procedures, nature of the work, technology and work organisation, styles of leadership, management systems, working conditions.
- **Environmental factors** include economic, social, technical and governmental influences.

These different factors all affect the job satisfaction of certain individuals in a given set of circumstances but not necessarily in others. For example, in times of economic depression and fears of high unemployment, job security is likely to be a prominent concern. A survey by the Chartered Management Institute found that organisational culture and values emerged as very strong motivational drivers, and managers' relationship with their line manager had a powerful impact on job satisfaction and related measures.[52] The FreshMinds survey (**discussed in Chapter** 3), suggests that when it comes to job satisfaction it pays to be older. Apparently 100 per cent of older baby-boomers (born between 1946 and 1963) are satisfied with their job, but only 66 per cent of Generation Y (typified by travel first, then a career) feel the same way. And Generation Y want more at work, such as gym membership and sabbaticals.[53]

According to *De Vita,* well-being at work pays because employees who are happy and healthy take fewer days off sick, are more productive and more likely to stay with their organisation. The starting point to supporting and promoting well-being in the workplace has to be good people management and effective work organisation. Good line management is the most important of the characteristics of a high-quality workplace that has high levels of commitment and low absence rates.[54]

An increasingly important issue affecting job satisfaction and efficiency is the nature of the work environment and workplace facilities (**discussed in Chapter** 11).

Over the years, a number of different surveys suggest good interpersonal relationships with colleagues is more important to enjoying your work than a high salary. In 2014, a Cabinet Office survey of life satisfaction of 274 different occupations found members of the clergy, farmers, fitness instructors, school secretaries, dental nurses and farm workers among those with modest salaries but high personal job satisfaction.[55]

Alienation at work

One main approach to job satisfaction is in terms of frustration and alienation at work. Job satisfaction can be seen as the obverse of frustration at work (**discussed above**). **Alienation** refers to the detachment of the person from their work role. The concept of alienation at work is associated originally with the views of *Marx*.[56] He saw the division of labour in pursuit of profit, and exploitation by employers, as a denial of the workers' need for self-expression. Workers become estranged from the product of their work. Work no longer provides a satisfying experience in itself, but represents a means of satisfying other external demands.

The concept of alienation has been extended by *Blauner*.[57] He describes alienation in terms of four dimensions: powerlessness, meaninglessness, isolation and self-estrangement.

- **Powerlessness** denotes the workers' lack of control over management policy, immediate work processes, or conditions of employment.
- **Meaninglessness** stems from standardisation and division of labour. It denotes the inability to see the purpose of work done or to identify with the total production process or finished product.
- **Isolation** is not belonging to an integrated work group or to the social work organisation and not being guided by group norms of behaviour.
- **Self-estrangement** is the failure to see work as an end in itself or as a central life issue. Workers experience a depersonalised detachment and work is seen solely as a means to an end.

In recent years attention to job satisfaction has also become more closely associated with broader approaches to improved job design and work organisation (**discussed in Chapter 11**), and the quality of working life movement, and with stress and the work/life balance (**discussed in Chapter 3**).

Comprehensive model of job enrichment

Attempts to improve intrinsic motivation must not only include considerations of job characteristics, but also take account of individual differences and attributes, and people's orientation to work. A popular and comprehensive model of job enrichment has been developed by *Hackman and Oldham* (*see* Figure 7.15).[58] The model views job enrichment in terms of increasing five core job dimensions: skill variety, task identity, task significance, autonomy and feedback from the job.

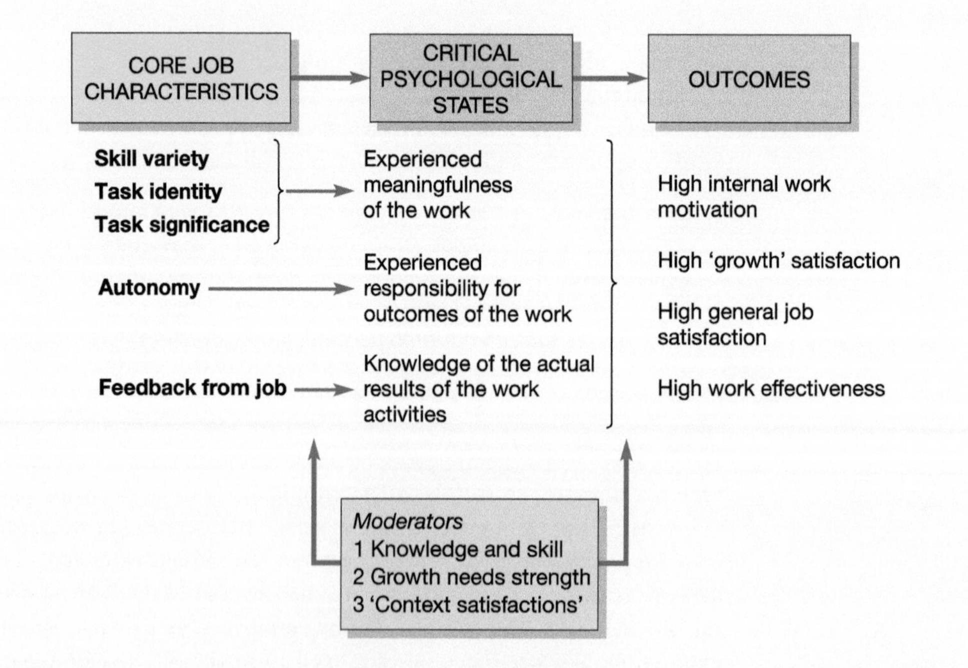

Figure 7.15 A job characteristics model of work motivation

Source: Hackman, J. R. and Oldham, G. R. *Work Redesign*, 1st ed., © 1980, Addison-Wesley Publishing Company, Inc. (1980), Figure 4.6, p. 90. Reprinted and electronically reproduced by permission of Pearson Education, Inc, New York.

Five core dimensions

The five core job dimensions can be summarised as follows:

- **skill variety** – the extent to which a job entails different activities and involves a range of skills and talents;
- **task identity** – the extent to which a job involves completion of a whole piece of work with a visible outcome;
- **task significance** – the extent to which a job has a meaningful impact on other people, either inside or outside the organisation;
- **autonomy** – the extent to which a job provides freedom, independence and discretion in planning the work and determining how to undertake it;
- **feedback** – the extent to which work activities result in direct and clear information on the effectiveness of job performance.

The extent of these core job dimensions create three critical psychological states based on the individual's perception of:

- experienced value and meaningfulness of the work;
- experienced personal responsibility for the outcomes of the work; and
- clear knowledge of actual results of work activities and level of performance.

An example of a job with little enrichment could be that of a production assembly line worker or a kitchen porter, where all five core characteristics are likely to score low. An example of an enriched job could be that of a parish priest who draws upon a wide range of social skills and talents, who can usually identify with the whole task and whose job has clear and important meaning and significance. There is a very high level of autonomy and likely to be direct and clear feedback.

Motivating potential score

From these five core job dimensions, Hackman and Oldham have developed an equation that gives a single index of a person's job profile. By answering a questionnaire – the Job Diagnostic Survey (JDS) – and by giving a score (between 1 and 7) to each job dimension, the person can calculate an overall measure of job enrichment, called the motivating potential score (MPS).

Examples of questions from the JDS are:

- How much variety is there in your job?
- To what extent does your job involve doing a whole and identifiable piece of work?
- In general, how significant or important is your job?
- How much autonomy is there in your job?
- To what extent does doing the job itself provide you with information about your work performance?

$$\text{MPS} = \frac{\{\text{Skill variety} + \text{Task identity} + \text{Task significance}\}}{3} \times \text{Autonomy} \times \text{Feedback}$$

The first three job dimensions of skill variety, task identity and task significance are averaged, since it is the combination of these dimensions that contributes to experienced meaningfulness of work. The remaining two job dimensions, autonomy and feedback, stand on their own. Since scores for skill variety, task identity and task significance are additive, this means that the absence of one dimension can be partially offset by the presence of the other dimensions. However, if either autonomy or feedback is absent then, because of the multiplicative relationship, the MPS would be zero. The job would offer no potential to motivate the person.

From their studies, Hackman and Oldham claim that people with enriched jobs and high score levels on the JDS experienced more satisfaction and internal motivation. The core job dimensions of skill variety, task identity and task significance combined to predict the level of experienced meaningfulness of the work. The core dimensions of autonomy and feedback did not relate so clearly to experienced responsibility and knowledge of results

Based on integrating Hackman and Oldham's job characteristics model with Maslow's hierarchy of needs, *Roe et al.* propose a general model of work motivation, tested with Bulgarian, Hungarian and Dutch workers. The model indicates that situational characteristics lead to critical psychological factors, inducing two main motivational factors – job involvement and organisational commitment – which in turn lead to two proximal outcomes of work motivation – effort and job satisfaction – which affect performance, stress and tendency to leave the organisation. Although there were some differences that draw attention to cultural variables, there was also a large degree of similarity in results across the three countries.[59]

Critical review and reflection

Individuals have a variety of changing, and often conflicting, needs and expectations, which they attempt to satisfy in a number of ways at different times.

What are the most powerful influences on YOUR own potential work motivation and job satisfaction? How do YOU think these are likely to change in five years' time?

Ten key points to remember

1 The relationship between the organisation and its members is influenced by what motivates them to work, and the rewards and fulfilment derived from it.

2 Individuals have a variety of changing, and often competing, needs and expectations at work, which they attempt to satisfy in a number of ways.

3 A person's work motivation, satisfaction and performance are determined by the comparative strength of economic rewards, intrinsic satisfaction and social relationships.

4 There are many competing theories that attempt to explain motivation at work. They show there are many motives that influence people's behaviour and performance.

5 Content theories place emphasis on what actually motivates the individual at work. Main theories include those of Maslow, Alderfer, Nohria, Herzberg and McClelland.

6 Process theories are concerned with the dynamic variables that make up motivation. Major approaches include expectancy-based models, equity theory, goal theory and attribution theory.

7 Another possible approach to motivation is organisational behaviour modification and the application of learning principles to behaviour at work.

8 Understanding the nature of job satisfaction and links with work performance is not easy. Job satisfaction may affect motivation but this is not always the case.

9 Satisfaction is an internal state associated with a feeling of personal achievement. One approach is in terms of frustration and alienation at work.

10 Attention has also been given to a comprehensive model of job enrichment based on skill variety, task identity, task significance, autonomy and feedback.

Review and discussion questions

1 Explain fully what you understand by the underlying concept of motivation.

2 How would you attempt to summarise the main needs and expectations to be taken into account in considering the motivation of people at work?

3 Assess critically the practical value of Maslow's hierarchy of needs model. Give examples of the extent to which the theory could meaningfully be applied to university students and/or staff in your own organisation.

4 Explain your understanding of expectancy-based theories of motivation. Use a simple diagram to illustrate an expectancy theory of your choice. What implications do expectancy theories of motivation have for the manager?

5 Give detailed practical examples of situations in which each of the following theories of motivation might be appropriate: (i) achievement motivation; (ii) equity theory; (iii) goal theory.

6 To what extent do you see yourself as a knowledge worker? And to what extent are you motivated by a climate of creativity?

7 What do you understand by frustration-induced behaviour? Give a practical example, preferably from your experience, of each of the main forms of this behaviour.

8 Debate critically the validity of the contention that the motivation to work well depends on more than a high salary and good working conditions.

9 What exactly do you understand by job satisfaction and what are the main dimensions? Relate specific examples of situations that have influenced your own job satisfaction.

10 Evaluate critically how you see the relationship between motivation, job satisfaction and effective work performance. Give reasons in support of your views.

Assignment

Work with two partners chosen by your tutor.

a. In private, you each number **in rank order** the following 20 factors in terms of the extent to which they are likely to motivate you in *preferring* to work for a particular organisation.

	YOU	**PARTNER 1**	**PARTNER 2**
Contributory pension scheme			
Long-term job security			
Safe working environment			
Harmonious working relationships			
Personal development and career progression			
Attractive benefits package (and perks)			
Leisure and sports facilities			
Size of the organisation			
Location			
Average age of working colleagues			
Group or team working			
Flexible working hours			

→

	YOU	PARTNER 1	PARTNER 2
High basic salary			
Perceived status of the organisation and/or its work			
Wide diversity of members of staff			
Extent to which work involves high level of ICT			
Voluntary paid overtime			
Challenging work with a sense of achievement			
Autonomy on manner of undertaking tasks			
Employee share ownership scheme			

a. Record all three lists, and together compare and discuss your rankings.
b. Do any of the rankings surprise you or your colleagues?
c. To what extent do you think you would enjoy working together?

Personal skills and employability exercise

Objectives

Completing this exercise should help you to enhance the following skills:

- Review the nature of, and influences on, motivation to work.
- Take account of individual needs and expectations at work.
- Reflect upon your perceptions about the motives of other people.

Exercise – working in conjunction with a partner

1 FIRST, you each list, as far as possible in rank order, the specific needs and expectations that are most important to you as an individual. (Do *not* include basic physiological needs such as to satisfy thirst or hunger, or a *minimal* standard of accommodation.) Explain, briefly, to what extent these needs and expectations were met currently by any work experience that you have had – even a short-term or part-time job – and/or to what extent you anticipate they will be met by your future career ambitions. Exchange accounts with your partner before proceeding further.

2 NOW, you each describe fully two recent situations in which you felt:
(i) highly motivated, enthusiastic; and
(ii) when you lacked enthusiasm, felt half-hearted and found it difficult to put in much effort.
Both you and your partner attempt to interpret the events of both situations with possible reasons for the other person's behaviour, needs and motivation.

3 NEXT, refer back to Blanchard's eight critical employee needs described in the text of this chapter: meaningful work, collaboration, fairness, autonomy, recognition, growth, connectedness with leaders and connectedness with colleagues. Attempt to place in rank order the importance of each of these needs. Discuss with your partner, with supporting reasons where possible.

4 THEN, discuss together what conclusions you draw from this exercise, and what you have each learnt about work motivation.

Discussion

- How difficult was it to avoid generalisations about what motivates other people?
- In your discussions, how far were you able to distance your own motivations?
- To what extent can you relate responses to underlying theories of motivation?

Case study
Managers and motivation

Most people who work in an organisational setting find that, apart from their immediate colleagues, their line manager is perhaps the most significant influence on their life at work. Relationships with the immediate boss can affect individuals' performance, motivation and engagement with organisational aims and objectives, and because these managers usually work in close proximity with their staff, their strengths and limitations are often very visible. Almost everyone will have an opinion about their boss, who is likely to be somewhere in the middle between the team with its day-to-day tasks and those senior managers who make the big, strategic decisions. What exactly does it feel like to be a middle manager, and what are the challenges and rewards for those who put themselves in the managerial front line?

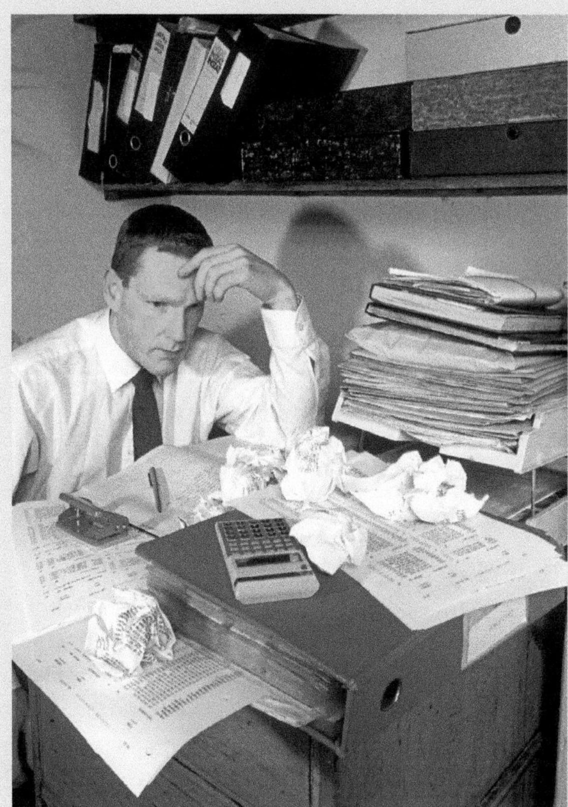

Are middle managers stressed out by bureaucracy and organisational politics, or inspired by their role and prospects?

Source: © Paul Ridsdale/Photofusion Picture Library

Middle managers: telling it like it is

In 2006 *Management Today* published the results of a survey into the experiences of middle managers.[60] Part of its purpose was to match a similar survey of top business leaders, which had taken place six months earlier, and to discover more about the role and nature of mid-ranking managers, many of whom might not have the ambition to become chief executives or captains of industry, but upon whom most organisations depend for the regular delivery of core activities. Over 1,000 managers took part in the survey, representing both public- and private-sector organisations, and a good 40 per cent of respondents were women. Some of the headline figures demonstrated a strong sense of job satisfaction, and in answer to a question about whether, if they had their time again, they would choose to become a manager, 92 per cent of respondents answered that they had not regretted their choice. A small majority, 54 per cent, were not actively seeking promotion and a significant majority, almost 69 per cent, did not want to step into their own boss's job. Clearly the picture here was one of broad satisfaction with the work and the nature of their managerial role. However, 43 per cent felt that they were not valued.

The survey seemed to highlight a number of common reasons why managers enjoyed their work. Chief among these were the following:

- Influence and achievement - the ability to see themselves making positive contributions to the organisation and the way it worked. A significant 88 per cent of those surveyed said that this was one of the strongest motivating factors for them.
- Autonomy - 79 per cent considered that a relative degree of autonomy was also a source of satisfaction. The managers who were happiest in their work were those whose own bosses were able to allow them a relatively free rein.
- Developing people - again, almost 80 per cent of the managers considered that their role in developing others, helping people to achieve better levels of performance and encouraging newer or younger workers to be a major source of work-related pleasure.

Things that managers reported as being de-motivating and that frustrated them in their jobs were the following:

- Bureaucracy - 48 per cent cited excessive and bureaucratic systems as being what they disliked most about their work.
- Pressure to do more with less - this was often what stressed managers most. As customers and clients

→

become more demanding, the lack of resources, coupled with increasing spans of control, were clearly putting managers under significant strain.

- Politics – 45 per cent of the survey respondents believed that office politics was damaging to their organisations.

There were some marked differences of opinion about how the question of organisational politics should be approached; one manager who was interviewed in detail for the *Management Today* report considered it was something that had to be understood and handled, but others were very critical of the sort of behaviour that caused different units or departments of (mostly larger) organisations to become close-knit and focused on protecting their own interests, often at the expense of overall organisational success. This problem surfaced again in 2007 when another CMI survey reported that 44 per cent of senior managers felt they were diverted from work by internal politics.[61]

Leading isn't easy

Becoming a manager means, for many, a significant change in role and perspective, and the transition causes a number of common problems for those who find themselves in 'the middle'. One aspect of their managerial work that many reported as problematic was the need to learn effective delegation, and to become a leader rather than a 'doer'. One respondent from Hewlett Packard illustrated this point:

> *When I first became a manager, I tried to do everything myself, my old job plus my new responsibilities, but I soon realised this was a mistake.*

She also noted that being judged on the success of her team, rather than on her individual performance, was difficult to get used to. This related to another problem – the difficulty of identifying and dealing with underperforming staff. While workers might believe their colleagues to be lazy, they also clearly felt that managers were not doing enough to tackle matters of poor performance.[62]

As Ruth Spellman, Chief Executive of IIP, observed in her commentary on the findings:

> *It is clear from the findings that UK managers are aware that dead wood is a problem that can damage their organisation – but are failing to do anything about it. However, left unchecked . . . [it] . . . can breed resentment amongst colleagues and cripple an organisation's productivity.*[63]

On the other hand, if this is set against the complaints of micro-management that many employees voiced, it becomes clear that the delicate balance between effective monitoring and interference is a difficult one to achieve.

Another common theme running through the *Management Today* and the CMI surveys was that of middle-manager stress. This arises partly from the causes highlighted above, but also from the ambiguity that often surrounds the role. Middle managers might be pivotal to the actual running of the day-to-day activities of the organisation, but while they are accountable to senior people who are often the strategic decision-makers, they are also embroiled in the minutiae of daily work. This results in two very different sets of demands from two different directions. A 2010 study by the mental health charity Mind found that the level of stress-related absence among middle managers was reportedly double that of company directors, with 29 per cent of those surveyed saying that they had lost their temper with colleagues, and 25 per cent reporting that they had cried at work. A contributory factor was certainly the amount of unpaid overtime, which seems to be the lot of the middle manager, and issues of work/life balance are problematic for them:[64]

> *middle managers are least satisfied with their work-life balance, most likely to say they are under excessive pressure every day, and also most likely to be looking for a new job. They also have least job security, with nearly one in three thinking it likely they could lose their job as a result of the economic downturn.*[65]

In some cases, managers felt not only that the additional stresses of taking on a managerial workload removed them from the work they enjoyed as specialists, but also that the additional pay was scarcely adequate to compensate for the added pressure. One respondent noted that:

> *There's only £2k difference in a managerial role pay and an analyst below, but the workload increases by 45%.*[66]

Similarly, while middle managers are the key players in organisational change and development, they report that they often find themselves driving through initiatives that have been developed and determined by those above them in the organisation, who are sometimes those who lack recent knowledge of the realities of life on the front line.

But what does the team think?

Finally, what do staff think about their managers? In its winter 2014–15 'Employee Outlook' survey, which focused on managers,[67] the Chartered Institute of Personnel and Development (CIPD) noted that, on the whole, employees are quite positive about their immediate managers, with 67 per cent of respondents reporting satisfactory relationships with their line manager. In particular, employees were happy that they were treated fairly (69 per cent), received support when they had problems (65 per cent), that their suggestions were listened to (64 per cent) and were clear about what was expected of them (61 per cent). They were less content with discussion of training and development (only 36 per cent of respondents reported that line managers talked with them about training needs) and even fewer (30 per cent) reported that they received coaching on the job.

The quality of the relationship with line managers can also be seen to underpin levels of employee commitment and engagement.

> *Both positive line manager behaviours and satisfaction with the relationship with the supervisor are positively associated with employees being motivated by their organisation's core purpose.*[68]

This echoes findings by *Purcell* and others, who discovered that the line manager's ability to consult staff, then communicate and explain decisions in a way that treats them respectfully, is an important factor in creating the sense of fairness that, in turn, supported engagement.[69]

So, however managers are feeling about their own work, one thing is clear: they continue to have a major influence on the way in which employees think about their jobs and the motivation and commitment they show towards the organisation where they work. And perhaps that is the most important finding of all.

Tasks

1 Using *either* the achievement motivation theory of McClelland *or* Porter and Lawler's expectancy model as the basis for your analysis, explain what might motivate someone to take on a line manager or supervisory role in an organisation for which they have worked for some time as a team member.

2 What are the main elements of job satisfaction that managers appear to experience? Which are most important, and why? What are the major frustrations, and how do you think a manager should deal with them?

3 To what extent do the results of the CIPD employee survey of winter 2014–15 indicate the motivational effect of job enrichment?

4 What lessons could managers take from the Hackman and Oldham model (Figure 7.15) of job enrichment, and how could a line manager use these ideas to improve employee commitment and engagement at work?

Notes and references

1. Krech, D., Crutchfield, R. S. and Ballachey, E. L. *Individual in Society,* McGraw-Hill (1962).
2. Mitchell, T. R. 'Motivation: New Directions for Theory, Research, and Practice', *Academy of Management Review,* vol. 7, no. 1, 1982, pp. 80–8.
3. 'Motivating Your Employees in a Time of Change', Checklist 068, Chartered Management Institute, August 2012.
4. Kreitner, R., Kinicki, A. and Buelens, M. *Organizational Behaviour,* first European edition, McGraw-Hill (1999).
5. Farren, C. 'Mastery: The Critical Advantage', in Chowdhury, S. (ed.) *Management 21C,* Financial Times Prentice Hall (2000), p. 95.
6. Weaver, T. 'Theory M: Motivating with Money', *Cornell HRA Quarterly,* vol. 29, no. 3, 1988, pp. 40–5.
7. Chamorro-Premuzic, T. and Fagan, P. 'Money Talks, But Do People Still Listen?', *Management Today,* November 2014, pp. 50–3.
8. See, for example, Rudolph, P. A. and Kleiner, B. H. 'The Art of Motivating Employees', *Journal of Managerial Psychology,* vol. 4, no. 5, 1989, pp. i–iv.
9. Sauermann, H. and Cohen, W. M. 'What Makes Them Tick? Employee Motives and Firm Innovation', Working Paper 1443, National Bureau of Economic Research. © 2008 Henry Sauermann and Wesley M. Cohen.
10. Gratton, L. *Hot Spots,* Financial Times Prentice Hall (2007), p. 133; Blanchard, K. 'Do you get passionate at work?', *Manager, The British Journal of Administrative Management,* Autumn 2011, p. 26.
11. Waller, D. 'Are You What You Do?', *Management Today,* October 2008, pp. 42–6.
12. Kets de Vries, M. 'Beyond Sloan: Trust is at the core of corporate values', in Pickford, J. (ed.) *Financial Times Mastering Management 2.0,* Financial Times Prentice Hall (2001), pp. 267–70.

13. Blanchard, K. 'Do you get passionate at work?', *Manager, The British Journal of Administrative Management,* Autumn 2011, p. 26.
14. For a fuller discussion, see Mullins, L. J. and Dossor, P. *Hospitality Management and Organisational Behaviour,* fifth edition, Pearson Education (2013).
15. Stewart, H. *The Happy Manifesto: Make Your Organisation a Great Place to Work – Now,* Happy (2012); see also Stewart, H. 'How to have a happy and productive office', *Management Today,* February 2012, pp. 38–41.
16. Maslow, A. H. 'A Theory of Human Motivation', *Psychological Review,* 50, July 1943, pp. 370–96; and Maslow, A. H. *Motivation and Personality,* third edition, Harper and Row (1987).
17. Steers, R. M. and Porter, L. W. *Motivation and Work Behaviour,* fifth edition, McGraw-Hill (1991).
18. Saunders, A. 'Keep Staff Sweet', *Management Today,* June 2003, p. 75.
19. Adair, J. *Leadership and Motivation,* Kogan Page (2006).
20. Alderfer, C. P. *Existence, Relatedness and Growth,* Collier Macmillan (1972).
21. Nohria, N., Groysberg, B. and Lee, L.-E. 'Employee Motivation: A Powerful New Model', *Harvard Business Review,* vol. 86, July 2008, pp. 78–84.
22. Herzberg, F., Mausner, B. and Snyderman, B. B. *The Motivation to Work,* second edition, Chapman and Hall (1959).
23. Crainer, S. and Dearlove, D. (eds) *Financial Times Handbook of Management,* second edition, Financial Times Prentice Hall (2001), p. 361.
24. McClelland, D. C. *Human Motivation,* Cambridge University Press (1988).
25. For examples of pictures, see Osland, J. S., Kolb, D. A. and Rubin, I. M. *Organizational Behaviour: An Experimental Approach,* seventh edition, Prentice Hall (2001).
26. McClelland, D. C. and Burnham, D. H. 'Power Is the Great Motivation', *Harvard Business Review,* vol. 54, March–April 1976, pp. 100–10.
27. Vroom, V. H. *Work and Motivation,* Wiley (1964); also published by Krieger (1982).
28. Porter, L. W. and Lawler, E. E. *Managerial Attitudes and Performance,* Irwin (1968).
29. Lawler, E. E. *Motivation in Work Organizations,* Brooks/Cole (1973).
30. Lundin, S., Paul, H. and Christensen, J. *Fish: A Remarkable Way to Boost Morale and Improve Results,* Hyperion Press (2001), p. 37.
31. CIPD 'Strategic reward and total reward', CIPD Factsheet, Chartered Institute of Personnel and Development, March 2014.
32. Adams, J. S. 'Injustice in Social Exchange', in Berkowitz, L. (ed.) *Advances in Experimental and Social Psychology,* Academic Press (1965); also abridged in Steers, R. M. and Porter, L. W. *Motivation and Work Behavior,* second edition, McGraw-Hill (1979), pp. 107–24.
33. Werner, G., Schmittberger, R. and Schwarze, B. 'An Experimental Analysis of Ultimatum Bargaining', *Journal of Economic Behavior and Organization,* vol. 3, no. 4, 1982, pp. 367–88.
34. Locke, E. A. 'Towards a Theory of Task Motivation and Incentives', *Organizational Behavior and Human Performance,* vol. 3, 1968, pp. 157–89.
35. Locke, E. A. 'Personal Attitudes and Motivation', *Annual Review of Psychology,* vol. 26, 1975, pp. 457–80.
36. Gratton, L. Living Strategy: Putting People at the Heart of Corporate Purpose, Financial Times Prentice Hall (2000), p. 193.
37. Hannagan, T. *Management,* fourth edition, Financial Times Prentice Hall (2005), p. 363.
38. 'Motivating Your Staff in a Time of Change', Management Checklist 068, Chartered Management Institute, August 2012.
39. Adair, J. *Leadership and Motivation,* Kogan Page (2006), p. 38.
40. See, for example, Cheng, T., Sculli, D. and Chan, F. S. 'Relationship Dominance – Rethinking Management Theories from the Perspective of Methodological Relationalism', *Journal of Managerial Psychology,* vol. 16, no. 2, 2001, pp. 97–105.
41. Francesco, A. M. and Gold, B. A. *International Organizational Behavior,* second edition, Pearson Prentice Hall (2005), p. 126.
42. Adler, N. J. *International Aspects of Organizational Behaviour,* third edition, South Western College Publishing (1997).
43. Luthans, F. and Kreitner, R. *Organisational Behavior Modification and Beyond,* second edition, Scott Foresman (1985), p. 36.
44. Stajkovic, A. D. and Luthans, F. 'Differential Effects of Incentive Motivators on Work Performance', *Academy of Management Journal,* vol. 44, no. 3, 2001, pp. 580–90.
45. Luthans, F., Stajkovic, A., Luthans, B. C. and Luthans, K. W. 'Applying Behavioral Management in Eastern Europe', *European Management Journal,* vol. 16, no. 4, 1998, pp. 466–74.
46. Tampoe, M. 'Knowledge Workers – The New Management Challenge', *Professional Manager,* November 1994, pp. 12–13.
47. Whitmore, Sir J. 'Breaking Down the Barriers to Management Creativity', *Manager, The British Journal of Administrative Management,* May/June 2002, pp. 24–6.
48. Matson, E. and Prusak, L. 'Boosting the productivity of knowledge workers', *Management Services,* vol. 57, no. 2, 2013, pp. 14–15.
49. Goffee, R. and Jones, G. 'How to harness the special talents of Clever People', *Management Today,* September 2009, pp. 56–60.

50. See, for example, Brown, J. A. C. *The Social Psychology of Industry*, Penguin (1954 and 1986).
51. Reeves, R. 'Reality Bites', *Management Today*, May 2003, p. 37.
52. Worrall, L. and Cooper, C. 'The Quality of Working Life 2007', Chartered Management Institute, October 2007.
53. Stern, S. 'My Generation', *Management Today*, March 2008, pp. 40–6.
54. De Vita, E. 'Best Fit,' *Management Today*, September 2008, pp. 54–8.
55. For the full list see **www.dailymail.co.uk/happiest_jobs** (accessed 22 March 2014).
56. Marx, K. 'The Notion of Alienation', in Coser, L. A. and Rosenburg, B. *Sociological Theory*, Collier Macmillan (1969), pp. 505–10.
57. Blauner, R. *Alienation and Freedom*, University of Chicago Press (1964).
58. Hackman, J. R. and Oldham, G. R. *Work Redesign*, Addison-Wesley (1980).
59. Roe, R. A., Zinovieva, I. L., Dienes, E. and Ten Horn, L. A. 'A Comparison of Work Motivation in Bulgaria, Hungary and the Netherlands: Test of a Model', *Applied Psychology: An International Review*, vol. 49, 2000, pp. 658–87.
60. Kennett, M. 'View from the Middle', *Management Today*, March 2006.
61. Peacock, L. 'Senior executives struggling to manage their workloads', *Personnel Today*, 2 November 2007.
62. BBC News, 19 August 2006, 'Staff brand colleagues as "lazy"', **http://news.bbc.co.uk** (accessed 23 February 2015).
63. IIP Press Release, 19 August 2005.
64. Waller, D. 'Stress hits middle managers the hardest', *Management Today*, 21 December 2010.
65. CIPD, *Employee Outlook Winter 2011–12*, p. 17, **www.cipd.co.uk** (accessed 23 February 2015).
66. Kennett, M. 'View from the Middle', op. cit., pp. 35–42.
67. CIPD, *Employee Outlook Winter 2014–15*, **www.cipd.co.uk** (accessed 23 February 2015).
68. Ibid., p. 4.
69. Purcell, J. 'Time to focus on employee voice as a prime antecedent of engagement: Rediscovering the black box', *The Future of Engagement Thought Piece Collection*, Institute for Employment Studies (2014).

Academic viewpoint

Below you will find the title and abstract of a recent article in an academic journal that explores a topic relevant to the chapters in Part 2.

Timming, A. R. 'Visible tattoos in the service sector: A new challenge to recruitment and selection', *Work, Employment and Society*, vol. 29, no. 1, 2015, pp. 60–78. doi: 10.1177/0950017014528402

Abstract

Drawing on 25 in-depth interviews with hiring managers and visibly tattooed respondents, this article explores the nature of prejudice surrounding body art in the service sector. It focuses on the impact of visible tattoos on employment chances. The study reveals a predominantly negative effect on selection, but the extent of employer prejudice is mitigated by: where the tattoo is located on the body; the organization or industry type; proximity of the role to customers; and the genre of the tattoo. Employer prejudice against tattoos is also driven largely by hiring managers' perceptions of consumer expectations regarding body art in the workplace.

Commentary

Andrew Timming notes that body art such as tattoos and piercings are becoming an increasingly popular and therefore common means of self-adornment among young people in Western societies. In particular he is concerned to investigate the degree to which visible tattoos - those on the face, arms or hands, for instance - have an impact on the way in which workers in the service sector are viewed by colleagues, managers and customers. This in turn is likely to affect their job prospects and relationships in the workplace. He explains that while anthropological studies of tattoos and body art are common, it is rare as a subject of employment-related research, and that attitudes to body art in the workplace, especially when they are hostile, could be examined as a form of prejudice and discrimination. The stigma arises from the perceived relationship between tattooing and anti-social behaviour. The study is based on a small number of case histories and examines managerial attitudes to

→

the tattooed subjects. It analyses the attitudes of hiring managers in relation to their personal views, their views about the expectation of customers and the way that these two might act together to disadvantage the prospects of a visibly tattooed job applicant.

The article might prompt you to consider some of the following questions

- Should recruiting managers take into account visible tattoos and other forms of body art when hiring people for customer-facing jobs?
- Is such body art likely to be more acceptable in certain industries and organisations than others, and does the nature of the tattoo itself make a difference? The article contrasts attitudes towards images of butterflies or flowers and those of politically loaded symbols such as swastikas.
- Should those with visible tattoos be included as a legally protected category with regard to workplace discrimination?
- Are you likely to be more favourably disposed to someone with a tattoo if you have one yourself?

Part 2 Case study

Philanthropy: the resurgence of personal social responsibility?

Something rather spectacular happened on 26 June 2006: Warren Buffett, then the world's second wealthiest man, announced that he intended to give 85 per cent of his fortune to the Bill and Melinda Gates Foundation. There, it will join the billions that Bill Gates, the world's wealthiest man, has already pledged, to make an enormous sum of money to support good works around the world. A few months earlier, Anita Roddick, who founded and built up Body Shop International, had announced her intention to give away half of her fortune. Philanthropy has long been a noble and admirable part of the capitalist tradition and seemed to be back in the news.

Why is this sort of philanthropy of interest to students of organisational behaviour? Several reasons can be suggested:

- Firstly, of course, the wealth that is given away is often the result of setting up and running an organisation that successfully fulfils its purpose over a long period: the profits that flow to the owner result from customers choosing and paying for its output.
- Also, the generosity of wealthy individuals makes an interesting contrast with the more familiar concept of 'corporate social responsibility', which sometimes involves donations of company, rather than personal, money.
- The charitable foundations, together with their external relationships, are of interest in their own right

The word 'philanthropy' is derived from the Greek and is defined as 'love of humankind; the disposition or effort to promote the happiness of and well-being of one's fellow-people'.[1] The practice of philanthropy was well established before that of capitalism of course, but the early stages of the growth of the US economy saw a significant surge in the social custom of philanthropy. Although it may have been no part of their aim, the names of some of the USA's most significant philanthropists are as well known for their giving as for the business careers that made the money. Two celebrated examples from the same era provide a view of the way a philanthropic life can be lived.

From Carnegie and Rockefeller to Bill and Melinda Gates

Andrew Carnegie (1835–1919) was born in Dunfermline, Scotland. He was the son of a weaver and the family emigrated to the USA in 1848. Like many at that time, Carnegie started work at the age of 13 doing a number of jobs until 1865, when he started his own business. This was to become the foundation of the steel industry in Pittsburgh and the origin of Carnegie's fortune. At the turn of the new century, Carnegie sold the business for $480 million and spent the rest of his life devoted to his philanthropic interests. These were diverse, but centred around the theme of the provision of public libraries and education.[2] Over his life, Carnegie gave away more than $350 million (multiply by about twenty for today's values). Some of the quotes attributed to him[3] show the combination of hard-nosed business acumen and the strong sense of social duty that characterises this type of philanthropist:

> *And while the law of competition may be sometimes hard for the individual, it is best for the race, because it ensures the survival of the fittest in every department.*

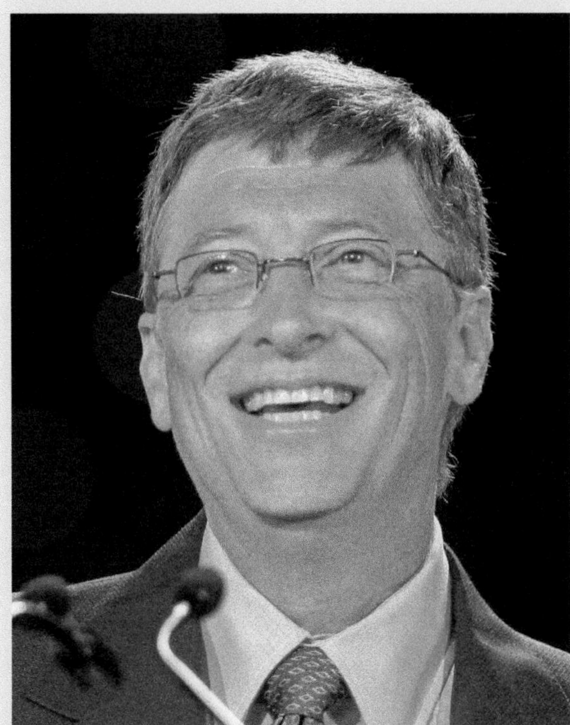

Bill Gates and his wife set up the Bill and Melinda Gates Foundation with part of the personal fortune he had earned from the success of Microsoft
Source: Adrian Wyld/AP/Press Association Images

> *Surplus wealth is a sacred trust which its possessor is bound to administer in his lifetime for the good of the community.*
>
> *I would as soon leave my son a curse as the almighty dollar.*

As will be seen, similar sentiments and values continue to motivate today's philanthropists.

John D. Rockefeller (1839–1937) was born in the USA to a farming family. In his business career, he founded and developed the Standard Oil Company, which became the leading force in the fast-growing oil industry. At the age of 57, Rockefeller decided that he should step aside from the day-to-day leadership of Standard Oil and devote himself to philanthropy. This had been important to him from his early life, but also because of his religious convictions and his approach to finance:

> *I believe it is every man's religious duty to get all he can honestly and to give all he can.*

Like Carnegie, his philanthropic interests centred on education, with substantial donations to found and develop universities and research institutes, as well as the establishment of trusts and foundations for the improvement of education at all levels. Over his life, he gave away some $550 million.[4] Again, some of the quotes attributed to the man[5] show a mixture of hard-headedness and generosity that is far from sentimental:

> *Charity is injurious unless it helps the recipient to become independent of it.*
>
> *I believe that every right implies a responsibility; every opportunity, an obligation; every possession, a duty.*

Both Carnegie and Rockefeller were members of the group of very powerful US business giants in the late 1800s known by some as 'robber barons'. John Kampfner's 2014 book[6] about the super-rich through history finds familiar themes in their behaviour, including their notable involvement in philanthropy later in their lives. For him, the educational foundations, art galleries and concert galleries are as much about 'reputation laundering' as philanthropy, something that has characterised the behaviour of the super-rich over the ages. In his view:

> *Wealth rarely buys peace of mind. The super-rich are consumed by what happens next. They fear for their legacies and for their children. Will the money they have made be safe in their hands? Will the standing they have acquired in society be frittered away? Will statues be cast in their image?*
>
> *They want to be remembered for more than making a fortune. What matters to them most is reputation.*
>
> *(Kampfner 2014, Prologue)*

Not everyone would share this level of cynicism about the motives of the givers, of course, but there is often a tension between the means through which fortunes are amassed and the great works that are funded by the philanthropy.

The emerging philanthropists of the twenty-first century have often made their money through businesses that were not even heard of in the lifetimes of Carnegie and Rockefeller. Bill Gates, for example, is one of the founders of the enormously successful Microsoft Corporation, whose information products are about as far from steel and oil as can be imagined. This case is mainly concerned with the Bill and Melinda Gates Foundation (BMGF), which was established in 1997 with an initial gift from the two founders.[7] It grew rapidly from 1999: in a list published in 2014[8] it was by a significant margin the largest foundation in the USA, in terms of both value of assets (about $37 billion at the end of 2012) and total giving (about $3 billion in year ending 2012). By 2014, total grants from the BMGF since its inception had grown to almost $33 billion and the organisation employed more than 1,200 people in eight locations

(Seattle, Washington DC, Delhi, Beijing and London, together with three offices in Africa: Addis Ababa, Abuja and Johannesburg).[9]

The organisation is organised around its four main priorities, which are: global development; global health; global policy and advocacy; and US programmes. In a letter published on the BMGF website,[10] Bill and Melinda Gates explain their aims in respect of global health, pointing out that health is fundamental to economic development:

> *Our friend and co-trustee Warren Buffett once gave us some great advice about philanthropy: 'Don't just go for safe projects,' he said. 'Take on the really tough problems.'*
>
> *We couldn't agree more. Our foundation is teaming up with partners around the world to take on some tough problems: extreme poverty and poor health in developing countries, the failures of America's education system. We focus on only a few issues because we think that's the best way to have great impact, and we focus on these issues in particular because we think they are the biggest barriers that prevent people from making the most of their lives.*
>
> *For each issue we work on, we fund innovative ideas that could help remove these barriers: new techniques to help farmers in developing countries grow more food and earn more money; new tools to prevent and treat deadly diseases; new methods to help students and teachers in the classroom. Some of the projects we fund will fail. We not only accept that, we expect it – because we think an essential role of philanthropy is to make bets on promising solutions that governments and businesses can't afford to make. As we learn which bets pay off, we have to adjust our strategies and share the results so everyone can benefit.*
>
> *We're both optimists. We believe by doing these things – focusing on a few big goals and working with our partners on innovative solutions – we can help every person get the chance to live a healthy, productive life.*

In the world of business, as opposed to philanthropic foundations, there has been growing interest in recent years in the subject of corporate governance: what the business is aiming to do and how it can be sure that its actions are consistent with those aims. It has been common for wealthy individuals to adopt a corporate format in making good works happen, often by setting up and then directing a dedicated foundation to look after both the strategic and operational aspects of the task. This seems to acknowledge the benefits of the corporate approach in terms of efficiency and the ability to recruit and apply specialist skills, while still retaining control by the founder or the founding family. It is also easy to appreciate how focused and effective such an organisation can be in pursuing the goals of the founder, and to acknowledge the possibility that an effective philanthropic foundation may be at least as effective as, say, a government or international agency.

As will already be clear, some of the world's philanthropic foundations have multinational corporation-sized (even government-sized) budgets, meaning that the issue of governance is rightly of some concern to the society within which these organisations operate. One does not need to be a fan of James Bond movies to appreciate that very rich individuals using their wealth to pursue their private aims is not in itself guaranteed to be in the general interest.

In fact, foundations often go to some lengths to communicate their values and aims publicly. For example, the BMGF website sets out some key principles in the section 'Who We Are', whose subheadings are as follows:[11]

- We seek to unlock the possibility inside every individual.
- We are focused on the areas of greatest need, on the ways in which we can do the most good.
- We are focused on results. Those that can be measured. And those measured in ways beyond numbers.
- We seek to drive change on a global scale.
- We are impatient optimists.

Warren Buffett and Anita Roddick

Warren Buffett's fortune was made through the Berkshire Hathaway organisation, which for many years has been very successful in providing investment management services for its clients. Buffett himself is famously moderate in his lifestyle, with a liking for a diet of burgers and Cherry Coke. His extraordinary wealth was recently augmented by his firm decision not to get involved in the late 1990s dotcom boom and subsequent bust: his policy has always been to concentrate on business fundamentals and to invest for the long term. He also has a long-standing reputation for pithy quotes and one attributed remark seemed to sum up the chaos caused by the collapse of rapid stock market growth and the series of corporate scandals that followed:

> *It's only when the tide goes out that you can see who's been swimming without their trunks on.*

From remarks made by Buffett since the announcement of his association with the BMGF,[12] it seems clear that he had been thinking about an involvement in philanthropy for some time. Some of his motivation is bound up with the American tradition of philanthropy by wealthy individuals, including the notion that there is something problematic about the idea that huge wealth should result from accidents of birth. As he has suggested, children should be left wealthy enough to do anything, but not enough to do nothing. He had also become very impressed by the approach taken by the BMGF and by Bill and Melinda themselves; the announcement coincided with that of the succession plans for Gates's leadership of Microsoft, which allowed Gates to devote more time to the BMGF. Buffett has become a trustee of the BMGF and jokingly promised at the launch not to assess Gates's efforts more than once a day. At the same meeting, both men acknowledged the inspirational value that the news of the donation could have: one questioner suggested that the success of organisations like the BMGF could do much to improve public confidence in charitable donation in general and perhaps increase the willingness of a far wider spectrum of people to give. Since 2010, Gates and Buffett have also turned their attention to persuading other very rich people to give their wealth away through their Giving Pledge campaign.[13] One notable feature of the annual Forbes Magazine list of the world's dollar billionaires[14] has been the arrival of more and more very wealthy people from the fast-emerging BRIC economies (e.g. the 2014 list showed three Brazilians in the top 100, along with six Russians, five Indians and nine from China/Hong Kong). It will be interesting to see how the practice of philanthropy develops in these and other emerging economies, where cultural traditions may differ from the West and where the local needs are often urgent.

The decision by the late UK entrepreneur Anita Roddick to join the ranks of business-based philanthropists adds some interesting features to the discussion. Roddick was something of a business celebrity for much of her career, having founded and built up the very successful Body Shop International, a business whose market appeal was always strongly centred on the values of its founder. Its campaigns against animal testing of cosmetics and in favour of fair trade, for example, became prominent during the 1990s. Explaining that she did not want to die rich, Roddick announced at the end of 2005[15] that she intended to give away half her £100 million fortune, much of which resulted from the sale of her business to L'Oreal. Sadly, she died suddenly aged just 64 in September 2007, but the Roddick Foundation survives her.[16]

In her lifetime, Anita Roddick was often sharply critical of some aspects of business life in the UK, especially where attitudes seemed to her to be selfish and

The world's most generous man? In 2006 Warren Buffet, the world's second wealthiest man, promised to give 85 per cent of his fortune to support good works around the world

Source: Seth Wenig/AP/Press Association Images

short-termist. But, in her view, the rich had to look after the poor, and:

> *I don't think in our society we have any understanding of that.*

A BBC article[17] commented at the time that personal philanthropy was less prominent in the UK than in the USA, possibly because people in the UK regard it as a government responsibility to look after the poor, with projects financed from general taxation and with additional contributions from companies under the heading of 'corporate social responsibility'. This is not to suggest that government programmes and corporate donations are by any means unimportant in the USA, but rather to emphasise how unusual personal philanthropy has been in the UK. However, one recent initiative in the UK made its appeal to people on ordinary incomes, rather than the world's billionaires. The organisation Giving What We Can[18] seeks pledgers to donate 10 per cent of personal incomes and offers guidance on the most cost-effective charities. As it points out, significant impacts can be made by donations at this level over the long term.

Corporate versus personal philanthropy

Many large businesses in the UK have made significant donations to charity from corporate funds, which may be partly motivated by a desire for approval from some stakeholder groups. As such, corporate philanthropy – and corporate social responsibility in general – has come in for criticism from some quarters, on the basis that it amounts to acts of generosity using other people's money (specifically, that of the shareholders, who own

the company). The economist Milton Friedman forcefully suggested for some decades that business should get on with the business of business: making money for its owners through successfully marketing products and services within the law. From this point of view, donations to charity by individuals making choices about their own funds are more desirable than acts of corporate generosity using other people's funds. In reality, public opinion seems to be sympathetic towards the idea of corporate donations to charity, whatever scepticism may sometimes be expressed about motives. However, from any reasonable point of view, there remains an important difference between giving personally and approving corporate gifts: the difference perhaps, between signing your own, rather than a company, cheque.

At the BMGF conference mentioned above, Bill Gates alluded to the celebrated work of Adam Smith, the Scottish economist who first explained the general benefits of free markets in identifying and providing for needs effectively and efficiently. From these ideas have come the modern economies that provided the context in which organisations such as Microsoft, Berkshire Hathaway and Body Shop International can generate large amounts of wealth, mainly through providing products and services that are attractive enough to cause people to choose to spend their own money on them. In short, this is the main reason why recent generations have in most cases been richer than their predecessors. The tradition of philanthropy on the part of wealthy individuals is by no means contrary to the desirability of free and fierce competition; rather, wealth generation and philanthropy can only go hand in hand.

What is generally less well known about Adam Smith is his significant contribution to moral philosophy. Perhaps the way to bring this discussion to a close is with a quote from the beginning of Adam Smith's *Theory of Moral Sentiments*, which was highlighted by Bill Gates in explaining the basic importance of philanthropy.

Anita Roddick, founder of the Body Shop, who built a business based on caring values, gave half of her wealth away.

Source: Jean/Empics Entertainment/Press Association Images

> *How selfish soever man may be supposed, there are evidently some principles in his nature which interest him in the fortune of others and render their happiness necessary to him though he derives nothing from it except the pleasure of seeing it.*

Philanthropic foundations are organisations that are interesting in their own right, in respect of the origin of their funds, in their interaction with other types of organisation and, of course, in the effects they have on the societies within which they operate.

Tasks

1. Not all successful business leaders become renowned philanthropists like Gates, Roddick and others. Using concepts from Chapter 4 as the basis for your analysis, suggest which aspects of individual personality might explain why some do and others do not.
2. Philanthropic foundations have often been created to transfer knowledge and skills from their countries of origin to people living in parts of the developing world. What challenges might those who work for such organisations face in achieving this task, and how could theories of learning help them?
3. To some extent, philanthropic foundations are engaged in the same types of social projects as government agencies. How might approaches to employee motivation differ between the two types of organisation? What could either type of organisation usefully learn from the other?

Notes and references

1 *New Shorter Oxford English Dictionary* (1993).
2 **http://www.carnegie.org/sub/about/biography.html** (accessed 23 February 2015).
3 **http://www.brainyquote.com/quotes/authors/a/andrew_carnegie.html** (accessed 23 February 2015).
4 **http://www.notablebiographies.com/Pu-Ro/Rockefeller-John-D.html** (accessed 23 February 2015).
5 **http://www.brainyquote.com/quotes/authors/j/john_d_rockefeller.html** (accessed 23 February 2015).
6 Kampfner, J. *The Rich – From Slaves to Super-Yachts: A 2000-Year History*, Little Brown (2014).
7 **http://www.gatesfoundation.org/about/Pages/foundation-timeline.aspx** (accessed 23 February 2015).
8 **http://foundationcenter.org/findfunders/topfunders/top100assets.html** (accessed 23 February 2015).
9 **http://www.gatesfoundation.org/about/Pages/foundation-fact-sheet.aspx** (accessed 23 February 2015).
10 **www.gatesfoundation.org/Who-We-Are/General-Information/Letter-from-Bill-and-Melinda-Gates** (accessed 23 February 2015).
11 **http://www.gatesfoundation.org/who-we-are** (accessed 23 February 2015).
12 **http://www.nytimes.com/2006/06/27/business/27friends.html?_r=1&** (accessed 23 February 2015).
13 **http://givingpledge.org/** (accessed 23 February 2015).
14 **http://www.forbes.com/billionaires/list/#tab:overall** (accessed 23 February 2015).
15 **http://news.bbc.co.uk/1/hi/business/4524046.stm** (accessed 23 February 2015).
16 **http://www.theroddickfoundation.org/** (accessed 23 February 2015).
17 **http://news.bbc.co.uk/1/hi/business/4524046.stm** (accessed 23 February 2015).
18 **http://www.givingwhatwecan.org/** (accessed 23 February 2015).

CHAPTER 8
Working in groups and teams

Work is a group-based activity and if the organisation is to function effectively it requires collaboration and co-operation among its members. Most activities of the organisation require at least some degree of co-ordination through groups and teamwork. Understanding the nature, operation and impact of groups and teams is vital if the manager is to influence the behaviour and performance of people in the work situation.

Learning outcomes

After completing this chapter you should have enhanced your ability to:

- explain the nature and significance of work groups and teams;
- relate the nature of informal groups and importance of group values and norms;
- examine factors that influence group cohesiveness and performance;
- identify characteristics of an effective work group and virtual teams;
- explain role structure of the organisation and individual role relationships;
- evaluate individual compared with group or team performance;
- review the importance and characteristics of successful groups or teams.

Critical review and reflection

Self-interest and opportunism are natural features of human behaviour and will always take preference over the demands and best interests of the group or teamwork.

To what extent can YOU present a counter point of view? How far are YOU prepared to put the interests of a work group or team before YOUR own interests?

The importance and significance of groups

Groups are a characteristic of all social situations. Individuals seldom work in isolation from others. The work organisation and its sub-units are made up of groups of people. **Groups** are an essential feature of any organisation and almost every member of staff will belong to one or more groups. Although there is no single accepted definition, most people will readily understand what constitutes a group. The essential feature is that its members regard themselves as belonging to the group. A popular definition defines the group in psychological terms as:

> *any number of people who (1) interact with one another; (2) are psychologically aware of one another; and (3) perceive themselves to be a group.*[1]

Another useful way of defining a work group is a collection of people who share most, if not all, of the following characteristics:

- a definable membership;
- group consciousness;
- a sense of shared purpose;
- interdependence;
- interaction;
- ability to act in a unitary manner.[2]

Members of a group must co-operate in order for work to be carried out, and managers themselves will work within these groups. The working of groups and the influence they exert over their membership is an essential feature of management and organisational behaviour. People in groups influence each other in many ways and groups develop their own hierarchies and leaders. Group pressures can have a major influence over the behaviour of individual members and their work performance.

Peterson and colleagues discuss the importance of morale as an indicator of group well-being. The attention of positive psychology to promote good life (**discussed in Chapter** 1) should include not only individuals but also groups within which individuals live, work, love and play. Groups should be a primary focus of research into health and well-being.[3]

Groups and teams

The use of the word 'teams' has become increasingly fashionable in recent years. In common usage and literature, including in this book, there is a tendency for the terms 'groups' and 'teams' to be used interchangeably and based on personal preference. It is not easy to distinguish clearly between a group and a team. According to ACAS:

> *Teams have been around for as long as anyone can remember and there can be few organisations that have not used the term in one sense or another. It is common to hear of management teams, production teams, service teams or even whole organisations referred to as teams . . . The term 'team' is used loosely to describe many different groupings and a variety of labels are given to the types of teams . . . It is doubtful whether any definition of types of teams would be universally acceptable.*[4]

Holpp poses the question 'Why do you want teams?' While many people are still paying homage to teams, teamwork, empowerment and self-management, others have become disillusioned.

> *If teams are just a convenient way to group under one manager a lot of people who used to work for several downsized supervisors, don't bother. But if teams can truly take ownership of work areas and provide the kind of up-close knowledge that's unavailable elsewhere, then full speed ahead.*[5]

Cane suggests that organisations are sometimes unsure whether they have teams or simply groups of people working together.

> *It is certainly true to say that any group of people who do not know they are a team cannot be one. To become a team, a group of individuals needs to have a strong common purpose and to work towards that purpose rather than individually. They need also to believe that they will achieve more by co-operation than working individually.*[6]

Teamwork as a fashionable term

Belbin points out that to the extent that teamwork was becoming a fashionable term, it began to replace the more usual reference to groups and every activity was now being described as 'teamwork'. He questions whether it matters whether one is talking about groups or teams and maintains that the confusion in vocabulary should be addressed if the principles of good teamwork are to be retained. Belbin suggests there are several factors that characterise the difference between groups and teams (*see* Figure 8.1). The best differentiator is size: groups can comprise any number of people but teams are smaller with a membership between (ideally) four and six. The quintessential feature of a small, well-balanced team is that leadership is shared or rotates, whereas large groups typically throw up solo leaders.[7]

While acknowledging the work of Belbin, it appears that the term 'group' is often used in a more general sense and 'team' in a more specific context. We continue to refer to 'group' or 'team' according to the particular focus of attention and the vocabulary of the quoted authors. **Whereas all teams are, by definition, groups, it does not necessarily follow that all groups are teams.** The Chartered Management Institute maintains that a team is more than just a group of people who happen to work together.

> *It is a group of people working towards common goals and objectives and sharing responsibility for the outcomes. Team building is the process of selecting and grouping team members effectively and developing good working relationships and practices enabling the team to steer and develop the work and reach their goals. Increasingly, a team may be composed of people drawn from different functions, departments and disciplines whom have been brought together for a specific project.*[8]

	Team	Group
Size	Limited	Medium or large
Selection	Crucial	Immaterial
Leadership	Shared or rotating	Solo
Perception	Mutual knowledge understanding	Focus on leader
Style	Role-spread co-ordination	Convergence conformism
Spirit	Dynamic interaction	Togetherness persecution of opponents

Figure 8.1 Differences between a team and a group

Source: Belbin, R. M. *Beyond the Team*, Butterworth-Heinemann (2000). Copyright © 2000. Reproduced with permission from Belbin, www.belbin.com.

Whatever the debate on 'groups' or 'teams', what is clear is the increasing popularity of teamworking and the importance to organisations of effective group working or teamworking.

Critical review and reflection

It is almost impossible to distinguish clearly or in any meaningful way between work groups and teams. Attempting to do so is a vain, and pointless, quest. It is a waste of study time.

What is YOUR reaction to this assertion? How do YOU distinguish between a work group and team?

Formal and informal groups

Groups are formed as a consequence of the pattern of organisation structure and arrangements for the division of work, for example the grouping together of common activities into divisions or sections. **Formal groups** are created to achieve specific organisational objectives and are concerned with the **co-ordination of work activities.** People are brought together on the basis of defined roles within the structure of the organisation. The nature of the tasks to be undertaken is a predominant feature of the formal group. Goals are identified by management, and certain rules, relationships and norms of behaviour established.

Groups may result from the nature of technology employed and the way in which work is carried out, for example bringing together a number of people to carry out a sequence of operations on an assembly line. Groups may also develop when a number of people of the same level or status within the organisation see themselves as a group, for example departmental heads of an industrial organisation or chief officers of a local authority. Formal groups tend to be relatively permanent, although there may be changes in actual membership. However, temporary formal groups may also be created by management, as with, for example, the use of project teams in a matrix organisation. (**See also matrix organisation in Chapter 11.**)

Informal groups

The formal structure of the organisation, and system of role relationships, rules and procedures, will be augmented by interpretation and development at the informal level. Groups will also arise from social processes and the informal organisation (**discussed in Chapter 3**).

Informal groups are based more on personal relationships and agreement of group members than on defined role relationships. They serve to satisfy psychological and social needs not related necessarily to the tasks to be undertaken. Informal groups may devise ways of attempting to satisfy members' affiliation and other social motivations lacking in the work situation. Membership can cut across the formal structure. These groups may comprise individuals from different parts of the organisation and/or from different levels of the organisation, both vertically and diagonally, as well as from the same horizontal level. An informal group could also be the same as the formal group, or it might comprise a part only of the formal group (*see* Figure 8.2).

Members of an informal group may appoint their own leader who exercises authority by consent of the members themselves. The informal leader may be chosen as the person who reflects the attitudes and values of the members, helps to resolve conflict, leads the group in satisfying its goals, or liaises with management or other people outside the group. The informal leader may change according to the particular situation facing the group. Although not usually the case, it is possible for the informal leader to be the same person as the formal leader appointed officially by management.

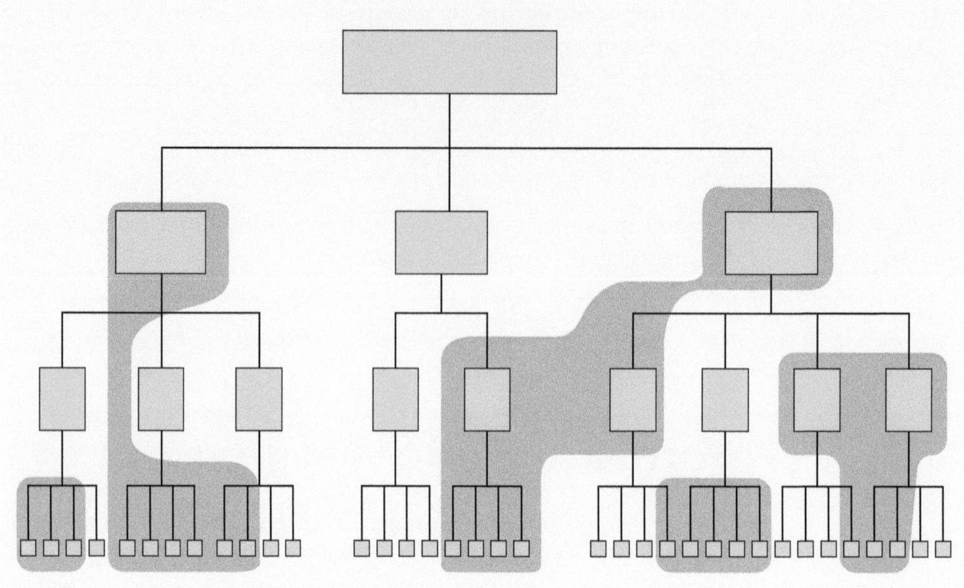

Figure 8.2 Examples of informal groups within the formal structure of an organisation

Major functions of informal groups

Lysons suggests four main reasons for informal groups:

- **Perpetuation of the informal group 'culture'.** Culture in this context means a set of values, norms and beliefs that form a guide to group acceptance and group behaviour. Unless you broadly subscribe to the group culture, you will not belong and will be an 'outsider' or 'isolate'.
- **Maintenance of a communication system.** Groups want all the information that affects their welfare, either negatively or positively. If groups are not apprised of policies and motives behind actions, they will seek to tap into formal communication channels and spread information among group members.
- **Implementation of social control.** Conformity to group culture is enforced by such techniques as ridicule, ostracism and violence. This is illustrated, for example, by the enforcement of group norms in the bank wiring room discussed in the next section.
- **Provision of interest and fun in work-life.** Many jobs are monotonous and fail to hold workers' attention. Work may also offer few prospects. Workers may try to compensate by interpersonal relations provided by the group and in such activities as time wasting by talking, gambling, practical joking and drinking.[9]

As *Law* reminds us:

> *We humans are a gregarious lot. We like to gather together and establish our own social networks, which are often the real key to creativity and innovation in organisations . . . But many managers are unaware that seemingly pointless social networking does in fact play a crucial part in the way people interact with each other and get work done.*[10]

Group values and norms

The classical approach to organisation and management tended to ignore the importance of groups and the social factors at work. The human relations approach, however (**discussed in Chapter 2**), gave recognition to the work organisation as a social organisation and to the importance of the group, and group values and norms, in influencing behaviour at work.

In the Hawthorne studies, one experiment involved the observation of a group of fourteen men working in the bank wiring room who formed their own sub-groups or cliques, with natural leaders emerging with the consent of the members. Despite a financial incentive scheme for the more work they did, the group decided on a level of output well below what they were capable of achieving. Group pressures on individual workers were stronger than financial incentives offered by management.

Informal social relations

The group developed its own pattern of informal social relations and codes and practices ('norms') of what constituted proper group behaviour.

- **Not to be a 'rate buster'** – Not to produce at too high a rate of output compared with other members or to exceed the production restriction of the group.
- **Not to be a 'chiseller'** – Not to shirk production or to produce at too low a rate of output compared with other members of the group.
- **Not to be a 'squealer'** – Not to say anything to the supervisor or management that might be harmful to other members of the group.
- **Not to be 'officious'** – People with authority over members of the group, for example inspectors, should not take advantage of their seniority or maintain a social distance from the group.

The group had its own system of sanctions including sarcasm, damaging completed work, hiding tools, playing tricks on the inspectors and ostracising those members who did not conform to the **group norms.** Threats of physical violence were also made and the group developed a system of punishing offenders by 'binging', which involved striking someone a fairly hard blow on the upper part of the arm. This process of binging also became a recognised method of controlling conflict within the group.

Importance of social norms

According to *Riches*, one way to improve team performance is to establish agreed norms or rules for how the team is to operate and rigorously stick to them. Norms could address the obligations of individual members to the team, how it will assess its performance, how it will work together, what motivation systems will be used, how it will relate to customers, and the mechanisms to facilitate an honest exchange about the team norms and behaviour.[11]

A study by the Economic & Social Research Council draws attention to the importance of social norms among employees and questions whether employees are guided not only by monetary incentives, but also by peer pressure towards social efficiency for the workers as a group: 'Intuitively, social norms among workers must be important if they work in teams where bonuses are dependent on group rather than individual effort.'[12] (You may see some similarity here with the bank wiring room experiment, discussed above.)

A concept map of group norms is set out in Figure 8.3.

Reasons for formation of groups or teams

Individuals have varying expectations of the benefits from group membership, both formal and informal, relating to both work performance and social processes.

- **Certain tasks can be performed only through the combined efforts of a number of individuals working together.** The variety of experience, knowledge and expertise among members provides a synergetic effect that can be applied to the increasingly complex problems of modern organisations.
- **Collusion between members** in order to modify formal working arrangements more to their liking – for example, by sharing or rotating unpopular tasks. Membership therefore provides the individual with opportunities for initiative and creativity.

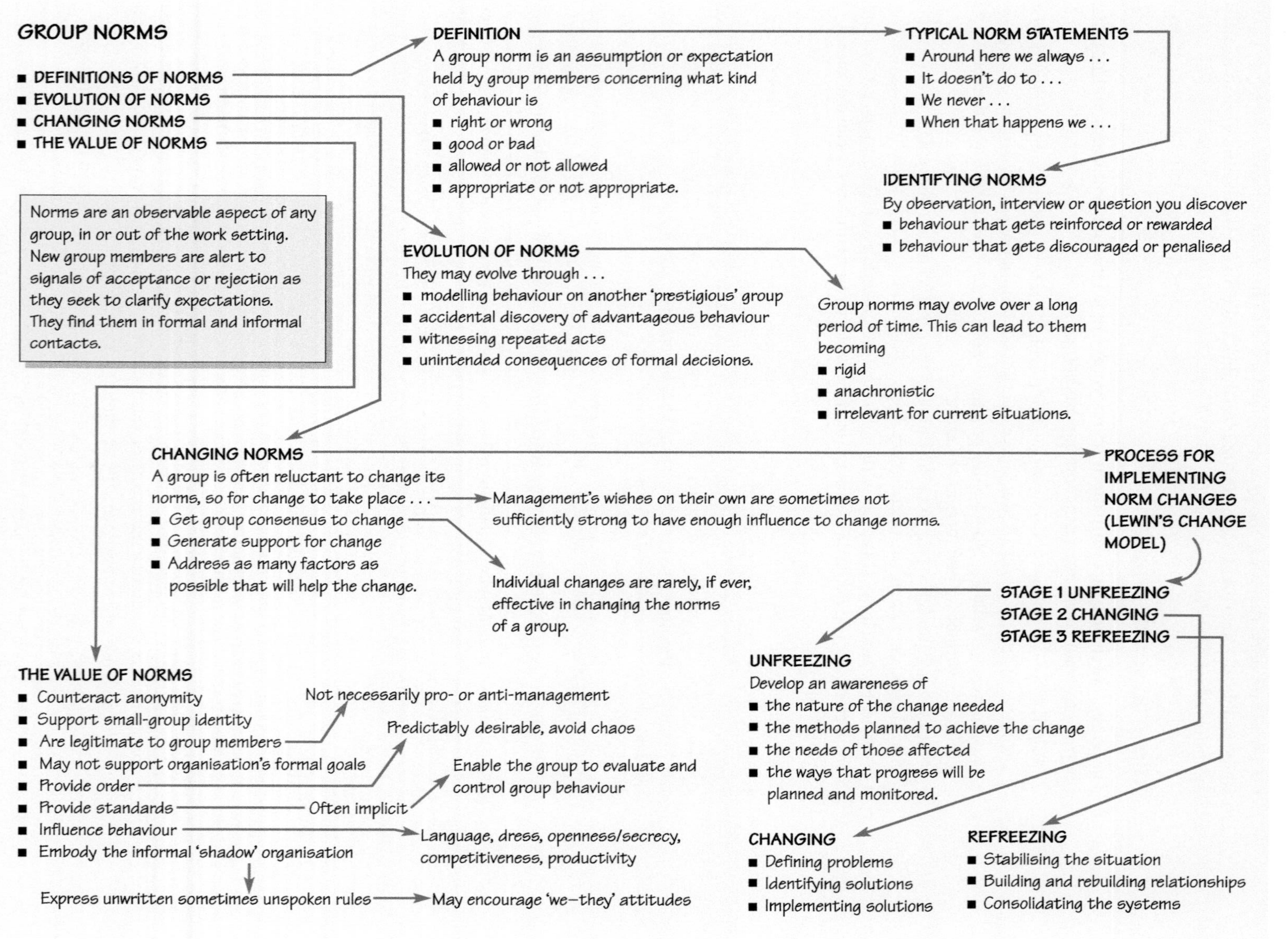

Figure 8.3 Concept map of group norms

Source: Copyright © 2008 The Virtual Learning Materials Workshop. Reproduced with permission.

- **Companionship and a source of mutual understanding and support from colleagues.** This can help in solving work problems and also to militate against stressful or demanding working conditions.
- **Membership provides the individual with a sense of belonging.** It provides a feeling of identity and the chance to acquire role recognition and status within the group or team. (**See the discussion on social identity theory below.**)
- **Guidelines on generally acceptable behaviour.** These help to clarify ambiguous situations, such as the extent to which official rules and regulations are expected to be adhered to in practice, the rules of the game and what is seen as the correct actual behaviour. Allegiance to the group or team can serve as a means of control over individual behaviour and individuals who contravene the norms may be disciplined.
- **Protection for its membership.** Group or team members collaborate to protect their interests from outside pressures or threats.

Critical review and reflection

Given the importance of social interactions and interpersonal relationships for morale, job satisfaction and work performance, the main focus of your studies should be on the operations and management of the informal organisation.

Can YOU present a counterargument to this contention? How much have YOU learned about the importance and influence of the informal organisation?

Group cohesiveness and performance

Social interaction is a natural feature of human behaviour and work organisation but ensuring harmonious working relationships and effective teamwork is not an easy task. Co-operation is likely to be greater in a united, cohesive group. Membership can be a rewarding experience for the individual, contribute to the promotion of morale and aid release of creativity and energy. Members of a high-morale group are more likely to think of themselves as a group and work together effectively. Strong and cohesive work groups can, therefore, have beneficial effects for the organisation. There are many factors that affect group cohesiveness and performance, which can be summarised under four broad headings, as shown in Figure 8.4.

Membership

Size of the group

As a group increases in size, problems arise with communications and co-ordination. Large groups are more difficult to handle and require a higher level of supervision. Absenteeism also tends to be higher. When a group becomes too large it may split into smaller units and friction may develop between the sub-groups. It is difficult to put a precise figure on the ideal size of a work group. Much will depend upon other variables, but it seems to be generally accepted that cohesiveness becomes more difficult to achieve when a group exceeds ten to twelve members.[13] Beyond this size the group tends to split into sub-groups. A figure of between five and seven is often quoted as an apparent optimum size for full participation within the group.

Cane asks the question: 'How many people should be in a team?'

> *The answers from different organisations as to what is the perfect number vary from between four and fifteen depending on a whole range of variables. Fifteen is about the maximum*

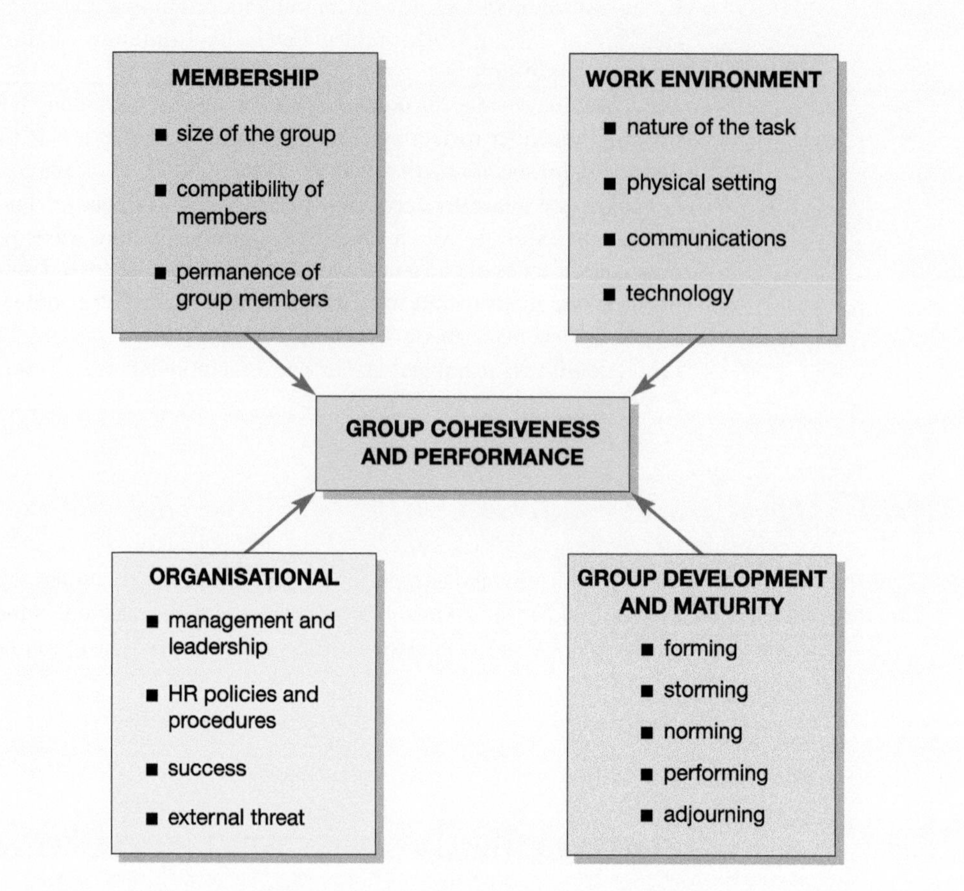

Figure 8.4 Factors contributing to group cohesiveness and performance

number of people anyone can communicate with without having to raise their voice significantly and any less than four has a restriction in the amount of creativity and variety that can be produced. It is interesting to note that these figures range between the maximum and minimum numbers of sports teams – perhaps less of a coincidence than it seems.[14]

Compatibility of members

The more homogeneous the group in terms of such features as shared backgrounds, interests, attitudes and values of its members, the easier it is usually to promote cohesiveness. Variations in other individual differences, such as personality or skills of members, may serve to complement each other and help make for a cohesive group. However, such differences may be the cause of disruption and conflict. Conflict can also arise in a homogeneous group where members are in competition with each other. Individual incentive payment schemes, for example, may be a source of conflict.

Permanence of group members

Group spirit and relationships take time to develop. Cohesiveness is more likely when members of a group are together for a reasonable length of time and changes occur only slowly. A frequent turnover of members is likely to have an adverse effect on morale and on the cohesiveness of the group.

Work environment

Nature of the task

Where workers are involved in similar work, share a common task or face the same problems, this may assist cohesiveness. The nature of the task may serve to bring people together when it is necessary to communicate and interact regularly – for example, members of a research and development team. Even if members of a group normally work at different locations they may still experience a feeling of cohesiveness if the nature of the task requires frequent communication and interaction – for example, security guards patrolling separate areas who need to check with each other on a regular basis.

Physical setting

Where members of a group work in the same location or in close physical proximity to each other this may generally help cohesiveness. However, this is not always the case. For example, in large open-plan offices staff often tend to segregate themselves from colleagues and create barriers through the strategic siting of such items as filing cabinets, bookcases or indoor plants. The size of the office and the number of staff in it are, of course, important considerations in this case. Isolation from other groups of workers will also tend to build cohesiveness. This often applies to a smaller number of workers on a night shift.

Communications

The more easily members can communicate freely with each other, the greater the likelihood of group cohesiveness. Communications are affected by the work environment, by nature of the task and technology. For example, difficulties in communication can arise with production systems where workers are stationed continuously at a particular point with limited freedom of movement. Even when opportunities exist for interaction with colleagues, physical conditions may limit effective communication. For example, the technological layout and high level of noise with some assembly line work can limit contact between workers. Changes in the nature of work, including increasing demand for flexible working arrangements, may restrict opportunities for social interaction and hamper internal group unity.[15]

Technology

Technology is clearly a major influence on patterns of group operation and behaviour. ACAS draws attention to technological advances and how new technology enables production to be tailored quickly to customer requirements, often on an individual basis.

> *Mass production techniques, where jobs are broken down into simple tasks, are not suitable for the new customer focused manufacturing nor the expectations of an educated workforce. Organisations need workers to be more flexible, to co-operate with other workers, supervisors and managers throughout the organisation, to operate sophisticated technology and to be more adaptable. In addition, the sheer complexity of operations in industry, commerce and the services places them beyond the expertise and control of any one individual. In these circumstances some form of teamwork becomes not just desirable but essential.*[16]

The impact of IT demands new patterns of work organisation and affects the formation and structure of groups. Improvements in telecommunications mean that support staff need no longer be located within the main production unit. Individuals may work more on their own, from their homes, shared offices or hotels, or work more with machines than with other people.

Organisational

Management and leadership

Teams tend to be a mirror image of their leaders. The form of management and style of leadership adopted are major determinants of group cohesiveness. In general terms, cohesiveness will be affected by such things as the manner in which the manager gives support, guidance and encouragement to the group, provides opportunities for participation, attempts to resolve conflicts and gives attention to both employee relations and task problems.

McKenna and Maister draw attention to the importance of the group leader establishing a level of trust among the group by helping its members understand the behaviours that build trust: 'The job of the group leader is to encourage people to earn the trust of others in their group and then show them how it can translate into greater commitment, greater creativity, greater professional satisfaction, and better performance.'[17] *Farrell* makes the point that managers are ultimately responsible for creating a balance in the workplace and should take the lead in setting standards of behaviour in teams.[18]

HR policies and procedures

Harmony and cohesiveness within the group are more likely to be achieved if HR policies and procedures are well developed and perceived to be equitable, with fair treatment for all members. Attention should be given to the effects that appraisal systems, discipline, promotion and rewards and opportunities for personal development have on members of the group.

Success

Success is usually a strong motivational influence on cohesiveness and level of work performance. Success or reward as a positive motivator can be perceived by group members in a number of ways – for example, the satisfactory completion of a task through co-operative action, praise from management, a feeling of high status, achievement in competition with other groups or benefits gained, such as high wage payments from a group bonus incentive scheme.

External threat

Cohesiveness may be enhanced by members co-operating with one another when faced with a common external threat, such as changes in their method of work or the appointment of a new manager. Even if the threat is subsequently removed, the group may continue to have a greater degree of cohesiveness than before the threat arose. Conflict between groups will also tend to increase the cohesiveness of each group and the boundaries of the group become drawn more clearly.

Group development and maturity

The degree of cohesiveness is affected also by the manner in which groups progress through the various stages of development and maturity before getting down to the real tasks in hand. This process can take time and is often traumatic for the members. A popular model by *Tuckman* identifies five main successive stages of group development and relationships: **forming, storming, norming, performing** and **adjourning.**[19]

- **Stage 1 – forming.** This concerns initial formation of the group and bringing together individuals who identify, tentatively, the purpose of the group, its composition and terms of reference. Consideration is given to the hierarchical structure of the group, pattern of leadership, individual roles and responsibilities and codes of conduct. There is likely to be considerable anxiety as members attempt to create an impression, test each other and establish their personal identity within the group.

- **Stage 2 – storming.** As members of the group get to know each other better they will put forward their views more openly and forcefully. Disagreements will be expressed and challenges offered on the nature of the task and arrangements made in the earlier stage of development. This may lead to conflict and hostility. The storming stage is important because, if successful, there will be discussions on reforming arrangements for the working and operation of the group, and agreement on more meaningful structures and procedures.
- **Stage 3 – norming.** As conflict and hostility start to be controlled, members of the group will establish guidelines and standards and develop their own norms of acceptable behaviour. The norming stage is important in establishing the need for members to co-operate in order to plan, agree standards of performance and fulfil the purpose of the group.
- **Stage 4 – performing.** When the group has progressed successfully through the three earlier stages of development it will have created structure and cohesiveness to work effectively as a team. At this stage the group can concentrate on the attainment of its purpose and performance of the common task is likely to be at its most effective.
- **Stage 5 – adjourning.** This refers to the adjourning or disbanding of the group because of, for example, completion of the task, members leaving the organisation or moving on to other tasks. Some members may feel a compelling sense of loss at the end of a major or lengthy group project and their return to independence is characterised by sadness and anxiety. Managers may need to prepare for future group tasks and engendering team effort.

Another writer suggests that new groups go through the following five stages:

- the polite stage;
- the why are we here, what are we doing stage;
- the power stage, which dominant person will emerge;
- the constructive stage when sharing begins; and
- the unity stage – this often takes weeks, eating together, talking together.[20]

Critical review and reflection

Modern systems of communication, such as email and the increasing use of social media, restrict personal interaction and have only a negative effect on group development, cohesiveness and performance.

To what extent do YOU believe this fair comment? How has email or social media affected YOUR experience of group membership?

Creative leadership and group development

In an examination of creative leadership and team effectiveness, *Rickards and Moger* propose a modification to the Tuckman model and suggest a two-barrier model of group development. From their empirical studies of small groups and project teams, Rickards and Moger put forward two challenges to the prevailing model of team development:

1. Weak teams posed the question 'What is happening if a team fails to develop beyond the storm stage?'.
2. The exceptional teams posed the question 'What happens if a team breaks out of the performance norms developed?'.

The suggestion is that teams are differentiated by two barriers to performance. The weak barrier is behavioural and defeated a minority of teams; the strong barrier was a block to creativity or innovation, and defeated the majority of those teams who passed through the weak barrier. The two-barrier model provides a starting point for exploring the impact and influence of a team leader on the performance of teams. Rickards and Moger identified seven factors through which a leader might influence effective team development:

- building a platform of understanding;
- creating a shared vision;
- providing a creative climate;
- showing a commitment to idea ownership;
- resilience to setbacks;
- developing networking skills;
- learning from experience.[21]

Social identity theory

Within work organisations there will be a number of different but overlapping groups representing a variety of functions, departments, occupations, technologies, project teams, locations or hierarchical levels. Organisational effectiveness will be dependent upon the extent to which these groups co-operate, but often the different groupings are part of a network of complex relationships resulting in competitiveness and conflict. A feature of the importance and significance of group membership is the concept of social identity theory. *Tajfel and Turner* originally developed the idea of **social identity theory** as a means of understanding the psychological basis of inter-group discrimination.[22] Individuals are perceived as having not just one 'personal self' but a number of 'selves' derived from different social contexts and membership of groups.

Because of the need for a clear sense of personal identity, the groups or social categories with which we associate are an integral part of our self-concept (social identity). A natural process of human interaction is social categorisation, by which we classify both ourselves and other people through reference to our own social identity. For example, membership of high-status groups can increase a person's perceived self-esteem. According to *Guirdham*, 'self-categorisation is the process that transforms a number of individuals into a group'.[23] *See* Figure 8.5.

Haslam refers to the relationship between individuals and groups in an understanding of organisational behaviour, and argues that:

> *in order to understand perception and interaction in organizational contexts we must do more than just study the psychology of individuals as individuals. Instead, we need to understand how social interaction is bound up with individuals' social identities – their definition of themselves in terms of group memberships.*[24]

Identification with social groupings

We identify ourselves in terms of membership of certain social groupings and differentiate ourselves from other social groupings. This leads to minimising differences between members of our own groupings (in-groups) and maximising differences from other groupings (out-groups). Over time the sense of shared identity with the in-group increases a feeling of what is right and proper and highlights differences from the out-groups.[25] As a result, this reinforces both social identity with our own category and the projection of negative perceptions and stereotypes towards out-groups.

Stereotyping can lead to shared attitudes to out-groups and to increased conflict among work groups. The examples of group stereotyping (**discussed in Chapter 6**) are associated with social identity theory. Tajfel and Turner suggest that the mere act of individuals categorising themselves as group members leads them to exhibit in-group favouritism. *Hewstone et al.*

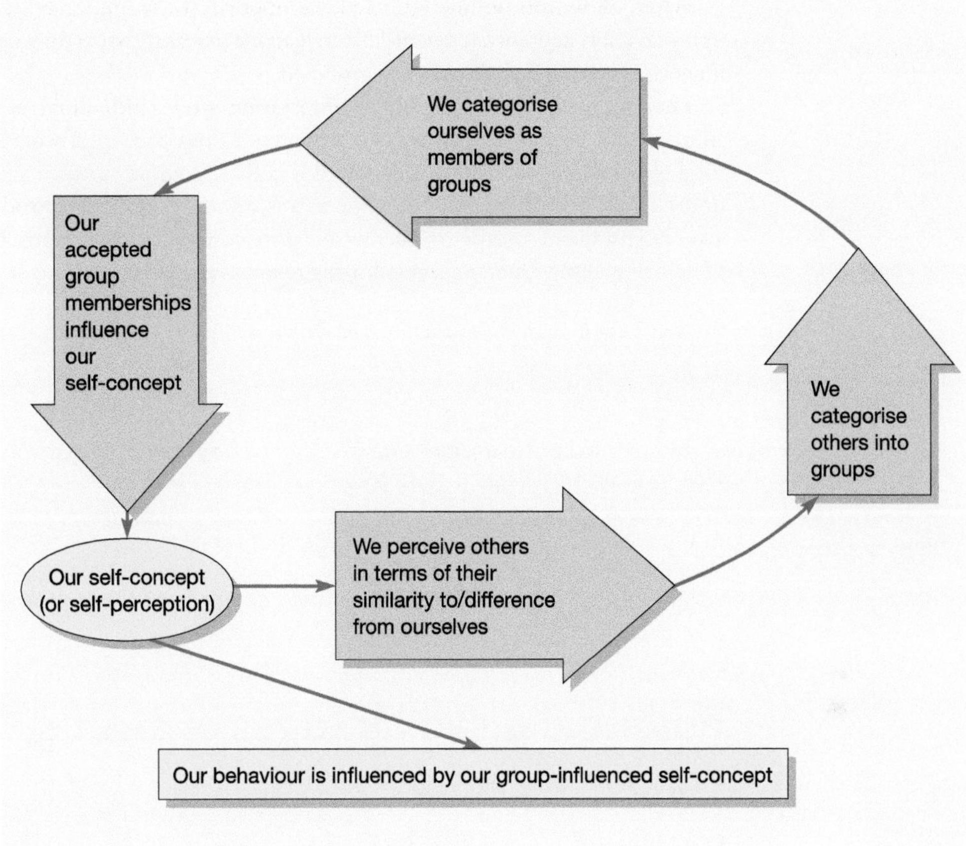

Figure 8.5 Processes of social and self-categorisation

Source: Guirdham, M. *Interactive Behaviour at Work*, third edition, Financial Times Prentice Hall (2002), p. 119. Reproduced with permission of Pearson Education Ltd.

suggest that, even without realising it, we tend usually to favour the groupings we belong to more than denigrate out-groups. Successful inter-group bias enhances self-esteem.[26] (**See also the discussion on social exchange theory in Chapter 1 and possible effects on group membership, norms and control.**)

Characteristics of an effective work group

The characteristics of an effective work group are not always easy to isolate clearly. The underlying feature is a spirit of co-operation in which members work well together as a united team and with harmonious and supportive relationships. This may be evidenced when members of a group exhibit:

- belief in shared aims and objectives;
- sense of commitment to the group;
- acceptance of group values and norms;
- feeling of mutual trust and dependency;
- full participation by all members and decision-making by consensus;
- free flow of information and communications;
- open expression of feelings and disagreements;
- resolution of conflict by the members themselves;
- lower level of staff turnover, absenteeism, accidents, errors and complaints.

However, as *Brooks* points out, as teams operate at the higher order of group dynamics this list is arguably more reflective of 'effective *work teams* rather than work groups and this is how it should be – these are teams not groups'.[27]

Musical ensembles make for an interesting study. Individual members may be brilliant soloists and often noted for their temperament, but their performance is as much about the total blend and working noticeably well together as about musical ability. By comparison, it is noticeable how managers of sporting teams often deliberately introduce new players, even to a successful team, in order to further increase competition or rivalry for places, with the hope of achieving even greater success for the team as a whole.

Critical review and reflection

To gain a greater appreciation of effective teamwork, attention should be given in the classroom to the management and functioning of successful musical ensembles and successful sports teams.

To what extent do YOU believe an understanding of musical ensembles or sports teams relates in a meaningful way to the work organisation?

Potential disadvantages of strong, cohesive groups

If the manager is to develop effective work groups, attention should be given to those factors that influence the creation of group identity and cohesiveness. This may result in greater interaction between members, mutual help and social satisfaction, lower turnover and absenteeism, and often higher production.[28] However, strong and cohesive groups also present potential disadvantages for management. Working in groups may result in members spending too much time talking among themselves. Cohesive groups do not necessarily produce a higher level of output. It may be remembered that in the bank wiring room experiment of the Hawthorne studies the level of output was restricted to a standard acceptable as a norm by the group.

Once a group has become fully developed, created cohesiveness and established its own culture, it is more difficult for the manager successfully to change attitudes and behaviour of the group. It is important that the manager attempts to influence the group during the norming stage, when members are establishing their own guidelines and standards and their own norms of acceptable behaviour.

Inter-group conflict

Strong, cohesive groups may develop a critical or even hostile attitude towards people outside the group or members of other groups. Groups may also compete against each other in a non-productive manner. This can be the case, for example, when group cohesiveness is based on common status, qualifications, technical expertise or professional standing. As a result, resentment and inter-group conflict may arise to the detriment of the organisation as a whole. (**Recall the discussion on social identity theory, above.**) In order to help prevent, or overcome, unconstructive inter-group conflict, the manager should attempt to stimulate a high level of communication and interaction between groups.

Yet, inter-group rivalry may be deliberately encouraged as a means of building stronger within-group cohesiveness. The idea is that a competitive element may help to promote unity within a group. However, inter-group rivalry and competition need to be handled carefully to avoid development of 'win–lose' situations. Emphasis should be placed on overall objectives of the organisation and superordinate goals. These are goals over and above the issues at conflict and which, if they are to be achieved, require the co-operation of the competing groups.

Virtual teams

The combination of increasing globalisation, competition and widespread developments in ICT has given greater emphasis to the opportunities for, and need of, **virtual teams.** Instead of involving face-to-face proximity, virtual teams are a collection of people who are geographically separated but still need to work together closely. The primary interaction among members is by some electronic information and communication process. This enables organisations to function away from traditional working hours and the physical availability of staff. Computer-based information systems and increased wireless connectivity further the opportunities for virtual working. By their very nature, virtual teams are likely to be largely self-managed.

According to *Hall*, the virtual team is a potential future compromise between fully fledged teams and well-managed groups.

> *I am watching the rise of this idea with interest but am sceptical that it will actually create a 'third way'. Real teams can only be forged in the crucible of personal interaction: videoconferences and Net communications are still poor substitutes for this. Of course, once a team has formed it can use these media, as members will know each other well, but that's not the important bit. It's the forming, norming and storming that make a team.*[29]

Virtual teams may lead to an increase in productivity through a reduction in commute time and greater personal flexibility. Organisations are able to establish a greater worldwide presence. Virtual teams can comprise people with different types of knowledge, help to reduce discrimination and provide wider employment opportunities. A potential difficulty is maintaining effective communications, bearing in mind the lack of body language and non-verbal communication (**discussed in Chapter 6**). Virtual teams demand good leadership and management, including competence in ICT. Virtual working is not always to the initial liking of all people and it is important to have a remote working strategy.

Some people seem clearly to welcome virtual working with its feeling of autonomy, freedom from distractions and interruptions and less time and stress on commuting. However, despite the increase in remote working, it does not appeal to everyone. Not everyone enjoys working on their own and they miss group membership, social structure, contact and interaction. They may feel ignored by the organisation and experience an increasing feeling of isolation. For some people, trust is difficult when they cannot see the other person. Without direct personal interaction some people find it difficult to motivate themselves. A sense of discipline and self-motivation is important for effective remote working.

Leadership and motivation

Symons considers that one advantage of virtual teamworking is the clarity and richness of contributions when respondents are removed from the urgency of immediate interaction, and that this can be particularly relevant in cross-cultural groups. However, as the leader cannot influence by physical presence, and as hierarchies fade online, managing dispersed teams requires a range of subtly different leadership skills. It is important to develop mutual trust and a democratic approach of shared control and decision-making, and adopt the role and style of a coach: 'The leader has to establish and maintain "credit" with the group, as "position power" has little or no currency in virtual working.'[30]

Garrett maintains that collaborating with other people in different cities or countries is not always a successful arrangement and lists the following suggestions for helping to organise the virtual team:

- **Say hello** – The most successful teams spend time during their formation period face to face, getting to know each other.
- **Build trust** – This holds the team together so that you can depend on other team members and feel comfortable opening up to them.
- **Recruit with care** – People who can communicate in the right way at the right time are more likely to be successful in virtual teams.
- **Do not rely on email** – The written word is easily misunderstood so supplement its use with other forms of communication.
- **Encourage dissent** – Without face-to-face meetings people become reluctant to speak out, but a healthy organisation needs people to speak out and challenge leaders and each other.
- **Use technology thoughtfully** – Used badly, sophisticated tools can be a disaster, and people need to be trained to use the technology, not simply have it imposed on them.
- **Measure outcomes** – Focus on the outcomes rather than time management, find a personal way to appraise performance, rather than email, and hold regular chats with members.
- **Do say** – 'By proactively creating virtual teams we can go where talent is, extend our reach and work more efficiently.'
- **Do not say** – 'We call them a virtual team because they're not quite the real thing.'[31]

Cultural diversity

One reason for the growth in virtual teams is increasing globalisation and team members working and living in different countries. This gives rise to potential difficulties of cultural diversity. As *Francesco and Gold* point out:

> *The more culturally diverse the members, the more difficult it is to manage a virtual team. Cultural diversity, which will be increasingly common, adds to the complexity of managing virtual teams because different values, customs, and traditions require more leadership under conditions that reduce the ability to use direct leadership.*[32]

And, according to *Murray,* although virtual working presents some unexpected benefits, if managing diversity in the workplace is a tough task for business leaders, the challenges of keeping executives from different backgrounds working together in various parts of the world is even more difficult. Virtual working does not eradicate the sort of cultural misunderstandings that can arise in a face-to-face situation.

> *Cultural or behavioural differences that can manifest themselves in face-to-face working situations can be exacerbated in virtual team working, particularly when the group has members from different backgrounds.*[33]

Hazlehurst points out that the rise of the virtual organisation is not a universal development.

> *In emerging economies, the office is still a novelty and young people are clamouring to work in them. It may seem hard to understand to westerners with generations of travel-weary commuters in their family tree, but if you are the first person in your family to move from a village to a city, an office job is alive with exciting possibilities, as well as being a potent symbol of personal success.*[34]

Critical review and reflection

With continuing globalisation and advances in ICT, the days of people spending most of their time working together in physical contact with colleagues are gone. Global virtual teams are the way forward.

How far do YOU agree? What difficulties and problems do YOU foresee? Are YOU concerned about the prospect of virtual teamworking?

Management and organisational behaviour in action case study
Remote teamworking

Joanne Mooney, Customer Journey and Online Experience Manager, British Gas, based in Stockport, and her boss, **Lucy Shadholt,** Head of Channel Development for British Gas New Energy, based in Staines

In the two years she's been working remotely for British Gas, Joanne Mooney has enjoyed the flexibility and greater access to her young family, and feels she mostly gets the balance right.

> *You have to know when to switch off. At home, define your space, define your roles in the house, be disciplined in your working day, when it starts and stops. It's not always fair to the family – they know mummy's working, so they have to talk in hushed tones and that seems restrictive to them in their own home.*

She had managed a call centre of 150 people and sometimes misses the banter: 'When I started, I was 100% working from home. I prefer the mix of the new role, where I'm getting out and meeting people. It's easier to build the relationship over the phone if you've met the person.'

Lucy Shadbolt is Mooney's boss. Since taking on the role in October she has built a team of ten, all of whom work at least part of the time remotely, including herself. 'It suits me; I get so much more done. The whole team love it,' she says. Shadbolt runs weekly meetings from the Staines office and is in regular contact with each team member. 'Some things are not suitable for conference calls. If I have to have a difficult conversation it needs to be face to face.' She's confident she's getting good performance from each of them:

> *You have to trust them. I make it clear with new team members that working from home is a privilege. If you give clear objectives it's easy to monitor output. People don't work 9 to 5, they work longer. It's not unusual to send an email at 10 pm. Work is where your laptop is.*

Shadbolt acknowledges some aspects of her own career development are more difficult to achieve at arm's length – such as getting the ear of the boss. 'When I go into the office, where we hot-desk, I have to make an effort to position myself near my boss. You need to consciously build relationships when you don't have those water-cooler moments naturally occurring.'

Source: 'Remote control - how to manage homeworkers - Take-home lessons: Tips from remote workers and their bosses', *Management Today*, March 2011, p. 49 (www.managementtoday.com). Reproduced with permission.

Tasks

1. What particular problems do you envisage with remote teamworking?
2. Explain how would you attempt to establish mutual trust when you cannot see the other person.
3. Discuss fully the extent to which you would be happy as a remote teamworker.

Role structure of the organisation

In order for the organisation to achieve its goals and objectives, the work of individual members must be linked into coherent patterns of activities and relationships. This is achieved through the 'role structure' of the organisation.

A **role** is the expected pattern of behaviours associated with members occupying a particular position within the structure of the organisation. It also describes how a person perceives their own situation. The concept of role differentiation helps to clarify structure and define the pattern of complex relationships within the group.

The role, or roles, that the individual plays within the group is influenced by a combination of:

- **situational factors** such as the requirements of the task, nature of technology employed, time scales, style of leadership, position in the communication network; and
- **personal factors** such as values, culture, attitudes, motivation, ability and personality.

However, everyone within a group is expected to behave in a particular manner and to fulfil certain role expectations. The formal organisational relationships (line, functional, staff or lateral) – **discussed in Chapter 11** – can be seen as forms of role relationships that determine the pattern of interaction with other roles.

A person's role set

In addition to the role relationships with members of their own group – peers, superiors, subordinates – the individual will have a number of role-related relationships with outsiders, for example members of other work groups, trade union officials, suppliers, consumers. This is a person's **role set**. The role set comprises the range of associations or contacts with whom the individual has meaningful interactions in connection with the performance of the role (*see* Figure 8.6).

Role incongruence

An important feature of role relationship is the concept of **role incongruence**. This arises when a member of staff is perceived as having a high and responsible position in one respect but a low standing in another respect. Difficulties with role incongruence can arise from the nature of groupings and formal relationships within the structure of the organisation. There are a number of work-related relationships, such as doctor and nurse, chef and waiter, senior manager and personal assistant, which can give rise to a potential imbalance of authority and responsibility.

Difficulties with role incongruence can also arise in line-staff relationships: for instance, a relatively junior member of the HR department informing a senior departmental manager that a certain proposed action is contrary to the policies of the organisation. Another example with staff relationships is where a person establishes themselves in the role of 'gatekeeper' to the boss[35] – for instance, where a comparatively junior personal assistant passes on the manager's instructions to one of the manager's more senior subordinates.

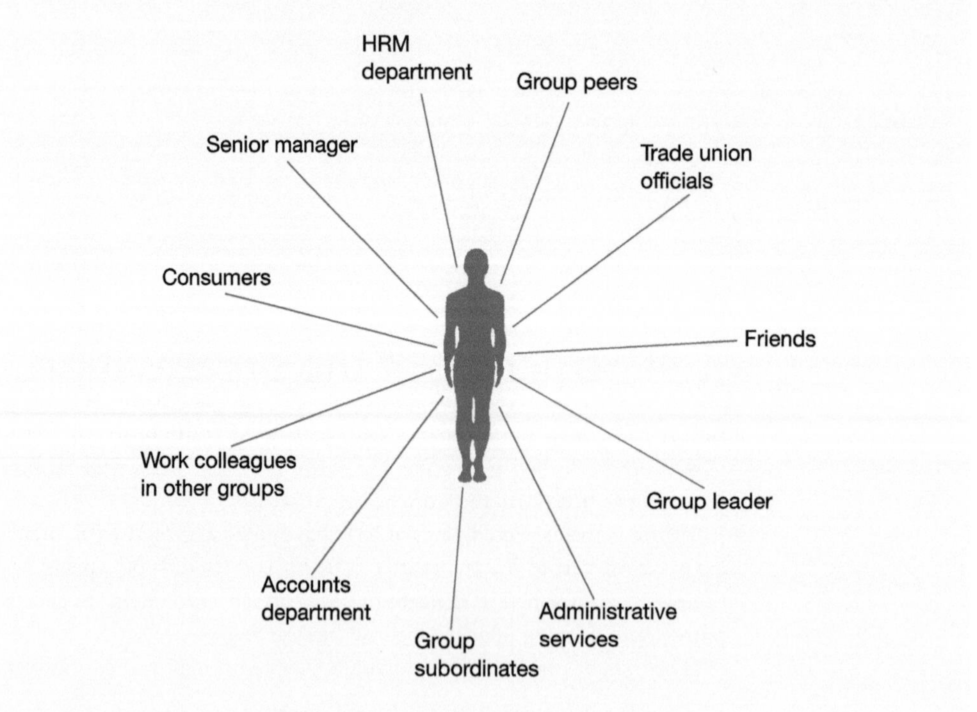

Figure 8.6 Representation of a possible role set in the work situation

Role expectations

Many **role expectations** are prescribed formally and indicate what the person is expected to do, their duties and obligations, and provide guidelines for expected behaviours. Examples are written contracts of employment, rules and regulations, standing orders, policy decisions, job descriptions, or directives from superiors. Formal role expectations may also be derived clearly from the nature of the task. They may, in part at least, be defined legally: for example, under Health and Safety at Work legislation; obligations of a company secretary under the Companies Acts; or responsibilities of a district auditor under the Local Government Acts.

Not all role expectations are prescribed formally, however. There will be certain patterns of behaviour which, although not specified formally, will nonetheless be expected of members. These informal role expectations may be imposed by the group itself, or at least communicated to a person by other members of the group. Examples include general conduct, mutual support to co-members, attitudes towards superiors, means of communicating, dress and appearance. Members may not always be consciously aware of these informal expectations, yet they still serve as important determinants of behaviour. Under this heading could be included the concept of a psychological contract (**discussed in Chapter 1**).

Self-established roles

Some members may have the opportunity to determine largely their own role expectations, where, for example, formal expectations are specified loosely or only in very general terms. Opportunities for **self-established roles** are more likely in senior positions, but also occur within certain professional, technical or scientific groups, for example senior research staff, or where there is a demand for creativity or artistic flair, for example head chefs. Such opportunities may be greater within an 'organic' organisation and will also be influenced by the style of leadership adopted – for example, where a laissez-faire approach is adopted.

Critical review and reflection

Despite apparent advantages of group working, the reality is that most people prefer the freedom of working on their own. Individuals have varying and often conflicting expectations of the benefits from group membership and this distracts from effective work performance.

To what extent do YOU feel this is a valid contention? Would YOU really prefer working on your own?

Role conflict

Patterns of behaviour result from both the person's role and personality. The concept of role focuses attention on aspects of behaviour existing independently of an individual's personality. **Role conflict** arises from inadequate or inappropriate role definition and needs to be distinguished from personality clashes. These arise from incompatibility between two or more people as individuals, even though their roles may be defined clearly and understood fully. In practice, the manner in which a person actually behaves may not be consistent with their expected pattern of behaviours. This inconsistency may be a result of role conflict. Role conflict as a generic term can include:

- role incompatibility
- role ambiguity
- role overload
- role underload.

These are all problem areas associated with the creation of role expectations (*see* Figure 8.7).

- **Role incompatibility** arises when a person faces a situation in which simultaneous different or contradictory expectations create conflict or inconsistency. Compliance with one set of expectations makes it difficult or impossible to comply with other expectations. A typical example concerns the person 'in the middle', such as the supervisor or section head, who faces opposing expectations from workers and from management. Another example might be the situation of a manager who believes in a relaxed, participative style of behaviour but whose superior expects a more formal and directive style of behaviour.
- **Role ambiguity** occurs when there is lack of insufficient information or clarity as to the precise requirements of the role and the person is unsure what to do. The person's perception of their role may differ from the expectations of others. It is likely to arise in large, diverse groups or at times of constant change. Uncertainty often relates to such matters as method of performing tasks, extent of the person's authority and responsibility, standards of work, time for completion, and evaluation and appraisal of performance.
- **Role overload** is when a person faces too many separate roles or too great a variety of expectations. The person is unable to meet satisfactorily all expectations and some must be neglected in order to satisfy others. This leads to a conflict of priority and potential stress. Some writers distinguish between role overload and work overload. Role overload is seen in terms of the total

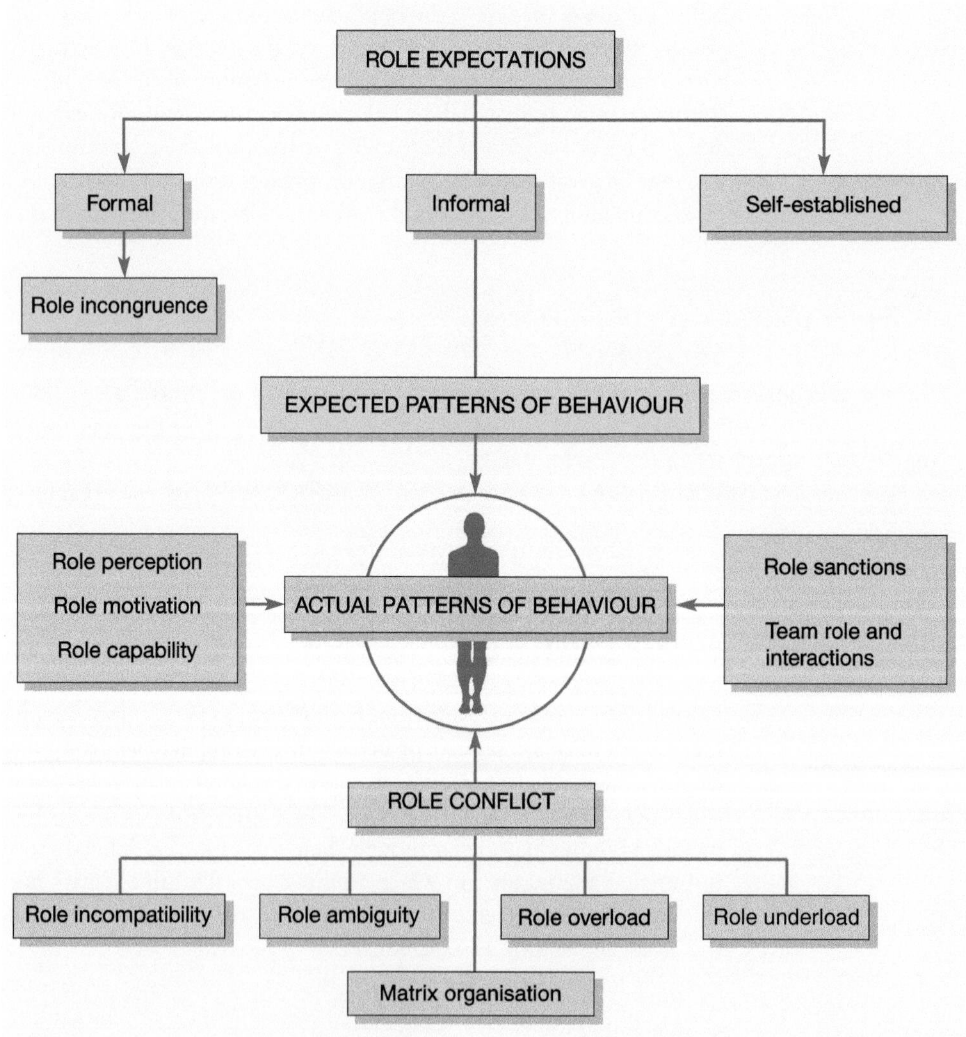

Figure 8.7 Role relationships and conflicts
Source: based on Miner, J. B. *Management Theory*, Macmillan (1971), p. 47.

role set and implies that the person has too many separate roles to handle. Where there are too many expectations of a single role – that is, a problem of quantity – this is work overload.

- **Role underload** can arise when the prescribed role expectations fall short of the person's perception of their role. The person may feel their role is not demanding enough and that they have the capacity to undertake a larger or more varied role, or an increased number of roles. Role underload may arise, for example, when a new member of staff is first appointed or from the initial effects of empowerment.

Role conflict and matrix organisation

Problems of role conflict can often arise from the matrix form of organisation (**discussed in Chapter 11**) and, for example, from the use of flexible project teams. Where staff are assigned temporarily, and perhaps on a part-time basis, from other groups this creates a two-way flow of authority and responsibility.

Unless role differentiations are defined clearly, this can result in conflicting expectations from the manager of the person's own functional grouping and from the manager of the project team (role incompatibility). It can also lead to uncertainty about the exact requirements of the part the person is expected to play as a member of the project team (role ambiguity). The combinations of expectations from both managers may also result in role overload.

Other influences on behaviour

Even if there is an absence of role conflict and role stress, a person's actual behaviour may still be inconsistent with their expected pattern of behaviours. *Miner* gives three reasons that may account for this disparity:

- The person does not perceive their job in the way the role prescriptions specify. This is a form of role ambiguity but may arise not because the role prescriptions themselves are unclear, but because the person misunderstands or distorts them.
- Motivation is lacking and the person does not want to behave in the way prescribed.
- The person does not have the capabilities – knowledge, mental ability or physical skills – required to behave in the way the role prescriptions specify.[36]

Application of sanctions

Organisations apply a number of both positive and negative sanctions as inducements for members to contribute and behave in accordance with their prescribed roles. Typical examples are: an increase in salary or wages; promotion; upgrading to the latest equipment or technology; a sideways or downwards move in the organisation structure; and the threat of dismissal. There are also a number of less direct sanctions that may be adopted. These include the size of office or work area, the allocation of unpopular tasks, giving opportunities for paid overtime work, priority for holiday rotas, level of supervision or empowerment, the amount of information given or the extent of consultation and granting or withholding privileges. Role sanctions may also be applied through the operation of the informal organisation. Members of the group may impose their own sanctions and discipline individuals who contravene the norms of the group or expected standards of behaviour.

Interactions among members

Whatever an individual's role within the structure of an organisation, if groups are to be successful and perform effectively, there must be a spirit of unity and co-operation. As Crainer reminds us, in most teams people will contribute individual skills, many of which will be different. However, referring to the work of *Obeng*,[37] *Crainer* points out that it is not enough to have a rag-bag collection of individual skills.

The various behaviours of the team members must mesh together in order to achieve objectives. For people to work successfully in teams, you need people to behave in certain ways. You need some people to concentrate on the task at hand (doers). You need some people to provide specialist knowledge (knowers) and some to solve problems as they arise (solvers). You need some people to make sure that it is going as well as it can and that the whole team is contributing fully (checkers). And you need some people to make sure that the team is operating as a cohesive social unit (carers).[38]

Individual team roles

One of the most popular analyses of individual roles within a work group or team is that developed by *Belbin,* who concludes that groups composed entirely of clever people, or of people with similar personalities, display a number of negative results and lack creativity. The most consistently successful groups comprise a range of roles undertaken by various members. The constitution of the group itself is an important variable in its success.[39]

A **team role** is a pattern of behaviour, characteristic of the way in which one team member interacts with another whose performance serves to facilitate the progress of the team as a whole.[40] Strength of contribution in any one role is commonly associated with particular weaknesses. These are called allowable weaknesses. Members are seldom strong in all nine team roles. A description of the evolved nine team roles is given in Table 8.1.

Table 8.1 Belbin's evolved nine team roles

Roles and descriptions - team-role contribution		Allowable weaknesses
Plant	Creative, imaginative, free-thinking. Generates ideas and solves difficult problems	Ignores incidentals. Too preoccupied to communicate effectively
Resource investigator	Outgoing, enthusiastic, communicative. Explores opportunities and develops contacts	Over-optimistic. Loses interest once initial enthusiasm has passed
Co-ordinator	Mature, confident, identifies talent. Clarifies goals. Delegates effectively	Can be seen as manipulative. Offloads own share of the work
Shaper	Challenging, dynamic, thrives on pressure. Has the drive and courage to overcome obstacles	Prone to provocation. Offends people's feelings
Monitor-evaluator	Sober, strategic and discerning. Sees all options and judges accurately	Lacks drive and ability to inspire others. Can be overly critical
Teamworker	Co-operative, perceptive and diplomatic. Listens and averts friction	Indecisive in crunch situations. Avoids confrontation
Implementer	Practical, reliable, efficient. Turns ideas into actions and organises work that needs to be done	Somewhat inflexible. Slow to respond to new possibilities
Completer-finisher	Painstaking, conscientious, anxious. Searches out errors. Polishes and perfects	Inclined to worry unduly. Reluctant to delegate
Specialist	Single-minded, self-sharing, dedicated. Provides knowledge and skills in rare supply	Contributes on only a narrow front. Dwells on technicalities

Source: Belbin © 2015, www.belbin.com.

An extensive study by *Aritzeta et al.* points to a number of critical assessments of Belbin's work, such as:

- concerns about the theoretical basis of the inventory;
- questions concerning the relationship between the role of personality and team roles;
- lack of clear differentiation among the nine team roles;
- insufficient account of the type of task undertaken by the group;
- influence of organisational factors such as strategy, resources, structure, leadership and management style;
- a dominant psychological approach to understanding teamwork that needs to be complemented by socio-technical considerations

However, despite negative criticisms the authors do not think it justifiable to suggest the team-role theory is flawed. While evidence is mixed they conclude, on balance, that the model and accompanying inventory have adequate convergent validity.[41]

Critical review and reflection

The study of evolved team roles has little practical value. Behaviour does not fit into neat categories and most people do not acknowledge allowable weaknesses. The two most important roles for effective teamwork are a competent, decisive and fair leader, and a humourist to make people laugh and reduce tension.

What is YOUR honest opinion of this contention? How would YOU explain your role as a team member?

Analysis of individual behaviour

In order to understand and to influence the functioning and operation of a group or team, it is necessary to study patterns of interaction and the parts played by individual members. Not all skilled and capable individuals are necessarily good team players and, for example, it may sometimes be an advantage to have someone with a more sceptical attitude and open to change. The basic assumption behind the analysis of individual behaviour in groups is from the viewpoint of its function.

A popular classification of member roles in the study of group behaviour is that devised originally by *Benne and Sheats*.[42] The description of member roles performed in well-functioning groups is classified into three broad headings: group task roles, group building and maintenance roles, and individual roles.

- **Group task roles** – These assume that the task of the group is to select, define and solve common problems. For example, initiator–contributor, opinion seeker, co-ordinator, evaluator, recorder.
- **Group building and maintenance roles** – The analysis of member functions is orientated towards activities that build group-centred attitudes or maintain group-centred behaviour. For example, encourager, gatekeeper, standard setter, group commentator.
- **Individual roles** – These are directed towards the satisfaction of personal needs. Their purpose is not related either to group task or to the group functioning. For example, aggressor, blocker, dominator, help-seeker.

Sociometry

Originally developed by *Moreno* in 1953, **sociometry** is a method of indicating the feelings of acceptance or rejection among members of a group.[43] The basis of sociometry is usually 'buddy rating' or 'peer rating'. Each member is asked to nominate or to rate, privately, other members in terms of some given context or characteristic – for example, with whom they communicate, or how influential or how likeable they are. Questions may relate to either work or social activities. For example:

- Who would you most prefer or least prefer to work with closely?
- Who would make a good leader?
- With whom would you choose and not choose to have a drink in the pub or to go on holiday?

Positive and negative choices may be recorded for each person, although sometimes positive choices only are required. Sometimes individuals may be asked to rank their choices.

A sociogram is a diagrammatical illustration of the pattern of interpersonal relationships derived from sociometry and depicts choices, preferences, likes or dislikes and interactions between individual members. An advantage of a diagrammatical illustration is that it can also display a visual description of the structure of the group. It can indicate cliques and sub-groups, compatibility, and members who are popular, isolated or who act as links. Figure 8.8 gives a simple illustration of an actual sociogram for a group of fifteen members with single, positive choices only.

1. G and M are popular (the stars) and most often chosen by members.
2. M is the link between two overlapping cliques, KML and MNO.
3. H and P are unpopular (isolated) and chosen least by members.
4. JKMO is a chain.
5. ABCD is a sub-group and separated from the rest of the members.

There are several methods of compiling and drawing sociograms, and a number of potential criticisms and limitations. Problems also arise over how to draw the sociogram and how to interpret the roles of individual members. However, if handled sensitively it can serve to encourage meaningful discussions on patterns of social interactions, group behaviour and the perceptions of individual members towards each other. This can serve as a useful basis for the development of both employability and wider social skills.

Self-insight and the Johari window

A simple framework for looking at self-insight is the **Johari window**[44] (*see* Figure 8.9). This classifies behaviour in matrix form between what is known–unknown to self and what is known–unknown to others in order to encourage a reduction of the individual's 'hidden' behaviour through self-disclosure and of the 'blind' behaviour through feedback from others.

- **Hidden behaviour** is that which the individual wishes to conceal from, or not to communicate to, other group members. It is part of the private self. An important role of the group is to establish whether members conceal too much, or too little, about themselves from other members.

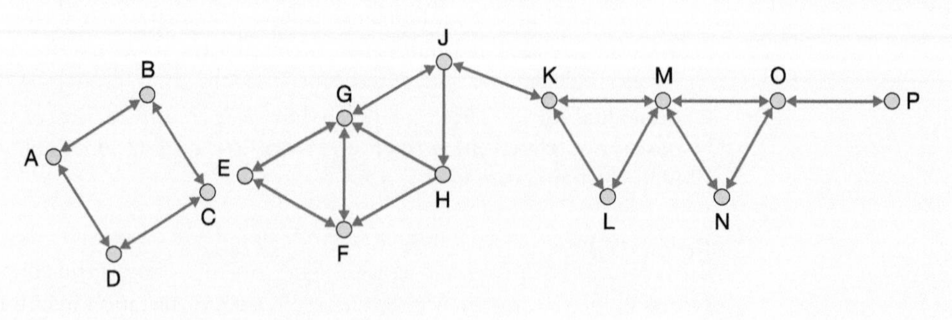

Figure 8.8 A simple illustration of a sociogram

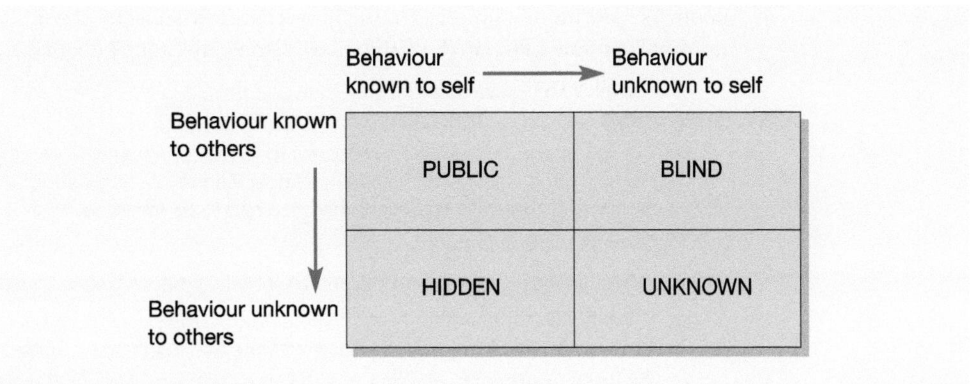

Figure 8.9 The Johari window

- **The blind area** (i.e. behaviour known to others but unknown to self) includes mannerisms, gestures and tone of voice, and represents behaviour of the impact on others of which the individual is unaware. This is sometimes referred to as the 'bad breath' area.

Members must establish an atmosphere of openness and trust in order that hidden and blind behaviours are reduced and the public behaviour enhanced. (**Recall also the comment in Chapter 4 on making public people's private attitudes.**)

Balance between team and individual

Group performance and the satisfaction derived by individuals are influenced by the interactions among members of the group. Individuals in groups interact extensively with each other and with other groups in the organisation. Although everyone operates fundamentally as a loner at work, *James* draws attention to the need in most jobs for teamworking.

> *Effective teams need equilibrium, no matter how uneasy. The perfect team will have balance, with each member aware of their role and happy to add that value to the task. The natural leaders for any given job will be in charge and their leadership will be cherished by mutual consent. Being a perfect team member means commitment to the task and overrides personal ambition and glory. Unfortunately this is rarely achieved in the workplace.*[45]

Working in a group is likely to be both a psychologically rewarding and a potentially demanding experience for the individual. As an example of this, Figure 8.10 gives an unsolicited commentary from five final-year business studies degree students after completing a group-based assignment.

Friendships and relationships at work

Increasing attention has been given to the possible effects of friendships and relationships at work, and potential conflict between personal freedom and team performance. While work may be one of the best sources of friends as well as the most desirable place to have them, the trouble is that friendships at work are full of ambiguities. For friendships, the trouble with work is that you are there to be useful: to do something for a client, team or boss. Professional friendships will always be influenced and possibly determined by the utility factor.[46] Romance in the workplace presents managers with an interesting problem: 'On the one hand, you seek to shape a team with close bonds; a degree of flirtation may well accompany, even promote this. On the other; an ill-starred liaison that jeopardises harmony and risks litigation is emphatically to be avoided'.[47]

WHAT WE FEEL WE HAVE LEARNED FROM WORKING IN A GROUP

1 'We learned that we has to listen to everybody's points of view and take these into consideration.'
2 'We found that we had to be prepared to make certain sacrifices and adopted a democratic decision process. However, if an individual felt very strongly about a specific point and persisted with a valid argument then this had to be included.'
3 'We often felt frustrated.'
4 'It was time-consuming and difficult to schedule meetings due to differences in timetables and preferences in working hours.'
5 'We learned that it is good to pool resources because this increased the overall standard of the piece of work. We feel this was only because we all set high personal standards and expected these from our fellow group members. We learned that it is possible to work in other less productive groups where individual levels of achievement may decrease.'
6 'We learned that it is better to work in a smaller and not a larger group, as there is a tendency for individual ideas to be diluted.'
7 'Groups formed on the basis of friendship are not as effective as groups formed with work as the major influence. The former tend to be unproductive.'
8 'We found that it was good to get positive response, encouragement and fedback from team members. Likewise, it was demotivating to receive a negative response.'
9 'We learned a lot about our individual personalities.'
10 'We benefited from sharing peresonal experiences from our industrial placements.'
11 'It is important to separate work and personal relationships.'

Figure 8.10 Unsolicited commentary from students after completing a group-based assignment

Critical review and reflection

Students would learn much about themselves and how they are perceived by others through regular participation in a sociometry exercise with members of their classmates. Possible difficulties are outweighed by potential benefits.

To what extent do YOU agree? How specifically would YOU expect to benefit from sociometry exercises?

Individual compared with group or team performance

Despite apparent advantages of group working, it is difficult to draw any firm conclusions from a comparison between individual and group or team performance. Group decision-making can be frustrating and stressful as well as costly and time consuming. According to *Hall*, there is a danger of elevating teams into a 'silver bullet' – a magic solution to all business problems.

> *It is not that I don't think teams work. They clearly do and it would be difficult to run an organisation of any size if you couldn't create and manage a team . . . The truth is that teams are not always the right answer to a problem. Often a well-briefed and well-managed group of individuals will do a task fine . . . A further point is that some very skilled individuals are not good team players.*[48]

However, the general feeling appears to be that the collective power of a group outshines individual performance.[49] 'Even though individuals working on their own are capable of phenomenal ingenuity, working together as a team can produce astounding results and a better decision.'[50] *Guirdham* believes that: 'Compared with individuals, groups can make objectively better decisions to which people feel more commitment, while teams can perform functions and carry out projects better and more efficiently. This can only happen, however, if the people have the special skills and abilities needed.'[51]

One might expect, therefore, a higher standard of decision-making to result from group discussion. There are, however, particular features of individual versus team performance, including:

- social loafing
- risky-shift phenomenon
- groupthink
- brainstorming.

Social loafing

The concept of **social loafing (or the Ringelmann effect)** is the tendency for individual members of a group to expend less effort than if they were working on their own. A German psychologist, Maximilien Ringelmann, compared results of individual and group performance on a rope-pulling task. Workers were asked to pull as hard as they could on a rope, performing the task first individually and then with others in groups of varying size. A meter measured the strength of each pull. Although the total amount of force did increase with the size of the work group, the effort expended by each individual member decreased with the result that the total group effort was less than the expected sum of the individual contributions.[52] Replications of the Ringelmann effect have generally been supportive of the original findings.[53]

The risky-shift phenomenon

This suggests that instead of the group taking fewer risks and making safer or more conservative decisions, the reverse is often the case. Pressures for conformity mean there is a tendency for groups to make more risky decisions than would individual members of the group on their own. People are arguably less averse to risk when there is an emotional bond with others in the group. Studies suggest that people working in groups generally advocate more risky alternatives than if they were making an individual decision on the same problem.[54] Presumably, this is because members do not feel the same sense of responsibility for group decisions or their outcomes: 'A decision which is everyone's is the responsibility of no one.'

Other explanations offered for the **risky-shift** phenomenon include the following:

- People inclined to take risks are more influential in group discussions than more conservative people.
- Risk-taking is regarded as a desirable cultural characteristic that is more likely to be expressed in a social situation such as group working.[55]

However, groups do appear to work well in the evaluation of ideas and to be more effective than individuals for problem-solving tasks requiring a range of knowledge and expertise. From a review of the research, *Shaw* suggests that evidence supports the view that groups produce more solutions and better solutions to problems than do individuals.[56]

'Groupthink'

The effectiveness of group behaviour and performance can be adversely affected by the idea of **groupthink**. From an examination of some well-known government policy-making groups, *Janis* concluded that decisions can be characterised by groupthink, which he defines as 'a deterioration of mental efficiency, reality testing, and moral judgment that results from in-group pressures'.[57] Groupthink results in the propensity for the group just to drift along. It is a generalised feature and can be apparent in any organisational situation where groups are relied upon to make important decisions.

Janis identifies a number of specific symptoms of groupthink, including: an illusion of invulnerability; discrediting of negative feedback that contradicts group consensus; an unquestioned belief in the inherent morality of the group; negative stereotyping of opponents or people outside the group, or to the acceptance of change; and pressure on individual members to conform and reach consensus so that minority or unpopular ideas may be suppressed.

Brainstorming

A **brainstorming approach** (sometimes referred to as **thought showers** or 'cloud bursting' in order not to offend people with conditions such as epilepsy) involves a group of between six and ten members adopting a 'freewheeling' attitude and generating as many ideas as possible, the more wild or apparently far-fetched, the better.[58]As an illustrative exercise a group may be asked to generate as many and varied possible uses as they can for, for example, a man or woman's leather belt. Brainstorming is based on encouraging members to suspend judgement, the assumption that creative thinking is achieved best by encouraging the natural inclinations of group members, and free association of ideas. The quantity of ideas will lead to quality of ideas.

There are a number of basic procedures for brainstorming:

- Maximum freedom of expression with a totally relaxed and informal approach. Members are encouraged to elaborate or build on ideas expressed by others and to bounce suggestions off one another.
- Initial emphasis is on the quantity of ideas generated, not the quality of ideas. No individual ideas are criticised or rejected at this stage, however wild or fanciful they may appear.
- Need for good reporting of all the ideas either in writing and/or by tape or video recording.

An interesting and popular exercise to help illustrate the suspension of initial perceived barriers and the encouragement of creative thinking is given in Figure 8.11. This exercise may also be used to compare individual and group/team-based performance. Your tutor will provide an answer. There may be others that the author is unaware of!

One might reasonably expect that members of a brainstorming group would produce more creative problem-solving ideas than if the same members worked alone as individuals. Availability of time is an important factor. Over a longer period of time the group may produce more ideas through brainstorming than individuals could. Perhaps surprisingly, there appears to be doubt about the effectiveness of brainstorming groups over an individual working under the same conditions. However, any procedure that aids the process of creativity (**discussed in Chapter 5**) should be welcomed, and there are a number of potential positive achievements in terms of related structural techniques for stimulating innovation.

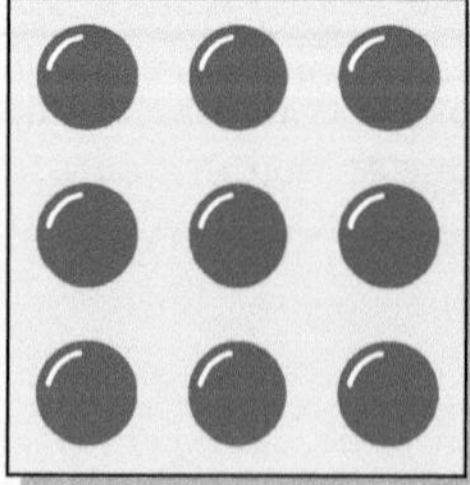

The task is to see if it is possible to touch each of the nine spots using only four straight, interconnected lines.

Figure 8.11 An example of creative thinking

Building effective teams

Whatever the debate about individual and group or team performance, effective teamworking is of increasing importance in modern organisations. The Chartered Management Institute points out that teams can play a key role in organisational success, but the development of good working relationships is vital to team performance.

> *A team is more than just a group of people who happen to work together. It is a group of people working towards common goals and objectives and sharing responsibility for the outcomes. Team building is the process of selecting and grouping team members effectively and developing good working relationships and practices enabling the team to steer and develop the work and reach their goals. Increasingly, a team may be composed of people drawn from different functions, departments and disciplines who have been brought together for a specific project.*[59]

Yukl refers to the purpose of team building as being to increase cohesiveness, mutual co-operation, and identification with the group. Based on research, theory and practice, Yukl identifies eight team-building procedures:

- **Emphasise common interests and values** – collective identification is stronger when members agree about objectives, values, priorities, strategies and the need for co-operation.
- **Use ceremonies and rituals** – to increase identification with the group and make membership appear special. The use of rituals for initiation and retirement, and ceremonies for special occasions or events.
- **Use symbols to develop identification with the group** – such as team name, logo, insignia, emblem or particular colour to help create a special identity for the team.
- **Encourage and facilitate social interaction** – development of a cohesive group is more likely when members get to know each other on a personal basis and find social interactions satisfying.
- **Tell people about group activities and achievements** – keeping members informed about the plans, activities and achievements and how their work contributes to the success of the mission.
- **Conduct process analysis sessions** – frank and open discussions of interpersonal relationships and group processes, including suggestions on how to improve effectiveness.
- **Conduct alignment sessions** – to increase mutual understanding among team members and to overcome negative stereotypes and attributions.
- **Increase incentives for mutual co-operation** – incentives based not individually but on group performance to encourage co-operation, such as bonus based on team performance.[60]

'Away days'

Another approach to team building is the use of activity-based exercises undertaken as part of corporate bonding, usually referred to as **away days**. The main objective is often the building of team spirit and working relationships involving formal team dynamics and assessment, although this may also be linked with a social purpose, for example to develop interactions with colleagues, improve motivation or to thank and reward staff. The idea of away days is subject to frequent criticism and even ridicule. Individuals may feel pressurised into participating for fear of not appearing to support management initiative or their group colleagues.

Baroness Kingsmill suggests that of course there is a case to be made for getting away from day-to-day routines and pressures and spending time with colleagues: 'Fostering relationships, encouraging creativity and innovative thinking and promoting better communication are all desirable goals. It is just that it is usually done so badly and is often a waste of time and resource. Companies spend millions on away-days every year but rarely do they make much difference to the way the business is run.' A successful away day should be small, with perhaps no more than twenty participants, provide an opportunity for wide-ranging and out-of-the-box thinking and conversation, be accompanied by some social activity to foster relationships and, if it involves sleeping away from home, have comfortable surroundings.[61]

Critical review and reflection

The nature of the hierarchical structure and inevitable role conflicts, power struggles, politics and personality clashes mean that individuals working on their own will usually complete a task more quickly and effectively than a group or team.

To what extent do YOU think this is fair comment? What has been YOUR own experience? Do YOU prefer to work on YOUR own or as a member of a group/team?

Skills of successful teamwork

How people behave and perform as members of a group is as important as their behaviour or performance as individuals. Harmonious working relationships and good teamwork help make for a high level of staff morale and work performance. Teamwork is important in any organisation but may be especially significant in emergency and caring industries or service industries such as hospitality organisations, where there is a direct effect on customer satisfaction.[62]

According to *Guirdham*, the growth of teamwork has led to the increased interest in interface skills at work.

> *More and more tasks of contemporary organisations, particularly those in high technology and service businesses, require teamwork. Taskforces, project teams and committees are key elements in the modern workplace. Teamwork depends not just on technical competence of the individuals composing the team, but on their ability to 'gel'. To work well together, the team members must have more than just team spirit. They also need collaborative skills – they must be able to support one another and to handle conflict in such a way that it becomes constructive rather than destructive.*[63]

Peeling maintains that to build good teams you need a wide pool of staff with different talents to draw upon.

> *Good managers should delight in the diversity and excellence of their staff and know that one of their main jobs is to manage the problems that come with any diverse group of talented people. In any group of talented people you will naturally get interpersonal tensions. It is important that you show you respect all the different skills and personalities in your team.*[64]

Autonomous working groups

An important development in work redesign and job enrichment is a form of work organisation based on autonomous work groups (or self-managed work groups) who are encouraged to manage their own work and working practices. The group operates without direct supervision and decides for itself how work should be distributed and carried out. Members of the group assume greater autonomy and responsibility for the effective performance of the work.

With greater empowerment the belief is that members will feel more committed to the objectives and operations of the group.

Key features of the self-managed work group include the following:

- Specific goals are set for the group but members decide the best means by which these goals are to be achieved and have greater freedom and wider discretion over the planning, execution and control of their work.
- Collectively members of the group have the necessary variety of expertise and skills to undertake the tasks of the group successfully.
- The level of external supervision is reduced and the role of supervisor becomes more one of giving advice and support to the group. Feedback and evaluation are related to the performance of the group as a whole.

ACAS strongly supports autonomous work groups for both increased competitiveness and for the quality of working life.

> *The concept of autonomous teams may be misleading as teams will always be answerable to management and rely on the provision of resources and other support. Nevertheless, one of the best ways to ensure that teams continue to develop is to move towards self-regulation - an important way of monitoring the progress of teams is to assess the level of dependence on management. It is for management to encourage progress by helping the teams develop greater independence. Reorganising the workforce into teams is not easy but when successfully developed, team working has been shown to be a way of improving competitiveness and at the same time enhancing the quality of working life for employees.*[65]

Autonomous working groups are not free of potential difficulties. With greater independence there may be a resistance to change and the acceptance of new ideas or responsibilities. With less management control internal battles over authority may develop within the group. A self-managed group is more likely to establish its own values and norms, including the pace of work, that may be at variance with those of the organisation. Developments in ICT and the growth of remote teamworking enable individuals to work collaboratively despite physical distance.

Skills to build self-managed teams

Cloke and Goldsmith refer to the special skills required for successful teamwork and list ten skills team members can develop in order to build innovative self-managing teams. All of these skills are interrelated, mutually reinforcing and dependent upon each of the others.[66]

- **Skill of self-management** – Overcoming obstacles together, and building a sense of ownership, responsibility, commitment and efficiency within each team member.
- **Skill of communication** – Collaboratively developing skills in becoming better listeners, communicating honestly about things that really matter.
- **Skill of leadership** – Creating opportunities for each member to be skilled in order to serve as leader.
- **Skill of responsibility** – Personal responsibility not only for their own work but for the work of every other member of the team in order to become self-managing.
- **Skill of supportive diversity** – Allowing team members to overcome prejudices and biases and not create winners and losers, reject outsiders or mistrust people who are different.
- **Skills of feedback and evaluation** – Essential to improving learning, team communication and the quality of products, processes and relationships.
- **Skill of strategic planning** – Identifying challenges and opportunities collaboratively. Think long term, be proactive and focus on solutions rather than problems.
- **Skill of shaping successful meetings** – Team meetings can be streamlined and made shorter, more satisfying and more productive, and result in expanded consensus.

- **Skill of resolving conflicts** – Encouraging members to improve skills in problem-solving, collaborative negotiation, responding to difficult behaviour and conflict resolution.
- **Skill of enjoyment** – Most team members enjoy working together to accomplish difficult tasks, meeting high-performance challenges and producing results that benefit themselves and their teams, organisations and communities.

The Margerison 'Team Wheel'

From work with teams in major oil companies, Charles Margerison concluded that they lacked a common teamwork language to deal with team issues or for learning and development. After further work with Dick McCann in a range of other organisations, *Margerison* identified nine major skills necessary in every business and team that can improve work contribution. The key to the system is the 'Team Wheel' (*see* Figure 8.12).

The nine key factors cover all aspects of teamwork in every organisation. Linking is the all-encompassing area of co-ordination, and organisation success depends on how effectively members of the team link to achieve objectives:

- **Advising** – Gathering and reporting information.
- **Innovating** – Creating and experimenting with ideas.
- **Promoting** – Exploring and presenting opportunities.
- **Developing** – Assessing and planning applications.
- **Organising** – Organising staff and resources.
- **Producing** – Concluding and delivering output.
- **Inspecting** – Controlling and auditing contracts and procedures.
- **Maintaining** – Upholding and safeguarding standards and values.
- **Linking** – Co-ordinating and integrating the work of others.

The 'Team Wheel' can also be used as a focus for reviewing both internal links between each member of the team and external linking with other teams and key stakeholders such as clients.[67]

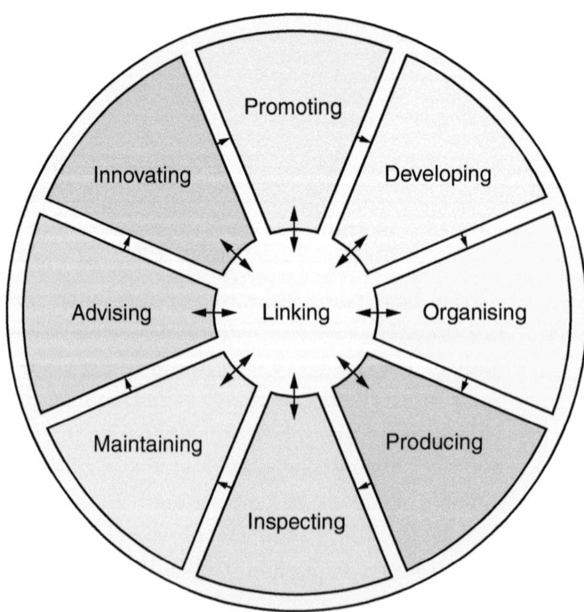

Figure 8.12 Margerison 'Team Wheel'

Source: Charles J Margerison, *Team Leadership: A guide to success with Team Management Systems*, Thomson (2002), p. 8.

The role of team leader

Building successful teams requires effective leadership with an emphasis on trust, clear communications, full participation and self-management: 'The influence and usefulness of team leaders comes, not from their delivery of traditional supervisory and control methods, but from their ability to lead from the front and in training, coaching and counselling their team members to high standards of performance.'[68]

In her discussion of the 'democratic enterprise' (organisations that can flourish economically and can also be places of excitement and stimulation, fulfilment and tranquillity), *Gratton* maintains that it is the leaders of the teams across the organisation who make the company vision a reality on a day-to-day basis. The team leaders are the creators of space in which choice and freedom can be exercised; they delineate the obligations and accountabilities contained within the business goals; they become role models for how members should behave; and they bring the philosophy of autonomy and personal development to realisation by the manner in which they act as mentors and coaches.[69]

According to *Powell*, if you want to see the efficacy of a leader and his or her leadership style, then you need to look no further than the team he or she leads.

> *A team rarely demonstrates more passion or behaves more positively than its leader. Similarly, cynical leaders produce, and therefore deserve, cynical teams. Innovative, creative and developmental leaders help to produce creative, innovative and developed followers. A team that is enthusiastic, energetic and innovative will have at its heart a leader who is correspondingly so.*[70]

With the football business as an example, *Brady* refers to the importance for any organisation, especially with a people business, of bringing staff with you, building a team around you and how team ethic leads to success.

> *The reason it works is because of the respect we have for each other. We all know each other's strengths and weaknesses and we work around them. We don't step into each other's territories. We leave each one to each role, but we support them instead.*[71]

Continuous improvement and innovation

The requirement for continual development and improvement is a necessary part of effective teamwork. The ACAS advisory booklet concludes that although self-regulation is necessary if the potential of teamworking is to be realised, teams will always need some degree of management direction. The task of management is to oversee the development of teams and provide the necessary support and training. Even when in place, teams will need constant monitoring and development. Teamworking is not a finite project but a process of continuous improvement and innovation.

> *The introduction of team working is a major step for an organisation to take. It is important that management, trade unions and employees ensure they know how team working will contribute to their business strategy and that it is likely to involve a long-term transformation . . . The early challenge and excitement of establishing teams may fade and it is easy for organisations to accept a level of performance which is short of optimum . . . In order to achieve high performance, teams require regular changes and challenges. These may include: changes to team personnel; new tasks; re-examining the contribution the team makes to the overall business aims; and ensuring that the team has regular dealings with other teams.*[72]

Critical review and reflection

Discussion about building successful teams sounds fine in the classroom. But it ignores the reality of the work environment, for example managing groups of people in a restaurant kitchen, a production assembly line, a gay pub, an orchestra, or professionals such as lecturers.

What do YOU think? Give YOUR own examples of the reality of teamworking in a specific environment.

Ten key points to remember

1 Groups are characteristic of all social situations. Individuals seldom work in isolation, and groups and teams are a major feature of the work organisation.

2 The terms 'groups' and 'teams' are to be used interchangeably. Whereas all teams are groups, it does not necessarily follow that all groups are teams.

3 Formal groups are concerned with co-ordination of work activities. Within the formal structure informal groups develop to satisfy psychological and social needs.

4 The manager's main concern is that members work together as a united, cohesive team with supportive relationships and to prevent unconstructive inter-group conflict.

5 Continuing globalisation and developments in ICT have given emphasis to the virtual teams. Members are geographically separated but still need to work together closely.

6 The role structure of the organisation, interactions among members and individual team roles are important to an understanding of group processes and behaviour.

7 In order to understand and influence the working of groups it is necessary to understand patterns of interactions and parts played by individual members.

8 Working in groups would appear to offer advantages to performance but it is difficult to draw any firm conclusion from comparison with individual performance.

9 The growth of teamwork has led to increased interest in attention to social skills, competencies and leadership in order to build and develop effective teams.

10 How to behave and perform as members of a group is as important as their actions as individuals. Continual development and improvement is a necessary part of effective teamwork.

Review and discussion questions

1 How would you distinguish between a 'group' and a 'team'? To what extent do you believe the distinction has practical significance for managers?

2 Distinguish between formal and informal groups. Explain the importance and influence of group values and norms and give practical examples from within your own university and/or organisation.

3 Explain fully the extent to which you prefer working on your own or as part of a group. What benefits would you expect both to give up and to receive from group membership?

4 Identify different stages in group development and maturity. What other factors influence the cohesiveness of work groups? Give examples by reference to a work group to which you belong.

5 Set out in detail the advantages and potential difficulties of virtual teams. Explain how you believe virtual team-working is likely to develop in the future.

6 What is meant by the role structure of an organisation? Construct a diagram that shows your own role set within your university or any work situation. Give examples of informal role expectations to which you are, or have been, a party.

7 Discuss critically what you believe could be learnt in the classroom from a study of successful music ensembles *and* sporting teams.

8 Explain fully your understanding of (a) groupthink; (b) the risky-shift phenomenon; and (c) brainstorming. Assess critically the likely standard of individual performance compared with group or team performance.

9 Discuss potential benefits and limitations of team-building exercises including 'away days'. Where possible relate to your own experiences.

10 Detail fully what you believe are the essential characteristics of a successful work group or team. As a manager, explain how you would attempt to develop effective group/team relationships and performance.

Assignment

Working in small self-selecting teams, you are required to design and present an 'ice-breaker' exercise as a fun way to help groups of new students (or other new members or delegates) to get to know and interact with each other. The exercise should be **simple, easy to understand and undertake, entertaining, something to which all members of the team/group can contribute, and that can be completed within thirty minutes.**

Your tutor will be asked to decide which team has come up with the most novel, engaging and appropriate exercise.

- If possible, attempt to employ the chosen exercise in a real-life situation. How successful was the exercise?

Personal skills and employability exercise

Objectives

Completing this exercise should help you to enhance the following skills:

- Evaluate the role(s) you play within the team and the contribution you make.
- Explore your relationships with other members of the team.
- Receive and give honest feedback about strengths and personal weaknesses.

In order to work well with other people you need to know and understand yourself and be prepared to receive honest feedback from your colleagues. The effectiveness of a team can be enhanced by a genuine openness among its members.

Exercise

For this exercise, work in pairs with another team member – if possible from a different ethnicity, culture, gender or age group. You should both agree to honour confidentiality and to conduct the exercise as a means of providing constructive feedback.

Part 1

Refer to Belbin's nine team roles (Table 8.1 in the text of this chapter) and ask the following question of each other:

1 For what role do you think I am most suited – and why?

Next refer to the Margerison 'Team Wheel' (Figure 8.12 in the text) and ask the following question of each other:

2 In what ways can I contribute more to the work of the team?

Part 2

Now ask the follow-up questions, below, of each other:

1. Which member of the team do you believe I am most close to and which member most distant from?
2. What do you see as my major strengths and personal weaknesses as a member of the team?
3. What is it about me that you find most annoying?
4. In what ways could we help each other in our work?
5. How can I be a better all-round member of the team?

Discussion

After you have both completed these questions, consider carefully and honestly:

- What have you learned about yourself from this activity?
- What response from your colleague surprised you the most?
- To what extent has this exercise helped you to understand how well you work as a team member? Put this in writing as an aid to discipline and for your personal reflection.

Case study
The Red Arrows

In the spring of 2014 the Queen celebrated her 88th birthday in the year that also marked the 50th anniversary of the D-Day Normandy landings during the Second World War. As part of this event one of the most spectacular examples of teams at work was seen - and heard - in the skies above London. The nine pilots of the Royal Air Force Aerobatic Team, better known as the Red Arrows, combine extraordinarily high levels of individual skill with strongly disciplined teamwork to mount displays that can be breathtaking, in terms of both the expertise on show and the balletic quality of the patterns and images that they paint in the air.

Source: Graham Taylor/Shutterstock.com

The full display team comprises nine pilots, and many of the manoeuvres that are part of the Red Arrows display involve all of them. However, some of the formations require smaller configurations, and the nine are divided into two sub-teams: a team of five (Reds 1-5) called 'Enid' (named after the Enid Blyton characters the Famous Five), who fly at the front of the characteristic V-formation; and a further team of four (Reds 6-9) called, for reasons lost in the mists of time, 'Gypo', who fly at the rear.[73] Two members of team Gypo (Reds 6 and 7) also fly as the 'Synchro Pair', undertaking specific 'opposition' manoeuvres such as describing patterns of loops or hearts in the air using the aircrafts' smoke trails.

The nine pilots of the Hawk T1 jet aircraft are the mere tip of the Red Arrows iceberg. Each pilot is accompanied to and from displays by their personal flight engineer, whose job is to service the aircraft and to ensure peak performance during flights. These flight engineers (who are known collectively as the 'Circus') work with their specified pilots and aircraft throughout the summer display season. The full technical support team on the ground numbers over 100 and is distinguishable by its blue overalls, contrasting with the pilots' red ones. Among the support team's number is another specialist group, the 'Dye Team' - six personnel who have the specific responsibility for replenishing the diesel and dye mix that the pilots use to create the dramatic red, white and blue vapour trails that enhance the displays. These trails also serve a technical safety purpose, as they help Red 1 to judge wind speed and direction, thereby ensuring that the display team can adjust to variations on the day.

In 2009, Flight Lieutenant Kirsty Moore made history when she became the first female pilot to join the Red Arrows. The selection criteria are very demanding: no pilots can even be shortlisted until they have been assessed as above average during their flying career, have a minimum of 1,500 flying hours' experience and have completed at least one operational tour. But individual excellence and celebrity cannot be allowed to get in the way of teamwork; as the then Red 1, Wing Commander Jas Hawker, pointed out during an interview in 2009:

> *there's zero place in the Red Arrows for an egoist even though we do get associated with pop-star lifestyle. I think if there were big egos around they'd be stamped out by the team.*[74]

Building the team

Many of the team's set pieces look scarily dangerous and many an amateur photographer has caught what he or she believed to be a near miss on film. The choreography often requires the Hawk jets to be very close in aeronautical terms and certainly the visual effect of two jets apparently hurtling towards each other on collision course at 400 mph (640 km/h) can be breathtaking. The key to this is, of course, a rigorous and continuous training programme, the start of which coincides with the selection of the next year's new pilots at the end of the display season. Three new recruits will take the places of three pilots whose time with the squad is finished; and only Red 1 will continue to fly in the same position, meaning that all the pilots need to learn new roles in an updated formation.

During the period from the end of the display season (September/October) to the following February, squad members fly three times a day from their HQ at RAF Scampton, wearing the normal green flying suits of any RAF pilot. They work individually, then in smaller groups of three or four, with intensive review using video footage and other debriefing methods to ensure that mistakes and errors are corrected. After both practice sessions and actual displays, the pilots watch recordings of their performance to identify flaws or moments when the formation was not as precisely aligned as the leader would like. In order to remove the personal aspects of criticism that might get in the way of focused analysis, the team adopts the simple psychological technique of referring to each other as numbers rather than by name when reviewing the performance of the members.[75] By March the nine are ready to begin flying as an entire team (starting with their classic formation, the 'Diamond Nine') and the more complex display work can be developed.

On the ground

During the months while the nine are consolidating their skill in the air, the aircraft themselves also have to be thoroughly overhauled. Maintenance and technical work is carried out in shifts, starting at 6.30 in the morning and continuing through to the early hours so that enough aircraft are ready for the first training flight of the day. Finally, in March, the whole operation moves to the RAF base of Akrotiri in Cyprus and the team puts the final touches to its programme. When judged sufficiently safe and professional in their performance, the nine are given formal permission to display by the Commander-in-Chief (Public Display Authority). Only then can they wear the characteristic red and blue overalls in recognition of this annual milestone, and as the next set of applicants begin their tests, the core team embarks on the summer display programme.

In addition to the flight and engineering co-ordination, the logistics of both training sessions and displays demand high levels of organisation and teamwork. During the summer the public display schedule dictates the life of the Circus. Technical staff, equipment, fuel and other resources must be available as necessary, wherever in the world the team is likely to be based for displays. This task is carried out by the Display Co-ordination and Administration Group and regularly briefed to all staff through a detailed schedule called WHAM (What's Happening According to the Manager). The image of the squadron has to be managed as well, not only to satisfy public interest in the team, but also to ensure that it retains popular support in an era of environmental concern and government austerity. A small group of RAF personnel handles enquiries from the public and press, runs the official website and organises publicity around the Reds' appearances. They are sometimes involved in charity events and challenges, such as their 'Jet Pull' in aid of the Soldiers, Sailors, Airmen and Families Association (SSAFA), when teams and individuals from the Circus compete to pull a Hawk T1 50 metres (Joe Tiley, one of the Blues, achieved this feat in 1 minute and 12 seconds in 2013).

Nevertheless, despite the rigorous and thorough training and close team co-ordination, very occasionally something goes terribly wrong. Fatalities are rare – only ten since the team was founded in 1965 – but 2011 was a tragic year. Two pilots, Jon Egging and Sean Cunningham, died in separate accidents, both of which were away from the crowds and neither of which was

→

the result of a display manoeuvre.[76] In March 2010 there was an incident during pre-season training when Reds 6 and 7, the 'Synchro Pair', struck each other during a practice flight. Red 7 was able to land safely, but the pilot of Red 6 had to eject from his plane, sustaining significant injuries to shoulder and knees that put him out of action for the 2010 display season. His aircraft was also seriously damaged; flight training was suspended until an accident investigation had been completed and the squad cleared to fly again. The immediate result for the team was the need, once the all-clear had been given, to integrate a new member since the majority of the Red Arrows' stunts require all nine aircraft. In this highly structured organisational environment the choice of replacement meant the recall of a previous Red 6.

In February 2015 Red 1 - David Montenegro - unveiled a new livery for the squadron's tailfins, and explained something of the philosophy behind the Arrows' work:

> *we aim to inspire young people by giving a tangible demonstration of what professionalism, hard work and teamwork can achieve - not just in the Armed Forces but in whatever career they choose for their future.*[77]

A Red Arrows display is, for many, a blend of sights and sounds that is not easily forgotten, and a powerful reminder of the possibilities opened up by effective teamwork.

Tasks

1 Explain the importance of group cohesiveness to the Red Arrows. How can cohesiveness be achieved when team members are so physically isolated as they train and perform?

2 Analyse the Red Arrows' yearly programme using Tuckman's model of group development and relationships. Explain how far the schedule reflects the model, and identify key transition points between the five stages.

3 Examine the whole team (including the pilots as well as the engineers and administration staff of the 'Circus') using Belbin's model of team roles. Where would you expect to find people with each of the characteristics Belbin identifies?

4 What do you think are the particular challenges facing Red 1 as leader of the display team? How might concepts outlined in the chapter help the leader understand and manage such challenges?

Notes and references

1. Schein, E. H. *Organizational Psychology,* third edition, Prentice Hall (1988), p. 145.
2. Adair, J. *Effective Teambuilding,* Gower (1986).
3. Peterson, C., Park, N and Sweeney, P. J. 'Group Well-Being: Morale from a Positive Psychology Perspective', *Applied Psychology: An International Review,* vol. 57, 2008, pp. 19–36.
4. ACAS *Teamwork: Success Through People,* advisory booklet, ACAS (2007), p. 24.
5. Holpp, L. 'Teams: It's All in the Planning', *Training & Development,* vol. 51, no. 4, 1997, pp. 44–7.
6. Cane, S. *Kaizen Strategies for Winning Through People,* Pitman (1996), p. 116.
7. Belbin, R. M. *Beyond the Team,* Butterworth–Heinemann (2000).
8. 'Steps in Successful Team Building', Checklist 088, Chartered Management Institute, June 2011.
9. Lysons, K. 'Organisational Analysis', *Supplement to The British Journal of Administrative Management,* no. 18, March/April 1997.
10. Law, S. 'Beyond the Water Cooler', *Professional Manager,* January 2005, pp. 26–8.
11. Riches, A. 'Emotionally Intelligent Teams', Organisational Change & Leadership Development, **www.anneriches.com.au** (accessed 5 March 2009).
12. Huck, S., Kubler, D. and Weibull, J. 'Social Norms and Economic Incentives in Firms', Economic & Social Research Council, 5 March 2003.
13. See, for example, Jay, A. *Corporation Man,* Penguin (1975). In an amusing historical account of the development of different forms of groups, Jay suggests that ten is the basic size of human grouping.
14. Cane, S. *Kaizen Strategies for Winning Through People,* Pitman (1996), p. 131.
15. Hazlehurst, J. 'The Way We Work Now', *Management Today,* June 2013, pp. 46–9.
16. ACAS *Teamwork: Success Through People,* advisory booklet, ACAS (2007), p. 8.
17. McKenna, P. J. and Maister, D. H. 'Building Team Trust', *Consulting to Management,* vol. 13, no. 4, 2002, pp. 51–3.

18. Farrell, E. 'Take the Lead in Setting Standards of Behaviour in Your Team', *Professional Manager,* vol. 19, no. 1, 2009, p. 14.
19. Tuckman, B. W. 'Development Sequence in Small Groups', *Psychological Bulletin,* vol. 63, 1965, pp. 384–99; and Tuckman, B. W. and Jensen, M. C. 'Stages of Small Group Development Revised', *Group and Organizational Studies,* vol. 2, no. 3, 1977, pp. 419–27.
20. Cited in Green, J. 'Are Your Teams and Groups at Work Successful?', *Administrator,* December 1993, p. 12.
21. Rickards, T. and Moger, S. T. 'Creative Leadership and Team Effectiveness: Empirical Evidence for a Two Barrier Model of Team Development', Working paper presented at the Advanced Seminar Series, University of Uppsala, Sweden, 3 March 2009; see also Rickards, T. and Moger, S. 'Creative Leadership Processes in Project Team Development: An Alternative to Tuckman's Stage Model?', *British Journal of Management,* Part 4, 2000, pp. 273–83.
22. Tajfel, H. and Turner, J. C. 'The Social Identity Theory of Intergroup Behavior', in Worchel, S. and Austin, L. W. (eds) *Psychology of Intergroup Relations,* Nelson-Hall (1986), pp. 7–24.
23. Guirdham, M. *Interactive Behaviour at Work,* third edition, Financial Times Prentice Hall (2002), p. 118.
24. Haslam, S. A. *Psychology in Organizations: The Social Identity Approach,* second edition, Sage (2004), p. 17.
25. See, for example, Flynn, F. J., Chatman, J. A. and Spataro, S. E. 'Getting to Know You: The Influence of Personality on Impressions and Performance of Demographically Different People in Organizations', *Administrative Science Quarterly,* vol. 46, 2001, pp. 414–42.
26. Hewstone, M., Ruibin, M. and Willis, H. 'Intergroup Bias', *Annual Review of Psychology,* vol. 53, 2002, pp. 575–604.
27. Brooks, I. *Organisational Behaviour: Individuals, Groups and Organisation,* fourth edition, Financial Times Prentice Hall (2009), p. 132.
28. Argyle, M. *The Social Psychology of Work,* second edition, Penguin (1989).
29. Hall, P. 'Team Solutions Need Not Be the Organisational Norm', *Professional Manager,* July 2001, p. 45
30. Symons, J. 'Taking Virtual Team Control', *Professional Manager,* vol. 12, no. 2, March 2003, p. 37.
31. Garrett, A. 'Crash Course in Managing a Virtual Team', *Management Today,* September 2007, p. 20.
32. Francesco, A. M. and Gold, B. A. *International Organizational Behavior,* second edition, Pearson Prentice Hall (2005), p. 118.
33. Murray, S. 'Virtual Teams: Global Harmony Is Their Dream', *Financial Times,* 11 May 2005.
34. Hazlehurst, J. 'The Way We Work Now', *Management Today,* June 2013, pp. 46–9.
35. See, for example, Lerner, P. M. 'Beware the Gatekeeper', *Amtrak Express,* July/August 1994, pp. 14–17.
36. Miner, J. B. *Management Theory,* Macmillan (1971).
37. Obeng, E. *All Change,* Pitman (1994).
38. Crainer, S. *Key Management Ideas: Thinkers That Changed the Management World,* third edition, Financial Times Prentice Hall (1998), p. 238.
39. Belbin, R. M. *Management Teams: Why They Succeed or Fail,* Butterworth–Heinemann (1981).
40. Belbin, R. M. *Team Roles at Work,* Butterworth–Heinemann (1993); see also Belbin, M. *The Belbin Guide to Succeeding at Work,* A & C Black (2009).
41. Aritzeta, A., Swailes, S, and Senior, B. 'Belbin's Team Role Model: Development, Validity and Applications for Team Building', *Journal of Management Studies,* vol. 44, no. 1, 2007, pp. 96–118.
42. Benne, K. D. and Sheats, P. 'Functional Roles of Group Members', *Journal of Social Issues,* vol. 4, 1948, pp. 41–9.
43. Moreno, J. L. *Who Shall Survive?* Beacon House (1953). See also Moreno, J. L. and Jennings, H. H. *The Sociometry Reader,* Free Press of Glencoe (1960).
44. Luft, J. *Group Processes: An Introduction to Group Dynamics,* second edition, National Press (1970). (The term 'Johari window' was derived from a combination of the first names of the original authors, Joseph Luft and Harry Ingham.)
45. James, J. *Body Talk at Work,* Piatkus (2001), p. 212.
46. Vernon, M. 'Office Friends: Who needs them?', *Management Today,* September 2005, pp. 59–61
47. Newman, R. 'Love Games', *Professional Manager,* September/October 2011, pp. 19–23
48. Hall, P. 'Team Solutions Need Not Be the Organisational Norm', *Professional Manager,* July 2001, p. 45.
49. See, for example, Blanchard, K. and Bowles, S. *High Five: None of Us Is As Smart As All of Us,* HarperCollins Business (2001).
50. Stanley, T. J. 'The Challenge of Managing a High-Performance Team', *SuperVision,* vol. 63, no. 7, 2002, pp. 10–12.
51. Guirdham, M. *Interactive Behaviour at Work,* third edition, Financial Times Prentice Hall (2002), p. 498.
52. Kravitz, D. A. and Martin, B. 'Ringelmann Rediscovered: The Original Article', *Journal of Personality and Social Psychology,* May 1986, pp. 936–41.
53. See, for example, Karau, S. J. and Williams, K. D. 'Social Loafing: A Meta-Analysis Review and Theoretical Integration', *Journal of Personality and Social Psychology,* October 1993, pp. 681–706; and Liden, R. C., Wayne, S. J., Jaworkski, R.A. and Bennett, N. 'Social loafing: a field investigation', *Journal of Management,* vol. 30, no. 2, 2004, pp. 285–304.
54. Kogan, N. and Wallach, M. A. 'Risk-Taking as a Function of the Situation, the Person and the Group', in Newcomb, T. M. (ed.) *New Directions in Psychology III,* Holt, Rinehart and Winston (1967).

55. For a comprehensive review of the 'risky-shift' phenomenon, see, for example, Clarke, R. D. 'Group Induced Shift Towards Risk: A Critical Appraisal', *Psychological Bulletin,* vol. 76, 1971, pp. 251–70; see also Vecchio, R. P. *Organizational Behavior,* third edition, Harcourt Brace (1995).
56. Shaw, M. E. *Group Dynamics,* McGraw-Hill (1976).
57. Janis, J. L. *Victims of Groupthink,* Houghton Mifflin (1972); and Janis, J. L. *Groupthink,* second edition, Houghton Mifflin (1982).
58. Osborn, A. F. *Applied Imagination: Principles and Procedures of Creative Thinking*, Scribner's (1963).
59. 'Steps in Successful Team Building', Checklist 088, Chartered Management Institute, June 2011.
60. Yukl, G. *Leadership in Organizations,* seventh edition, Pearson Prentice Hall (2010), pp. 374–7.
61. Baroness Kingsmill, 'Survive awayday season', *Management Today,* January 2010, p. 24.
62. See, for example, Mullins, L. J. and Dossor, P. *Hospitality Management and Organisational Behaviour,* fifth edition, Pearson Education (2013).
63. Guirdham, M. *Interactive Behaviour at Work,* third edition, Financial Times Prentice Hall (2002), p. 12.
64. Peeling, N. *Brilliant Manager: What the Best Managers Know, Do and Say,* Pearson Prentice Hall (2005), pp. 129–30.
65. ACAS *Teamwork: Success Through People,* advisory booklet, ACAS (2007), p. 30.
66. Cloke, K. and Goldsmith, J. *The End of Management and the Rise of Organizational Democracy*, Jossey-Bass (2002).
67. Margerison, C. J. *Team Leadership: A Guide to Success with Team Management Systems*, Thomson (2002).
68. ACAS *Teamwork: Success Through People,* advisory booklet, ACAS (2007), p. 31.
69. Gratton, L. *The Democratic Enterprise,* Financial Times Prentice Hall (2004).
70. Powell, N. 'Teams Are a Mirror Image of Their Leaders', *Professional Manager,* vol. 16, no. 5, 2007, p. 41.
71. Brady, K. in conversation with Webber, M. 'Team Focus', *Manager,* Spring 2013, pp. 36–8.
72. ACAS *Teamwork: Success Through People,* advisory booklet, ACAS (2007), p. 34.
73. The Red Arrows, **http://www.raf.mod.uk/reds** (accessed 2 March 2015).
74. Brown, I. 'The Red Arrows: aerial acrobats', *Telegraph,* 1September 2009.
75. BBC, *Inside the Bubble,* documentary broadcast by BBC2 on 27 July 2014.
76. Lowbridge, C. 'How dangerous is life as a Red Arrow?', BBC News, 2014, **http://www.bbc.co.uk/news/uk-england-lincolnshire-25763663** (accessed 2 March 2015).
77. The Red Arrows, **http://www.raf.mod.uk/reds/news/** (accessed 2 March 2015).

14 Conflict and Negotiation

Source: Taylor Hill/FilmMagic/Getty Images

LEARNING OBJECTIVES

After studying this chapter, you should be able to:

14-1 Describe the three types of conflict and the three loci of conflict.

14-2 Outline the conflict process.

14-3 Contrast distributive and integrative bargaining.

14-4 Apply the five steps of the negotiation process.

14-5 Show how individual differences influence negotiations.

14-6 Assess the roles and functions of third-party negotiations.

MyManagementLab®
Chapter Warm Up

If your professor has chosen to assign this, go to the Assignments section of **mymanagementlab.com** to complete the chapter warm up.

A CHANGE OF TUNE

While most of us are accustomed to instant access to nearly any music we want over the Internet, digital music distribution is actually a relatively new and volatile market. As recently as 2005, almost all music sales came from physical media like compact discs. By 2015, however, digital downloads overtook CDs in revenue and legal streaming services comprised nearly a third of the overall music market. In Sweden and South Korea, as an extreme example, streaming music services provided 90 percent of recorded music revenues. This rapid shift for the industry in a short period of time has created ongoing high-stakes negotiations.

When Daniel Ek (pictured here) started Spotify in 2006, now one of the most successful streaming services, the music producers were suspicious that his service would lower their revenues. Ek claimed his intention was not to cheat the system, but to beat music pirates at their own game by offering a service that made legally listening to tracks easier and more pleasant than illegal downloads. He noted, "It's not like people want to be pirates. They just want a great experience. So we started sketching what that would look like." Through many conflicts and negotiations, Ek maintained that Spotify offered greater profits for everyone in the music industry, and eventually the industry's players agreed.

The basic terms between record companies and Spotify are simple—Spotify acquires the right to distribute music to fans by paying royalties to the copyright holders. In turn, Spotify can make money from either running advertisements or charging users. To maintain legal access to the music, Ek must continually negotiate with all the recording companies that administer copyrights. Spotify remains completely responsible for ensuring adherence to copyright laws.

This seemingly straightforward negotiation process of exchanging rights for revenues is actually quite complex in practice, especially since pricing models are still being worked out by the players in the industry. Spotify also needs to demonstrate to recording companies that cooperating with streaming services creates better value for them than different music distribution methods, even as prices change. The possibilities for lucrative negotiations are high—but so are the possibilities for conflict.

A number of factors have strengthened Spotify's bargaining position. For one, any record label that walks away from a deal with Spotify risks losing access to many listeners who rely exclusively on streaming services for their music. For another, it's better for record labels to make money through an agreement with Spotify than to make nothing from pirated copies of their music.

At the same time, the major labels have their own bargaining resources. First and foremost, if media companies won't deal with Spotify, the service will quickly lose its appeal. Second and related to this, if Spotify cannot obtain music rights for popular artists, disappointed listeners may easily turn to other services and threaten its existence. The highest-profile defector so far is Taylor Swift, who moved from Spotify to another streaming service that offered her a higher rate of return on plays. The impact of the music star's defection isn't completely known but may be costly since the decision was very public in the media.

The stakes of these negotiations are high. One thing is for sure: in such a turbulent market, there will surely be a lot of time spent at the bargaining table in the years to come.

Sources: J. Seabrook, "Revenue Streams," *The New Yorker,* November 24, 2014, http://www.newyorker.com/magazine/2014/11/24/revenue-streams; S. Dredge, "Ministry of Sound Boss Attacks Major Labels for Streaming 'Short Termism,'" *The Guardian,* May 15, 2015, http://www.theguardian.com/technology/2015/may/15/ministry-of-sound-major-labels-music-streaming-spotify; and N. Prins "Spotify Racks Up a Streaming Milestone: Artists Settle in for the Fight," *Forbes,* May 14, 2015, http://www.forbes.com/sites/nomiprins/2015/05/14/spotify-racks-up-a-streaming-milestone-artists-settle-in-for-the-fight/.

As the music industry example demonstrates, forms of conflict and negotiation are often complex—and controversial—interpersonal processes. While we generally see conflict as a negative topic and negotiation as a positive one, what we deem positive or negative often depends on our perspective.

Conflict can turn personal. It can create chaotic conditions that make it nearly impossible for employees to work as a team. However, conflict also has a less well-known positive side. We'll explain the difference between negative and positive conflicts in this chapter and provide a guide to help you understand how conflicts develop. We'll also present the specifics about the topic closely akin to conflict: negotiation.

A Definition of Conflict

14-1 Describe the three types of conflict and the three loci of conflict.

conflict A process that begins when one party perceives that another party has negatively affected, or is about to negatively affect, something that the first party cares about.

There has been no shortage of definitions of *conflict*,[1] but common to most is the idea that conflict is a perception. If no one is aware of a conflict, then it is generally agreed no conflict exists. Also needed to begin the conflict process are opposition or incompatibility, and interaction.

We define **conflict** broadly as a process that begins when one party perceives another party has affected or is about to negatively affect something the first party cares about. Conflict describes the point in ongoing activity when interaction becomes disagreement. People experience a wide range of conflicts in organizations over an incompatibility of goals, differences in interpretations of facts, disagreements over behavioral expectations, and the like. Our definition covers the full range of conflict levels, from overt and violent acts to subtle forms of disagreement.

There is no consensus over the role of conflict in groups and organizations. In the past, researchers tended to argue about whether conflict was uniformly good or bad. Such simplistic views eventually gave way to approaches recognizing that not all conflicts are the same and that different types of conflict have different effects.

functional conflict Conflict that supports the goals of the group and improves its performance.

dysfunctional conflict Conflict that hinders group performance.

Contemporary perspectives differentiate types of conflict based on their effects. **Functional conflict** supports the goals of the group, improves its performance, and is thus a constructive form of conflict. For example, a debate among members of a work team about the most efficient way to improve production can be functional if unique points of view are discussed and compared openly. Conflict that hinders group performance is destructive or **dysfunctional conflict**. A highly personal struggle for control in a team that distracts from the task at hand is dysfunctional. Exhibit 14-1 provides an overview depicting the effect of levels of conflict. To understand different types of conflict, we will discuss next the *types* of conflict and the *loci* of conflict.

Types of Conflict

task conflict Conflict over content and goals of the work.

relationship conflict Conflict based on interpersonal relationships.

process conflict Conflict over how work gets done.

One means of understanding conflict is to identify the *type* of disagreement, or what the conflict is about. Is it a disagreement about goals? Is it about people who just rub one another the wrong way? Or is it about the best way to get things done? Although each conflict is unique, researchers have classified conflicts into three categories: task, relationship, or process. **Task conflict** relates to the content and goals of the work. **Relationship conflict** focuses on interpersonal relationships. **Process conflict** is about how the work gets done.

Studies demonstrate that relationship conflicts, at least in work settings, are almost always dysfunctional.[2] Why? It appears that the friction and interpersonal hostilities inherent in relationship conflicts increase personality clashes and decrease mutual understanding, which hinders the completion of organizational tasks. Of the three types, relationship conflicts also appear to be the most psychologically exhausting to individuals.[3] Because they tend to revolve around personalities, you can see how relationship conflicts can become destructive. After all, we can't expect to change our coworkers' personalities,

Exhibit 14-1 Conflict and Unit Performance

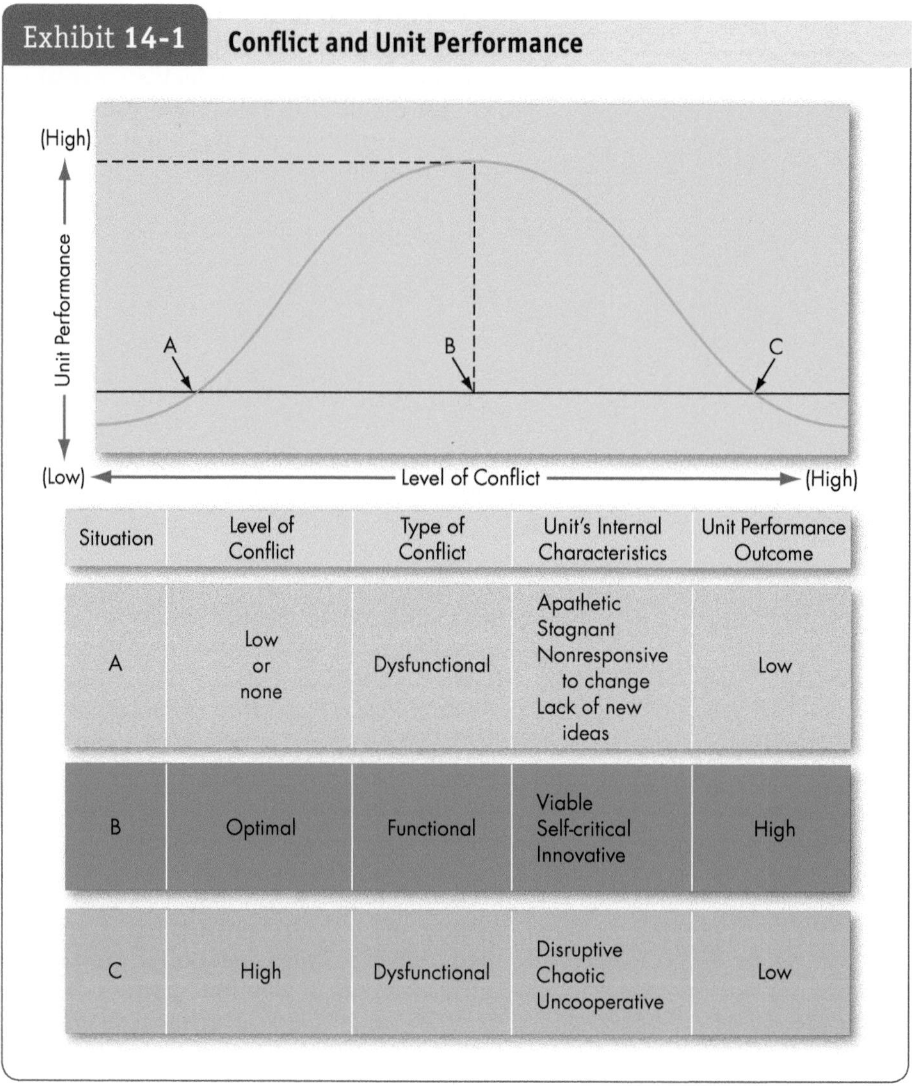

Situation	Level of Conflict	Type of Conflict	Unit's Internal Characteristics	Unit Performance Outcome
A	Low or none	Dysfunctional	Apathetic Stagnant Nonresponsive to change Lack of new ideas	Low
B	Optimal	Functional	Viable Self-critical Innovative	High
C	High	Dysfunctional	Disruptive Chaotic Uncooperative	Low

and we would generally take offense at criticisms directed at who we *are* as opposed to how we behave.

While scholars agree that relationship conflict is dysfunctional, there is considerably less agreement about whether task and process conflicts are functional. Early research suggested that task conflict within groups correlated to higher group performance, but a review of 116 studies found that generalized task conflict was essentially unrelated to group performance. However, there were factors of the conflict that could create a relationship between conflict and performance.[4]

One such factor was whether the conflict included top management or occurred lower in the organization. Task conflict among top management teams was positively associated with performance, whereas conflict lower in the organization was negatively associated with group performance, perhaps because people in top positions may not feel as threatened in their organizational roles by conflict. This review also found that it mattered whether other types of conflict were occurring at the same time. If task and relationship conflict occurred together, task conflict was more likely negative, whereas if task conflict occurred by itself, it more likely was positive. Also, some scholars have argued that the strength of conflict is important—if task conflict is very low, people aren't really engaged or addressing the important issues. If task conflict is too high, however, infighting will quickly degenerate into relationship conflict. Moderate levels of task conflict may thus be optimal. Supporting this argument, one study in China found that moderate levels of task conflict in the early development stage increased creativity in groups, but high levels decreased team performance.[5]

Finally, the personalities of the teams appear to matter. One study demonstrated that teams of individuals who are, on average, high in openness and emotional stability are better able to turn task conflict into increased group performance.[6] The reason may be that open and emotionally stable teams can put task conflict in perspective and focus on how the variance in ideas can help solve the problem, rather than letting it degenerate into relationship conflicts.

What about process conflict? Researchers found that process conflicts are about delegation and roles. Conflicts over delegation often revolve around the perception of some members as shirking, and conflicts over roles can leave some group members feeling marginalized. Thus, process conflicts often become highly personalized and quickly devolve into relationship conflicts. It's also true, of course, that arguing about how to do something takes time away from actually doing it. We've all been part of groups in which the arguments and debates about roles and responsibilities seem to go nowhere.

Loci of Conflict

dyadic conflict Conflict that occurs between two people.

intragroup conflict Conflict that occurs within a group or team.

intergroup conflict Conflict between different groups or teams.

Another way to understand conflict is to consider its *locus*, or the framework within which the conflict occurs. Here, too, there are three basic types. **Dyadic conflict** is conflict between two people. **Intragroup conflict** occurs *within* a group or team. **Intergroup conflict** is conflict *between* groups or teams.

Nearly all the literature on task, relationship, and process conflict considers intragroup conflict (within the group). That makes sense given that groups and teams often exist only to perform a particular task. However, it doesn't necessarily tell us all we need to know about the context and outcomes of conflict. For example, research has found that for intragroup task conflict to positively

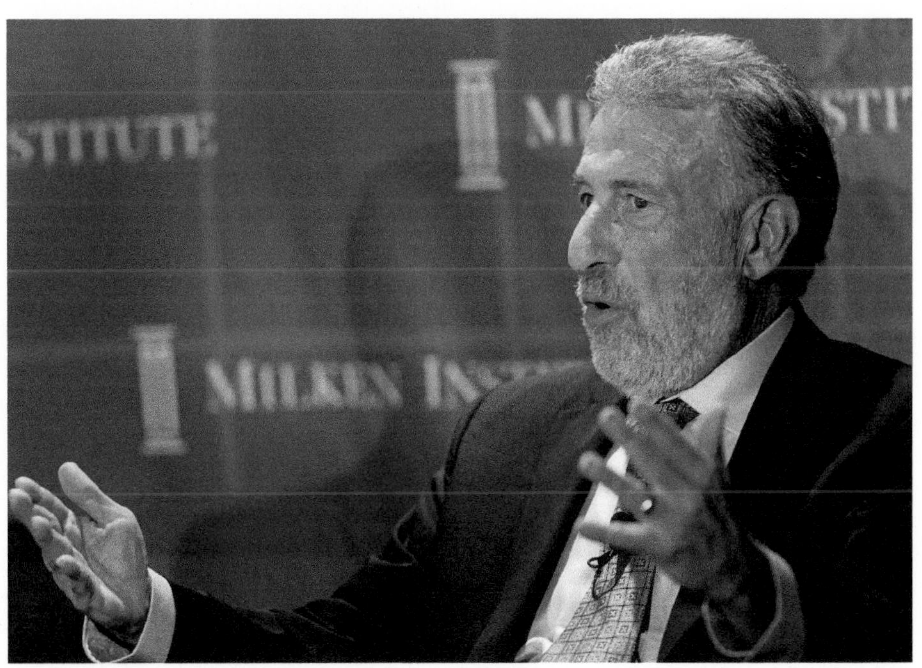

Under the leadership of George Zimmer as the founder and CEO of Men's Warehouse and its advertising spokesman, the retailer grew into a multi-million-dollar firm with 1,143 stores. After retiring as CEO, Zimmer served as executive chairman of MW's board until an intragroup conflict between him and other members resulted in his removal from the board.
Source: Patrick Fallon/Bloomberg/Getty Images

influence performance within the team, it is important that the team has a supportive climate in which mistakes aren't penalized and every team member "[has] the other's back."[7] But is this concept applicable to the effects of intergroup conflict? Think about, say, NFL football. As we said, for a team to adapt and improve, perhaps a certain amount of intragroup conflict (but not too much) is good for team performance, especially when the team members support one another. But would we care whether members from one team supported members from another team? Probably not. In fact, if groups are competing with one another so that only one team can "win," interteam conflict seems almost inevitable. Still, it must be managed. Intense intergroup conflict can be quite stressful to group members and might well affect the way they interact. One study found, for example, that high levels of conflict between teams caused individuals to focus on complying with norms within their teams.[8]

It may surprise you that individuals become most important in intergroup conflicts. One study that focused on intergroup conflict found an interplay between an individual's position within a group and the way that individual managed conflict between groups. Group members who were relatively peripheral in their own group were better at resolving conflicts between their group and another one. But this happened only when those peripheral members were still accountable to their group.[9] Thus, being at the core of your workgroup does not necessarily make you the best person to manage conflict with other groups.

Another intriguing question about loci is whether conflicts interact with or buffer one another. Assume, for example, that Jia and Marcus are on the same team. What happens if they don't get along interpersonally (dyadic conflict) *and* their team also has high task conflict? Progress might be halted. What happens to their team if two other team members, Shawna and Justin, do get along well? The team might still be dysfunctional, or the positive relationship might prevail.

Thus, understanding functional and dysfunctional conflict requires not only that we identify the type of conflict; we also need to know where it occurs. It's possible that while the concepts of task, relationship, and process conflict are useful in understanding intragroup or even dyadic conflict, they are less useful in explaining the effects of intergroup conflict. But how do we make conflict as productive as possible? A better understanding of the conflict process, discussed next, will provide insight about potential controllable variables.

The Conflict Process

14-2 Outline the conflict process.

conflict process A process that has five stages: potential opposition or incompatibility, cognition and personalization, intentions, behavior, and outcomes.

The **conflict process** has five stages: potential opposition or incompatibility, cognition and personalization, intentions, behavior, and outcomes (see Exhibit 14-2).

Stage I: Potential Opposition or Incompatibility

The first stage of conflict is the appearance of conditions—causes or sources—that create opportunities for it to arise. These conditions *need not* lead directly to conflict, but one of them is necessary if it is to surface. We group the conditions into three general categories: communication, structure, and personal variables.

Communication Susan had worked in supply chain management at Bristol-Myers Squibb for three years. She enjoyed her work largely because her manager, Harry, was a great boss. Then Harry was promoted and Chuck took his place. Six months later, Susan says her job is frustrating. "Harry and I were

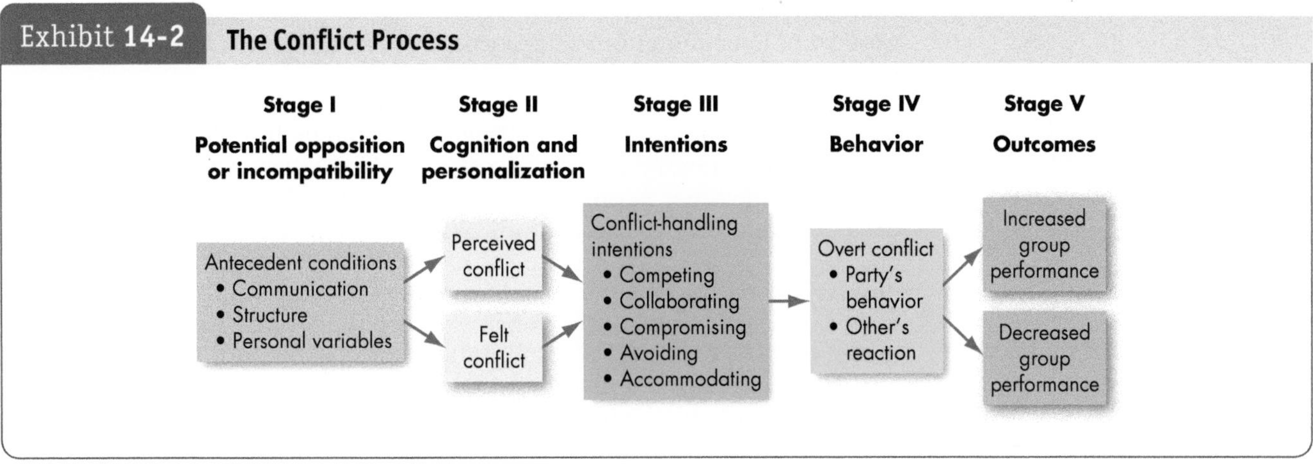

on the same wavelength. It's not that way with Chuck. He tells me something, and I do it. Then he tells me I did it wrong. I think he means one thing but says something else. It's been like this since the day he arrived. I don't think a day goes by when he isn't yelling at me for something. You know, there are some people you just find it easy to communicate with. Well, Chuck isn't one of those!"

Susan's comments illustrate that communication can be a source of conflict.[10] Her experience represents the opposing forces that arise from semantic difficulties, misunderstandings, and "noise" in the communication channel (see Chapter 11). These factors, along with jargon and insufficient information, can be barriers to communication and potential antecedent conditions to conflict. The potential for conflict has also been found to increase with too little or *too much* communication. Communication is functional up to a point, after which it is possible to overcommunicate, increasing the potential for conflict.

Structure Charlotte is a salesperson and Mercedes is the company credit manager at Portland Furniture Mart, a large discount furniture retailer. The women have known each other for years and have much in common: They live two blocks apart, and their oldest daughters attend the same middle school and are best friends. If Charlotte and Mercedes had different jobs, they might be friends, but at work they constantly disagree. Charlotte's job is to sell furniture, and she does it well. Most of her sales are made on credit. Because Mercedes's job is to minimize credit losses, she regularly has to turn down the credit applications of Charlotte's customers. It's nothing personal between the women; the requirements of their jobs just bring them into conflict.

The conflicts between Charlotte and Mercedes are structural in nature. The term *structure* in this context includes variables such as size of group, degree of specialization in tasks assigned to group members, jurisdictional clarity, member–goal compatibility, leadership styles, reward systems, and degree of dependence between groups. The larger the group and the more specialized its activities, the greater the likelihood of conflict. Tenure and conflict are inversely related, meaning that the longer a person stays with an organization, the less likely conflict becomes. Therefore, the potential for conflict is greatest when group members are younger and when turnover is high.

Personal Variables Have you ever met someone you immediately disliked? Perhaps you disagreed with most of his opinions. Even insignificant characteristics—his voice, facial expressions, or word choice—may have annoyed you. Sometimes our impressions are negative. When you have to work with people you don't like, the potential for conflict arises.

Our last category of potential sources of conflict is personal variables, which include personality, emotions, and values. People high in the personality traits of disagreeableness, neuroticism, or self-monitoring (see Chapter 5) are prone to tangle with other people more often—and to react poorly when conflicts occur.[11] Emotions can cause conflict even when they are not directed at others. An employee who shows up to work irate from her hectic morning commute may carry that anger into her workday, which can result in a tension-filled meeting.[12] Furthermore, differences in preferences and values can generate higher levels of conflict. For example, a study in Korea found that when group members didn't agree about their desired achievement levels, there was more task conflict; when group members didn't agree about their desired interpersonal closeness, there was more relationship conflict; and when group members didn't have similar desires for power, there was more conflict over status.[13]

Stage II: Cognition and Personalization

If the conditions cited in Stage I negatively affect something one party cares about, then the potential for opposition or incompatibility becomes actualized in the second stage.

As we noted in our definition of conflict, one or more of the parties must be aware that antecedent conditions exist. However, just because a disagreement is a **perceived conflict** does not mean it is personalized. It is at the **felt conflict** level, when individuals become emotionally involved, that they experience anxiety, tension, frustration, or hostility.

perceived conflict Awareness by one or more parties of the existence of conditions that create opportunities for conflict to arise.

felt conflict Emotional involvement in a conflict that creates anxiety, tenseness, frustration, or hostility.

Stage II is important because it's where conflict issues tend to be defined, where the parties decide what the conflict is about.[14] The definition of conflict is important because it delineates the set of possible settlements. Most evidence suggests that people tend to default to cooperative strategies in interpersonal interactions unless there is a clear signal that they are faced with a competitive person. However, if our salary disagreement is a zero-sum situation (the increase in pay you want means there will be that much less in the raise pool for me), I am going to be far less willing to compromise than if I can frame the conflict as a potential win–win situation (the dollars in the salary pool might be increased so both of us could get the added pay we want).

Second, emotions play a major role in shaping perceptions.[15] Negative emotions allow us to oversimplify issues, lose trust, and put negative interpretations on the other party's behavior.[16] In contrast, positive feelings increase our tendency to see potential relationships among elements of a problem, take a broader view of the situation, and develop innovative solutions.[17]

Stage III: Intentions

intentions Decisions to act in a given way.

Intentions intervene between people's perceptions and emotions, and their overt behavior. They are decisions to act in a given way.[18]

Intentions are a distinct stage because we have to infer the other's intent to know how to respond to behavior. Many conflicts escalate simply because one party attributes the wrong intentions to the other. There is slippage between intentions and behavior, so behavior does not always accurately reflect a person's intentions.

Exhibit 14-3 represents one way to identify the primary conflict-handling intentions. Using two dimensions—*assertiveness* (the degree to which one party attempts to satisfy his or her own concerns) and *cooperativeness* (the degree to

Exhibit 14-3 **Dimensions of Conflict-Handling Intentions**

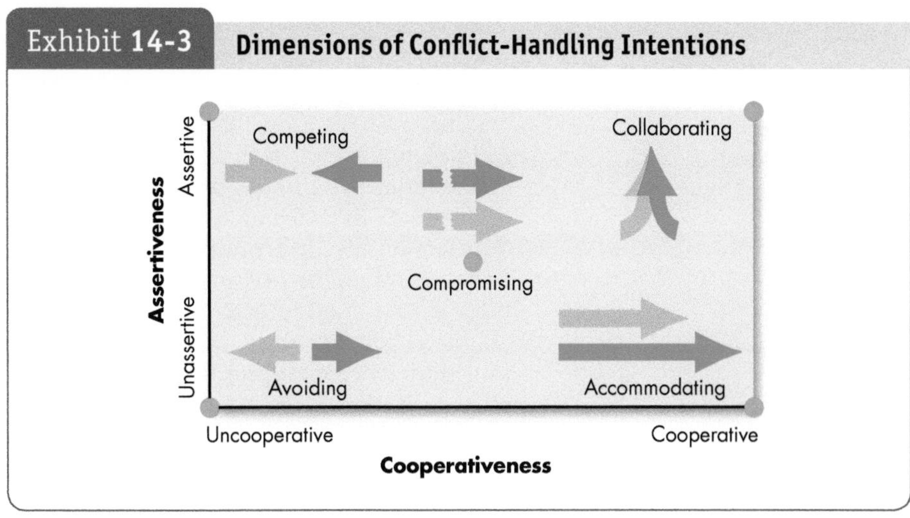

Source: Figure from "Conflict and Negotiation Processes in Organizations" by K. Thomas in M. D. Dunnette and L. M. Hough (eds.), *Handbook of Industrial and Organizational Psychology*, 2/e, vol. 3 (Palo Alto, CA: Consulting Psychologists Press, 1992), 668. Used with permission.

which one party attempts to satisfy the other party's concerns)—we can identify five conflict-handling intentions: *competing* (assertive and uncooperative), *collaborating* (assertive and cooperative), *avoiding* (unassertive and uncooperative), *accommodating* (unassertive and cooperative), and *compromising* (midrange on both assertiveness and cooperativeness).[19]

competing A desire to satisfy one's interests, regardless of the impact on the other party to the conflict.

Competing When one person seeks to satisfy his or her own interests regardless of the impact on the other parties in the conflict, that person is **competing**. We are more apt to compete when resources are scarce.

collaborating A situation in which the parties to a conflict each desire to satisfy fully the concerns of all parties.

Collaborating When parties in conflict each desire to fully satisfy the concerns of all parties, there is cooperation and a search for a mutually beneficial outcome. In **collaborating**, parties intend to solve a problem by clarifying differences rather than by accommodating various points of view. If you attempt to find a win–win solution that allows both parties' goals to be completely achieved, that's collaborating.

avoiding The desire to withdraw from or suppress a conflict.

Avoiding A person may recognize a conflict exists and want to withdraw from or suppress it. Examples of **avoiding** include trying to ignore a conflict and keeping away from others with whom you disagree.

accommodating The willingness of one party in a conflict to place the opponent's interests above his or her own.

Accommodating A party who seeks to appease an opponent may be willing to place the opponent's interests above his or her own, sacrificing to maintain the relationship. We refer to this intention as **accommodating**. Supporting someone else's opinion despite your reservations about it, for example, is accommodating.

compromising A situation in which each party to a conflict is willing to give up something.

Compromising In **compromising**, there is no winner or loser. Rather, there is a willingness to ration the object of the conflict and accept a solution with incomplete satisfaction of both parties' concerns. The distinguishing characteristic of compromising, therefore, is that each party intends to give up something.

Stage IV: Behavior

When most people think of conflict, they tend to focus on Stage IV because this is where conflicts become visible. The behavior stage includes statements, actions, and reactions made by conflicting parties, usually as overt attempts to implement their own intentions. As a result of miscalculations or unskilled enactments, overt behaviors sometimes deviate from original intentions.[20]

Stage IV is a dynamic process of interaction. For example, you make a demand on me, I respond by arguing, you threaten me, I threaten you back, and so on. Exhibit 14-4 provides a way of visualizing conflict behavior. All conflicts exist somewhere along this continuum. At the lower end are conflicts characterized by subtle, indirect, and highly controlled forms of tension, such as a student challenging a point the instructor has made. Conflict intensities escalate as they move upward along the continuum until they become highly destructive. Strikes, riots, and wars clearly fall in this upper range. Conflicts that reach the upper ranges of the continuum are almost always dysfunctional. Functional conflicts are typically confined to the lower range of the continuum.

Intentions that are brought into a conflict are eventually translated into behaviors. *Competing* brings out active attempts to contend with team members, and more individual effort to achieve ends without working together. *Collaborating* creates investigation of multiple solutions with other members of the team and trying to find a solution that satisfies all parties as much as possible. *Avoidance* is seen in behavior like refusals to discuss issues and reductions in effort toward group goals. People who *accommodate* put their relationships ahead of the issues in the conflict, deferring to others' opinions and sometimes acting as a subgroup with them. Finally, when people *compromise,* they both expect to (and do) sacrifice parts of their interests, hoping that if everyone does the same, an agreement will sift out.

A review that examined the effects of the four sets of behaviors across multiple studies found that openness and collaborating were both associated with superior group performance, whereas avoiding and competing strategies were associated with significantly worse group performance.[21] These effects were nearly as large as the effects of relationship conflict. This further demonstrates that it is not just the existence of conflict or even the type of conflict that creates problems, but rather the ways people respond to conflict and manage the process once conflicts arise.

If a conflict is dysfunctional, what can the parties do to de-escalate it? Or, conversely, what options exist if conflict is too low to be functional and

Exhibit 14-4 Conflict-Intensity Continuum

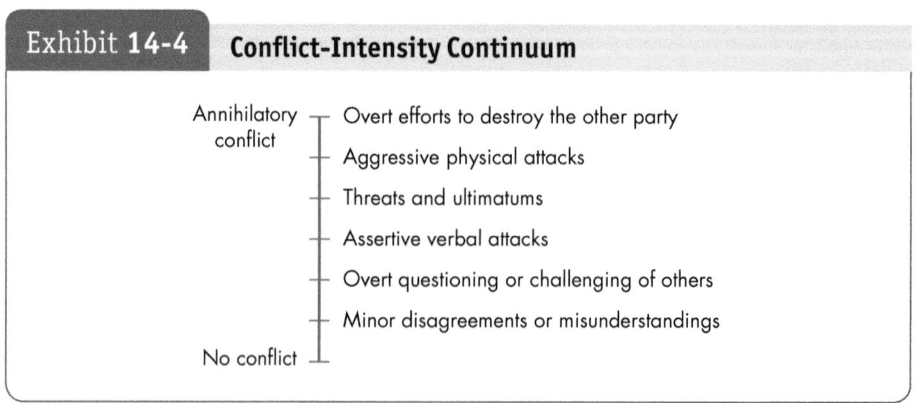

Sources: Based on S. P. Robbins, *Managing Organizational Conflict: A Nontraditional Approach* (Upper Saddle River, NJ: Prentice Hall, 1974), 93–97; and F. Glasi, "The Process of Conflict Escalation and the Roles of Third Parties," in G. B. J. Bomers and R. Peterson (eds.), *Conflict Management and Industrial Relations* (Boston: Kluwer-Nijhoff, 1982), 119–40.

Exhibit 14-5 **Conflict Management Techniques**

Conflict-Resolution Techniques	
Problem solving	Meeting face to face for the purpose of identifying the problem and resolving it through open discussion.
Superordinate goals	Creating a shared goal that cannot be attained without the cooperation of each of the conflicting parties.
Expansion of resources	Expanding the supply of a scarce resource (for example, money, promotion, opportunities, office space).
Avoidance	Withdrawing from or suppressing the conflict.
Smoothing	Playing down differences while emphasizing common interests between the conflicting parties.
Compromise	Having each party to the conflict give up something of value.
Authoritative command	Letting management use its formal authority to resolve the conflict and then communicating its desires to the parties involved.
Altering the human variable	Using behavioral change techniques such as human relations training to alter attitudes and behaviors that cause conflict.
Altering the structural variables	Changing the formal organization structure and the interaction patterns of conflicting parties through job redesign, transfers, creation of coordinating positions, and the like.
Conflict-Stimulation Techniques	
Communication	Using ambiguous or threatening messages to increase conflict levels.
Bringing in outsiders	Adding employees to a group whose backgrounds, values, attitudes, or managerial styles differ from those of present members.
Restructuring the organization	Realigning work groups, altering rules and regulations, increasing interdependence, and making similar structural changes to disrupt the status quo.
Appointing a devil's advocate	Designating a critic to purposely argue against the majority positions held by the group.

Source: Based on S. P. Robbins, *Managing Organizational Conflict: A Nontraditional Approach* (Upper Saddle River, NJ: Prentice Hall, 1974), 59–89.

conflict management The use of resolution and stimulation techniques to achieve the desired level of conflict.

needs to be increased? This brings us to techniques of **conflict management.** Exhibit 14-5 lists the major resolution and stimulation techniques that allow managers to control conflict levels. We have already described several as conflict-handling intentions. Under ideal conditions, a person's intentions should translate into comparable behaviors.

Stage V: Outcomes

The action–reaction interplay between conflicting parties creates consequences. As our model demonstrates (see Exhibit 14-1), these outcomes may be functional if the conflict improves the group's performance, or dysfunctional if it hinders performance.

Functional Outcomes How might conflict act as a force to increase group performance? It is hard to visualize a situation in which open or violent aggression could be functional. But it's possible to see how low or moderate levels of conflict could improve group effectiveness. Note that all our examples focus on task and process conflicts and exclude the relationship variety.

Conflict is constructive when it improves the quality of decisions, stimulates creativity and innovation, encourages interest and curiosity among group members, provides the medium for problems to be aired and tensions released, and fosters self-evaluation and change. Mild conflicts also may generate energizing emotions so members of groups become more active, energized, and engaged in their work.[22]

IBM encourages employees to engage in functional conflict that results in innovations, such as the Watson supercomputer designed to learn through the same process human brains use. For innovation to flourish, IBM relies on the creative tension from employees' different ideas and skills and provides a work environment that promotes risk taking and outside-the-box thinking.
Source: Jon Simon/Feature Photo Service/Newscom

Dysfunctional Outcomes The destructive consequences of conflict on the performance of a group or an organization are generally well known: Uncontrolled opposition breeds discontent, which acts to dissolve common ties and eventually leads to the destruction of the group. And, of course, a substantial body of literature documents how dysfunctional conflicts can reduce group effectiveness.[23] Among the undesirable consequences are poor communication, reductions in group cohesiveness, and subordination of group goals to the primacy of infighting among members. All forms of conflict—even the functional varieties—appear to reduce group member satisfaction and trust.[24] When active discussions turn into open conflicts between members, information sharing between members decreases significantly.[25] At the extreme, conflict can bring group functioning to a halt and threaten the group's survival.

Managing Functional Conflict If managers recognize that in some situations conflict can be beneficial, what can they do to manage conflict effectively in their organizations? In addition to knowing the principles of conflict motivation we just discussed, there are some practical guidelines for managers.

First, one of the keys to minimizing counterproductive conflicts is recognizing when there really is a disagreement. Many apparent conflicts are due to people using different verbiage to discuss the same general course of action. For example, someone in marketing might focus on "distribution problems," while someone from operations will talk about "supply chain management" to describe essentially the same issue. Successful conflict management recognizes these different approaches and attempts to resolve them by encouraging open, frank discussion focused on interests rather than issues. Another approach is to have opposing groups pick parts of the solution that are most important to them and then focus on how each side can get its top needs satisfied. Neither side may get exactly what it wants, but each side will achieve the most important parts of its agenda.[26]

Third, groups that resolve conflicts successfully discuss differences of opinion openly and are prepared to manage conflict when it arises.[27] The most disruptive conflicts are those that are never addressed directly. An open discussion makes it much easier to develop a shared perception of the problems at hand; it also allows groups to work toward a mutually acceptable solution. Fourth, managers need to emphasize shared interests in resolving conflicts, so groups that disagree with one another don't become too entrenched in their points of view and start to take the conflicts personally. Groups with cooperative conflict styles and a strong underlying identification with the overall group goals are more effective than groups with a competitive style.[28]

Differences across countries in conflict resolution strategies may be based on collectivistic tendencies and motives.[29] Collectivist cultures see people as deeply embedded in social situations, whereas individualist cultures see them as autonomous. As a result, collectivists are more likely to seek to preserve relationships and promote the good of the group as a whole. They will avoid the direct expression of conflict, preferring indirect methods for resolving differences of opinion. Collectivists may also be more interested in demonstrations of concern and working through third parties to resolve disputes, whereas individualists will be more likely to confront differences of opinion directly and openly.

Some research supports this theory. Compared to collectivist Japanese negotiators, their more individualist U.S. counterparts are more likely to see offers as unfair and to reject them. Another study revealed that whereas U.S. managers were more likely to use competing tactics in the face of conflicts, compromising and avoiding were the most preferred methods of conflict management in China.[30] Interview data, however, suggest that top management teams in Chinese high-technology firms prefer collaboration even more than compromising and avoiding.[31]

Cross-cultural negotiations can also create issues of trust.[32] One study of Indian and U.S. negotiators found that respondents reported having less trust in their cross-culture negotiation counterparts. The lower level of trust was associated with less discovery of common interests between parties, which occurred because cross-culture negotiators were less willing to disclose and solicit information. Another study found that both U.S. and Chinese negotiators tended to have an ingroup bias, which led them to favor negotiating partners from their own cultures. For Chinese negotiators, this was particularly true when accountability requirements were high.

Having considered conflict—its nature, causes, and consequences—we now turn to negotiation, which often resolves conflict.

WATCH IT!
If your professor has assigned this, go to the Assignments section of **mymanagementlab.com** to complete the video exercise titled ***Gordon Law Group: Conflict and Negotiation***.

Negotiation

14-3 Contrast distributive and integrative bargaining.

Negotiation permeates the interactions of almost everyone in groups and organizations. There's the obvious: Labor bargains with management. There's the not-so-obvious: Managers negotiate with employees, peers, and bosses;

salespeople negotiate with customers; purchasing agents negotiate with suppliers. And there's the subtle: An employee agrees to cover for a colleague for a few minutes in exchange for a future benefit. In today's loosely structured organizations, in which members work with colleagues over whom they have no direct authority and with whom they may not even share a common boss, negotiation skills are critical.

negotiation A process in which two or more parties exchange goods or services and attempt to agree on the exchange rate for them.

We can define **negotiation** as a process that occurs when two or more parties decide how to allocate scarce resources.[33] Although we commonly think of the outcomes of negotiation in one-shot economic terms, like negotiating over the price of a car, every negotiation in organizations also affects the relationship between negotiators and the way negotiators feel about themselves.[34] Depending on how much the parties are going to interact with one another, sometimes maintaining the social relationship and behaving ethically will be just as important as achieving an immediate outcome of bargaining. Note that we use the terms *negotiation* and *bargaining* interchangeably.

Bargaining Strategies

There are two general approaches to negotiation—*distributive bargaining* and *integrative bargaining*.[35] As Exhibit 14-6 shows, they differ in their goal and motivation, focus, interests, information sharing, and duration of relationship. Let's define each and illustrate the differences.

distributive bargaining Negotiation that seeks to divide up a fixed amount of resources; a win-lose situation.

fixed pie The belief that there is only a set amount of goods or services to be divvied up between the parties.

Distributive Bargaining You see a used car advertised for sale online that looks great. You go see the car. It's perfect, and you want it. The owner tells you the asking price. You don't want to pay that much. The two of you negotiate. The negotiating strategy you're engaging in is called **distributive bargaining**. Its identifying feature is that it operates under zero-sum conditions—that is, any gain I make is at your expense, and vice versa. Every dollar you can get the seller to cut from the car's price is a dollar you save, and every dollar the seller can get from you comes at your expense. The essence of distributive bargaining is negotiating over who gets what share of a fixed pie. By **fixed pie**, we mean a set amount of goods or services to be divvied up. When the pie is fixed, or the parties believe it is, they tend to bargain distributively.

Exhibit 14-6 Distributive versus Integrative Bargaining

Bargaining Characteristic	Distributive Bargaining	Integrative Bargaining
Goal	Get as much of the pie as possible	Expand the pie so that both parties are satisfied
Motivation	Win–lose	Win–win
Focus	Positions ("I can't go beyond this point on this issue.")	Interests ("Can you explain why this issue is so important to you?")
Interests	Opposed	Congruent
Information sharing	Low (Sharing information will only allow other party to take advantage)	High (Sharing information will allow each party to find ways to satisfy interests of each party)
Duration of relationship	Short term	Long term

Exhibit 14-7 Staking Out the Bargaining Zone

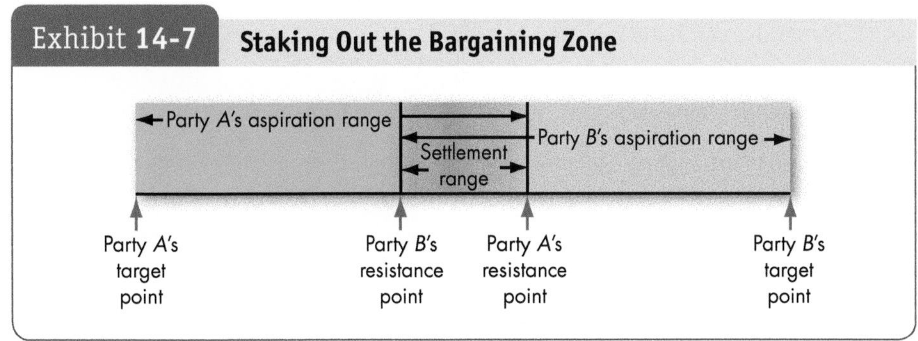

The essence of distributive bargaining is depicted in Exhibit 14-7. Parties *A* and *B* represent two negotiators. Each has a *target point* that defines what he or she would like to achieve. Each also has a *resistance point,* which marks the lowest acceptable outcome—the point beyond which the party would break off negotiations rather than accept a less favorable settlement. The area between these two points makes up each party's *aspiration range.* As long as there is some overlap between *A*'s and *B*'s aspiration ranges, there exists a settlement range in which each one's aspirations can be met.

When you are engaged in distributive bargaining, one of the best things you can do is make the first offer, and make it an aggressive one. Making the first offer shows power; individuals in power are much more likely to make initial offers, speak first at meetings, and thereby gain the advantage. Another reason this is a good strategy is the anchoring bias, mentioned in Chapter 6. People tend to fixate on initial information. Once that anchoring point has been set, they fail to adequately adjust it based on subsequent information. A savvy negotiator sets an anchor with the initial offer, and scores of negotiation studies show that such anchors greatly favor the person who sets them.[36]

Say you have a job offer, and your prospective employer asks you what sort of starting salary you want. You've just been given a gift—you have a chance to set the anchor, meaning you should ask for the highest salary you think the employer could reasonably offer. Asking for a million dollars is only going to make most of us look ridiculous, which is why we suggest being on the high end of what you think is *reasonable.* Too often, we err on the side of caution, afraid of scaring off the employer and thus settling for far too little. It *is* possible to scare off an employer, and it's true employers don't like candidates to be assertive in salary negotiations, but liking isn't the same as doing what it takes to hire or retain someone.[37] What happens much more often is that we ask for less than we could have obtained.

Integrative Bargaining Jake was a Chicago luxury boutique owned by Jim Wetzel and Lance Lawson. In the early days of the business, Wetzel and Lawson moved millions of dollars of merchandise from many up-and-coming designers. They developed such a good rapport that many designers would send allotments to Jake without requiring advance payment. When the economy soured in 2008, Jake had trouble selling inventory, and designers were not being paid for what they had shipped to the store. Despite the fact that many designers were willing to work with the store on a delayed payment plan, Wetzel and Lawson stopped returning their calls. Lamented one designer, Doo-Ri Chung, "You kind of feel this familiarity with people who supported you for so long. When they have cash-flow issues, you want to make sure you

Officials of General Motors and United Auto Workers participate in the ceremonial handshake that opens new contract negotiations. They are committed to integrative bargaining and work toward negotiating win–win settlements that boost GM's competitiveness. From left are GM CEO Mary Barra, UAW president Dennis Williams, GM VP Cathy Clegg, and UAW VP Cindy Estrada.
Source: Paul Sancya/AP Images

integrative bargaining Negotiation that seeks one or more settlements that can create a win–win solution.

are there for them as well."[38] Chung's attitude shows the promise of **integrative bargaining**. In contrast to distributive bargaining, integrative bargaining assumes that one or more of the possible settlements can create a win–win solution. Of course, as the Jake example shows, both parties must be engaged for integrative bargaining to work.

In terms of intraorganizational behavior, integrative bargaining is preferable to distributive bargaining because the former builds long-term relationships. Integrative bargaining bonds negotiators and allows them to leave the bargaining table feeling they have achieved a victory. Distributive bargaining, however, leaves one party a loser. It tends to build animosity and deepen divisions when people have to work together on an ongoing basis. Research shows that over repeated bargaining episodes, a losing party who feels positively about the negotiation outcome is much more likely to bargain cooperatively in subsequent negotiations.

Why, then, don't we see more integrative bargaining in organizations? The answer lies in the conditions necessary for it to succeed. These include opposing parties who are open with information and candid about concerns, are sensitive to the other's needs and trust, and maintain flexibility.[39] Because these conditions seldom exist in organizations, negotiations often take a win-at-any-cost dynamic.

Compromise may be your worst enemy in negotiating a win–win agreement. Compromising reduces the pressure to bargain integratively. After all, if you or your opponent caves in easily, no one needs to be creative to reach a settlement. People then settle for less than they could have obtained if they had been forced to consider the other party's interests, trade off issues, and be creative.[40] Consider a classic example in which two siblings are arguing over who gets an orange. Unknown to them, one sibling wants the orange to drink the juice, whereas the other wants the orange peel to bake a cake. If one capitulates and gives the other the orange, they will not be forced to explore their reasons for wanting the orange, and thus they will never find the win–win solution: They could *each* have the orange because they want different parts.

Myth or Science?

Teams Negotiate Better Than Individuals in Collectivistic Cultures

According to a recent study, this statement appears to be false.

In general, the literature has suggested that teams negotiate more effectively than individuals negotiating alone. Some evidence indicates that team negotiations create more ambitious goals, and that teams communicate more with each other than individual negotiators do.

Common sense suggests that if this is indeed the case, it is especially true in collectivistic cultures, where individuals are more likely to think of collective goals and be more comfortable working in teams. A study of the negotiation of teams in the United States and in Taiwan, however, suggests that this common sense is wrong. The researchers conducted two studies comparing two-person teams with individual negotiators. They defined negotiating effectiveness as the degree to which the negotiation produced an optimal outcome for both sides. U.S. teams did better than solo individuals in both studies. In Taiwan, solo individuals did better than teams.

Why did this happen? The researchers determined that in Taiwan norms respecting harmony already exist, and negotiating in teams only amplifies that tendency. This poses a problem because when norms for cooperation are exceptionally high, teams "satisfice" (settle for a satisfactory, but less than optimal, solution) to avoid conflict. When Taiwanese individuals negotiate solo, at least they can clearly represent their own interests. In contrast, because the United States is individualistic, solo negotiators may focus on their own interests, which makes reaching integrative solutions more difficult. When Americans negotiate in teams, they become less inclined to focus on individual interests and therefore can reach solutions.

Overall, these findings suggest that negotiating individually works best in collectivistic cultures, and negotiating in teams works best in individualistic cultures.

Sources: Based on M. J. Gelfand et al., "Toward a Culture-by-Context Perspective on Negotiation: Negotiating Teams in the United States and Taiwan," *Journal of Applied Psychology* 98 (2013): 504–13; and A. Graf, S. T. Koeszegi, and E.-M. Pesendorfer, "Electronic Negotiations in Intercultural Interfirm Relationships," *Journal of Managerial Psychology* 25 (2010): 495–512.

The Negotiation Process

14-4 Apply the five steps of the negotiation process.

Exhibit 14-8 provides a simplified model of the negotiation process. It views negotiation as made up of five steps: (1) preparation and planning, (2) definition of ground rules, (3) clarification and justification, (4) bargaining and problem solving, and (5) closure and implementation.[41]

Preparation and Planning Before you start negotiating, do your homework. What's the nature of the conflict? What's the history leading up to this negotiation? Who's involved and what are their perceptions of the conflict? What do you want from the negotiation? What are *your* goals? If you're a supply manager at Dell Computer, for instance, and your goal is to get a significant cost reduction from your keyboard supplier, make sure this goal stays paramount in discussions and doesn't get overshadowed by other issues. It helps to put your goals in writing and develop a range of outcomes—from "most hopeful" to "minimally acceptable"—to keep your attention focused.

You should also assess what you think are the other party's goals. What are they likely to ask? How entrenched is their position likely to be? What intangible or hidden interests may be important to them? On what might they be willing to settle? When you can anticipate your opponent's position, you are better equipped to counter arguments with facts and figures that support your position.

Relationships change as a result of negotiation, so take that into consideration. If you could "win" a negotiation but push the other side into resentment

Exhibit 14-8 The Negotiation

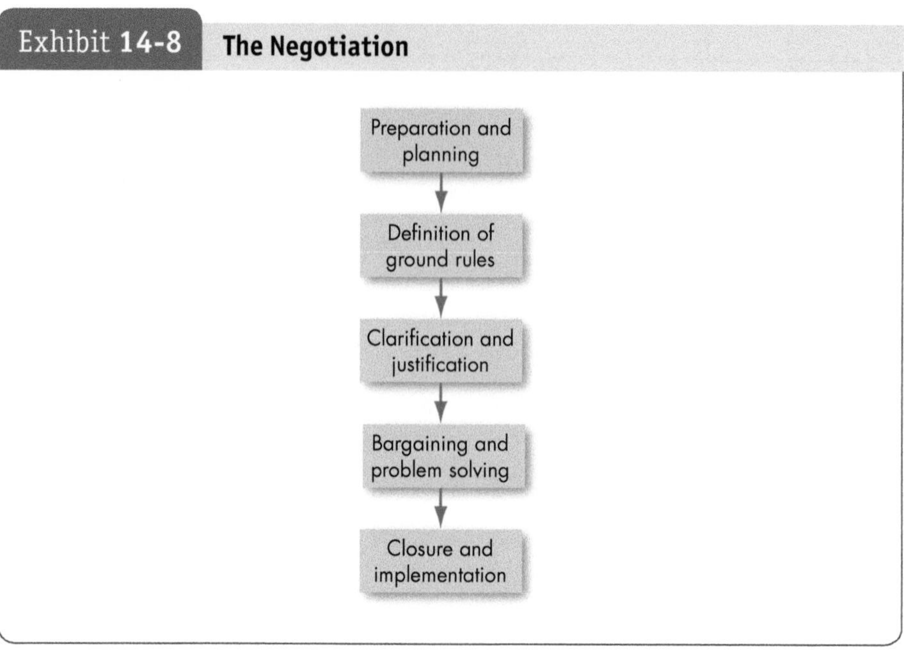

or animosity, it might be wiser to pursue a more compromising style. If preserving the relationship will make you seem easily exploited, you may consider a more aggressive style. As an example of how the tone of a relationship in negotiations matters, people who feel good about the *process* of a job offer negotiation are more satisfied with their jobs and less likely to turn over a year later regardless of their actual *outcomes* from these negotiations.[42]

Once you've gathered your information, develop a strategy. You should determine your and the other side's **b**est **a**lternative **t**o a **n**egotiated **a**greement, or **BATNA**. Your BATNA determines the lowest value acceptable to you for a negotiated agreement. Any offer you receive that is higher than your BATNA is better than an impasse.

BATNA The **b**est **a**lternative **t**o a **n**egotiated **a**greement; the least the individual should accept.

In nearly all cases, the party with superior alternatives will do better in a negotiation, so experts advise negotiators to solidify their BATNA prior to any interaction.[43] There is an interesting exception to this general rule—negotiators with absolutely no alternative to a negotiated agreement sometimes "go for broke" since they don't even consider what would happen if the negotiation falls through.[44] Think carefully about what the other side is willing to give up. People who underestimate their opponent's willingness to give on key issues before the negotiation even starts end up with lower outcomes.[45] Conversely, you shouldn't expect success in your negotiation effort unless you're able to make the other side an offer it finds more attractive than its BATNA.

Definition of Ground Rules Once you've done your planning and developed a strategy, you're ready to define with the other party the ground rules and procedures of the negotiation itself. Who will do the negotiating? Where will it take place? What time constraints, if any, will apply? To what issues will negotiation be limited? Will you follow a specific procedure if an impasse is reached? During this phase, the parties will exchange their initial proposals or demands.

Clarification and Justification When you have exchanged initial positions, you and the other party will explain, amplify, clarify, bolster, and justify your original demands. This step needn't be confrontational. Rather, it's an opportunity for educating each other on the issues, why they are important, and how you arrived at your initial demands. Provide the other party with any documentation that supports your position.

Bargaining and Problem Solving The essence of the negotiation process is the actual give-and-take in trying to hash out an agreement. This is where both parties need to make concessions.

Closure and Implementation The final step in the negotiation process is formalizing your agreement and developing procedures necessary for implementing and monitoring it. For major negotiations—from labor–management negotiations to bargaining over lease terms—this requires hammering out the specifics in a formal contract. For other cases, closure of the negotiation process is nothing more formal than a handshake.

Individual Differences in Negotiation Effectiveness

14-5 Show how individual differences influence negotiations.

Are some people better negotiators than others? The answer is complex. Four factors influence how effectively individuals negotiate: personality, mood/emotions, culture, and gender.

Personality Traits in Negotiations Can you predict an opponent's negotiating tactics if you know something about his or her personality? Because personality and negotiation outcomes are related but only weakly, the answer is, at best, "sort of."[46] Most research has focused on the Big Five trait of agreeableness, for obvious reasons—agreeable individuals are cooperative, compliant, kind, and conflict-averse. We might think such characteristics make agreeable individuals easy prey in negotiations, especially distributive ones. The evidence suggests, however, that overall agreeableness is weakly related to negotiation outcomes. Why is this the case?

It appears that the degree to which agreeableness, and personality more generally, affects negotiation outcomes depends on the situation. The importance of being extraverted in negotiations, for example, will very much depend on how the other party reacts to someone who is assertive and enthusiastic. One complicating factor for agreeableness is that it has two facets: The tendency to be cooperative and compliant is one, but so is the tendency to be warm and empathetic.[47] It may be that while the former is a hindrance to negotiating favorable outcomes, the latter helps. Empathy, after all, is the ability to take the perspective of another person and gain insight/understanding of him or her. We know perspective-taking benefits integrative negotiations, so perhaps the null effect for agreeableness is due to the two tendencies pulling against one another. If this is the case, then the best negotiator is a competitive but empathetic one, and the worst is a gentle but empathetic one.

The type of negotiations may matter as well. In one study, agreeable individuals reacted more positively and felt less stress (measured by their cortisol levels) in integrative negotiations than in distributive ones. Low levels of stress, in turn, made for more effective negotiation outcomes.[48] Similarly, in "hard-edged" distributive negotiations, where giving away information leads to a disadvantage, extraverted negotiators do less well because they tend to share more information than they should.[49]

Career OBjectives

How can I get a better job?

I feel like my career is at a standstill, and I want to talk to my boss about getting a more developmental assignment. How can I negotiate effectively for a better job position?

— Wei

Dear Wei:

You're certainly starting out on the right foot. A lot of people focus on a salary as a way to achieve success and negotiate for the best short-run offer. There's obviously an advantage to this strategy in the short run, but sustained career growth has better payoffs in the long run. Developing skills can help put you on track for multiple salary increases. A strong skill set from developmental assignments will also give you a better position for future negotiations because you will have more career options.

Long-term career negotiations based on developmental assignments also often are easier to bring up with a supervisor. That's because salary negotiations are often a zero-sum situation, but career development negotiations can bring positive outcomes to both sides. When negotiating for a developmental assignment, make sure you emphasize a few points with your supervisor:

- *When it comes to salary negotiations, either you get the money, or the company keeps the money.* Given that, your interests and the interests of your managers are directly opposed. On the other hand, negotiating for developmental assignments usually means finding ways to improve not just your skills, but also your contribution to the company's bottom line. You can, in complete honesty, frame the discussion around these mutual benefits.
- *Let your supervisor know that you are interested in getting better at your job, and that you are motivated to improve through a developmental assignment.* Asking your supervisor for opportunities to grow is a clear sign that you are an employee worth investing in.
- *Be open to creative solutions.* It's possible that there are some idiosyncratic solutions (also called "I-deals") for enhancing both your interests and those of your supervisor. One of the best things about an integrative bargaining situation like this is that you and your negotiation partner can find novel solutions that neither would have imagined separately.

Think strategically about your career, and you'll likely find you can negotiate not just for a better paycheck tomorrow, but for a paycheck that keeps increasing in the years to come.

Sources: Y. Rofcanin, T. Kiefer, and K. Strauss, "How I-Deals Build Resources to Facilitate Reciprocation: Mediating Role of Positive Affective States," *Academy of Management Proceedings,* August, 2014, DOI: 10.5465/AMBPP.2014.16096abstract; C. Liao, S. J. Wayne, and D. M. Rousseau, "Idiosyncratic Deals in Contemporary Organizations: A Qualitative and Meta-Analytical Review," *Journal of Organizational Behavior,* October 16, 2014, DOI: 10.1002/job.1959; and V. Brenninkmeijer and M. Hekkert-Koning, "To Craft or Not to Craft," *Career Development International* 20 (2015): 147–62.

Self-efficacy is one individual-difference variable that consistently seems to relate to negotiation outcomes.[50] This is a fairly intuitive finding—it isn't too surprising to hear that those who believe they will be more successful in negotiation situations tend to perform more effectively. It may be that individuals who are more confident stake out stronger claims, are less likely to back down from their positions, and exhibit confidence that intimidates others. Although the exact mechanism is not yet clear, it does seem that negotiators may benefit from trying to get a boost in confidence before going to the bargaining table.

Research suggests intelligence predicts negotiation effectiveness, but, as with personality, the effects aren't especially strong.[51] In a sense, these weak links mean you're not severely disadvantaged, even if you're an agreeable extravert, when it's time to negotiate. We all can learn to be better negotiators.[52]

Moods/Emotions in Negotiations Do moods and emotions influence negotiation? They do, but the way they work depends on the emotion as well as the

An Ethical Choice

Using Empathy to Negotiate More Ethically

You may have noticed that much of our advice for negotiating effectively depends on understanding the perspective and goals of the person with whom you are negotiating. Preparing checklists of your negotiation partner's interests, likely tactics, and BATNA have all been shown to improve negotiation outcomes. Can these steps make you a more ethical negotiator as well? Studies suggest that they might.

Researchers asked respondents to indicate how much they tended to think about other people's feelings and emotions and to describe the types of tactics they engaged in during a negotiation exercise. More empathetic individuals consistently engaged in fewer unethical negotiation behaviors like making false promises and manipulating information and emotions.

When considering how to improve your ethical negotiation behavior, follow these guidelines:

1. **Try to understand your negotiation partner's perspective.** This isn't just by understanding cognitively what the other person wants, but by empathizing with the emotional reaction he or she will likely have to the possible outcomes.
2. **Be aware of your own emotions, because many moral reactions are fundamentally emotional.** One study found that engaging in unethical negotiation strategies increased feelings of guilt, so by extension, feeling guilty in a negotiation may mean you are engaging in behavior you'll regret later.
3. **Beware of empathizing so much that you work against your own interests.** Just because you try to understand the motives and emotional reactions of the other side does not mean you have to assume the other person is going to be honest and fair in return. So be on guard.

Sources: Based on T. R. Cohen, "Moral Emotions and Unethical Bargaining: The Differential Effects of Empathy and Perspective Taking in Deterring Deceitful Negotiation," *Journal of Business Ethics* 94, no. 4 (2010): 569–79; and R. Volkema, D. Fleck, and A. Hofmeister, "Predicting Competitive-Unethical Negotiating Behavior and Its Consequences," *Negotiation Journal* 26, no. 3 (2010): 263–86.

context. A negotiator who shows anger can induce concessions, for instance, because the other negotiator believes no further concessions from the angry party are possible. One factor that governs this outcome, however, is power—you should show anger in negotiations only if you have at least as much power as your counterpart. If you have less, showing anger actually seems to provoke "hardball" reactions from the other side.[53]

Another factor is how genuine your anger is—"faked" anger, or anger produced from surface acting (see Chapter 4), is not effective, but showing anger that is genuine (deep acting) is.[54] It also appears that having a history of showing anger, rather than sowing the seeds of revenge, actually induces more concessions because the other party perceives the negotiator as "tough."[55] Finally, culture seems to matter. For instance, one study found that when East Asian participants showed anger, it induced more concessions than when the negotiator expressing anger was from the United States or Europe, perhaps because of the stereotype of East Asians as refusing to show anger.[56]

Another relevant emotion is disappointment. Generally, a negotiator who perceives disappointment from his or her counterpart concedes more. In one study, Dutch students were given 100 chips to bargain over. Negotiators who expressed disappointment were offered 14 more chips than those who didn't. In a second study, showing disappointment yielded an average concession of 12 chips. Unlike a show of anger, the relative power of the negotiators made no difference in either study.[57]

Anxiety also appears to have an impact on negotiation. For example, one study found that individuals who experienced more anxiety about a negotiation used more deceptions in dealing with others.[58] Another study found that anxious negotiators expect lower outcomes, respond to offers more quickly, and exit the bargaining process more quickly, leading them to obtain worse outcomes.[59]

People generally negotiate more effectively within cultures than between them. Politeness and positivity characterize the typical conflict-avoidant negotiations in Japan, such as with labor union leader Hidekazu Kitagawa (right), shown here presenting wage and benefits demands to Ikuo Mori, president of Fuji Heavy Industries, which makes Subaru vehicles.
Source: Kyodo/Newscom

As you can see, emotions—especially negative ones—matter to negotiation. Even emotional unpredictability affects outcomes; researchers have found that negotiators who express positive and negative emotions in an unpredictable way extract more concessions because this behavior makes the other party feel less in control.[60] As one negotiator put it, "Out of the blue, you may have to react to something you have been working on in one way, and then something entirely new is introduced, and you have to veer off and refocus."[61]

Culture in Negotiations Do people from different cultures negotiate differently? The simple answer is the obvious one: Yes, they do. However, there are many nuances in the way this works. It isn't as simple as "these negotiators are the best"; indeed, success in negotiations depends on the context.

So what can we say about culture and negotiations? First, it appears that people generally negotiate more effectively within cultures than between them. For example, a Colombian is apt to do better negotiating with a Colombian than with a Sri Lankan. Second, it appears that in cross-cultural negotiations, it is especially important that the negotiators be high in openness. This suggests a good strategy is to choose cross-cultural negotiators who are high on openness to experience, and to avoid factors such as time pressure that tend to inhibit learning about the other party.[62]

Finally, because emotions are culturally sensitive, negotiators need to be especially aware of the emotional dynamics in cross-cultural negotiation. One study, for example, explicitly compared how U.S. and Chinese negotiators reacted to an angry counterpart. Chinese negotiators increased their use of distributive negotiating tactics, whereas U.S. negotiators decreased their use of these tactics. That is, Chinese negotiators began to drive a harder bargain once they saw that their negotiation partner was becoming angry, whereas U.S. negotiators capitulated somewhat in the face of angry demands. Why the difference? It may be that individuals from East Asian cultures feel that using anger to get their way in a negotiation is not a legitimate tactic, so they refuse to cooperate when their opponents become upset.[63]

Gender Differences in Negotiations There are many areas of organizational behavior (OB) in which men and women are not that different. Negotiation

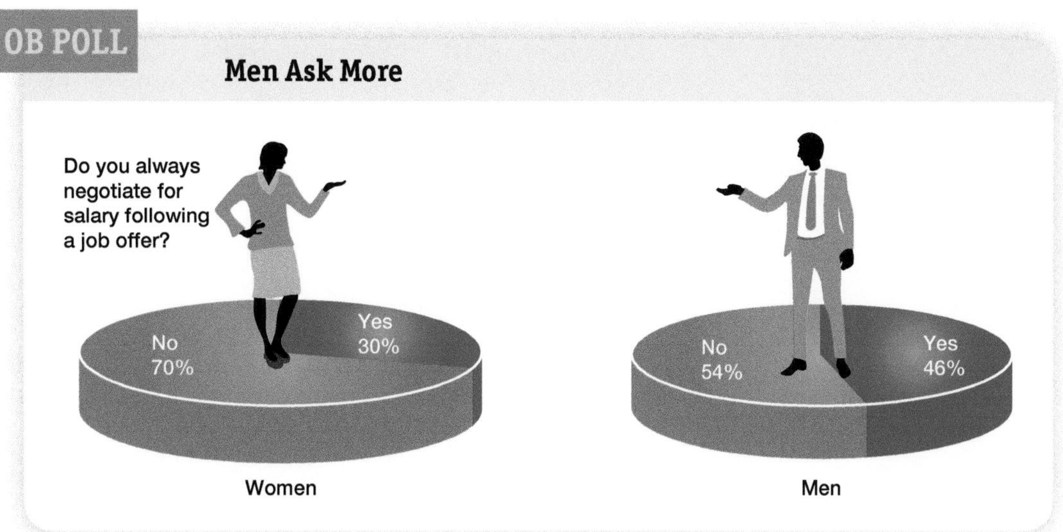

Source: A. Gouveia, "Why Americans Are Too Scared to Negotiate Salary," *San Francisco Chronicle*, April 3, 2013, downloaded May 30, 2013 from http://www.sfgate.com/jobs/.

is not one of them. It seems fairly clear that men and women negotiate differently, men and women are treated differently by negotiation partners, and these differences affect outcomes (see OB Poll).

A popular stereotype is that women are more cooperative and pleasant in negotiations than men. Though this is controversial, there is some merit to it. Men tend to place a higher value on status, power, and recognition, whereas women tend to place a higher value on compassion and altruism. Moreover, women do tend to value relationship outcomes more than men, and men tend to value economic outcomes more than women.[64]

These differences affect both negotiation behavior and negotiation outcomes. Compared to men, women tend to behave in a less assertive, less self-interested, and more accommodating manner. As one review concluded, women "are more reluctant to initiate negotiations, and when they do initiate negotiations, they ask for less, are more willing to accept [the] offer, and make more generous offers to their negotiation partners than men do."[65] A study of MBA students at Carnegie-Mellon University found that the male students took the step of negotiating their first offer 57 percent of the time, compared to 4 percent for the female students. The net result? A $4,000 difference in starting salaries.[66]

One comprehensive literature review suggests that the tendency for men to receive better negotiation outcomes in some situations does not cover *all* situations.[67] Indeed, evidence suggested women and men bargained more equally in certain situations, women sometimes outperformed men, and men and women obtained more nearly equal outcomes when negotiating on behalf of someone else. In other words, everyone was better at advocating for others than they were at advocating for themselves.

Factors that increased the predictability of negotiations also tended to reduce gender differences. When the range of negotiation settlements was well defined, men and women were more equal in outcomes. When more experienced negotiators were at the table, men and women were also more nearly equivalent. The study authors proposed that when situations are more ambiguous, with less well-defined terms and less experienced negotiators, stereotypes may have stronger effects, leading to larger gender differences in outcomes.

So what can be done to change this troublesome state of affairs? First, organizational culture plays a role. If an organization, even unwittingly, reinforces gender-stereotypic behaviors (men negotiating competitively, women negotiating cooperatively), it will negatively affect negotiations when anyone goes against stereotype. Men and women need to know that it is acceptable for each to show a full range of negotiating behaviors. Thus, a female negotiator who behaves competitively and a male negotiator who behaves cooperatively need to know that they are not violating expectations. Making sure negotiations are designed to focus on well-defined and work-related terms also has promise for reducing gender differences by minimizing the ambiguous space for stereotypes to operate. This focus on structure and work relevance also obviously helps focus negotiations on factors that will improve the organization's performance.

Research is less clear on whether women can improve their outcomes by showing some gender-stereotypic behaviors. Researchers Laura Kray and colleagues suggested that female negotiators who were instructed to behave with "feminine charm" (be animated in body movements, make frequent eye contact with their partners, smile, laugh, be playful, and frequently compliment their partners) did better in negotiations than women not so instructed. These behaviors didn't work for men.[68]

Other researchers disagree and argue that what can best benefit women is to break down gender stereotypes for the individuals who hold them.[69] It's possible this is a short-term/long-term situation: In the short term, women can gain an advantage in negotiation by being both assertive and charming, but in the long term, their interests are best served by eliminating these sorts of sex role stereotypes.

Evidence suggests women's own attitudes and behaviors hurt them in negotiations. Managerial women demonstrate less confidence than men in anticipation of negotiating and are less satisfied with their performance afterward, even when their performance and the outcomes they achieve are similar to those for men.[70] Women are also less likely to see an ambiguous situation as an opportunity for negotiation. Women may unduly penalize themselves by failing to engage in negotiations that would be in their best interests. Some research suggests that women are less aggressive in negotiations because they are worried about backlash from others.

Negotiating in a Social Context

14-6 Assess the roles and functions of third-party negotiations.

We have mostly been discussing negotiations that occur among parties that meet only once, and in isolation from other individuals. However, in organizations, many negotiations are open-ended and public. When you are trying to figure out who in a work group should do a tedious task, negotiating with your boss to get a chance to travel internationally, or asking for more money for a project, there's a social component to the negotiation. You are probably negotiating with someone you already know and will work with again, and the negotiation and its outcome are likely to be topics people will talk about. To really understand negotiations in practice, then, we must consider the social factors of reputation and relationships.

Reputation Your reputation is the way other people think and talk about you. When it comes to negotiation, having a reputation for being trustworthy matters. In short, trust in a negotiation process opens the door to many forms of integrative negotiation strategies that benefit both parties.[71] The most effective way to build trust is to behave in an honest way across repeated interactions. Then, others feel more comfortable making open-ended offers with many different outcomes. This helps to achieve win-win outcomes, since both parties can work to achieve what is most important to themselves while still benefitting the other party.

Sometimes we either trust or distrust people based on word-of-mouth about a person's characteristics. What type of characteristics help a person develop a trustworthy reputation? A combination of competence and integrity.[72] Negotiators higher in self-confidence and cognitive ability are seen as more competent by negotiation partners.[73] They are also considered better able to accurately describe a situation and their own resources, and more credible when they make suggestions for creative solutions to impasses. Individuals who have a reputation for integrity can also be more effective in negotiations.[74] They are seen as more likely to keep their promises and present information accurately, so others are more willing to accept their promises as part of a bargain. This opens many options for the negotiator that wouldn't be available to someone who is not seen as trustworthy. Finally, individuals who have higher reputations are better liked and have more friends and allies—in other words, they have more social resources, which may give them more understood power in negotiations.

Relationships There is more to repeated negotiations than just reputation. The social, interpersonal component of relationships with repeated negotiations means that individuals go beyond valuing what is simply good for themselves and instead start to think about what is best for the other party and the relationship as a whole.[75] Repeated negotiations built on a foundation of trust also broaden the range of options, since a favor or concession today can be offered in return for some repayment further down the road.[76] Repeated negotiations also facilitate integrative problem solving. This occurs partly because people begin to see their negotiation partners in a more personal way over time and come to share emotional bonds.[77] Repeated negotiations also make integrative approaches more workable because a sense of trust and reliability has been built up.[78]

In sum, it's clear that an effective negotiator needs to think about more than just the outcomes of a single interaction. Negotiators who consistently act in a way that demonstrates competence, honesty, and integrity will usually have better outcomes in the long run.

Third-Party Negotiations

To this point, we've discussed bargaining in terms of direct negotiations. Occasionally, however, individuals or group representatives reach a stalemate and are unable to resolve their differences through direct negotiations. In such cases, they may turn to a third party to help them find a solution. There are three basic third-party roles: mediator, arbitrator, and conciliator.

mediator A neutral third party who facilitates a negotiated solution by using reasoning, persuasion, and suggestions for alternatives.

A **mediator** is a neutral third party who facilitates a negotiated solution by using reasoning and persuasion, suggesting alternatives, and the like. Mediators are widely used in labor–management negotiations and in civil court disputes. Their overall effectiveness is fairly impressive. For example, the Equal Employment Opportunity Commission (EEOC) reported a settlement rate through mediation at 72.1 percent.[79] But the situation is the key to whether mediation will succeed; the conflicting parties must be motivated to bargain and resolve their conflict. In addition, conflict intensity can't be too high; mediation is most effective under moderate levels of conflict. Finally, perceptions of the mediator are important; to be effective, the mediator must be perceived as neutral and noncoercive.

arbitrator A third party to a negotiation who has the authority to dictate an agreement.

An **arbitrator** is a third party with the authority to dictate an agreement. Arbitration can be voluntary (requested by the parties) or compulsory (forced on the parties by law or contract). The big plus of arbitration over mediation is that it always results in a settlement. Whether there is a downside depends on how heavy-handed the arbitrator appears. If one party is left feeling overwhelmingly defeated, that party is certain to be dissatisfied and the conflict may resurface at a later time.

conciliator A trusted third party who provides an informal communication link between the negotiator and the opponent.

A **conciliator** is a trusted third party who provides an informal communication link between the negotiator and the opponent. This role was made famous by Robert Duval in the first *Godfather* film. As Don Corleone's adopted son and a lawyer by training, Duval acted as an intermediary between the Corleones and the other Mafioso families. Comparing conciliation to mediation in terms of effectiveness has proven difficult because the two overlap a great deal. In practice, conciliators typically act as more than mere communication conduits. They also engage in fact-finding, interpret messages, and persuade disputants to develop agreements.

Summary

While many people assume conflict lowers group and organizational performance, this assumption is frequently incorrect. Conflict can be either constructive or destructive to the functioning of a group or unit. Levels of conflict can be either too high or too low to be constructive. Either extreme hinders performance. An optimal level is one that prevents stagnation, stimulates creativity, allows tensions to be released, and initiates the seeds of change without being disruptive or preventing the coordination of activities.

Implications for Managers

- Choose an authoritarian management style in emergencies, when unpopular actions need to be implemented (such as cost cutting, enforcement of unpopular rules, discipline), and when the issue is vital to the organization's welfare. Be certain to communicate your logic when possible to make certain others remain engaged and productive.
- Seek integrative solutions when your objective is to learn, when you want to merge insights from people with different perspectives, when you need to gain commitment by incorporating concerns into a consensus, and when you need to work through feelings that have interfered with a relationship.
- You can build trust by accommodating others when you find you're wrong, when you need to demonstrate reasonableness, when other positions need to be heard, when issues are more important to others than to yourself, when you want to satisfy others and maintain cooperation, when you can build social credits for later issues, to minimize loss when you are outmatched and losing, and when others should learn from their own mistakes.
- Consider compromising when goals are important but not worth potential disruption, when opponents with equal power are committed to mutually exclusive goals, and when you need temporary settlements to complex issues.
- Distributive bargaining can resolve disputes, but it often reduces the satisfaction of one or more negotiators because it is confrontational and focused on the short term. Integrative bargaining, in contrast, tends to provide outcomes that satisfy all parties and build lasting relationships.

PERSONAL INVENTORY ASSESSMENTS

Strategies for Handling Conflict

We all handle conflict, but few of us may have actual strategies in place. Take this PIA to further explore ways to handle conflict.

Pro Sports Strikes Are Caused by Greedy Owners

POINT

I'm as sick as anyone of the constant strikes, lockouts, and back-and-forth negotiations between sports teams and the players' unions. Of the major pro sports leagues, Major League Baseball (MLB) is the only one without a strike since 1995—and it had eight in its history. You've got to wonder why this keeps happening. Here's why: Owners' greed knows no limit.

In nearly every recent strike or lockout, the main issue was money and how to divide it. When the National Hockey League (NHL) locked out the players during the 2012-2013 season, the owners were the instigators. They wanted to reduce the players' share of hockey revenues. They wanted to eliminate salary arbitration. They wanted to introduce term limits to contracts. They wanted to change free-agency rules and eliminate signing bonuses. On a philosophical level, some of these proposals are interesting because they reveal that owners want to restrict competition when it suits them and increase it when it benefits them.

While the owners were whining about the unfairness of long-term contracts, the Minnesota Wild's owner Craig Leipold, a noted negotiations hawk, signed Zach Parise and Ryan Suter to identical 13-year, $98 million contracts. Contracts like these suggest that owners want the players' union to save them from themselves.

Perhaps some of this behavior would make sense if the owners were losing money hand over fist, but that is hardly the case. The NHL has three teams worth over $1 billion each, and few are worth less than $200 million. The owners aren't hurting, either. Most are millionaires many times over. Los Angeles Kings owner Philip Anschutz is reported to have a net worth of $12 billion.

Forbes reports the average NFL team is now worth more than $1.43 billion and the Dallas Cowboys are worth $3.2 billion; even low-earning and poorly run teams make money. Take the Jacksonville Jaguars. Wayne Weaver paid $208 million for the team in 1993. It has never made it to the Super Bowl and is almost always an also-ran in its division. Did the team's ineffectiveness really cost Weaver? He sold the club for $770 million in 2012.

In essence, what we have are rich owners trying to negotiate rules that keep them from competing with one another for players. It's a bald-faced and hypocritical attempt to use their own kind of union to negotiate favorable agreements, all the while criticizing the players' unions.

COUNTERPOINT

Major league owners are an easy target. But they have the most to lose from work stoppages. It's the players and their unions who push the envelope.

It's true that most major league players are well rewarded for their exceptional talents and the risks they take. It's also true that owners who are able to invest in teams are wealthy—investors usually are. But the fault for disputes lies with spoiled players—and the union leaders who burnish their credentials and garner the limelight by fanning the flames of discontent.

On this latter point, give all the credit in the world to the union negotiators (paid millions themselves), who do nothing if not hawk publicity and use hardball negotiating tactics. Take the NHL players' union boss Donald Fehr. For a "negotiation" set to begin at 10 A.M., he arrived at 11:15. At exactly 12:00, he announced he had a lunch meeting uptown and left.

As for the players, pro athletes are entitled almost by definition. For example, one retired NFL player and union representative, Chester Pitts, was commenting about how he had to settle for an $85,000 Mercedes instead of a $250,000 car. Well, we all have to make sacrifices. One rookie, Jets' quarterback Geno Smith, fired his agent after signing "only" a four-year contract for roughly $4.99 million. Smith called the contract "hard to stomach." I see a future in the players' union for this guy.

Do we really need labor unions for workers whose average salaries are $2 million (NFL), $2.58 million (NHL), $3.82 million (MLB), and $4.9 million (NBA)? NHL clubs spent 76 percent of their gross revenues on players' salaries and collectively lost $273 million the year before the most recent lockout. It's not much better in the NBA, where many teams lose money. Take the Dallas Mavericks, who have rarely made money since 2002, despite playing in the fourth-most populous metro area and winning the NBA title in 2011.

It's easy to argue that major league sports have an unusual number of labor disputes, but that's not necessarily accurate. Did you hear about the 2015 largest strike of oil refinery workers in decades or the ongoing worldwide strikes by low-paid workers in the fast-food industry? Somehow these strikes don't always make the news or our collective consciousness as much as sports strikes. Sports strikes interest us, but we shouldn't fall into the trap of blaming these on the owners.

Sources: #104 Philip Anschutz, *Forbes* real time net worth, http://www.forbes.com/profile/philip-anschutz/, downloaded June 9, 2015; T. Cary, "The 3 NHL Teams That Are Worth a Billion Dollars," *Sports Cheat Sheet,* June 6, 2015; K. Badenhausen, "Average MLB Player Salary Nearly Double NFL's, but Still Trails NBA's," *Forbes,* January 23, 2015, http://www.forbes.com/sites/kurtbadenhausen/2015/01/23/average-mlb-salary-nearly-double-nfls-but-trails-nba-players/; J. Feinstein, "In the NHL Lockout, the Owners Have It All Wrong," *Washington Post,* December 25, 2012, downloaded May 29, 2013, from http://articles.washingtonpost.com/; R. Cimini, "Geno Smith's Maturity Questioned," ESPN, May 3, 2013, downloaded May 3, 2013, from http://espn.go.com/; K. Campbell, "Thanks to Donald Fehr, NHL Negotiating against Itself ... and Losing," *The Hockey News,* December 29, 2012, downloaded May 29, 2013, from http://sports.yahoo.com/; B. Murphy, "20 Years of Peace and Prosperity Have Followed MLB's Last Strike," *Twin Cities,* July 5, 2014, http://www.twincities.com/sports/ci_26095630/peace-that-lasts-since-1994-season-ending-strike; and E. Seba, "Oil Refinery Strike Widens to Largest U.S. Plant," *Huffington Post,* February 21, 2015, http://www.huffingtonpost.com/2015/02/21/us-refinery-strike-wide_n_6727736.html.

CHAPTER REVIEW

MyManagementLab

Go to **mymanagementlab.com** to complete the problems marked with this icon.

QUESTIONS FOR REVIEW

14-1 What are the three types of conflict and the three loci of conflict?

14-2 What are the steps in the conflict process?

14-3 What are the differences between distributive and integrative bargaining?

14-4 What are the five steps in the negotiation process?

14-5 How do individual differences influence negotiations?

14-6 What are the roles and functions of third-party negotiations?

EXPERIENTIAL EXERCISE A Negotiation Role-Play

There are two scenarios to consider for this case; one is more distributive, the other more integrative. Within your group of two, one of you takes the role of the engineering director, while the other takes the role of the marketing director. Read only your own side's specific information for the two negotiation processes. The overall situation is the same for both scenarios, but the priorities and outlook for the parties change depending on whether the group is doing the "contested resources" scenario or the "combined future" scenario.

The Case

Cytrix develops integrated bicycle and running performance systems. Runners and bikers wear the Cytrix watch, which uses GPS signals to identify their location and the distance they've covered. This information can then be uploaded to Cytrix Challenge website, where users record their performance over time. Social media tools also allow them to compare their performance relative to that of friends. The majority of users are either amateur student athletes or committed adult hobbyists like marathon runners.

The organization needs to determine how to allocate a fixed pool of resources for future development between the marketing and engineering groups. Rather than making an executive decision about resource allocation, the top management team has asked the respective teams to allocate $30 million dollars for planned future development and decide who will run different parts of the project.

Marketing Group Specific Information (only the marketing manager should read this)

The marketing group has been tracking the major areas of sales and has come to the conclusion that Cytrix has saturated the market. New sources of customers will need to be considered for future growth, especially general consumers who are interested in health but are not committed athletes. Research into sales of competitive products and areas where competitors are failing to meet consumer demands is needed. The marketing group's primary goal is to allocate sufficient resources to finance the research. The group also wants to retain control over which new products will be developed. Marketing would prefer to see engineering act in a consulting role, determining how best to manufacture the devices that fit the needs identified above.

Engineering Group Specific Information (only the engineering manager should read this)

The engineering group has recently been tracking the development of new hardware that will improve the accuracy of distance and speed estimates in remote areas. Several other companies are already experimenting with similar designs. To fully realize this improvement, engineering believes it will be necessary to further develop the technology so it is both lightweight and inexpensive to produce. The engineering group's primary goal is to allocate sufficient resources to develop these new technologies. The engineers would prefer to see marketing act in a consulting role, determining how best to advertise and deliver the new devices.

Contested Resources Scenario

The marketing and engineering departments are locked in a struggle for power. Your side (either marketing or engineering) should try to direct the largest possible proportion of both money and authority toward your proposed program. You still need to come up with a solution in which the other side ultimately agrees to assist you in implementing the program. If you can't reach an agreement for shared resources, the CEO will appoint new directors for both groups.

Combined Future Scenario

The marketing and engineering departments are eager to find a positive solution. Both sides should endeavor to see that the company's future needs are met. You know that to achieve success everyone needs to work together, so you'd like to find a way to divide the money and resources that benefits both marketing and engineering. Plans can incorporate multiple techniques for sharing and collaborating with resources.

The Negotiation

At the start of the negotiation, the instructor randomly assigns half the groups to the contested resources scenario, and the other half to the combined future scenario. Begin the process by outlining the goals and resources for your side of the negotiation. Then negotiate over the terms described in your scenario, attempting to advocate for a solution that matches your perspective.

Debriefing

Afterward, get the class together to discuss the processes used. Especially consider the differences in outcomes between the contested resources and combined future scenarios. Either scenario could arise in a real work environment, so think about how different negotiation situations give rise to different strategies, tactics, and outcomes.

ETHICAL DILEMMA The Lowball Applicant

Consider this first-person account:

> I am a human resource manager, so I interview people every day. Sometimes the managers in my company ask me to prescreen candidates, which I do after discussing the job at length with the manager. I usually start the candidate screening with a few personality–job fit tests; then conduct an interview, following a list of job-specific questions the manager has given me; and finally discuss the job requirements, our company, and the pay/benefits. By that time in the process, the candidate usually has a good idea of the job and is eager to suggest a level of pay at the top of the advertised bracket or, often, above the pay bracket. However, this isn't always the case. One time in particular, an excellent candidate with outstanding qualifications surprised me by saying that since she wanted flextime, she would accept a rate below the pay bracket. Confused, I asked her whether she wanted a reduction in hours below full-time. She said no, she expected to work full-time and only wanted to come in a little late and would leave a little late to make up the time. I guess she figured this was a concession worth slashing her salary for, but our company has flextime. In fact, she could have asked for 5 fewer hours per week, still have been considered full-time by our company policies, and negotiated for salary above the advertised pay grade.

I knew the manager would be highly interested in this candidate and that he could probably get her to work the longer full-time hours at a lower rate of pay. That outcome might be best for the company, or it might not. The candidate obviously didn't fully understand the company policies in her favor, and she was unsophisticated about her worth in the marketplace. What should I have done?

Questions

14-7. If the human resource manager coached the applicant to request a higher salary, did the coaching work against the interests of the organization? Was the responsibility of the human resource (HR) manager to put the organization's financial interests first?

14-8. What do you see as the potential downside of the HR manager's abstaining from discussing the pay issue further with the candidate?

14-9. If the candidate were hired at the reduced rate she proposed, how might the situation play out over the next year when she gets to know the organization and its pay standards better?

CASE INCIDENT 1 Disorderly Conduct

The sound of Matt and Peter's arguing is familiar to everyone in the office by now. In an effort to make the best use of space and ensure a free flow of discussion and ideas, the founder of Markay Design had decided to convert the one-floor office of the company to an open plan with no walls between workers. The goal of such a layout is to eliminate boundaries and enhance creativity. But for Matt and Peter, the new arrangement creates a growing sense of tension.

The argument boils down to the question of workspace order and organization. Peter prefers to keep his desk completely clean and clear, and he keeps a stack of cleaning wipes in a drawer to eliminate any dust or dirt. Matt, on the other hand, likes to keep all his work visible on his desk, so sketches, plans, magazines, and photos are scattered everywhere, alongside boxes of crackers and coffee cups. Peter finds it hard to concentrate when he sees Matt's piles of materials everywhere, while Matt feels he can be more creative and free flowing when he's not forced to clean and organize constantly. Many of Matt and Peter's coworkers wish they'd just let the issue drop. The men enjoyed a good working relationship in the past, with Peter's attention to detail and thorough planning serving to rein in some of Matt's wild inspirations. But of late, their collaborations have been derailed in disputes.

Everyone knows it's not productive to engage in conflicts over every small irritant in the workplace. However, completely avoiding conflict can be equally negative. An emerging body of research has examined "conflict cultures" in organizations. The findings suggest having a culture that actively avoids and suppresses conflicts is associated with lower levels of creativity. Moreover, cultures that push conflict underground but do not succeed in reducing the underlying tensions can become passive-aggressive, marked by underhanded behavior against other coworkers.

Ultimately, finding a way through the clutter dispute is probably going to be an ongoing process to find a balance between perspectives. Both Matt and Peter worry that if they can't find a solution, their usually positive work relationship will be too contentious to bear. And that would be a real mess.

Questions

14-10. What could Peter and Matt's manager do to help them resolving their conflict?

14-11. The case suggests that there is research to support the notion that avoiding conflict stifles creativity. Is there such research, and do you agree?

14-12. How can Matt and Peter develop an active problem-solving discussion to resolve this conflict? What could effectively be changed, and what is probably going to just remain a problem?

Sources: S. Shellenbarger, "Clashing over Office Clutter," *Wall Street Journal,* March 19, 2014, http://www.wsj.com/articles/SB10001424052702304747404579447331212245004; S. Shellenbarger, "To Fight or Not to Fight? When to Pick Workplace Battles," *Wall Street Journal,* December 17, 2014, http://www.wsj.com/articles/picking-your-workplace-battles-1418772621; and M. J. Gelfand, J. R. Harrington, and L. M. Leslie, "Conflict Cultures: A New Frontier for Conflict Management Research and Practice," in N. M. Ashkanasy, O. B. Ayoko, and K. A. Jehn (eds.), *Handbook of Conflict Management Research,* 2014, 109–35.

CASE INCIDENT 2 Is More Cash Worth the Clash?

With 3,700 hotels located in 92 countries, Accor's revenues total more than $6 billion. About 180,000 people currently work for Accor's internationally renowned brands, including Sofitel, Novotel, and Ibis in Europe, the Middle-East, and Africa, and Huazhu, Grand Mercure (through domestic brands Mei Jue, Maha Cipta, and Manee Pura), and Sebel in Asia, Australia, and Latin America. Because Accor is opening one hotel every two days, it will employ even more people over the next few years directly and via subcontracting temporary work agencies. Not only does it mean negotiating an increasing number of employment contracts with individuals, but it also involves local negotiations with subcontractors. Work conditions and pay are often at the core of most of these negotiations.

In European hotels, labor costs represent almost 50% of revenues. Thus, human capital is either a competitive advantage you might invest in or a resource you may save money on. There is often a clash between shareholders, whose goal is to increase profit by lowering costs and generating more cash, and employees, who expect a higher pay from their company's growth.

In France, over the last five years, there have been hundreds of room attendants working for Accor hotels who publicly went on strike, complaining in the media about their pay and work conditions. These room attendants were not directly employed by Accor, but by subcontractors who paid them less than the industry minima and imposed higher production-rates on them (for example, to clean four rooms an hour) than room attendants directly employed by Accor, whose unions negotiated work conditions (three rooms an hour is the key-performance indicator used in Ibis hotels). Although the conflict occurred between temporary workers and their employing agencies, Accor had to play a role, because room attendants on strike could not be replaced on the spot and remaining employees could not accept more supplementary hours.

To foster its engagement in CSR and to solve the conflict, Accor signed a protocol with its subcontractors and the room attendants went back to work.

Unions may play a role in such labor-management conflicts. While it has excellent relationships with French unions, Accor was actually warned by the French Organisation for Economic Co-operation and Development (OECD) national contact point (NCP) in 2012 after a complaint about the violation of international guidelines was brought against it in 2010 by the International Union of Food, Agricultural, Hotel, Restaurant, Catering, Tobacco and Allied Workers' Associations (IUF), which represents over 12 million workers. The IUF stated that Accor Group Accor Group had denied the right of its employees to join collective negotiation in one hotel in Benin and to establish trade unions in three hotels in Canada. Because local unions and hotels' managers were unable to come to any agreement for years, the social conflict reached a global level with the IUF. In 2014, the French OECD NCP eventually thanked Accor for their involvement in resolving the conflicts with the IUF, and in deploying training plans to nurture hotels' franchisees and managers' sense of CSR.

Yet such conflicts should have been avoided, for Accor is strongly committed to developing compensation systems and work conditions that exceed the requirements of local legislation. In 2014, Accor signed non-discretionary profit-sharing agreements in countries like Mexico, Russia, Turkey, and the United Arab Emirates. Gender-neutral compensation and equal opportunity programs are also vital to Accor, which created a Women at Accor Generation (WAAG) network designed to help women to evolve within the group. A Singaporean general counsel states that she had to face cultural pressures that compelled her to focus on family commitments rather than to work, but WAAG assisted her in solving work–life conflicts and advancing within Accor. In Dubai, where hotel managerial positions are usually held by men, the director of two hotels spoke of how WAAG helped her with training courses and Webinars, which also covered gender-related challenges, to assume her responsibilities as a female manager.

Questions

14-13. Labor–management negotiations might be characterized as more distributive than integrative. Do you agree? Why do you think this is the case? What, if anything, would you do about it?

14-14. Be they dyadic, intragroup, or intergroup ones, labor–management conflicts are too often considered as dysfunctional while neglecting the role of third-parties that could make them more functional. Do you agree? Why?

14-15. If you were advising union and management representatives about how to solve their conflicts, drawing from the artefacts in the UIF-Accor case and the concepts in this chapter, what would you tell them?

14-16. What kind of conflicts do the Accor employees involved in WAAG networks face? Imagine, describe, and analyze both the conflict process and the negotiation process that one of them might have experienced.

Sources: P. Rosenzweig, "Accor: Global Excellence through People," *International Institute for Management Development Case*, 1999; F. Rivaud, "Comment Bazin veut faire d'Accor le meilleur groupe hôtelier du monde," *Challenges*, December 2014; Accor & Autorité des Marchés Financiers, "Enhancing Your Hotel Experience," *2014 Registration Document and Annual Financial Report*, March 2015; Direction de la Communication et des Relations Extérieures Accor, "Nous réinventons votre séjour," *Rapport d'activité 2014*, 2015; S. Stabile, "Women's Words," *Women at Accor Generation WAAG*, February 2015; European Trade Union Institute for Research, "European Trade Unions and Sustainable Development," 2008; accorhotels-group.com; oecd.org; tresor.economie.gouv.fr; uif.org; cfdt-accor.org; hrinasia.com; hotelmagazine.com; e-hotelier.com; "Hotel Industry in Benin and Canada," OECD Guidelines for Multinational Enterprises, https://mneguidelines.oecd.org/database/instances/fr0013.htm; http://www.tresor.economie.gouv.fr/File/411552.

MyManagementLab

Go to **mymanagementlab.com** for the following Assisted-graded writing questions:

14-16. In regard to Case Incident 1, how do you think modern, open workspaces contribute to or inhibit employee conflicts?

14-17. From your reading of Case Incident 2 and the text, how do you think unions have changed organizational negotiation practices?

14-18. **MyManagementLab Only** – comprehensive writing assignment for this chapter.

ENDNOTES

[1]See, for instance, D. Tjosvold, A. S. H. Wong, and N. Y. F. Chen, "Constructively Managing Conflicts in Organizations," *Annual Review of Organizational Psychology and Organizational Behavior* 1 (March 2014): 545–68; and M. A. Korsgaard, S. S. Jeong, D. M. Mahony, and A. H. Pitariu, "A Multilevel View of Intragroup Conflict," *Journal of Management* 34, no. 6 (2008): 1222–52.
[2]F. R. C. de Wit, L. L. Greer, and K. A. Jehn, "The Paradox of Intragroup Conflict: A Meta-Analysis," *Journal of Applied Psychology* 97, no. 2 (2012): 360–90; and N. Gamero, V. González-Romá, and J. M. Peiró, "The Influence of Intra-Team Conflict on Work Teams' Affective Climate: A Longitudinal Study," *Journal of Occupational and Organizational Psychology* 81, no. 1 (2008): 47–69.
[3]N. Halevy, E. Y. Chou, and A. D. Galinsky, "Exhausting or Exhilarating? Conflict as Threat to Interests, Relationships and Identities," *Journal of Experimental Social Psychology* 48 (2012): 530–37.
[4]F. R. C. de Wit, L. L. Greer, and K. A. Jehn, "The Paradox of Intragroup Conflict: A Meta-Analysis," *Journal of Applied Psychology* 97 (2012): 360–90.
[5]J. Farh, C. Lee, and C. I. C. Farh, "Task Conflict and Team Creativity: A Question of How Much and When," *Journal of Applied Psychology* 95, no. 6 (2010): 1173–80.
[6]B. H. Bradley, A. C. Klotz, B. F. Postlethwaite, and K. G. Brown, "Ready to Rumble: How Team Personality Composition and Task Conflict Interact to Improve Performance," *Journal of Applied Psychology* 98 (2013): 385–92.
[7]B. H. Bradley, B. F. Postlethwaite, A. C. Klotz, M. R. Hamdani, and K. G. Brown, "Reaping the Benefits of Task Conflict in Teams: The Critical Role of Team Psychological Safety Climate," *Journal of Applied Psychology* 97 (2012), 151–58.
[8]S. Benard, "Cohesion from Conflict: Does Intergroup Conflict Motivate Intragroup Norm Enforcement and Support for Centralized Leadership?" *Social Psychology Quarterly* 75 (2012): 107–30.
[9]G. A. Van Kleef, W. Steinel, and A. C. Homan, "On Being Peripheral and Paying Attention: Prototypicality and Information Processing in Intergroup Conflict," *Journal of Applied Psychology* 98 (2013): 63–79.
[10]R. S. Peterson and K. J. Behfar, "The Dynamic Relationship between Performance Feedback, Trust, and Conflict in Groups: A Longitudinal Study," *Organizational Behavior & Human Decision Processes*, September–November 2003, 102–12.
[11]T. M. Glomb and H. Liao, "Interpersonal Aggression in Work Groups: Social Influence, Reciprocal, and Individual Effects," *Academy of Management Journal* 46, no. 4 (2003): 486–96; and V. Venkataramani and R. S. Dalal, "Who Helps and Harms Whom? Relational Aspects of Interpersonal Helping and Harming in Organizations," *Journal of Applied Psychology* 92, no. 4 (2007): 952–66.
[12]R. Friedman, C. Anderson, J. Brett, M. Olekalns, N. Goates, and C. C. Lisco, "The Positive and Negative Effects of Anger on Dispute Resolution: Evidence from Electronically Mediated Disputes," *Journal of Applied Psychology*, April 2004, 369–76.
[13]J. S. Chun, and J. N. Choi, "Members' Needs, Intragroup Conflict, and Group Performance," *Journal of Applied Psychology* 99 (2014): 437–50.
[14]See, for instance, J. R. Curhan, "What Do People Value When They Negotiate? Mapping the Domain of Subjective Value in Negotiation," *Journal of Personality and Social Psychology*, September 2006, 117–26; N. Halevy, E. Chou, and J. K. Murnighan, "Mind Games: The Mental Representation of Conflict," *Journal of Personality and Social Psychology* 102 (2012): 132–48.
[15]A. M. Isen, A. A. Labroo, and P. Durlach, "An Influence of Product and Brand Name on Positive Affect: Implicit and Explicit Measures," *Motivation & Emotion*, March 2004, 43–63.
[16]Ibid.
[17]C. Montes, D. Rodriguez, and G. Serrano, "Affective Choice of Conflict Management Styles," *International Journal of Conflict Management* 23 (2012): 6–18.
[18]M. A. Rahim, *Managing Conflict in Organizations*, 4th ed. (New Brunswick, NJ: Transaction Publishers, 2011).
[19]Ibid.
[20]Ibid.
[21]L. A. DeChurch, J. R. Mesmer-Magnus, and D. Doty, "Moving beyond Relationship and Task Conflict: Toward a Process-State Perspective," *Journal of Applied Psychology* 98 (2013): 559–78.
[22]G. Todorova, J. B. Bear, and L. R. Weingart, "Can Conflict Be Energizing? A Study of Task Conflict, Positive Emotions, and Job Satisfaction," *Journal of Applied Psychology* 99 (2014): 451–67.
[23]P. J. Hinds and D. E. Bailey, "Out of Sight, Out of Sync: Understanding Conflict in Distributed Teams," *Organization Science*, November–December 2003, 615–32.
[24]K. A. Jehn, L. Greer, S. Levine, and G. Szulanski, "The Effects of Conflict Types, Dimensions, and Emergent States on Group Outcomes," *Group Decision and Negotiation* 17, no. 6 (2005): 777–96.
[25]Zellmer-Bruhn, Maloney, Bhappu, and Salvador, "When and How Do Differences Matter?"
[26]J. Fried, "I Know You Are, but What Am I?" *Inc.*, July/August 2010, 39–40.
[27]K. J. Behfar, R. S. Peterson, E. A. Mannix, and W. M. K. Trochim, "The Critical Role of Conflict Resolution in Teams: A Close Look at the Links between Conflict Type, Conflict Management Strategies, and Team Outcomes," *Journal of Applied Psychology* 93, no. 1 (2008):. 170–88; A. G. Tekleab, N. R. Quigley, and P. E. Tesluk, "A Longitudinal Study of Team Conflict, Conflict Management, Cohesion, and Team Effectiveness," *Group and Organization Management* 34, no. 2 (2009): 170–205.
[28]A. Somech, H. S. Desivilya, and H. Lidogoster, "Team Conflict Management and Team Effectiveness: The Effects of Task Interdependence and Team Identification," *Journal of Organizational Behavior* 30, no. 3 (2009): 359–78.
[29]H. Ren and B. Gray, "Repairing Relationship Conflict: How Violation Types and Culture Influence the Effectiveness of Restoration Rituals," *Academy of Management Review* 34, no. 1 (2009): 105–26.
[30]M. J. Gelfand, M. Higgins, L. H. Nishii, J. L. Raver, A. Dominguez, F. Murakami, S. Yamaguchi, and M. Toyama, "Culture and Egocentric Perceptions of Fairness in Conflict and Negotiation," *Journal of Applied Psychology*, October 2002, 833–45; and Z. Ma, "Chinese Conflict Management Styles and Negotiation Behaviours: An Empirical Test," *International Journal of Cross Cultural Management*, April 2007, 101–19.
[31]P. P. Fu, X. H. Yan, Y. Li, E. Wang, and S. Peng, "Examining Conflict-Handling Approaches by Chinese Top Management Teams in IT Firms," *International Journal of Conflict Management* 19, no. 3 (2008): 188–209.
[32]W. Liu, R. Friedman, and Y. Hong, "Culture and Accountability in Negotiation: Recognizing the Importance of In-Group Relations," *Organizational Behavior and Human Decision Processes* 117 (2012): 221–34; and B. C. Gunia, J. M. Brett, A. K. Nandkeolyar, and D. Kamdar, "Paying a Price: Culture, Trust, and Negotiation Consequences," *Journal of Applied Psychology* 96, no. 4 (2010): 774–89
[33]M. H. Bazerman, J. R. Curhan, D. A. Moore, and K. L. Valley, "Negotiation," *Annual Review of Psychology* 51 (2000): 279–314.
[34]See, for example, D. R. Ames, "Assertiveness Expectancies: How Hard People Push Depends on the Consequences They Predict," *Journal of Personality and Social Psychology* 95, no. 6 (2008): 1541–57; and J. R. Curhan, H. A. Elfenbein, and H. Xu, "What Do People Value When They Negotiate? Mapping the Domain of Subjective Value in Negotiation," *Journal of Personality and Social Psychology* 91, no. 3 (2006): 493–512.
[35]R. Lewicki, D. Saunders, and B. Barry, *Negotiation*, 6th ed. (New York: McGraw-Hill/Irwin, 2009).
[36]J. C. Magee, A. D. Galinsky, and D. H. Gruenfeld, "Power, Propensity to Negotiate, and Moving First in Competitive Interactions," *Personality and Social Psychology Bulletin*, February 2007, 200–12.
[37]H. R. Bowles, L. Babcock, and L. Lei, "Social Incentives for Gender Differences in the Propensity to Initiative Negotiations: Sometimes It Does Hurt to Ask," *Organizational Behavior and Human Decision Processes* 103 (2007): 84–103.
[38]E. Wilson, "The Trouble with Jake," *The New York Times*, July 15, 2009, www.nytimes.com.
[39]Rahim, *Managing Conflict in Organizations.*
[40]C. K. W. De Dreu, L. R. Weingart, and S. Kwon, "Influence of Social Motives on Integrative Negotiation: A Meta-Analytic Review

and Test of Two Theories," *Journal of Personality & Social Psychology,* May 2000, 889–905.
[41]This model is based on R. J. Lewicki, D. Saunders, and B. Barry, *Negotiation,* 7th ed. (New York: McGraw Hill, 2014).
[42]J. R. Curhan, H. A. Elfenbein, and G. J. Kilduff, "Getting off on the Right Foot: Subjective Value versus Economic Value in Predicting Longitudinal Job Outcomes from Job Offer Negotiations," *Journal of Applied Psychology* 94, no. 2 (2009): 524–34.
[43]L. L. Thompson, J. Wang, and B. C. Gunia. "Negotiation," *Annual Review of Psychology* 61, (2010): 491–515.
[44]Michael Schaerer, Roderick I. Swaab, and Adam D. Galinsky, "Anchors Weigh More Than Power: Why Absolute Powerlessness Liberates Negotiators to Achieve Better Outcomes," *Psychological Science,* December, 2014, doi:10.1177/0956797614558718.
[45]R. P. Larrick and G. Wu, "Claiming a Large Slice of a Small Pie: Asymmetric Disconfirmation in Negotiation," *Journal of Personality and Social Psychology* 93, no. 2 (2007): 212–33.
[46]H. A. Elfenbein, "Individual Difference in Negotiation: A Nearly Abandoned Pursuit Revived," *Current Directions in Psychological Science* 24 (2015): 131–36.
[47]T. A. Judge, B. A. Livingston, and C. Hurst, "Do Nice Guys—and Gals—Really Finish Last? The Joint Effects of Sex and Agreeableness on Income," *Journal of Personality and Social Psychology* 102 (2012): 390–407.
[48]N. Dimotakis, D. E. Conlon, and R. Ilies, "The Mind and Heart (Literally) of the Negotiator: Personality and Contextual Determinants of Experiential Reactions and Economic Outcomes in Negotiation," *Journal of Applied Psychology* 97 (2012): 183–93.
[49]E. T. Amanatullah, M. W. Morris, and J. R. Curhan, "Negotiators Who Give Too Much: Unmitigated Communion, Relational Anxieties, and Economic Costs in Distributive and Integrative Bargaining," *Journal of Personality and Social Psychology* 95, no. 3 (2008): 723–38; and D. S. DeRue, D. E. Conlon, H. Moon, and H. W. Willaby, "When Is Straightforwardness a Liability in Negotiations? The Role of Integrative Potential and Structural Power," *Journal of Applied Psychology* 94, no. 4 (2009): 1032–47.
[50]S. Sharma, W. Bottom, and H. A. Elfenbein, "On the Role of Personality, Cognitive Ability, and Emotional Intelligence in Predicting Negotiation Outcomes: A Meta-Analysis," *Organizational Psychology Review* 3 (2013): 293–336.
[51]H. A. Elfenbein, J. R. Curhan, N. Eisenkraft, A. Shirako, and L. Baccaro, "Are Some Negotiators Better Than Others? Individual Differences in Bargaining Outcomes," *Journal of Research in Personality,* December 2008, 1463–75.
[52]A. Zerres, J. Hüffmeier, P. A. Freund, K. Backhaus, and G. Hertel, "Does It Take Two to Tango? Longitudinal Effects of Unilaterial and Bilateral Integrative Negotiation Training," *Journal of Applied Psychology* 98 (2013): 478–91.
[53]G. Lelieveld, E. Van Dijk, I. Van Beest, and G. A. Van Kleef, "Why Anger and Disappointment Affect Other's Bargaining Behavior Differently: The Moderating Role of Power and the Mediating Role of Reciprocal Complementary Emotions," *Personality and Social Psychology Bulletin* 38 (2012): 1209–21.
[54]S. Côté, I. Hideg, and G. A. van Kleef, "The Consequences of Faking Anger in Negotiations," *Journal of Experimental Social Psychology* 49 (2013): 453–63.
[55]G. A. Van Kleef and C. K. W. De Dreu, "Longer-Term Consequences of Anger Expression in Negotiation: Retaliation or Spillover?" *Journal of Experimental Social Psychology* 46, no. 5 (2010): 753–60.
[56]H. Adam and A. Shirako, "Not All Anger Is Created Equal: The Impact of the Expresser's Culture on the Social Effects of Anger in Negotiations," *Journal of Applied Psychology,* 2013.
[57]Lelieveld, Van Dijk, Van Beest, and Van Kleef, "Why Anger and Disappointment Affect Other's Bargaining Behavior Differently."
[58]M. Olekalns and P. L Smith, "Mutually Dependent: Power, Trust, Affect, and the Use of Deception in Negotiation," *Journal of Business Ethics* 85, no. 3 (2009): 347–65.
[59]A. W. Brooks and M. E. Schweitzer, "Can Nervous Nellie Negotiate? How Anxiety Causes Negotiators to Make Low First Offers, Exit Early, and Earn Less Profit," *Organizational Behavior and Human Decision Processes* 115, no. 1 (2011): 43–54.
[60]M. Sinaceur, H. Adam, G. A. Van Kleef, and A. D. Galinsky, "The Advantages of Being Unpredictable: How Emotional Inconsistency Extracts Concessions in Negotiation," *Journal of Experimental Social Psychology* 49 (2013): 498–508.
[61]K. Leary, J. Pillemer, and M. Wheeler, "Negotiating with Emotion," *Harvard Business Review,* January–February 2013, 96–103.
[62]L. A. Liu, R. Friedman, B. Barry, M. J. Gelfand, and Z. Zhang, "The Dynamics of Consensus Building in Intracultural and Intercultural Negotiations," *Administrative Science Quarterly* 57 (2012): 269–304.
[63]M. Liu, "The Intrapersonal and Interpersonal Effects of Anger on Negotiation Strategies: A Cross-Cultural Investigation," *Human Communication Research* 35, no. 1 (2009): 148–69; and H. Adam, A. Shirako, and W. W. Maddux, "Cultural Variance in the Interpersonal Effects of Anger in Negotiations," *Psychological Science* 21, no. 6 (2010): 882–89.
[64]P. D. Trapnell and D. L. Paulhus, "Agentic and Communal Values: Their Scope and Measurement," *Journal of Personality Assessment* 94 (2012): 39–52.
[65]C. T. Kulik and M. Olekalns, "Negotiating the Gender Divide: Lessons from the Negotiation and Organizational Behavior Literatures," *Journal of Management* 38 (2012): 1387–415.
[66]C. Suddath, "The Art of Haggling," *Bloomberg Businessweek,* November 26, 2012, 98.
[67]J. Mazei, J. Hüffmeier, P. A. Freund, A. F. Stuhlmacher, L. Bilke, and G. Hertel, "A Meta-Analysis on Gender Differences in Negotiation Outcomes and Their Moderators," *Psychological Bulletin* 141 (2015): 85–104.
[68]L. J. Kray, C. C. Locke, and A B. Van Zant, "Feminine Charm: An Experimental Analysis of its Costs and Benefits in Negotiations," *Personality and Social Psychology Bulletin* 38 (2012): 1343–57.
[69]S. de Lemus, R. Spears, M. Bukowski, M. Moya, and J. Lupiáñez, "Reversing Implicit Gender Stereotype Activation as a Function of Exposure to Traditional Gender Roles," *Social Psychology* 44 (2013): 109–16.
[70]D. A. Small, M. Gelfand, L. Babcock, and H. Gettman, "Who Goes to the Bargaining Table? The Influence of Gender and Framing on the Initiation of Negotiation," *Journal of Personality and Social Psychology* 93, no. 4 (2007): 600–13.
[71]D. T. Kong, K. T. Dirks, and D. L. Ferrin, "Interpersonal Trust within Negotiations: Meta-Analytic Evidence, Critical Contingencies, and Directions for Future Research," *Academy of Management Journal* 57 (2014): 1235–55.
[72]G. R. Ferris, J. N. Harris, Z. A. Russell, B. P. Ellen, A. D. Martinez, and F. R. Blass, "The Role of Reputation in the Organizational Sciences: A Multilevel Review, Construct Assessment, and Research Directions," *Research in Personnel and Human Resources Management* 32 (2014): 241–303.
[73]R. Zinko, G. R. Ferris, S. E. Humphrey, C. J. Meyer, and F. Aime, "Personal Reputation in Organizations: Two-Study Constructive Replication and Extension of Antecedents and Consequences," *Journal of Occupational and Organizational Psychology* 85 (2012): 156–80.
[74]A. Hinshaw, P. Reilly, and A. Kupfer Schneider, "Attorneys and Negotiation Ethics: A Material Misunderstanding?" *Negotiation Journal* 29 (2013): 265–87; N. A. Welsh, "The Reputational Advantages of Demonstrating Trustworthiness: Using the Reputation Index with Law Students," *Negotiation Journal* 28 (2012): 117–45.
[75]J. R. Curhan, H. A. Elfenbein, and X. Heng, "What Do People Value When They Negotiate? Mapping the Domain of Subjective Value in Negotiation," *Journal of Personality and Social Psychology* 91 (2006): 493–512.
[76]W. E. Baker and N. Bulkley, "Paying It Forward vs. Rewarding Reputation: Mechanisms of Generalized Reciprocity," *Organization Science* 25 (June 17, 2014): 1493–510.
[77]G. A. Van Kleef, C. K. W. De Dreu, and A. S. R. Manstead, "An Interpersonal Approach to Emotion in Social Decision Making: The Emotions as Social Information Model," *Advances in Experimental Social Psychology* 42 (2010): 45–96.
[78]F. Lumineau and J. E. Henderson, "The Influence of Relational Experience and Contractual Governance on the Negotiation Strategy in Buyer–supplier Disputes," *Journal of Operations Management* 30 (2012): 382–95.
[79]U.S. Equal Employment Opportunity Commission, http://www.eeoc.gov/eeoc/mediation/qanda.cfm, accessed June 9, 2015.

CHAPTER 9
Leadership in organisations

An essential element of management and organisational behaviour is co-ordinating the activities of people and guiding their efforts towards the goals and objectives of the organisation. This involves the process of leadership and the choice of an appropriate form of behaviour and action. The manager needs to understand the nature and influence of leadership and factors that determine the effectiveness of the leadership relationship.

Learning outcomes

After completing this chapter you should have enhanced your ability to:

- explain the meaning and significance of leadership in work organisations;
- contrast main approaches to, and studies of, leadership;
- explore different styles and forms of leadership;
- detail situational forces and variables in the style of leadership adopted;
- explain the leadership relationship, and power and leadership influence;
- examine the variables affecting effective leadership;
- review the nature and importance of leadership development.

Critical review and reflection

Leadership is one of the holy grails of management and organisational behaviour. However complex or nebulous the subject area may appear, an understanding of leadership is an essential part of your studies.

What benefits do YOU expect to achieve from YOUR study of leadership?

The significance of leadership

The changing nature of work organisations involves moving away from an emphasis on command and getting results by the close control of the workforce and towards an environment of teamwork coaching, support and empowerment. This places an ever-growing importance on leadership. The leader–follower relationship is reciprocal, and effective leadership is a two-way process that influences both individual and organisational performance. Leadership is related to motivation and interpersonal behaviour.[1] A CBI report makes the point that: 'Effective leaders, who can inspire their people to realise their personal and collective potential, are often the deciding factor between a company being good at what it does and achieving greatness.'[2]

Leadership and management

What is the relationship between leadership and management? Although the two terms are often used interchangeably, management may be viewed as relating to people working within a structured organisation and with prescribed roles, in order to achieve stated organisational objectives (**see Chapter 10**). The emphasis of leadership is on interpersonal behaviour in a broader context. It is often associated with the willing and enthusiastic behaviour of followers.

Arguably there are differences between leadership and management. For example, *Zaleznik* explores difference in attitudes towards goals, conceptions of work, relations with others, self-perception and development:

- Managers tend to adopt impersonal or passive attitudes towards goals. Leaders adopt a more personal and active attitude towards goals.
- In order to get people to accept solutions, the manager needs continually to co-ordinate and balance in order to compromise conflicting values. The leader creates excitement in work and develops choices that give substance to images that excite people.
- In their relationships with other people, managers maintain a low level of emotional involvement. Leaders have empathy with other people and give attention to what events and actions mean.
- Managers see themselves more as conservators and regulators of the existing order of affairs with which they identify and from which they gain rewards. Leaders work in, but do not belong to, the organisation. Their sense of identity does not depend upon membership or work roles and they search out opportunities for change.[3]

Summarising the views of scholars who have attempted to differentiate between leading and managing, *Kent* draws attention to the following characteristics:

- managers do things right; leaders do the right things;
- managing is an authority relationship; leading is an influence relationship; and
- managing creates stability; leading creates change.

Kent suggests that although the ideas are provocative and stimulating, they provide a basis for a deeper understanding of the dynamics behind the two processes.[4]

Leadership role not defined

The key point about leadership is that it does not necessarily take place within the hierarchical structure of the organisation. It can occur at different levels and be manifested in different ways. Many people operate as leaders without their role ever being clearly established or defined.

For example, *Belbin* suggests that:

> *there is a clear implication that leadership is not part of the job but a quality that can be brought to a job . . . The work that leadership encompasses in the context clearly is not assigned but comes about spontaneously.*[5]

Radcliffe maintains that leadership is not mysterious, it is completely natural. Leadership is plain and simple. The only qualification to be a leader is the desire to grow. It absolutely does not matter where you are in an organisation.

> *This 'leadership stuff' really needn't be complicated. I believe that leading is a natural, human activity that is part of all of us. You don't need a certain IQ or job title to be a leader.*

There are only three aspects to leading: Future, Engage, Deliver.

- First, leading always starts in the Future.
- Second, if you want the help of others to create that Future, you need to Engage them.
- Third, in Deliver, you make things happen.[6]

Different perspectives

Despite continuing debate on differences between management and leadership, there is a close relationship and it is not easy to separate them as distinct activities. There appears to be an increasing tendency to emphasise the interrelationship between management and leadership and to see them more as synonymous. Many methods of management training can also be used as a means of measuring leadership style. For example, the Leadership Grid® (**discussed in Chapter** 10) was until recently known as the Managerial Grid®.

Mintzberg does not accept a distinction between the manager or the leader and poses the questions: 'How would you like to be managed by someone who doesn't lead; or why would you want to be led by someone who doesn't manage?'

> *Frankly, I don't understand what this distinction means in the everyday life of organizations. Sure, we can separate leading and managing conceptually. But can we separate them in practice? Or, more to the point, should we even try?*[7]

Moorcroft suggests two perspectives on the debate between leadership and management:

> *The debate between Leadership and Management is well rehearsed, and usually produces shades of two perspectives, presented here as extremes: A hierarchical relationship with Leadership at the top; Leadership and Management equal in status, but at opposite ends of a continuum. Frankly, there is little evidence to support one view over the other. But there is overwhelming evidence that people like the idea of being a 'leader'. Indeed this may be the reason why the debate still rages, as it fulfils a need for differentiation.*[8]

Critical review and reflection

In universities, many lecturers inspire students and are viewed usually as leaders not managers. In sport, we hear frequent talk about great leaders who are not managers of the team. There appears to be a clear and accepted distinction between leadership and management.

Why do YOU think this distinction does not appear to apply in the same way within business organisations? How do YOU distinguish between leadership and management?

Approaches to leadership

There are many ways of looking at **leadership** and interpretations of its meaning. Leadership might be interpreted in simple terms, such as 'getting others to follow' or 'getting people to do things willingly', or interpreted more specifically, for example as 'the use of authority in decision-making'. It may be exercised as an attribute of position or because of personal knowledge or wisdom. Leadership might be based on a function of personality or it can be seen as a behavioural category. It may also be viewed in terms of the role of the leaders and their ability to achieve effective performance from others. Leadership can also be discussed in terms of a form of persuasion or power relationship. It is difficult, therefore, to generalise about leadership, but essentially it is a **relationship through which one person influences the behaviour or actions of other people.** This means that the process of leadership cannot be separated from the activities of groups and effective team building.

Due to its complex and variable nature, there are many alternative ways of analysing leadership. It is helpful, therefore, to have some framework in which to consider different approaches to study of the subject.

One way is to examine managerial leadership in terms of:

- a qualities or traits approach;
- a functional or group approach, including action-centred leadership;
- styles of leadership;
- contingency theories;
- transitional or transformational leadership;
- inspirational or visionary leadership; and
- servant leadership. (*See* Figure 9.1.)

Qualities or traits approach

This approach assumes that leaders are born and not made. Leadership consists of certain inherited characteristics, or personality traits, which distinguish leaders from their followers. The **qualities (traits) approach** focuses attention on the man or woman in the job and not on the job itself. It suggests that attention is given to the selection of leaders rather than to training for leadership.

Drucker (writing originally in 1955) makes the point that:

> *Leadership is of utmost importance. Indeed there is no substitute for it. But leadership cannot be created or promoted. It cannot be taught or learned.*[9]

However, attempts at identifying common personality, or physical and mental, characteristics of different 'good' or 'successful' leaders have met with little success.[10] Investigations have identified lists of traits that tend to be overlapping, contradictory or with little correlation for most features. It is noticeable that 'individuality' or 'originality' usually features in the list. This suggests there is little in common between specific personality traits of different leaders. It is perhaps possible therefore to identify general characteristics of leadership ability, such as self-confidence, initiative, intelligence and belief in one's actions, but research into this area has revealed little more than this.

Limitations of the traits approach

There are three further limitations with this approach:

- There is bound to be some subjective judgement in determining who is regarded as a 'good' or 'successful' leader. (This can make for an interesting class discussion.)
- The lists of possible traits tend to be very long and there is not always agreement on the most important.
- It ignores the situational factors.

Even if it were possible to identify an agreed list of more specific qualities, this would provide little explanation of the nature of leadership or the development and training of future leaders. The qualities or traits approach gives rise to the questions of whether leaders are born or made and whether leadership is an art or a science. The important point, however, is that **these**

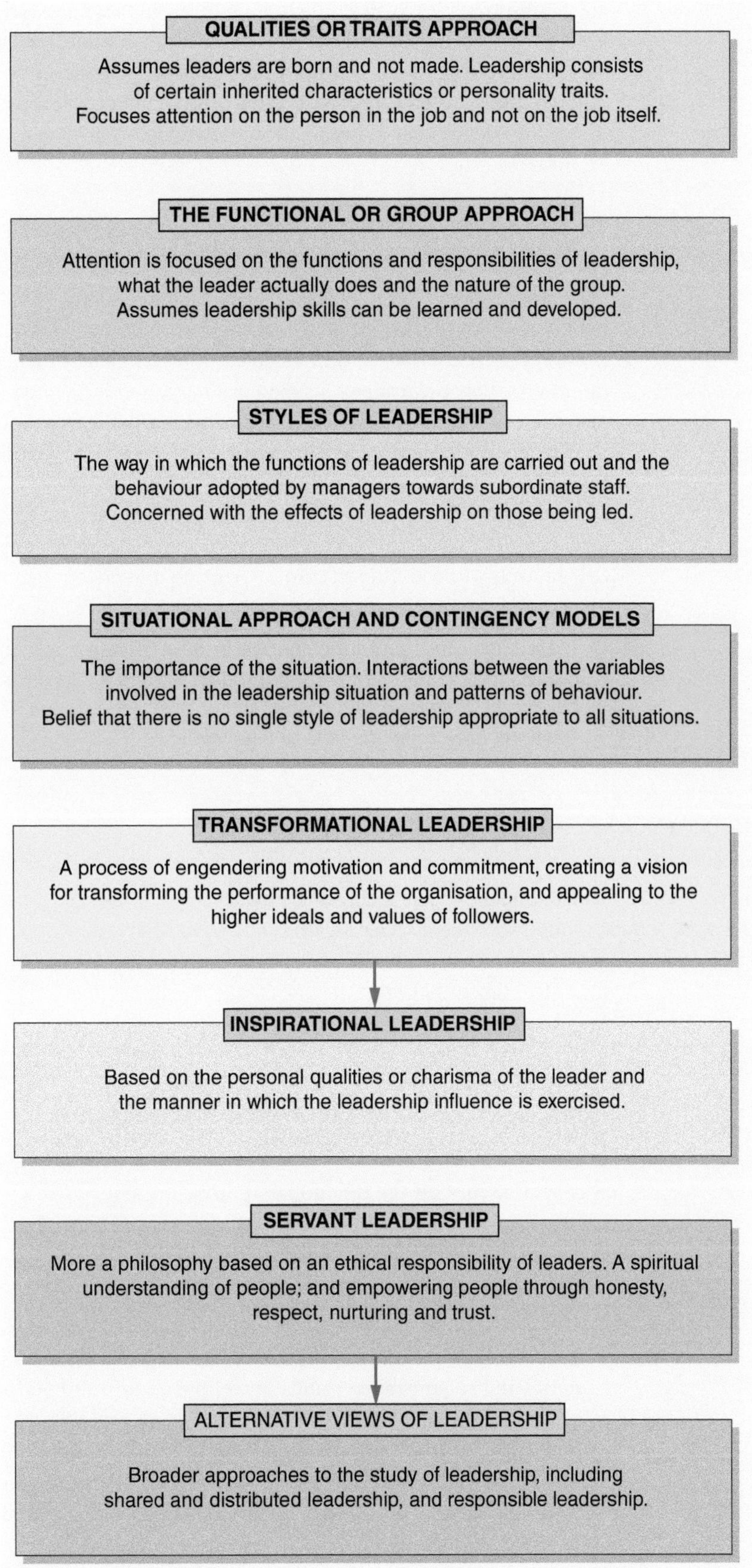

QUALITIES OR TRAITS APPROACH

Assumes leaders are born and not made. Leadership consists of certain inherited characteristics or personality traits. Focuses attention on the person in the job and not on the job itself.

THE FUNCTIONAL OR GROUP APPROACH

Attention is focused on the functions and responsibilities of leadership, what the leader actually does and the nature of the group. Assumes leadership skills can be learned and developed.

STYLES OF LEADERSHIP

The way in which the functions of leadership are carried out and the behaviour adopted by managers towards subordinate staff. Concerned with the effects of leadership on those being led.

SITUATIONAL APPROACH AND CONTINGENCY MODELS

The importance of the situation. Interactions between the variables involved in the leadership situation and patterns of behaviour. Belief that there is no single style of leadership appropriate to all situations.

TRANSFORMATIONAL LEADERSHIP

A process of engendering motivation and commitment, creating a vision for transforming the performance of the organisation, and appealing to the higher ideals and values of followers.

↓

INSPIRATIONAL LEADERSHIP

Based on the personal qualities or charisma of the leader and the manner in which the leadership influence is exercised.

SERVANT LEADERSHIP

More a philosophy based on an ethical responsibility of leaders. A spiritual understanding of people; and empowering people through honesty, respect, nurturing and trust.

↓

ALTERNATIVE VIEWS OF LEADERSHIP

Broader approaches to the study of leadership, including shared and distributed leadership, and responsible leadership.

Figure 9.1 Framework for study of managerial leadership

are not mutually exclusive alternatives. Even if there are certain inborn qualities that make for a good leader, these natural talents need encouragement and development. Even if leadership is something of an art, it still requires the application of special skills and techniques. Although there is still limited interest in the qualities or traits approach, attention has been directed more to other approaches to leadership.

Functional (or group) approach

This approach to leadership focuses attention not on the personality of the leader, nor on the man or woman in the job, per se, but on the contents or **functions of leadership**. Leadership is always present in any group engaged in a task. The functional approach views leadership in terms of how the leader's behaviour affects, and is affected by, the group of followers. This approach concentrates on the nature of the group, the followers or subordinates.

The functional approach believes the skills of leadership can be learned, developed and perfected. In contrast to the view of Drucker (referred to above), *Kotter* makes the point that successful companies do not wait for leaders to come along: 'They actively seek out people with leadership potential and expose them to career experiences designed to develop that potential. Indeed, with careful selection, nurturing and encouragement, dozens of people can play important leadership roles in a business organisation.'[11] A similar point is made by *Whitehead:*

> *There has been a dramatic change in how management thinkers regard leadership today. Leaders are not born, they say, but made. And the good news is everyone can do it. You don't have to be promoted to a management position. You can be a leader whatever job you do. You don't have to be the boss to be a leader.*[12]

Critical review and reflection

Leadership is all about determination, personality and innate ability at the right time for a particular competitive situation. Many effective business leaders have no formal academic qualifications and each has their own individual leadership style.

Does this suggest to YOU that successful leaders are more likely born rather than trained? Do YOU believe YOU would make a successful leader?

Action-centred leadership

A general theory on the functional approach is associated with the work of *John Adair* and his ideas on **action-centred leadership**, which focuses on what leaders actually *do*.[13] The effectiveness of the leader is dependent upon meeting three areas of need: the need to achieve the common **task;** the need for **team maintenance;** and the **individual needs** of group members – symbolised by three overlapping circles (*see* Figure 9.2).

- **Task needs** involve achieving objectives and defining group tasks, organising the work, duties and responsibilities and controlling quality and performance.
- **Team maintenance needs** involve maintaining morale and team spirit, maintaining standards and discipline, and training and communication within the group.
- **Individual needs** involve meeting needs of individual members and attending to personal problems, giving praise and status, and reconciling conflicts between group needs and needs of the individual.

Action by the leader in any one area of need will affect one or both of the other areas. The ideal position is where complete integration of the three areas of need is achieved.

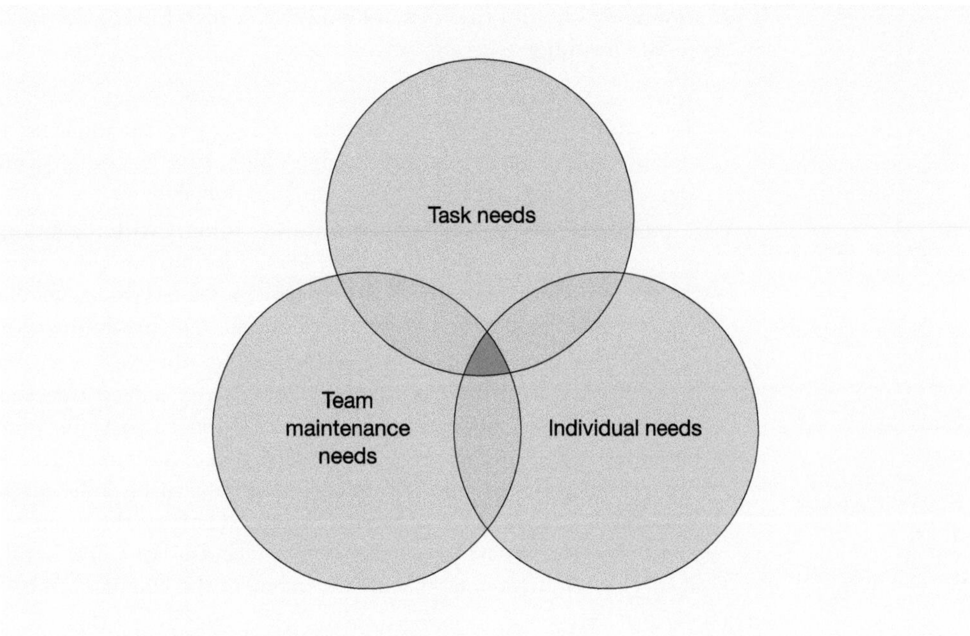

Figure 9.2 Interaction of needs within the group
Source: Adair, J. *Action-Centred Leadership*, Gower Press (1979), p. 10. Reproduced with permission from John Adair.

Are leaders born or made?

There are times when leadership comes out of all of us. A few years ago, some of my team and I were caught up in the terrorist attack on the Taj Hotel in Mumbai. We were stuck inside, debris was falling and people were screaming. But a young member of staff rose to the situation and took care of us. This 22 year-old woman guided us through the hotel and led us to safety. Nothing in her training had ever taught her how to respond in a situation like that, but she was calm, composed and unflappable. The way she exerted her authority was amazing. She showed me a lesson in leadership - you can lead in a moment, with your heart.

Source: Leena Nair, 'Debate: The Changing Face of the Leader', *Management Today*, 3 June 2013, p. 53.

Styles of leadership

In the work situation it has become increasingly clear that managers can no longer rely solely on the use of their position in the hierarchical structure. To get the best results from subordinates the manager must also have regard for the need to encourage high morale, a spirit of involvement and co-operation, and a willingness to work. This gives rise to consideration of the style of leadership and provides another heading under which to analyse leadership behaviour.

Leadership style is the way in which the functions of leadership are carried out, the way in which the manager typically behaves towards members of the group. There are many possible ways of describing leadership style, such as abdicatorial, benevolent, bureaucratic, charismatic, consultative, dictatorial, inspirational, participative, servant or unitary. With so many potential descriptions of leadership styles it is useful to have a broad framework in which to focus attention and study. The style of managerial leadership towards subordinate staff and the focus of power can therefore be considered within a simplified three-fold heading:

- **Authoritarian (autocratic) style**, where the focus of power is with the manager and interactions within the group move towards the manager. The manager alone exercises decision-making and authority for determining policy, procedures for achieving goals, work tasks and relationships and control of rewards or punishments.
- **Democratic style**, where the focus of power is more with the group as a whole and there is greater interaction within the group. The leadership functions are shared with members of the group and the manager is more part of a team. Group members have a greater say in decision-making, determination of policy and implementation of systems and procedures.
- **Laissez-faire (genuine) style**, where the manager observes members of the group are working well on their own. The manager consciously makes a decision to pass the focus of power to members, allow them freedom of action 'to do as they think best', not to interfere but to be readily available if help is needed. There is often confusion over this style of leadership. The word 'genuine' is emphasised because this is to be contrasted with the manager who could not care, who deliberately keeps away from the trouble spots and does not want to get involved. Members are then left to face decisions that rightly belong with the manager. This is more a non-style of leadership, or it could perhaps be labelled as abdication.

Continuum of leadership behaviour

One of the best-known works on leadership style is that by *Tannenbaum and Schmidt* (see Figure 9.3).[14] Originally written in 1958 and updated in 1973, their work suggests a continuum of possible leadership behaviour available to a manager. The continuum presents a range of action related to the degree of authority used by the manager and to the area of freedom available to non-managers in arriving at decisions.

Four main styles of leadership

Moving along the continuum, the manager may be characterised according to the degree of control that is maintained. Neither extreme of the continuum is absolute as there is always some limitation on authority and on freedom. This approach can be seen as identifying four main styles of leadership by the manager: tells, sells, consults, joins.

- **Tells** – The manager identifies a problem, makes a decision and announces this to subordinates, expecting them to implement it without an opportunity for participation.
- **Sells** – The manager still makes a decision but recognises the possibility of some resistance from those faced with the decision and attempts to persuade subordinates to accept it.
- **Consults** – The manager identifies the problem but does not make a decision until the problem is presented to the group, and the manager has listened to the advice and solutions suggested by subordinates.
- **Joins** – The manager defines the problem and the limits within which the decision must be made and then passes to the group, with the manager as a member, the right to make decisions.

Three main forces

Tannenbaum and Schmidt suggest that there are three factors, or forces, of particular importance in deciding what types of leadership are practicable and desirable. These are: forces in the manager, forces in the subordinate and forces in the situation.

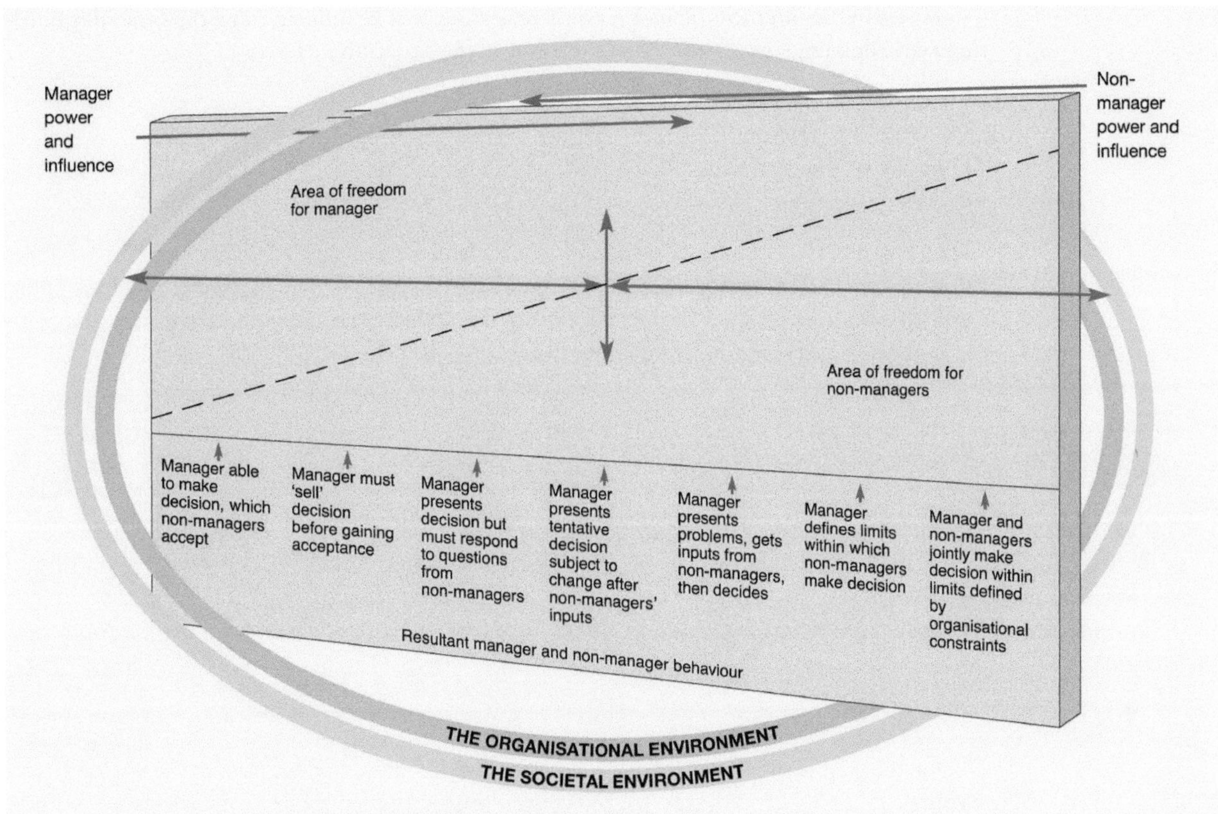

Figure 9.3 Continuum of manager–non-manager behaviour

Source: From Tannenbaum, R. and Schmidt, W. H. 'How to Choose a Leadership Pattern', *Harvard Business Review*, May/June 1973, p. 167.

Forces in the manager. The manager's behaviour will be influenced by his or her personality, background, knowledge and experiences. These internal forces will include:

- value-systems;
- confidence in subordinates;
- leadership inclinations;
- feelings of security in an uncertain situation.

Forces in the subordinate. Subordinates are influenced by many personality variables and their individual set of expectations about their relationship with the manager. Characteristics of the subordinate are:

- strength of the need for independence;
- readiness to assume responsibility for decision-making;
- degree of tolerance for ambiguity;
- interest in the problem and feelings as to its importance;
- understanding and identification with the goals of the organisation;
- necessary knowledge and experience to deal with the problem;
- extent of learning to expect to share in decision-making.

The greater the positive response to these characteristics, the greater freedom of action can be allowed by the manager.

Forces in the situation. The manager's behaviour will be influenced by the general situation and environmental pressures. Characteristics in the situation include:

- type of organisation;
- group effectiveness;
- nature of the problem;
- pressure of time.

Tannenbaum and Schmidt conclude that successful leaders are keenly aware of those forces that are most relevant to their behaviour at a particular time. They are able to behave appropriately in terms of their understanding of themselves, the individuals and the group, the organisation and environmental influences.

Critical review and reflection

The Tannenbaum and Schmidt continuum is the single most relevant study of leadership. Successful managers need to be consistent in both personality and behaviour, yet adaptable to forces that continually influence their leadership style and decision-making.

To what extent can YOU argue against this assertion? What do YOU think is the single most important study of leadership?

Contingency theories of leadership

The continuum of leadership behaviour draws attention to forces in the situation as one of the main forces influencing the nature of managerial behaviour. The **contingency or situational approach** emphasises the situation as the dominant feature in considering the characteristics of effective leadership. There are, however, limitations to this approach. There are people who possess the appropriate knowledge and skills and appear to be the most suitable leaders in a given situation, but who do not emerge as effective leaders. Also, in the work organisation, it is not usually practicable to allow the situation continually to determine who should act as the leader.

Despite limitations of the contingency approach, situational factors are important in considering the characteristics of leadership. Contingency models focus on the interactions between the variables involved in a leadership situation and patterns of leadership behaviour. Major contingency models of leadership include:

- Favourability of leadership situation – Fiedler
- Quality and acceptance of leader's decision – Vroom and Yetton
- **Path–goal theory** – House, and House and Dessler
- Readiness level of followers – Hersey and Blanchard.

Fiedler's contingency model

One of the first leader–situation models was developed by *Fiedler* in his contingency theory of leadership effectiveness.[15] In order to measure the attitudes of the leader, Fiedler developed a 'least preferred co-worker' (LPC) scale. This measures the rating given by leaders about the person with whom they could work least well. The questionnaire contains up to twenty items. Examples of items in the LPC scale are pleasant/unpleasant, friendly/unfriendly, helpful/frustrating, distant/close, co-operative/unco-operative, boring/interesting, self-assured/hesitant, open/guarded.

Each item is given a single ranking of between 1 and 8 points, with 8 points indicating the most favourable rating. For example:

Pleasant	:	:	:	:	:	:	:	:	Unpleasant
	8	7	6	5	4	3	2	1	

The LPC score is the sum of the numerical ratings on all the items for the 'least preferred co-worker'. The original interpretation of the LPC scale was that the leader with a high LPC score derived most satisfaction from interpersonal relationships. The leader with a low LPC score derived most satisfaction from performance of the task and achieving objectives. However, the interpretation of LPC has changed a number of times and there is still uncertainty about its actual meaning.

Favourability of the leadership situation

Fiedler suggests that leadership behaviour is dependent upon the favourability of the leadership situation. There are three major variables that determine the favourability of the situation and that affect the leader's role and influence:

- **Leader–member relations** – degree to which the leader is trusted and liked by group members, and their willingness to follow the leader's guidance.
- **The task structure** – degree to which the task is clearly defined for the group and the extent to which it can be carried out by detailed instructions or standard procedures.
- **Position power** – power of the leader by virtue of position in the organisation, and the degree to which the leader can exercise authority to influence (for example) rewards and punishments, or promotions and demotions.

From these three variables, Fiedler constructed eight combinations of group–task situations through which to relate leadership style (*see* Figure 9.4).

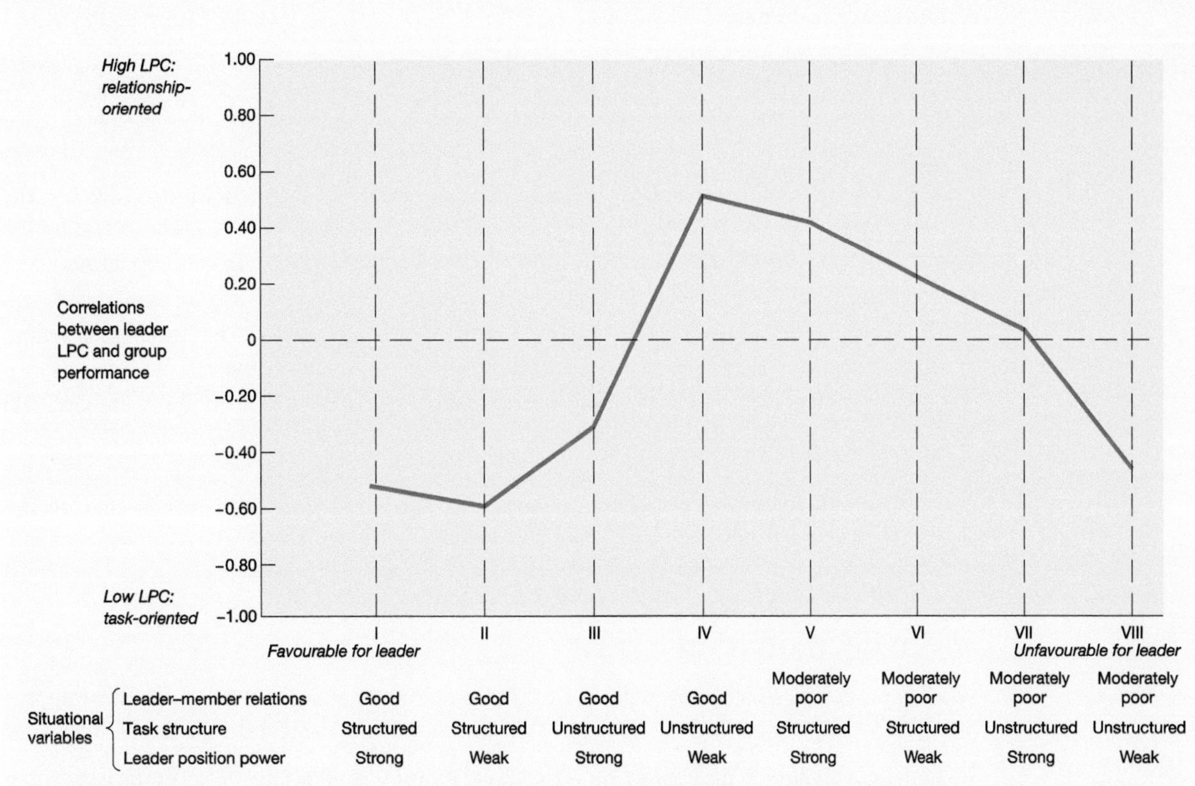

Figure 9.4 Correlations between leader's LPC scores and group effectiveness

Source: Adapted from Fiedler, F. E. A *Theory of Leadership Effectiveness*, McGraw-Hill (1967), p. 146. Reproduced with permission from Fred E. Fiedler.

When the situation is **very favourable** (good leader–member relations, structured task, strong position power) or **very unfavourable** (poor leader–member relations, unstructured task, weak position power), then a **task-oriented leader** (low LPC score) with a directive, controlling style will be more effective.

When the situation is **moderately favourable** and the variables are mixed, then the leader with an **interpersonal relationship orientation** (high LPC score) and a participative approach will be more effective.

Fiedler argues that leadership effectiveness may be improved by changing the leadership situation. Position power, task structure and leader–member relations can be changed to make the situation more compatible with the characteristics of the leader.

Fiedler's work has been subject to much debate and criticism but it does provide a further dimension to the study of leadership.[16] It brings into consideration the organisational variables that affect leadership effectiveness and suggests that in given situations a task-oriented, or structured, style of leadership is most appropriate. The 'best' styles of leadership will be dependent upon the variable factors in the leadership situation.

Vroom and Yetton contingency model

Vroom and Yetton base their analysis on two main aspects of a leader's decision: its quality and its acceptance.[17]

- **Decision quality, or rationality,** is the effect that the decision has on group performance.
- **Decision acceptance** refers to the motivation and commitment of group members in implementing the decision.

A third consideration is:

- **the amount of time** required to make the decision.

The Vroom and Yetton model suggests five main management decision styles:

- Autocratic
  - Leader solves the problem or makes the decision alone using information available at the time.
  - Leader obtains information from subordinates but then decides on solution alone.
- Consultative
  - The problem is shared with relevant subordinates, individually. The leader then makes the decision that may or may not reflect the influence of subordinates.
  - The problem is shared with subordinates as a group. The leader then makes the decision that may or may not reflect the influence of subordinates.
- Group
  - The problem is shared with subordinates as a group. The leader acts as chairperson rather than an advocate. Together the leader and subordinates generate and evaluate alternatives and attempt to reach group consensus on a solution.

Seven decision rules

Vroom and Yetton suggest seven decision rules to help the manager discover the most appropriate leadership style in a given situation. The first three rules protect the **quality of decisions.**

1. Is there a quality requirement such that one solution is likely to be more rational than another?
2. Is there sufficient information to make a high-quality decision?
3. Is the problem structured?

The last four rules protect the **acceptance of decisions.**

1. Is acceptance of the decision by subordinates critical to effective implementation?
2. If you were to make the decision yourself, is it reasonably certain that it would be accepted by subordinates?
3. Do subordinates share the organisational goals to be obtained in solving the problem?
4. Is conflict among subordinates likely in preferred solutions?

These rules indicate decision styles that the manager should **avoid** in a given situation and indicate the use of others. Decision-tree charts can be produced to help in the application of the rules and to relate the situation to the appropriate leadership style.

Path-goal theory

A third contingency model of leadership is the **path-goal theory**, the main work on which has been undertaken by *House*[18] and by *House and Dessler.*[19] The model is based on the belief that the individual's motivation is dependent upon expectations that increased effort to achieve an improved level of performance will be successful, and expectations that improved performance will be instrumental in obtaining positive rewards and avoiding negative outcomes. This is the 'expectancy' theory of motivation (**discussed in Chapter** 7).

Path–goal theory of leadership suggests that the performance of subordinates is affected by the extent to which the manager satisfies their expectations. Subordinates see leadership behaviour as a motivating influence to the extent that it means:

- satisfaction of their needs is dependent upon effective performance; and
- the necessary direction, guidance, training and support, which would otherwise be lacking, are provided.

Main types of leadership behaviour

House identifies four main types of leadership behaviour:

- **Directive leadership** – letting subordinates know exactly what is expected of them and giving specific directions. Subordinates are expected to follow rules and regulations. This type of behaviour is similar to 'initiating structure' in the Ohio State Leadership Studies.
- **Supportive leadership** – having a friendly and approachable manner and displaying concern for the needs and welfare of subordinates. This type of behaviour is similar to 'consideration' in the Ohio State Leadership Studies.
- **Participative leadership** – consulting with subordinates and the evaluation of their opinions and suggestions before the manager makes the decision.
- **Achievement-oriented leadership** – setting challenging goals for subordinates, seeking improvement in their performance and showing confidence in subordinates' ability to perform well.

Path–goal theory suggests that the different types of behaviour can be practised by the same person at different times in varying situations. By using one of the four styles of leadership behaviour the manager attempts to influence subordinates' perceptions and motivation, and smooth the path to their goals (*see* Figure 9.5).

Two main situational factors

Leadership behaviour is determined by two main situational factors: personal characteristics of subordinates and nature of the task.

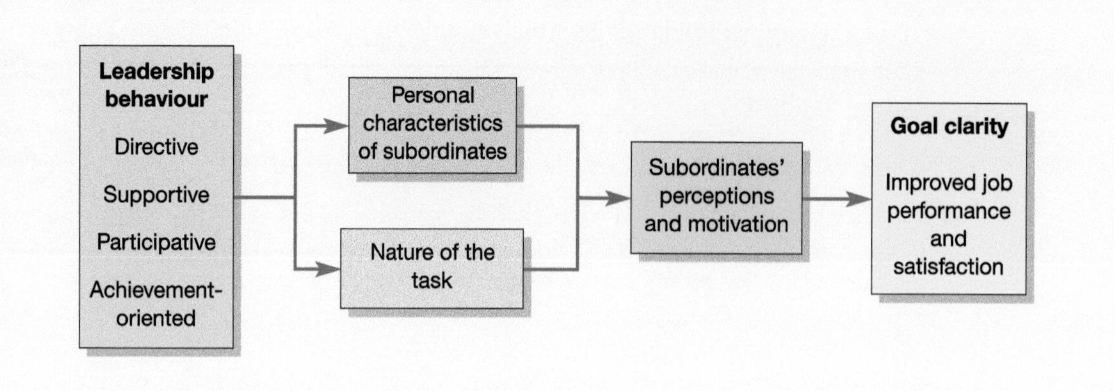

Figure 9.5 Representation of the path–goal theory of leadership

- **Personal characteristics of subordinates** determine how they will react to the manager's behaviour and the extent to which they see such behaviour as an immediate or potential source of need satisfaction.
- **Nature of the task** relates to the extent that it is routine and structured or non-routine and unstructured.

Effective leadership behaviour is based, therefore, on both the willingness of the manager to help subordinates and the needs of subordinates for help. Leadership behaviour will be motivational to the extent that it provides necessary direction, guidance and support, helps clarify path–goal relationships and removes any obstacles that hinder attainment of goals. For example, when a task is highly structured, the goals readily apparent and subordinates are confident, attempts to further explain the job or to give directions are likely to be viewed as unacceptable behaviour. However, when a task is highly unstructured, the nature of the goals is not clear and subordinates lack experience, a more directive style of leadership behaviour is likely to be welcomed by subordinates.

Critical review and reflection

Common sense suggests that situational factors are clearly a major determinant of the most appropriate leadership style. But, realistically, contingency models appeal only to teachers rather than practitioners of management.

What do YOU think? Can YOU relate any practical example of the apparent application of a contingency model of leadership?

Readiness of the followers or group

A major variable in the style of leadership adopted by the manager is the nature of subordinate staff. This view is developed by *Hersey and Blanchard*, who present a form of situational leadership based on the 'readiness' level of the people the leader is attempting to influence. Readiness is the extent to which followers have the ability and willingness to accomplish a specific task. It is not a personal characteristic of the individual but how ready the individual is to perform a particular task.[20]

Readiness (R) is divided into a continuum of four levels: R1 (low), R2 and R3 (moderate) and R4 (high):

- **R1 – low follower readiness** – refers to followers who are both *unable and unwilling* and who lack commitment and motivation, or who are *unable and insecure.*
- **R2 – low to moderate follower readiness** – refers to followers who are *unable but willing* and who lack ability but are motivated to make an effort, or who are *unable but confident.*
- **R3 – moderate to high follower readiness** – refers to followers who are *able but unwilling,* and who have the ability to perform but are unwilling to apply their ability, or who are *able but insecure.*
- **R4 – high follower readiness** – refers to followers who are both *able and willing* and who have the ability and commitment to perform, or who are *able and confident.*

Task behaviour and relationship behaviour

For each of the four levels of maturity, the appropriate style of leadership is a combination of task behaviour and relationship behaviour:

- **Task behaviour** is the extent to which the leader provides directions for the actions of followers, sets goals for them and defines their roles and how to undertake them.
- **Relationship behaviour** is the extent to which the leader engages in two-way communication with followers, listens to them and provides support and encouragement.

From the combination of task behaviour and relationship behaviour four leadership styles (S) are derived: telling (S1), selling (S2), participating (S3) and delegating (S4). The appropriate leadership style corresponds with the readiness of the followers (*see* Figure 9.6).

- **S1 – telling** – emphasises high amounts of guidance (task behaviour) but limited supportive (relationship) behaviour. This style is most appropriate for *low follower readiness* (R1).
- **S2 – selling** – emphasises high amounts of both directive (task) and relationship behaviours. This style is most appropriate for *low to moderate follower readiness* (R2).
- **S3 – participating** – emphasises a high amount of two-way communication and supportive (relationship) behaviour but low amounts of guidance (task behaviour). This style is most appropriate for *moderate to high follower readiness* (R3).
- **S4 – delegating** – emphasises little direction or support with low levels of both task and relationship behaviours. This style is most appropriate for *high follower readiness* (R4).

Development of subordinates

Hersey and Blanchard suggest the key to using situational leadership is that any leader behaviour may be more or less effective according to the readiness of the person the leader is attempting to influence. The model draws attention to the importance of developing the

S1 – TELLING – emphasises high amounts of guidance (task behaviour) but limited supportive (relationship) behaviour. This style is most appropriate for ***low follower readiness*** **(R1).**
Leadership behaviour based on detailed instructions and close supervision

S2 – SELLING – emphasises high amounts of both directive (task) and relationalship behaviours. This style is most appropriate for ***low to moderate follower readiness*** **(R2).**
Leadership behaviour based on explanation and discussion of decision

S3 – PARTICIPATING – emphasises high amounts of two-way communication and supportive (relationship) behaviour but low amounts of guidance (task behaviour). This style is most appropriate for ***moderate to high follower readiness*** **(R3).**
Leadership behaviour based on sharing ideas and facilitating decision-making

S4 – DELEGATING – emphasises little direction or support with low levels of both task and relationship behaviour. This style is most appropriate for ***high follower readiness*** **(R4).**
Leadership behaviour based on delegation of responsibility for decisions

Figure 9.6 Hersey and Blanchard's four leadership styles

ability, confidence and commitment of subordinates. The manager should help subordinates to develop in readiness to the extent that they are able and willing to go. This development should take place by adjusting leadership behaviour through the four styles of telling, selling, participating and delegating.

Transformational leadership

Increasing business competitiveness and need for the most effective use of human resources have resulted in writers on management focusing attention on how leaders revitalise or transform organisations. Based on the work of writers such as *Burns*, this has given rise to a distinction between two fundamental forms of leadership: transactional leadership and transformational (or creative) leadership.[21]

- **Transactional leadership** is based on legitimate authority within the bureaucratic structure of the organisation. The emphasis is on the clarification of goals and objectives, work task and outcomes, and organisational rewards and punishments. Transactional leadership appeals to the self-interest of followers. It is based on a relationship of mutual dependence and an exchange process of 'I will give you this, if you do that.'
- **Transformational (or creative) leadership,** by contrast, is a process of engendering higher levels of motivation and commitment among followers. The emphasis is on generating a vision for the organisation and the leader's ability to appeal to higher ideals and values of followers, and creating a feeling of justice, loyalty and trust. In the organisational sense, transformational leadership is about transforming the performance or fortunes of a business.

Components of transformational leadership

Applying the ideas of Burns to organisational management, *Bass* proposed a theory of transformational leadership that argues that the leader transforms and motivates followers by:

1. Generating greater awareness of the importance of the purpose of the organisation and task outcomes.
2. Inducing them to transcend their own self-interests for the sake of the organisation or team.
3. Activating their higher-level needs.[22]

Transformational leadership comprises four basic components:

- **idealised influence** – the charisma of the leader, and the respect and admiration of the followers;
- **inspirational motivation** – the behaviour of the leader, which provides meaning and challenge to the work of the followers;
- **intellectual stimulation** – leaders who solicit new and novel approaches for the performance of work and creative problem solutions from followers; and
- **individualised consideration** – leaders who listen and give special concern to the growth and developmental needs of the followers.[23]

Set of guidelines

Yukl provides a set of guidelines for transformational leadership:

- **Articulate a clear and appealing vision** of what the organisation could accomplish or become to help people understand the purpose, objectives and priorities of the organisation, and to help guide the actions and decisions of members.
- **Explain how the vision can be attained** and establish a clear link between the vision and a credible conventional yet straightforward strategy for attaining it.
- **Act confident and optimistic** about likely success, demonstrate self-confidence and conviction and emphasise positive aspects of the vision rather than the obstacles and dangers.

- **Express confidence in followers** and their ability to carry out the strategy for accomplishing the vision, especially when the task is difficult or dangerous, or when members lack confidence in themselves.
- **Use dramatic, symbolic actions** to emphasise key values and demonstrate leadership behaviour through dramatic, highly visible actions including risking personal loss, self-sacrifice or acting unconventionally.
- **Lead by example** by recognising actions speak louder than words, through exemplary behaviour in day-to-day interactions with subordinates and by demonstrating consistency in daily behaviour.[24]

Critical review and reflection

Transactional and transformational leadership should not be seen as alternatives. Any effective leader will clearly use a balance of both legitimate authority and attention to higher ideals and values of followers.

To what extent do YOU agree? How difficult do YOU think it is to apply this balance in practice? What would be the most likely problem areas?

Inspirational or visionary leadership

Many writers see transformational leadership as the same thing as charismatic, visionary or inspirational leadership. *Kreitner et al.* refer to charismatic leadership as transforming employees to pursue organisational goals over self-interests:

> *Charismatic leaders transform followers by creating changes in their goals, values, needs, beliefs, and aspirations. They accomplish this transformation by appealing to followers' self-concepts - namely, their values and personal identity.*[25]

Successful transformational leaders are usually identified in terms of providing a strong vision and sense of mission, arousing strong emotions in followers and a sense of identification with the leader. Leadership today is increasingly associated with the concept of creating a vision with which others can identify, getting along with other people and the concept of inspiration. This might be considered as part of transformational leadership or arguably it has given rise to a new approach to leadership – that of **inspirational or visionary leadership**. Inspirational leadership is not concerned so much with the theory of leadership but more with the skills of motivating and inspiring people.

In her discussion of the creation of the democratic enterprise (organisations that can flourish economically and can also be places of excitement and stimulation, fulfilment and tranquillity), *Gratton* maintains that it is the creation of a shared purpose and the role of the leadership team that are most vital. The role of the leader as visionary is fundamental to creating the broad philosophical context of democracy and as the architect of shared purpose.[26]

Goffee and Jones point out that the need for visionary leadership is becoming increasingly important. Traditional business hierarchies gave managers and workers a sense of their own position and what was expected of them. Now, as these hierarchies break down, it is leaders themselves who must fill the void, helping subordinates to understand their place and purpose. Personal leadership is beginning to replace organisation structure.[27]

Personal qualities or charisma

Leadership may be based on the personal qualities, or charisma, of the leader and the manner in which influence is exercised. The concept of charismatic or inspirational leadership is not new and has been applied in the organisational context by writers such as Max Weber

(1864–1920).[28] The importance of charisma for effective leadership today is emphasised by *Conger*, who also believes that many of the traits that make a successful leader can be taught, including charisma.

> *Now the big question is whether you are born with charisma or whether you can develop it. I believe you can develop elements of it. For example, you can take courses to improve your speaking skills. You can learn to stage events that send powerful messages. You can learn to think more critically about the status quo and its shortcomings. You can do more on a daily basis to motivate your team. What you simply cannot learn is how to be passionate about what you do. You have to discover that for yourself, and passion is a big part of what drives a charismatic leader. It is also what motivates and inspires those who work for the charismatic leader.*[29]

However, the extent to which charismatic or inspirational leadership helps bring about improvement in organisational performance is open to debate. Conger also draws attention to the danger that the leader's vision, dynamism and inspirational nature are highly attractive to followers, which leads to a natural dependence. Staff see this extraordinary figure as a model to be emulated and the leader's abilities become the yardstick by which they measure their own performance. This is a potential source of leadership derailment. Dependence makes the followers more susceptible to deception.[30]

Leadership not about the leader

Adair argues that to be a truly inspirational leader one must understand the spirit within. All people have the potential for greatness. The inspirational leader connects with the led, appreciates the capabilities of others and through trust will unlock the powers in others. Adair refers to 'the inspired moment' – a recognition and seizure of a brief window of opportunity that can act as a powerful catalyst that inspires both the leader and the led.[31]

> *Leadership is not about the leader, it is about how he or she builds the confidence of everyone else. Leaders are responsible for both the big structures that serve as the cornerstone of confidence, and for the human touches that shape a positive emotional climate to inspire and motivate people . . . Leaders deliver confidence by espousing high standards in their messages, exemplifying these standards in the conduct they model and establishing formal mechanisms to provide a structure for acting on those standards.*[32]

Kingsmill suggests that the belief that real change and transformation will come from a charismatic visionary may have an immediate appeal to some but all too often this can prove to be a shallow myth rather than a reality.

> *Frequently, boards of companies that are in trouble look for a corporate saviour from outside rather than choose the internal candidate who may have a better understanding of the problems and how to solve them. Grand strategies that never come to fruition, demoralised people whose voices are not heard and innovations that are stifled are all too often the real result of this preoccupation with the hero leader.*[33]

Critical review and reflection

Charisma and the ability to inspire and move loyal followers in the desired direction are among the most controversial leadership qualities. Despite the apparent attraction of charisma by itself, it is unlikely to lead to a noticeable improvement in organisational performance.

To what extent do YOU believe in the organisational benefits of charismatic leadership? To what extent do YOU possess, or would you like to possess, charisma?

Servant leadership

In recent years renewed attention has been given to the idea of **servant leadership**, originally proposed in 1970 by *Robert Greenleaf*.[34, 35]

> *The servant-leader is servant first . . . It begins with the natural feeling that one wants to serve, to serve first. Then conscious choice brings one to aspire to lead. That person is sharply different from one who is leader first, perhaps because of the need to assuage power drive or to acquire material possessions . . . The difference manifests itself in the care taken by the servant-first to make sure that other people's highest priority needs are being served.*[36]

Rather than the use of position power, servant leadership is more a philosophy based on an ethical responsibility of leaders, a spiritual understanding of people and empowering people through honesty, respect, nurturing and trust. A servant leader gives attention to the needs of people and the promotion of their personal development. The focus of leadership is on a supportive and participative style of management. A test of servant leadership is the extent to which the followers, that is those served, benefit. It might therefore be particularly appropriate in service organisations such as in the hospitality industry.[37] Servant leadership can be associated with the idea of positive psychology with an emphasis on human strengths, how things go right and how to enhance people's satisfaction and well-being (**discussed in Chapter 1**).

Critical characteristics

A set of ten critical characteristics central to servant leadership has been identified by *Spears*:

- Good communication skills and the motivation to **listen actively**
- Understanding and **empathy** with others
- Ability to **heal** oneself and others
- **Self-awareness** and to view situations from a holistic position
- Rely on **persuasion** as opposed to the use of power or status
- Able to **conceptualise** and think beyond day-to-day realities and focus on long-term goals
- **Foreseeing** likely outcomes, learning from the past and identifying consequences of future decisions
- **Stewardship** of their organisations for the greater good of society
- Commitment to the personal, professional and **spiritual growth** of people
- Building a strong organisational **community.**[38]

According to *Yukl*, the values emphasised in servant leadership are primarily about helping people and fostering a relationship of trust and cooperation. Yukl lists seven key values and examples of how these might be expressed in a leader's behaviour:

- **Integrity** – open and honest communications, keeps promises and commitments, accepts responsibility for mistakes.
- **Altruism** – helps others and puts their need before your own, willing to takes risks and make sacrifices to benefit others.
- **Humility** – treats others with respect, avoids status symbols and privileges, modest about achievements, emphasises contributions of others.
- **Empathy and healing** – helps others cope with emotional distress, acts as mediator, encourages reconciliation.
- **Personal growth** – encourages development of individual confidence and ability, provides learning opportunities and mentoring and coaching.
- **Fairness and justice** – encourages and supports fair treatment, speaks out against unfair and unjust practices or policies.
- **Empowerment**– consults with others about decisions that affect them, provides autonomy and discretion, encourages expression of dissenting views.[39]

The focus of servant leadership

According to *Wong*, the focus of leadership needs to shift from process and outcome to people and the future. Servant leadership represents a radical approach – it is humanistic and spiritual rather than rational and mechanistic. Command and control leadership no longer works because leaders must earn people's respect and trust. New types of leaders are needed to create new futures, and the challenge for management and leadership education is to:

- develop workers and unleash their creative potential;
- create a positive workplace that will attract and retain knowledge workers; and
- reinforce innovations and risk-taking to adapt to an uncertain future.

However, Wong acknowledges common criticism of servant leadership including that it is too restrictive, too unrealistic and impractical and would not work in situations such as military operations or prison systems. It is too idealistic and naive, too closely related to Christian spirituality and too foreign to a preferred alternative leadership style.[40]

A summary of leadership and management is set out in the concept map in Figure 9.7.

Power and leadership influence

Leadership influence is a social process and may be seen in terms of the type of power that the leader can exercise over the behaviour and actions of others. An early view of social power upon which the influence of the leader is based has been presented by *French and Raven*, who identify five main sources: reward power, coercive power, legitimate power, referent power and expert power.[41] We shall consider these in terms of the manager (as a leader) and subordinate relationship. It is important to note that these sources of power are based on the subordinates' perception of the influence of the leader, whether it is real or not.

- **Reward power** is based on the subordinate's *perception* that the leader has the ability and resources to obtain rewards for those who comply with directives – for example, pay, promotion, praise, recognition, increased responsibilities, allocation and arrangement of work and granting of privileges.
- **Coercive power** is based on fear and the subordinate's *perception* that the leader has the ability to punish or to bring about undesirable outcomes for those who do not comply with directives – for example, withholding pay rises, promotion or privileges, allocation of undesirable duties or responsibilities, withdrawal of friendship or support and formal reprimands or possibly dismissal. This is in effect the opposite of reward power.
- **Legitimate power** is based on the subordinate's *perception* that the leader has a right to exercise influence because of the leader's role or position in the organisation. Legitimate power is based on authority – for example, that of managers and supervisors within the hierarchical structure of an organisation. Legitimate power is therefore 'position' power because it is based on the role of the leader in the organisation, and not on the nature of the personal relationship with others.
- **Referent power** is based on the subordinate's *identification* with the leader. The leader exercises influence because of perceived attractiveness, personal characteristics, reputation or what is called 'charisma'. For example, a particular manager may not be in a position to reward or punish certain subordinates, but may still exercise power over the subordinates because the manager commands their respect or esteem.
- **Expert power** is based on the subordinate's *perception* of the leader as someone who is competent and who has some special knowledge or expertise in a given area. Expert power is based on credibility and clear evidence of knowledge or expertise, including 'functional' specialists such as the management accountant or systems analyst.

French and Raven point out that the five sources of power are interrelated and the use of one type of power (e.g. coercive) may affect the ability to use another type of power (e.g. referent).

LEADERSHIP AND MANAGEMENT

- MANAGEMENT → Leadership by function
- LEADERSHIP → Leadership by personality

Managers have to ensure their subordinates collectively or separately reach their goals

No single trait or group of characteristics has been isolated which sets off the leader from members of groups (Jenkins)

MANAGERS have the authority to direct work and behaviour
LEADERS have influence through example, persuading, motivating, teaching

Leadership may be situationally governed
– arising due to a set of circumstances
Some managers are more suitable to operate in one set of situations than others

LEADERSHIP
– the ability to ensure subordinates perform their tasks and duties up to the standards required, by inspiration or inducement

Leaders cannot achieve the goals by themselves
Subordinates require direction to obtain the goals

Therefore co-operation or coercion required
– Leaders are those individuals who are perceived most frequently to perform those roles and functions which initiate or control behaviour of others towards the achievement of group goals or sub goals (Gibb)

Charisma ⟷ Technocrat

FOUR VARIABLES
1 Characteristics/traits of the leader
2 Attitudes of the followers
3 Organisation purpose, technology, ethos, values, structure
4 Social economic and political milieu (McGregor) between countries between cultures

- Group tasks usually complex
- Organisations require stability not continuous change in leader
- Situational Theory Leadership is specific to the situation under investigation, i.e. a leader emerges in response to the problem or challenge
- Personnel with highly technical skills possessing wide sapiential (knowledge) gives authority/leadership

LEADERSHIP TRAITS
- Intelligence
- Self-confidence
- Initiative taking
- Empathy
- Self-awareness
- Objectivity (human relationships)

THE ESSENTIALS OF LEADERSHIP
– Social skills
– Ability to communicate
– Flexibility/judgement as to which management style to adopt

ACTION-CENTRED LEADERSHIP (ADAIR)

INDIVIDUAL NEEDS
– Concern for the individual
- fairness and consistency in disciplinary matters
- help with training, career prospects with …
  preparation for retirement
  recognition of performance
- good or adequate with …
- commendation or helpful criticism

– Job enrichment
– Giving status

Group Needs
Individual Needs
Task Needs

GROUP NEEDS
Defence of the group needs
– laterally and vertically
Building up teamwork, recognising informal groups
Protection of interests which may lead to disruption e.g. relocation to another site; uneven work loads; accomodation; pay differentials

TASK NEEDS
Task definition
Planning
Allocating work and resources
Controlling quality, pace of work
Monitoring
Amending the plans
Co-ordinating with other groups
Obtaining resources required

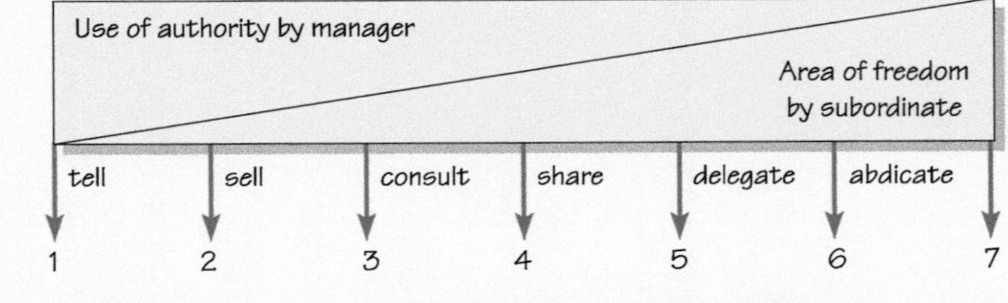

1 Tell them
2 Tell them and sell it to them
3 Tell them and talk about it
4 Tentative decision and talk
5 Problem – talk and manager decides
6 Manager gives limits; all discuss, group decides
7 Manager gives limits; group discusses and decides

- Organisational leadership
- Personal leadership … contribution by the individual in the post showing – charisma/energy/vision

Authoritarian ⟷ Democratic

KINDS OF LEADERSHIP
Formal
– appointed in the hierarchy by the management
Informal
– exercises influence but is not in formal position; can initiate or block actions; can be in conflict with the formal leader; can set the group norms

Figure 9.7 Concept map of leadership and management
Source: Copyright © 2008 The Virtual Learning Materials Workshop. Reproduced with permission.

Furthermore, the same person may exercise different types of power, in particular circumstances and at different times.

Yukl suggests that a further relevant source of power is **control over information.**[42]

The leadership relationship

Whatever the perceived approach to leadership, an underlying feature of leadership is *the manner* in which the leader influences the behaviour and actions of other people. Leadership is a dynamic form of behaviour and there are a number of variables that affect the leadership relationship. For example, *Bass* reviews leadership influence in terms of persuasion, a power relation, an instrument of goal achievement, an emerging effect of interaction and the initiation of structure.[43] Four major variables are identified by *McGregor* as:

- the characteristics of the leader;
- the attitude, needs and other personal characteristics of the followers;
- the nature of the organisation, such as its purpose, its structure and the tasks to be performed; and
- the social, economic and political environment.

McGregor concludes that 'leadership is not a property of the individual, but a complex relationship among these variables'.[44]

According to *Kouzes and Posner,* 'credibility is the foundation of leadership'. From extensive research in over thirty countries and response to the question of what people 'look for and admire in a leader, in a person whose direction they would willingly follow', people have consistently replied that they want:

> *leaders who exemplify four qualities: they want them to be honest, forward-looking, inspiring and competent. In our research our respondents strongly agree that they want leaders with integrity and trustworthiness, with vision and a sense of direction, with enthusiasm and passion, and with expertise and a track record for getting things done.*[45]

Fullan refers to the importance of relationship building as a basic component of the change process and effective leadership: 'Leaders must be consummate relationship builders with diverse people and groups – especially with people different from themselves. Effective leaders constantly foster purposeful interaction and problem solving, and are wary of easy consensus.'[46]

Roddick makes the point that:

> *You have to look at leadership through the eyes of the followers and you have to live the message. What I have learned is that people become motivated when you guide them to the source of their own power and when you make heroes out of employees who personify what you want to see in the organisation.*[47]

Power, responsibility and wisdom

Lloyd suggests that the way we think about leadership is a contributory factor to the leadership crisis. Leadership has traditionally been associated with those who have power and there is a need to re-examine the core relationship between power and responsibility. Rather than gaining and keeping power for ourselves, more emphasis should be given to unifying consideration of the two concepts together with greater attention to the subject of wisdom.

> *The new agenda moves us from that narrow focus to a much broader concept of leadership that is more concerned with how power is used, i.e. in whose interest power is used. This explicitly recognises that the use of power is deeply values driven . . . We need to give much greater attention to the values agenda by exploring wisdom, then seeing that emphasis reflected as wise leadership.*[48]

Critical review and reflection

Whatever the debate on leadership relationship and ideas such as servant leadership, the harsh reality is that influence exercised by a leader depends on the amount of power and authority the leader can exert over other people.

Can YOU present a strong argument against this assertion? What form of leadership influence best describes YOUR relationship with tutors or senior administrative staff?

Culture as a contingent factor?

The contribution of contingency approaches to understanding leadership suggests that contrasting types and styles of leadership may be more or less appropriate in different situations. A consistent view expressed within the literature is that a major variable influencing choice of leadership style may be national culture. We should be wary of stereotyping the behaviour of leaders or subordinates, and many myths appear to have grown around notions of 'orderly' German, 'undisciplined' Italian and even 'obstructive' British workers. However, there are reasons to suggest that there may indeed be national cultural differences that are relevant to an understanding of leadership.

Global Leadership and Organizational Behavior Effectiveness (GLOBE)

Project GLOBE was a large-scale research project that sought to identify those leader behaviours and attributes that would be accepted and therefore effective in all societies and, contrastingly, those that would only be accepted and effective in some cultural contexts. This study was conducted by an international team of researchers led by *Robert House* and encompassed sixty-two countries across the world, including some that had not always featured in cross-cultural study – for example, newly capitalist states in Eastern Europe. The GLOBE study commenced in 1991 and led to a series of publications in the early twenty-first century.[49]

The results, according to the GLOBE researchers, are some significant variations in leadership style, attributes and behaviour. Charismatic and team-orientated leaders were shown to be globally endorsed – and hence universally effective. Leaders who displayed high levels of trust, integrity and vision were supported by subordinates in all societies. It was also found that there were so-called universal impediments to success: for example, *self-protective* leaders characterised by malevolence and 'face-saving' were viewed negatively by subordinates in all cultures.

There were some aspects of leadership that varied between societies. In common with Hofstede (**see Chapter 1**), the GLOBE study identifies clusters of societies with important points of commonality. To take one example, in a situation that might imply a directive style of leadership, subordinates in the 'Anglo' cluster of societies (in effect, the main English-speaking countries) would prefer some degree of informality on the part of the leader and as much of a participative style as the situation allowed.

The GLOBE study recognises that strategic organisational contingencies such as the sector an organisation operates in will affect leadership style and behaviour. However, the GLOBE researchers concluded that such factors would be moderated by the national cultural context. Leader effectiveness will be influenced by the interaction between leaders and subordinates, which is dependent on the nature of power relations within the particular culture, and organisational contingencies applying in all societies.[50]

Differences or shared values?

According to *Walker,* too much focus in recent decades has been on Western approaches to leadership and that a study of alternative methods can help inspire leaders – wherever they are. In the Far East, for example, face-to-face contact and relationship building are prized more highly than here. Walker suggests that new thinking sees Asian business culture not as a challenge to be overcome but as a source of leadership inspiration.[51]

However, in response to the question of whether different business cultures affect how we view good leadership, *Murray* refers to the importance of shared company values overriding any cultural differences.

> *A shared set of company values is the glue that binds people, builds trust and enables an organisation to function across cultural barriers . . . While expectations on leaders might not be the same everywhere, and may have cultural variations, there is no doubt employees have a general desire to be respected, valued and involved. This is a trend that transcends geographical and cultural barriers. Leaders must respond to this demand, wherever they are.*[52]

Leadership effectiveness

Attention to style of leadership has come about because of a greater understanding of the needs and expectations of people at work. It has also been influenced by such factors as: broader standards of education and training and advances in scientific and technical knowledge; pressure for a greater social responsibility towards employees, for example through schemes of participation in decision-making and work/life balance; legislation, for example in the areas of employment protection; and influence of the European Union.

These factors have combined to create resistance against purely autocratic styles of leadership. There is an assumption that subordinates are more likely to work effectively for managers who adopt a certain style of leadership than for managers who adopt alternative styles.

Goleman reports that the most effective executives use a collection of distinct leadership styles, each in the right measure, at just the right time. Although the authoritative style of leadership can be occasionally overbearing, it was found to be most effective and can motivate and inspire commitment to the goals of the organisation. The affiliative style has potential to create harmony within teams and can be used in conjunction with the authoritative style. The democratic approach was seen as positive, and encourages input from staff and helps build consensus through participation. The coaching style, although the least frequently used, can help staff identify their strengths and encourage long-term development goals. The study concludes that the most effective leaders rely on more than one leadership style and were able to master a mixture of authoritative, democratic, affiliative and coaching styles. Leaders with the best results use most of the styles in a given week – seamlessly and in different measure – depending on the business situation.[53]

The shadow of leadership

Leadership is clearly a major feature of effective teamwork. Good leaders surround themselves with talented and capable members of staff, and their behaviour and actions serve as a role model. *McCabe* suggests that leaders who want to transform their performance and the effectiveness of the team should look at how their own shadow could be getting in the way. Leaders focus on what they see as important and they are typically quite unconscious of the unintended but massive impact they are having on their colleagues, teams and clients. All leaders cast a shadow, and whatever a particular leadership style, the shadow will affect others and can compromise people's engagement at work and business effectiveness. Leaders need to be fully aware of the shadow they cast and the impact they have on others.

> *To be successful, leaders today have to find ways to engage people's ideas, energy and inspiration and this means they will have to build much stronger relationships - and what will prevent such relationships from occurring is their shadow.*[54]

Authority without arrogance

In his discussion on the skills of clear leadership, and sustaining collaboration and partnership at work, *Bushe* draws attention to the importance of authority. Collaborative work systems may flatten hierarchies and reduce command and control but do not decrease or eliminate authority.

Authority and hierarchy are two separate things. In collaborative organisations authority is widely spread and more people are authorised to make decisions and take actions. Authority is the power to make and enforce decisions. This is one reason why these organisations need people using the skills of clear leadership: self-awareness, descriptiveness, curiosity and appreciation.[55]

The turbulent and uncertain economic situation of recent times has resulted in many commentators drawing attention to the expectations for clear, decisive and authoritative leadership. For example, *Masson* refers to the leadership attribute of self-assurance, being authentic and comfortable with whom you are. What leaders need is an acute self-awareness and to avoid arrogance.

> *That self-assurance needs to come with an honest assessment of oneself. The whole idea of perfection in leadership is outdated and unhelpful, and leaders who don't open themselves to feedback, and don't reflect on their own behavior, come across as arrogant. Part of being 'authentic' is being open to vulnerability and admitting to one's mistakes.*[56]

Reeves and Knell suggest that being a successful leader is less about who you are or what you do than about what you know. This includes four pieces of knowledge: where the organisation is heading; what is going on; who they are; and how to build a strong team. Leaders in the most successful organisations are authoritative but their secret is that they use their authority without arrogance. Successful leaders:

- build a 'culture of discipline' and are about getting things done, controlling costs and marshalling resources;
- keep in touch with how people are feeling – they do not waste time worrying if everyone is happy but understand the emotional temperament of the organisation and emotional responses from people;
- know where they are strong but also know their weaknesses and display a fierce humility;
- are motivated by what they build, such as great teams and talented people, rather than what they get;
- have a clear sense of where the organisation is going, but very often this is the result of collective decision-making in a talent team.[57]

No one best form of leadership

We have seen that there are many alternative forms and styles of managerial leadership. Within an organisation different individuals may fulfil the functions of leadership and there are many different styles of leadership. A potential danger with the contingency approach is that the manager may appear to lack consistency in leadership style. However, although subordinates may reasonably expect some degree of consistency from the manager in approaching the same type of problem with the same style, this is not to say that different types of problems should be approached in the same manner. Subordinates would ordinarily expect a different style of managerial leadership according to the contingencies of the situation.

Variables affecting leadership effectiveness

Clearly, there is no one 'best' form of leadership that will result in the maintenance of morale among group members and high work performance. Three main aspects to be considered in determining the most appropriate style of leadership are the manager, the group and the work environment. However, there are many variables that underlie the effectiveness of leadership in work organisations. More specifically, these include the following:

- **characteristics of the manager** – personality, attitudes, abilities, value-system and personal credibility;
- **type of power of the manager** and basis of the leadership relationship;
- **characteristics of the followers** – diversity, needs and expectations, attitudes, knowledge, confidence and experience, and motivation and commitment;
- type and nature of the organisation, organisation culture and structure;
- nature of the tasks to be achieved and time scales;

- technology, systems of communication and methods of work organisation;
- **informal organisation,** and the psychological contract;
- nature and influence of the external environment and national culture.

In addition there is an argument that physical attributes, such as height, can be associated with good leadership (**discussed in Chapter 6**).

Right style for the right situation

An effective manager will clearly recognise that different styles of leadership are called for in different situations. As an extreme example, emergency situations demand an assertive, directive style of action. (Recall the actual example of the Mumbai hotel attack given above.) As *Rajan* also points out: 'Of course, different leadership styles are needed to cope with different situations: for example, the autocratic style makes sense when an organisation is in deep trouble and needs to achieve a rapid turn-around. That style would be counter-productive when the organisation is in a growth situation.'[58]

And *Stern* maintains that although in more carefree times business gurus exalted leaders who admitted to frailty, this is not so any more. The task of sustaining growth in a sluggish market calls for driven, leather-skinned bosses. Instead of touchy-feely management the quality of 'mental toughness' is needed to help elite performers to prevail.[59]

Different types of leadership may also be most appropriate at different stages in the development of a business organisation. Leadership can also vary between public and private sectors and depend upon the size of the organisation. A primary challenge for organisational leaders in promoting innovation is to:

> *Recognise and develop appropriate leadership for the different stages of the innovation process. How leaders are selected, supported, evaluated, motivated and developed is likely to differ depending upon the stage of the innovation process they are responsible for. For instance, transformational leadership skills may be more useful in early-stage innovation activity, such as R & D and product development, but transactional leadership skills are also essential to the smooth functioning of commercialisation.*[60]

Critical review and reflection

There is much commentary on the need for less hierarchical structures and a changed culture of leadership based on skills and competencies throughout the organisation as a whole.

How realistic do YOU think this is? How do YOU believe leadership potential can best be developed? And what do YOU see as the future of leadership?

Alternative views of leadership

In recent years the changing nature of the work organisation, referred to at the start of this chapter, has drawn attention to different, broader approaches to the study of leadership, including shared and distributed leadership and responsible leadership.

Shared and distributed leadership

As with servant leadership, discussed earlier, the original idea of distributed leadership can be traced back many years. For example, *Mary Parker Follet,* writing in 1941, envisioned management responsibility not just concentrated at the top of the hierarchy, but diffused throughout the organisation from the depersonalising of orders and obeying the law of the situation.[61, 62]

Rather than a traditional view of a single, all-powerful and visionary appointed leader, the underlying concept of **shared and distributed leadership** is of multiple leaders throughout the organisation. As opposed to hierarchical leadership, distributed leadership gives recognition to the sharing of the leadership function, power and decision-making among staff at all levels and positions including the role of the informal organisation (**discussed in Chapter 3**). *Day et al.* suggest that collective leadership from many different members of the organisation is of more importance than the actions of any individual leader.[63]

With the continuing pace of change, developments in ICT and uncertain economic environment, leadership functions will evolve and leadership roles change according to the situation. With increasing emphasis on teamwork, attention has been focused on the significance of the leadership function for team performance. Greater awareness of the benefits from a more diverse workforce has also encouraged distributed leadership. *Hewlett et al.* draw attention to the wider community leadership roles of ethnic minority staff who may hold only junior positions in the organisation.[64]

Responsible leadership

The term **responsible leadership** has emerged as an organisation's approach to governance, social responsibilities and business ethics. According to Business In The Community, the challenge for business leaders is to ensure the wider responsibilities of business are understood within their organisation and in society to demonstrate how a responsible approach to business will create value.

> *Business leaders must be seen to act and demonstrate their commitment to creating a fairer society and a more sustainable future by fostering a culture that will encourage innovation, reward the right behaviours and regain trust. In short, leaders must write a new contract with society into their own business.*[65]

However, as the *Financial Times* points out:

> *Responsible Leadership, as a business school subject area, is less about ethical theory and more about ethical practice based on case studies. The practice has a particular focus on an individual's values system and the pragmatic application of an individual's values in the real-life challenging dilemmas of business.*[66]

Corporate responsibility and ethics are the subject of Chapter 14.

Management and organisational behaviour in action case study

The Post Office – Women in Leadership Programme

The Post Office is a commercial organisation with a social purpose. Its network of around 11,800 branches delivers over 170 products and services, serves 18 million customers per week and has 7,845 employees. Facing a specific challenge of declining female representation (March 2013: 61.4 per cent of frontline positions/43.8 per cent of first-line management/35.5 per cent of senior management/22.2 per cent of senior leadership), and a quarter of roles were part-time (90 per cent filled by women), it needed to increase females in senior teams. Initiatives included:

The Women in Leadership Programme

Senior Leadership Endorsement – the female chair and chief executive both acted as figure-heads. Sponsored by the Chief Executive, Paula Vennells, who attended each event to provide an introduction and undertake a question and answer session.

→

Transparent Diversity Targets - For 2013–14 the business set a target of appointing women into 40 per cent of its senior leadership and senior management roles, a 7 per cent increase on the 2012–13 out-turn.

Line Manager Support - workshops for seventy senior managers were run to explain the target and what people could do to support it. Sessions focused on the business case and unconscious bias.

Each event brings together eighty of the organisation's high-potential women identified through existing performance and potential data. The events take place every three months with the objectives of:

1. Profiling female role models (internal and external).
2. Working on real business problems (a recent event focused on our female SME customer proposition).
3. Networking (our full Executive is invited to the events so our aspiring female leaders can meet them informally).

Regular Follow-Up Communication - Bi-annual Women in Leadership events where high-potential women met role models, networked and worked on real business problems. Launch of a communications campaign called '3 minutes with' featuring an interview with someone in the Post Office with a diverse perspective. Feedback for the event has been very positive with an average rating of 9.5 out of 10. The outcome resulted in 45.7 per cent of women appointed into senior management roles. The senior leadership team is now 28.3 per cent female.

This activity is supporting the business to achieve a greater level of customer excellence and business engagement. The employee survey saw a 2 per cent increase in the level of customer understanding. The senior management talent programme identified 40 per cent female members, over 4 per cent above the wider female representation at that level and a female engagement index of 58 per cent- currently 7 per cent above the organisational norm.

Source: Aidan Alston, Talent and Diversity Manager, Post Office Ltd. Reproduced with permission.

Tasks

1. Give your views on the Women in Leadership Programme. What in particular do you think has contributed to the success of the programme?
2. Explain why you think there has been an under-representation of women in senior leadership positions.
3. Comment critically on the representation, and actual responsibilities, of women in senior leadership positions in your own university and/or other organisation with which you are familiar.

Leadership development

Education and training in management needs to emphasise not only interpersonal skills, but also a flexibility of approach, diagnostic ability and realisation that the most effective form of leadership behaviour is a product of the total leadership situation. *Melville-Ross* refers to the importance of developing leadership skills in everyone, not just those at the top.[67] Even people in the most junior positions can play a leadership role. It is about the dissemination of ideas, taking the initiative and encouraging others to see it that way. For this to happen, there has to be an open leadership culture that runs right through the organisation. People are encouraged to take personal responsibility and are not afraid to speak up with ideas or take risks.

The leadership jigsaw

Cutler has designed a 'jigsaw' of best practice. There are six interlinking pieces: vision, example, relationships, motivation, empowerment and communications as a guide to the measurement and development of leadership skills. Cutler believes that leadership is not such a difficult role if condensed to these essential elements and has devised a set of questions to help aspiring leaders to find out if they have all the necessary pieces of the jigsaw (*see* Figure 9.8).[68]

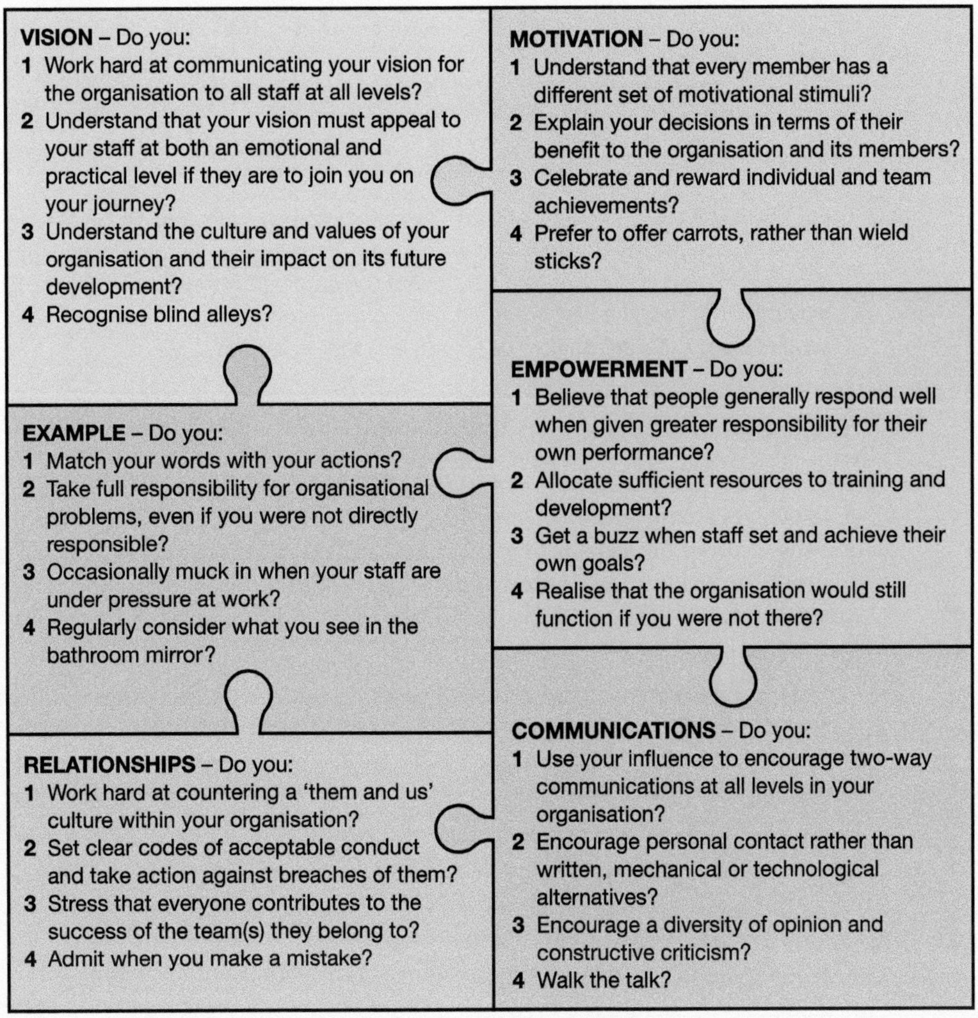

VISION – Do you:
1 Work hard at communicating your vision for the organisation to all staff at all levels?
2 Understand that your vision must appeal to your staff at both an emotional and practical level if they are to join you on your journey?
3 Understand the culture and values of your organisation and their impact on its future development?
4 Recognise blind alleys?

MOTIVATION – Do you:
1 Understand that every member has a different set of motivational stimuli?
2 Explain your decisions in terms of their benefit to the organisation and its members?
3 Celebrate and reward individual and team achievements?
4 Prefer to offer carrots, rather than wield sticks?

EXAMPLE – Do you:
1 Match your words with your actions?
2 Take full responsibility for organisational problems, even if you were not directly responsible?
3 Occasionally muck in when your staff are under pressure at work?
4 Regularly consider what you see in the bathroom mirror?

EMPOWERMENT – Do you:
1 Believe that people generally respond well when given greater responsibility for their own performance?
2 Allocate sufficient resources to training and development?
3 Get a buzz when staff set and achieve their own goals?
4 Realise that the organisation would still function if you were not there?

RELATIONSHIPS – Do you:
1 Work hard at countering a 'them and us' culture within your organisation?
2 Set clear codes of acceptable conduct and take action against breaches of them?
3 Stress that everyone contributes to the success of the team(s) they belong to?
4 Admit when you make a mistake?

COMMUNICATIONS – Do you:
1 Use your influence to encourage two-way communications at all levels in your organisation?
2 Encourage personal contact rather than written, mechanical or technological alternatives?
3 Encourage a diversity of opinion and constructive criticism?
4 Walk the talk?

Figure 9.8 The leadership 'jigsaw'

Source: Cutler, A. 'A Good Fit Is Essential', *Professional Manager*, vol. 15, no. 3, May 2005, p. 38. Reproduced with permission from Chartered Management Institute and Alan Cutler.

Seven principles for developing leaders

Referring to his action-centred leadership model (discussed earlier in this chapter), *Adair* identifies seven key principles of leadership development that can be applied successfully in different kinds of organisations in both the public and private sectors.

- **Development of a strategy for leadership development** for each of the three levels of leadership – operational, strategic and team.
- **Selection** of those with high potential for becoming effective leaders.
- **Training for leadership** that implies instruction with a specific end in view. Identify your business training needs in the leadership context and assign them priorities.
- **Career development** through giving a person the right job at the right time. People grow as leaders through the actual practice of leading.

- **Line managers as leadership developers** by developing the individual's potential and sharing their knowledge of leadership.
- **Corporate culture** that is valued at all levels and should encourage a climate of self-development in leadership.
- **The chief executive** who should be leading from the front and who owns the problem of growing leaders.

The seven principles are complementary and are likely to have a synergetic effect if applied as a whole. Although a simple framework, Adair maintains the seven principles form the first coherent and effective approach for growing leaders.[69]

> *We are not born as leaders, but we are born with the potential to become a leader. This potential has to be worked on and we have to go through a learning experience to equip us to become leaders. Sometimes the potential is realised and sometimes it is not. Opportunities play a part in this; the best organisations seem to grow their own leaders. The best, the very good and the excellent do give priority to developing leaders.*[70]

Intuitive intelligence in leadership

According to *Bacon,* a critical factor in leadership development is the intuitive intelligence of leaders, especially when it comes to decision-making. We use our instinct and intuition in many facets of our personal lives, but Bacon questions if we underutilise one of the most powerful leadership tools at work. Much credence is given to emotional intelligence (**discussed in Chapter 4**) but perhaps the greatest weapon for business decision-making is intuitive intelligence.

> *Many people feel that intuition has little or no place in business, that decisions should be based on empirical evidence rather than on trusting your gut feeling. But there is increasing evidence that intuition is more than merely a feeling. Many scientists now believe that it is, in fact, the result of our brains piecing together information and experiences to come to different, and less obvious conclusions.*

Bacon maintains that intuitive intelligence can be trained, and the best leaders have learned not only to just trust their instincts but to obey them by listening to one's own internal voice. Situations in which leaders rely most consistently on their intuitive intelligence include:

- **in a crisis** when rapid response is required;
- **high-speed change** when situations are changing rapidly without warning;
- **in a messy situation** when a problem or challenge is poorly constructed;
- **in an ambiguous situation** when there are contradictory factors to consider.[71]

Importance of self-awareness

An underlying feature of effective leadership is self-awareness: understanding who you are, and what you are thinking and feeling. *Benjamin* sees a leader simply as someone who takes the lead and whom other people are inclined to follow willingly. The sense of who you are is so important because leadership is, at heart, about leading people.

> *Approaching leadership with a clear sense of self will give you the strength to work with others respectfully but also the confidence to challenge another's opinion or authority because you know what you stand for, and what your principles and beliefs are.*[72]

Blanchard believes that all good leadership starts with a shared vision. The best and most respected leaders share not just their visions for the future of their organisations with their people, but also their personal beliefs about how and why they lead as they do. Blanchard suggests clarifying and sharing your leadership point of view means answering seven questions:

1. Who are the people who have influenced you in your life?
2. What is your life purpose?

3. What core values will guide your behaviour as you live your life 'on purpose'?
4. What are your beliefs about leading and motivating people?
5. What can people expect of you?
6. What do you expect from your people?
7. How will you set an example?[73]

In his discussion on the future of management, *Hamel* argues the point that in any constitutional democracy success does not depend upon brilliant leadership. If democracies are more resilient than large companies it is not because they are better led. In a democracy, the pace of change depends only tangentially on the vision and moral courage of those in power: 'The real challenge, then, isn't to hire or grow great leaders, but to build companies that can thrive with less-than-perfect leaders.'[74]

Critical review and reflection

Despite vast amounts of writing on the subject, it is extremely difficult to give a precise and agreed meaning of leadership. Nor is there agreement on one best model or style of leadership, or how leadership potential can best be developed.

Do YOU find this confusing and a hindrance to your studies? What do YOU believe are the essential and distinctive characteristics that make for an effective leader?

Ten key points to remember

1 There are many ways of looking at leadership but essentially it is a relationship through which one person influences the behaviour or actions of other people.

2 There is arguably a close relationship between leadership and management. However, it does not follow that every leader is a manager.

3 Due to its complex and variable nature, there are many alternative ways of analysing leadership and different approaches to study of the subject area.

4 A simple threefold heading of leadership behaviour is authoritarian, democratic or laissez-faire. Four main styles of leadership are tells, sells, consults and joins.

5 Contingency theories draw attention to major variables and forces in the situation as one of the main forces influencing the nature of managerial behaviour.

6 Attention has been focused on charisma, leaders creating a vision with which others can identify, and inspiring followers to improve organisational performance.

7 Leadership is a dynamic form of behaviour. The leadership relationship is a social process dependent upon the type of power and influence exercised over other people.

8 Attention needs to be given to the criteria for leadership effectiveness and sets of skills to work within less hierarchical-based systems of command and control.

9 There is no one 'best' form or style of leadership. There are many variables that underlie the effectiveness of leadership, including national culture.

10 Leadership development needs to emphasise interpersonal skills and recognise that successful leadership behaviour is a product of the total leadership situation.

Review and discussion questions

1 Explain clearly what you understand by the meaning of leadership and give your own definition. To what extent do you believe leadership differs from management?

2 Distinguish between different approaches to the study of leadership and discuss critically what you see as the relevance today of each of these approaches.

3 Using the Tannenbaum and Schmidt continuum, identify, with reasons, what would be your preferred style of leadership.

4 Assess the practical value to the manager of: (i) Fiedler's contingency model of leadership effectiveness; and (ii) Hersey and Blanchard's readiness of the followers or group situational model.

5 Discuss critically the contention that in times of uncertainty or economic depression a confident, authoritarian style of leadership is likely to be the most effective.

6 Explain clearly the nature and main features of transformational leadership. Give your own examples of people you would regard as transformational leaders. Discuss critically the relevance of personality and charisma for effective leadership.

7 Discuss the main sources of power and leadership influence. Give a practical example of each of these main sources of power and influence within your own university or organisation.

8 Explain why self-awareness is increasingly highlighted as an important feature of leadership. To what extent are you aware of who you are, and what you are thinking and feeling?

9 If you were a consultant on leadership, what areas of needs would you include in designing a leadership development programme for managers in a large work organisation? Justify your ideas.

10 Discuss the main situational forces and variables likely to influence the most appropriate form of managerial leadership. Give an example of when a particular style of leadership is likely to be most effective.

Assignment

Prepare to lead a seminar discussion in which you:

a. Explain fully a situation from university and/or any work experience where you have been inspired by a person through their charisma and natural leadership authority.
b. Identify clearly the specific personal qualities exhibited by the person.
c. Describe how the experience has influenced your views on the nature of leadership.
d. Debate the extent to which it is possible to learn charisma and the ability to inspire other people.
e. Write a short paper in which you summarise conclusions from the discussion.

Personal skills and employability exercise

Objectives

Completing this exercise should help you to enhance the following skills:

- Recognise your self-awareness and understanding of who you are.
- Explore attributes associated with leadership.
- Evaluate your readiness for a leadership role.

Exercise

Self-knowledge about who you are, and what you are thinking and feeling, is crucial if you are to be an effective and inspiring leader. Work together in small groups.

To gain maximum benefit from this exercise it is important to be completely honest with yourself.

First, for each of the following twenty-five items, consider honestly and fully the extent to which you:

1. Have a strong work ethic
2. Are adaptable to changes in the work situation
3. Place emphasis on service to others over self-interest
4. Stretch yourself to meet objectives
5. Take time in connecting with group members
6. Set yourself clear goals and criteria for success
7. Believe in doing things right the first time
8. Have strong moral values
9. Think leadership is simple if you have the right personality
10. Find it easy to compliment fellow colleagues
11. Are competitive and take pride in winning
12. Communicate easily your ideas, thoughts or concerns to others
13. Tolerate genuine mistakes by others that affect your work
14. Believe respect for superiors is more important than popularity
15. Enjoy others relying on you or coming to you for help
16. Respect hierarchical authority and chain of command
17. Believe leadership depends on confidence and courage
18. Are prepared to place trust in your fellow colleagues
19. Believe everyone is responsible for their own actions and behaviour
20. Get upset by disagreements or confrontation with your peers
21. Simplify and explain complex situations to others
22. Tend naturally to take the initiative in group situations
23. Encourage challenging debate and dialogue
24. Do not put off for tomorrow what can be done now
25. Believe you would make an effective leader

There are no right or wrong answers, but score and record each item from 1 to 10 with 10 as the highest.
Second, share and discuss fully and openly your scoring among other members of the group.

Discussion

- How difficult was it for you to complete this exercise? How well do you think you know yourself?
- To what extent do colleagues agree with your own scoring, including an honest evaluation of your perceived readiness for a leadership role?
- What benefits have you gained from this exercise and what have you learned about yourself as a potential leader?

Case study
A change of leadership at Barclays Bank

On 4 July 2012, Bob Diamond, the former Group Chief Executive (GCE) of Barclays, who had resigned a few days earlier, was asked by Labour MP John Mann at a Treasury Select Committee hearing whether he could name the three Quaker values that had inspired the founders of Barclays. He could not, prompting this retort from Mann:

> *Honesty. Integrity. Plain dealing. That's the ethos of the bank you've just spent two hours telling us is doing so well – in fact so well that I wonder why you've not received an extra bonus rather than the sack.*[75]

Diamond's replacement was Antony Jenkins, who was appointed in August 2012. The appointment was hailed

Source: Tupungato/Shutterstock.com

as a new chapter for the beleaguered bank, with press reports highlighting Jenkins' career experience at Barclays and Citibank,[76] his distinctly unflashy image and his solid track record of effectiveness, most recently at Barclaycard.[77]

Barclays under Diamond

The events that led to this remarkable transition can be briefly summarised. Bob Diamond had joined Barclays in 1996 and rose to head Barclays Capital, its investment banking[78] arm. An American by birth, his earlier career in the banking industry with Morgan Stanley and CS First Boston was in investment banking. Investment banking is mainly concerned with assisting individuals, businesses and governments to raise capital. These operations are important for the creation and growth of businesses, and although they are relatively risky, they can generate very high rewards. Retail or 'personal' banking, by contrast, involves providing banking services such as current and savings accounts, mortgages, loans, credit card operations, etc., directly to individual or business customers. Risks are lower, but so are potential profits. Barclays was a straightforward retail bank until the 1980s when changes to banking regulations gave it the opportunity to move into investment banking, which it did with some limited success.

When Diamond became CEO his priorities reflected his career background; his ambition for the company was to grow Barclays Capital into an operation that could rival the global banks of Wall Street. Following the financial crash of 2008, Barclays acquired the remains of Lehman Brothers' US operations for what looked (at the time) like a bargain price. In 2011, he was appointed GCE of Barclays, and in the same year delivered the BBC inaugural Today Business Lecture in which he argued for the importance of investment banking to the growth and development of businesses and economies.[79] However, Diamond's style at Barclays was not universally popular and he was criticised for his very high pay levels and his apparent lack of humility; however, those criticisms became more focused as a series of scandals emerged in the banking industry. Many of these scandals - for example, the mis-selling of Payment Protection Insurance - involved a wide range of banks, but the UK's Financial Services Authority's report into the manipulation of the key interest rate known as LIBOR[80] was particularly critical of the behaviour of Barclays employees. By the summer of 2012, in the face of pressure from both the Bank of England and the Financial Services Authority,[81] the Barclays board bowed to the inevitable and Diamond resigned. In his evidence to the Select Committee, he remained adamant that he had not known about much of the malpractice, which led John Mann to suggest that:

> *He was either in there doing it or deliberately turned a blind eye, or he was so useless that he couldn't see fiddling on his own trading floor [. . .] I think he must have known what was going on.*[82]

Barclays under Jenkins

It is probably fair to say that the job of a bank CEO in the wake of such scandal is not only difficult, but also carried out under fairly hostile public scrutiny. Leading a successful organisation might be a tough job, but what are the leadership challenges faced by those attempting to restore damaged and unpopular organisations, and what qualities and behaviours are needed in such circumstances?

When Antony Jenkins became CEO in 2012 there were reports that the bank had struggled to find a successor, and that two of the most credible candidates had already turned down the job before Jenkins was approached. Unusually for a bank CEO, he is not an investment banker; he ran Barclays credit card operations and had also managed the retail arm of the business. The contrast with Diamond was clear:

> *In Jenkins you've got the archetypal English CEO who is seen as rather safe, compared with the typically aggressive US investment banker that was Bob Diamond. His appointment signals that the bank is not going to be as brazen as it has been in the past.*[83]

He has been described as the 'nice guy' of banking, a calm, softly spoken and mild-mannered individual who, nevertheless, could be 'scary'. He explains this by saying:

> *What that means is you don't have to raise your voice or thump the table to get your point across. When you have a very measured style, you don't need to shout.*

You just need to make your point a little more directly and people notice.[84]

In an early move to signal his views about the bank's road ahead, Jenkins circulated a letter to all 140,000 staff emphasising his commitment to restoring its integrity and reputation by a return to five 'core' values: respect, integrity, service, excellence and stewardship. He warned that:

There might be some who don't feel they can fully buy into an approach which so squarely links performance to the upholding of our values. My message to those people is simply: Barclays is not the place for you. The rules have changed. You won't feel comfortable at Barclays and, to be frank, we won't feel comfortable with you as colleagues.[85]

The strategy is known as the 'TRANSFORM'[86] programme, which aims to reinvigorate the bank not only morally but also commercially. To that end he has said that he would not indulge underperforming parts of the company, essentially the investment bank for which Diamond had such great ambitions. In 2014 Jenkins announced a three-year programme of job cuts that would see Barclays Capital lose 7,000 staff - a quarter of its workforce - as part of a general restructuring and simplification programme.

In the future, Barclays will be leaner, stronger, much better balanced and well positioned to deliver lower volatility, higher returns, and growth.[87]

In 2015 he continued to assert that he would not be 'patient' with poor returns from any part of the bank; again it was Barclays Capital that was underperforming and that seemed most under threat, and its relatively poor performance will clearly not be allowed to drag the bank down either in shareholder value or in reputation.[88]

Another contrast with the Diamond years was Jenkins' decision not to take the usual banker's bonus for his first two years in post. Whereas Diamond famously received £17 million total reward in 2011,[89] the jazz-loving Jenkins took the relatively modest sum of £5.4 million for his third year as CEO, including a £1.1 million bonus payment. Even so, some commentators considered that he had not yet fully earned this perk as the group's overall performance remained weak, particularly that of Barclays Capital. Additionally profits have been undermined by the need to set aside significant sums to cover the cost of litigation and potential regulatory fines as yet more scandals from earlier years come to light.[90]

Jenkins is seen as the 'clean-up guy' at Barclays. He has made a number of painful and important changes but the company is not yet out of the woods. It is still one of the most complained-about banks in the UK, the investment arm remains under serious threat and the shadows of its past misbehaviour still loom large. The challenge for Barclays continues, and it remains to be seen whether Jenkins' leadership can restore its good name and commercial fortunes.*

Tasks

1. To what extent could it be argued that Diamond was a leader but Jenkins is a manager? Explain your view with reference to concepts from the chapter.
2. Examine the tasks facing each of the two CEOs of Barclays at different points in the company's history. How did the business environment affect the requirements of leadership? Use one of the contingency models outlined in the chapter to explain your view.
3. Discuss the proposition that although Jenkins has adopted a strategy of transformation at Barclays, he is in fact a transactional, not a transformational, leader.
4. How many of the characteristics and behaviours of servant leadership (as identified by Spears and Yukl) can be identified in Jenkins' approach at Barclays? Explain which you think are present, and which are missing.
5. How far do you think cultural difference between the American and British approaches to banking and business contributed to the problems encountered by Diamond?

* The Barclays story continues to get more interesting, and you might like to catch up with the events of July 2015 when Jenkins was fired by the new Chairman, John McFarlane (see, for instance, the summary by Kamal Ahmed, Business Editor for the BBC, on 8 July 2015, **http://www.bbc.co.uk/news/business-33438914**).

Notes and references

1. See, for example, Adair, J. *Leadership and Motivation,* Kogan Page (2006).
2. *CBI The Path to Leadership: Developing a Sustainable Model within Organisations*, Caspian Publishing (2005), p. 4.
3. Zaleznik, A. 'Managers and Leaders: Are They Different?', *Harvard Business Review,* May–June 1977, pp. 67–78.
4. Kent, T. W. 'Leading and Managing: It Takes Two to Tango', *Management Decision,* vol. 43, no. 7/8, 2005, pp. 1010–17.
5. Belbin, R. M. *Changing the Way We Work,* Butterworth–Heinemann (1997), p. 98.
6. Radcliffe, S. *Leadership: Plain and Simple,* Financial Times Prentice Hall (2010).
7. Mintzberg, H. *Managing,* Financial Times Prentice Hall (2009), p.8.
8. Moorcroft, R. 'To Lead or to Manage? That Is the Question', *Manager, The British Journal of Administrative Management,* November 2005, p. 4.
9. Drucker, P. F. *The Practice of Management,* Heinemann Professional (1989), p. 156.
10. See, for example, Bryman, A. 'Leadership in Organisations', in Clegg, S. Hardy, C. and Nord, W. (eds) *Managing Organsations: Current Issues,* Sage (1999), pp. 26–62.
11. Kotter, J. P. 'What Leaders Really Do', *Harvard Business Review,* May–June 1990, p. 103.
12. Whitehead, M. 'Everyone's a Leader Now', *Supply Management,* 25 April 2002, pp. 22–4.
13. Adair, J. *Action-Centred Leadership,* Gower (1979); see also Adair, J. *The Skills of Leadership,* Gower (1984).
14. Tannenbaum, R. and Schmidt, W. H. 'How to Choose a Leadership Pattern', *Harvard Business Review,* May–June 1973, pp. 162–75, 178–80.
15. Fiedler, F. E. *A Theory of Leadership Effectiveness,* McGraw-Hill (1967).
16. See, for example, Yukl, G. *Leadership in Organizations,* fifth edition, Prentice Hall (2002).
17. Vroom, V. H. and Yetton, P. W. *Leadership and Decision-Making,* University of Pittsburgh Press (1973).
18. House, R. J. 'A Path–Goal Theory of Leadership Effectiveness', *Administrative Science Quarterly*, vol. 16, September 1971, pp. 321–38.
19. House, R. J. and Dessler, G. 'The Path–Goal Theory of Leadership', in Hunt, J. G. and Larson, L. L. (eds) *Contingency Approaches to Leadership,* Southern Illinois University Press (1974).
20. Hersey, P. and Blanchard, K. H. *Management of Organizational Behavior: Utilizing Human Resources,* sixth edition, Prentice Hall (1993).
21. Burns, J. M. *Leadership,* Harper & Row (1978).
22. Bass, B. M. *Leadership and Performance Beyond Expectations*, Free Press (1985).
23. Bass, B. M. and Avolio, B. J. *Improving Organizational Performance Through Transformational Leadership*, Sage (1994).
24. Yukl, G. *Leadership in Organizations,* sixth edition, Pearson (2006).
25. Kreitner, R., Kinicki, A. and Buelens, M. *Organizational Behaviour,* First European edition, McGraw-Hill (1999), p. 487.
26. Gratton, L. *The Democratic Enterprise,* Financial Times Prentice Hall (2004).
27. Goffee, R. and Jones, G. *Why Should Anyone Be Led By You?,* Harvard Business School Press (2006).
28. Weber, M. *The Theory of Social and Economic Organization,* Oxford University Press (1947).
29. Conger, J. 'Charisma and How to Grow It', *Management Today,* December 1999, pp. 78–81.
30. Conger, J. 'The Danger of Delusion', *Financial Times,* 29 November 2002.
31. Adair, J. *The Inspirational Leader: How to Motivate, Encourage and Achieve Success*, Kogan Page (2003).
32. Kanter, R. M. *Confidence: Leadership and the Psychology of Turnarounds*, Random House (2004), pp. 325–6.
33. Kingsmill, D. ' Leaders who can recruit and reward teams for their unique skills will always achieve the best results', *Management Today,* September 2014, p. 20.
34. Greenleaf, R. K., *Servant Leadership: A Journey into the Nature of Legitimate Power and Greatness*, Paulist Press (1977); see also, for example, Spears, L. C. and Lawrence, M. (eds.) *Practicing servant leadership: Succeeding through trust, bravery and forgiveness*, Jossey-Bass (2004).
35. See also, for example, Smith, B. N., Montagno, R. V. and Kuzmenko, T. N. 'Transformational and servant leadership: Content and contextual comparisons', *Journal of Leadership & Organizational Studies,* vol. 10, no. 4, 2004, pp. 80–91.
36. 'What is Servant Leadership?', Greenleaf Centre for Servant Leadership, **www.Greenleaf.org** (accessed 2 September 2011).
37. See, for example, Brownell, J. 'Leadership in the Service of Hospitality', *Cornell Hospitality Quarterly,* vol. 51, no. 3, 2010, pp. 363–78.
38. Spears, L. C. (ed.) *Reflections on Leadership,* Wiley (1997).
39. Yukl, G. *Leadership in Organizations,* seventh edition, Pearson (2010).
40. Wong, P. T. P. 'Best Practices in Servant Leadership', *School of Global Leadership & Entrepreneurship,* Regent University, July 2007, pp. 1–15.

41. French, J. R. P. and Raven, B. 'The Bases of Social Power', in Cartwright, D. and Zander, A. F. (eds) *Group Dynamics: Research and Theory,* third edition, Harper & Row (1968).
42. Yukl, G. *Leadership in Organizations,* sixth edition, Pearson Prentice Hall (2006).
43. Bass, B. M. *Handbook of Leadership: Theory, Research and Managerial Applications*, third edition, Free Press (1990), p. 11.
44. McGregor, D. *The Human Side of Enterprise,* Penguin (1987), p. 182.
45. Kouzes, J. M. and Posner, B. Z. 'The Janusian Leader', in Chowdhury, S. (ed.) *Management 21C,* Financial Times Prentice Hall (2000), p. 18.
46. Fullan, M. *Leading in a Culture of Change,* Jossey-Bass (2001), p. 5.
47. Roddick, A. *Body and Soul,* Ebury Press (1991), p. 214.
48. Lloyd, B. 'Balancing Power with Responsibility and Wisdom', *Professional Manager,* vol. 17, no. 3, 2008, p. 37.
49. House, R. J., Hanges, P. J., Javidan, M., Dorfman, P. J. and Gupta, V. (eds) *Culture, Leadership, and Organizations: The GLOBE Study of 62 Societies,* Sage (2004).
50. For a fuller account of Project GLOBE see French, R. *Cross-Cultural Management,* second edition, Chartered Institute of Personnel and Development (2010).
51. Walker, B. 'Feast On The East', *Professional Manager,* Spring 2014, pp. 46–9.
52. Murray, K. in conversation with Benner, V. 'Is good leadership the same around the world?', *Professional Manager,* September/October 2012, p. 24.
53. Goleman, D. 'Leadership That Gets Results', *Harvard Business Review,* vol. 78, no. 2, March–April 2000, pp. 78–90.
54. McCabe, B. 'The Disabling Shadow of Leadership', *Manager, The British Journal of Administrative Management,* April/May 2005, pp. 16–17.
55. Bushe, G. R. *Clear Leadership,* Davies-Black (2009). For a short extract, see *Manager, The British Journal of Administrative Management,* Summer 2009, pp. 26–7.
56. Masson, L. 'Leading through Turbulent Times', *Chartered Secretary,* June 2008, p. 16.
57. Reeves, R. and Knell, J. 'Your Mini MBA', *Management Today,* March 2009, pp. 60–4.
58. Rajan, A. 'Meaning of Leadership in 2002', *Professional Manager,* March 2002, p. 33.
59. Stern, S. 'If You Think You're Hard Enough', *Management Today,* March 2003, pp. 46–51.
60. 'Leadership for Innovation', Advanced Institute of Management Research, March 2005.
61. Metcalfe, H and Urwick, L (eds), *Dynamic Adnministration – The collected papers of Mary Parker Follett,* Harper (1941).
62. See also Semler, R. 'Managing without managers', *Harvard Business Review,* September–October 1989, pp. 76–84.
63. Day, D. V., Gronn, P. and Salas, E., 'Leadership capacity in teams', *Leadership Quarterly,* vol. 15, 2004, pp. 857–80.
64. Hewlett, S.A., Luce, C. B. and West, C., 'Leadership in your midst: Tapping the hidden strengths of minority executives', *Harvard Business Review,* vol. 83, 2005, pp. 74–82.
65. 'Responsible leadership', Business In The Community, **www.bitc.org.uk/issues/responsibleleadership** (accessed 3 October 2014).
66. 'Responsible leadership', *Financial Times,* **http://lexicon.ft.com/=responsible-leadership** (accessed 4 October 2014).
67. Melville-Ross, T. 'A Leadership Culture has to Run Right Through an Organisation', *Professional Manager,* vol. 16, no. 1, 2007, pp. 18-21.
68. Cutler, A. 'A Good Fit Is Essential', *Professional Manager,* vol. 14, no. 3, 2005, p. 38.
69. Adair, J. *How to Grow Leaders,* Kogan Page (2005).
70. 'A Conversation with John Adair', *Manager,* April/May 2007, p. 20.
71. Bacon, B. 'Intuitive intelligence in leadership', *Governance + Compliance,* September 2013, pp. 24–5.
72. Benjamin, D. 'In my opinion', *Management Today,* May 2011, p. 58.
73. Blanchard, K 'Developing your leadership point of view', *Manager, The British Journal of Administrative Management,* Spring 2010, p. 15.
74. Hamel, G. with Breen, B. *The Future of Management,* Harvard Business School Press (2007), p. 169.
75. Transcript available at **http://www.parliament.uk/documents/commons-committees/treasury/Treasury-Committee-04-July-12-Bob-Diamond.pdf** (accessed 4 March 2015).
76. **http://m.bbc.co.uk/news/business-19421534** (accessed 4 March 2015).
77. **http://www.bloomberg.com/bw/articles/2012-09-06/barclays-gets-a-quiet-leader-for-a-change** (accessed 4 March 2015)
78. Investment banking is defined at **http://www.investopedia.com/terms/i/investment-banking.asp** It is usually defined in contrast to 'retail' banking, which provides the more familiar services such as bank account management, lending, savings products and taking deposits.
79. BBC Today Business Lecture 2011, **http://news.bbc.co.uk/today/hi/today/newsid_9630000/9630673.stm** (accessed 5 March 2015).
80. LIBOR, or the London Interbank Offer Rate, determines the rate of interest at which banks lend money to each other on the open market. A number of banks had been colluding in what was essentially a price-fixing exercise, and Barclays was the first to be investigated and fined by the then Financial Services Authority.

81. **http://m.bbc.co.uk/news/business-18690102** (accessed 4 March 2015).
82. The Telegraph online, **http://www.telegraph.co.uk/finance/newsbysector/banksandfinance/9374516/Bob-Diamond-questioned-by-MPs-on-Barclays-Libor-scandal-as-it-happened.html** (accessed 5 March 2015).
83. **http://www.bloomberg.com/bw/articles/2012-09-06/barclays-gets-a-quiet-leader-for-a-change** (accessed 4 March 2015).
84. **http://www.telegraph.co.uk/finance/6591628/Nice-guy-of-banking-Antony-Jenkins-is-the-big-winner-at-Barclays.html** (accessed 5 March 2015).
85. Moore, J. 'Can Antony Jenkins get rid of Bob Diamond's legacy at Barclays?', *Independent,* 17 January 2013, **http://www.independent.co.uk/news/business/analysis-and-features/can-antony-jenkins-get-rid-of-bob-diamonds-legacy-at-barclays-8456614.html** (accessed 5 March 2015).
86. Turnaround, Return Acceptable Numbers, Sustain FORward Momentum.
87. **http://www.telegraph.co.uk/finance/newsbysector/banksandfinance/10815350/Barclays-cuts-7000-investment-bank-jobs-in-overhaul.html** (accessed 5 March 2015).
88. **http://www.telegraph.co.uk/finance/newsbysector/banksandfinance/11445210/Barclays-sets-aside-another-750m-for-FX-rigging-fines.html** (accessed 5 March 2015).
89. **http://www.theguardian.com/business/2012/mar/09/barclays-chief-bob-diamond-pay** (accessed 5 March 2015).
90. Guthrie, J. 'Barclays: Antony Jenkins's L'Oréal moment', Ft.com, **http://www.ft.com/cms/s/0/48dc4866-c184-11e4-8b74-00144feab7de.html#axzz3TWh45dva** (accessed 5 March 2015).

CHAPTER 11

Organisation structure and design

It is by means of structure that the work of the organisation is carried out. Structure provides the framework of an organisation and its pattern of management. Some structure is necessary to make possible the effective performance of key activities and to support the efforts of staff. The manager needs to understand the importance and effects of structure, and the variables that influence the most appropriate structure for a particular organisation.

Learning outcomes

After completing this chapter you should have enhanced your ability to:

- detail the purpose and importance of good structure and consequences of a deficient structure;
- explore the underlying dimensions and design features of organisation structure;
- explain formal organisational relationships that exist between individuals;
- explore situational variables influencing patterns of structure;
- review the nature of the contingency approach and main contingency models;
- assess the changing nature of the workplace and demand for flexibility;
- debate realities of structure and organisational behaviour.

Critical review and reflection

Structure is the defining feature of a work organisation. However good the goals and objectives, systems of management or quality of its members, an organisation will not achieve optimum performance without a sound and appropriate structure.

Give YOUR critical view of this assertion. What do YOU expect to learn from YOUR study of organisation structure?

The purpose and importance of structure

The purpose of structure is the division of work among members of the organisation and the co-ordination of their activities so they are directed towards the goals and objectives of the organisation. Structure makes possible the application of the process of management and creates a framework of order and command through which the activities of the organisation can be planned, organised, directed and controlled. The structure defines tasks and responsibilities, work roles and relationships, and channels of communication.

Underlying the effective management of people is the requirement for a clear understanding of the nature of the business in which the organisation is engaged. If the organisation is to be successful then its structure must be related to its objectives and to its strategy. Structure must be designed to be appropriate to environmental influences, the continued development of the business and the management of opportunities and risks. There is obviously a close relationship between organisation structure and corporate strategy (**discussed in Chapter 14**). It is by means of the organisation's structure that its goals and objectives are attained.

Structure is clearly important for any organisation, whatever its size. However, in the smaller organisations there are likely to be fewer problems of structure. The distribution of tasks, the definition of authority and responsibility, and the relationship between members of the organisation can be established on a more personal and informal basis. With increasing size, however, there is greater need for a carefully designed and purposeful form of organisation. There is need for a formal **organisation structure**. There is also need for a continual review of structure to ensure that it is the most appropriate form for the particular organisation, and in keeping with its growth and development.

Structure provides the framework for the activities of the organisation and must harmonise with its goals and objectives. The purpose of structure may be summarised as to provide for:

- economic and efficient performance of the organisation and level of resource utilisation;
- monitoring activities of the organisation;
- accountability for areas of work undertaken by groups and individual members of the organisation;
- co-ordination of different parts of the organisation and different areas of work;
- flexibility in order to respond to future demands and developments, and to adapt to changing environmental influences; and
- social satisfaction of members working in the organisation.[1]

Structure, though, is not an end in itself but a means of improving organisational performance. According to *Drucker,* it is the correct design of structure that is of most significance in determining organisational performance.

> *Good organisation structure does not by itself produce good performance. But a poor organisation structure makes good performance impossible, no matter how good the individual managers may be. To improve organisation structure . . . will therefore always improve performance.*[2]

The importance of good structure is also emphasised by *Child:*

> *In the final resort, it is vital that we understand what organization is, what it does, and the grounds on which it can be justified because it is not just a means to achieving better economic performance but also exerts a profound influence on the societies in which we live . . . The form of organization we employ transports values back into society and carries a message about how to treat other people.*[3]

The human element

The functions of the formal structure, and the activities and defined relationships within it, exist independently of the members of the organisation who carry out the work. Structure should be designed, therefore, so as to encourage both the willing participation of members of the organisation and effective organisational performance. *Lord Forte*, for example, has drawn attention to the importance of the human element in organisation structure:

> *The human aspect in a business is vital: you can keep drawing squares and lines, but within these squares you must have people and they must be deeply involved with the business. If this does not happen, then the lines and squares and the diagrams mean nothing.*[4]

One of the strongest critics of the formal organisation is *Argyris*. He claims that the formal, bureaucratic organisation restricts individual growth and self-fulfilment and, in the psychologically healthy person, causes a feeling of failure, frustration and conflict. Argyris argues that the organisation should provide a more 'authentic' relationship for its members. Managers need to consider how structural design and methods of work organisation influence the behaviour and performance of members of the organisation.[5]

Lucas points out that rigid structures are all very well but they can and do inhibit free thinking, which is vital for creativity. Referring to the parallels between 'the stage' and working life, Lucas reports on the use of improvisation as a means of helping managers work together better in teams, release creativity and improve their presentation skills.[6]

Critical review and reflection

Personalities are an important part of the work organisation. Whatever its formal structure, in practice the actual operations of the organisation and success in meeting its objectives will depend upon the behaviour and actions of people within the structure.

To what extent do YOU think people give shape and personality to the formal structure of YOUR university or organisation?

Levels of organisation

Determination of policy and decision-making, the execution of work, and the exercise of authority and responsibility are carried out by different people at varying levels of seniority throughout the structure. In small organisations, these activities tend to be less distinct, but in the larger organisations it is possible to look at organisations in terms of three broad interrelated levels in the hierarchical structure: the **technical level**, the **managerial level** and the **community level**.[7] These last two levels are often referred to as middle management and senior management.

The **technical level** is concerned with specific operations and discrete tasks, with the actual job or tasks to be done, and with performance of the technical function. Examples are the physical production of goods in a manufacturing firm, administrative processes giving direct service to the public in government departments and the actual process of teaching in an educational establishment. The technical level interrelates with the **managerial** (or organisational) **level**, concerned with the co-ordination and integration of work at the technical level. Decisions at the managerial level relate to the resources necessary for performance of the technical function and to the beneficiaries of the products or services provided.

In turn, the managerial level interrelates with the **community** (or institutional) **level,** concerned with broad objectives and the work of the organisation as a whole. Decisions at the community level will be concerned with the selection of operations and the development of the organisation in relation to the wider social environment. Examples of the community level within organisations are the board of directors of joint-stock companies, governing bodies of educational establishments that include external representatives, and trustees of non-profit organisations. Such bodies provide a mediating link between the managerial organisation and co-ordination of work of the technical organisation and the wider community interests.

Divide between senior and middle management

Rawson draws attention to the increasing absence of mutuality between senior and middle managers in both the public and private sector.

> *Traditionally, senior managers have been concerned with setting the strategic direction and objectives for the organisation; middle managers with making it happen – resourcing and managing the changes. The corollary is that senior managers are concerned with results and middle managers with how these are achieved. The divide appears as middle levels complain that their seniors are solely concerned with short-term financial results and as seniors reply that the middle strata devote more effort to voicing problems than to finding solutions. In both sectors the delayering of organisations has dramatically reduced the resources available to middle managers. The divide deepens as each accuses the other of pursuing their own personal rather than organisational ends. Middle accuse senior of being concerned with their own career advancement: senior accuse middle of directing their efforts to protecting their positions.*[8]

Blurring of differentiation

In practice, there is no clear division between determination of policy and decision-making, co-ordination of activities and the actual execution of work. Most decisions are taken with reference to the execution of wider decisions, and most execution of work involves decision. Decisions taken at the institutional level determine objectives for the managerial level, and decisions at the managerial level set objectives for the technical level (*see* Figure 11.1). Movement towards more democratic organisations, empowerment, an increase in knowledge workers and technological advances have contributed to lack of a clear distinction between policy, management and the execution of work. Flatter structures, the dismantling

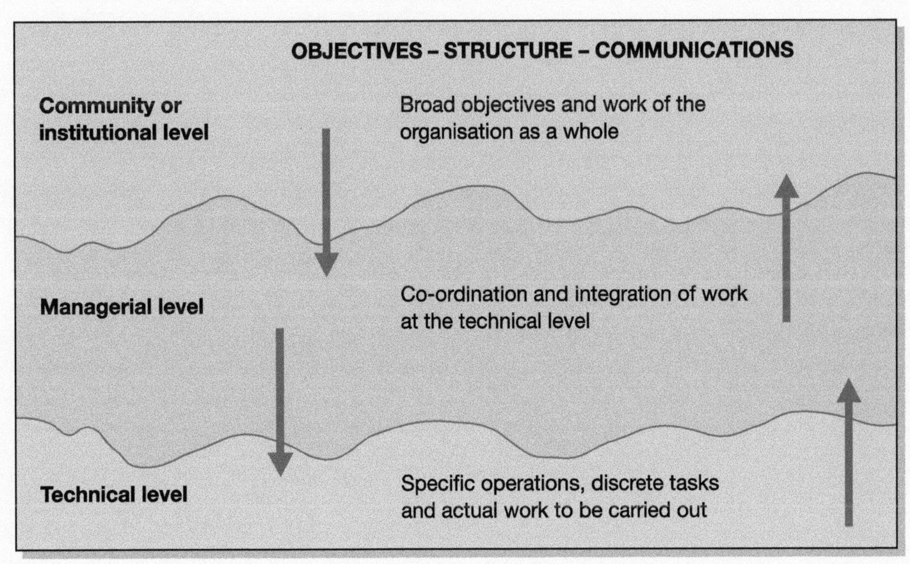

Figure 11.1 Interrelated levels of organisation

of hierarchies and virtual teams all contribute to a further blurring of differentiation. The three broad levels do, however, provide a basis for a critical analysis of the interrelated activities of the organisation.

Underlying dimensions of organisation structure

There are many variables that influence the most appropriate organisation structure and system of management. There is nevertheless an underlying need to establish a framework of order and system of command by which the work to be undertaken is accomplished successfully. **These principles and considerations are not prescriptive but present a series of initial important decision points for design of organisation structure, or in reviewing the effectiveness of an existing structure (*see* Figure 11.2).**

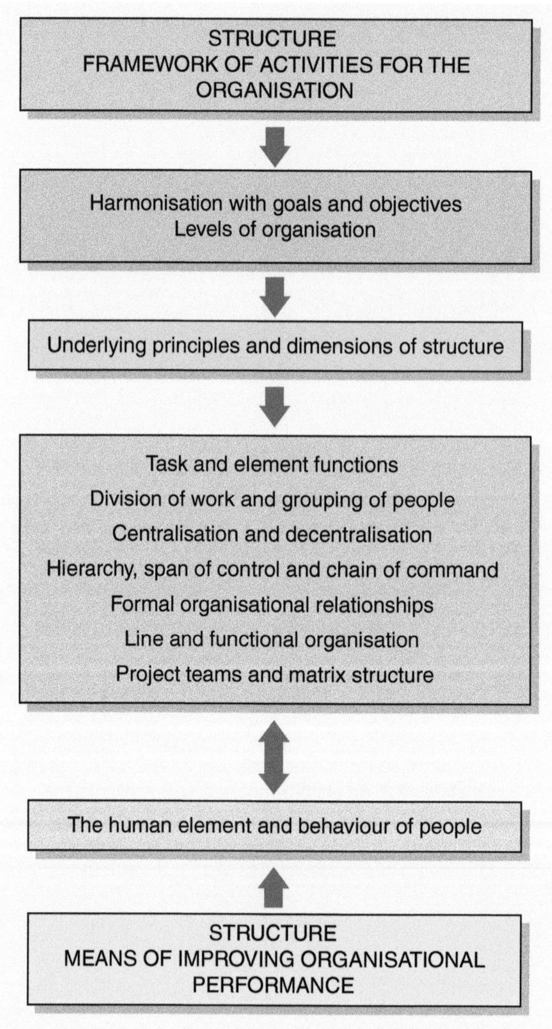

Figure 11.2 Considerations in design of organisation structure

Task and element functions

In order to produce some product, or provide some service, there are four essential functions that the organisation must perform:

1. The product or service must be developed.
2. Something of value must be created – the production or manufacture of a product or provision of a service.
3. The product or services must be marketed, and distributed or made available to those who are to use them.
4. Finance is needed in order to make available resources for the development, creation and distribution of the products or services provided.

These essential functions, what *Woodward* refers to as the **'task' functions**, are the basic activities of the organisation related to the actual completion of the productive process and directed towards specific and definable end results.[9] Other activities of the organisation not directed towards specific and definable ends are supportive of the task functions and an intrinsic part of the management process. These are referred to as **'element' functions** and include, for example, human resources, planning, management services, public relations, quality control and maintenance. In the majority of organisations, the HR function does not normally have any direct accountability for the performance of a specific end-task. In certain organisations, however, noticeably in service industries involving direct customer contact, HR management can arguably be seen as closely associated with a task function.[10]

Failure to distinguish between the two types of functions can lead to confusion in the planning of structure and in the relationship between members of the organisation. For example, in her study of the management organisation of firms in this country, Woodward comments on the bad relationships between accountants and other managers referred to during the study. One reason for this hostility was the bringing together of two quite separate financial functions essential to the efficient operation of a business.

> *People concerned with works accounting tended to assume responsibility for end results that was not properly theirs; they saw their role as a controlling and sanctioning one rather than as a servicing and supportive one. Line managers resented this attitude and retaliated by becoming aggressive and obstructive.*[11]

According to Woodward, activities concerned with raising funds for the business, keeping accounts and determination of financial policy are task functions. Management accounting, however, concerned with prediction and control of production administration, is an element function, and is primarily a servicing and supportive one. Relationships between the accountants and other managers seemed better when the two functions were organisationally separate.

Critical review and reflection

Many organisational conflicts arise through element functions, such as human resource management, overstepping responsibilities and failure to recognise the primary purpose as support to the essential task functions of the organisation.

How valid do YOU think the distinction is between task and element functions? To what extent can YOU see conflict between the two functions in YOUR university or organisation?

Division of work and grouping of people

Within the formal structure, work has to be divided among its members and different jobs related to each other. The division of work and the grouping together of people should, wherever possible, be organised by reference to some common characteristic that forms a logical link between the activities involved. Work can be divided, and activities linked together, in a variety of ways.

Major purpose or function

The most common basis for grouping activities is according to specialisation, the use of the same set of resources, or the shared expertise of members of staff. It is a matter for decision in each organisation as to which activities are important enough to be organised into separate functions, departments or sections. Work may be departmentalised and based, for example, on differentiation between task and element functions, discussed above (*see* Figure 11.3).

Product or service

Contributions of different specialists are integrated into separate, semi-autonomous units with collective responsibility for a major part of the business process or for a complete cycle of work. This form of grouping is more common in the larger diversified organisations and may be used as a means of sub-dividing departments into sections. An example is the bringing together of all activities concerned with a particular production line, product or service (*see* Figure 11.4). Another example is a hospital where medical and support staff are grouped together in different units dealing with particular treatments such as accidents and emergency, medical or surgery. With grouping by product or service there is a danger that the divisions may attempt to become too autonomous, presenting management with a problem of co-ordination and control.

Location

Different services are provided by area or geographical boundaries according to particular needs or demands, the convenience of consumers, or for ease of administration (*see* Figure 11.5). Examples are the provision of local authority services for people living in a particular locality, sales territories for business firms or the grouping of a number of retail shops under an area manager. Another example is provided by organisations with multi-site working and the grouping of a range of similar activities or functions located together on one site. Improvement

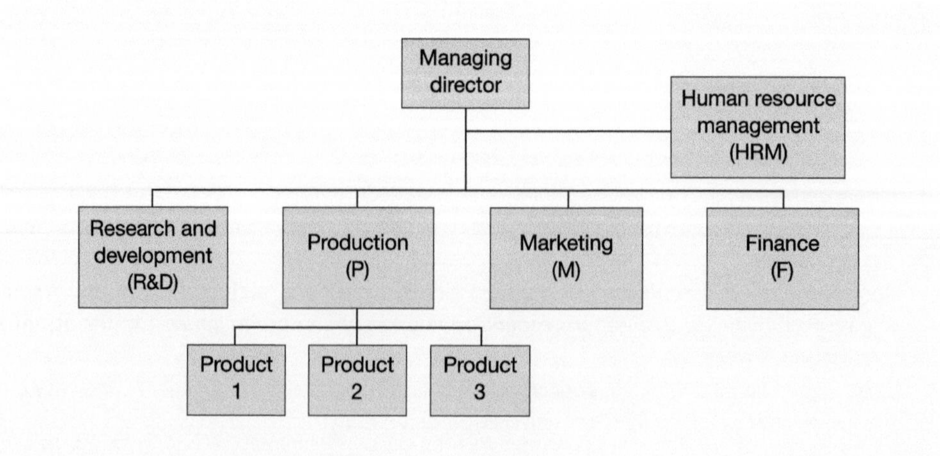

Figure 11.3 Division of work by major purpose or function

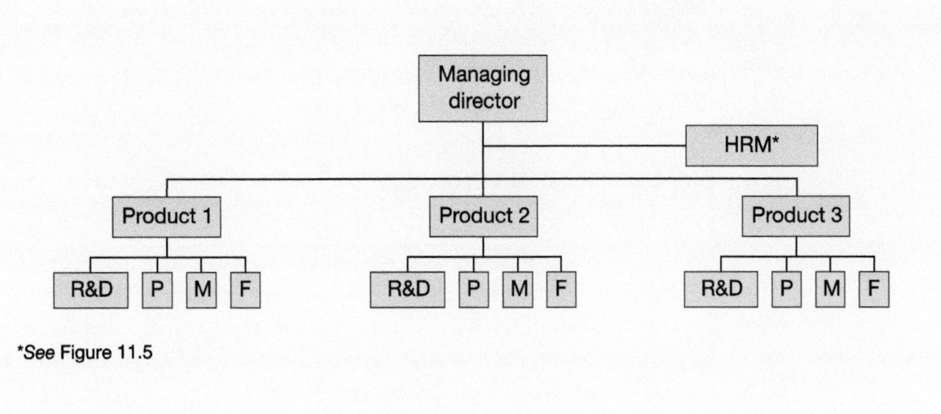

Figure 11.4 Division of work by product or service

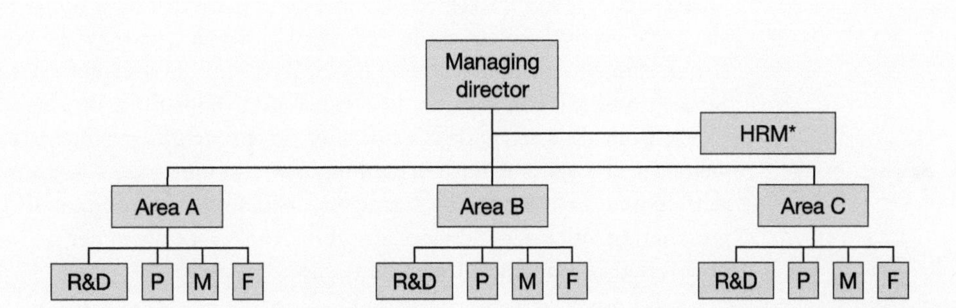

*In the case of division of work by product or service, or by geographical location, it is possible that certain aspects of support services, such as human resource management, may also be assigned to individual units of the organisation. However, the main responsibility of the HRM manager, as a separate entity, is to provide a specialist advisory service to all unit managers and to ensure implementation of HRM policy throughout the organisation as a whole. Responsibility for the main aspects of the HRM function is likely to remain, therefore, in a direct line of authority from top management.

Figure 11.5 Division of work by location

in telecommunications tends, however, to reduce the importance of location. For example, administrative staff may no longer need to be located within the main production unit.

Nature of work performed

This is division according to the nature of work performed where there is some special common feature of the work, such as the need for speedy decisions, accuracy, confidentiality/security, or where local conditions require first-hand knowledge not immediately available elsewhere. Another example may be the grouping of equipment or machinery that is noisy or produces dust, fumes or unpleasant odours. When common processes are used in a range of different activities, this may also be used as the basis of division. This method of grouping includes, for example, the decision as to whether to establish a centralised resource centre for all departments of the organisation or to allow each department to have its own service.

Common time scales

Division according to time scales, for example shift working. In a further education college there may be separate departments or groupings to deal with the different needs of full-time day and part-time evening students. Another example is in a hotel. Activities in the kitchen tend to be short term, especially when guests in the restaurant are waiting to be served, and a range of different tasks have to be co-ordinated very quickly. Other activities, for example market research and forecasting future room occupancy, are longer-term decisions and subject to different organisational requirements.

Nature of staff employed

Division based on a particular skill, special qualification or responsibility – for example, the division of work between surgeons, doctors and nurses, or between barristers, solicitors and legal executives. In smaller organisations the allocation of work may be on an ad hoc, personal basis according to the knowledge and skills contributed by individuals. Work may also be planned deliberately to give a variety of tasks and responsibilities to provide improved job satisfaction or to assist in the training of staff.

Customers or clients to be served

Separate groups may be established to deal with different consumer requirements – for example, the division between trade and retail customers or between home and export sales. In hospitals there are different groupings dealing with, for example, patients in the gynaecology, geriatric and children's wards. In large clothes shops there may be separate departments for men's, women's and children's clothing. Government departments are often grouped by this method and work is divided according to whom the services are provided – for example, the unemployed, low-pay families, students, people or senior citizens. A further example is the provision of restaurant services according to type of customer or customer demand such as price, range or standard of meals and speed of service.

Centralisation and decentralisation

The balance between centralisation and decentralisation is one of the major debates in organisation structure. Most organisations necessarily involve a degree of **decentralisation** arising from such features as an increase in size, the geographical separation of different parts of the organisation, or the need to extend activities or services to remote areas. Our main concern is with decentralisation or devolution in terms of specific delegation or empowerment to sub-units or groups within the organisation such that they enjoy a measure of autonomy or independence.

Advantages often claimed for centralisation tend to relate to economic and administrative considerations. However, such advantages frequently are not realised fully and do not lead to an actual improvement in service. There are a number of contrary arguments against centralisation, including the criticism that it creates a more mechanistic structure and may result in lengthening the chain of command. There are also positive arguments, which tend to relate more to behavioural considerations, in favour of decentralisation (*see* Figure 11.6).

Extent of decentralisation

Growing emphasis on participation and empowerment suggests a focus of attention on the principles of decentralisation, yet senior management still need to maintain effective co-ordination and overall control of the activities of the organisation as a whole. The balance between centralisation and decentralisation will be affected by such factors as the importance of decision-making, the urgency of the situation and time scales, and also by technological developments, changes in structure, the prevailing organisational climate and the nature of staff employed. Decentralisation generally tends to be easier to implement in

Advantages of centralisation

- the easier implementation of a common policy for the organisation as a whole;
- provides a consistent strategy across the organisation;
- prevents sub-units from becoming too independent;
- makes for easier co-ordination and management control;
- improved economies of scale and a reduction in overhead costs;
- greater use of specialisation, including better facilities and equipment;
- improved decision-making, which might otherwise be slower and a result of compromise because of diffused authority.

Advantages of decentralisation

- enables decisions to be made closer to the operational level of work;
- increased responsiveness to local circumstances;
- improved level of personal customer service;
- more in keeping with developments in flatter and more flexible structures;
- support services, such as adminstration, are more likely to be effective if provided as close as possible to the activities they are intended to serve;
- provides opportunities for training and development in management;
- usually, it has an encouraging effect on the motivation and morale of staff.

Figure 11.6 Advantages of centralisation or decentralisation

private-sector organisations than in public-sector organisations, where there is a greater demand for the accountability of their operations, regularity of procedures and uniformity of treatment.

Critical review and reflection

Attention to basic principles and considerations in the design of structure, such as division of work, grouping of people and extent of decentralisation, is essential for effective management and organisational performance.

To what extent do YOU support this contention? How well are these design principles applied to the structure of YOUR university or organisation?

Principles of organisation

As mentioned earlier (**Chapter 2**), the classical writers placed emphasis on the requirements of the formal organisation and the search for a common set of principles applicable to all circumstances. The idea of common sets of principles on organisation and management has been subject to much criticism. Statements are expressed in non-operational terms and give little basis for specific managerial action, and tend to view people as a given rather than as a variable in the system. However, it is difficult to argue against the principles providing general guidance on the structuring of organisations. The basic concepts can be of value to the practical manager, **if modified to suit the demands of the particular situation,** including the nature of staffing in the organisation. The proper application of these principles is likely to help improve organisational performance. Three of the more specific principles of general interest in the structuring of organisations are: (i) the hierarchy; (ii) the span of control; and (iii) the chain of command.

Importance of the hierarchy

Early writers on management drew attention to the importance of the **hierarchy**. That is, clearly delineated levels of management authority as a means of co-ordination and control. However, the changing nature of work has led to discussion on the continuing role and importance role of the hierarchy and the extent to which managers can rely solely on their perceived formal authority within the structure of the organisation.

The importance of the hierarchy is emphasised strongly by *Drucker,* who asserts: 'One hears a great deal today about "the end of the hierarchy". This is blatant nonsense. In any institution there has to be a final authority, that is, a "boss" – someone who can make the final decisions and who can expect them to be obeyed.'[12]

However, contrary to the view of Drucker, *Cloke and Goldsmith* question whether we are accustomed to and have accepted the hierarchy, rules and managers as an essential part of organisational life. Have managers been seduced by the apparent power over others that a hierarchical organisation offers and by the disproportionate rewards it can provide to those at the top? If so, this is depriving individuals of the chance to develop themselves to their full potential and cluttering organisations with wasteful and counterproductive processes.[13]

Gratton has maintained that, more than at any other point in time, there is a chance to create the democratic enterprise.

> *Over the last decade it has become increasingly clear that through the forces of globalization, competition and more demanding customers, the structure of many companies has become flatter, less hierarchical, more fluid and virtual. The breakdown of hierarchies provides us with fertile ground on which to create a more democratic way of working.*[14]

Note, however, that *Child* maintains: 'despite the widespread disparagement of hierarchy, most companies find it very difficult to avoid it once they have grown beyond a very small size'.[15]

Span of control

Span of control refers to the number of subordinates who report directly to a given manager or supervisor. It does not refer to the total of subordinate operating staff, that is those who report first to another person. Hence the term 'span of responsibility' or 'span of supervision' is sometimes considered to be more appropriate. *Graicunas* developed a mathematical formula for the span of control.[16] The limitation of the number of subordinates who can effectively be supervised is based on the total of direct and cross-relationships

$$R = n\left\{\frac{2^n}{2} + n - 1\right\}$$

where n is the number of subordinates and R is the number of interrelationships. For example, with five subordinates the total number of interrelationships requiring the attention of the manager is 100; with six subordinates the number of interrelationships is 222.

If the span of control is *too wide,* it becomes difficult to supervise subordinates effectively and this places more stress on the manager. With larger groupings, informal leaders and subgroups or cliques are more likely to develop. If the span of control is *too narrow,* this may present a problem of co-ordination and consistency in decision-making and hinder effective communications. Morale and initiative of subordinates may suffer as a result of too close a level of supervision. Narrow spans of control can lead to additional levels of authority in the organisation, creating an unnecessarily long chain of command.

Chain of command

This refers to the number of different levels in the structure of the organisation. The **chain of command** establishes the vertical graduation of authority and responsibility, and the framework for superior–subordinate relationships in an unbroken line down from the top of the organisation. Every person should know their position within the structure of the organisation. Most organisation charts demonstrate that this principle is used widely as a basis for organisation design. A clear line of authority and responsibility is necessary for the effective operation of the organisation.

It seems generally accepted that for reasons of morale and to help decision-making and communications, there should be as few levels as possible in the chain of command. There is danger in adding to the structure in such a way that it results in increased hierarchical authority and control, and leads to the risk of empire building and the creation of unnecessary work in justification of the new position. However, if efforts are made to reduce the number of levels this may bring about an increase in the span of control.

Need for a balanced structure

The balance of span of control and chain of command determines the overall pyramid shape of the organisation and whether the hierarchical structure is 'flat' or 'tall' (*see* Figure 11.7). Broader spans of control and fewer levels of authority result in a **flat hierarchical structure** as tends to be found, for example, in universities. Narrower spans of control and more levels of authority result in a **tall hierarchical structure** as tends to be found, for example, in the civil service or the armed forces. There is no one, ideal combination of span of control and scalar chain. This depends upon the particular situation for each organisation, but it is important to provide an appropriate, balanced structure.

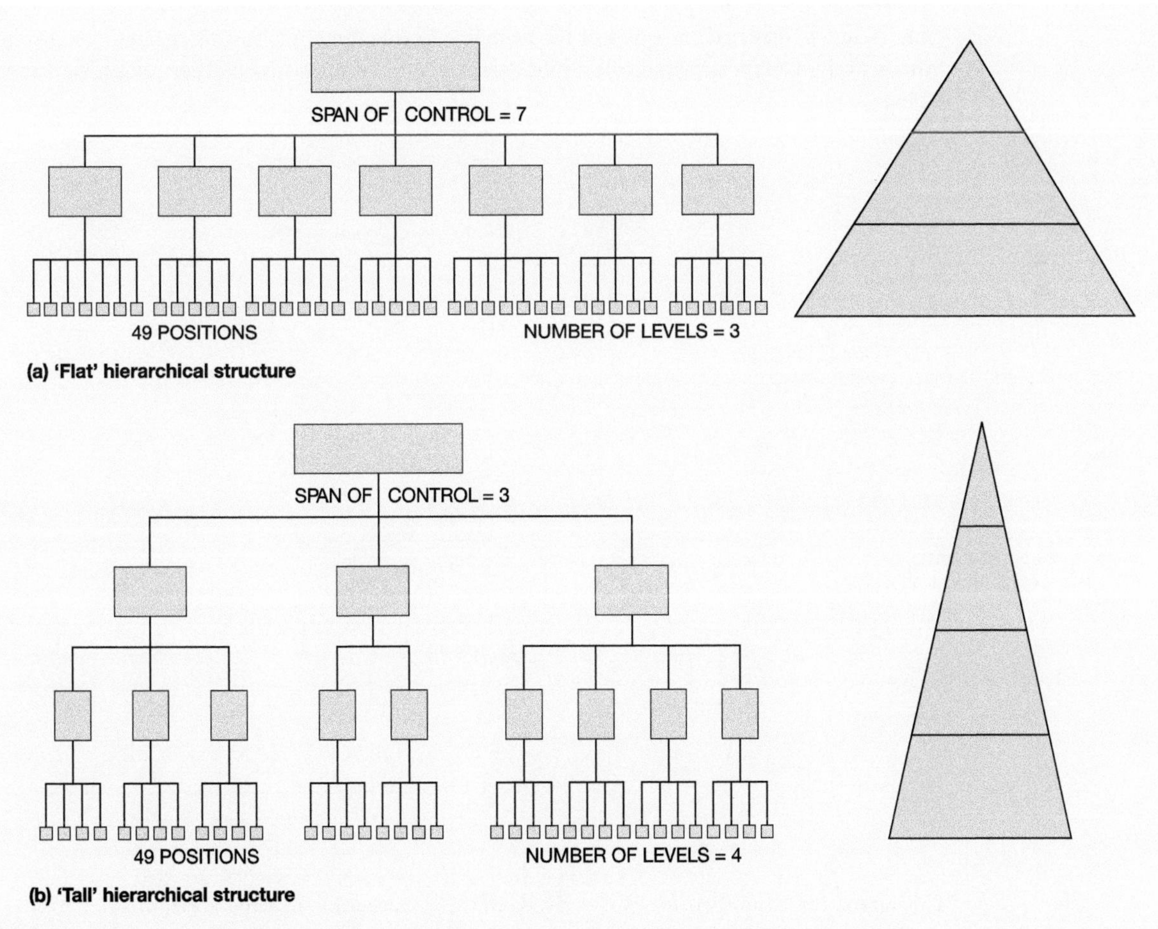

Figure 11.7 How span of control affects organisation structure

Critical review and reflection

Advancement through the hierarchy is seen as an indicator of career progression, recognition of merit and reward for achievement. Organisations are a form of social stratification. Removing the hierarchy will only cause lack of ambition and dissatisfaction.

To what extent do YOU think this statement has validity for modern work organisations? How do YOU feel about working in an organisation with little or no hierarchy?

Formal organisational relationships

In any organisation structure, certain formal relationships between individuals will arise from the defined pattern of responsibilities. There is often confusion over the meaning of different terms and their implications for organisation structure, but these **individual relationships** may be identified as:

- line;
- functional;
- staff; or
- lateral (*see* Figure 11.8).

The design of structure in terms of the principle of line, functional, staff or lateral determines the pattern of organisational role relationships and interactions with other roles (**discussed in Chapter 8**).

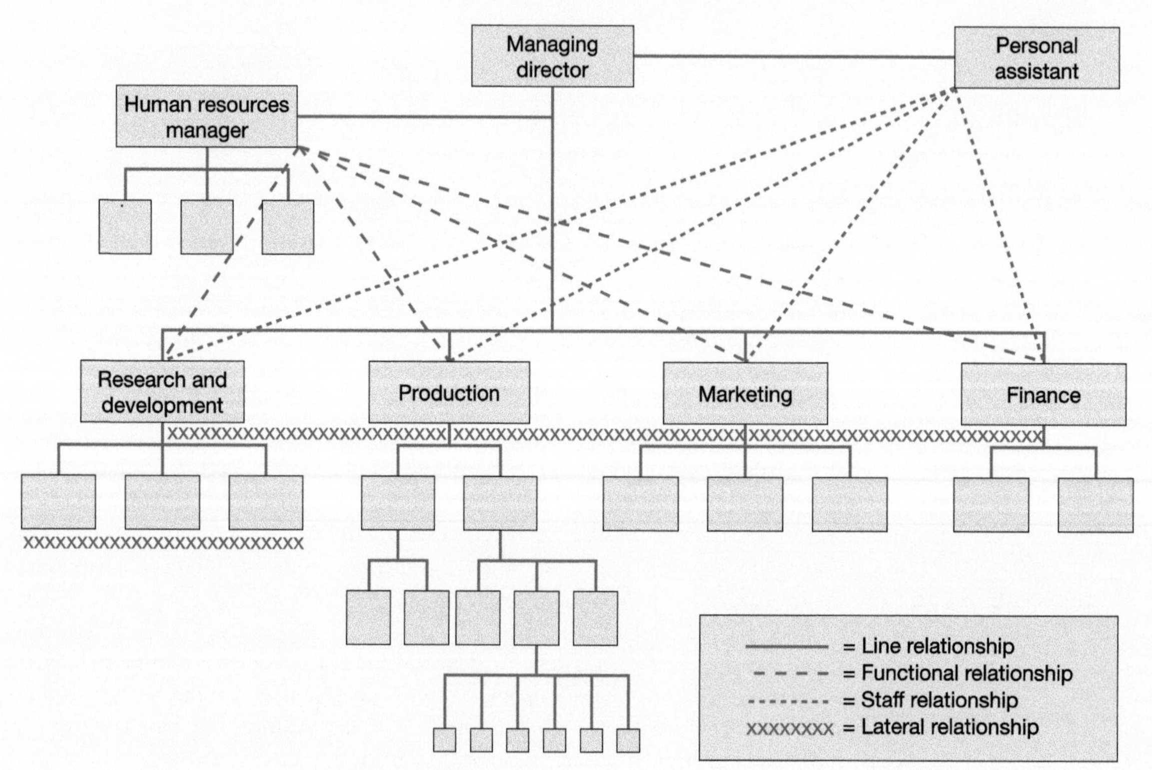

Figure 11.8 Illustration of formal organisational relationships

In **line relationships**, authority flows vertically down through the structure – the chain of command. There is a direct relationship between superior and subordinate, with each subordinate responsible to only one person. Line relationships are associated with functional or departmental division of work and organisational control. Line managers have authority and responsibility for all matters and activities within their own department.

Functional relationships apply to people in specialist or advisory positions, and line managers and their subordinates. The specialist offers a common service throughout all departments of the organisation, but has no direct authority over those who make use of the service. For example, the HR manager has no authority over staff in other departments – this is the responsibility of the line manager. However, as the position and role of the HR manager would have been sanctioned by top management, other staff might be expected to accept the advice that is given. The HR manager, however, could be assigned some direct, executive authority for certain specified responsibilities such as health and safety matters throughout the whole organisation.

Staff relationships arise from the appointment of personal assistants to senior members of staff. There is no formal relationship between the personal assistant and other staff except where delegated authority and responsibility have been given for some specific activity. They exercise only 'representative' authority and often act in a 'gatekeeper' role. In practice, however, personal assistants often have influence over other staff. This may be because of the close relationship between the personal assistant and the superior, the knowledge and experience of the assistant, or the strength of the assistant's personality.

> *In business and governmental agencies, from doctors' offices to licensing and regulatory boards, one may come face to face with people who have established themselves as gatekeeper to the boss. Gatekeepers aspire to and are rewarded with various titles, like administrative assistant, office manager or special assistant to such-and-such. But the essential role is usually that of secretary to the boss . . . Aspiring gatekeepers typically evoke polarised reactions among the office staff . . . Peers, unlike the boss, quickly recognise the individual's lack of integrity and willingness to step on all toes en route to the position of guardian and the gate.*[17]

Lateral relationships exist between individuals in different departments or sections, especially individuals on the same level. These lateral relationships are based on contact and consultation and are necessary to maintain co-ordination and effective organisational performance. Lateral relationships may be specified formally but in practice they depend upon the co-operation of staff and, in effect, are a type of informal relationship.

Line and functional organisation

As organisations develop in size and work becomes more complex, the range of activities and functions undertaken increases. People with specialist knowledge have to be integrated into the managerial structure. **Line and functional organisation** provides a means of making full use of specialists while maintaining the concept of line authority. It creates a type of informal matrix structure (*see* Figure 11.9).

The distinction between a line manager and a functional manager is not absolute. With the increasing complexity of organisations and the rise of specialist services it becomes harder to distinguish clearly between what is directly essential to the operation of the organisation and what might be regarded only as an auxiliary function. Functional managers may feel that their difficulties and work problems are not appreciated fully by the line managers. Functional managers often complain about resistance to their attempts to provide assistance and co-ordination, and the unnecessary demands for departmental independence by line managers. A major source of difficulty is to persuade line managers to accept, and act upon, the advice and recommendations that are offered. The line and functional relationship can also give rise to problems of 'role incongruence' (**discussed in Chapter 8**).

Keohane refers to the challenge of achieving the potential benefits of a more integrated approach.

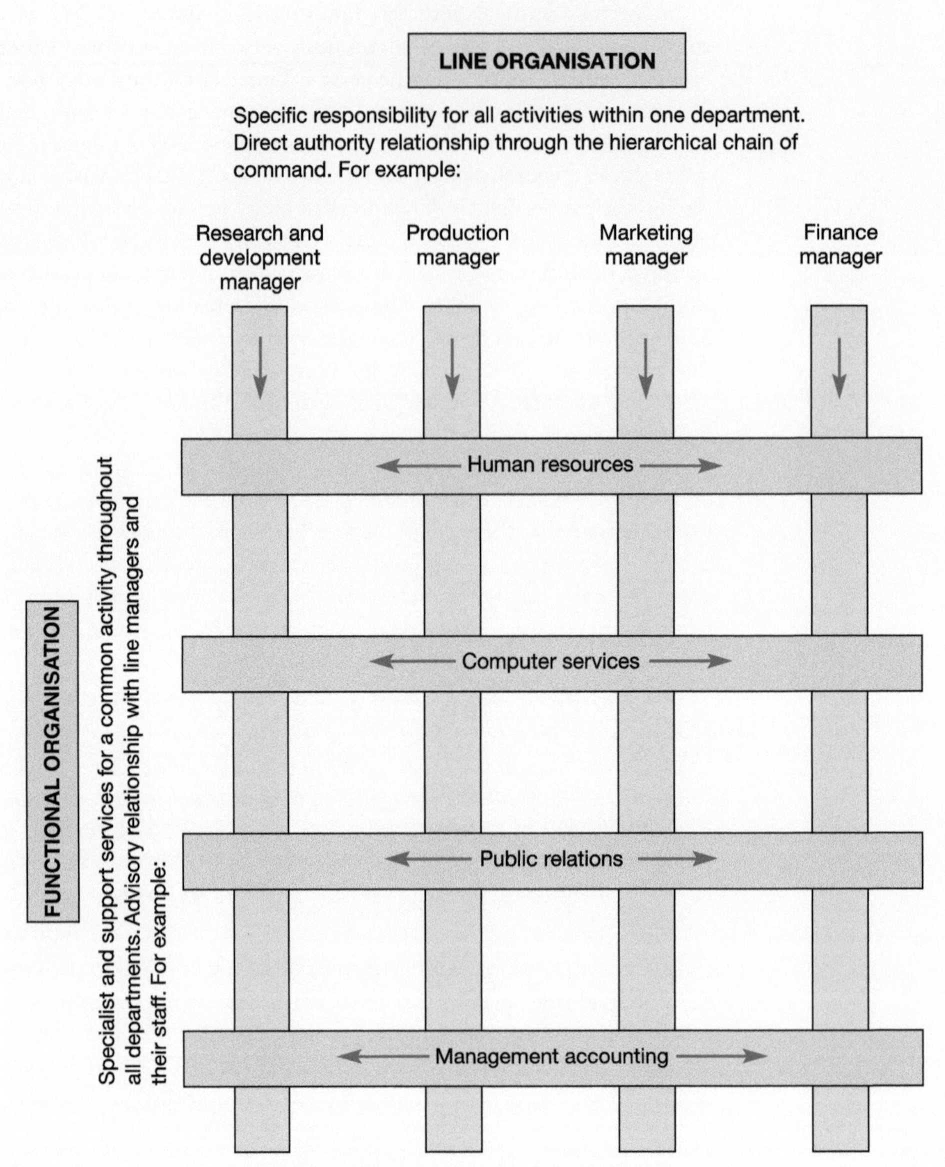

Figure 11.9 Representation of line and functional organisation

Why is that? It's because organisations, quite logically, shape themselves around specialist functional expertise. That's sensible, but it becomes less sensible when the agenda of the specialist function begins to overshadow that of the organisation. All too often the functional agenda elevates its own views, methods, systems and terminology at the expense of a more outcome-focused, clear and simple approach.[18]

Project teams and matrix organisation

The division of work and methods of grouping described earlier tend to be relatively permanent forms of structure. With growth of newer, complex and technologically advanced systems it has become necessary for organisations to provide greater integration of a wide range of functional activities. Although bureaucratic structures and hierarchies still exist in many organisations, increasing attention has been given to the creation of groupings based on project teams and matrix organisation. Members of staff from different departments or sections are assigned to the team for the duration of a particular project.

A **project team** may be set up as a separate unit on a temporary basis for the attainment of a particular task. When this task is completed the project team is disbanded or members of the unit are reassigned to a new task. Project teams may be used for people working together on a common task or to co-ordinate work on a specific project such as the design and development, production and testing of a new product; or the design and implementation of a new system or procedure. For example, project teams have been used in many military systems, aeronautics and space programmes.

The matrix structure

The matrix structure is a combination of:

- departments that provide a stable base for specialised activities and a permanent location for members of staff; and
- units that integrate various activities of different functions on a project team, product, programme, geographical or systems basis.

A **matrix structure** might be adopted in a university or college, for example, with grouping both by common subject specialism and by association with particular courses or programmes of study. The matrix organisation therefore establishes a grid, or matrix, with a two-way flow of authority and responsibility (*see* Figure 11.10). Within the functional departments authority and responsibility flow vertically down the line, but the authority and responsibility of the 'project' manager (or course programme manager) flow horizontally across the organisation structure.

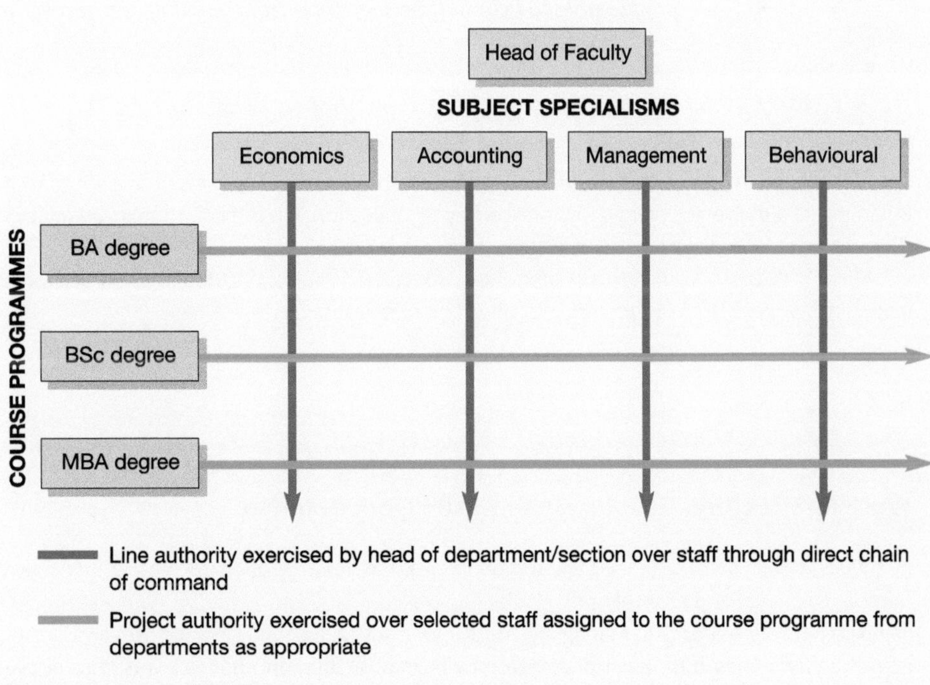

Figure 11.10 Outline of a matrix structure in a university

A matrix design might be adopted in the following circumstances:

1. **More than one critical orientation to the operations of the organisation.** For example, an insurance company has to respond simultaneously to both functional differentiation (such as life, fire, marine, motor) and different geographical areas.
2. **A need to process simultaneously large amounts of information.** For example, a local authority's social services department seeking help for an individual will need to know where to contact help from outside agencies (such as police, priest, community relations officer) and at the same time who to contact from internal resources within the organisation (such as the appropriate social worker, health visitor or housing officer).
3. **The need for sharing of resources.** This could be justified only on a total organisational basis, such as the occasional or part-time use by individual departments of specialist staff or services.

Developing an effective matrix organisation, however, takes time and a willingness to learn new roles and behaviour; this means that matrix structures are often difficult for management to implement effectively.[19]

Difficulties with matrix structures

The matrix structure offers the advantages of flexibility, greater security and control of project information, and opportunities for staff development. There are, however, a number of potential difficulties and problem areas. The matrix structure can result in a more complex structure. By using two methods of grouping it sacrifices the unity of command and can cause problems of co-ordination. An underlying difficulty with matrix structures is that of divided loyalties and role conflict, with individuals reporting simultaneously to two managers; this highlights the importance of effective teamwork. *Senior and Swailes* make the point that:

> *Matrix structures rely heavily on teamwork with managers needing high-level people management skills. The focus is on solving problems through team action. In a mature matrix structure, team members are managed simultaneously by two different managers – one is their functional line manager and the other the team or project leader. This type of organizational arrangement, therefore, requires a culture of co-operation, with supportive training programmes to help staff develop their team working and conflict-resolution skills.*[20]

Critical review and reflection

The idea of a matrix structure may appeal to those critical of a so-called prescriptive approach to organisation design. But in reality a matrix structure is an unnecessary complication. It is difficult to manage effectively, hard for people to shine and creates more potential problems than it answers.

What do YOU see as the benefits of a matrix structure? What is YOUR impression of organisation design in YOUR university? Would YOU be comfortable working in a matrix structure?

Management and organisational behaviour in action case study

Working structure: Geoplan Spatial Intelligence Limited

In 2000 Geoplan, a consultancy organisation in Yorkshire and Humberside, was in meltdown. As well as a growing number of market and technological challenges, the company was grappling with a structure that did not work and in which all roads led back to Managing Director John Taylor. Finance Director Sara McCartney explains: 'John would go out and win new business, which created a buzz of excitement. But this was quickly overtaken by a feeling of dread about how we were going to deliver on that promise.'

John and Sara realised that they had to find a better way of working. This meant finding a way of decentralising the business to get away from a line management structure that put John – and everyone else – under huge pressure. They also recognised that they needed to invest in developing their people if they were going to succeed.

Initially Geoplan used a facilitator to help John share his vision and mission for the company, something he found difficult: 'It felt like being in a padded cell, kicking it around until it all came out.' But, ultimately, Investors in People gave the team a 'Geoplan way of working'. Next, Geoplan used Investors in People to help them develop a new 'matrix' structure for the company. This meant that the business became increasingly self-managed and anyone – rather than just John – could lead a project. John credits the leadership and management criteria in the Investors in People framework with helping him to realise that everyone could be a leader at some point in their role. But now Geoplan's staff had to step up to that challenge. As Sara said: 'We've worked very hard to develop an Investors in People framework that helps people to understand their own competences. That knowledge has given them confidence that they know their stuff and can deliver to global businesses.'

Now people focus on outputs and the value they add to the business. Effective planning and organisation, teamwork and prioritisation have delivered a significant increase in performance.

In 2003, Geoplan was making a loss of nearly half a million pounds a year. In 2011, it made a profit of £400,000. The value of the average contract has risen from £20,000 to £150,000–£200,000, and productivity has gone up from £56,000 per head in 2002 to £93,000 per head in 2011. Geoplan puts its improved results down to the increased confidence and ability of its people, who now form project teams to win new business and work much more closely with clients. They win and retain more customers, and their improved performance has enabled them to move from 'data assembly' work to large, bespoke jobs where Geoplan can add value. This consultancy approach is also more profitable.

Involving all staff in management and strategy has also enabled Geoplan to cope with rapid technological change in its sector. This meant Geoplan had to change from being a desktop-based business used by specialists, to online systems used by a wide range of business customers and sectors. This change has also enabled it to expand from being a UK business to working with global clients such as TNT and KFC owners Yum! Brands. John says that Investors in People also helps Geoplan 'to explain to a billion-pound business why they should work with you rather than a big company'.

Source: For case study: Investors in People content provided by the UK Commission for Employment and Skills. **www.investorsinpeople.co.uk**

Tasks

1. Discuss potential problem areas in decentralising a business away from a line management structure.
2. What do you see as the advantages of a matrix structure with a business becoming more self-managed?
3. Discuss the implications for organisation structure with a change from desktop-based business to online systems.

Boundaryless organisation

The idea of boundaryless organisation originated with Jack Welch, former Chairman of General Electric, in the 1990s. Despite the enormous size of the organisation, the idea was to eliminate internal barriers: both vertical boundaries between different levels of the management hierarchy and horizontal boundaries between different departments; and external barriers between the company, suppliers and customers. The concept has been popularised by *Ashkenas* and colleagues.[21] A number of organisations have since attempted to follow this idea.

Francesco and Gold refer to the globalisation of the economy that has created new types of structures such as the 'boundaryless organization', which breaks the traditional demarcations of authority and task specialisation associated with bureaucracies and other structures: 'Features of a boundaryless organization include a widespread use of project teams, interfunctional teams, networks, and similar structural mechanisms, thus reducing boundaries that typically separate organizational functions and hierarchical levels.' A key management challenge is the socialisation and training of members of the organisation away from the effects of the bureaucratic mentality. Although there is still some form of authority structure, and task and political boundaries, such boundaries are flexible and unlike the rigid horizontal and vertical dimensions of traditional organisations.[22]

Advances in ICT and the growth of social networking together with the general movement towards less rigid chains of command and empowered teamwork have given impetus to the boundaryless organisation. However, as *Nicholson* points out:

> *Of course, no organisation can function without boundaries - they just sometimes become less visible. Neither might it be desirable - boundaries can actually foster freedom by making people safe.*[23]

Effects of a deficient organisation structure

It is not easy to describe, in a positive manner, what constitutes a 'good' or effective organisation structure, although the negative effects of a poorly designed structure can be identified more easily. In his discussion on the principles of organisation and co-ordination, *Urwick* (writing in 1947) suggests that 'lack of design is Illogical, Cruel, Wasteful and Inefficient'.

> *In short, a very large proportion of the friction and confusion in current society, with its manifest consequences in human suffering, may be traced back directly to faulty organisation in the structural sense.*[24]

Urwick's emphasis on the logical design of organisation structure rather than the development around personalities is typical of the classical approach to organisation and management. Despite this rather narrow view, more recent writers have drawn similar conclusions as to the consequences of badly designed structure. For example, *Child* points out the consequences of structure deficiencies:

> *Certain problems arise time and time again in struggling companies. Even at the best of times they can point to incipient dangers that have to be dealt with. Deficiencies in organisation can play a part in exacerbating each of these problems. High on the list are (1) low motivation and morale, (2) late and inappropriate decisions, (3) conflict and lack of co-ordination, (4) a generally poor response to new opportunities and external change, and (5) rising costs.*[25]

Organisation charts

The structure of an organisation may be depicted in the form of a chart that provides a pictorial representation of the overall shape and structural framework of the organisation. Some charts are very sketchy and give only a minimum amount of information. Other charts give varying amounts of additional detail, such as an indication of the broad nature of duties and responsibilities of the various units.

Charts are usually displayed in a traditional, vertical form such as those already depicted in Figures 11.5 and 11.6. They can, however, be displayed either horizontally with the information reading from left to right, or concentrically with top management at the centre. Organisation charts are useful in explaining the outline structure of an organisation. They may be used as a basis for the analysis and review of structure, and for formulating changes. The chart may indicate **apparent weaknesses** in structure such as, for example:

- too wide a span of control;
- overlapping areas of authority;
- too long a chain of command;
- unclear reporting relationships and/or lines of communication;
- unstaffed functions.

Probably the most immediate and accessible way to describe any formal organisation is to outline its structure. For the student of organisations, knowledge of its structure is indispensable as a first step to understanding the processes which occur within it. When asked to describe their organisation, managers will frequently sketch an organisation chart to show how their organisation 'works'.[26]

Limitations of organisation charts

There are, however, a number of limitations with traditional organisation charts. They depict only a static view of the organisation, and show how it looks and what the structure should be. Charts do not show the comparative authority and responsibility of positions on the same level, or lateral contacts and informal relations. Neither do charts show the extent of personal delegation from superior to subordinates, or the precise relationships between line and staff positions. Organisation charts can become out of date quickly and are often slow to be amended to reflect changes in the actual structure.

While acknowledging that organisation charts have some uses, *Townsend* likens them to 'rigor mortis' and advises that they should be drawn in pencil.

Never formalize, print and circulate them. Good organizations are living bodies that grow new muscles to meet challenges. A chart demoralizes people. Nobody thinks of himself as below other people. And in a good company he isn't. Yet on paper there it is . . . In the best organizations, people see themselves working in a circle as if around one table.[27]

Critical review and reflection

Although no longer common in many organisations, and despite their weaknesses, a chart portraying a clear representation of the overall shape and structure of an organisation with indication of broad duties and responsibilities of various units can serve many useful features.

Have YOU seen an organisation chart for YOUR own university or department? If so, how helpful was it? If not, in what ways would a chart be beneficial to YOU?

A summary of formal organisations and organisation charts is set out in the concept map in Figure 11.11.

Variables influencing organisation structure

Earlier approaches to organisation and management (**discussed in Chapter 2**) believed in one best form of structure and tended to concentrate on limited aspects of organisation. They also tended to study the organisation in isolation from its environment. According to *Bouchikhi and Kimberly,* a feature that differentiates the nineteenth-, twentieth- and twenty-first-century management paradigms is that as customers and shareholders have been more proactive, market-driven strategies and flexible organisations have developed as a consequence. The changing nature of the work environment, the increasing demands for flexibility and concerns with the contextual factors influencing structure have drawn attention to the contingency approach to organisation design.[28]

Contingency approach

The **contingency approach** can be seen as a development of the systems approach; it goes a stage further in relating the environment, and other variables, to specific structures of organisation. The contingency approach takes the view that there is no one best, universal structure.

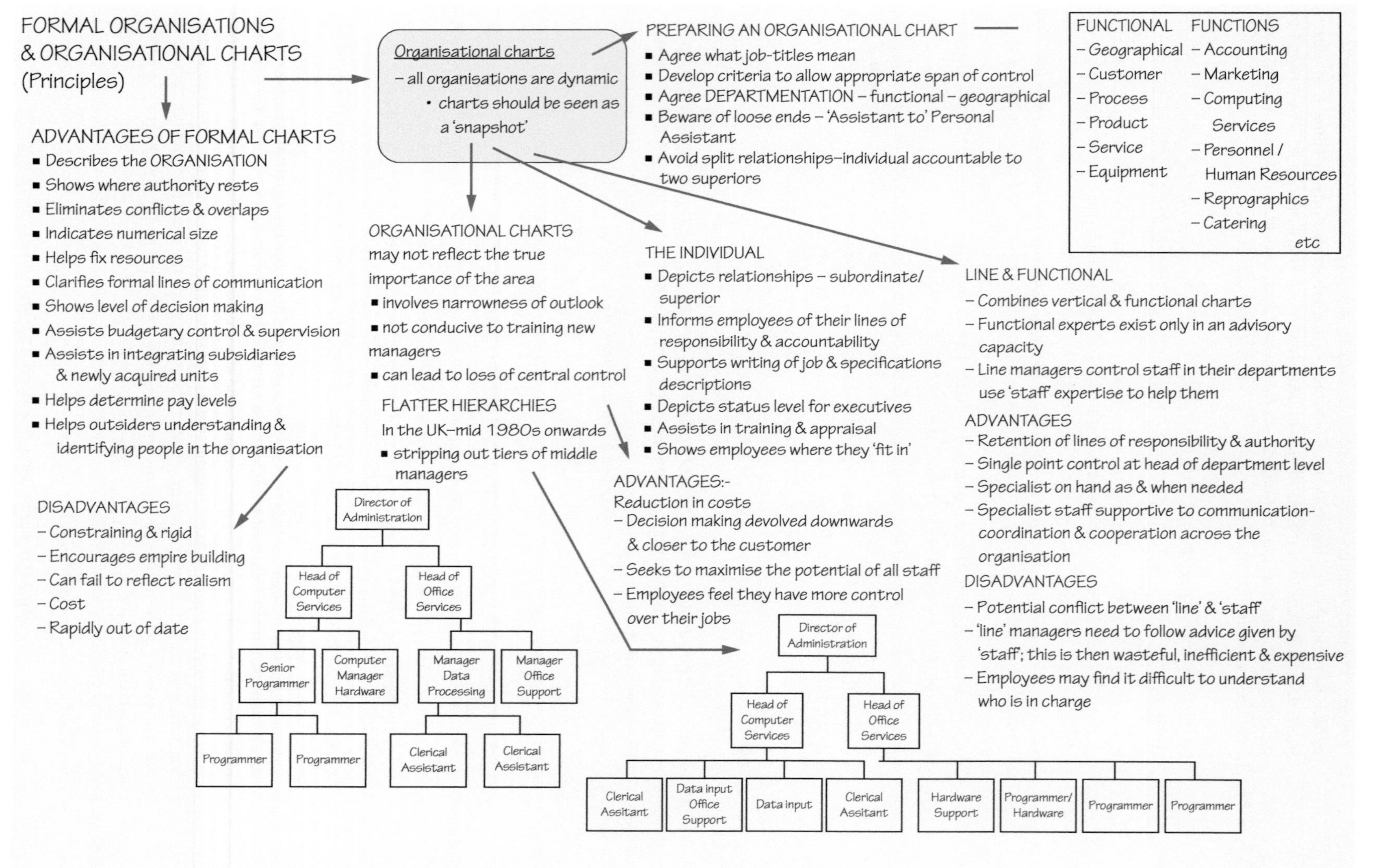

Figure 11.11 Formal organisations and organisation charts

Source: Copyright ©2012 The Virtual Learning Materials Workshop. Reproduced with permission.

There are a large number of variables, or situational factors, that influence organisation design and performance. The contingency approach emphasises the need for flexibility.

As *Vecchio* puts it: 'The goal of the contingency view is to explain how differences in the contextual and structural dimensions are related. As the term *contingency* implies, this approach does not seek universal principles that can be used for every situation, but instead seeks to explain how one attribute or characteristic depends upon another.'[29] The most appropriate structure is dependent, therefore, upon the contingencies of the situation for each individual organisation. These situational factors account for variations in the structure of different organisations.

Lynch points out that 'Every organisation is unique in size, products or services, people, leadership and culture' and provides helpful examples of some of the possible implications for organisation design (*see* Figure 11.12).[30]

Situational factors may be identified in a number of ways. Obvious bases for comparison include the type of organisation and its purpose, history, and the characteristics of the members of the organisation such as their abilities, skills and experience. Other important variables are **size, technology** and **environment.** A number of studies have been carried out into the extent to which these contingency factors influence organisation design and effectiveness.

Size of organisation

Size has clear implications for organisation structure. In the very small organisations there is little need for a formal structure. With increasing size, however, and associated problems of execution of work and management of staff, there are likely to be more formalised relationships and greater use of rules and standardised procedures. Size explains best many of the characteristics of organisation structure, for example bureaucracy and the importance

Purpose	Implications for organisation design
• 'Ideas factory' such as an advertising or promotions agency	• Loose, fluid structure with limited formalised relationships. As it grows in size, however, more formal structures are usually inevitable
• Multinational company in branded goods	• Major linkage and resource issues that need carefully co-ordinated structures, e.g. on common suppliers or common supermarket customers for separate product ranges
• Government civil service	• Strict controls on procedures and authorisations. Strong formal structures to handle major policy directions and legal issues
• Non-profit-making charity with a strong sense of mission	• Reliance on voluntary members and their voluntary contributions may require a flexible organisation with responsibility devolved to individuals
• Major service company such as a retail bank or electricity generating company	• Formal structures but supported by some flexibility so that variations in demand can be met quickly
• Small business attempting to survive and grow	• Informal, willingness to undertake several business functions such as selling or production, depending on the short-term circumstances
• Health service with strong professional service ethics, standards and quality	• Formalised structure that reflects the seniority and professional status of those involved while delivering the crucial complex service provisions
• Holding company with subsidiaries involved in diverse markets	• Small centralised headquarters acting largely as a banker, with the main strategic management being undertaken in individual companies

Figure 11.12 Examples of the connection between purpose and organisational design

Source: Lynch, R. *Strategic Management*, sixth edition, Pearson Education (2012), p. 464. Reprinted by permission of Pearson Education Ltd.

of standardisation through rules and procedures as a mechanism for co-ordination in larger organisations.

Size, however, is not a simple variable. It can be defined and measured in different ways, although a common indication is the number of persons employed. There is the problem of distinguishing the effects of size from other organisational variables. Furthermore, there is conflicting evidence on the relationship of size to the structure and operation of the organisation. There is a continuing debate about the comparative advantages of large and small organisations, or whether 'bigger is best' or 'small is beautiful'. The conclusion appears to be that complexity rather than size may be a more influential variable.[31]

Global companies and size

Birkinshaw draws attention to size as a particular feature of the structures of global companies: 'The reality is that global companies end up being perceived as complex, slow-moving and bureaucratic. The challenge for top managers lies in minimizing these liabilities, while retaining the benefits of size.' The pure matrix with equal stress on two lines of accountability does not work. Attention must be given to strong but informal horizontal relationships and country managers in developing markets. The organisation of a global company depends on a host of factors including number of businesses and countries in which it operates, the type of industry, location of major customers and its own heritage.[32]

Technology

Two major studies concerning technology are those by:

- Woodward – patterns of organisation, production technology and business success; and
- Perrow – main dimensions of technology and organisation structure.

Woodward – structure and production technology

A major study of the effects of technology on organisation structure was carried out by *Joan Woodward* in the 1950s.[33] Her pioneering work presents the results of empirical study of 100 manufacturing firms in southeast Essex and the relationships between the application of principles of organisation and business success. The main thesis was:

> *that industrial organisations which design their formal organisational structures to fit the type of production technology they employ are likely to be commercially successful.*[34]

Firms were divided into nine different types of production systems, from least to most technological complexity, with three main groupings of:

- unit and small-batch production;
- large-batch and mass production;
- process production.

The firms varied considerably in their organisation structure and many of the variations appeared to be linked closely with differences in manufacturing techniques.

Patterns of organisation and business success

There appeared to be no direct link between principles of organisation and business success. There was, however, a stronger relationship between organisation structure and success within each of the three main groupings of production systems. Organisational patterns were found

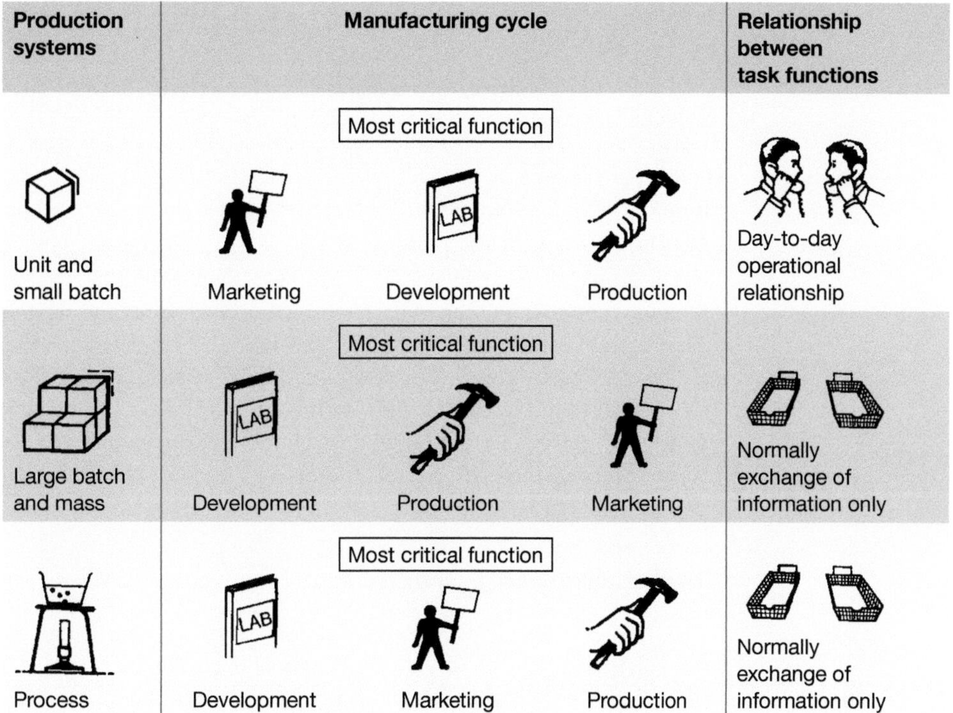

Figure 11.13 Characteristics of production systems

Source: Woodward, J. *Industrial Organization: Theory and Practice*, second edition, Oxford University Press (1980), p. 128. Reproduced with permission from Oxford University Press.

to be related more to similarity of objectives and production techniques than to size, type of industry or the business success of the firm. Woodward acknowledges that technology is not the only variable that affects organisation, but is one that could be isolated more easily for study. She does, however, draw attention to the importance of technology, organisation and business success.

Another important finding of Woodward's study was the nature of the actual cycle of manufacturing and the relationship between three key 'task' functions of development, production and marketing. The most critical of these functions varied according to the type of production system (*see* Figure 11.13).

- **Unit and small batch.** Production was based on firm orders only, with marketing the first activity. Greater stress was laid on technical expertise, and the quality and efficiency of the product. Research and development were the second, and most critical, activities. The need for flexibility, close integration of functions and frequent personal contacts meant that an organic structure was required.
- **Large batch and mass.** Production schedules were not dependent directly on firm orders. The first phase of manufacturing was product development, followed by production, which was the most important function, and thirdly by marketing. The three functions were more independent and did not rely so much on close operational relationships among people responsible for development, production and sales.
- **Process.** The importance of securing a market meant that marketing was the central and critical activity. Products were either impossible or difficult to store, or capacity for storage was very limited. The flow of production was directly determined, therefore, by the market situation. The emphasis of technical knowledge was more on how products could be used than on how they could be made.

Perrow – major dimensions of technology

The work by Woodward was extended by *Perrow*, who drew attention to two major dimensions of technology:

- the extent to which the work task is predictable or variable; and
- the extent to which technology can be analysed.[35]

Variability refers to the number of exceptional or unpredictable cases and the extent to which problems are familiar. For example, a mass-production factory is likely to have only a few exceptions, but the manufacture of a designer range of clothing would have many exceptional and unpredictable cases. The **analysis of technology** refers to the extent to which the task functions are broken down and highly specified, and the extent to which problems can be solved in recognised ways or by the use of routine procedures. Combining the two dimensions provides a continuum of technology from routine to non-routine. With non-routine technology there are a large number of exceptional cases involving difficult and varied problem-solving.

Technology and structure

The classification of each type of technology relates to a particular organisation structure. Perrow suggests that by classifying organisations according to their technology and predictability of work tasks, we should be able to predict the most effective form of structure. Variables such as the discretion and power of sub-groups, the basis of co-ordination and the interdependence of groups result from the use of different technologies.

In the **routine type of organisation** there is minimum discretion at both the technical and supervisory levels, but the power of the middle management level is high, co-ordination is based on planning and there is likely to be low interdependence between the two groups. This arrangement approaches a bureaucratic structure. In the **non-routine type of organisation** there is a high level of discretion and power at both the technical and supervisory levels, co-ordination is through feedback and there is high group interdependence. This model resembles an organic structure.

Uncertain external environment

Two important studies that focused not just on technology but also on the effects of uncertainty and a changing external environment on the organisation, and its management and structure, are those by:

- Burns and Stalker – divergent systems of management practice, 'mechanistic' and 'organic'; and
- Lawrence and Lorsch – the organisation of specific departments, and the extent of 'differentiation' and 'integration'.

Burns and Stalker – mechanistic and organic structures

The study by *Burns and Stalker* was an analysis of twenty industrial firms in the UK and the effects of the external environment on their pattern of management and economic performance. The firms were drawn from a number of industries: a rayon manufacturer, a large engineering company, Scottish firms attempting to enter the electronics field and English firms operating in varying sectors of the electronics industry.[36]

From an examination of the settings in which the firms operated, Burns and Stalker distinguished five different kinds of environments ranging from 'stable' to 'least predictable'. They also identified two divergent systems of management practice and structure – the 'mechanistic' system and the 'organic' system.

The **mechanistic system** is a more rigid structure that is unable to deal adequately with rapid change; it is therefore more appropriate for stable environmental conditions. The characteristics of a mechanistic management system are similar to those of bureaucracy. An example might be a traditional high-class and expensive hotel operating along classical lines with an established reputation and type of customer. However, major fast food chains that tend to operate along the lines of scientific management (**discussed in Chapter 2**) also require a mechanistic structure.

The **organic system** is a more fluid structure appropriate to changing conditions. It appears to be required when new problems and unforeseen circumstances arise constantly and require actions outside defined roles in the hierarchical structure. A holiday or tourist hotel with an unpredictable demand, offering a range of functions and with many different types of customers, requires an organic structure.

A summary of the characteristics of mechanistic and organic organisations is provided by *Litterer* (*see* Table 11.1).[37]

Burns and Stalker point out that there are intermediate stages between the two extreme systems that represent not a dichotomy but a polarity. The relationship between the mechanistic and organic systems is not rigid. An organisation moving between a relatively stable and a relatively changing environment may also move between the two systems.

'Mixed' forms of organisation structure

Organisations *tend* towards mechanistic or organic, and many will be hybrid – that is, a mix of both mechanistic and organic structures – and often this is an uneasy mix that can lead to tension and conflict. For example, a group of people engaged on a set of broad functional activities might prefer, and perform best in, an organic structure, while another group tends to prefer a mechanistic structure and to work within established rules, systems and procedures. Different preferences for organisational styles and working methods present a particular challenge to management.

Table 11.1 Characteristics of mechanistic and organic organisations

Mechanistic		Organic
High, many and sharp differentiations	SPECIALISATION	Low, no hard boundaries, relatively few different jobs
High, methods spelled out	STANDARDISATION	Low, individuals decide own methods
Means	ORIENTATION OF MEMBERS	Goals
By superior	CONFLICT RESOLUTION	Interaction
Hierarchical, based on implied contractual relation	PATTERN OF AUTHORITY CONTROL AND COMMUNICATION	Wide net based upon common commitment
At top of organisation	LOCUS OF SUPERIOR COMPETENCE	Wherever there is skill and competence
Vertical	INTERACTION	Lateral
Directions, orders	COMMUNICATION CONTENT	Advice, information
To organisation	LOYALTY	To project and group
From organisational position	PRESTIGE	From personal contribution

Source: Litterer, J. A. *The Analysis of Organizations*, second edition, John Wiley & Sons (1973), p. 339. Reproduced with permission from the estate of Joseph A. Litterer.

A typical example of a hybrid organisation could be a university with differences in perception between academic staff and non-teaching staff. Academic staff may feel they can work effectively only within an organic structure, and tend to see non-teaching staff as bureaucratic and resistant to novel or different ideas. Non-teaching staff have an important function in helping to keep the organisation operational and working effectively, and may fail to understand why academics appear to find it difficult, or resent, working within prescribed administrative systems and procedures. Universities may also tend to be more mechanistic at top management level, with an apparent proliferation of committees and sub-committees, because of their dealings with, for example, government bodies and other external agencies.

Critical review and reflection

Students of organisational behaviour often express a strong preference for working within an organic organisation. But then many express concerns about possible lack of superior competence, clear direction and strong management.

Why do YOU think this is? In which type of structure would YOU prefer to work, and why?

Lawrence and Lorsch – differentiation and integration

Lawrence and Lorsch undertook a study of six firms in the plastics industry followed by a further study of two firms in the container industry and two firms in the consumer food industry. They extended the work of Burns and Stalker and examined not only the overall structure, but also the way in which specific departments were organised to meet different aspects of the firm's external environment. The internal structures of the firms were analysed in terms of 'differentiation' and 'integration'.[38]

Differentiation describes 'the difference in cognitive and emotional orientation among managers in different functional departments' with respect to goal orientation, time orientation, interpersonal relations and formality of structure.

Integration describes 'the quality of the state of collaboration that exists among departments that are required to achieve unity of effort by the demands of the environment'. It is the degree of co-ordination and co-operation between different departments with interdependent tasks. Lawrence and Lorsch's view of integration was not the minimising of differences between departments and the provision of a common outlook. It was the recognition that different departments could have their own distinctive form of structure according to the nature of their task, and the use of mediating devices to co-ordinate the different outlooks of departments.

This view of differentiation and integration was confirmed in the subsequent study of firms in the container and consumer food industries. It was concluded that the extent of differentiation and integration in effective organisations will vary according to the demands of the particular environment:

- The more diverse and dynamic the environment, the more the effective organisation will be differentiated and highly integrated.
- In more stable environments, less differentiation will be required but a high degree of integration is still required. Differences in the environment will require different methods of achieving integration.
- Given the possibility that different demands of the environment are characterised by different levels of uncertainty, it follows that individual departments may develop different structures.

Integrating mechanisms

Mechanisms used to achieve integration depend on the amount of integration required and the difficulty in achieving it. In mechanistic structures, integration may be attempted through the use of policies, rules and procedures. In organic structures, integration may be attempted through teamwork and mutual co-operation. As the requirements for the amount of integration increase, additional means may be adopted, such as formal lateral relations, committees and project teams. It is important, however, to achieve the right balance of integration. Too high a level of integration may involve costs that are likely to exceed possible benefits. Too low a level of integration is likely to result in departments 'doing their own thing', poorer-quality decisions and failure to make the best use of resources.[39]

Evaluation of contingency approach

The contingency approach draws attention to situational factors that influence variations in the structure of organisations. It is more concerned with differences among organisations than with similarities, and rejects assumptions of the classical and human relations approaches and the idea of one best form of structure. For its part, however, the contingency approach tends to assume that organisational performance is dependent upon the degree to which the structure of the organisation matches the prevailing contingencies.

Hunt explains the concept of contingency as follows:

> *The concept of contingency also implies that there is no one, absolute 'best' design; rather, there is a multitude of possibilities and the best or preferred choice will be contingent on the situation being analysed. Universal models designed to suit all situations are therefore rejected. This is consistent with the fact that most organizations are networks of a variety of bits of design rather than conforming, as one entity, to a particular model. So we might find units of bureaucracy, units of matrix structures, units with project teams, units with extremely loose, almost ad hoc structures – and all these within, say, the same oil company. In this sense, the contingency theorists merely reflected the findings of hundreds of researchers. There are common elements in the hierarchies of different organizations but there are also very many differences peculiar to the local situation.*[40]

Not every situation is unique

According to *Robey*, modern contingency theory defines variables ignored in earlier work, and directs attention of the manager to contingencies to be considered in the design of organisation structure. However, the contingency approach runs the risk of concluding that 'it all depends on everything', and the greatest danger is the over-emphasis on differences between organisations and the exclusion of similarities. If the contingency approach is to be useful in guiding organisation design it should not treat every situation as being unique: 'Rather it must strike a balance between universal prescriptions and the statement that all situations are different (which is really no theory at all). Thus, modern theory uses a limited number of contingencies to help explain structural differences between organizations.'[41]

Organisation structure and culture

The pervasive nature of culture in terms of both external influences and 'how things are done around here' and common values, beliefs and attitudes will have a significant effect on organisational processes including the design of structure.

Schneider and Barsoux suggest that while managers are ready to accept national culture as an influence on the way people relate to each other, they are less convinced of its real effect on the structure, systems and process of the organisation. However, the emerging approaches to management reflect different cultural assumptions, and models of management have diffused across countries at different rates in different ways. Historical and societal context needs to be considered to understand the adoption and diffusion of different forms of organisation across countries. Schneider and Barsoux discuss the multidimensional impact of culture on organisations and management and maintain that it would be a mistake to base a prediction regarding structure or process on a single cultural dimension.

> *Managers need to recognise that the relationships between cultural dimensions and structure (or processes) are not simple cause–effect links, but instead, are multidetermined. Similar approaches may exist for the same reason. Thus formalized rules and procedures or participative management approaches may have a different raison d'être on different sides of the national border.*[42]

Watson suggests that we must be careful not to treat structures or cultures as if they were solid 'things' existing separately from the processes and relationships that the two concepts are intended to help us make sense of. The structure of work organisations also involves the wider context of societal structures and cultures: 'Societal structures both contribute to and result from organisational structures.' Watson also refers to the closeness and overlap of structure and culture: 'Many of the processes and practices we observe in an organisation could as readily be said to be part of the structure of the organisation as part of its culture.'[43]

An interesting set of caricatures for organisation charts of different countries is given in Figure 11.14.

Critical review and reflection

According to the contingency approach, different situational variables may have some relevance for certain types of organisations at certain times given a particular set of circumstances. This *it all depends* approach is too vague to have any practical benefit for managers.

How would YOU attempt to defend the value of the contingency approach? To what extent have YOU seen applications of contingency theory in YOUR university or organisation?

The changing face of the workplace

Birchall refers to the changing world of organisations and its impact on management. Much of the work undertaken by middle management no longer requires the considerable layers of management. Tasks that used to take up a great deal of management time in hierarchical structures are now possible with minimal supervision or intervention. Much of the organisation's work is carried out in projects. Many managers will find themselves managing people who spend much of their time outside the office. There is a strong move towards the use of consultants. Managers will need to be familiar with electronic networks, the operation of dispersed teams and virtual organisations.[44]

A similar point is made by *Cloke and Goldsmith*, who maintain that management is an idea whose time is up and the days of military command structures are over.

> *Rather than building fixed structures with layers of middle management, many innovative organizations function as matrixed webs of association, networks, and fast-forming high-performance teams . . . The most significant trends we see in the theory and history of management are the decline of the hierarchical, bureaucratic, autocratic management and the expansion of collaborative self-management and organizational democracy.*[45]

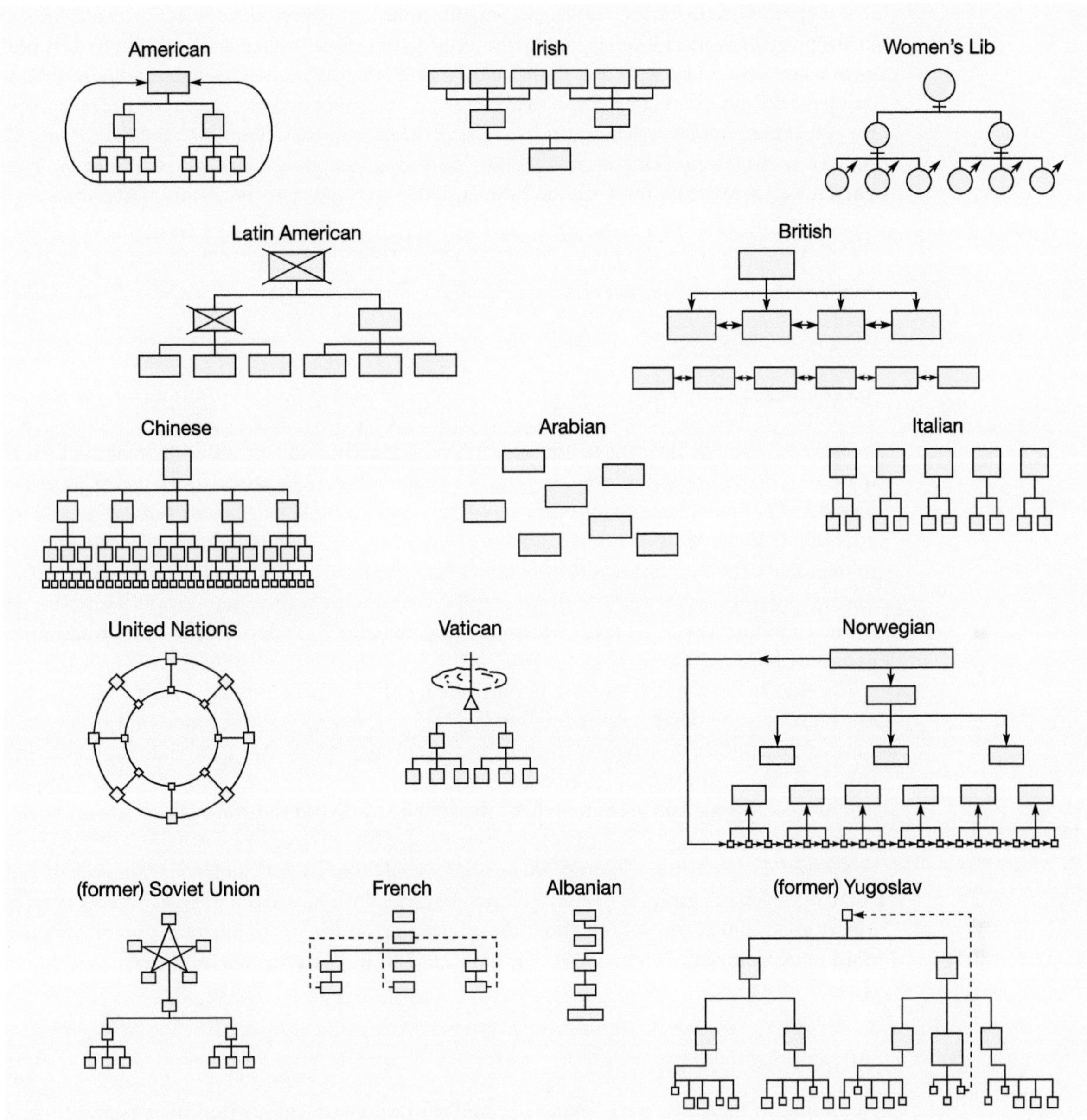

Figure 11.14 Caricatures of organisation charts for different countries

Source: Copyright © Reed Business Information, reprinted with permission.

Information technology

The impact of information technology has significant effects on the structure, management and functioning of most organisations. IT influences the need for restructuring the organisation and changes to lines of command and authority. Computer-based information and decision-support systems influence choices in design of production or service activities, hierarchical levels and organisation of support staffs. IT may influence the centralisation/decentralisation of decision-making and control systems. New technology has typically resulted in a 'flatter' organisational pyramid with fewer levels of management required. In the case of new office technology it allows the potential for staff at clerical/operator level to carry out a wider range of functions and to check their own work. The result is a change in the traditional supervisory function and a demand for fewer supervisors.

Most manufacturing and industrial organisations still require the physical presence of staff at the place of work. However, for many service or creative organisations such physical presence is not always necessary. For knowledge workers their work can be undertaken from home or where there is access to a computer. For example, *Fisher* points out that as the technology for achieving remote working gets better and cheaper, expectations for remote working are rocketing. Mobile working is increasingly hard to ignore and, facing global demands, companies and individuals must decide how available they want to be. Nine-to-five working is no longer enough. Some businesses will be able to dispense with fixed premises altogether.[46] **Recall also the earlier discussion on information technology and remote teamworking** (see Chapter 8).

Outsourcing

In order to free management to concentrate on core activities, businesses are making increasing use of outsourcing and a wider range of non-core services provided by specialist service providers. A Management Consultancies Association and *Management Today* survey drew attention to a changing relationship between organisations and individuals. The survey refers to the significant increase in outsourcing, with some of the highest growth in business process outsourcing (BPO) where entire functions are moved outside the organisation. However, one of the consequences of increased outsourcing is that the boundaries of the organisation are becoming blurred.[47]

Thomas reports on the increase in outsourcing of legal and company secretarial activities. Outsourcing can address cost reduction, lack of expertise or work that does not make a full-time role, but it is a very radical answer to cost cutting. It may cause more difficulties than it solves. When a company outsources an activity, it cannot just forget about it. The company and its directors are still accountable for the activity, and need to review and monitor the outsourced work.[48]

Overell suggests that although there is a lack of hard evidence of consequences of outsourcing, there are grounds for prospective concern. With outsourcing, power seems to be no longer about direct control but about the ability to co-ordinate an intricate web of organisations, contractors, subcontractors, bit-part players and intermediaries known as a supply chain.[49]

What to outsource?

According to the CMI, outsourcing has evolved into a strategic option for businesses of all sizes. Often seen as a threat by employees and an opportunity by organisations, outsourcing has nonetheless become standard practice in many businesses.

> *On the surface, the benefits of outsourcing may seem both straightforward and considerable. However, in addition to cost-savings, there are many other factors that lead managers to consider outsourcing. These include access to skills and new technology, the desire to expand globally, and the need for flexibility both to deal with rises and falls in product development demand and to improve ways of delivering products or services . . . If you focus on identifying the core competencies of your organisation and on what differentiates the company and makes it unique, then those areas which make up the support, administration, routine and internal serving of the organisation will become potential areas for outsourcing.*[50]

In the public sector there have been a number of recent high-profile problems associated with outsourcing of major government services. According to *Hazlehurst*, 'Outsourcing firms seem to stagger from one scandal to the next, with even their Government paymasters putting the boot in at times.' However, as Hazlehurst points out, outsourcing is not privatisation, and it is not going away.

Outsourcing makes sense . . . we don't expect local councils to design and build their own street-sweeping machines. They buy them from Volvo. So why shouldn't they buy services from experts too?[51]

Demand for flexibility

The nature of work is being redefined and this has created strong pressures for greater flexibility in patterns of work organisation and in the workforce. A report from ACAS examines the need for work/life balance and flexible working:

> *The hours and times people work have always been subject to change but the pace of this change is now more rapid than ever because: customers expect to have goods and services outside traditional working hours; organisations want to match their business needs with the way their employees work; individuals want to achieve a better balance between work and home life . . . Flexible patterns of work can help address these pressures by maximizing the available labour and improving customer service. Flexible working can also help to reduce absenteeism and increase productivity, employee commitment and loyalty.*[52]

Flexible working arrangements

Flexible working arrangements are a range of options designed to help employees balance work and home life and can describe the place of work or the contract of employment. There is a wide range of flexible working practices, which in many instances can be used in a wide variety of workplaces:

- part-time working;
- annual hours;
- staggered hours;
- job sharing;
- time off in lieu;
- flexitime;
- work at or from home;
- self-rostering;
- mobile working/teleworking.
- compressed working hours;
- shift swapping;
- term-time working;
- career breaks from work.

Telecommuting

Recent advances in computerisation and telecommunications have had a further significant effect on opportunities for flexible working. People can work from almost any geographic location: from head office, a satellite office, a shared access telecentre; or from their home, hotel room or car. An increasingly popular means of teleworking is **telecommuting**, where staff work from home with a computer network, telephone, etc.

Lucas reports on underlying resistance from organisations to flexible working. Despite the well-documented benefits, there are many organisations where it is just not happening on the front line. Workplace cultures make it too difficult for employees to ask and a 'can't do' attitude is the status quo. There is a different perspective between line managers and the HR department. The biggest hurdle is often concerns of line managers about the practicalities of a flexible working arrangement and worries over managing performance. However, objections often raised are not insurmountable. Managers need proper training on how to manage flexible working practices to make telecommuting a success in their team.[53]

Homeworking

A noticeable feature of the changing nature of the workplace is the growth in homeworking. Most commentators suggest that the benefits outweigh the drawbacks.[54] Figures from the ONS in June 2014 show homeworkers account for 14 per cent of the national workforce.[55] ACAS, however, points out that relatively few homeworkers, approximately 5 per cent of the workforce, carry out *all* or even *the majority* of their work at home. The greatest barrier to homeworking success is that of trust, and the traditional managerial attitude about employees needing to be seen to be considered productive.

> *If we accept as axiomatic the fact that not all job roles nor job holders will be suited to homeworking and that exclusive homeworking is not universally appropriate, the question that follows is what is the optimum balance between office and home? In one sense this is a futile question since any satisfactory answer will be specific to each organisation. But the question is helpful insofar as it reminds us that homeworking is an arrangement based on balance and not a binary practice, with staff being located either solely at home or entirely in an office.*[56]

Working from home does not appeal to everyone and it needs to be managed well, especially for full-time homeworkers. An increasing number of homeworkers report a feeling of detachment from the work situation and miss the interaction with colleagues. Homeworkers may struggle to escape the strains of domestic life and often report a feeling of exhaustion and increased conflict from demands of balancing work and family.

Critical review and reflection

Remote working, telecommuting and homeworking are clearly the way forward and should be the main feature of organisation design. Attention to traditional views on formal structure, and managerial authority and control, are no longer of significance.

How would YOU attempt to present a counterargument? To what extent would YOU be comfortable being employed by an organisation based largely on remote working and telecommuting?

Structure and organisational behaviour

It is clear, then, that it is essential to give full attention to the structure of an organisation. However, this is not always an easy task. Structuring an organisation involves balancing a series of trade-offs. In analysing the effectiveness of structure, consideration should be given to the formal and technological requirements, to principles of design and to social factors, and to the needs and demands of the human part of the organisation. Structure should be designed so as to maintain the balance of the socio-technical system and to encourage the willing participation of members and effective organisational performance.

> *An organisation can be separated into two parts or structures which can then be examined. One section is a definable structure that will be present in every company, the other is the structure caused by human intervention. The latter provides the company with its distinctive appearance, and may be regarded as the manager's particular response to the design requirements of organised behaviour. Essentially the effectiveness of an organisation depends on how accurately human design matches the structure of organised behaviour.*[57]

Trends towards flatter hierarchies, teamwork, empowerment and flexible working have reduced significantly the importance of formal structures. What really matters is that individuals know what is expected of them, work well with other people and perform their tasks successfully.

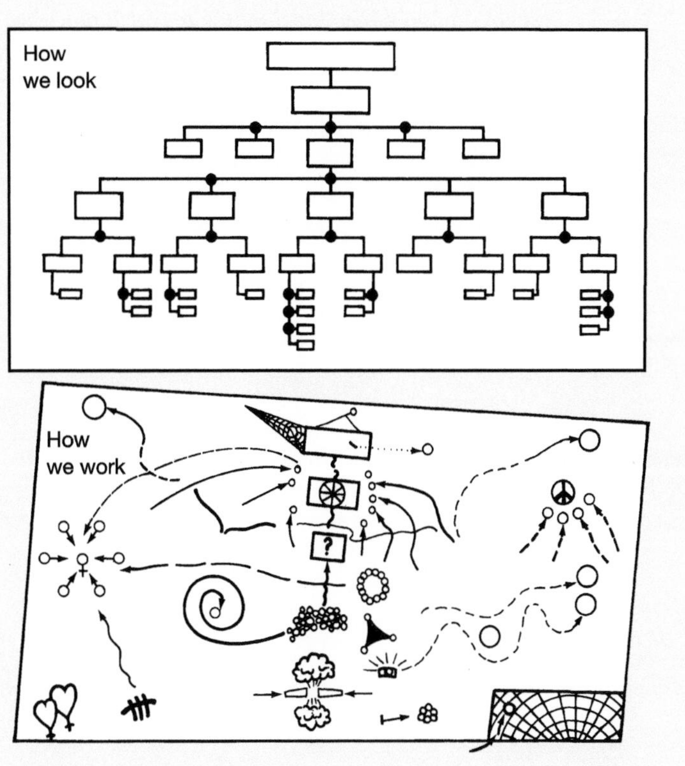

Figure 11.15 How the organisation should be, compared with how it actually works

Source: Gray, J. L. and Starke, F. A. *Organizational Behavior: Concepts and Applications*, fourth edition, © 1988. Reprinted and electronically reproduced by permission of Pearson Education, Inc., New York.

'Realities' of organisational behaviour

The structure or charts do not describe what really happens in work organisations. Individuals differ and people bring their own perceptions, feelings and attitudes towards the organisation, styles of management and their duties and responsibilities. The behaviour of people cannot be studied in isolation and we need to understand interrelationships with other variables that comprise the total organisation, including the social context of the work organisation and the importance of the informal organisation.

Gray and Starke provide a humorous but perhaps realistic illustration of how an organisation actually works (*see* Figure 11.15).[58] *Heller* also refers to 'the gap between the aims of big company organisations and what actually happens. Organisational form and organisational behaviour are not one and the same thing.'[59]

No perfect structure

As *Owen* points out, there is no such thing as the perfect organisation structure. Every structure is a trade-off between competing priorities. Building an effective organisation is becoming harder. With increasing size and complexity, challenges of co-ordination grow. Firms are becoming more complicated for two reasons: the rise of the global firm and re-engineering. The real problems of the cross-border team are about trust, power, belonging and identity. The structural revolution is more far-reaching and complicated than simply turning the pyramid on its head. The pyramid has been turned on its side and completely reconfigured.

> *The simplicity and certainty of the functional organisation has given way to the complexity of a multi-dimensional matrix in which processes count as much as functions . . . The challenge is to make the current style of organisation work. Many firms manage new style structures with old systems, then wonder why it does not work.*[60]

Whatever its structure, the various operations of the organisation have to be distributed among its members. It is necessary to plan, organise, direct and control their activities. The demand for flexibility and greater freedom and autonomy for individuals raises questions about the extent and nature of delegation and empowerment, the manager–subordinate relationship and the maintenance of management control within the formal structure of the organisation. (**This is discussed more fully in Chapter 13.**)

Critical review and reflection

We trained very hard, but it seemed every time we were beginning to form into teams we would be reorganised. I was to learn later in life that we tend to meet any new situation by reorganising and a wonderful method it can be for creating the illusion of progress while producing confusion, inefficiency and demoralisation.

(Gaius Petronius, AD 66)

To what extent do YOU think this is still true for a modern work organisation? Can YOU relate an example of reorganisation in YOUR university or organisation that has been clearly beneficial?

Ten key points to remember

1. The purpose of structure is the division of work among members of the organisation, and the means by which its goals and objectives are achieved.
2. Structure makes possible application of the process of management and creates a framework of order and system of command for the activities of the organisation.
3. Attention is focused on certain underlying dimensions in the design of organisation structure. These are not prescriptive but provide important decision points.
4. Critical decisions arise from division of work and grouping of activities, centralisation and decentralisation, role of the hierarchy and formal organisational relationships.
5. The need to integrate a wide range of activities has focused attention on more flexible forms of structure, such as line and functional, project teams and matrix organisation.
6. The contingency approach suggests there is no one best structure but a number of situational variables influencing organisation design and performance.
7. Situation variables may be identified in a number of ways, including size, technology and external environment, and arguably the influence of culture.
8. The changing nature of the workplace has drawn attention to influences such as information technology and demands for flexibility on organisation structure.
9. It is essential to give full attention to structuring an organisation but this is not an easy task. Consideration should be given to the realities of organisational behaviour.
10. There is no perfect structure. Organisation design involves balancing a series of trade-offs and attention to both the needs of staff and effective performance.

Review and discussion questions

1 Discuss the interrelationships between organisation structure and corporate strategy.

2 Give your views on the purpose and importance of structure. To what extent do you think there are clearly identified different levels in the structure of an organisation?

3 Explain the main determinants in design of an effective organisation structure. How effective do you think the structure is in your own university?

4 Discuss critically the continuing importance of the hierarchy.

5 Prepare your own diagrams to help explain: (i) line and functional organisation; and (ii) a matrix form of organisation structure. What are the reasons for adopting each of these forms of structure and what problem areas might arise?

6 Explain how the contingency approach differs from other approaches to organisation and management.

7 Contrast 'mechanistic' and 'organic' systems of management practice and structure. What is the significance of this distinction?

8 What are *your* views on the influence of advances in computerisation and telecommunications for patterns of structure and work organisation?

9 Discuss critically questions raised by increased demands for flexibility and greater freedom of choice for individuals at work.

10 To what extent would you agree with the contention that a logical structure for organisation is better for efficiency and morale than a structure allowed to develop around personalities? What are the likely consequences of a poorly designed structure?

Assignment

To cope with the changing nature of the workplace many writers are calling for more creative forms of organisation structure.

a. Explain how you believe the structure of your university, or other organisation with which you are familiar, affects your level of motivation and performance.
b. Detail fully, with supporting reasons, how you would design a more creative form of organisation structure.
c. Where appropriate, prepare a revised organisation chart.
d. Be prepared to lead a class discussion, including a question-and-answer session, to discuss your findings.

Personal skills and employability exercise

Objectives

Completing this exercise should help you to enhance the following skills:

- Diagnose specific features of structure within your university.
- Evaluate the significance and effects of structure on people within the university.
- Act as a senior manager.

→

Exercise

Remind yourself of key features in the text of this chapter relating to:

- centralisation and decentralisation;
- line and functional organisation;
- matrix structures; and
- mechanistic and organic structures of organisation.

1 Prepare a detailed report with specific examples on the manner in which these features are manifested in your university (and/or some other organisation well known to you).
2 Comment on how these features impact upon the apparent effectiveness of structure and influence various activities of the university, styles of management, the people employed and you as students.
3 Give examples of tensions and conflicts that arise from the implementation of these features, *for example* from a mix of mechanistic and organic structures.
4 As a senior manager, explain fully what changes you would recommend to organisation structure and actions to help overcome these tensions and conflicts.

Discussion

- To what extent does organisation structure influence the actions, behaviour and effectiveness of: (i) senior management; (ii) members of staff; and (iii) students?
- Who should realistically be involved in decision-making relating to structure?
- To what extent would you expect to see changes in the structure of your university in, say, the next five to ten years? And why?

Case study
John Lewis and Waitrose: distinctively successful

> *The John Lewis Partnership is a visionary and successful way of doing business, boldly putting the happiness of Partners at the centre of everything it does. It's the embodiment of an ideal, the outcome of nearly a century of endeavour to create a different sort of company, owned by Partners dedicated to serving customers with flair and fairness. All 90,000 permanent staff are Partners who own over 40 John Lewis shops across the UK, over 300 Waitrose supermarkets (***www.waitrose.com***), an online and catalogue business,* **johnlewis.com***, a production unit and a farm. The business has annual gross sales of over £10bn. Partners share in the benefits and profits of a business that puts them first.*[61]

John Lewis opened his Oxford Street department store for business in 1864. In its early days it was a traditional family-owned business, and his two sons followed him into the firm. John Spedan Lewis, later to found the John Lewis Partnership, became Director of a second store (Peter Jones' in Sloane Square) in 1905. When he inherited the whole enterprise in 1928, Spedan Lewis drew up the First Trust Settlement, which left him in control of the business but gave employees shares in its profits. Shortly before the Second World War the business acquired the Waite, Rose and Taylor grocery stores, and in 1950 the Second Trust Settlement created the John Lewis Partnership (JLP) as it is today, owned and run entirely by its employees. John Spedan Lewis died in 1963.

As a business, the John Lewis Partnership is therefore organisationally very different to its major rivals in the UK. It operates in a variety of highly competitive business environments: the UK food retail business is dominated by Tesco, Sainsbury's and Walmart (Asda); and John Lewis department stores compete not only with other department stores, but also with specialist high-street retailers of clothing, electrical goods, furniture and furnishings. Success in these markets requires very high standards of efficiency and effectiveness, and it is interesting to consider the extent to which JLP's distinctive organisation and culture explain its success.

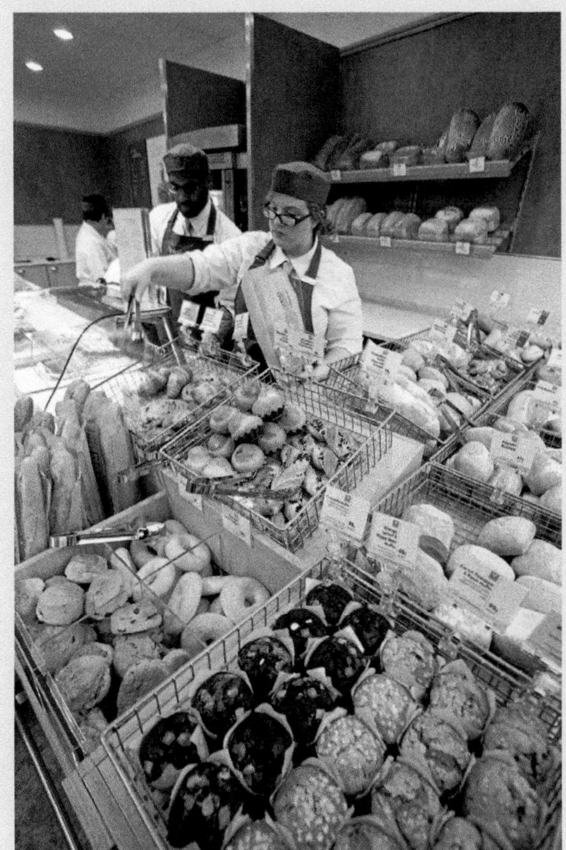

The John Lewis Partnership, including Waitrose, has a unique organisation structure, which has contributed to its business success

Source: Courtesy of Waitrose Ltd

How successful is it, and how is it successful?

> *The Constitution states that 'the happiness of its members' is the Partnership's ultimate purpose, recognising that such happiness depends on having a satisfying job in a successful business. It establishes a system of 'rights and responsibilities', which places on all Partners the obligation to work for the improvement of our business in the knowledge that we share the rewards of success.*[62]

These words set an unusual objective for a business organisation. While many commercial organisations consider the happiness of the workforce as one among several key aims, few hold it to be an overriding one. JLP's structure is an example of representative democracy: all partners elect representatives to the governing Partnership Council; elected representatives account for 80 per cent of Council members, with the remaining 20 per cent appointed by the Chairman. The Chairman and senior directors are required to give an annual account of their stewardship at a full Council meeting. Further means of communication and decision-making include branch forums and divisional councils, which reflect the various operating units including warehouses and factories as well as stores. Partners can therefore influence decisions and affect the company's activities; also, there is a direct pay-off in the shape of an annual bonus based on the company's profits. The Chairman and other directors must ensure the continuing solvency of the business as well as keeping funds available for growth, but, beyond whatever is necessary for these purposes, the annual profits are redistributed to members. All partners receive bonuses, which are calculated as a percentage of their base pay; in the financial year 2013–14 this resulted in £202.5 million of profit being redistributed at a rate of 15 per cent of salary.[63] In some years this has gone as high as 22 per cent, although a range of 9–15 per cent appears to be more usual. This direct form of 'industrial democracy' and high level of worker participation means that the management of the JLP does not recognise or negotiate with trade unions.

A further aspect of the objective of 'partner happiness' is the extensive range of benefits and services that the JLP provides to its workforce. There is a non-contributory final-salary pension scheme and many direct forms of assistance including a loans scheme. Holiday entitlements are generous, as are discounts on purchases, and the JLP owns social and sporting amenities as well as several estates that provide leisure activities and accommodation for Partners and their families.

Its commercial success, as we have noted, depends on performance in some very tough markets. How has the JLP maintained and grown its business?

Keeping the customer satisfied

> *Today, the John Lewis Partnership is the largest employee-owned business in the UK. Our Partnership model is admired across both the private and public sectors. Co-ownership gives us a distinctive culture – and a competitive advantage.*[64]

In 2014 John Lewis was voted the UK's favourite overall retailer for the sixth time in seven years in a regular Verdict[65] survey of customer satisfaction, and Waitrose also topped the poll in the food and grocery category. Like most retail businesses, the JLP experienced a drop in operating profits during the economic downturn of 2008–9, although the company remained robust and rode the downturn better than many of its competitors.[66]

The introduction of its 'essential' range and the pledge to match Tesco on the prices of branded goods has helped drive up sales and keep customers during the recession. Part of its strength has to be the company's focus on quality and to offer value for money; John Spedan Lewis introduced the 'never knowingly undersold' principle in 1925.

Taking Waitrose as the main example, this has meant a defining principle of 'Quality food, honestly priced'. The effect can be seen in a number of ways, including a relatively early decision to integrate local products into its range (many major food retailers have preferred to stock only products that can be made available at all their stores nationally), thus anticipating a growing interest in localism and the environmental problems associated with long-distance haulage (food miles). In 2001 its television advertising campaign announced that it was selling only free-range eggs, and it has gone on to establish links with farmers whose meat and poultry are produced according to high standards of animal welfare. In 2014 all Waitrose fresh beef, pork, chicken, hens' eggs and milk were produced in the UK, and it works with feed companies to reduce farmers' reliance on overseas sources of animal feed. In recent years it has become an advocate for better standards of employment for migrant agricultural workers in the UK through links with the Gangmasters Licensing Authority and the charity Migrant Help.[67]

In 2005, and as part of a broader approach to corporate social responsibility, the JLP launched the Waitrose Foundation, which runs parallel to its commitment to fair trade. Operating in South Africa, Ghana and Kenya where the company has supply chain links, the Foundation supports local education, training and healthcare projects. This was followed, in 2010, by the creation of a similar organisation, The John Lewis Foundation, which has focused on projects to develop sustainable cotton farming in Gujarat. It aims to uphold the International Labour Organization standards within its supply chain, and JLP buyers are trained to ensure suppliers treat their workers fairly and uphold human rights and well-being.[68]

Getting the message across

These initiatives are supported by distinctive and superior advertising campaigns. The Waitrose advertisements generally focus on the provenance of the products and the lives and work of individual producers and suppliers in a way that emphasises the relationship between producer and consumer, and positions the company as a discreet intermediary between the two rather than a dominant brand. The John Lewis Christmas advertisements have become something of a national institution; the breakthrough came with the 2011 television advert 'The Long Wait', which featured a little boy waiting impatiently for the Big Day, with the final reveal that he was eager to give his parents their gift (rather than get his own presents). It went viral almost immediately, causing a media frenzy in which even hard-bitten journalists admitted that it had made them cry.[69] More recently the snowman searching for a scarf and hat for his snow-lady friend (2012) and Monty the Penguin's surprise present (2014) similarly tugged at middle-class heartstrings. Delia Smith and Heston Blumenthal - two very different types of celebrity chef - have also helped promote both ingredients and ready meals, further widening the brand's appeal.

And so?

Any company can start spending money on corporate social responsibility (CSR) ventures; all the main supermarkets do and many publicly announce a specific percentage of profits for the purpose. What appears to make the JLP different is the coherence and integration of a number of features, including:

- Structure, systems and culture (the Partnership, its consultative councils).
- Segmentation and positioning (its market is clearly identified as middle-class educated professionals in metropolitan and suburban areas).
- Product strategy and upstream relationships (high quality, locally sourced, Fairtrade).
- Customer service (universally appreciated in surveys and delivered by people who have every reason to care about the difference between adequate and very good).
- Specific CSR initiatives (the Waitrose and John Lewis Foundations, the 'model' estate farm at Leckford in Hampshire).
- Marketing communications (innovative, engaging, memorable, perfectly targeted and understated).

Twenty years ago, the JLP and Waitrose were admirable but not very exciting. Today, the brand is cool, with a seemingly effortless stylishness that makes some of the others look flatfooted, loud and desperate. It has formed a strong bond with a very profitable niche market of customers who love being treated that way. And it only works because the offering as a whole fits together and is utterly credible.

Tasks

1 Using the Litterer model summarised in Table 11.1 as the basis for analysis, identify the degree to which the John Lewis Partnership and Waitrose reflect mechanistic and organic structures of organisation.

2 Critically review the governing structure of the John Lewis Partnership. What are the strengths and weaknesses of such a structure in a fast-moving competitive environment?

3 Discuss and evaluate the possible impact of this democratic style of organisation on the role and behaviour of managers. How is it likely to differ from the role and behaviour of managers in a more traditional, shareholder-owned company?

4 The John Lewis Partnership is a UK-based organisation with a global supply chain. What cultural challenges might it face in attempting to ensure that its values are upheld by overseas suppliers? How might its structure influence its effectiveness in dealing with producers in, for instance, Africa and Asia?

Notes and references

1. Adapted from Knight, K. (ed.) *Matrix Management: A Cross-Functional Approach to Organization,* Gower (1977), pp. 114–15.
2. Drucker, P. F. *The Practice of Management,* Heinemann Professional (1989), p. 223.
3. Child, J. *Organization: Contemporary Principles and Practice,* Blackwell (2005), p. 399.
4. Forte, C. (Lord Forte) *Forte: The Autobiography of Charles Forte,* Sidgwick and Jackson (1986), p. 122.
5. Argyris, C. *Integrating the Individual and the Organization,* Wiley (1964).
6. Lucas, E. 'Work: Unlimited', *Professional Manager,* vol. 19, no. 4, 2010, pp. 22–55.
7. Parsons, T. 'Some Ingredients of a General Theory of Formal Organization', in Litterer, J. A. *Organizations: Structure and Behaviour,* third edition, Wiley (1980).
8. Rawson, M. 'Whose Side Are You On?', *Professional Manager,* November 1997, p. 3.
9. Woodward, J. *Industrial Organization: Theory and Practice,* second edition, Oxford University Press (1980).
10. See, for example, Mullins, L. J. and Dossor, P. *Hospitality Management and Organisational Behaviour,* fifth edition, Pearson Education (2013).
11. Woodward, J. *Industrial Organization: Theory and Practice,* second edition, Oxford University Press (1980), p. 113.
12. Drucker, P. F. *Management Challenges for the 21st Century,* Butterworth–Heinemann (1999), p. 11.
13. Cloke, K. and Goldsmith, J. *The End of Management and the Rise of Organizational Democracy,* Jossey-Bass (2002).
14. Gratton, L. *The Democratic Enterprise,* Financial Times Prentice Hall (2004), pp. xii–xiv.
15. Child, J. *Organization: Contemporary Principles and Practice,* Blackwell (2005), p. 76.
16. Graicunas, V. A. 'Relationship in Organization', in *Papers on the Science of Administration,* University of Columbia (1937).
17. Learner, P. M. 'Beware the Gatekeeper', *Amtrak Express,* July/August 1994, pp. 14–17.
18. Keohane, K. 'Get your brand and talent right', *Training Journal,* 1 May 2014, p. 29.
19. Adapted from Kolondy, H. F. 'Managing in a Matrix', *Business Horizons,* March/April 1981, pp. 17–24.
20. Senior, B. and Swailes, S. *Organizational Change,* fourth edition, Financial Times Prentice Hall (2010), p. 84.
21. Ashkenas, R., Ulrich, D., Jick, T. and Kerr, S. *The Boundaryless Organization: Breaking the Chains of Organizational Structure,* second edition, Jossey-Bass (2002).
22. Francesco, A. M. and Gold, B. A. *International Organizational Behavior,* second edition, Pearson Prentice Hall (2005), p. 246.
23. Nicholson, N. 'What's the big idea? Boundaryless organisation', *Management Today,* November 2010, p. 16.
24. Urwick, L. *The Elements of Administration,* second edition, Pitman (1947), pp. 38–9.
25. Child, J. *Organization: Contemporary Principles and Practice,* Blackwell (2005), p. 17.
26. Rosenfeld, R. H. and Wilson, D. C. *Managing Organizations: Text, Readings and Cases,* second edition, McGraw-Hill (1999), p. 255.
27. Townsend, R. *Further Up The Organisation,* Coronet Books (1985), p. 159.
28. Bouchikhi, H. and Kimberly, J. R. 'The Customised Workplace', in Chowdhury, S. (ed.) *Management 21C,* Financial Times Prentice Hall (2000), pp. 207–19.

29. Vecchio, R. P. *Organizational Behavior: Core Concepts,* fourth edition, Dryden Press (2000), p. 338.
30. Lynch, R. *Corporate Strategy,* fourth edition, Financial Times Prentice Hall (2006), p. 582.
31. See, for example, McKinley, W. 'Decreasing Organisational Size: To Untangle or Not to Untangle?', *Academy of Management Review,* January 1992, pp. 112–23; Shapiro, E. 'Power, Not Size Counts', *Management Review,* September 1996.
32. Birkinshaw, J. 'The Structures behind Global Companies', in Pickford, J. (ed.) *Mastering Management 2.0,* Financial Times Prentice Hall (2001), pp. 75–80.
33. Woodward, J. *Industrial Organization: Theory and Practice,* second edition, Oxford University Press (1980).
34. Dawson, S. and Wedderburn, D. 'Introduction' to Woodward, J. *Industrial Organization: Theory and Practice,* second edition, Oxford University Press (1980), p. xiii.
35. Perrow, C. *Organisational Analysis: A Sociological View,* Tavistock (1970).
36. Burns, T. and Stalker, G. M. *The Management of Innovation,* Tavistock (1966).
37. Litterer, J. A. *The Analysis of Organizations,* second edition, Wiley (1973).
38. Lawrence, P. R. and Lorsch, J. W. *Organisation and Environment,* Irwin (1969).
39. Boschken, H. L. 'Strategy and Structure: Reconceiving the Relationship', *Journal of Management,* vol. 16, no. 1, 1990, pp. 135–50.
40. Hunt, J. W. *Managing People at Work: A Manager's Guide to Behaviour in Organizations,* third edition, McGraw-Hill (1992), p. 170.
41. Robey, D. *Designing Organizations,* Irwin (1982), p. 59. See, for example, Fincham, R. and Rhodes, P. S. *The Individual, Work and Organization,* second edition, Weidenfeld & Nicolson (1992).
42. Schneider, S. C. and Barsoux, J. *Managing Across Cultures,* second edition, Financial Times Prentice Hall (2003), p. 101.
43. Watson, T. *Organising and Managing Work,* second edition, Financial Times Prentice Hall (2006), pp. 254–62.
44. Birchall, D. W. 'What Managers Do', in Crainer, S. and Dearlove, D. (eds) *Financial Times Handbook of Management,* second edition, Financial Times Prentice Hall (2001), pp. 110–31.
45. Cloke, K. and Goldsmith, J. *The End of Management and the Rise of Organizational Democracy,* Jossey-Bass (2002), p. 41.
46. Fisher, P. 'Truly Seamless Mobility', *Management Today,* May 2008, pp. 55–8.
47. Czerniawska, F. 'From Bottlenecks to Blackberries: How the Relationship between Organisations and Individuals is Changing', Management Consultancies Association (September 2005).
48. Thomas, A. 'At arm's length', *Chartered Secretary,* June 2010, pp. 28–9.
49. Overell, S. 'The Blurring of Control and Responsibility', ACAS, December 2012.
50. 'Deciding Whether to Outsource', Checklist 079, Chartered Management Institute, September 2014.
51. Hazlehurst, J. 'A New Deal for Public Services', *Management Today,* April 2014, pp. 42–5.
52. 'Flexible Working and Work-Life Balance', ACAS, September 2010.
53. Lucas, E. 'Underlying resistance to flexible working', *Professional Manager,* vol. 19, no. 6, 2010, pp. 26–8.
54. See, for example, Willis, B. 'Out Of Office', *Professional Manager,* Summer 2014, pp. 66–8.
55. 'Characteristic of Home Workers', Office for National Statistics, June 2014, **http://www.ons.gov.uk/ons/search/index.html?newquery=Characteristics+of+home+workers** (accessed 12 October 2014).
56. Sutherland, A. 'Agile but fragile: The changing face of UK homeworking – what works best for whom?', ACAS, July 2014.
57. Dunderdale, P. 'Analysing Effective Organisations', *Professional Manager,* September 1994, pp. 23–4.
58. Gray, J. L. and Starke, F. A. *Organizational Behavior: Concepts and Applications,* fourth edition, Merrill Publishing, an imprint of Macmillan (1988).
59. Heller, R. *In Search of European Excellence,* HarperCollins Business (1997), p. 4.
60. Owen, J. *The Death of Modern Management: How to lead in the new world disorder,* Wiley (2009), p. 175.
61. John Lewis Partnership, 'About Us', **http://www.johnlewispartnership.co.uk/** (accessed 20 February 2015).
62. The Constitution of the John Lewis Partnership, **http://www.johnlewispartnership.co.uk/about/our-constitution.html** (accessed 24 February 2015).
63. John Lewis Partnership Annual Report and Accounts 2014.
64. Ibid.
65. Verdict Retail, **http://www.verdictretail.com/john-lewis-retains-title-of-the-uks-best-retailer/** (accessed 20 February 2015).
66. John Lewis Partnership Annual Report and Accounts 2014.
67. John Lewis Partnership Sustainability Review, 2014.
68. Ibid.
69. BBC News, 22 November 2011, 'Ad breakdown: The John Lewis Christmas ad'. Recordings of all the John Lewis Christmas adverts can be found on the Marketing Magazine website, **http://www.marketingmagazine.co.uk/article/1320008/john-lewis-christmas-ads-2007-2014-humble-roots-national-event** (accessed 24 February 2015).

CHAPTER 15

Organisational culture and change

A central feature of the successful organisation is the diagnosis of its culture, health and performance, and the ability of the organisation to adapt to change. It involves the applications of organisational behaviour and recognition of the social processes of the organisation. The manager needs to understand the nature and importance of organisational culture and climate, and the successful implementation and management of organisational change.

Learning outcomes

After completing this chapter you should have enhanced your ability to:

- detail the nature, types and main features of organisational culture;
- evaluate influences on the development and importance of culture;
- debate the importance and characteristic features of a healthy organisational climate;
- explain the nature and forces of organisational change;
- explore the nature of, and reasons for, resistance to change;
- examine the management of change, and human and social factors of change;
- review relationships between organisation culture and control.

Critical review and reflection

The socialisation of new members into an organisation's culture and climate is no more than a management control system and manipulation of the individual. It is therefore unethical and should be condemned.

How would YOU challenge the validity of this statement? What has been YOUR personal experience of socialisation into YOUR university or organisation?

Adapting to change

In order to thrive in an increasingly competitive, global environment with new technologies, an organisation must pay attention to its continual effectiveness and development. An underlying feature of the successful organisation is the ability to adapt to change. This involves the applications of organisational behaviour and recognition of the social processes of the organisation. No two organisations are the same. Each organisation has its own types of problems and most appropriate remedies. For an organisation to perform well and develop, the process of change must be in harmony with organisational culture. Successful management of change is dependent upon a culture of openness, participation and acceptance of new ideas. Sustained organisational improvement can only be achieved through involvement of people, who are the organisation.

> *'Rapid technological changes create huge opportunities for companies bold enough to seize them.*
>
> *(Attributed to Jeff Bezos, founder and CEO, Amazon)*

Organisational culture

Although most of us will understand in our own minds what is meant by **organisational culture**, it is a general concept with many different meanings and difficult to define or explain precisely. There is also sometimes confusion over the difference between the interpretation of organisational culture and organisational climate (discussed below). Although people may not be aware consciously of culture, it still has a pervasive influence over their behaviour and actions. There is, however, no consensus on its meaning or its applications to the analysis of work organisations. A popular and simple way of defining culture is 'how things are done around here'. For example, *Atkinson* explains organisational culture as reflecting the underlying assumptions about the way work is performed; what is 'acceptable and not acceptable'; and what behaviour and actions are encouraged and discouraged.[1]

A more detailed definition from *Rachael Johnson,* Editor of *Governance & Compliance* magazine, is:

> *In its broadest sense, our understanding of workplace culture is that it embodies the ethos and values of a particular organisation, which are expressed through the way it operates and the practices it undertakes. If the latter are deemed to be wrong, then the former needs to be addressed in order for any issues to be resolved effectively. Anything else would be superficial change and unlikely to have a lasting impact.*[2]

The culture of an organisation is also often likened to the personality of an individual[3] (**see the Assignment at the end of this chapter**).

Relationship between culture and change

The pervasive nature of organisational culture means that if change is to be brought about successfully, this is likely to involve changes to culture. For example, *Stewart* makes the following comment on the relationship between culture and change:

> *In recent years attention has shifted from the effects of the organization of work on people's behaviour to how behaviour is influenced by the organizational culture. What is much more common today is the widespread recognition that organizational change is not just, or even necessarily mainly, about changing the structure but often requires changing the culture too.*[4]

A similar view is held by *Naylor,* who points out that: 'In the holistic system, any change will affect the culture and the culture will affect or constrain the change . . . Cultural change is intimately bound up with the process of organisational change.'[5]

However, although attention is often given to shifting the prevailing activities and atmosphere of an organisation to a brighter future, changing the ethos and culture of an organisation is not easy. In practice, organisations usually appear to alter their underlying ethos only on a gradual basis and the complexity of environmental pressures may itself hinder rapid change. Culture is often deep-rooted, and commitment to the objectives and policies of the organisation, people's cognitive limitations and their uncertainties and fears may mean a reluctance to accept a change in behaviour. Culture is reinforced through the system of rites and rituals, patterns of communication, the informal organisation, expected patterns of behaviour and perceptions of the psychological contract. (**Organisational change is discussed below.**)

A depiction of the way elements of culture can support and/or defend against change is given in Figure 15.1.

Critical review and reflection

It seems generally accepted that any organisational change will affect culture and that one of the main hurdles to effective adaption to change is the culture of the organisation. Culture and change are linked.

To what extent do YOU support this contention? How would YOU explain the interrelationship between organisational culture and change?

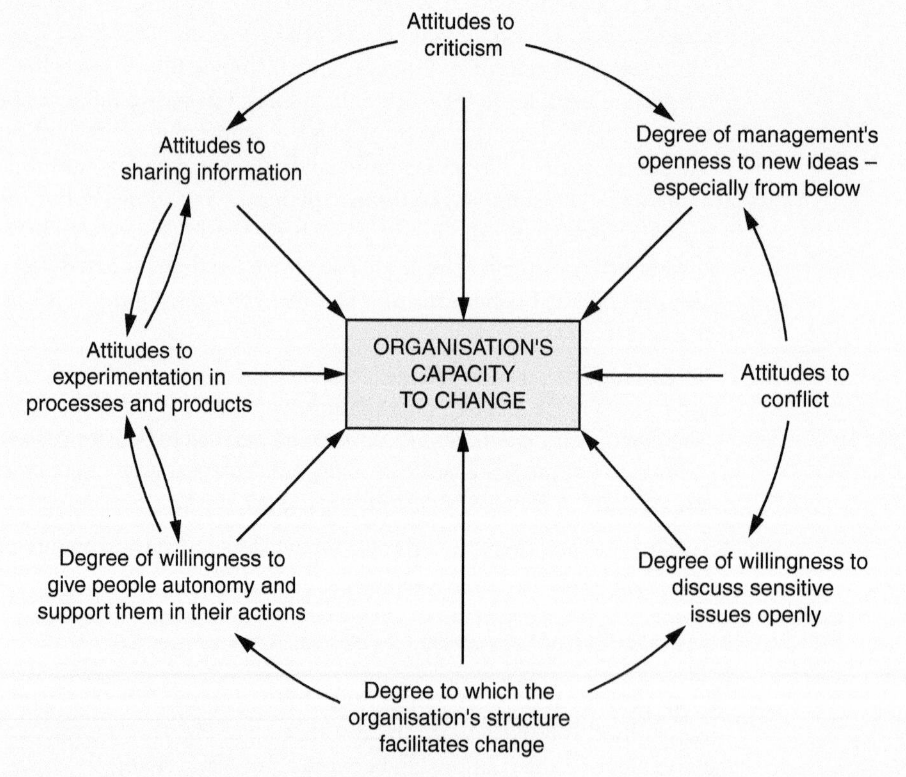

Figure 15.1 Organisational culture and change

Source: Senior, B. and Swailes, S. *Organizational Change*, fourth edition, Financial Times Prentice Hall (2010), p. 161, Pearson Education Ltd

Levels of culture

Schein suggests a view of organisational culture based on distinguishing three levels of culture, from the shallowest to the deepest: artefacts and creations; values; and basic assumptions.[6]

- **Level 1: Artefacts.** The most visible level of the culture is artefacts and creations – the constructed physical and social environment. This includes physical space and layout, the technological output, written and spoken language and the overt behaviour of group members.
- **Level 2: Espoused beliefs and values.** Cultural learning reflects someone's original values. Solutions about how to deal with a new task, issue or problem are based on convictions of reality. If the solution works, the value can transform into a belief. Values and beliefs become part of the conceptual process by which group members justify actions and behaviour.
- **Level 3: Basic underlying assumptions.** When a solution to a problem works repeatedly, it comes to be taken for granted. Basic assumptions are unconsciously held learned responses. They are implicit assumptions that actually guide behaviour and determine how group members perceive, think and feel about things.

Schein suggests that the basic assumptions are treated as the essence – what culture really is – and values and behaviours are treated as observed manifestations of the culture essence. See Figure 15.2.

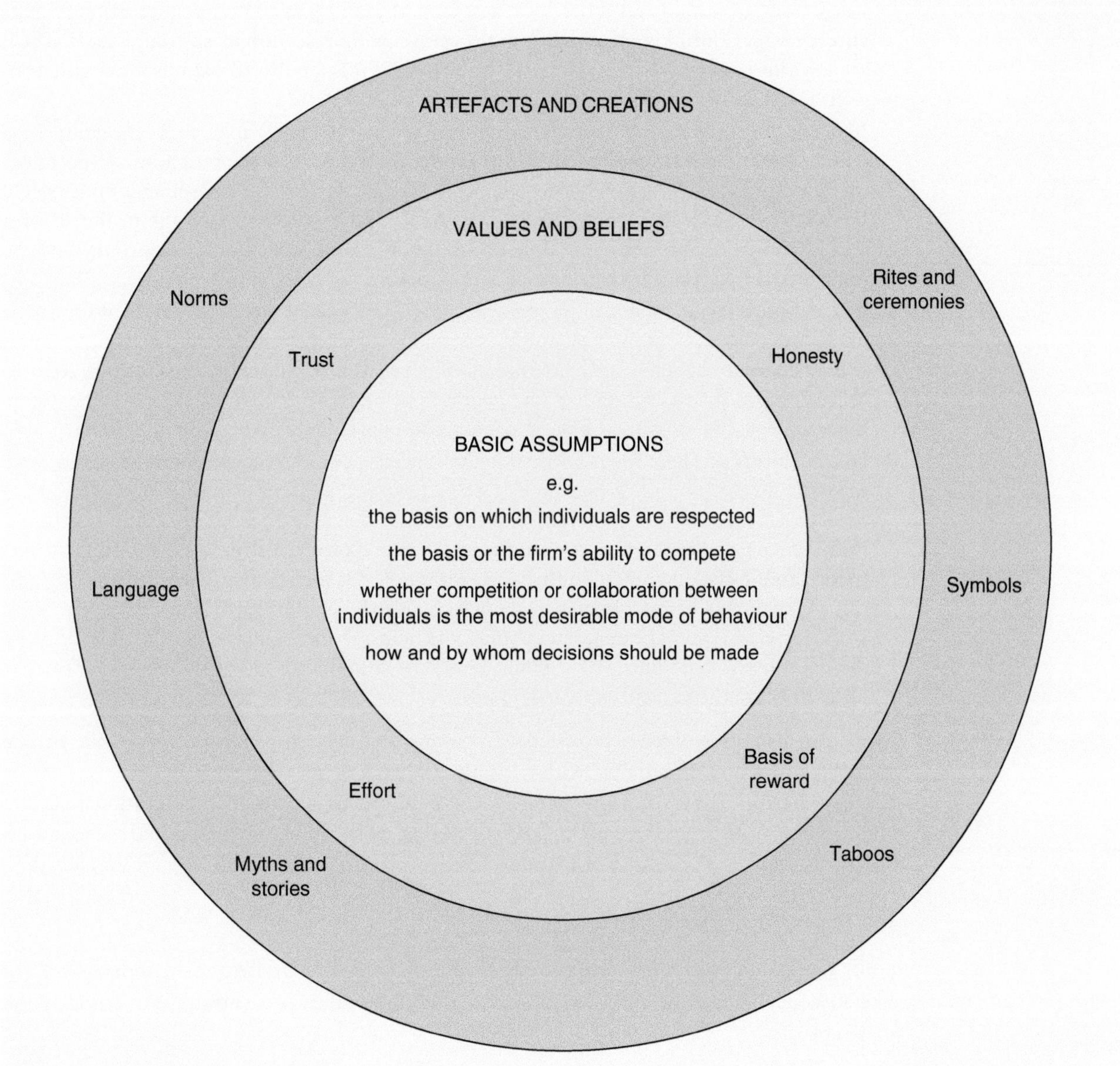

Figure 15.2 Schein's levels of culture

Source: Rollinson, D. *Organisational Behaviour and Analysis: An Integrated Approach*, fourth edition, Financial Times Prentice Hall (2008), p. 592, Pearson Education Ltd

Naylor suggests that seeing quite what forms organisational culture is difficult, and to make a start we need to recognise both the visible and invisible layers. On the surface is the visible layer made up of elements such as artefacts, symbols, languages, stories and activities, which can be collected, compared and assembled into a description of the organisation. Underpinning this 'visible culture' is the invisible layer of beliefs, values, norms, basic assumptions and understanding.[7]

Types of organisational culture

There are a number of ways to classify different types of organisational culture. Two common classifications are those by Handy and by Deal and Kennedy. Developing the ideas of *Harrison*,[8] *Handy* describes four main types of organisational cultures: power culture; role culture; task culture; and person culture.[9]

- **Power culture** depends on a central power source with rays of influence from the central figure throughout the organisation. A power culture is frequently found in small entrepreneurial organisations and relies on trust, empathy and personal communications for its effectiveness. Control is exercised from the centre by the selection of key individuals. There are few rules and procedures, and little bureaucracy. It is a political organisation with decisions taken largely on the balance of influence.
- **Role culture** is often stereotyped as a bureaucracy and works by logic and rationality. Role culture rests on the strength of strong organisational 'pillars' – the functions of specialists in, for example, finance, purchasing and production. The work of, and interaction between, the pillars is controlled by procedures and rules, and co-ordinated by the pediment of a small band of senior managers. Role or job description is often more important than the individual, and position is the main source of power.
- **Task culture** is job orientated or project orientated. In terms of structure, the task culture can be likened to a net, some strands of which are stronger than others, and with much of the power and influence at the interstices. An example is the matrix organisation. Task culture seeks to bring together the right resources and people, and utilises the unifying power of the group. Influence is widely spread and based more on expert power than on position or personal power.
- **Person culture** is where the individual is the central focus and any structure exists to serve the individuals within it. When a group of people decide that it is in their own interests to band together to do their own thing and share office space, equipment or clerical assistance, then the resulting organisation would have a person culture. Examples are groups of barristers, architects, doctors or consultants. Although it is found in only a few organisations, many individuals have a preference for person culture – for example, university professors and specialists. Management hierarchies and control mechanisms are possible only by mutual consent. Individuals have almost complete autonomy and any influence over them is likely to be on the basis of personal power.

Every organisation will have its own unique culture and most large businesses are likely to be something of a mix of cultures, with examples for each of the four types in varying areas of the organisation. Different people enjoy working in different types of organisational culture and they are more likely to be happy and satisfied at work if their attributes and personalities are consistent with the culture of that part of the organisation in which they are employed.

Four generic types of culture

From an examination of hundreds of business organisations and their environments, *Deal and Kennedy* categorise corporate cultures according to two determining factors in the marketplace:

- the degree of risk associated with the organisation's activities; and
- the speed at which organisations and their employees receive feedback on the success of decisions or strategies.

These factors give rise to four generic types of culture: the tough-guy, macho culture; the work-hard/play-hard culture; the bet-your-company culture; and the process culture.[10]

- **Tough-guy, macho culture** – an organisation of individualists who frequently take high risks and receive quick feedback on the right or wrong of their actions. Examples cited include police departments, surgeons, construction, cosmetics, management consulting and the entertainment industry. Financial stakes are high and there is a focus on speed. The intense pressure and frenetic pace often result in early 'burnout'. Internal competition and conflict are normal, stars are temperamental but tolerated. A high staff turnover can create difficulties in building a strong cohesive culture.
- **Work-hard/play-hard culture** – characterised by fun and action where employees take few risks, all with quick feedback. There is a high level of relatively low-risk activity. Examples include sales organisations such as estate agents and computer companies, mass-consumer companies such as McDonald's, office equipment manufacturers and retail stores. Organisations tend to be highly dynamic and the primary value centres on customers and their needs. It is the team that produces the volume, and the culture encourages games, meetings, promotions and conventions to help maintain motivation. However, although a lot gets done, volume can be at the expense of quality.
- **Bet-your-company culture** – where there are large-stake decisions with a high risk but slow feedback so that it may be years before employees know if decisions were successful. Examples include oil companies, investment banks, architectural firms and the military. The focus is on the future and the importance of investing in it. There is a sense of deliberateness throughout the organisation, typified by the ritual of the business meeting. There is a hierarchical system of authority, with decision-making from the top down. The culture leads to high-quality inventions and scientific breakthroughs, but moves only very slowly and is vulnerable to short-term fluctuations.
- **Process culture** – a low-risk, slow-feedback culture where employees find difficulty in measuring what they do. Typical examples include insurance companies, financial services and the civil service. The individual financial stakes are low and employees get very little feedback on their effectiveness. Their memos and reports seem to disappear into a void. Lack of feedback forces employees to focus on how they do something, not what they do. People tend to develop a 'cover your back' mentality. Bureaucracy results, with attention to trivial events, minor detail, formality and technical perfection. Process cultures can be effective when there is a need for order and predictability.

Criticisms of cultural typologies

Some writers are critical of the generic typologies of culture that suggest organisations have a single overriding cultural environment representative of management ideology and all stakeholders. The complex nature of organisations may give rise to many different cultures and overlapping and/or conflicting sub-cultures, including ways in which members of staff distinguish themselves within the organisation.

A notable critic of a unitary approach to a dominate culture imposed by senior management is *Smircich,* who uses the metaphor of a plant root. Culture is something that 'is' and has developed and spread (like plant roots), together with an organisation's history, structure and staff. It is culture that drives organisations and shapes their structure and interactions. Smircich views culture as usually defined hierarchically and is elevated as a critical variable that controls the nature of organisational life, and determines its performance and effectiveness.[11]

Martin contrasts an integrationist perspective of a single unified culture as a basis for organisational effectiveness with a differentiation or pluralistic perspective that views organisational culture in terms of diverse interest groups within their own objectives.[12] *Parker* also suggests that rather than a strong single culture, organisations possess multiple sub-cultures that may overlap or contradict each other. An organisation's culture may also be perceived differently in terms of either the formal or informal structure (**see Chapter 3**).[13]

Critical review and reflection

Attempting to analyse culture in terms of different levels or generic typologies is too simplistic and prescriptive. It serves no useful purpose in evaluating applications of management and organisational behaviour.

What do YOU think? How would YOU analyse the culture of YOUR own university or organisation?

Influences on the development of culture

The culture and structure of an organisation develop over time and in response to a complex set of factors. We can, however, identify a number of key influences that are likely to play an important role in the development of any corporate culture. These include history, primary function and technology, strategy, size, location, management and leadership, and the environment.[14]

- **History.** The reason and manner in which the organisation was originally formed, its age and the philosophy and values of its owners and first senior managers will affect culture. A key event in the organisation's history such as a merger or major reorganisation, or a new generation of top management, may bring about a change in culture. Corporate history can be an effective induction tool to assist a growth programme, and to help integrate acquisitions and new employees by infusion with the organisation's culture and identity.[15] Failure in mergers and acquisitions can arise from cultural clashes and failure to integrate different cultures.[16]
- **Primary function and technology.** The nature of the organisation's 'business' and its primary function have an important influence on its culture. This includes the range and quality of products and services provided, the importance of reputation and the type of customers. The primary function of the organisation will determine the nature of the technological processes and methods of undertaking work, which in turn also affect structure and culture.
- **Strategy.** Although a business organisation may pursue profitability, this is not by itself very clear or a sufficient criterion for its effective management. For example, to what extent is emphasis placed on long-term survival or growth and development? How much attention is given to avoiding risks and uncertainties? Or how much concern is shown for broader social responsibilities? The organisation must give attention to objectives in all key areas of its operations. The combination of objectives and resultant strategies will influence culture, and may itself be influenced by changes in culture. (**See also Chapter 14.**)
- **Size.** Usually larger organisations have more formalised structures and cultures. Increased size is likely to result in separate departments and possibly split-site operations. This may cause difficulties in communication and interdepartmental rivalries, with the need for effective co-ordination. A rapid expansion, or decline, in size and rate of growth, and resultant changes in staffing, will influence structure and culture.
- **Location.** Geographical location and physical characteristics can have a major influence on culture – for example, whether an organisation is located in a quiet rural location or a busy city centre can influence the types of customers and the staff employed. An example could be a hotel or restaurant. Location can also affect the nature of services provided, the sense of 'boundary' and distinctive identity, and opportunities for development.
- **Management and leadership.** Top executives can have considerable influence on the nature of corporate culture. Examples are the key roles played by Sir Richard Branson, Anita Roddick, founder of The Body Shop, and Marjorie Scardino and her change of style when she took over as the new chief executive of Pearson.

Her candour works . . . As an example of straight talking winning over a sceptical City and press, it is brilliant. As an example of just how much a company's culture can change under a new chief executive, it is breathtaking.[17]

Another example is *Louis Gerstner*, who remade the ossified culture of computing giant IBM bred by the company's success, rebuilt the leadership team and gave the workforce a renewed sense of purpose.[18] A further example is Harriet Green, who between 2012 and 2014 completely transformed the financial fortunes of travel operator Thomas Cook. Before her appointment as CEO, Thomas Cook was described by the Financial Times as 'a near-death experience'. Such was the impact of Harriet Green that after her sudden departure £360 million was wiped off the share price of the company.

However, all members of staff help to shape the dominant culture of an organisation, irrespective of what senior management feel it should be. Culture is also determined by the nature of staff employed and the extent to which they accept management philosophy and policies or pay only 'lip service'. Another important influence is the match between corporate culture and employees' perception of the psychological contract (**discussed in Chapter 1**).

- **The environment.** In order to be effective, the organisation must be responsive to external environmental influences. For example, if the organisation operates within a dynamic environment it requires a structure and culture that are sensitive and readily adaptable to change. An organic structure is more likely to respond effectively to new opportunities and challenges, and risks and limitations presented by the external environment. (**Recall the discussion on mechanistic and organic systems in Chapter 11.**)

The cultural web

In order to help describe and understand the culture of an organisation, *Johnson et al.* present a cultural web, which brings together different aspects for the analysis of organisational culture (*see* Figure 15.3).

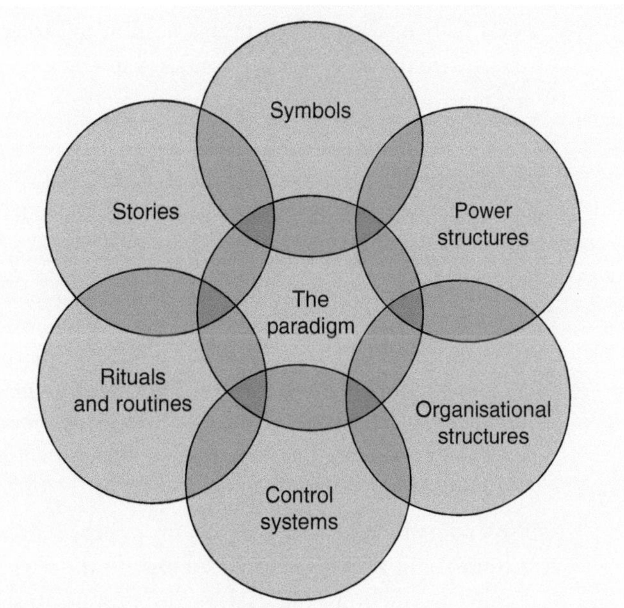

Figure 15.3 The cultural web

Source: Johnson, G., Whittington, R., Scholes, K., Angwin, D. and Regnér, P. *Exploring Strategy*, tenth edition, Pearson Education Ltd (2014), p. 156

- **Routine behaviours** – the ways in which members of the organisation behave towards each other and towards those outside the organisation and that make up how things are done or how things should happen.
- **Rituals** – the particular activities or special events through which the organisation emphasises what is particularly important; can include formal organisational processes and informal processes.
- **Stories** told by members of the organisation that embed the present and flag up important events and personalities, and typically have to do with successes, failures, heroes, villains and mavericks.
- **Symbols** – such as logos, offices, cars, titles, type of language or terminology commonly used, which become a shorthand representation of the nature of the organisation.
- **Power structures** – the power of the most powerful individuals or groups in the organisation, which may be based on management position and seniority, but in some organisations power can be lodged with other levels or functions.
- **Control systems** – the measurement and reward systems that emphasise what it is important to monitor, and to focus attention and activity upon, for example, stewardship of funds or quality of service.
- **Organisational structure** – which reflects power structures and delineates important relationships and activities within the organisation, and involves both formal structure and control and less formal systems.
- **The paradigm** of the organisation, which encapsulates and reinforces the behaviours observed in other elements of the cultural web.[19]

Culture and organisational control

A number of writers have referred to an alternative view of culture as a means of organisational control. For example, *Cartwright* sees culture as a system of management authority. When accepted by employees, cultural values increase the power and authority of management in three ways. Employees:

- identify themselves with their organisation and accept its rules when 'it is the right thing to do';
- internalise the organisation's values when they believe they are right; and
- are motivated to achieve the organisation's objectives.[20]

Egan refers to culture as the largest organisational control system that dictates how crazy or idiosyncratic people can be. Companies and institutions have both an overt and covert culture that influences both business and organisational behaviour.

> *The covert set can be quite dysfunctional and costly. Culture – the assumptions, beliefs, values and norms that drive 'the way we do things here' – is the largest and most controlling of the systems because it affects not only overt organisational behaviour but also the shadow-side behaviour . . . Culture lays down norms for the social system. In one institution you had to be an engineer to rise to the top. There was no published rule, of course, it was just the way things were. In one bank you could never be made an officer of the company if you wore polyester clothes. Culture tells us what kind of politics is allowed and just how members of an organisation are allowed to play the political game.*[21]

Watson refers to the cultural design of an organisation and the link between direct and indirect controls. In a highly centralised organisation with a tight bureaucratic structure and culture, there would be an emphasis on direct controls with prescribed rules and procedures, and a low level of psychological commitment from employees. In a less centralised organisation with a loosely bureaucratic structure and culture, there would be more attention to indirect controls with relatively loose rules and procedures, greater flexibility and discretion, and a culture of high-level commitment.[22]

Critical review and reflection

The idea that culture is a form of management control over the behaviour and identities of individuals is far too nebulous. It all depends on the personality and actions of immediate supervisors and/or senior managers.

What is YOUR considered opinion? To what extent do YOU believe your organisation's culture asserts control over YOUR behaviour?

Two different forms of culture

ACAS distinguishes two different organisational cultures and different ways of doing things:

- control culture with the emphasis on rules and procedures, control and compliance with precedent providing guidelines; and
- quality of working life culture with the emphasis on core values, with mission statements providing guidance and commitment via shared goals, values and traditions.[23]

Kershaw contrasts rules-based or values-based culture.

> *In rules-based cultures, people follow the rules and procedures assuming they are in place for good reasons and will achieve results. Examples of this type of organisation are the emergency services and the military. However, some companies may have a rules-based bias as a result of the regulatory nature of the work they undertake, or even because of a particular management style. In value-driven organisations, there is a 'code of conduct' made up of a number of values that set out expected behaviours. People should understand the values of the organisation so that they know how to behave and perform to achieve objectives. . . Diverse organisations need a mix of 'command and control' and 'culture and values' to be successful.*[24]

The importance of culture

Applications of organisational behaviour and effective management of people are dependent not only upon the nature of the industry or business, but also upon the characteristic features of the individual organisation – and its culture. The pervasive nature of culture in terms of 'how things are done around here' and common values, beliefs and attitudes will therefore have a significant effect on organisational processes such as decision-making, design of structure, group behaviour, work organisation, motivation and job satisfaction, and management control. With increasing globalisation, work organisations are becoming even more complex and internationally based. There is greater emphasis on the understanding and management of a diverse group of people from different nationalities into a coherent culture.

Reigle refers to culture as an important factor in successful technology implementation, innovation, mergers, acquisitions, job satisfaction, organisational success and team effectiveness, and to the importance of determining whether organisations exhibit organic or mechanistic cultures.[25]

Culture and work ethic

Culture can influence people's attitudes and behaviour at work. *Bunting* draws attention to the link between work ethic (**discussed in Chapter 1**) and culture, and the extent to which people have a choice over how hard they work. Although some people have no choice, for the vast majority of people there is a degree of choice but the choices are not made in isolation:

> *they are the product of the particular organisational culture of our workplaces, which promote concepts of success, of team spirit so that we don't let colleagues down, and a powerful work ethic. We are also influenced by a culture that reinforces that work ethic and its cycle of continual achievement and consumption as measures of self-worth.*

Bunting maintains that it is through work that we seek to satisfy our craving for a sense of control, mastery and security, and that clever organisations exploit this cultural context by designing corporate cultures that meet the emotional needs of their employees.[26]

The culture of the organisation is also important in determining the behaviour of managers and how well the organisation works. *Brodbeck* refers to a blame culture that exists in many organisations and where the brickbats fly more often than the bouquets. Such organisations are a very unhealthy environment in which to work. For example, an organisation may see low reports of errors as a healthy sign but in reality this is because individuals are worried about reporting mistakes. Improving the safety culture and a climate of proactive error management will encourage individuals to see the benefits when errors are pinpointed.[27]

The Core Partnership suggests that the kind of culture existing within an organisation can be gauged by the amount of time employees are expected to work past their core hours. This is often considered as an unwritten law. A culture that encourages bottom-sharing of new ideas contributes to employee morale.[28]

The competitive environment and concerns about job security have contributed to a prevailing work culture of 'presenteeism'. In many organisations working long hours is seen as a necessary feature of acceptable behaviour and career progression. Presenteeism does not necessarily imply physical presence at your place of work, but ready availability at most hours, including weekends and evenings, by email and mobile.

National cultural environment (**discussed in Chapter 1**) can have a noticeable effect on presenteeism. As the author experienced for himself in Australia, work-related activities are often undertaken comfortably away from the workplace, in local coffee houses for example, without concern about not being seen by management. This is in contrast to the typical work ethic throughout much of the USA, where again the author experienced the almost obsessive concern for always being seen about the place.

Culture and organisational performance

Culture is clearly an important ingredient of effective organisational performance. *Stanford* suggests that although people have difficulty in explaining why, intuitively they know that 'yes, of course' culture matters. It is an intangible asset that is both distinctive to that organisation and adds value to it (or diminishes value). Ten typical characteristics that form the typical organisation culture are: a story or stories, a purpose, a set of values, an attitude to people, a global mindset, a relationship network, a digital presence, a reputation, a customer proposition and a horizon-scanning ability. Although links between culture and business success are difficult to prove, Stanford maintains that even when there is a strong and healthy culture, a business cannot be successful if there is a flawed business model. However, with a strong and healthy culture there is less likelihood of a flawed business model.[29]

Hilton believes there is a stronger link and that companies succeed because of their culture. Most management systems, such as risk management, neglect the importance of culture and treat business as a mechanical operation when its outcomes depend fundamentally on the way people behave and interact.

> *The key to understanding any business is to understand its culture, yet often it is the most neglected and taken for granted part. Companies succeed because of their culture, they*

decline because of their culture and if there were to be any single reason advanced for the failure of two thirds of mergers and acquisitions, it would probably be the incompatibility in culture of the businesses.[30]

As *Clifton* points out, an organisation's culture, whether officially defined and promoted or just established organically, will determine a whole range of performance indicators. A happy and engaged workforce is widely acknowledged to outperform one where negativity and office politics thrive: 'Business leaders should re-evaluate the importance of culture when embarking on any change management programme focused on performance improvement.'[31]

Critical review and reflection

The extent to which an individual's needs and expectations at work are compatible with the culture of an organisation is probably the most important determinant of motivation and job satisfaction.

Are YOU able to challenge this assertion? How important is the culture of YOUR university to YOUR general state of well-being and to your studies?

National and international culture

With greater global competition, an understanding of national culture has become of increasing importance for managers. *Schneider and Barsoux* suggest that cultural beliefs and values influence the meaning of management and also show up differences in conceptions of organisations. National differences and cultural reasons raise concerns about the transferability of organisational structures, systems and processes, and question the logic of universal 'best practice'.[32] *Cheng et al.* also question the universality of theories of management and organisational behaviour on the grounds that they have not adequately addressed the factor of culture.[33]

According to *Francesco and Gold*, culture has recently been accepted as an explanation of organisational behaviour. One reason is the increase in competitiveness of nations and a second reason is that managers encounter different cultures in their contacts with people from other nations. However, there are limits to the use of culture to explain organisational behaviour, and the relationship between national cultural values and actual behaviour in organisations is complex.[34]

Menzies points out that understanding the culture of doing business in a particular country can give you the upper hand. While the cultural differences in doing business abroad represent one of the biggest barriers to efficient working, these barriers can be easily overcome by taking the time to understand the nuances of business culture, including different legal frameworks and local business culture and language.[35]

The CIPD points out that an increase in travel and technology and the international broadcasting of television channels has led to a blurring of some distinctions of culture. However, there are still clearly definable differences in culture between different countries and ethnic groups.

Although the outward signs of work (dress, technology, etc.) might be increasingly similar regardless of the country of origin, there are many ways in which people can be offended, and business propositions damaged, if there is not an understanding of the culture of the country in which the activities are being conducted.[36]

See the discussion on language as part of culture in Chapter 6, and culture as a contingent factor of leadership in Chapter 9. See also the case study on Brazil below.

A generic model of cultural categorisation

With the wide range of national cultures and regional variations, and a world of rapidly globalising business, *Lewis* draws attention to the importance of cross-cultural training and a generic model of cultural categorisation. His model classifies cultures under three main headings: linear-actives; multi-actives; and reactives (*see* Figure 15.4).

- **Linear-active people** tend to be task-orientated, highly organised planners who complete action chains doing one thing at a time. They prefer straightforward and direct discussion, adhere to logic rather than emotion, have faith in rules and regulations, honour written contracts and are process orientated.
- **Multi-active people** are emotional, loquacious and impulsive, and attach great importance to family, feelings and relationships. They like to do many things at the same time. Relationships and connections are more important than products. They have limited respect for authority, often procrastinate, are flexible and often change their plans.
- **Reactive people** are listeners who rarely initiate action or discussion. They concentrate on what is being said, listen before they leap and show respect. Reactives are introverts and adept at non-verbal communications. Silence is regarded as a meaningful part of discourse. Smalltalk is not easy and lack of eye contact is typical.[37]

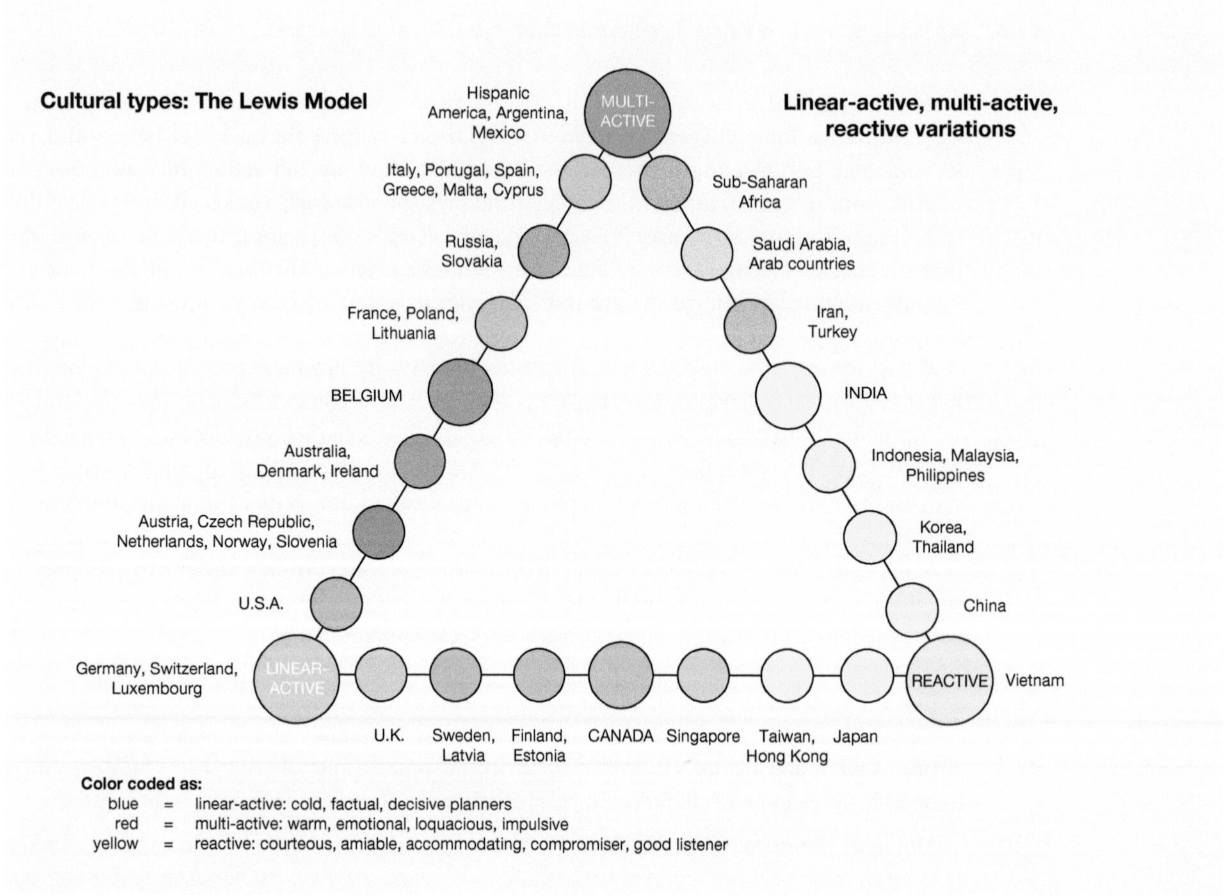

Figure 15.4 Cultural categorisation

Source: from The Cultural Imperative: Global Trends in the 21st Century, Nicholas Brealey (Lewis, R.D. 2007) © 2003 Richard Lewis. Reproduced by permission of Nicholas Brealey Publishing.

Case study
Brazil

Full of colour and rhythm, Brazil has become the new land of opportunity in South America. Currently the seventh largest economy in the world, Brazil is wrought by its diverse culture and geography. Its growing economy is a thriving fusion of Portuguese, African and indigenous Indian influences, all of which have left their mark on Brazilian society. When in Brazil to do business, having an understanding of the diversity of its society and the unique values and attitudes of its citizens will help you to develop better relationships and do business more successfully with your Brazilian colleagues.

Under its motto 'Ordem e Progresso', Brazilian culture is known for its hospitality, openness and traditional events, such as the carnival. The climate of Brazil comprises a wide range of weather conditions across a large area and a varied topography, but most of the country is tropical. It is important to appreciate that the Brazilian football team is a key component of national pride. As such you shouldn't schedule a business meeting during a soccer match and you should always comment about the game when on a conference call.

In Brazil family is at the centre of the social structure. Families in Brazil tend to be large and close-knit, providing members with security and connections. The importance of family is also evident in Brazilian business culture, where family members will often be found working for the same company, whether or not it is family-owned.

Relationships are one of the most important elements of Brazilian business culture. It is essential therefore to spend time getting to know your Brazilian counterparts, both personally and professionally. By cultivating close personal relationships and building trust, you will have a greater chance of successfully doing business in Brazil.

When you meet someone for the first time, it is polite to say 'muito prazer' (my pleasure). Expressions such as 'como vai' and 'tudo bem' are common forms of saying hello once you know someone and can demonstrate that you are making an effort to develop a relationship with a person. The use of titles and first names varies across Brazilian society. It is polite to address your Brazilian counterpart with their title and surname at the first meeting or when writing to them. Once you know them, it is common to use just first names, or else their title followed by their first name.

Advancing your company's relationship with a Brazilian company may rest upon your ability to gain trust. So, on your next meeting, remember to make eye contact, as this shows you are paying attention and are interested and honest. Make sure to accept any food or coffee that is offered to you, saying no can be seen as insulting. Do not show feelings of frustration or impatience as this will reflect poorly on you as an individual. Brazilians pride themselves on their ability to be in control, so acting in a similar fashion will improve your relationship with your Brazilian counterparts.

You should bear in mind that Brazilian companies tend to have vertical hierarchies, where managers at the top make most of the decisions. These positions tend to be dominated by men, but women are slowly gaining employment in executive roles.

Time in Brazil is approached in a flexible manner; punctuality and defined plans are not common. This carries over into business, which can result in negotiations taking much longer than scheduled. Meetings are also often delayed or cancelled without any prior warning.

Finally, Fique tranquilo, if Brazilians value any single trait, it's optimism and being able to solve problems. If the problem can't be fixed, you should just relax and forget about it. At the first signs of someone becoming stressed, a Brazilian will often say: Fique tranquilo (fee-kee kdang-kwee-loh), which means don't worry; it has a very calming effect.

Paola Fonseca, Manager at TMF Costa Rica

Source: This case was published originally in ICSA Global Outlook, a supplement to the May 2011 issue of *Chartered Secretary* magazine.

Critical review and reflection

The proliferation of definitions and explanations of culture, its anthropological origins and lack of clarity undermine its value to our understanding of organisational behaviour. It is too ambiguous a concept for the effective day-to-day management of the organisation.

Do YOU agree? What role do YOU think culture plays in the management of YOUR own university or work organisation?

Organisational climate

In addition to arrangements for the carrying out of organisational processes, management have a responsibility for creating a climate in which people are motivated to work willingly and effectively. Organisational climate is another general concept and difficult to define precisely. It is more something that is felt. It is often likened to our description of the weather and the way in which the climate of a geographical region results from the combination of environmental forces. Some of these forces are better understood than others. In a similar way that culture was defined simply as 'how things are done around here', climate can be defined as 'how it feels to work around here'.

Both culture and climate relate to the value-system of the organisation and both have an influence on the behaviour of its members. **Organisational climate** can be said to relate to the prevailing atmosphere surrounding the organisation, to the level of morale and to the strength of feelings of belonging, care and goodwill among members. Climate will influence the attitudes that members of the organisation bring to bear on their work performance and personal relationships. The extent to which employees accept the culture of the organisation will have a significant effect on climate. Whereas organisational culture describes what the organisation is about, organisational climate is an indication of the employees' feelings and beliefs of what the organisation is about. According to *Tagiuri and Litwin,* climate is based on the perceptions of members towards the organisation.

> *Organizational climate is a relatively enduring quality of the internal environment of an organization that (a) is experienced by its members, (b) influences their behavior, and (c) can be described in terms of the values of a particular set of characteristics (or attributes) of the organization.*[38]

Characteristics of a healthy organisational climate

Organisational climate is characterised, therefore, by the nature of the people–organisation relationship and the superior–subordinate relationship. These relationships are determined by interactions among goals and objectives, formal structure, the process of management, styles of leadership and the behaviour of people. Although similar types of organisations will share certain common features and norms, each organisation will have its own different and distinctive features. In general terms, however, a healthy organisational climate might be expected to exhibit such characteristic features as set out in Figure 15.5.

A healthy climate will not by itself guarantee improved organisational effectiveness. However, an organisation is most unlikely to attain optimum operational performance unless the climate evokes a spirit of support and co-operation throughout the organisation, and is conducive to motivating members to work willingly and effectively. *Gray* maintains from his research to have found a clear correlation between successful workplace outcomes and a range of climate characteristics and that a climate conducive to successful outcomes also tends to be

The extent to which members of staff believe there is:

- acceptance of the psychological contract between the organisation and its members
- managerial and leadership behaviour appropriate to the particular work situation
- mutual trust, consideration and support among different levels of the organisation
- easy access to senior staff with open channels of communication
- respect for individual differences, diversity, equality and inclusion
- attention to work environment and reduction of alienation or frustration at work
- genuine concern for flexibility and work/life balance
- opportunities for personal development and career progression
- democratic functioning of the organisation and opportunities for participation
- recognition of trade unions or staff representatives
- open discussion of conflict with attempt to avoid confrontation
- a sense of identity within the organisation
- a feeling of being a valued and appreciated member of the organisation

Figure 15.5 Characteristic features of a healthy organisational climate

conducive to individual happiness. The climate of an organisation has a significant impact on the quality and quantity of work that gets done and on the well-being of employees.[39]

Six dimensions of climate

Atkinson and Frechette of Forum Corporation maintain there is a direct correlation between organisational climate and financial results. A healthy climate increases employee motivation, catalysing more effective performance. Research by Forum identifies six dimensions that influence the work environment and employee motivation:

- **Clarity** – people's degree of understanding of the organisation's goals and policies, as well as the requirement of their job.
- **Commitment** – the expression of continuing dedication to a common purpose and to achieving goals.
- **Standards** – the emphasis management place on high-performance standards and the amount of pressure it exerts on teams to improve performance.
- **Responsibility** – the degree to which people feel personally responsible for their work.
- **Recognition** – the feeling that people are recognised and rewarded for doing good work, and that they receive accurate performance feedback.
- **Teamwork** – the feeling of belonging to an organisation characterised by cohesion, mutual support, trust and pride.

A corporate imperative now is to cultivate a positive organisational climate in a negative economic one. Successful leaders take pains to ignite a chain reaction that improves climate, increases motivation and enhances performance. Strong leaders have the motivation and influence skills to develop the workforce in these six measurable dimensions.[40]

Organisational change

Change is an inevitable and constant feature. It is an inescapable part of both social and organisational life and we are all subject to continual change of one form or another. Like it or not, change happens. Change is also a pervasive influence and much of the following discussion provides links with other topics in other chapters. The effects of change can be studied over different time scales, from weeks to hundreds of years, and studied at different levels. Change can be studied in terms of its effects at the individual, group, organisation, society, national or international level. However, because of its pervasive nature, change at any one level is interrelated with changes at other levels, and it is difficult to study one area of change in isolation.

At the individual level there could, for example, be a **personal transformational change** where circumstances have not changed, but because of some emotional or spiritual happening the individual was transformed or changed. This transformation may have some effect on the individual's behaviour and actions at work and relationships with colleagues. But our main focus of attention is on the management of organisational change. Organisational change can be initiated deliberately by managers, it can evolve slowly within a department, it can be imposed by specific changes in policy or procedures, or it can arise through external pressures. Change can affect all aspects of the operation and functioning of the organisation.[41]

Forces of change

An organisation can perform effectively only through interactions with the broader external environment of which it is part. The structure and functioning of the organisation must reflect, therefore, the nature of the environment in which it is operating. Factors that create an increasingly volatile environment include:

- uncertain economic conditions;
- globalisation and fierce world competition;
- the level of government intervention;
- EU influences and social legislation;
- political interests;
- scarcity of natural resources;
- rapid developments in new technologies and the information age.

In order to help ensure its survival and future success the organisation must be readily adaptable to the external demands placed upon it. The organisation must be responsive to change. Other major forces of change include:

- increased demands for quality and high levels of customer service and satisfaction;
- greater flexibility in the structure of work organisations and patterns of management;
- the changing nature and composition of the workforce;
- social and cultural influences such as diversity, equality and inclusion;
- conflict from within the organisation.

According to Dan *Wagner*, change is good:

> *It is the whole dynamic that creates successful companies in the first place, whether you are trying to do something differently or more efficiently, or something that leverages the technology that has become prevalent to do something better.*

And according to Duncan *Tait:*

> *It is always better to lead change than react to it, in my experience, because the later you leave it to react to change, the more severe your actions have to be.*[42]

Economic change in the EU

The European Commission points out that today all economic sectors face the permanent effects of economic change, which may be cyclical, structural or related to globalisation. In the past companies have had to change to adapt to specific events such as new technology or manufacturing process, but now change no longer constitutes a response to a specific crisis. Change has become permanent.

Economic change cannot be managed by preserving old practices but requires the development of common approaches and modern practices, and to generalise a proactive culture of anticipating change. In order to reflect the changed and changing environment, the EU is likely to face a number of challenges including finding the necessary skills to allow the European economy to remain competitive in the global market. The EU makes a range of funds available to Member States in order to support restructuring and works within a body of legislation, including information and consultation of workers on changes likely to affect them.[43]

Critical review and reflection

Continuing organisational change is inevitable. It is nothing new and a simple fact of life. There is no point in dwelling on the subject. It is easier just to accept the need to adapt to change as part of your working life.

To what extent are YOU in agreement? How readily are YOU able to adapt to change?

Planned organisational change

Change also originates within the organisation itself. Much of this change is part of a natural process of ageing – for example: as material resources such as buildings, equipment or machinery deteriorate or lose efficiency; or as human resources get older; or as skills and abilities become outdated. Some of this change can be managed through careful planning – for example, regular repairs and maintenance, choice of introducing new technology or methods of work, effective HR planning to prevent a large number of staff retiring at the same time, and management succession planning – training and staff development. However, the main pressure of change is usually from external forces. The organisation must be properly prepared to face the demands of a changing environment. It must give attention to its future development and success; this includes public-sector organisations and the armed forces.

A concept map of sources of organisational change is presented in Figure 15.6.

Most planned organisational change is triggered by the need to respond to new challenges or opportunities presented by the external environment, or in anticipation of the need to cope with potential future problems, for example uncertain economic conditions, intended government legislation, new product development by a major competitor or further technological advances. Planned change represents an intentional attempt to improve, in some important way, the operational effectiveness of the organisation.

The basic underlying objectives can be seen in general terms as:

- modifying the behavioural patterns of members of the organisation; and
- improving the ability of the organisation to cope with changes in its environment.

Behaviour modification

A programme of planned change and improved performance developed by *Lewin* involves the management of a three-phase process of behaviour modification:

- **unfreezing** – reducing those forces that maintain behaviour in its present form, recognition of the need for change and improvement to occur;
- **movement** – development of new attitudes or behaviour and the implementation of the change;
- **refreezing** – stabilising change at the new level and reinforcement through supporting mechanisms, for example policies, structure or norms.[44]

French et al. list eight specific components of a planned-change effort related to the above process (*see* Figure 15.7).[45]

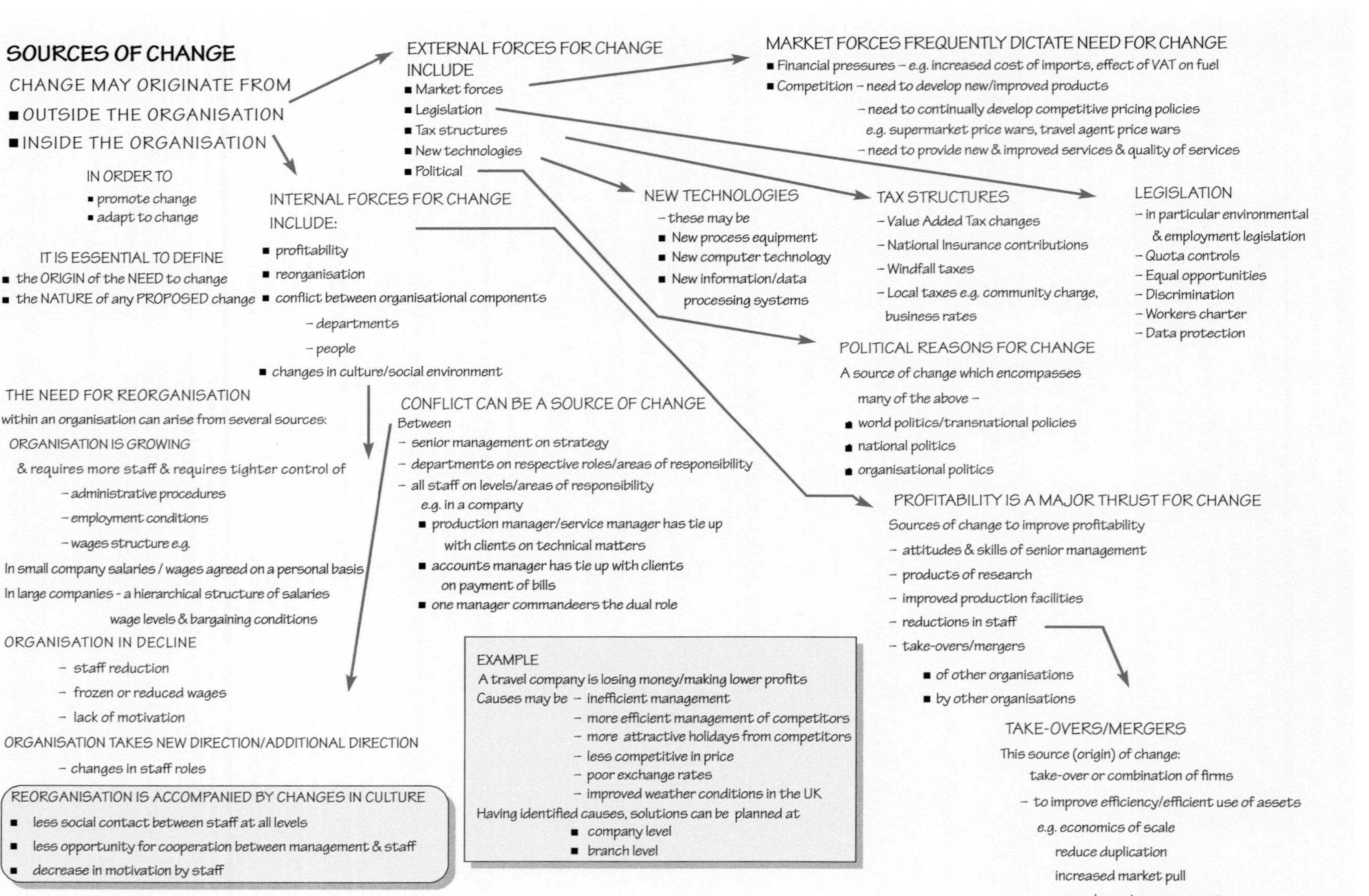

Figure 15.6 Sources of change

Source: Copyright © 2011 The Virtual Learning Materials Workshop. Reproduced with permission.

French, Kast and Rosenzweig refer to eight specific stages of a planned-change effort related to the above process.

- **Unfreezing** relates to the stages of (1) initial problem identification and (2) obtaining data.
- **Movement** relates also to stage (2) obtaining data; and stages (3) problem diagnosis, (4) action planning, (5) implementation, (6) follow-up and stabilisation, and (7) assessment of consequences.
- **Refreezing** relates also to stage (7) assessment of consequences; and (8) learning from the process.

Figure 15.7 Stages in a planned-change effort
Source: based on French, W. L., Kast, F. E. and Rosenzweig, J. E. *Understanding Human Behavior in Organizations*, Harper and Row (1985), p. 9.

Management and organisational behaviour in action case study: MANAGEMENT 2020

HARRIET GREEN
CHIEF EXECUTIVE
THOMAS COOK

Harriet Green told the Commission about her personal 'transformation toolkit', which she has used to overhaul a number of organisations on different continents, including Thomas Cook.

'Driving transformation is a 24/7 job,' she said. 'Organisations are like living organisms and, when looking to transform them, you need to consider all elements, whilst addressing the most urgent priorities.' The critical three elements are:

The psychology: how people think, feel and act – in other words, the organisation's culture, values, ways of working and 'the way we get things done round here'.

The physiology: the systems and processes that underpin and connect the business, like nerve endings and blood flows.

And, finally, *its anatomy*: the organisational structure. Businesses need to create a lean, agile structure as befits a digitally enabled business, supporting fast decision-making, and reducing the layers of management between the CEO and customers.

Harriet believes a CEO must lead change in all three areas to truly transform the organisation. An effective CEO today needs to operate at the centre of the vortex – not from the top of the pyramid in a historical, hierarchical construct – and has to gather information from all the organisation's communities, both internal and external. *'Organisations are like living organisms and, when looking to transform them, you need to consider all elements, whilst addressing the most urgent priorities.'*

Harriet described some of the key 'tools' in her personal leadership toolkit that are helping her to drive the ongoing turnaround at Thomas Cook.

Investigate the problem

On her first day as CEO, Harriet sent a survey to everyone in the business asking what was wrong with it. In under a month, over 8,000 people had replied. Those at the frontline usually know what's not working and have a passion for fixing it.

Be visible

Communicate often, update the organisation regularly, and use different media, like video. Be available and reply quickly. Be visible, share honestly and celebrate success.

Be open

Ensure you are open to feedback from employees. At Thomas Cook, Harriet developed an 'Ask Harriet' email address, so employees could email in confidence on any issue. At its peak, Harriet received 200 emails a day and prides herself on replying to everyone.

→

Identify talent

Leaders need to identify their talented performers quickly. Engage with people across the organisation – meet the key players in every area, know their direct reports, and meet with up and coming talent. Identify quickly those who are not 'on the bus'—make decisions quickly. When transforming an organisation, moving at pace is essential—don't waste time trying to convert those managers and leaders who don't want to change and who make it clear that they will never support the new ways. Give everyone a fair chance to change but then take the tough decisions. Middle-management is often a big part of the problem—and also the solution. By engaging and fostering belief at the top and the bottom of the organisation, those in the middle who might be slower to change begin to feel the squeeze and move forward positively.

Build a winning team

Bringing in fresh talent, different industry experience and a different perspective is vitally important, as is identifying the skills and knowledge gaps early on. At Thomas Cook, Harriet personally recruited close to 80 people, believing that, when transforming the leadership of an organisation, the principle of 'a third, a third and a third' is usually the right balance: keep one-third of the original leadership team, promote one-third from within and bring in one-third to give fresh perspective and learnings from other industries, and then involve and engage them to work together as one aligned team.

Develop the culture

From the very start, focus on the culture. Develop and agree together the values and the ways of working. Create a strong code of conduct and involve the whole organisation. Everyone needs to clearly know what the organisation believes in, how it works and 'how we do things round here'. Together, these will create a culture and build trust. Every employee needs to see themselves and their beliefs reflected in the culture to succeed—like a flamingo looking into a pool. Develop clear leadership competencies to measure the performance of your leaders and enforce the code of conduct fairly and clearly for everyone without exception. Lead with integrity and by example every day. Be a role model.

Break down barriers

Silos and organisational politics have no place in transformations—build new teams, share best practice and encourage openness.

Celebrate success

Remember to take time to celebrate success—it's an important part of rebuilding belief, particularly in an organisation that's been through a tough time. Pride in the company, its performance, its products and its services is important for everyone.

Listen to stakeholders

Never stop listening to your customers. Never be so remote or so arrogant to think you can stop listening to any of your key stakeholders.

Source: 'MANAGEMENT 2020', Commission on The Future of Management and Leadership, Chartered Management Institute, July 2014, p.33, www.managers.org.uk/management2020. Reproduced with permission.

Tasks

1. Explain fully what you understand by transformational change. Give your own views on Harriet Green's 'transformation toolkit'.
2. To what extent do you believe sending a survey to everyone in the business is *ordinarily* likely to produce constructive and meaningful feedback? How well do you think this would work in your own university?
3. What particular problems do you foresee in attempting to 'create a strong code of conduct and involve the whole organisation'?

Transformational change

Organisations may be faced with the need for large-scale **transformational change** involving a fundamental shift in the culture, conduct of business and working practices of the organisation. Transformational change is often enacted over a **period** of time. The CIPD reports on the increasing demand for transformational change programmes as organisations emerge from the recession and once again seek more growth and development-orientated opportunities. Investment in change capability and capacity is essential for organisations wishing to have an ability to effect transformational change.[46] **See the Management and organisational behaviour in action case study.**

The challenge of e-business

Whatever the future of e-business, it will continue to bring tremendous change. One of the biggest changes for managers, especially within large organisations, is learning how to get to grips with an increasingly flexible workforce. As a result of the e-business environment many people can work at any time, anywhere and at any place. Many employees work at home but although the virtual office may help organisations to cut costs, it also poses many management challenges, including the challenge to put structures in place to ensure regular meetings take place. Flexible working calls for flexible managers. This means that the traditional line managers need to become leaders, coaches and facilitators. Given the accelerating rate of change, particularly with the Internet, it is essential that organisations invest in and develop their managers to succeed with this change.

Continuous organisational change and burnout

Rees and Rumbles point out that the pace and scope of change have been unprecedented and they examine the extent to which continuous organisational change leads to organisational burnout. Organisational causes of burnout include excessive workload, lack of autonomy and authority, insufficient reward, and disparity between personal and organisational values. Burnout may also have a 'spillover' effect on people's home lives. Rees and Rumbles question the extent to which organisations 'care' about the amount of stress that occurs during change and whether organisations can assess whether their human capital is close to burnout.

In terms of practical intervention, organisations must firstly have measures of measuring and evaluating organisational stress, and an understanding of the potential for organisational burnout. Organisations also need to determine how to get out of the burnout rut by becoming more resilient to change and engaging employees in a positive and productive manner in order to ensure long-term success. The involvement of managers in both preventing and dealing with the symptoms of burnout is paramount.[47] (**Organisational stress is discussed in Chapter 3.**)

Resistance to change

Despite the potential positive outcomes, change is often resisted at both the individual and the organisational level. Resistance to change – or the thought of the implications of the change – appears to be a common phenomenon. As long ago as 1970, *Toffler* wrote about the psychological dimension of 'future shock', and that people are naturally wary of change: 'Among many there is an uneasy mood – a suspicion that change is out of control.'[48]

Resistance to change can take many forms and it is often difficult to pinpoint the exact reasons. The forces against change in work organisations include: ignoring the needs and expectations of members; when members have insufficient information about the nature of the change; or if they do not perceive the need for change. Fears may be expressed over such matters as employment levels and job security, de-skilling of work, loss of job satisfaction, wage-rate differentials, changes to social structures and working conditions, loss of individual control over work and greater management control.

Change is reciprocal, and changing organisations will affect the nature of managerial work. *Lockhead* maintains that 'most successful organisations develop a culture that welcomes change and the opportunities it brings'.[49] However, according to *Crainer*, many managers refuse to accept the necessity of change. Instead of being proactive, change is often reactive, the last resort.

> *Research repeatedly shows that it is managers who are the chief stumbling block to making change happen. Changing organizational structures and managerial thinking challenges and undercuts traditional power bases . . . For the manager reared on the old functional certainties, the new world organization is very difficult to manage. Indeed, the vast majority of managers are neither trained nor equipped to manage in such an environment.*[50]

The impact of change on work organisations and their management draws attention to the importance of lifelong learning and self-development (**discussed in Chapter 5**).

Individual resistance

Some common reasons for individual resistance to change within organisations include the following:

- **Selective perception.** People's interpretation of stimuli presents a unique picture or image of the 'real' world. This can result in selective perception and lead to a biased view of a particular situation, which fits most comfortably into a person's own perception of reality, and can cause resistance to change. For example, trade unionists may have a stereotyped view of management as untrustworthy and therefore oppose any management change, however well founded the intention might have been. Managers exposed to different theories or ideas may tend to categorise these as either those they already practise and have no need to worry about, or those that are of no practical value and that can be discarded as of no concern to them.
- **Habit.** People tend to respond to situations in an established and accustomed manner. Habits may serve as a means of comfort and security, and as a guide for easy decision-making. Old patterns are seductive. Proposed changes to habits, especially if the habits are well established and require little effort, may well be resisted. However, if there is a clearly perceived advantage, for example a reduction in working hours without loss of pay, there is likely to be less, if any, resistance to the change, although some people may, because of habit, still find it difficult to adjust to the new times.
- **Inconvenience or loss of freedom.** If the change is seen as likely to prove inconvenient, make life more difficult, reduce freedom of action or result in increased control, there will be resistance.
- **Economic implications.** People are likely to resist change that is perceived as reducing either directly or indirectly their pay or other rewards, requiring an increase in work for the same level of pay or acting as a threat to their job security. People tend to have established patterns of working and a vested interest in maintaining the status quo.
- **Security in the past.** There is a tendency for some people to find a sense of security in the past. In times of frustration or difficulty, or when faced with new or unfamiliar ideas or methods, people may reflect on the past. There is a wish to retain old and comfortable ways. For example, in bureaucratic organisations officials often tend to place faith in well-established ('tried and trusted') procedures and cling to these as giving a feeling of security.
- **Fear of the unknown.** Changes that confront people with the unknown tend to cause anxiety or fear. Many major changes in a work organisation present a degree of uncertainty, for example the introduction of new technology or methods of working. A person may resist promotion because of uncertainty over changes in responsibilities or the increased social demands of the higher position.

Critical review and reflection

Some people actively thrive on new challenges and constant change, while others prefer the comfort of the status quo and strongly resist any change. It is all down to the personality of the individual and there is little management can do about resistance to change.

What is YOUR attitude to change? To what extent do YOU welcome and accept, rather than resist, change?

Organisational resistance

Although organisations have to adapt to their environment, they tend to feel comfortable operating within the structure, policies and procedures that have been formulated to deal with a range of present situations. To ensure operational effectiveness, organisations often set up defences against change and prefer to concentrate on the routine things they perform well. Some of the main reasons for organisational resistance against change are as follows:

- **Organisational culture.** Recall that the culture of an organisation develops over time and may not be easy to change. The pervasive nature of culture in terms of 'how things are done around here' also has a significant effect on organisational processes and the behaviour of staff. An outdated culture may result in a lack of flexibility for, or acceptance of, change.
- **Maintaining stability.** Organisations, especially large-scale ones, pay much attention to maintaining stability and predictability. The need for formal structure and the division of work, narrow definitions of assigned duties and responsibilities, established rules, procedures and methods of work, can result in resistance to change. The more mechanistic or bureaucratic the structure, the less likely it is that the organisation will be responsive to change.
- **Investment in resources.** Change often requires large resources that may already be committed to investments in other areas or strategies. Assets such as buildings, technology, equipment and people cannot easily be altered. For example, a manufacturer may not find it easy to change to a socio-technical approach and the use of autonomous work groups because it cannot afford the cost of a new purpose-built plant and specialised equipment.
- **Past contracts or agreements.** Organisations enter into contracts or agreements with other parties, such as the government, other organisations, trade unions, suppliers and customers. These contracts and agreements can limit changes in behaviour – for example, organisations operating under a special licence or permit, or a fixed-price contract to supply goods/services to a government agency. Another example might be an agreement with unions that limits the opportunity to introduce redundancies, or the introduction of new technology or working practices.
- **Threats to power or influence.** Change may be seen as a threat to the power or influence of certain groups within the organisation, such as their control over decisions, resources or information. For example, managers may resist the introduction of worker-directors because they see this as increasing the role and influence of non-managerial staff, and a threat to the power in their own positions. Where a group of people have, over a period of time, established what they perceive as their 'territorial rights', they are likely to resist change.

Perceptions and change

Although change is often resisted, *Cunningham* maintains that one of the greatest myths in management is the generalisation that people resist change. In fact people love change. The commonest reason for resistance is where people perceive a potential loss. For example, because of negative rumour-mongering, people may perceive that they will be worse off from a proposed change even if the opposite is in fact true. In a different context, changes that result, for example, in the loss of one's job can create real, fact-based resistance. While people welcome change that they want, they have to be careful about the pace of change. In a more general context people may be enthusiastic for change, for example in large organisations where some people want to see changes and improvements in communication.

> *What seems to get in the way is the continual chanting of the untrue generalisation that 'people resist change'. People resist some change – if they perceive that they are going to lose out. People welcome change that makes things better.*[51]

Managing change

The successful management of change is clearly essential for continued economic performance and competitiveness and is the life-blood of business success. New ideas and innovations should not be perceived as threats by members of the organisation. Efforts to maintain the balance of the socio-technical system will influence people's attitudes, the behaviour of individuals and groups, and thereby the level of organisational performance and effectiveness.

Many books and articles refer to the steps or actions to be taken to secure successful and sustainable change.[52] The CMI provides a thirteen-point action checklist for the implementation of an effective change programme:

1. Agree the implementation strategy.
2. Agree timeframes.
3. Draw up detailed implementation plans.
4. Set up a team of change champions.
5. Establish good programme management practices.
6. Communicate clearly.
7. Ensure participation and help to minimise stress.
8. Personalise the case for change.
9. Be prepared for conflict and manage it effectively.
10. Motivate your employees.
11. Develop skills.
12. Maintain momentum.
13. Monitor and evaluate.

The checklist aims to provide some generic guidance. It assumes a sound business case for change has been made, and the scope and objectives clearly defined. The detailed schedule for implementing change will vary according to both the type of organisation and the nature and scope of the changes planned.[53]

Toterhi and Recardo report that many business leaders continue to struggle with navigating their organisation through a change initiative. Despite increased awareness of change management processes, principles and practices, challenges from nine common blunders can significantly impede progress in achieving project goals:

Blunder 1. Accepting lucklustre leadership.
Blunder 2. Setting fire to perfectly good platforms.
Blunder 3. Treating change management as a separate workstream.
Blunder 4. Failing to align the organisation to support the change.
Blunder 5. Tolerating weak project management.
Blunder 6. Tolerating soft deadlines and weak metrics.
Blunder 7. Creating a convoluted plot.
Blunder 8. Failure to buy a warranty.
Blunder 9. Letting culture hold you hostage.

Toterhi and Recardo propose a road map of change, methodology, essential tasks and guidelines for change management.[54]

Minimising problems of change

People are the key factor in the successful management of change. If change is to work, it must change the perceptions, attitudes and behaviour of people. The effective management of change must be based on a clear understanding of human behaviour at work. Most people are not detached from their work but experience a range of emotional involvements through their membership of the organisation, and they feel threatened and disoriented by the challenge of change. Emotions such as uncertainty, frustration or fear are common reactions. It is understandable, therefore, that people often adopt a defensive and negative attitude, and demonstrate resistance to change. It is important to remember that change is a complex and powerful psychological experience, and that individuals react internally to change.

According to *Atkinson,* a major problem in driving change in organisations is dealing with and managing the resistance that will be encountered – but that resistance should be welcomed as a healthy response. Resistance is natural and should not be viewed only as a negative response to change. In the absence of really positive benefits from the proposed change, the 'default' response of resistance is acceptable.

> *It is unusual for any change not to attract some resistance. Even with foresight, pre-planning and all the apparent logic behind the need to change, you should expect some resistance as the norm. Recognise and welcome it as a healthy response and an opportunity to openly debate possibilities and treat resistance as a powerful ally in facilitating the learning process.*[55]

Taylor points out that one of the most stressful aspects of change is often the sense of loss of control that accompanies it. The individual can feel powerless and helpless. Many organisations spend a great deal of attention and energy focusing on the operational outcomes of proposed changes but often pay scant attention to enabling employees to adapt psychologically to the new situation.[56] *Reeves and Knell* suggest that 'knowledge leaders understand that change provokes an emotional response, that successful change involves allowing people to feel angry, resentful and afraid as well as excited, hopeful and energised'.[57]

Activities managed on the basis of economic or technical efficiency alone are unlikely to lead to optimum improvement in organisational performance. One of the most important factors in the successful implementation of organisational change is the style of managerial behaviour. Some members may actually prefer, and respond better, to a directed and controlled style of management. (**Recall, for example, the discussion on Theory X and Theory Y styles of managerial behaviour in Chapter 10.**) In most cases, however, the introduction of change is more likely to be effective with a participative style of managerial behaviour. If staff are kept fully informed of proposals, are encouraged to adopt a positive attitude and have personal involvement in the implementation of the change, there is a greater likelihood of their acceptance of the change.

- An important priority is to create an environment of trust and shared commitment, and to involve staff in decisions and actions that affect them. It is important that members of staff understand fully the reasons for change. Organisations should try to avoid change for the sake of change as this can both be disruptive and lead to mistrust. However, considerations of the need to change arising from advances in IT simply cannot be ignored. There should be full and genuine participation of all staff concerned as early as possible, preferably well before the actual introduction of new equipment or systems. Information about proposed change, its implications and potential benefits should be communicated clearly to all interested parties. Staff should be actively encouraged to contribute their own ideas, suggestions and experiences, and to voice openly their worries or concerns.
- Team management, a co-operative spirit among staff and a genuine feeling of shared involvement will help create a greater willingness to accept change. A participative style of managerial behaviour that encourages supportive relationships between managers and subordinates, and group methods of organisation, decision-making and supervision, are more likely to lead to a sustained improvement in work performance. There is an assumption that most people will direct and control themselves more willingly if they share in the setting of their objectives.
- As part of the pre-planning for new technology there should be a carefully designed 'human resource management action programme'. The action programme should be directed to a review of recruitment and selection, natural wastage of staff, potential for training, retraining and the development of new skills, and other strategies to reduce the possible level of redundancies or other harmful effects on staff. There should be full and meaningful consultation with trade unions and staff associations. Where appropriate, arrangements for greater flexibility or a shorter working week, and redeployment of staff, should be developed in full consultation with those concerned.

Critical review and reflection

The biggest difficulty with change is the associated fear and uncertainty. This is a natural reaction for most people. However, a participative style of management with full and open continuous communications throughout the change would noticeably minimise problems.

What is YOUR view? To what extent are YOU fearful and uncertain about organisational change?

Getting people to accept change

Anne Riches, an internationally recognised leader in neuro-scientific research, questions why some organisations struggle to change and applies an interesting approach to resistance to change based on a neuro-scientific understanding. Whether consolidating a merger, reengineering business processes, restructuring, changing value propositions, introducing new IT systems, relocating premises or changing the culture – all too often the process is derailed by the resistance of employees. Resistance to change is one of the most powerful drivers of human behaviour, and the key to dealing with it effectively is to understand both its physical and emotional components. Most organisations make two fatal errors when dealing with resistance. Firstly, they underestimate the strength of current patterns that employees are comfortable and familiar with. Secondly, they underestimate what will be required to change those patterns and deal with the automatic, though sometimes subtle, fight or flight responses that occur when employees interpret changes as threats.

The amygdala and The Almond Effect®

According to Riches, our brains are hard-wired to do three things: match patterns, resist or fight any threats to survival and respond first with emotion over logic. Our neural pathways and amygdalae are the key players in these reactions. The amygdala is an almond-shaped piece of the brain that triggers the 'fight or flight' reaction. Your brain has two amygdalae, and they play a fundamental role in ensuring your survival. Sometimes, though, the amygdalae set off a false alarm. This is what Riches calls The Almond Effect®. Put simply, you act without thinking and get it wrong. You can probably think of many times when this has happened, times when you said or did something in the heat of the moment and almost immediately afterwards regretted it.

At work, The Almond Effect often gets in the way. It is the reason why, all too often, human beings automatically react to change with resistance, even before they fully understand the nature of the change. The amygdala has activated the fear response based on previous memories of change (old neural pathways) associated with, for example, job losses, more work, new skills required, change of roster, cost cutting and so on. Stress hormones are released as part of the inbuilt flight/fight mechanism and show up at work as anger, anxiety, lethargy, poor performance and reluctance to change.

Mechanisms of change

Riches points out that people do not change behaviours easily. This is especially true in workplaces with cultures and histories that are slow and resistant to change. The nature and intensity of our motivation to change will differ in various circumstances but regardless of our reasons for wanting to change behaviours or thought patterns, we will have to create new neural pathways and then use them in preference to the old ones.

When we have to change, and even if we are strongly motivated to do so, we need to stay actively focused on changing our behaviours. If not, you may find yourself in a situation where the old behaviours are triggered automatically and reappear. Many managers seem to overlook this. They become frustrated and impatient with the time it takes for people to adopt change at work. They get tired of answering questions like: 'But what about . . . ?', 'What's wrong with the existing way?' and 'We've tried this before; what makes you think it will work this time?'. Many questions are rationally based, yet many more have an emotional basis.

It is worth remembering that:

- Humans are hard-wired for survival above all else.
- Our default thinking is habitual and self-perpetuating.
- Everyone is the product of their own experiences with different motivations and unique memories.
- Change can be frustratingly slow because it is hard brain work to rewire – even if it is logical and in the best interests.

Managers striving for commitment to change require people to respond to those emotion-based concerns even though they are under time pressures and deadlines. Failure to address the emotionally based questions results in delayed or failed change efforts. These questions are triggered by our amygdalae, which are concerned with anything that does not fit the existing patterns we know are 'safe'. **Successful change leaders know this.**[58]

Responsibilities of top management

The successful management of change is a key factor of organisational performance and effectiveness and should emanate from the top of the organisation. Top management have a responsibility for the underlying philosophy and attitudes of the organisation, for creating and sustaining a healthy climate and for establishing appropriate and supportive organisational processes. The successful implementation of change demands positive action from top management and a style of transformational leadership in order to gain a commitment to change. *Yukl* points out that, contrary to common assumptions, major changes are not always initiated by top management, who may not become involved until the process is well underway. However, large-scale change is unlikely to be successful without the support of top management.[59]

Leading IT change

A report published jointly by the CMI, the British Computer Society and the Change Leadership Network refers to challenges facing senior executives to ensure they are better prepared to lead technological change. Change always involves risk and on the basis of examination of ten detailed organisational case studies the report identifies five key challenges in obtaining best value from IT-enabled change:

- Creating transformational value rather than just implementing IT projects.
- Building capability for ongoing change. Being able to predict future business needs and how IT can help shape new business models and deliver the desired benefits.
- Creating a climate of open communication.
- Managing confidence and trust – understanding the impact of external changes.
- Building personal capability, learning and confidence.[60]

Change leaders

An interesting proposition is put forward by *Drucker,* who contends that 'one cannot manage change. One can only be ahead of it. Everyone now accepts that change is unavoidable.'

> *But in a period of upheavals, such as the one we are living in, change is the norm. To be sure, it is painful and risky, and above all it requires a great deal of very hard work. But unless it is seen as the task of the organization to lead change, the organization – whether business, university, hospital and so on – will not survive. In a period of rapid structural change, the only*

ones who survive are the Change Leaders. It is therefore a central 21st-century challenge for management that its organization becomes a change leader. A change leader sees change as opportunity. A change leader looks for change, knows how to find the right changes and knows how to make them effective both outside the organization and inside it. This requires:

1. *Policies to make the future.*
2. *Systematic methods to look for and to anticipate change.*
3. *The right way to introduce change, both within and outside the organization.*
4. *Policies to balance change and continuity.*[61]

Culture and change

Katzenbach et al. suggest that when a major change runs aground, leaders often blame their company's culture for pushing it off course. Too often culture becomes an excuse and diversion rather than an accelerator and energiser. Leaders see cultural initiatives as a last resort, except for top-down exhortations to change.

Must cultures are too well entrenched to be jettisoned. The secret is to stop fighting your culture – and to work with and within it, until it evolves in the right direction.[62]

Critical review and reflection

An organisation cannot develop, or change. It is the people comprising the organisation who determine the culture of the organisation, and who develop and change. The study of organisational culture and change should therefore concentrate priority on the actions, behaviour and effectiveness of individuals.

What is YOUR considered view? How realistic do YOU believe this contention to be?

Ten key points to remember

1 A central feature of the successful organisation is the diagnosis of its culture, health and performance, and the ability of the organisation to adapt to change.

2 Culture describes what the organisation is all about and helps to explain its underlying values and how things are performed in different organisations.

3 Culture is a general concept, and difficult to explain precisely. There are a number of ways to classify different types of organisational culture.

4 The culture of an organisation develops over time and in response to a complex set of factors. One view of culture is as a means of organisational control.

5 Culture has an important effect on the behaviour and actions of individuals, on the process of management and on organisational performance.

6 Organisational climate is based on the perception of members towards the organisation, and is the state of mutual trust and understanding among its members.

7 Organisations operate within an increasingly volatile environment. Change is a pervasive influence and an inescapable part of social and organisational life.

8 Planned organisational change involves a process of behaviour modification. Change is reciprocal and changing organisations may affect the nature of managerial work.

9 Change is often resisted at both the individual and organisational level. Resistance to change can take many forms and it is not always easy to pinpoint exact reasons.

10 The successful initiation and management of change must be based on a clear understanding of social factors and human behaviour at work.

Review and discussion questions

1 Explain how you would attempt to explain the concept of organisational culture. What factors do you believe influence the development of culture?

2 Discuss critically how you view the relationships between organisational culture and change.

3 To what extent do you believe the culture of an organisation can be likened to the personality of an individual?

4 What value do you place on different typologies of organisational culture?

5 Discuss critically the extent to which the climate within your own university has influenced the enjoyment of, and motivation towards, your course of study.

6 Explain fully how you see the main subject and focus of change.

7 Give specific examples of major change confronting management today and probable implications for your university and/or an organisation of your choice.

8 Explain fully why you think many people appear to exhibit a strong resistance to change. Where possible support your answer with actual examples.

9 Discuss critically your view of The Almond Effect® and a neuro-scientific understanding in overcoming individual resistance to change.

10 Explain fully what you believe are the most important features in the successful implementation and management of organisational change.

Assignment *Understanding your organisation's personality*

An important part of any manager's, salesperson's or front-line staff's role is to be an ambassador for the organisation. This means representing its values, its image and its style in a variety of situations.

In each case, you represent the personality not only of yourself, but of your organisation – and one of the most effective ways to explore the personality of your organisation is by describing it as if it were a person.

Ask yourself the following questions about your organisation:

- What gender would it be?
- How old would it be?
- Where would it live?
- Where would it prefer to holiday?
- What car would it drive?
- What interests or hobbies would it have?
- If it were to win the lottery, what would it do?

Source: Understanding Your Organisation's Image and Style, www.learningmatters.com

Compare and discuss your answers with colleagues. (Feedback may be given by your tutor.)

→

Personal skills and employability exercise

Objectives

Completing this exercise should help you to:

- Work together effectively in a small group.
- Evaluate organisational culture and its application to management and organisational behaviour.
- Undertake a critical review of the socialisation process.

Exercise

The socialisation of new members of staff into the culture of the organisation is an important aspect of management and organisational behaviour.

Working in small groups, you are required to undertake a detailed review of the socialisation of new members into the culture of your own university (or organisation). Comment critically, with supporting examples where possible, on the extent to which the socialisation process successfully addresses such topics as, for example:

- Design and nature of the induction programme
- Introduction to top management and key members of staff
- Expected patterns of behaviour
- Unwritten codes of behaviour, including dress codes
- Attempts to build cohesiveness among close working colleagues
- Mentoring relationships
- Responsibilities for human resource management
- Nature of discipline and grievance procedures
- Social facilities and activities
- Housekeeping arrangements such as canteen and refreshment facilities, car parking
- Opportunities for further studies, training and development, career progression.

Discussion

- How successfully did the socialisation process indoctrinate new members into the ways of the university or organisation and its cultural norms? What changes would you recommend?
- How much did you learn about the informal organisation or how things really work?
- To what extent did the socialisation process help generate an initial feeling of engagement with the university or organisation?

Case study

Changing priorities: ActionAid

The charity ActionAid was created by Albert Cecil Cole, a successful entrepreneur, in 1972. It was one of several philanthropic organisations (including Oxfam) either founded or supported by Cole, and in its first incarnation (as Action in Distress) its aim was to provide direct sponsorship of education; initially eighty-eight UK sponsors committed to the funding for eighty-eight children in India and Kenya. For the first ten years of its history it focused on creating similar long-term programmes of educational sponsorship in other African and Asian countries, but also gradually came to include projects related to health, sanitation and agricultural improvements in its range of activities. The educational sponsorship scheme is still a major part of its work: 60,000 children were sponsored during 2012, and the donors receive annual messages and photographs from their sponsored child together with reports from ActionAid staff on their progress.[63] Nevertheless, the organisation has changed considerably in its approach, structure and focus as the needs of developing countries themselves

Source: Marco Luzzani/Stringer/Getty Images

have changed. Such change is common in business organisations, which have to adapt to the market, but can be controversial and difficult for charities and other non-governmental organisations (NGOs) like ActionAid.

Charity, politics and human rights

The traditional model of organisations such as ActionAid, which attempt to address issues of poverty in developing countries, is a familiar one. It involves appealing to people's sense of altruism as a means of attracting both donors and workers. Money or effort is then directed at a specific problem, be it a major emergency (such as a flood or earthquake) or a more general issue (providing medical services, organising building projects, creating clean water supplies or shipping equipment and materials to where they are needed). The governments of most developed countries have also considered it important to contribute to such problems, and many earmark a percentage of national tax revenue for overseas aid. As a result of this, the governments of poor and developing countries have often found themselves heavily reliant on grants and loans from the developed world when trying to improve living conditions and reduce poverty. However well intentioned, aid does not necessarily lead to lasting change and, at worst, can result in a sort of dependency trap with money grants tied to the use of goods and services provided by the donor country. The traditional model of aid as charity and the responsibility of the developed world, even when it is effective on the ground, can be seen as having some important limitations and drawbacks.

The human rights-based approach (HRBA)[64] to issues of world poverty sees issues such as access to education as part of a wider picture - that of universal human rights. This is based on a very different philosophy from the familiar charity/aid approach. For example, if free basic education is considered as a universal human right by the international community (as it is under Article 26 of the United Nations Universal Declaration of Human Rights)[65] then any government that fails to provide it is technically in breach of international law. NGOs that adopt the HRBA to their work believe that this means they have a responsibility to pressurise governments in the developing world to engage with these failures and to correct them. Furthermore, this pressure has to come from below. The people whose human rights are being breached should both understand that this is the case and be encouraged and enabled to campaign on their own behalf. Therefore the work of aid organisations has to include empowering and facilitating these campaigns, not simply providing materials or services.

From welfare to human rights activism

In its original form, ActionAid, like many charities and NGOs, adopted the 'traditional' model, which focused on providing the education that was seen as fundamental to enabling poor people to improve their situation. Educational programmes were organised and delivered locally, meaning that ActionAid developed a structure and system of governance that is largely decentralised and federalised:

> *We are a federation. That means that every country has an equal share in decisions. The same applies to our work on the ground. ActionAid staff are local people, and we never impose our own solutions on the communities we work with.*[66]

In the late 1990s ActionAid began a significant process of change. Firstly, it relocated its headquarters from London to Johannesburg and since 2003 it has been the only organisation of its kind that is based in a developing country. This move was one manifestation of a major ideological change: the adoption of the HRBA to its work. This new approach resulted from changing perceptions of how poverty could be alleviated on a sustainable basis, and involved a more controversial and overtly political attitude to development work.

In 2010 the organisation published a document that both consolidated its new philosophy and offered practical advice to its workers that would help embed a new way of working in its organisational culture and activities: *Action on Rights: Human Rights Based Approach Resource Book*.[67] This text was aimed at staff and was intended to offer both guidance and inspiration to programme workers. It gave a clear articulation of the new approach and traced its development back to the 1970s, telling three stories to illustrate three phases of change. The stories, about an education programme in Kenya, are summarised in a table that could be easily recognised by ActionAid workers, enabling them to understand the cultural change and to set it in a familiar context. For example, one extract from the table is about ActionAid's changing role:

→

Approach	Features of needs-based (with elements of welfare) approach to development	Features of a participatory-empowerment approach to development	Features of ActionAid's HRBA to development
ActionAid's role	Story 1 Direct implementation of basic services	Story 2 Working in partnership with the community and in some cases with government to meet the basic needs of poor and excluded people	Story 3 Working to empower rights holder organisations, build solidarity between rights holders and allies, and supporting campaigns to hold the state accountable to poor and excluded people

This represented a significant change: where previously the organisation had focussed on providing educational services to 'needy' populations, it was now focussing on helping these populations assert their right to publicly funded education.[68]

The resource book was used as part of a major initiative throughout the organisation to communicate and install the HRBA. This programme included training for key staff who could then run retreats and national training programmes for field staff in each country where ActionAid was operating. This intense communication and development programme was essential to achieving culture change:

Approaching development interventions as an instance of human rights work rather than need-based charitable work is a monumental shift in thinking and requires an overhaul of how staff and partners operate in the field. One could not expect such a transition to proceed easily or automatically.[69]

Longer-term support for the new strategy involved coaching, quality circles and a staff exchange programme. Workers had the opportunity to give feedback, which would, in turn, inform the organisation's strategy for the period 2012–17. The strategy, together with a further and more detailed resource book, was published in 2012.[70] One of the key purposes of these documents was to align the work of a decentralised organisation where power did not emanate from the top:

This resource book is designed to be relevant for all ActionAid staff and partners. It aims to help staff and partners design and implement local, national and international rights programmes that are aligned with our collectively agreed strategy. It aims to be relevant to programme specialists and policy analysts, to campaigners and communications staff, to managers and trustees, to frontline workers and fundraisers, to administrators and activists.[71]

Despite this effort, there is some evidence that grassroots staff were reluctant to abandon a 'service delivery' approach. Perhaps it is a measure of the organisation's growing confidence in the cultural change that has been achieved that ActionAid's International Education Team has felt able to reframe its approach by integrating service provision into the HRBA rather than seeing them as in opposition to each other.[72] Today ActionAid is viewed as one of the most progressive and radical NGOs working in the development sector. As Joanna Kerr, the Chief Executive, explains on the organisation's website:

The work we are doing is truly different because of the way we mobilise communities to defend their own rights.[73]

Tasks

1 Examine the culture change at ActionAid using Senior and Swailes' model (Figure 15.1). Which of the elements supported change, and which hampered it?

2 Using the concept of the cultural web (Figure 15.3), explain how ActionAid's management team used each of the elements to encourage the culture change that was needed when adopting the human rights-based approach (HRBA) to alleviating poverty.

3 What types of resistance to change might be expected in this case, and how could they be overcome? Examine the problem from the point of view of the following major stakeholders:

- Aid workers 'on the ground' in the host countries.
- The communities receiving ActionAid support.
- The governments of the countries where ActionAid is active.
- Sponsors and donors to the charity in the UK and other Western countries.

4 To what extent has ActionAid followed the CMI thirteen-point plan for the effective management of change? Explain your view.

Notes and references

1. Atkinson, P. E. 'Creating Cultural Change', *Management Services,* vol. 34, no. 7, 1990, pp. 6–10.
2. Johnson, R. 'Changing corporate culture', *Governance & Compliance,* June 2013, p. 3.
3. See, for example, Oswick, C., Lowe, S. and Jones, P. 'Organisational Culture as Personality: Lessons from Psychology?', in Oswick, C. and Grant, D. (eds) *Organisation Development: Metaphorical Explorations,* Pitman (1996), pp. 106–20.
4. Stewart, R. *The Reality of Management,* third edition, Butterworth–Heinemann (1999), p. 123.
5. Naylor, J. *Management,* second edition, Financial Times Prentice Hall (2004), p. 79.
6. Schein, E. H. *Organizational Culture and Leadership,* fourth edition, Jossey-Bass (2010).
7. Naylor, J. *Management,* second edition, Financial Times Prentice Hall (2004).
8. Harrison, R. 'Understanding Your Organization's Character', *Harvard Business Review,* vol. 50, May/June 1972, pp. 119–28.
9. Handy, C. B. *Understanding Organizations,* fourth edition, Penguin (1993).
10. Deal, T. E. and Kennedy, A. A. *Corporate Cultures: The Rites and Rituals of Corporate Life*, Penguin (1982).
11. Smircich, L. 'Concepts of culture and organizational analysis', *Administrative Science Quarterly,* vol. 28, no. 3, 1983, pp. 339–58.
12. Martin, J. *Cultures and Organizations: Three Perspectives,* Oxford University Press (1992).
13. See, for example, Parker, M. *Organizational Culture and Identity: Unity and Division at Work*, Sage (2000).
14. See, for example, Handy, C. B. *Understanding Organizations,* fourth edition, Penguin (1993); and McLean, A. and Marshall, J. *Cultures at Work,* Local Government Training Board (1988).
15. Kransdorff, A. 'History – A Powerful Management Tool', *Administrator,* October 1991, p. 23.
16. See, for example, Beckett-Hughes, M. 'How to Integrate Two Cultures', *People Management,* vol. 11, no. 5, 2005, pp. 50–1.
17. Blackhurst, C. 'Up Front at Pearson', *Management Today,* May 1997, pp. 50–7.
18. Gerstner, L. V. Jr Who Says Elephants Can't Dance? Inside IBM's Historic Turnabout, HarperBusiness (2002).
19. Johnson, G. et. al. *Exploring Strategy,* tenth edition, Pearson Education (2014).
20. Cartwright, J. *Cultural Transformation,* Financial Times Prentice Hall (1999), p. 34.
21. Egan, G. 'The Shadow Side', *Management Today,* September 1993, p. 37.
22. Watson, T. J. *Organising and Managing Work,* second edition, FT Prentice Hall (2006).
23. 'Effective Organisations: The People Factor', Advisory Booklet, ACAS, November 2001.
24. Kershaw, P. 'Culture and control', *Governance & Compliance,* July 2014, p. 4.
25. Reigle, R. F. 'Measuring Organic and Mechanistic Cultures', *Engineering Management Journal,* vol. 13, no. 4, 2001, pp. 3–8.
26. Bunting, M. *Willing Slaves,* HarperCollins (2004), p. xxiii.
27. Brodbeck, F. 'The More We Blame, the Less We Gain', *Professional Manager,* vol. 13, no. 6, 2004, p. 37.
28. The Core Partnership, 'A culture of openness and acceptance of new ideas may not be consistent', *Governance & Compliance,* June 2014, p. 35.
29. Stanford, N. *Organisation Culture: Getting it right,* The Economist/Profile Books (2010).
30. Hilton, A. 'Hearts and minds', *Chartered Secretary,* April 2011, p. 14.
31. Clifton, K. 'Values Added', *Manager,* Autumn 2012, p. 14.

32. Schneider, S. C. and Barsoux, J. *Managing Across Cultures,* second edition, Financial Times Prentice Hall (2003).
33. Cheng, T., Sculli, D. and Chan, F. 'Relationship Dominance – Rethinking Management Theories from the Perspective of Methodological Relationalism', *Journal of Managerial Psychology,* vol. 16, no. 2, 2001, pp. 97–105.
34. Francesco, A. M. and Gold, B. A. *International Organizational Behavior,* second edition, Pearson Prentice Hall (2005).
35. Menzies, J. 'Cultural advantage', *Global Outlook, Chartered Secretary,* May 2011, pp. 10–12.
36. 'International Culture Factsheet', CIPD, June 2013.
37. Lewis, R. D. *The Cultural Imperative: Global Trends in the 21st Century*, Nicholas Brealey (2007).
38. Tagiuri, R. and Litwin, G. H. (eds) *Organizational Climate,* Graduate School of Business Administration, Harvard University (1968), p. 27.
39. Gray, R. *A Climate of Success,* Butterworth–Heinemann (2007).
40. Atkinson, T. and Frechette, H. 'Creating a Positive Organizational Climate in a Negative Economic One', *Forum Corporation,* **www.trainingindustry.com/media** (accessed 8 October 2011).
41. For a discussion of change in relation to the complexities of organisational life, see Senior, B. and Swailes, S. *Organizational Change,* fourth edition, Financial Times Prentice Hall (2010).
42. In conversation with Saunders, A. 'How to cope with a changing world', *Management Today,* October 2012, pp. 52–5.
43. 'Adapting to change – The EU approach to restructuring', *Social Agenda: The European Commission's Magazine,* July 2011, pp. 15–20.
44. Lewin, K. *Field Theory in Social Science,* Harper and Row (1951).
45. French, W. L., Kast, F. E. and Rosenzweig, J. E. *Understanding Human Behavior in Organizations,* Harper and Row (1985).
46. 'Leading transformational change', Research report, CIPD, September 2014.
47. Rees, G and Rumbles, S. 'Continuous Organizational Change and Burnout', *International Journal of Knowledge, Culture & Change Management,* vol. 11, 2012, pp. 1–16.
48. Toffler, A. *Future Shock,* Pan (1970), p. 27.
49. Lockhead, Sir M. 'In My Opinion', *Management Today,* September 2008, p. 12.
50. Crainer, S. *Key Management Ideas: Thinkers That Changed the Management World,* third edition, Financial Times Prentice Hall (1998), pp. 144–5.
51. Cunningham, I. 'Influencing People's Attitudes to Change', *Professional Manager,* vol. 14, no. 3, May 2005, p. 37.
52. See, for example, Yukl, G. *Leadership in Organizations,* seventh edition, Pearson Education (2012).
53. 'Implementing an Effective Change Programme', Management Checklist 040, Chartered Management Institute, September 2014.
54. Toterhi, T. and Recardo, R. 'Managing change: Nine common blunders and how to avoid them', *Global Business and Organizational Excellence,* vol. 31, no. 5, 2012, pp. 54–69.
55. Atkinson, P. 'Managing Resistance to Change', *Management Services,* Spring 2005, p. 15.
56. Taylor, G. 'Managing the Situational and Psychological Pressures Brought About by Change', *Professional Manager,* vol. 16, no. 4, 2007, p. 14.
57. Reeves, R. and Knell, J. 'Your Mini MBA', *Management Today,* March 2009, pp. 60–4.
58. Material in this section reproduced with kind permission of Anne Riches, creator of The Almond Effect® and author of 'CLUES: Tips, strategies and examples for change leaders'. For further information see **www.AnneRiches.com**
59. Yukl, G. *Leadership in Organizations,* seventh edition, Pearson Education (2012).
60. Tranfield, D. and Braganza, A. *Business Leadership of Technological Change: Five Key Challenges Facing CEOs,* Chartered Management Institute (2007).
61. Drucker, P. F. *Management Challenges for the 21st Century,* Butterworth–Heinemann (1999), p. 73.
62. Katzenbach, J. R., Steffen, I. and Kronley, C. 'Cultural Change That Sticks', *Harvard Business Review,* vol. 90, July/August 2012, pp. 110–17.
63. ActionAid, **http://www.actionaid.org.uk/40th#campaigns** (accessed 16 March 2015).
64. Sometimes abbreviated to 'rights based approach' or RBA in the literature.
65. United Nations, **http://www.un.org/en/documents/udhr/** (accessed 31 March 2015).
66. ActionAid, '40 Years of Fighting Poverty', **http://www.actionaid.org.uk/40th** (accessed 31 March 2015).
67. ActionAid, 2010, *Action on Rights: Human Rights Based Approach Resource Book,* available for download from **http://www.actionaid.org/sites/files/actionaid/hrba_resourcebook_11nov2010.pdf** (accessed 10 April 2015).
68. Magrath, B. 'Global norms, organisational change: framing the rights-based approach at ActionAid', *Third World Quarterly,* vol. 35, no. 7, 2014, pp. 5–6. doi:10.1080/01436597.2014.926117
69. Ibid., p. 1.
70. ActionAid, 2012, 'People's Action In Practice: ActionAid's Human Rights Based Approach 2.0', **http://www.actionaid.org/sites/files/actionaid/1._peoples_action_in_practice_final_20_07_2012.pdf** (accessed 10 April 2015).
71. Ibid., p. 11.
72. Magrath, op. cit., p. 10.
73. ActionAid, '40 Years of Fighting Poverty', op. cit.

CHAPTER 14
Strategy, corporate responsibility and ethics

The overall direction of an organisation is determined by the nature of its corporate strategy. Strategy links structure, the process of management and applications of organisational behaviour. Organisations play a major and increasingly important role in the lives of us all and have a responsibility to multiple stakeholders. The power and influence of a business organisation must be tempered by decisions relating to its broader social obligations and ethical responsibilities.

Learning outcomes

After completing this chapter you should have enhanced your ability to:

- explain the nature and importance of organisation strategy;
- assess the significance of organisational goals, objectives and policy;
- debate the significance of organisational ideologies, principles and values;
- review the concept and scope of corporate social responsibilities;
- detail approaches to the consideration of organisational values and ethics;
- evaluate the importance of ethics and corporate purpose and business ethics;
- review the nature and impact of codes of conduct or ethics.

Critical review and reflection

The most successful and enduring organisations are also those that give the greatest attention to the well-being of their staff and to their broader social and ethical responsibilities.

To what extent do YOU agree? What examples can YOU quote to support YOUR view? What would YOU say about YOUR university or organisation?

The importance of strategy

Underlying the effective management of people is the requirement for a clear understanding of the nature of the business that the organisation is engaged in and how best to provide customer or consumer satisfaction. We saw earlier (**Chapter 3**) that the context of the organisational setting is central to the application of organisational behaviour and the process of management. It is the interaction of people in order to achieve objectives that forms the basis of the particular organisation. An integral feature of the study of organisational behaviour is an understanding of the nature of corporate strategy for the formal organisation as a whole.

What is strategy?

Definitions of strategy vary. For example *Johnson et al.* view strategy in simple terms as about key issues for the future of organisations and the long-term direction of an organisation.[1] Some writers distinguish different terms and various levels of 'strategy', but **corporate strategy** is seen here as a generic term relating to the underlying purpose of the organisation and embracing links among structure, the process of management and applications of organisational behaviour. For some writers, such as *Andrews*, 'strategic management' is emerging as a more popular term than corporate strategy.

> *Strategic management is the pattern of major objectives, purposes or goals and essential policies or plans for achieving those goals, stated in such a way as to define what business the company is in or is to be in and the kind of company it is or is to be.*[2]

Strategy and structure

There is obviously a close relationship between strategy and organisation structure (**discussed in Chapter 11**). It is by means of the organisation's structure that its goals and objectives are attained. *Lynch* suggests that the nature of this relationship, and whether structure follows strategy or strategy follows structure, is not clear.

> *A major debate has been taking place over the last 30 years regarding the relationship between the strategy and the structure of the organisation. In the past, it was considered that the strategy was decided first and the organisation structure then followed . . . Recent research has questioned this approach and taken the view that strategy and structure are interrelated . . . Although it may not be possible to define which comes first, there is a need to ensure that strategy and structure are consistent with each other.*[3]

Strategy and people

Allen and Helms suggest that different types of reward practices may more closely complement different generic strategies and are significantly related to higher levels of perceived organisational performance.[4] According to *Stern,* it seems acceptable again to acknowledge the human factor in business: 'Niceness is back in vogue, at least for some of the time. People are talking about strategy not just in visionary terms but also in emotional ones.'[5] *Gratton* draws attention to people at the centre of business success and the importance of people-centred strategies.

> *Creating people-centred strategies is one of the means by which the organization balances the needs of the short term with those of the long term, as well as balancing financial capital with human potential. Creative and engaging people strategies have, at their core, an understanding of how the vision and business goals can be delivered through people, and of the specific actions which need to be taken in the short and longer term to bridge from reality to aspirations.*[6]

Strategy and culture

Schneider and Barsoux discuss the close link between culture and strategy and address such questions as: how does national culture affect strategy; how do different approaches to strategy reflect different underlying cultural assumptions; how do managers from different cultures respond to similar business environments; and in what ways does culture affect the content and process of decision-making? Among the examples quoted by Schneider and Barsoux are Japanese companies that challenge the Western view of strategic management and adopt a broader notion of strategy; managers from Nordic and Anglo countries who are less likely to see environments as uncertain; and managers from countries within Latin Europe or Asia who are likely to perceive greater uncertainty when faced with similar environments and perceive less control over what will happen.[7]

Critical review and reflection

Understandably, much attention is given to the importance of corporate strategy but not enough attention is normally given to the human factor or how the strategy impacts on people in the organisation.

To what extent can YOU identify with the strategy of YOUR university and/or organisation and how does it impact on YOUR actions or behaviour?

Organisational goals

The activities of the organisation are directed to the attainment of its goals. A goal is a future expectation, some desired future state, something the organisation is striving to accomplish. Goals are therefore an important feature of work organisations. **Organisational goals** are more specific than the function of an organisation. Goals will determine the nature of its inputs and outputs, the series of activities through which the outputs are achieved and interactions with its external environment. The extent to which an organisation is successful in attaining its goals is a basis for the evaluation of organisational performance and effectiveness.

To be effective, goals should be emphasised, stated clearly and communicated to all members of the organisation. At the individual level, the attainment of goals is the underlying influence on motivation. Movement towards greater delegation and empowerment through the hierarchy means that staff at all levels must be aware of their key tasks and actions, and exactly what is expected of them and their department/section. For example, goal-setting theory (**discussed in Chapter 7**) is widely recognised as a successful means of increasing work motivation and performance.[8]

According to *Reeves,* a few well-chosen aims in goal-setting can sharpen focus and boost productivity, but too many can lead to stress and even disaster. Clear objectives expressed as specific goals should improve performance, but measurement should not be confused with target-setting, and problems occur when there are too many targets and they are closely attached to individual performance.

> *The more freedom an individual has over the way their job is done, the higher the productivity and the bigger the rewards reaped by the firm for which they work. People need to know the objectives of their organisation and how their performance contributes to them. Employee engagement is much more likely to follow from autonomy than from a battery of management-dictated targets.*[9]

Objectives and policy

In addition to performing some function, all organisations have some incentive for their existence and for their operations. The goals of the organisation are translated into objectives and policy. Use of the two terms varies but objectives are seen here as the 'what' and policy as the 'how', 'where' and 'when' – the means that follow the objectives:

- **Objectives** set out more specifically the goals of the organisation, the aims to be achieved and the desired end results.
- **Policy** is developed within the framework of objectives. It provides the basis for decision-making and the course of action to follow in order to achieve objectives.

Choice of objectives is an essential part of corporate strategy and the decision-making process involving future courses of action. Objectives may be just implicit, but formal, explicit definition will assist communications and reduce misunderstandings, and provide more meaningful criteria for evaluating organisational performance. Clearly stated, good objectives can help provide unity of direction and aid employee engagement and commitment. However, objectives should not be stated in such a way that they detract from the recognition of possible new opportunities, potential danger areas, the initiative of staff or the need for innovation or change.

Policy is a guideline for organisational action and the implementation of goals and objectives. Policy is translated into rules, plans and procedures; it relates to all activities of the organisation and all levels of the organisation. Clearly stated, policy can help reinforce main functions of the organisation, make for consistency and reduce dependency on actions of individual managers. Policy clarifies roles and responsibilities of managers and other members of staff and provides guidelines for managerial behaviour. Some policy decisions are directly influenced by external factors – for example, government legislation on equal opportunities and diversity.

Corporate guidelines

Whatever the type of organisation, formulation of objectives and policy is a necessary function in every organisation and an integral part of the process of management. In terms of a systems approach, the objectives of an organisation are related to the input–conversion–output cycle. In order to achieve its objectives and satisfy its goals, the organisation takes inputs from the environment, through a series of activities transforms or converts these inputs into outputs and returns them to the environment as inputs to other systems. The organisation operates within a dynamic setting and success in achieving its goals will be influenced by a multiplicity of interactions with the environment (*see* Figure 14.1).

Together, objectives and policy provide corporate guidelines for the operations and management of the organisation. Clearly defined and agreed objectives are the first stage in the design of organisation structure and help facilitate systems of interaction and communication between different parts of the organisation. A commonly used mnemonic to summarise the characteristics of good objectives is 'SMART':

Specific – clear, detailed and understandable as to what is required
Measurable – to monitor and measure progress towards achievement of the objective
Achievable – challenging but obtainable by a competent person
Realistic – relevant to the goals of the organisation with a focus on outcomes of achievement
Timebound – outcomes to be achieved within an agreed time scale.

But note the observations from *Dryburgh:*

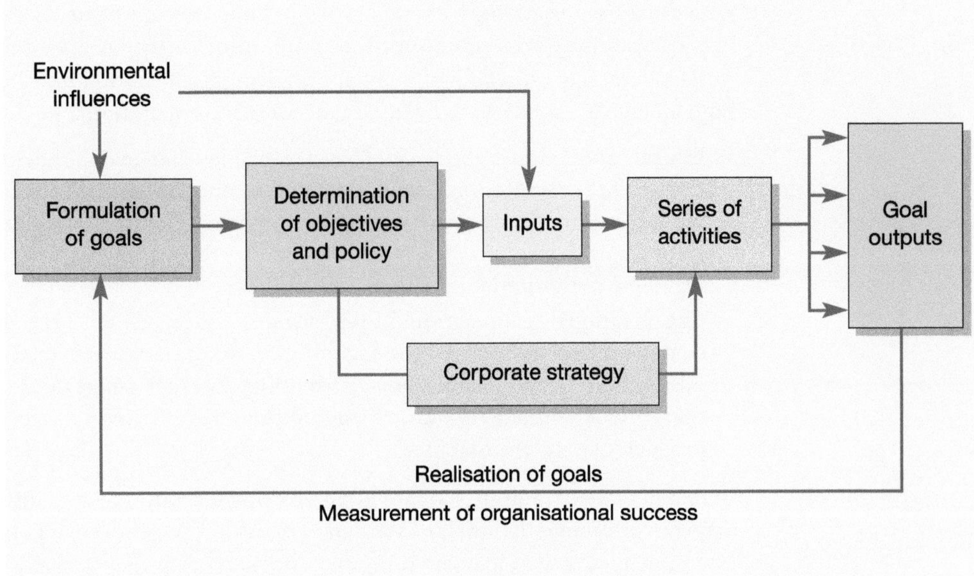

Figure 14.1 A systems view of organisational goals and objectives

Why SMART objectives are really DUMB

Alastair Dryburgh

We have all read about how objectives should be SMART - Specific, Measurable, Achievable, Realistic and Timed. This is well meaning but profoundly limiting. Let's take the points one by one and see where they lead us.

- **Specific.** Why is this a good thing, when it excludes objectives such as 'insanely great technology' (Apple), 'a totally new way of seeing' (Picasso) or 'customer service that gets customers raving about how good it is' (anyone? I wish someone would)?
- **Measurable.** Same problem as specific. Mediocrity is easy to measure, but greatness is harder - you know it when you see it.
- **Achievable and Realistic.** This is where the real problem occurs. I don't know, cannot know, how much I can achieve. If I want to set myself a goal that I know I can achieve, I have to set something that is much less than I could achieve. That's a recipe for mediocrity, at best. The worst thing that can happen with such a goal is that we do meet it, and we stop short of what we could have achieved. Consider instead the value of an impossible goal like 'be the world's greatest X'. It helps and inspires us. It sets a direction. We may never get there, but every day we know what to do to move closer.
- **Timed.** This creates the dangerous illusion that we make changes in order to arrive at a steady state at some defined point in the future. That's not how the world works - it keeps changing, and we need to keep changing with it.

SMART objectives are part of an obsolete management paradigm that assumes that we know what the future will look like (much like the present) and know how we will survive and thrive in that future. If Mother Nature had used SMART objectives instead of natural selection, we would still be no more than slightly improved monkeys.[10]

Organisational ideologies and principles

The goals of the organisation may be pursued in accordance with an underlying ideology, or philosophy, based on beliefs, values and attitudes. This **organisational ideology** determines the 'culture' of the organisation and provides a set of principles that govern the overall conduct of the organisation's operations, codes of behaviour, the management of people and dealings with other organisations.[11] These sets of principles may be recognised and implemented informally as 'accepted conventions' of the organisation or they may be stated formally in writing.

Forty years ago, *Brech* wrote about the ideology of an organisation related to the idea of both an ethical foundation and an organisational or operational foundation:

- **Ethical foundation** embodies the basic principles that govern the external and internal relations of the organisation. External relations concern standards of fair trading and relations with, for example, customers, suppliers and the general public. Internal relations are concerned with fair standards of employment and relations with members of the organisation, including authorised union representatives.
- **Organisational or operational foundation** is concerned with the structure, operation and conduct of the activities of the organisation. External aspects relate to, for example, methods of trading and channels of distribution. Internal aspects include methods of production, use of equipment and managerial practices relating to organisational performance, productivity and profitability.[12]

In recent years organisations have given growing attention to a set of stated corporate values displayed prominently for all to see. *Lucas* questions whether such grand statements of corporate principles really mean anything and concludes that they actually have a point and values can be used with success: 'A set of values is obviously a nice thing for an organisation to have; something to pin on the notice board. But for those organisations that have learned to walk the talk, deeply embedded values can attract the right people, underpin the business in times of crisis and provide direction for the future.'[13]

Cloke and Goldsmith contend that organisations can increase their integrity, coherence and integration, and improve their performance by reaching consensus on shared values. They can bolster value-based relationships by recognising and encouraging behaviours that uphold their values; communicate and publicise their values, and encourage individual and team responsibility for implementing them; and develop methods for monitoring compliance with values, providing feedback and identifying potential conflicts of interest. Most importantly, consensus on shared values means organisations can accomplish these goals without moralising, preaching, excusing or imposing their values on others.[14]

An organisation's 'signature' ideology

Certain aspects of an organisation's philosophy may be so dominant that they become the 'hallmark' of that organisation and place constraints on other areas or forms of activities. For example, the highest-quality hallmark of Rolls-Royce cars would presumably prevent entry into the cheaper mass-production market. With the Walt Disney Company, quality service is embedded deeply within its corporate culture.

Gratton refers to 'signature' processes of highly successful companies that are a direct embodiment of the history and values of the company and its top executive team, and their potential to create the energy to drive high performance. These signature processes, which differ significantly from general views of best practice, are acceptable within the companies in which they develop because of their association with the passion and value of the executive team, and are part of the fabric and ways of behaving.[15]A clear example of the point made by Gratton is Apple, with a signature that has survived the ultimate demise of its founder.

Critical review and reflection

Successful and enduring organisations may well have a clear ideology and idealistic motivation but members of staff are more likely to be committed to the goals and performance of the organisation by job security, high wages and good working conditions.

To what extent do YOU think core ideology and shared values are the hallmark of a successful organisation? Can YOU identify with the idea of a core ideology in YOUR university?

Vision and mission statements

It has become increasingly popular for an organisation to produce a **mission statement** and/or its 'vision' that sets out the purpose and general direction for the organisation. There is sometimes an apparent uncertainty over the distinction between the terms 'mission' and 'vision', which tend to be used interchangeably. It seems to be generally accepted that the vision provides the overall frame of reference of what the organisation would like to reach and how it will look. Within this vision the mission statement defines what the organisation aims to achieve, and its core business and activities.

Value of mission statements

The desire to identify with as many stakeholders as possible means that many mission statements are all-embracing with bland and abstract wording. The value of a mission statement is dependent, however, upon the extent to which it is understood and accepted throughout the organisation, and translated in meaningful terms to all members of staff including those at the operational level. A mission statement is only likely to be of any value if the organisation actually practises what it preaches. The purpose (strategy) and guiding principles of the John Lewis Partnership are set out below.

The John Lewis Partnership - defining principles

- **Purpose** - The Partnership's ultimate purpose is the happiness of all its members, through their worthwhile and satisfying employment in a successful business. Because the Partnership is owned in trust for its members, they share the responsibilities of ownership as well as its rewards of profit, knowledge and power.
- **Power** - Our Partners are able to influence their business at all levels of the Partnership through the democratic structure and the representative bodies which are defined in our **constitution**. Power in the Partnership is shared between three governing authorities: the **Partnership Council**, the **Partnership Board** and the **Chairman**.
- **Profit** - The Partnership aims to make sufficient profit from its trading operations to sustain its commercial vitality and finance its continued development, to enable it to undertake other activities consistent with its ultimate purpose and to distribute a share of those profits each year to its members. Our success relies on the collaboration and contribution of our Partners who receive a share of profits in the form of Partnership Bonus.
- **Knowledge** - We provide our Partners with the knowledge they need to carry out their responsibilities effectively as co-owners of the Partnership.
- **Members** - The Partnership aims to employ people of ability and integrity who are committed to working together and to supporting its Principles. Relationships are based on mutual respect and courtesy, with as much equality between its members as differences of responsibility permit. The Partnership aims to recognise their individual contributions and reward them fairly.
- **Customers** - The Partnership aims to deal honestly with its customers and secure their loyalty and trust by providing outstanding choice, value and service.
- **Business relationships** - The Partnership aims to conduct all its business relationships with integrity and courtesy and to honour scrupulously every business agreement.
- **The community** - The Partnership aims to obey the spirit as well as the letter of the law and to contribute to the wellbeing of the communities where it operates.

The profit objective - not a sufficient criterion

For business organisations, the objective of profit maximisation is undoubtedly of great importance but it is not, by itself, a sufficient criterion for effective management. There are many other considerations and motivations that influence assumptions underlying the economic theory of the firm. The meaning of 'profit maximisation' is not, by itself, very clear. Consideration has to be given to the range and quality of an organisation's products or services, and to environmental influences. Reducing attention to longer-term 'investments', such as quality and after-sales service, research and development, sales promotion, management development and employment conditions of staff, may increase profitability in the short term but is likely to jeopardise future growth and development, and possibly even the ultimate survival of the organisation.

This argument can be clarified to some extent by redefining the business goal as the maximisation of owner (shareholder) value, instead of 'profit'. The concept of value is defined as incorporating the short, medium and long term through the process of discounting (reducing the value of) future cash flows back to a present value. Thus managers seeking to maximise value have good reason to make investments in business activities that will yield profit in the future, even if the costs are immediate and the benefits are some years away.

A business organisation has to provide some commodity or service by which it contributes to the economic and/or social needs of the community. It also has broader social responsibilities to society (discussed later below). Profit can be seen as the incentive for an organisation to carry out its activities effectively. Profit does at least provide some broad measure of effectiveness and highlights the difficulty in evaluating the effectiveness of not-for-profit organisations, such as NHS hospitals, prisons or universities.

Fallacy of the single objective

The reality is that managers are usually faced with the challenge of several, often competing and/or conflicting objectives. *Drucker* has referred to the fallacy of the single objective of a business. The search for the one, right objective is not only unlikely to be productive, but also certain to harm and misdirect the business enterprise.

> *To emphasize only profit, for instance, misdirects managers to the point where they may endanger the survival of the business. To obtain profit today they tend to undermine the future . . . To manage a business is to balance a variety of needs and goals . . . the very nature of business enterprise requires multiple objectives which are needed in every area where performance and results directly and vitally affect the survival and prosperity of the business.*[16]

Drucker goes on to suggest eight key areas in which objectives should be set in terms of performance and results:

1. **Market standing** – for example, share of market standing; range of products and markets; distribution; pricing; customer loyalty and satisfaction.
2. **Innovation** – for example, innovations to reach marketing goals; developments arising from technological advancements; new processes and improvements in major areas of organisational activity.
3. **Productivity** – for example, optimum use of resources; use of techniques such as operational research to help decide alternative courses of action; the ratio of 'contributed value' to total revenue.
4. **Physical and financial resources** – such as plant, machines, offices and replacement of facilities; supply of capital and budgeting; planning for the money needed; provision of supplies.
5. **Profitability** – for example, profitability forecasts and anticipated time scales; capital investment policy; yardsticks for measurement of profitability.
6. **Manager performance and development** – for example, the direction of managers and setting up their jobs; the structure of management; the development of future managers.
7. **Worker performance and attitude** – for example, union relations; the organisation of work; employee relations.
8. **Public responsibility** – for example, demands made upon the organisation, such as by law or public opinion; responsibilities to society and the public interest.

Critical review and reflection

The single, most important objective for the business organisation is profit maximisation, ideally combined with high monetary rewards for members of staff. This is the bottom line and the only realistic criterion by which organisational effectiveness can be judged.

How would YOU attempt to challenge this assertion? How would YOU define the single, most important objective for a non-profit organisation such as YOUR university?

Organisational values and behaviour

Gidoomal maintains that we have taken it for granted that the ethical values and norms of society are there but they need to be spelled out.

> *It's almost a pity to say we need training in ethics. We should be brought up with it through the education system and the values taught at home and church. When you learn ethics and values as a kid you have learnt them for life. We have to be proud of our integrity and blow the whistle when things don't go right.*

Gidoomal also maintains that the ethical business dimension cannot be separated from the diversity issue (**discussed in Chapter 4**) and, while acknowledging that more and more companies now have diversity policies, wonders if they are just lying on a shelf gathering dust.[17]

The Institute of Chartered Secretaries and Administrators draws attention to the importance of creating a culture of integrity and raising awareness of the benefits of ethical behaviour within organisations.

> *Ethical behaviour touches every part of the organisation . . . in terms of a licence to operate such as Health and Safety, to control for example anti-bribery laws, and the most important piece – creating a culture with the expectation that you will do it right.*[18]

Ethical leadership

The importance of ethical behaviour, integrity and trust calls into question the extent to which managers should attempt to change the underlying values and beliefs of individual followers. (**See discussion on transformational leadership in Chapter 10.**) For example, *Yukl* discusses the controversy whereby some writers contend that this type of leader influence is clearly unethical even when intended to benefit followers as well as the organisation. A contrary view is that leaders have an important responsibility to implement major changes when necessary to ensure survival and effectiveness. Large-scale change would not be successful without some changes in member beliefs and perceptions.

> *The traditional perspective is that managers in business organizations are agents who represent the interest of the owners in achieving economic success for the organization. From this perspective, ethical leadership is satisfied by maximizing economic outcomes that benefit owners while not doing anything strictly prohibited by laws and moral standards . . . A very different perspective is that managers should serve multiple stakeholders inside and outside the organization.*[19]

According to a recent report from the Institute of Leadership and Management, despite the high level of public focus on ethics, managers are still placed under increased pressure from facing frequent ethical dilemmas at work. Although the majority of managers say their organisations have a statement of values, it is clear that they are not effective enough at influencing behaviour. Values need to be linked with strategy.

> *Building a set of values that do not link with targets is an ineffective way to influence behaviour. If values are contrary or irrelevant to the business goals, managers find themselves pulled in different directions trying to achieve both. But when values tie into the strategic objectives of an organisation, the way people are expected to behave and the goals they are required to achieve work in tandem.*[20]

The core values of Red Carnation Hotels are set out below.

Red Carnation Hotels - core values

Our core values reflect what is really important and matters to us as a company and group of individuals. They are the solid foundation and main principles of our company culture. By consistently working hard to maintain our values, we endeavour to preserve what makes Red Carnation Hotels so special - a sincere and deep commitment to each other, our guests whom we serve every day and the communities within which we work and live.

To give personalised, warm and consistently exceptional service We appreciate the myriad of choices and alternatives our customers have to choose from, and therefore set the bar high for ourselves, to provide the highest quality services and products we possibly can. We constantly challenge ourselves to update and enhance. Innovation, constant training and refurbishment help create an environment whereby our guests and our employees refer to our properties as their home from home.

To value, respect and support each other We believe that care comes from caring and so provide a level of care for our team members that inspires by example, generates trust, respect, open and honest communication and appreciation.

To create positive, memorable experiences for every guest We work hard to meet or exceed our customers' expectations on every visit or touch point they have with us. By delighting and satisfying our customers, we ensure the longevity of our business and employment for our team. By serving our customers with very personable, proficient, friendly, competent service, and listening to their needs we create memorable and distinctive experiences as well as loyal, returning guests.

To care about and give back to our local communities We recognize and appreciate our responsibility to be active participants in our local communities. We believe in trying to also give of our time to community and service organizations. We believe that it is important to give something back and make a difference. In a world of shrinking natural resources, we must endeavour to conserve, reuse and care about those around us.

All of our hotels make it an ongoing priority to support and contribute positively to a variety of charitable organizations within their respective communities. The charities we support in England include The Starlight Foundation, Great Ormond Street Children's Hospital, Action Against Hunger, the National Autistic Society and the Cystic Fibrosis Trust. In Geneva we have provided help for The Red Cross and in South Africa we support the Nelson Mandela Children's Fund, and our bath amenities are purchased from Charlotte Rhys, a Founding Member of the Proudly South African Organisation, dedicated to the support of disadvantaged women and men in South Africa. Recycling efforts continue to be reviewed and improved upon wherever possible.

Our guests, staff, and suppliers have been wonderfully sympathetic to our aims, assisting us with their wholehearted support, and we would like to send a sincere 'thank you' to every one of them. While we believe our collective contributions do make a difference we are not content to sit back, and constantly challenge ourselves to increase our involvement with the global community. We welcome ideas and input from our customers, staff and suppliers.

Jonathan Raggett
Managing Director, Red Carnation Hotels

Corporate social responsibilities

Organisations play a major and increasingly important role in the lives of us all, especially with the growth of large-scale business and expanding globalisation. The decisions and actions of management in organisations have an increasing impact on individuals, other organisations and the community. Organisations make a contribution to the quality of life and to the well-being of the community. The power and influence that many business organisations now exercise should be tempered, therefore, by an attitude of responsibility by management.

Organisational survival is dependent upon a series of continual interactions and exchanges between the organisation and its environment that give rise to a number of broader responsibilities to society in general. These broader responsibilities, which are both internal and external to the organisation, are usually referred to as **corporate social responsibility** (CSR).

Growing attention to social responsibilities

There has been growing attention given to the subject of CSR and an increasing amount of literature on the subject and on a new work ethic. According to The Chartered Management Institute, CSR is now an important and increasingly specialised aspect of strategy and management. Over recent decades, it has become a necessity rather than a choice, due to:

- legal changes that have made some aspects of CSR compulsory;
- increased public interest in environmental and ethical issues;
- a convincing business case linking CSR to better performance;
- shareholder pressure on businesses to show they operate ethically.

> *CSR is concerned with building integrity and fairness into corporate policies, strategies and decision-making. CSR policies can benefit an organisation by developing and enhancing relationships with customers and suppliers, help to attract and retain a strong workforce, and improve a business's reputation and standing. To be effective, it must be: embedded into everyone's thinking and behaviour, particularly that of leaders; integrated into organisational culture, policies and procedures; and built into organisational operations and activities at all levels.*[21]

Pearce suggests that many companies were involved in CSR simply because it was the right thing to do, but the story now is very different.

> *The pure motives behind and areas of action in regard to corporate social responsibility have been blurred. There are now so many strands, aspects, viewpoints and stakeholders involved in CSR that it can be difficult for companies to get a grip on precisely what it is they are, or should, be doing. This is not something that can be shrugged off, or put on the back burner – those companies that fail to adequately address CSR issues could be putting themselves in the line of fire.*[22]

Critical review and reflection

An NHS Trust chairperson was heavily criticised for maintaining that the primary loyalty of doctors was owed to their employers and that their duty to patients came third, after themselves.

What is YOUR reaction to this point of view? Do YOU believe owing first loyalty to YOUR organisation is such a bad thing?

Management and organisational behaviour in action case study

Corporate social responsibility: Graham McWilliam, BSkyB

CSR is good for brands

It always strikes me as surprising, when talking to my peers at other companies, how many of them talk about the substantial time they have to spend lobbying their colleagues to take CSR seriously.

Maybe one of the problems is the phrase itself - corporate social responsibility - which implies a commitment without a return; something you have to do, but from which you can derive little value. And why, in tough economic times, would companies prioritise something that doesn't help the bottom line? Why indeed.

At Sky, we look at things a little differently. We don't talk about CSR. Instead, we concentrate on long-term value creation, grounded in a focus on what really counts for customers. Looking at things from this angle, it makes perfect commercial sense to act responsibly day to day and to contribute broadly to the communities around you.

After all, like it or not, your brand isn't only created by what you say about yourself. It's built on what others say and think about you, which itself is built on their experience of what you do. For good or bad, that influences customer loyalty, employee engagement, investor sentiment and the regulatory and political climate.

This point is increasingly important in business. All those stakeholder groups now have fast and easy access to a wealth of information and commentary about your company, from news reports to social media conversations. Segmenting your audiences and controlling the message is becoming an impossible task. And, anyway, all the research shows people are more likely to trust what they hear through their informal networks than what they hear directly from you.

Don't just say it, do it

So, focus first on doing, rather than saying, the right things. Set it all in the context of long-term value creation, and you'll find it's no longer an unwanted responsibility to be discharged, but a positive opportunity to build trust, encourage reappraisal and open up new commercial avenues.

At Sky, we're proud of the positive contribution that our business makes to the communities around us, from bringing choice in TV to consumers, to the jobs that have been created for the 16,500 people who work at Sky.

But we want to do more, because we know it's what our customers and employees expect of us, and because we know that it drives positive reappraisal of our brand by those who haven't yet joined Sky.

So we've chosen three areas which we know our customers care about and where we think we can make the biggest difference: using our relationships with 10 million families across the UK and Ireland to inspire action on climate change, encourage participation in sport and open up the arts to more people.

How CSR creates opportunity

Our work in sport, for example, builds on our strong history and credibility in sports broadcasting to get more people active. Within this, our partnership with British Cycling takes a three-pronged approach: support for the GB cycling team, enabling our elite cyclists to be the very best they can be; the creation of Team Sky, the UK's only professional road racing team, to inspire a whole new generation of cyclists to get on their bikes; and Sky Ride, a series of mass summer cycling events across the UK, free to all and free of traffic, which more than 200,000 people took part in last year.

The long-term commercial benefits of such activity are clear to us at Sky, but are equally easy to see at a large and growing number of other successful UK companies. For such brands, CSR isn't about responsibility. It's about opportunity, creating sustainable value over the long term. And, if you want to be around for years to come, that's hard to argue with.

Source: Management Today, May 2011. p. 69. www.managementtoday.co.uk. Reproduced with permission.

Tasks

1. To what extent do you associate CSR as a commitment without a return?
2. Discuss Sky's approach of CSR as central to strategy and long-term value creation.
3. Give your own examples of how CSR can create opportunity and commercial benefits for an organisation.

Organisational stakeholders

Social responsibilities are often viewed in terms of **organisational stakeholders** – that is, those individuals or groups who have an interest in and/or are affected by the goals, operations or activities of the organisation or the behaviour of its members. Stakeholders include a wide variety of potential interests and may be considered under a number of headings. For example, drawing on the work of *Donaldson and Preston,*[23] *Rollinson* suggests a comprehensive view of stakeholders in terms of the potential harm and benefits approach.[24] See Figure 14.2.

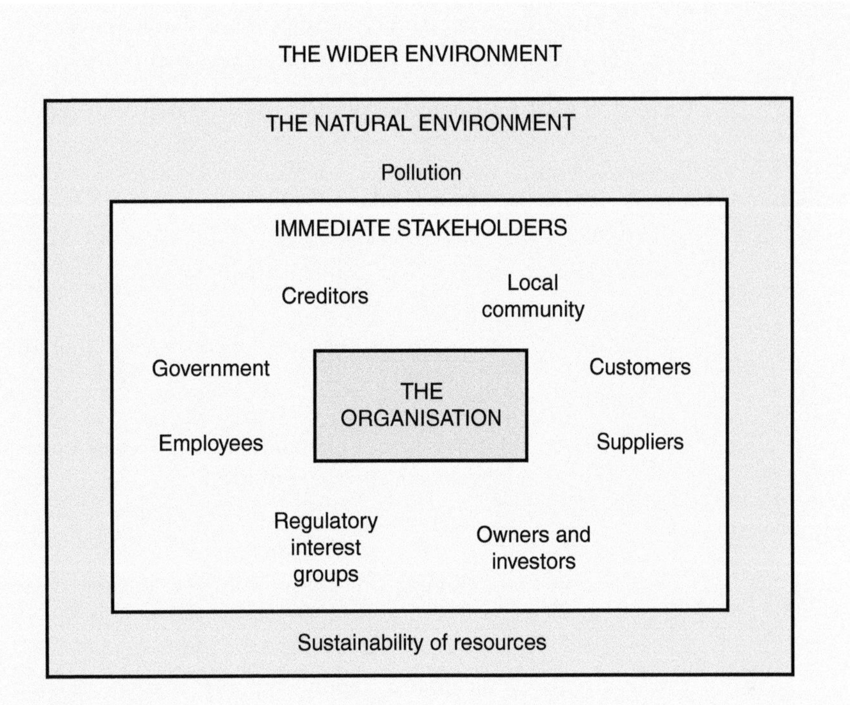

Figure 14.2 Areas of organisational social responsibilities
Source: Rollinson, D. *Organisational Behaviour and Analysis*, fourth edition, Financial Times Prentice Hall (2008), p. 56, Pearson Education Ltd.

A blurred distinction

Arguably, there is still something of blurred distinction between the exercise of a genuine social responsibility, on the one hand, and actions taken in pursuit of good business practice and the search for organisational efficiency on the other. One approach is that attention to social responsibilities arises out of a moral or ethical motivation and the dictates of conscience – that is, out of genuine philanthropic objectives. An alternative approach is that the motivation is through no more than enlightened self-interest and the belief that, in the long term, attention to social responsibilities is simply good business sense. In practice, it is a matter of degree and balance, of combining sound economic management with an appropriate concern for broader responsibilities to society.

The UN Global Compact

The United Nations Global Compact is a call to companies to align strategies and operations with universal principles on human rights, labour, environment and anti-corruption, and to take actions that advance societal goals. The UN Global Compact is a leadership platform for the development, implementation and disclosure of responsible corporate policies and practices. Launched in 2000, it is the world's largest voluntary corporate sustainability initiative, with over 12,000 signatories from business and key stakeholder groups based in 145 countries (**www.unglobalcompact.org**).

The UN Global Compact's ten principles in the areas of human rights, labour, the environment and anti-corruption enjoy universal consensus and are derived from:

- The Universal Declaration of Human Rights
- The International Labour Organization's Declaration on Fundamental Principles and Rights at Work
- The Rio Declaration on Environment and Development
- The United Nations Convention Against Corruption

The UN Global Compact asks companies to embrace, support and enact, within their sphere of influence, a set of core values in the areas of human rights, labour standards, the environment and anti-corruption:

Human rights

- **Principle 1:** Businesses should support and respect the protection of internationally proclaimed human rights; and
- **Principle 2:** make sure that they are not complicit in human rights abuses.

Labour

- **Principle 3:** Businesses should uphold the freedom of association and the effective recognition of the right to collective bargaining;
- **Principle 4:** the elimination of all forms of forced and compulsory labour;
- **Principle 5:** the effective abolition of child labour; and
- **Principle 6:** the elimination of discrimination in respect of employment and occupation.

Environment

- **Principle 7:** Businesses should support a precautionary approach to environmental challenges;
- **Principle 8:** undertake initiatives to promote greater environmental responsibility; and
- **Principle 9:** encourage the development and diffusion of environmentally friendly technologies.

Anti-corruption

- **Principle 10:** Businesses should work against corruption in all its forms, including extortion and bribery.[25]

Critical review and reflection

In George Bernard Shaw's play *Pygmalion* (which later became the basis for the very successful musical *My Fair Lady*), Eliza Doolittle's father complains that he is too poor to afford 'morals'.

In a similar vein, do YOU think that ideas of business ethics and corporate social responsibility can be argued to be mainly of relevance to larger corporations, because only they have the financial and other resources to behave in this way?

Values and ethics

The question of values and ethics in business has been thrown into sharp focus in the years following the financial crisis of 2007–8. Since the dramatic events of autumn 2008 that followed the collapse of prominent US investment bank Lehman Brothers, many of the major economies in the world have faced an extended period of low or negative growth, with rising unemployment and very low levels of business and consumer confidence, all of which made an early resumption of growth less likely. Some economists have published books suggesting that we must learn to accept, or even embrace, a future with much lower economic growth.[26]

Many governments have had to attempt to rein in public spending, with growing levels of resentment and disillusionment in some countries. In a number of parts of Europe, this has been linked with increased support for new political parties with populist agendas, whose manifestos often reflect a sense of unease at the effects of globalisation, together with a view that governments should intervene more, rather than less, to protect the interests of ordinary people. Unsurprisingly, given the origins of the 2008 crisis, bankers – or at least highly paid senior managers in global banks – were the initial focus of public opprobrium, but dissatisfaction with business and with capitalism has spread more broadly.

One consequence has been a growing focus in political discussions on inequality or, more specifically, on the way in which greatly increased rewards for the so-called 'super rich' have led to growing inequality in recent decades. An example of this was the remarkable sales success in 2014 of French economist Thomas Piketty's 700-page volume *Capital in the Twenty-First Century,* which led to lively discussions in the media about the causes and implications of these developments.[27]A similar sense of scepticism about the turn-of-the-century enthusiasm for lightly regulated business was reflected in Harvard philosopher Michael Sandel's 2012 book,[28] which warned of the risks of allowing markets – with their logic of buying and selling – to spread into areas beyond the commercial supply of goods and services.

A further trend in recent years has been the increasingly insistent demands that businesses – and particularly multinational businesses with global operations – should pay 'fair' levels of tax to the countries in which they sell products and services, rather than actively seeking to minimise the amounts due.

Moral compass

Opinions as to exactly *what* went wrong in 2008 varied widely – and still do. For many, the problem was one of inadequate regulation – rules that are insufficiently detailed and/or ineffectively applied. However, commentators across the political spectrum have sometimes also alluded to a lack of moral awareness in business and public affairs – the absence of an intuitive sense of right and wrong (sometimes referred to as a **moral compass**). These two aspects of ethical business will be discussed in greater detail later, but it should already be clear that these questions can be complex. In this section, we outline the influence of ethical considerations in terms of the actions taken by the organisation in pursuit of its strategic objectives, together with the ethical implications of interpersonal interaction, both inside the organisation and between individuals across organisational boundaries.

Ethics and business

Ethics is concerned with the study of morality: practices and activities that are considered to be importantly right or wrong, together with the rules that govern those activities and the values to which those activities relate.[29] It seeks to understand what makes good things good, for example, in ways that can be generalised to other similar cases. Business ethics can be seen as an example of applied ethics – just as medical ethics is about the application of general ethics to the human activity called medicine, business ethics seeks to explore the implications of general ethics for the conduct of business. This apparently obvious point is important: by taking this stance, one rejects the view that moral principles have no bearing on business, or that 'the business of business is business', as the common saying has it.

This is not to say that it is easy, or uncontroversial, to apply ethics to business; on the contrary, this fast-growing subject is characterised by a range of sharply contrasting views. Some of this controversy is inherent in ethics itself – as will be discussed below, there is no single clear view of how to judge good and bad, and this must impact on any application such as business ethics. This particular application of ethics, however, is also complicated by the fact that ethics mainly deals with good or bad conduct on the part of individuals, resulting in possible difficulties in applying these ideas to impersonal corporate entities like companies. Is it appropriate to regard companies as if they were individual people and, if not, what allowances should be made? Or, can the subject be satisfactorily seen as relating to the conduct of individuals as employees of businesses? Clearly, for very small businesses, the two views merge into one, but for larger, corporate entities, the position is more complex.

A discussion of ethics in business organisations has to take account of the purpose of the organisation, as well as its strategy: what it is trying to achieve, usually in competition with other similar businesses. These two factors are important because of their influence on what the organisation chooses to do and thus on the consequences for people inside and outside the organisation. A decision by an airline, for example, to pursue a low-cost strategy will have significant impacts on what is required of its staff and how well that business fares in the market. A successful implementation of such a strategy may mean fast growth, with attractive career development opportunities for some staff, but also more negative consequences for others. On the other hand, the failure of a strategy can lead to the end of the organisation as an independent entity, with more widespread adverse consequences for the organisation's people.

Critical review and reflection

Of course guidelines on values and business ethics are important, but in times of economic recession organisation survival and obligations to the workforce should take precedence. It is understandable if a blind eye is turned to bribery and corruption.

To what extent do YOU believe such a view can ever be justified?

Ethics and CSR

One illustration of the complexity of issues in business ethics is the diversity of opinion on the issue of CSR (discussed above). On one side of the debate are those who would share *Milton Friedman*'s view that the social responsibility of business is to make as much money as possible for the shareholders, within the law and the rules of the game (fair competition, no deception or fraud and so on).[30] This **shareholder-centred view** sees the directors of a company as agents of the owners, who are duty bound to act so as to maximise the interests of those owners, this being taken as the reason for owners having made the investment in the first place.

A more recent development of this general approach is that of *Sternberg* who proposes a teleological view of business ethics, based upon the pursuit of the business purpose – that of maximising long-term owner wealth by selling products and services.[31] Actions by a firm that are consistent with this aim and that satisfy the additional tests of common decency (e.g.

refraining from stealing, cheating, coercion and so on) and distributive justice (i.e. ensuring that rewards are proportional to contributions made) are ethical. Actions that fail any one of these three tests are, in this model, unethical.

At the other end of the spectrum are some forms of **stakeholder theory**, which emphasise a much broader set of social responsibilities for business. *Cannon* suggests that:

> *There exists an implicit or explicit contract between business and the community in which it operates. Business is expected to create wealth; supply markets; generate employment; innovate and produce a sufficient surplus to sustain its activities and improve its competitiveness while contributing to the maintenance of the community in which it operates. Society is expected to provide an environment in which business can develop and prosper, allowing investors to earn returns while ensuring that the stakeholders and their dependants can enjoy the benefits of their involvement without fear of arbitrary or unjust action. The interdependence between society and business cannot be overstated.*[32]

Differing assumptions about a business

The two perspectives provide very different views of how a business should act, because of their differing assumptions concerning what a business is *for*. In the shareholder-centred view, a business is principally for the shareholders and its actions should mainly be judged on the criterion of maximising their interests. In the stakeholder view quoted above, a business is for its stakeholders (who are potentially a very large and diverse group) and its actions should be designed to balance stakeholder interests. From the point of view of business ethics – the study of good and bad conduct in business – this distinction is very important. The use of company resources to support a local community project, for example, might be seen as admirable in the stakeholder view but unethical in the shareholder-centred view, in that it would be a misapplication of funds that belong to the owners (unless, of course, such an investment could be shown to be consistent with the shareholders' best interests).

'Goodness' of proposed action

Each of the two approaches adopts a different yardstick for judging the 'goodness' of a proposed action by a company. In the shareholder-centred view, the action has to be shown to be consistent with the duty of maximising owner wealth, which is conceptually relatively simple, but which necessarily involves assumptions concerning the likely effect of the proposed action (or, more precisely, the difference between taking the proposed action and not taking it). In the stakeholder view (or, at least in those versions of the stakeholder view that emphasise an accountability to stakeholders), the task of management is to balance stakeholder interests. However, managers seeking to do this – often in the face of loud opposing claims from the various interests – will very quickly encounter the practical problem of how that 'balance' should be defined and recognised.

Although difficult to reconcile in practice, the two approaches are not completely incompatible: to a stakeholder theorist, shareholders count as one type of stakeholder, but not the only type to which duties are owed by the firm. Likewise, *Sternberg* acknowledges the importance of understanding and remaining aware of the various stakeholder groups and of actively managing relationships between the company and these groups, because doing so is likely to be consistent with maximising owner wealth. As she points out, however, 'taking account' of something is importantly different from 'being accountable' to it.[33]

Intelligent self-interest

It is also worth emphasising that a company seeking to maximise its owners' long-term wealth may well do very good things for its 'stakeholders', not necessarily through any direct intent but in pursuit of its main duty. Providing customers with excellent products and services is the central example, of course, but this form of intelligent self-interest may also – for example – drive a firm to build strong, trusting relationships with its suppliers and distributors (because it will be better off as a result), or an attractive working environment for its employees (because it wishes to recruit and keep the best, in order to be able to compete more effectively).

Even beyond its immediate commercial relationships, an intelligently self-interested company may deliberately set out to build strong relationships with other stakeholders, or to take a principled stance on an issue such as the use of child labour, because to do so is to maximise owner value. The 'value' in question is not just next year's dividends, but refers to the value of the investment as a whole and thus obliges the management to think long term as well as short term and to consider the impact of company actions as broadly as possible.

Offshoring example

By way of an illustration of the two approaches, we could imagine how a UK-based company might think about an opportunity to 'offshore' part of its operation to a lower-cost Anglophone country. The shareholder-centred view would place emphasis on the unit cost savings to be achieved by moving the operation to a lower-cost area, provided that the required quality of service can be maintained. Other things being equal, lower unit costs obviously allow higher margins and improved rewards to shareholders. However, the assessment would also take into account the possibility of additional risks to be managed, such as security and quality control issues. Furthermore, this view would also consider the competitive implications of the decision: if other suppliers all outsource and reduce their prices to customers, a decision *not* to do the same could damage the company. On the other hand, being different could be a viable competitive stance for one or more competitors, particularly if some customers are concerned about reduced quality of service from offshoring; at one point, NatWest in the UK seemed to take this stance in its advertising.

A stakeholder-centred company would place more emphasis on the impacts of the decision on the various stakeholder groups, notably including UK employees in this case. Although the decision to offshore might still be seen as competitively necessary by such a company, it might feel impelled to make more generous arrangements for those whose jobs are to be replaced, both out of a sense of long-term obligation and to preserve its image in the UK labour market. The question as to whether the group defined as 'those that the company has not yet recruited in the offshore location' should also be considered to be a stakeholder group – with a legitimate claim for attention – is one of the numerous judgements to be made in this approach.

In the UK, the report of the RSA Inquiry 'Tomorrow's Company' referred to the concept of an imaginary 'operating licence' granted to a company by the public, which can be effectively suspended or withdrawn if a company appears to be behaving badly.[34] Doing business effectively and well relies upon hundreds, sometimes thousands, of transactions every day of the year. If some of these transactions become more difficult because trust has been squandered and co-operation has been withdrawn, then the firm will start to lose out to its better-behaved competitors and its owners' wealth will start to suffer.

Critical review and reflection

The stakeholder view of a business may appear ethically attractive but is too idealistic. The shareholder-centred view consistent with maximising owner wealth makes more sense. Without this wealth people would be reluctant to invest in a business and it would not be possible to satisfy fully the demands of the diverse group of stakeholders.

What do YOU see as the criticisms of this point of view? How would YOU prepare a counterargument?

Ethics and corporate purpose

How do these issues relate to the question of ethics and the corporate purpose? To return to the problems of the global financial services industry, events since 2008 have provided a stark example of a collapse in public trust of many formerly respected institutions.

There is much lively discussion of what went so badly wrong and what should be done in the future, but there is a general agreement that global banks under 'light-touch' regulation did not manage to act in ways that were consistent with their shareholders' interest (to put it mildly). In the years leading up to the autumn 2008 crisis, many banks grew rapidly and took risks that with hindsight were not well managed. When these risks turned bad – triggered by the problems in the US housing market – the damage turned out to be uncontainable for some and also exposed the extra risk represented by the interconnectedness of modern global financial services institutions. One notable quote came from Alan Greenspan, the former Chairman of the US Federal Reserve:

> *I made a mistake in presuming that the self-interest of organisations, specifically banks and others, were such that they were best capable of protecting their own shareholders and their equity in the firms . . . Those of us who have looked to the self-interest of lending institutions to protect shareholders' equity (myself especially) are in a state of shocked disbelief.*

These comments were made by Greenspan to a Congressional Committee in October 2008.[35] They are notable because Greenspan had been a lifelong believer in free markets and the leading advocate of light-touch regulation, and had been widely admired as such during the good years. His frank admission of a mistaken assumption about the behaviour of senior executives is particularly telling because it appears to cast doubt on one of the main foundations of Friedman's view of the corporate purpose – that society is best served by encouraging businesses to compete with each other within the law, with minimal further regulation.

The hugely expensive bailouts and nationalisations that resulted from the crisis have been followed by further revelations of questionable practice by banks: in the UK, for example, major banks were obliged by the courts to set aside billions of pounds to cover the expected cost of compensation for the mis-selling of Payment Protection Insurance (PPI) to large numbers of customers over a period of years.[36] This counted as 'mis-selling' because the products were unsuitable (i.e. of little or no value) to a number of groups – the self-employed, for example, or those with pre-existing health conditions. Most of the major banks were involved in this market, with strong pressure on staff to sell these profitable products wherever possible.

With hindsight, we can see that it should have been possible for senior managers to work out that this type of selling could eventually lead to claims against the bank that would outweigh any profits from the sales. Had this been done, some of the problems might have been averted. But there is perhaps something further to be said here: it hardly requires a degree in moral philosophy to work out that selling products to customers who quite foreseeably cannot benefit from them is an abuse of trust and something that a bank – or any other business – simply *should not do*. This is a clear example of the importance of the 'moral compass' mentioned earlier.

Reliance on regulators

The PPI example also leads to a further question about relying on regulations to govern the behaviour of companies: whether it is realistic to aim at regulations that completely rule out any bad or undesirable practice. This is difficult enough in its own right, but the risk is that increasingly detailed regulations will be taken by some as a list of things that may not be done, with the corollary that anything not expressly forbidden is potentially worth considering. This sort of cat-and-mouse game between regulators and regulated is an unhealthy use of energy and talent, partly because regulators will necessarily need time to absorb and respond to market innovations, but also because the quiet and insistent voice of the moral compass (*'we just shouldn't do this'*) may be drowned out entirely.

The PPI mis-selling scandal is not the only cause for concern – other reported problems have involved the mis-selling of interest rate hedging products, as well as the substantial fines imposed by US and UK regulators for attempts to manipulate the LIBOR inter-bank settlement rate. In 2014, some six years after the onset of the global financial crisis, UK and US regulators imposed fines totalling £2.6 billion on six prominent global banks in respect of attempts by traders to manipulate benchmark foreign exchange rates, whose levels are used every day to value a range of assets in world trade. Notably – and perhaps depressingly – this misbehaviour was reported by the UK's Financial Conduct Authority to have been going on between 2008 and 2013, that is to say *after* the injection of enormous sums of taxpayers' money into ailing banks in both countries.[37]

The prevalence of problems of this sort – whose consequences should have been all too predictable – in the industry may cause some to wonder whether the problems in some major banks are actually cultural at root, rather than arising from localised and temporary misbehaviour.

Moral reflection in ethical decision-making

The importance of active moral reflection in ethical decision-making in business would probably have come as no surprise to Adam Smith, the founder of the discipline of economics. Smith's 1776 work *The Wealth of Nations* was the first to set out clearly how markets work and how self-interested individuals competing in markets are guided by an 'invisible hand' to benefit society, even though this may be no part of their intention. Thus self-interest, mediated through the mechanism of the market, can be to the general advantage. But Smith's original discipline was not economics, but moral philosophy – his first major work, *The Theory of Moral Sentiments,* was published in 1759. The point here is that markets are best understood as very efficient systems for organising the supply of products and services to meet the demands of buyers. Beyond this very useful function, markets can offer no moral guidance, nor any guarantee that market outcomes will be ethically desirable. This gap can only be closed by the application of moral sense by actors in the market. In the 1930s this seemed to be very clear to bankers, as is evident in the famous statement made by J. P. Morgan Jr to a US Senate Sub-Committee in 1933:[38]

> *I should state that at all times the idea of doing only first-class business, and that in a first-class way, has been before our minds. We have never been satisfied with simply keeping within the law, but have constantly sought so to act that we might fully observe the professional code, and so maintain the credit and reputation which has been handed down to us from our predecessors in the firm.*

Of course, banking and the regulation of banking have become far more complex since the 1930s, but the basic sense of right and wrong is just as important today as it was then. The 2012 BBC Reith lecturer Niall Ferguson used one of his lectures[39] to express doubt about whether more complex and detailed regulation would provide an answer to the problems experienced in the financial services industry. It might be better, he suggested, to re-examine the approach described by Walter Bagehot's 1873 work *Lombard Street,* with a very powerful central bank exercising control based upon discretion, rather than detailed rules, and with the clear sanction of imprisonment for serious transgressions.

One further comment can be made in passing – it is not entirely clear that a greater stakeholder focus on the part of banks would have led to a very different outcome by 2008. Many of the banks badly damaged by the crisis were engaged in significant CSR programmes, as their websites at the start of 2009 made clear. With the benefit of hindsight, many stakeholders might have opted for more thoughtful and principled management of banks, rather than the benefits of bank CSR programmes. Increasingly, the phrase 'corporate social responsibility (CSR)' is being replaced by 'corporate responsibility (CR)'. If this signifies a more comprehensive assessment of a corporation's effect on society, routinely making full use of a moral compass, then this seems to be a welcome step forward.

Business ethics

The large-scale issues of CSR are to do with how a company should conduct itself within society; these questions certainly have an ethical aspect, as has been discussed, but they are not the whole of business ethics. Day-to-day decisions made by individual managers are not usually made on the basis of some detailed calculation of the consequences for shareholder value (however theoretically desirable that might be) and more general ethical considerations must play a part in resolving the dilemmas that sometimes arise in practice.

No single view of right or wrong

These questions can be complex, since there is no single view in general ethics of what makes something right or wrong. One school of thought emphasises **duties,** things that must be done (or refrained from) irrespective of the consequences. This deontological point of view holds that goodness or badness is evident only in the action itself: that, for example, lying is bad because it is bad in itself. By contrast, a **consequentialist** view of ethics holds that the goodness or badness of a proposed action is evident only in the consequences of that action: whether a lie is good or bad depends upon the consequences of that particular lie at the time. Utilitarianism, for example, is a consequentialist theory, in that it seeks to maximise the net happiness for everyone affected by a particular action ('the greatest good for the greatest number', as it is sometimes expressed). Both of the perspectives on CSR discussed in the previous section are also to some extent consequentialist, in that they are mainly concerned with an assessment of the effects of a firm's actions. We can also note that the idea of a moral compass typical of a duties-based approach to ethics – the sense that we just shouldn't do this – is one that is not reliant on any calculation of the consequences.

Both duties and consequences are plainly important in the way we deal with ethical issues in everyday life. Unfortunately, however, they are very different ways of reasoning, which can lead to contradictory outcomes in some cases. An exclusively duty-based view of ethics, for example, must sooner or later run into problems such as absolutism, or the difficulty of deciding which duty should take precedence over others in a particular situation. If, for example, both lying and killing are held to be inherently wrong, is it acceptable to lie in order to avoid a killing? And whatever answer is given, how do we know?

Informing our views

Nonetheless, duties and principles clearly do inform our views of how people should treat each other at work. An exclusively consequentialist view of ethics is likely to entail methodological problems of forecasting reliably what the consequences of an action may be and of deciding how to measure those consequences. Some forms of utilitarianism can be very unjust to small minorities, by allowing their unhappiness (i.e. as a result of some proposed action) to be offset by the increased happiness of a much larger number. Again, however, we can hardly deny that our assessment of the likely consequences of different actions plays a part in our view of acceptable and unacceptable behaviour in an organisation.

To return briefly to the earlier example of offshoring, a deontological approach to the ethics of offshoring would focus on aspects of the proposal that might be in breach of clear principles and duties. While no business can reasonably accept a general duty to keep existing employees on the payroll for ever, a contemplation of duties might cause a company to do as much as reasonably possible to soften the impact of the job losses, including the possibility of internal transfer, retraining, outplacement and more-than-minimum redundancy packages.

A utilitarian analysis would seek to identify all who would be affected – anywhere in the world – by the proposed offshoring decision and then assess the impact (positive or negative) on each person (or, more realistically, group). This would allow a sort of 'trial balance' of the consequences to be drawn up and an evaluation of the net impact on aggregate happiness. Necessarily in this method, the reduction in happiness for others, such as those who are made involuntarily redundant, is offset by the extra happiness created for some – those who get the offshore jobs, for example. Obviously, this is of little comfort to the former group, which illustrates one of the important criticisms of the utilitarian approach.

Ethical decision-making at work

How, then, are ethical choices to be made by people working for organisations? No simple and universal answer is available – ethical awareness is something that can be cultivated and the different perspectives will often help to shed light on a particular dilemma. Some perspectives may appear to be better suited to particular situations: whereas, for example, it is difficult to avoid some sort of consequentialist component in thinking about how a company should act, it is also clear that duty-based (or 'moral compass') arguments must also weigh heavily in thinking about the ethical treatment of people such as employees. The German philosopher Kant's view that we should always treat other people as ends in themselves and never simply as means is surely an important principle for ethical and decent HRM and one that would often be seen as more important than the prospect of short-term gain.[40]

Critical review and reflection

Provided companies comply fully with the laws of the land it is unfair to criticise them for behaving in a manner that benefits them most, even if this might be regarded as a breach of their social responsibilities.

To what extent do YOU feel able to justify this point of view as reasonable business practice?

Personal integrity and individual values are important elements in ethical decision-making at work, but the increasingly common company, professional or industry codes of conduct may also provide support and guidance (notice also the reference to the professional code in the 1933 quote from J. P. Morgan above). This is not to say that these ethical 'resources' will always provide clear and comfortable guidance – sometimes, people in organisations will experience tension between the conflicting demands of, say, their own personal values and the demands placed on them by their organisation. If these conflicts become intolerable and cannot be resolved through normal means, then an individual may decide to become a 'whistle-blower' in the public interest, by taking the high-risk approach of placing the problem in the public domain for resolution. Codes of conduct can help to reduce the risk of painful situations like this by providing a published set of values to which the individual can appeal, rather than taking the risk wholly personally.

A concept map outlining some issues of ethics at work is given in Figure 14.3.

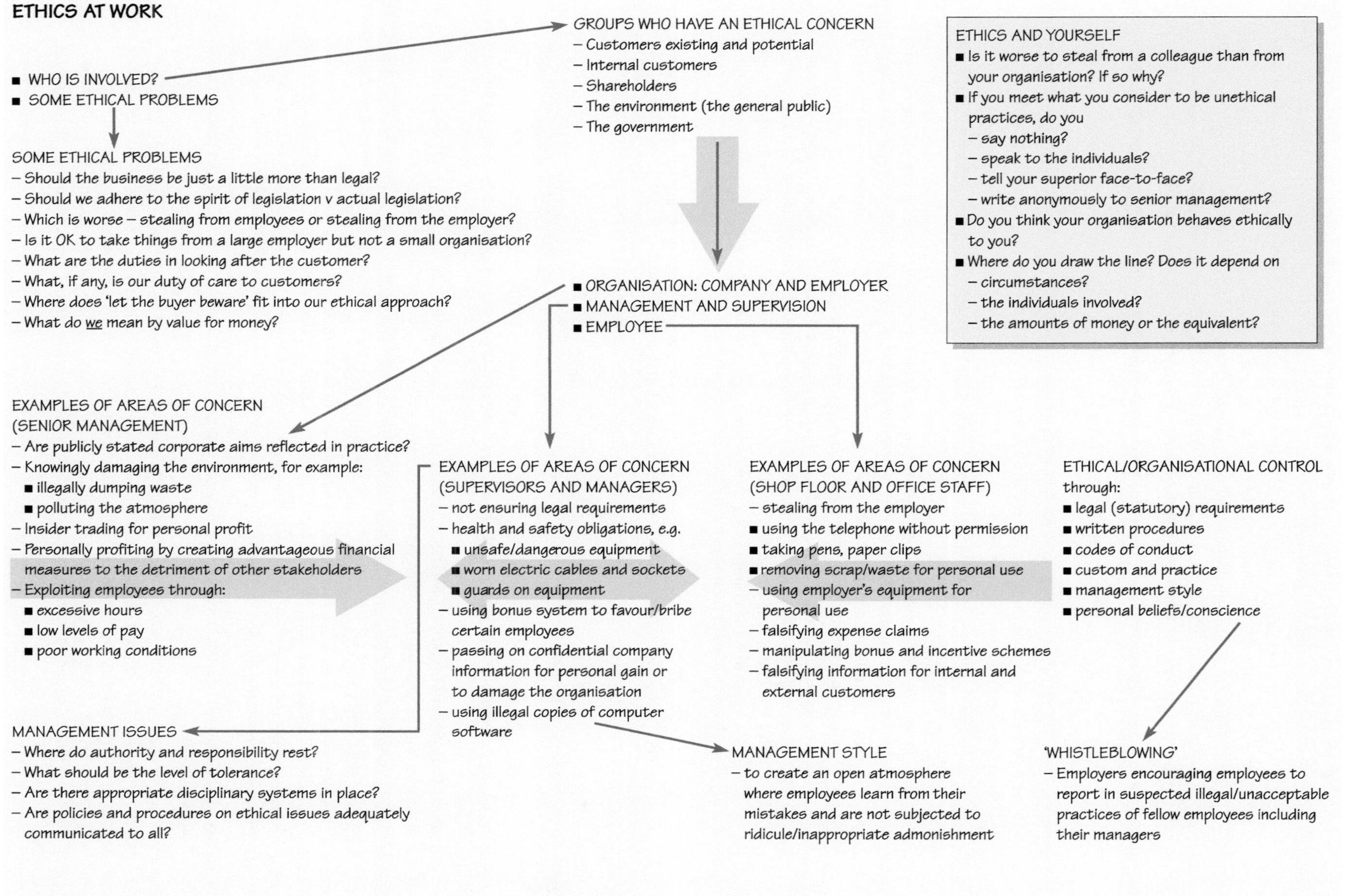

Figure 14.3 Concept map of ethics at work

Source: Copyright © 2008 The Virtual Learning Materials Workshop. Reproduced with permission.

Codes of business conduct (or ethics)

The previous section has suggested that detailed regulations, laws or codes may not by themselves guarantee ethical conduct if they are not accompanied by a clear moral sense on the part of the businesses making decisions about how to behave. Codes of conduct may, however, play a very important role in fostering ethical conduct in organisations, by sending clear guidance to employees about what is expected of them and to the outside world about the standards by which the organisation wishes to be judged. In some cases, concise and clear codes of conduct may also arise from a distillation of the knowledge and experience of the organisation over many years, which may be particularly helpful to junior or less experienced staff in their day-to-day work.

In US and Canadian organisations, codes of conduct are very common and in many cases members of the organisation are required to sign to indicate formally their acceptance. Codes may be updated on a regular basis.

IBM publishes a comprehensive document of business conduct guidelines relating to the ethical practices and values of the company.

> *IBM's Business Conduct Guidelines are, at the most basic level, a description of the conduct we establish for all IBMers to comply with laws and ethical practices wherever we do business. It is a living document that we regularly review and update, as business and the world at large become more complex. But the BCGs have always been about more than compliance and ethics. By establishing these guidelines decades ago and giving them weight of a governing document, we have embraced the proposition that our choices and actions define IBM for others. And we have sought to ensure that our relationships - with clients, investors, colleagues and the communities in which we live and work - are built on our core value of trust and personal responsibility.*[41]

The document includes a comprehensive set of guidelines on: Speaking Up; In the Workplace; In the Marketplace; On Your Own Time; Further Guidance.

Codes of conduct or ethics

In the UK an increasing number of organisations, of all types, also now publish a code of conduct or code of ethics. For example:

The Chartered Management Institute (CMI) has a Code of Conduct and Practice that is binding on all members. The code encapsulates, with supporting examples, six key principles:

- Behaving in an open, honest and trustworthy manner.
- Acting in the best interest of your organisation, customers, clients and/or partners.
- Continually developing and maintaining professional knowledge and competence.
- Respecting the people with whom you work.
- Creating a positive impact on society.
- Upholding the reputation of the profession and the institute.[42]

The University of Portsmouth has a detailed 'Ethics Policy' (as approved by Academic Council, 12 November 2013) and under 'Values' includes:

> *The University's Strategy 2012-2017 includes a statement of values which should be reflected in all the policies and practices of the University. The Strategy states: 'We will be a socially responsible university, serious about inclusivity and committed to improving social mobility. We will maintain the highest levels of academic and professional integrity and will ensure that we deliver our obligations in relation to corporate social responsibility. Our strategy will be driven by values of equality, openness, tolerance and respect. We will demonstrate and expect of others ethical and responsible behaviours.*[43]

An integrated approach

The late *Anita Roddick* suggested that business leaders should make ethics part of their heritage.

> *We need to develop a corporate code of conduct, a formal, articulated and well-defined set of principles which all global businesses agree to live up to. A broadly kept code of conduct would shut down the excuse about the competition making ethical behaviour impossible once and for all. We must all agree not to compete in ways that destroy communities or the environment. We must all embrace the principles of socially responsible business, because the decisions of business leaders not only affect economies, but societies. Unless businesses understand that they have responsibilities they must live up to, in terms of world poverty, the environment and human rights, the future for us all is pretty bleak.*[44]

According to *Philippa Foster Back*, OBE (Director, Institute of Business Ethics), the globalisation of business has raised questions of applying ethical values to the different cultures and societies in which organisations operate. The challenge for everyone concerned with ethics now is to ensure that values are embedded throughout an organisation. A code of ethics needs to be translated into reality through training and enforcement and driven from the top.[45]

McEwan summarises the separate histories of CSR, business ethics and corporate governance, and suggests a method of enquiry that attempts to integrate these different perspectives on business through three broad levels of enquiry:

- a **descriptive** approach that draws attention to the values and beliefs of people from different cultures and societies that influence their attitudes towards the various activities of business in their home countries and abroad;
- a **normative** approach that identifies sets of values and beliefs as a basis for making ethical decisions at the individual, group or senior management level in an organisation;
- an **analytical** approach that attempts to explore the relationship between these normative values and beliefs and other value-systems or ideologies, such as political or religious beliefs and culture or other social customs.[46]

A culture of ethics, integrity and compliance

Bennett points out that a culture of integrity focused on outstanding quality and business outcomes must be intentionally shaped and build on the values and principles of the organisation. This involves seven steps of: (1) designate a compliance owner; (2) implement written standards and procedures; (3) conduct appropriate training; (4) develop open lines of communication; (5) centrally manage all reports and allegations; (6) respond consistently and appropriately to alleged offences; (7) audit, monitor and adapt as needed. Bennett also points out the need for an integrated effort.

> *Achieving an effective ethics and compliance programme requires more than simply adding rules and additional layers of controls. There must be an integrated effort that aligns financial and compliance requirements with the organisation's mission and values.*[47]

Related legislation

As part of the growing attention to the concept of CSR there are a number of pieces of recent legislation that arguably relate to the concept of business ethics and organisational accountability. Although it is not in the scope of this book to provide detailed aspects of legal provisions, we should recognise the existence of such legislation, including the Human Rights Act 1998, the Public Interest Disclosure Act 1998, the Local Government Act 2000, the Freedom of Information Act 2000, the Corporate Manslaughter and Corporate Homicide Act 2007, the Bribery Act 2010 and the Equality Act 2010.

The **Human Rights Act 1998** came into force on 2 October 2000 and incorporates into English law rights and liberties enshrined in the European Convention on Human Rights. The provisions apply to the acts of 'public authorities' and make it unlawful for them to act in a way incompatible with a right under the Convention. The Act is designed to provide greater protection for individuals, and to protect them from unlawful and unnecessary interference. Everyone has the right to respect for their private and family life, their home and their correspondence. The Act has a significant effect on people both as citizens and at work.

The **Public Interest Disclosure Act 1998,** which has become known widely as the 'Whistleblower's Act', is designed to protect people who expose wrongdoing at their workplace, to provide reassurance that there is a safe alternative to silence and to provide a safeguard against retaliation. Employers need to establish clear internal procedures by which members of staff can raise any matters of personal concern.

The **Local Government Act 2000,** the so-called 'New Ethical Framework', requires all local authorities to provide codes of conduct to promote high standards of behaviour. The government has distinguished between general principles of conduct in public service and the code of conduct containing specific actions and prohibitions that demonstrate the principles are being observed.

The **Freedom of Information Act 2000** gives the public one simple right to access information held by public authorities. Under the Act, the public have a 'right to know'.

The **Corporate Manslaughter and Corporate Homicide Act 2007,** which came into force on 6 April 2008, clarifies the criminal liabilities of companies including large organisations where serious failures in the management of health and safety result in a fatality. For the first time, companies and organisations can be found guilty of corporate manslaughter as a result of serious management failures resulting in a gross breach of a duty of care.

The **Bribery Act 2010** consolidates and modernises the law on bribery and provides a more effective framework to combat bribery in both the private and public sectors. The Act creates a number of new offences relating to promising or giving an advantage or to bribes, and introduces anti-corruption regulations.

The **Equality Act 2010** covers areas of discrimination and bans unfair treatment and helps achieve equal opportunities in the workplace and in wider society.

Critical review and reflection

The harsh truth is that without EU intervention, government legislation and the threat of adverse press or television reports, the majority of organisations would give little regard to their social responsibilities or to business ethics.

To what extent do YOU support this contention? What has been YOUR experience of genuine concerns by organisations in general for their social responsibilities and ethical behaviour?

Ten key points to remember

1 Underlying the study of management and organisational behaviour is the nature of corporate strategy (or strategic management) for the organisation as a whole.

2 Strategy highlights the overall direction of an organisation, its goal, objectives and policy. The profit objective is not, by itself, a sufficient criterion for effective management.

3 The goals and objectives of the organisation may be pursued in accordance with an underlying ideology that determines the culture and conduct of the organisation.

4 Strategy gives rise to the consideration of organisational values and beliefs that draw attention to the importance of integrity and trust and ethical leadership.

5 The organisation cannot operate in isolation from interactions with its external environment and this gives rise to broader corporate social responsibilities.

6 Increasing attention is given to values and ethics and business. Ethics is concerned with the study of morality and understanding what makes things good or bad.

7 Two differing perspectives on ethics and corporate social responsibility, and how a business should act, are a shareholder-centred view and a stakeholder-theory view.

8 The scope of business ethics is very broad and gives rise to a number of questions including ethics and corporate purpose, and ethical decision-making at work.

9 An increasing number of organisations of all types publish a code of business (or professional) conduct, or ethics, which sets out their practices and values.

10 The globalisation of business highlights calls for an integrated approach to the application of ethical values. Related legislation arguably gives support to the importance of organisational accountability.

Review and discussion questions

1 Explain fully the nature, purpose and importance of corporate strategy.

2 Identify examples of objectives and policy in your own university or organisation. To what extent do you agree with Dryburgh's assertion that SMART objectives are really dumb?

3 To what extent do you believe profit maximisation is a realistic criterion for the effective management of a business organisation? What other indicators might be applied in terms of organisational performance and results?

4 Discuss critically the practical worth of value or mission statements and the extent to which they are likely to inspire members of staff. Support your answer with actual examples.

5 Explain fully the concept and ramifications of corporate social responsibility (CSR).

6 How would you attempt to explain the meaning and significance of organisational values and business ethics?

7 Compare and contrast the shareholder-centred and stakeholder approaches to social responsibilities for business. Which perspective do you tend to favour?

8 Comment critically on the code of ethics (or code of professional conduct) for your university or organisation; or if one does not exist, draw up your own suggested code.

9 Debate the extent to which you believe government legislation brings about a genuine advancement in the social responsibilities of organisations.

10 Give your own views on the importance of, and amount of attention you believe should be given to, corporate social responsibilities and ethical behaviour.

Assignment

a. Detail fully what you believe are the social responsibilities or obligations of your university (and/or other work organisation well known to you) and identify the major stakeholders.
b. Give specific examples of the ways in which the university has attempted to satisfy, and/or has failed to satisfy, responsibilities or obligations to these stakeholders.
c. Specify the extent to which attention has been given to values in the university, and to the principles, standards and expected practices or judgements of 'good' (ethical) behaviour.
d. Give your view on the code of conduct (or ethics) for your university.
e. Compare your observations with those of your colleagues and summarise what conclusions you draw.

Personal skills and employability exercise

Objectives

Completing this exercise should help you to enhance the following skills:

- Clarify the work values and beliefs that are important to you.
- Examine your sensitivity to, and dealings with, other people.
- Debate and justify with colleagues the nature of your values and beliefs.

Exercise

You are required to:
rate the following items according to the scale

5 (extremely important for me);
4 (very important for me);
3 (average importance for me);
2 (not important for me);
1 (I would oppose this).
What is required is your genuine beliefs and feelings about each item, not what others think or believe, but what you personally and honestly believe and feel about each item.

1 There should be clear allocation of objectives and accountability for them ____
2 We should be open and honest in all our dealings with each other ____
3 People's talents should be recognised, developed and correctly utilised ____
4 One should give acknowledgement and praise to those in authority ____
5 There are clear rules about what we should and should not do in getting the job done ____
6 Conflicts should be surfaced and resolved rather than allowed to simmer ____
7 The causes of problems should be directed away from oneself ____
8 Encouragement and support should be placed above criticism ____
9 Problems should be tackled and resolved in co-operation with others ____
10 What is right should be placed above who is right ____
11 Clear standard procedures should be in place for all important jobs ____
12 One should become visible and build up one's personal image ____
13 Equity and fairness should be applied to all, regardless of status or standing ____
14 Excellence should be our aim in all that we do, professionally and administratively ____
15 We give close attention to codes of conduct since this is what builds character ____

16 We should keep each other informed and practise open and friendly communication ____
17 We know who should be making the decisions and refer decisions to the right person ____
18 Everyone and their contribution should be treated with respect and dignity ____
19 We should meet all our commitments to one another - we do what we say we will do ____
20 One should form networks of support among those with influence ____
21 There are clear reporting relationships - who reports to whom - and we stick to them ____
22 People should take responsibility for their own decisions and actions ____
23 Everyone should be committed to personal growth and lifelong learning ____
24 Situations or events should be created so as to justify the advancement of one's goals ____
25 Performance should be assessed against objectives and standards declared up-front ____
26 Policies should be clear and not changed until there is proof that they need changing ____
27 Everyone's needs should be given equal standing regardless of their position or status ____
28 We should be committed to the service of others rather than ourselves ____
29 Positive relationships should be established with those who have influence ____
30 Warmth and affection should be demonstrated in our work relationships ____
31 Individual productivity and performance should be encouraged and actively promoted ____
32 We all know what our jobs are and we stick to our defined responsibilities ____
33 Those from disadvantaged backgrounds should be helped to catch up with others ____
34 One should expect to get support from those to whom we have given past support ____
35 Goals should be challenging and stretch people to higher levels of achievement ____

Source for the exercise: Misselhorn, A. *Head and Heart of Leadership*, (Reach Publishers, SA), (2012). p. 86. Reproduced with permission.

When you have completed the exercise, form into small groups to compare and discuss, frankly and openly, your ratings with those of your colleagues. Be prepared to justify your ratings but also listen with an open mind to the views of your colleagues.

Further information will be provided by your tutor.

Discussion

- How difficult was it for you to complete your ratings?
- How much agreement was there among members of your group? Did this surprise you?
- To what extent were you influenced to rethink your values or beliefs?

Case study

The Fairtrade Foundation

Over the last couple of decades, the ideals of fair trade have become prominent in UK retailing. The story of how this has come about shows how an organisation can make progress towards its own objectives through developing effective networks with other organisations, about the trade-offs that have to be managed along the way and about the realities of achieving improvements in business ethics.

The general concerns about unfairness in world trade are easy enough to set out. Firstly, the gap between the living standards of the richest and the poorest is distressingly wide and the scale of poverty enormous. The UN Development Programme pointed out in 2015 that although poverty rates halved between 1990 and 2010, there are still more than 1.2 billion people around the world - about one in five in developing regions - who live in extreme poverty.[48] Secondly, the fact that this gap is so wide is often felt to be something to do with the way in which international trade operates (although the definition of the actual problem is something on which experts differ sharply). Finally, there seems to be a growing sense that these are not just abstruse high-level policy problems, to be addressed by governments, experts and suchlike, but rather processes in which we *all* take

→

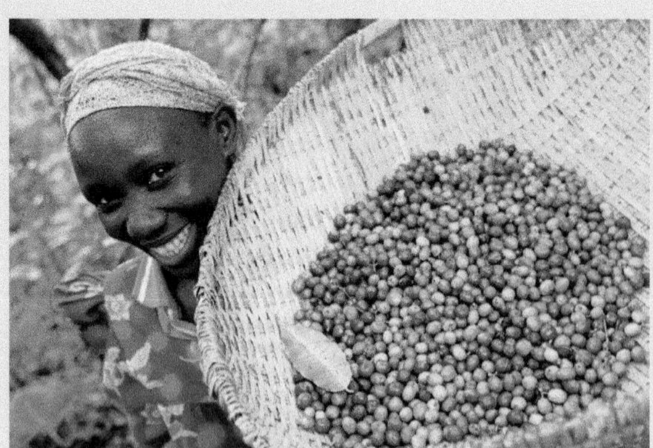

As the popularity of Fairtrade increases, is its growth sustainable or has commercialism resulted in a 'cleanwashing' of an idealistic movement?
Source: Simon Rawles/Alamy Images

part as a result of the choices we make when we buy and consume products and services. On the negative side, our demand for value for money in the shops may have unseen negative consequences for people in other countries who are in a much more parlous position than we are. More positively, consumer power may provide us with the means - if we take the trouble - to reduce the harm we do further along the supply chain and perhaps even create change for the better. The Fairtrade movement has sought to address these problems.

The Fairtrade movement is an international network of partners, who define fair trade as follows:

> *Fairtrade is about better prices, decent working conditions, local sustainability, and fair terms of trade for farmers and workers in the developing world. By requiring companies to pay sustainable prices (which must never fall lower than the market price), Fairtrade addresses the injustices of conventional trade, which traditionally discriminates against the poorest, weakest producers. It enables them to improve their position and have more control over their lives.*[49]

In the UK, the movement is centred around the Fairtrade Foundation, which was formed in 1992 by five prominent charities, later joined by the Women's Institute. Today, the Foundation has four main streams of activity:

- Providing independent certification of the trade chain and licensing use of the FAIRTRADE mark on products as a consumer guarantee.
- Help in growing demand for Fairtrade products and empowering producers to sell to traders and retailers.
- Working with partners to support producer organisations and their networks.
- Raising public awareness of the need for fair trade and the significant role of the FAIRTRADE mark in making trade fair.[50]

Launching the concept

As regular press reports make clear, Fairtrade in the UK has grown rapidly since its launch in 1992, from the first certified product (Green and Blacks' Maya Gold chocolate), through growth to include a wider range of products and then entry into the catering trade. Twenty years after launch, more than 4,500 Fairtrade products were on sale in the UK, with 2013 sales valued at £1.78 billon, up 14 per cent from the previous year.[51] For some years, percentage recognition of the Fairtrade mark has remained in the mid to high 70s,[52] a key factor in driving the growth of adoption by retailers. There is, however, plenty of scope for further growth: although the UK is an international leader in Fairtrade product penetration, these products still accounted for just 1.5 per cent of the overall UK food and drink market in 2013.[53]

The evolution of the Fairtrade approach has been the subject of a number of studies. *Davies*[54] suggests that three 'eras' can so far be distinguished:

- The 'solidarity' era (1970–90), in which sales were mainly in craft products, making use of alternative trading organisations such as not-for-profit and charity shops, specialist mail order and religious organisations. Product quality was inconsistent and sometimes poor, and branding very limited.
- The 'niche market' era (1990–2002), which saw a broadening of the range, with the growth of recognisable Fairtrade labelling and an appeal directed mainly at the ethical consumer, based upon public relations and press campaigns.
- The 'mass market' era (from 2002 onwards), distinguished by a rapid expansion of (mostly) food products into a wider range of mainstream outlets - most notably supermarkets, but also major chains of cafés and restaurants. Critically, Fairtrade decided to include large organisations in the scheme, allowing them to broaden the appeal to the mass-market customer.

In an earlier paper, *Jones et al.*[55] discussed some of the problems that had to be overcome when expanding into mass-market retail. For example, supermarkets need to secure adequate, consistent and regular supplies to maintain stocks, without which the growing consumer awareness will come to nothing. This is sometimes a challenge for smaller producers in the UK, but when the producer of the Fairtrade product lives in a remote part of a country with underdeveloped infrastructure, then the problem can be far greater. In the early stages, the willingness of a wider section of the market to pay a small price premium for a Fairtrade product was an area of uncertainty. Supermarkets had to play their part in consumer education in the early days via in-store leaflets and display materials and advertising campaigns.

Davies also addresses the question of how this development might continue in future, suggesting the possibility of more or less complete 'institutionalisation', in which the qualities of Fairtrade products become the norm for mainstream sales, rather than a specialised niche. Of course, this possibility only exists because Fairtrade products are now prominent in mass-market outlets. In future we may approach a tipping point where the average consumer will start to wonder why a particular brand on the supermarket shelf has *no* Fairtrade label. This could present a major management challenge for the Fairtrade Foundation: the label only works because it is widely recognised, understood and – above all – accepted as a trustworthy guarantee. That basic credibility is just as important for the supermarket retailer as for the consumer: if the reality starts to fall short of the promise in any respect, then things could quickly get difficult for the brand.

The issue of trust and credibility is becoming more complex for Fairtrade as its business grows: the FAIRTRADE logo has been joined in consumer consciousness by a number of other certification schemes. This increased emphasis on the ethics of products is in many respects a welcome development. For Fairtrade, it means greater competition for the public's attention, but it may also broaden the risk for the organisation and its image, since problems with any of these labelling schemes may damage credibility in ethical consumption more generally. Also, the range of issues covered by these schemes is more extensive than fair trade alone, raising the prospect of confusion about what exactly an individual label does guarantee and hence the risk of disappointment as a result of mistaken expectations.

Good or not; who decides?

As the Fairtrade movement has grown it has attracted criticism from both political wings. *Low and Davenport*,[56] for example, suggest that there are two dangers inherent in this growth: that of appropriation of the organisation by commercial interests in the process that the authors call 'cleanwashing'; and the transformation of the Fairtrade message into one of 'shopping for a better world', in which the movement's original radical values are watered down. A different critique arrived from the Right in 2008 when the free-market-championing Adam Smith Institute published its report 'Unfair Trade'.[57] Acknowledging the good intentions of the movement, it argued that the Fairtrade approach was far less effective in reducing poverty than global free trade would be, if rich countries were to abolish the trade barriers and domestic subsidies that make it hard for poor countries to sell to them. In 2010, the IEA also suggested that the Fairtrade approach could only benefit some producers; in particular, Fairtrade seemed not to focus its efforts on the poorest countries, but rather on middle-income countries, where Fairtrade penetration was higher.[58]

Those who work under a hot sun for low rates of pay could be forgiven a degree of impatience with these theoretical arguments: does it really matter if some of the greatly increased number of buyers of Fairtrade products do not fully grasp or agree with the radical agenda of the early days? Is it really better for poor people to wait for the arrival of the benefits of true free trade, given the glacial progress of international negotiations towards that end? As Voltaire remarked, are we not in danger of letting the best be the enemy of the good? Those who benefit from the Fairtrade system seem to have little doubt of the improved benefits it brings.[59]

The Fairtrade movement has managed to achieve very rapid growth from a specialised niche into the mainstream. It has created and communicated a prominent brand identity that provides consumers with a specific guarantee about the value chain that has brought the product to the shelf. To achieve and sustain this credibility, the Fairtrade Foundation has had to specify and manage what happens upstream, in order to use the immense power of the supermarkets to bring these products to the mainstream market. Many supermarkets have enthusiastically joined in the process of consumer education about Fairtrade products, possibly for normal commercial reasons of self-interest. Yet they have undoubtedly helped the idea to become firmly established in the minds of their customers and thus to ensure that ethics stays on the consumer agenda, even in difficult economic times.

→

Tasks

1. Who are the stakeholders of the Fairtrade Foundation? Using Figure 14.2 as a starting point, identify examples of each type of stakeholder. Who are the most powerful? Who the most important? Identify areas where the interests of stakeholders conflict as well as those where they coincide.
2. Explain what you think Low and Davenport mean by the term 'cleanwashing' and why this might be a danger to the values of the Fairtrade Foundation.
3. With reference to the decision to include major supermarkets and other large-scale retailers in the scheme, discuss whether you think that 'good' acts can result from selfish motives or not. Present the arguments on both sides.
4. How do you think the Fairtrade Foundation should present its message during an economic recession, when Western consumers might well be more motivated by price than other considerations?

Notes and references

1. Johnson, G., Whittington, R., Scholes, K., Angwin, D., and Regnér, P *Exploring Strategy,* tenth edition, Pearson Education (2014).
2. Andrews, K. 'The Concept of Corporate Strategy', Irwin (1971), in Lynch, R. *Strategic Management,* sixth edition, Pearson Education (2012), p. 7.
3. Lynch, R. *Strategic Management,* sixth edition, Pearson Education (2012), pp. 459, 462.
4. Allen, R. S. and Helms, M. M. 'Employee Perceptions of the Relationship between Strategy, Rewards and Organizational Performance', *Journal of Business Strategies,* vol. 19, no. 2, 2002, pp. 115–39.
5. Stern, S. 'The Next Big Thing', *Management Today,* April 2007, p. 50.
6. Gratton, L. *Living Strategy: Putting People at the Heart of Corporate Purpose,* Financial Times Prentice Hall (2000), p. 18.
7. Schneider, S. C. and Barsoux, J. *Managing Across Cultures,* second edition, Financial Times Prentice Hall (2003), ch. 5.
8. See, for example, Hannagan, T. *Management: Concepts & Practices,* fifth edition, Financial Times Prentice Hall (2008), p. 396.
9. Reeves, R. 'The Trouble with Targets', *Management Today,* January 2008, p. 29.
10. Dryburgh, A., **http://www.managementtoday.co.uk/features/1071164/dont-believe-it-its-smart-smart-objectives/** (accessed 8 June 2012).
11. See, for example, Brown, A. 'Organizational Culture: The Key to Effective Leadership and Organizational Development', *Leadership and Organization Development Journal,* vol. 13, no. 2, 1992, pp. 3–6.
12. Brech, E. F. L. (ed.) *The Principles and Practice of Management,* third edition, Longman (1975).
13. Lucas, E. 'Believe It Or Not, Values Can Make a Difference', *Professional Manager,* November 1999, pp. 10–12.
14. Cloke, K. and Goldsmith, J. *The End of Management and the Rise of Organizational Democracy,* Jossey-Bass (2002).
15. Gratton, L. *Hot Spots,* Financial Times Prentice Hall (2007).
16. Drucker, P. F. *The Practice of Management,* Heinemann Professional (1989), p. 59.
17. Mann, S., in conversation with Gidoomal, R. 'We Have to Be Proud of Our Integrity', *Professional Manager,* vol. 17, no. 5, 2007, pp. 18–21.
18. 'Creating a culture of integrity', *Governance & Compliance,* July 2014, pp. 26–8.
19. Yukl, G. *Leadership in Organizations,* seventh edition, Pearson Education (2010), p. 333.
20. 'Added values: The importance of ethical leadership', The Institute of Leadership and Management, June 2013.
21. 'Corporate Social Responsibility', Checklist 242, Chartered Management Institute, April 2013.
22. Pearce, G. 'Getting it straight', *Chartered Secretary,* August 2011, pp. 38–9.
23. Donaldson, T. and Preston, L. E. 'The stakeholder theory of the corporation: Concepts, evidence and implications, *Academy of Management Review,* vol. 20. no. 1, 1995, pp. 65–91.
24. Rollinson, D. *Organisational Behaviour and Analysis,* fourth edition, Financial Times Prentice Hall (2008).
25. Thanks to Ursula Wynhoven, **https://www.unglobalcompact.org/news/381-09-05-2013**

26. See, for example, Coyle, D. *The Economics of Enough: How to Run the Economy as If the Future Matters,* Princeton University Press (2011); and Skidelsky, R. and Skidelsky, E. *How Much is Enough? The Love of Money and the Case for a Good Life,* Allen Lane (2012).
27. Piketty, T. *Capital in the Twenty-First Century,* Harvard University Press (2014).
28. Sandel, M. *What Money Can't Buy: The Moral Limits of Markets,* Allen Lane (2012).
29. De George, R. T. *Business Ethics,* fifth edition, Prentice Hall (1999).
30. Friedman, M. 'The Social Responsibility of Business Is to Increase Its Profits', *New York Times Magazine,* 13 September 1970, pp. 32, 122–6.
31. Sternberg, E. *Just Business,* Little Brown (1994).
32. Cannon, T. *Corporate Responsibility,* Pitman (1994), pp. 32–3.
33. Sternberg, E. *Just Business,* Little Brown (1994).
34. RSA, *Tomorrow's Company – The Role of Business in a Changing World,* Royal Society for Arts, Manufactures and Commerce (1995).
35. *Guardian,* 24 October 2008, **http://www.guardian.co.uk/business/2008/oct/24/economics-creditcrunch-federal-reserve-greenspan** (accessed 8 August 2012).
36. Peston, R. 'The Big PPI Lessons For Banks', 9 May 2011, **http://www.bbc.co.uk/blogs/thereporters/robertpeston/2011/05/the_big_ppi_lesson_for_banks.html** (accessed 8 August 2012).
37. BBC News, 12 November 2014, 'Six banks fined £2.6bn by regulators over forex failings', **http://www.bbc.co.uk/news/business-30016007**; Ahmed, K. 'RBS boss admits – I cringed when I read forex chat room messages', BBC News, 12 November 2014, **http://www.bbc.co.uk/news/business-30027544**
38. A fuller version can be found at: **https://www.jpmorgan.com/cm/ContentServer?pagename=Chase/Href&urlname=jpmorgan/about/culture_new/fcb** (accessed 8 August 2012).
39. Full text at: **http://www.bbc.co.uk/programmes/b01jmxqp/features/transcript** (accessed 8 August 2012).
40. For a discussion, see De George, R. T. *Business Ethics,* fifth edition, Prentice Hall (1999).
41. Palmisano, S. 'IBM Business Conduct Guidelines', 2011, **www.ibm.com** (accessed 23 June 2012).
42. Chartered Management Institute, March 2011. For full details, see **www.managers.org.uk/code**
43. Available at: **http://www.port.ac.uk/accesstoinformation/policies/humanresources/filetodownload,88682,en.pdf** (accessed 23 November 2014).
44. Roddick, A. *Business As Unusual,* Thorsons (2000), p. 269.
45. Back, P. F. 'Taking a Proactive Approach to Ethics', *Professional Manager,* vol. 15, no. 3, 2006, p. 37.
46. McEwan, T. *Managing Values and Beliefs in Organisations,* Financial Times Prentice Hall (2001).
47. Bennett, M. 'Shaping the future', *Governance & Compliance,* June 2014, pp. 32–3.
48. **http://www.undp.org/content/undp/en/home/mdgoverview/mdg_goals/mdg1/** (accessed 10 February 2015).
49. **http://www.fairtrade.org.uk/what_is_fairtrade/faqs.aspx** (accessed 10 February 2015).
50. **http://www.fairtrade.org.uk/what_is_fairtrade/fairtrade_foundation.aspx** (accessed 10 February 2015).
51. **http://m.bbc.co.uk/news/business-26317759** (accessed 10 February 2015).
52. **http://www.fairtrade.org.uk/FTDoc/Fairtrade-Annual-Impact-Report-2013–14.pdf** (accessed 10 February 2015).
53. **http://www.theguardian.com/money/2013/mar/02/fairtrade-taste-growing-britain** (accessed 10 February 2015).
54. Davies, I. A. 'The eras and participants of fair trade: An industry structure/stakeholder perspective on the growth of the fair trade industry', *Corporate Governance,* vol. 7, no. 4, 2007, pp. 455–70.
55. Jones, P., Comfort, D. and Hillier, D. 'Developing customer relationships through fair trade: A case study from the retail market in the UK', *Management Research News,* vol. 27, no. 3, 2003, pp. 77–87.
56. Low, W. and Davenport, E. 'Has the medium (roast) become the message? The ethics of marketing fair trade in the mainstream', *International Marketing Review,* vol. 22, no. 5, 2005, pp. 494–511.
57. **http://www.adamsmith.org/blog/international/unfair-trade** (accessed 10 February 2015).
58. **http://www.iea.org.uk/in-the-media/press-release/new-research-finds-fair-trade-movement-is-a-distraction-not-a-solution** (accessed 10 February 2015).
59. See, for example, William Sutcliffe's 2004 *Guardian* article at **http://www.guardian.co.uk/lifeandstyle/2004/aug/07/foodanddrink.shopping2** (accessed 10 February 2015).

13 Power and Politics

Source: Robin Alam/Icon Sportswire/ AP Images

LEARNING OBJECTIVES

After studying this chapter, you should be able to:

13-1 Contrast leadership and power.

13-2 Explain the three bases of formal power and the two bases of personal power.

13-3 Explain the role of dependence in power relationships.

13-4 Identify power or influence tactics and their contingencies.

13-5 Identify the causes and consequences of abuse of power.

13-6 Describe how politics work in organizations.

13-7 Identify the causes, consequences, and ethics of political behavior.

If your professor has chosen to assign this, go to the Assignments section of **mymanagementlab.com** to complete the chapter warm up.

POWER IN COLLEGE SPORTS

Anyone who follows sports knows the huge media presence college football and basketball have. With all this attention comes big money: Estimates put direct revenues for college sports at $16 billion for the 2014–2015 academic year alone, with forecasts for subsequent increases. Revenues from successful sports are often sufficient to provide many scholarships and fund nearly all other athletic programs. TV coverage also draws massive media attention for the top-performing schools, enhancing their reputations and attracting donors. The resulting combination of large sums of money, complex power dynamics, and loose regulation systems creates a perfect environment for power struggles. It seems the lure of money and the pressure to compete at the stratospheric level are sometimes so great that college officials may become willing to subvert the rules and use political tactics to secure financial advantages for their institutions.

In this paradigm, coaches are often more powerful and highly paid than university presidents. Many observers worry that student athletes, who are not paid at all, might be the casualties of the intense politics. Their compensation is a good university education, which sometimes just doesn't happen. These students aren't always academically qualified

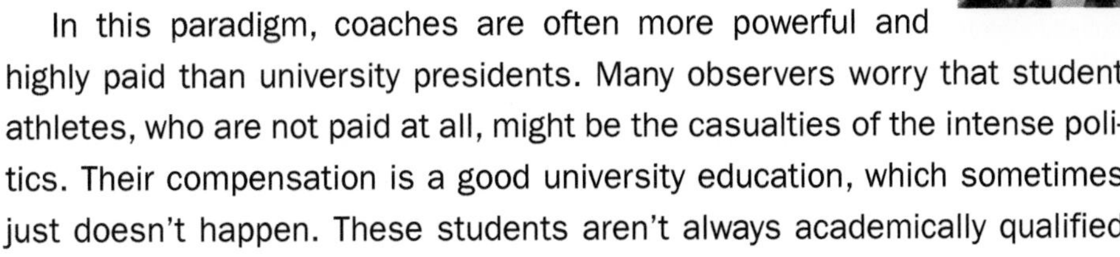

when they are recruited for their sports abilities, and are often not given the extra help needed to catch up. As researcher Richard Southall notes, "We pretend that it's feasible to recruit high school graduates with minimal academic qualifications, giving them a full-time job as a football or basketball player at a Division I NCAA school, and somehow have them get up to college-level reading and writing skills at the same time that they're enrolled in college-level classes."

The National Collegiate Athletic Association (NCAA), the governing body, requires that student athletes maintain certain grade point averages (GPAs) and graduation rates, but these metrics sometimes put university administrators, coaches, and professors in a power struggle. Administrators, alumni, and others who can influence the university's reputation or revenue stream can use their power to influence coaches and officials. Professors and tutors, feeling political pressure from coaches and students to pass student athletes, sometimes follow the path of least resistance, developing fictional classes with few requirements and top grades.

Few people in the chain are able to ignore the power players. In many cases, resisters and whistle-blowers even face retaliation. Athlete mentor from the University of Georgia Billy Hawkins asks, regarding students who have been pushed through the system, "Have they learned anything? Are they productive citizens now? That's a thing I worry about. To get a degree is one thing, to be functional with that degree is totally different."

The need to develop a workable solution for the power struggle in college sports is clear. Scandals like "paper classes" and/or falsified grading at Florida State University (2009), the University of Michigan (2008), Auburn University (2006), and the University of Georgia (2003) shed light on the problem. Media exposure and organizational politics can, if managed correctly, become part of the solution. Internal pressures from those who put a strong value on academic performance, as well as the desire of universities and the NCAA to preserve a positive face to external constituents, are creating much of the pressure to ensure student athletes truly receive the type of education that has been claimed.

Sources: P. M. Barrett, "The Insurgents Who Could Bring Down the NCAA," *Bloomberg Business,* August 21, 2014, http://www.bloomberg.com/bw/articles/2014-08-21/paying-ncaa-college-athletes-inside-the-legal-battle; P. M. Barrett, "In Fake Classes Scandal, UNC Fails Its Athletes—And Whistle Blower," *Bloomberg Business,* March 3, 2014, http://www.bloomberg.com/bw/articles/2014-02-27/in-fake-classes-scandal-unc-fails-its-athletes-whistle-blower; S. Ganim, "Some College Athletes Play Like Adults, Read Like 5th Graders," CNN, January 8, 2014, http://www.cnn.com/2014/01/07/us/ncaa-athletes-reading-scores/; and B. Wolverton, "NCAA Says It's Investigating Academic Fraud at 20 Colleges," *The Chronicle,* January 21, 2015, http://chronicle.com/article/NCAA-Says-It-s-Investigating/151315/.

As we can see in the opening story, politics can wreak havoc on an essentially good system—in this case, ensuring student athletes get a high-quality education. In both practice and research, *power* and *politics* have been described as dirty words. In fact, it is easier for most of us to talk about sex or money than about power or political behavior. People who have power deny it, people who want it try not to look like they're seeking it, and those who are good at getting it are secretive about how they do so.[1]

In this chapter, we show that power determines what goals people pursue, discuss how power works in organizations, and reveal the effects of political behavior. We begin by exploring our natural association of power with leadership.

WATCH IT!

If your professor has assigned this, go to the Assignments section of **mymanagementlab.com** to complete the video exercise titled ***Power and Political Behavior***.

Power and Leadership

13-1 Contrast leadership and power.

power A capacity that *A* has to influence the behavior of *B* so that *B* acts in accordance with *A*'s wishes.

dependence *B*'s relationship to *A* when *A* possesses something that *B* requires.

In organizational behavior (OB), **power** refers to a capacity that *A* has to influence the behavior of *B* so *B* acts in accordance with *A*'s wishes.[2] Someone can thus have power but not use it; it is a capacity or potential. Probably the most important aspect of power is that it is a function of **dependence**. The greater *B*'s dependence on *A*, the greater *A*'s power in the relationship. Dependence, in turn, is based on alternatives that *B* perceives and the importance *B* places on the alternative(s) *A* controls. A person can have power over you only if he or she controls something you desire. If you want a college degree and have to pass a certain course to get it, and your current instructor is the only faculty member in the college who teaches that course, she has power over you because your alternatives are highly limited and you place a high degree of importance on the outcome. Similarly, if you're attending college on funds provided by your parents, you probably recognize the power they hold over you. But once you're out of school, have a job, and are making a good income, your parents' power is reduced significantly.

Money is a powerful variable for dependence. Who among us has not heard of a rich relative who controls family members merely through the implicit or explicit threat of "writing them out of the will"? Another example is found on Wall Street, where portfolio manager Ping Jiang allegedly was able to coerce his subordinate, analyst Andrew Tong, into taking female hormones and wearing lipstick and makeup. Why such power? Jiang controlled Tong's access to day trading and thus his livelihood.[3]

A careful comparison of our description of power with our description of leadership in Chapter 12 reveals the concepts are closely intertwined. *Leaders* use *power* as a means of attaining group goals. How are the two terms different? Power does not require goal compatibility, just dependence. Leadership, on the other hand, requires some congruence between the goals of the leader and those being led. A second difference relates to the direction of influence. Leadership research focuses on the downward influence on followers. It minimizes the importance of lateral and upward influence patterns. Power research takes all factors into consideration. For a third difference, leadership research often emphasizes style. It seeks answers to questions such as: How supportive should a leader be? How much decision making should be shared with followers? In contrast, the research on power focuses on tactics for gaining compliance. Lastly, leadership concentrates on the individual leader's influence, while the study of power acknowledges that groups as well as individuals can use power to control other individuals or groups.

You may have noted that for a power situation to exist, one person or group needs to have control over resources the other person or group values. This is usually the case in established leadership situations. However, power relationships are possible in all areas of life, and power can be obtained in many ways. Let's explore the various sources of power next.

Bases of Power

13-2 Explain the three bases of formal power and the two bases of personal power.

Where does power come from? What gives an individual or a group influence over others? We answer by dividing the bases or sources of power into two general groupings—formal and personal—and breaking each of these down into more specific categories.[4]

Formal Power

Formal power is based on an individual's position in an organization. It can come from the ability to coerce or reward, or from formal authority.

coercive power A power base that is dependent on fear of the negative results from failing to comply.

Coercive Power The **coercive power** base depends on the target's fear of negative results from failing to comply. On the physical level, coercive power rests on the application, or the threat of application, of bodily distress through the infliction of pain, the restriction of movement, or the withholding of basic physiological or safety needs.

At the organizational level, *A* has coercive power over *B* if *A* can dismiss, suspend, or demote *B*, assuming *B* values her job. If *A* can assign *B* work activities *B* finds unpleasant, or treat *B* in a manner *B* finds embarrassing, *A* possesses coercive power over *B*. Coercive power comes also from withholding key information. People in an organization who have data or knowledge others need can make others dependent on them.

reward power Compliance achieved based on the ability to distribute rewards that others view as valuable.

Reward Power The opposite of coercive power is **reward power**, with which people comply because it produces positive benefits; someone who can distribute rewards others view as valuable will have power over them. These rewards can be financial—such as controlling pay rates, raises, and bonuses—or nonfinancial, including recognition, promotions, interesting work assignments, friendly colleagues, and preferred work shifts or sales territories.[5]

legitimate power The power a person receives as a result of his or her position in the formal hierarchy of an organization.

Legitimate Power In formal groups and organizations, probably the most common access to one or more of the power bases is through **legitimate power**. It represents the formal authority to control and use organizational resources based on the person's structural position in the organization.

Legitimate power is broader than the power to coerce and reward. Specifically, it includes members' acceptance of the authority of a hierarchical position. We associate power so closely with the concept of hierarchy that just drawing longer lines in an organization chart leads people to infer the leaders are especially powerful.[6] In general, when school principals, bank presidents, or army captains speak, teachers, tellers, and first lieutenants usually comply.

Personal Power

Many of the most competent and productive chip designers at Intel have power, but they aren't managers and they have no formal power. What they have is

Internet entrepreneur Mark Zuckerberg, co-founder and CEO of Facebook, has expert power. Shown here talking with employees, Zuckerberg earned the title "software guy" during college because of his expertise in computer programming. Today, Facebook depends on his expertise to achieve company goals.
Source: Tony Avelar/AP Images

personal power, which comes from an individual's unique characteristics. There are two bases of personal power: expertise and the respect and admiration of others. Personal power is not mutually exclusive from formal power, but it can be independent.

expert power Influence based on special skills or knowledge.

Expert Power **Expert power** is influence wielded as a result of expertise, special skills, or knowledge. As jobs become more specialized, we become dependent on experts to achieve goals. It is generally acknowledged that physicians have expertise and hence expert power: Most of us follow our doctor's advice. Computer specialists, tax accountants, economists, industrial psychologists, and other specialists wield power as a result of their expertise.

referent power Influence based on identification with a person who has desirable resources or personal traits.

Referent Power **Referent power** is based on identification with a person who has desirable resources or personal traits. If I like, respect, and admire you, you can exercise power over me because I want to please you.

Referent power develops out of admiration of another and a desire to be like that person. It helps explain, for instance, why celebrities are paid millions of dollars to endorse products in commercials. Marketing research shows people such as LeBron James and Tom Brady have the power to influence your choice of athletic shoes and credit cards. With a little practice, you and I could probably deliver as smooth a sales pitch as these celebrities, but the buying public doesn't identify with us. Some people who are not in formal leadership positions have referent power and exert influence over others because of their charismatic dynamism, likability, and emotional appeal.

Which Bases of Power Are Most Effective?

Of the three bases of formal power (coercive, reward, legitimate) and two bases of personal power (expert, referent), which are most important? Research suggests the personal sources of power are most effective. Both expert and referent power are positively related to employees' satisfaction with supervision, their organizational commitment, and their performance, whereas reward and legitimate power seem to be unrelated to these outcomes. One source of formal power—coercive power—can be damaging.

Referent power can be a powerful motivator. Consider Steve Stoute's company, Translation, which matches pop-star spokespersons with corporations that want to promote their brands. Stoute has paired Justin Timberlake with McDonald's, Beyoncé with Tommy Hilfiger, and Jay-Z with Reebok. Stoute's business seems to be all about referent power. His firm aims to use the credibility of artists and performers to reach youth culture.[7] The success of these well-known companies attests to Stoute's expectation that the buying public identifies with and emulates his spokespersons and therefore thinks highly of the represented brands.

Dependence: The Key to Power

13-3 Explain the role of dependence in power relationships.

The most important aspect of power is that it is a function of dependence. In this section, we show how understanding dependence helps us understand the degrees of power.

The General Dependence Postulate

Let's begin with a general postulate: *The greater* B*'s dependence on* A*, the more power* A *has over* B. When you possess anything others require that you alone control, you make them dependent on you, and therefore you gain power over them.[8] As the old saying goes, "In the land of the blind, the one-eyed man is king!" But if something is plentiful, possessing it will not increase your power. Therefore, the more you can expand your own options, the less power you place in the hands of others. This explains why most organizations develop multiple suppliers rather than give their business to only one. It also explains why so many people aspire to financial independence. Independence reduces the power others can wield to limit our access to opportunities and resources.

What Creates Dependence?

Dependence increases when the resource you control is important, scarce, and nonsubstitutable.[9]

Importance If nobody wants what you have, it's not going to create dependence. However, note that there are many degrees of importance, from needing the resource for survival to wanting a resource that is in fashion or adds to convenience.

Scarcity Ferruccio Lamborghini, who created the exotic supercars that still carry his name, understood the importance of scarcity and used it to his advantage during World War II. When Lamborghini was in Rhodes with the Italian army, his superiors were impressed with his mechanical skills because he demonstrated an almost uncanny ability to repair tanks and cars no one else could fix. After the war, he admitted his ability was largely due to his having been the first person on the island to receive the repair manuals, which he memorized and then destroyed so as to make himself indispensable.[10]

We see the scarcity–dependence relationship in the power situation of employment. Where the supply of labor is low relative to demand, workers can negotiate compensation and benefits packages far more attractive than those in occupations with an abundance of candidates. For example, college administrators have no problem today finding English instructors since there is a high supply and low demand. The market for network systems analysts, in contrast, is comparatively tight, with demand high and supply limited. The resulting

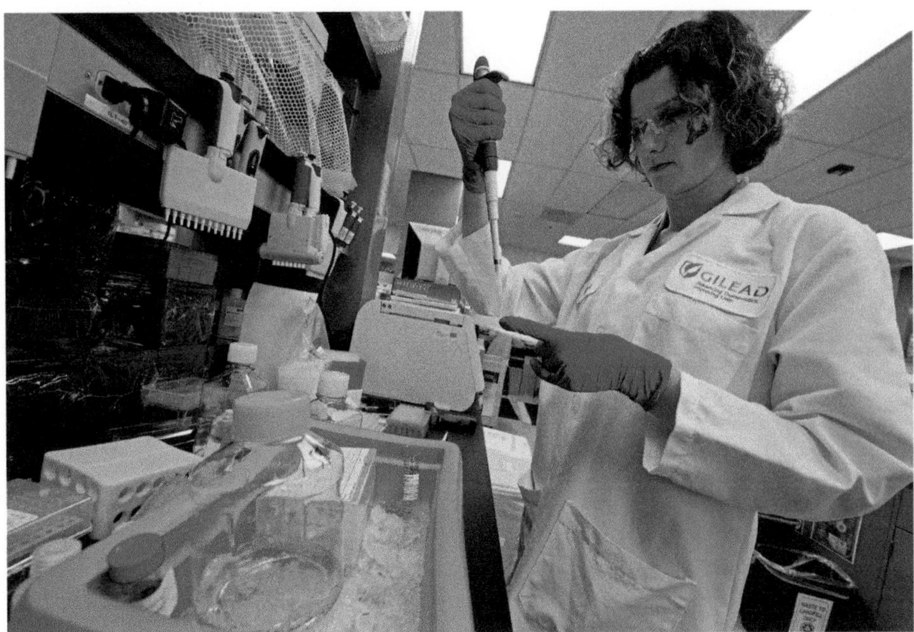

Scientist Maria Kovalenko is in a position of power at Gilead Sciences, a research-based biopharmaceutical firm. Scientists are in a powerful occupational group at Gilead because they discover and develop medicines that improve the lives of patients and contribute to Gilead's growth and success.
Source: David Paul Morris/Bloomberg/Getty Images

bargaining power of computer-engineering faculty allows them to negotiate higher salaries, lighter teaching loads, and other benefits.

Nonsubstitutability The fewer viable substitutes for a resource, the more power a person controlling that resource has. At universities that value faculty publishing, for example, the more recognition the faculty member receives through publication, the more control that person has because other universities want faculty who are highly published and visible.

Social Network Analysis: A Tool for Assessing Resources

One tool to assess the exchange of resources and dependencies within an organization is *social network analysis.*[11] This method examines patterns of communication among organizational members to identify how information flows between them. Within a social network, or connections between people who share professional interests, each individual or group is called a node, and the links between nodes are called ties. When nodes communicate or exchange resources frequently, they are said to have very strong ties. Other nodes that are not engaged in direct communication with one another achieve resource flows through intermediary nodes. In other words, some nodes act as brokers between otherwise unconnected nodes. A graphical illustration of the associations among individuals in a social network is called a *sociogram* and functions like an informal version of an organization chart. The difference is that a formal organization chart shows how authority is supposed to flow, whereas a sociogram shows how resources *really* flow in an organization. An example of a sociogram is in Exhibit 13-1.

Networks can create substantial power dynamics. Those in the position of brokers tend to have more power because they can leverage the unique resources they can acquire from different groups. In other words, many people are dependent upon brokers, which gives the brokers more power. For example, organizational culture changes such as corporate social responsibility (CSR) awareness will often begin in a single connected group of individuals, grow in strength, and then slowly move to other connected groups through brokers

Exhibit 13-1 An Organizational Sociogram

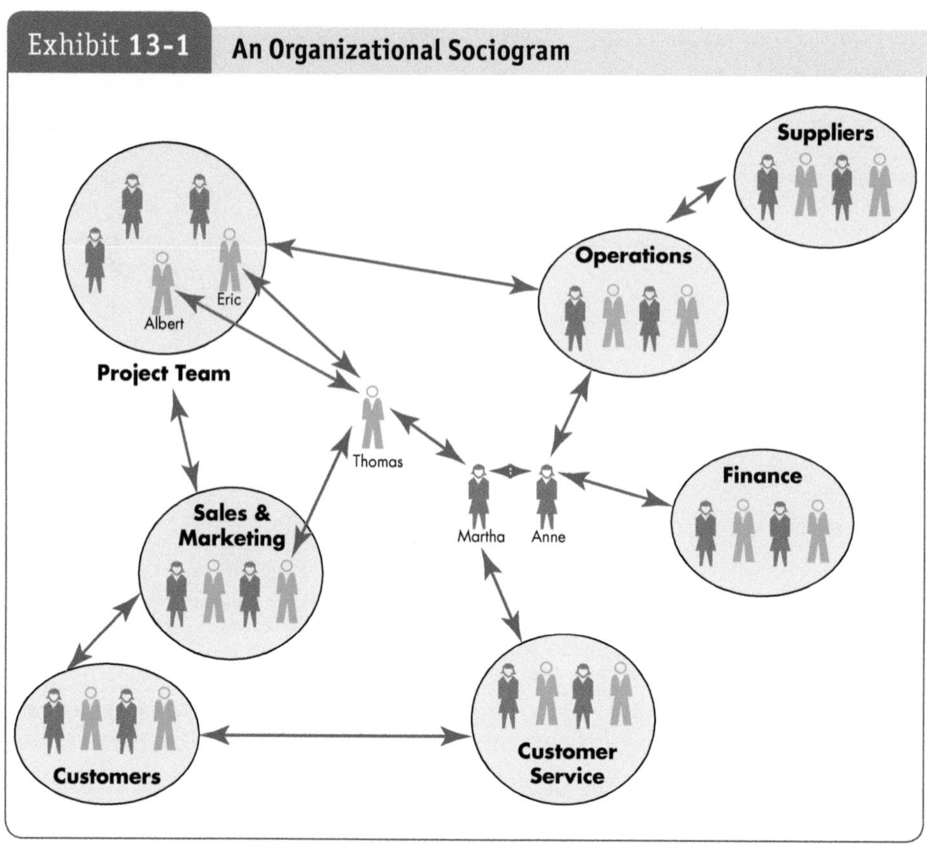

over time.[12] Data from the United Kingdom's National Health Service show that change agents—people entrusted with helping an organization to make a significant change—have more success if they are information brokers.[13] These functions are not without cost, however. One study found that people identified as central to advice networks were more likely to quit their jobs, possibly because they did a great deal of extra work without reward.[14]

There are many ways to implement a social network analysis in an organization.[15] Some organizations keep track of the flow of e-mail communications or document sharing across departments. These big-data tools are an easy way to gather objective information about how individuals exchange information. Other organizations look at data from human resources (HR) information systems, analyzing how supervisors and subordinates interact with one another. These data sources can produce sociograms showing how resources and power flow. Leaders can then identify powerful brokers who exert the strongest influence on many groups, and address these key individuals.

Power Tactics

13-4 Identify power or influence tactics and their contingencies.

power tactics Ways in which individuals translate power bases into specific actions.

What **power tactics** do people use to translate power bases into specific action? What options do they have for influencing their bosses, coworkers, or employees? Research has identified nine distinct influence tactics:[16]

- *Legitimacy.* Relying on your authority position or saying a request accords with organizational policies or rules.
- *Rational persuasion.* Presenting logical arguments and factual evidence to demonstrate a request is reasonable.

- *Inspirational appeals.* Developing emotional commitment by appealing to a target's values, needs, hopes, and aspirations.
- *Consultation.* Increasing support by involving the target in deciding how to accomplish your plan.
- *Exchange.* Rewarding the target with benefits or favors in exchange for acceding to a request.
- *Personal appeals.* Asking for compliance based on friendship or loyalty.
- *Ingratiation.* Using flattery, praise, or friendly behavior prior to making a request.
- *Pressure.* Using warnings, repeated demands, and threats.
- *Coalitions.* Enlisting the aid or support of others to persuade the target to agree.

Using Power Tactics

Some tactics are more effective than others. Rational persuasion, inspirational appeals, and consultation tend to be the most effective, especially when the audience is highly interested in the outcomes of a decision process. The pressure tactic tends to backfire and is typically the least effective of the nine.[17] You can increase your chance of success by using two or more tactics together or sequentially, as long as your choices are compatible.[18] Using ingratiation and legitimacy together can lessen negative reactions, but only when the audience does not really care about the outcome of a decision process or the policy is routine.[19]

Let's consider the most effective way of getting a raise. You can start with a rational approach—figure out how your pay compares to that of your organizational peers, land a competing job offer, gather data that testify to your performance, or use salary calculators like Salary.com to compare your pay with others in your occupation—then share your findings with your manager. The results can be impressive. Kitty Dunning, a vice president at Don Jagoda Associates, landed a 16 percent raise when she e-mailed her boss numbers showing she had increased sales.[20]

While rational persuasion may work in this situation, the effectiveness of some influence tactics depends on the direction of influence,[21] and of course on the audience. As Exhibit 13-2 shows, rational persuasion is the only tactic effective across organizational levels. Inspirational appeals work best as a downward-influencing tactic with subordinates. When pressure works, it's generally downward only. Personal appeals and coalitions are most effective as lateral influence. Other factors relating to the effectiveness of influence include the sequencing of tactics, a person's skill in using the tactic, and the organizational culture.

In general, you're more likely to be effective if you begin with "softer" tactics that rely on personal power, such as personal and inspirational appeals, rational persuasion, and consultation. If these fail, you can move to "harder" tactics,

Exhibit 13-2 Preferred Power Tactics by Influence Direction

Upward Influence	Downward Influence	Lateral Influence
Rational persuasion	Rational persuasion	Rational persuasion
	Inspirational appeals	Consultation
	Pressure	Ingratiation
	Consultation	Exchange
	Ingratiation	Legitimacy
	Exchange	Personal appeals
	Legitimacy	Coalitions

such as exchange, coalitions, and pressure, which emphasize formal power and incur greater costs and risks.[22] A single soft tactic is more effective than a single hard tactic, and combining two soft tactics or a soft tactic and rational persuasion is more effective than any single tactic or combination of hard tactics.[23]

As we mentioned, the effectiveness of tactics depends on the audience.[24] People especially likely to comply with soft power tactics tend to be more reflective and intrinsically motivated; they have high self-esteem and a greater desire for control. Those likely to comply with hard power tactics are more action-oriented and extrinsically motivated, and more focused on getting along with others than on getting their own way.

Cultural Preferences for Power Tactics

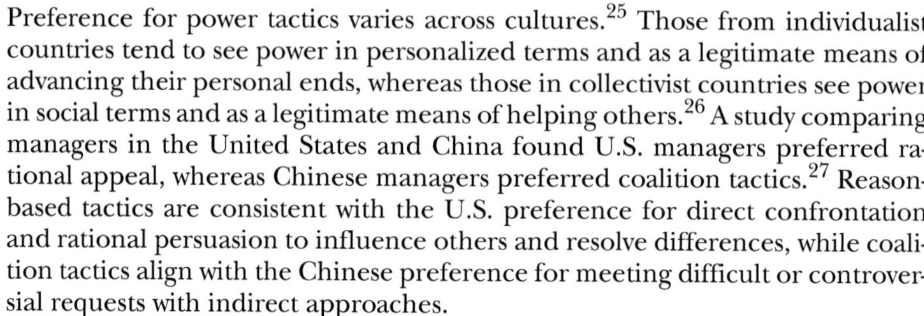

Preference for power tactics varies across cultures.[25] Those from individualist countries tend to see power in personalized terms and as a legitimate means of advancing their personal ends, whereas those in collectivist countries see power in social terms and as a legitimate means of helping others.[26] A study comparing managers in the United States and China found U.S. managers preferred rational appeal, whereas Chinese managers preferred coalition tactics.[27] Reason-based tactics are consistent with the U.S. preference for direct confrontation and rational persuasion to influence others and resolve differences, while coalition tactics align with the Chinese preference for meeting difficult or controversial requests with indirect approaches.

Applying Power Tactics

political skill The ability to influence others in such a way as to enhance one's objectives.

People differ in their **political skill**, or their ability to influence others to enhance their own objectives. The politically skilled are more effective users of all the influence tactics. Political skill is also more effective when the stakes are high, such as when the individual is accountable for important organizational outcomes. Finally, the politically skilled are able to exert their influence without others detecting it, a key element in effectiveness (it's damaging to be labeled political).[28] These individuals are able to use their political skills in environments with low levels of procedural and distributive justice. When an organization has fairly applied rules, free of favoritism or biases, political skill is actually negatively related to job performance ratings.[29]

Lastly, we know cultures within organizations differ markedly—some are warm, relaxed, and supportive; others are formal and conservative. Some encourage participation and consultation, some encourage reason, and still others rely on pressure. People who fit the culture of the organization tend to obtain more influence.[30] Specifically, extraverts tend to be more influential in team-oriented organizations, and highly conscientious people are more influential in organizations that value working alone on technical tasks. People who fit the culture are influential because they can perform especially well in the domains deemed most important for success. Thus, the organization itself will influence which subset of power tactics is viewed as acceptable for use.

How Power Affects People

13-5 Identify the causes and consequences of abuse of power.

To this point, we've discussed what power is and how it is acquired. But we've not yet answered one important question: Does power corrupt?

There is certainly evidence that there are corrupting aspects of power. Power leads people to place their own interests ahead of others' needs or goals. Why does this happen? Interestingly, power not only leads people to focus on their self-interests because they can, it liberates them to focus inward and thus come to place greater weight on their own aims and interests. Power also appears to lead individuals to "objectify" others (to see them as tools to obtain their instrumental goals) and to see relationships as more peripheral.[31]

That's not all. Powerful people react—especially negatively—to any threats to their competence. People in positions of power hold on to it when they can, and individuals who face threats to their power are exceptionally willing to take actions to retain it whether their actions harm others or not. Those given power are more likely to make self-interested decisions when faced with a moral hazard (such as when hedge fund managers take more risks with other people's money because they're rewarded for gains but less often punished for losses). People in power are more willing to denigrate others. Power also leads to overconfident decision making.[32]

Frank Lloyd Wright, perhaps the greatest U.S. architect, is a good example of power's corrupting effects. Early in his career, Wright worked for and was mentored by a renowned architect, Louis Sullivan (sometimes known as "the father of the skyscraper"). Before Wright achieved greatness, he was generous in his praise for Sullivan. Later in his career, that praise faded, and Wright even took credit for one of Sullivan's noted designs. Wright was never a benevolent man, but as his power accumulated, so did his potential to behave in a "monstrous" way toward others.[33]

Power Variables

As we've discussed, power does appear to have some important disturbing effects on us. But that is hardly the whole story—power is more complicated than that. It doesn't affect everyone in the same way, and there are even positive effects of power. Let's consider each of these in turn.

First, the toxic effects of power depend on the wielder's personality. Research suggests that if we have an anxious personality, power does not corrupt us because we are less likely to think that using power benefits us.[34] Second, the corrosive effect of power can be contained by organizational systems. One study found, for example, that while power made people behave in a self-serving manner, when accountability for this behavior was initiated, the self-serving behavior stopped. Third, we have the means to blunt the negative effects of power. One study showed that simply expressing gratitude toward powerful others makes them less likely to act aggressively against us. Finally, remember the saying that those with little power abuse what little they have? There seems to be some truth to this in that the people most likely to abuse power are those who start low in status and gain power. Why is this the case? It appears having low status is threatening, and the fear this creates is used in negative ways if power is later given.[35]

As you can see, some factors can moderate the negative effects of power. But there can be general positive effects. Power energizes and increases motivation to achieve goals. It also can enhance our motivation to help others. One study found, for example, that a desire to help others translated into actual work behavior when people felt a sense of power.[36]

This study points to an important insight about power. It is not so much that power corrupts as it *reveals what we value.* Supporting this line of reasoning, another study found that power led to self-interested behavior only in those with a weak moral identity (the degree to which morals are core to someone's identity). In those with a strong moral identity, power enhanced their moral awareness and willingness to act.[37]

Sexual Harassment: Unequal Power in the Workplace

sexual harassment Any unwanted activity of a sexual nature that affects an individual's employment and creates a hostile work environment.

Sexual harassment is defined as any unwanted activity of a sexual nature that affects an individual's employment or creates a hostile work environment. According to the U.S. Equal Employment Opportunity Commission (EEOC), sexual harassment happens when a person encounters "unwelcome sexual advances, requests for sexual favors, and other verbal or physical conduct of a sexual nature" on the job that disrupts work performance or that creates an "intimidating, hostile, or offensive" work environment.[38] Although the definition changes from country to country, most nations have at least some policies to protect workers. Whether the policies or laws are followed is another question, however. Equal employment opportunity legislation is established in Pakistan, Bangladesh, and Oman, for example, but studies suggest it might not be well implemented.[39]

Generally, sexual harassment is more prevalent in male-dominated societies. For example, a study in Pakistan found that up to 93 percent of female workers were sexually harassed.[40] In Singapore, up to 54 percent of workers (women and men) reported they were sexually harassed.[41] The percentages in the United States and some other countries are generally much lower but still troubling. Surveys indicate about one-quarter of U.S. women and 10 percent of men have been sexually harassed.[42] Data from the EEOC suggest that sexual harassment is decreasing: Sexual harassment claims now make up 10 percent of all discrimination claims, compared with 20 percent in the mid-1990s. Of this percentage, though, claims from men have increased from 11 percent of total claims in 1997 to 17.5 percent today.[43] Sexual harassment is disproportionately prevalent for women in certain types of jobs. In the restaurant industry, for instance, 80 percent of female wait staff reported having been sexually harassed by coworkers or customers, compared to 70 percent of male wait staff.[44]

Most studies confirm that power is central to understanding sexual harassment.[45] This seems true whether the harassment comes from a supervisor, coworker, or employee. And sexual harassment is more likely to occur when

A federal jury awarded this woman a $95 million judgment in a sexual harassment lawsuit against her employer for harassment from her supervisor that included unwanted physical contact. The jury found the supervisor guilty of assault and battery and the company liable for negligent supervision and sexual harassment.
Source: Bill Greenblatt/UPI/Newscom

there are large power differentials. The supervisor–employee dyad best characterizes an unequal power relationship, where formal power gives the supervisor the capacity to reward and coerce. Because employees want favorable performance reviews, salary increases, and the like, supervisors control resources most employees consider important and scarce. When there aren't effective controls to detect and prevent sexual harassment, abusers are more likely to act. For example, male respondents in one study in Switzerland who were high in hostile sexism reported higher intentions to sexually harass in organizations that had low levels of justice, suggesting that failure to have consistent policies and procedures for all employees might increase levels of sexual harassment.[46]

Sexual harassment can detrimentally impact individuals and the organization, but it can be avoided. The manager's role is critical:

1. *Make sure an active policy defines what constitutes sexual harassment, informs employees they can be fired for inappropriate behavior, and establishes procedures for making complaints.*
2. *Reassure employees they will not encounter retaliation if they file a complaint.*
3. *Investigate every complaint, and inform the legal and HR departments.*
4. *Make sure offenders are disciplined or terminated.*
5. *Set up in-house seminars to raise employee awareness of sexual harassment issues.*

The bottom line is that managers have a responsibility to protect their employees from a hostile work environment. They may easily be unaware that one of their employees is being sexually harassed, but being unaware does not protect them or their organization. If investigators believe a manager could have known about the harassment, both the manager and the company can be held liable.

Politics: Power in Action

13-6 Describe how politics work in organizations.

Whenever people get together in groups, power will be exerted. People in organizations want to carve out a niche to exert influence, earn rewards, and advance their careers. If they convert their power into action, we describe them as being engaged in *politics*. Those with good political skills have the ability to use their bases of power effectively.[47] Politics are not only inevitable; they might be essential, too (see OB Poll).

Definition of Organizational Politics

political behavior Activities that are not required as part of a person's formal role in the organization but that influence, or attempt to influence, the distribution of advantages and disadvantages within the organization.

There is no shortage of definitions of *organizational politics*. Essentially, this type of politics focuses on the use of power to affect decision making in an organization, sometimes for self-serving and organizationally unsanctioned behaviors.[48] For our purposes, **political behavior** in organizations consists of activities that are not required as part of an individual's formal role but that influence, or attempt to influence, the distribution of advantages and disadvantages within the organization.[49]

This definition encompasses what most people mean when they talk about organizational politics. Political behavior is outside specified job requirements. It requires some attempt to use power bases. It includes efforts to influence the goals, criteria, or processes used for decision making. Our definition is broad enough to include varied political behaviors such as withholding key information from decision makers, joining a coalition, whistle-blowing, spreading rumors, leaking confidential information to the media, exchanging favors with

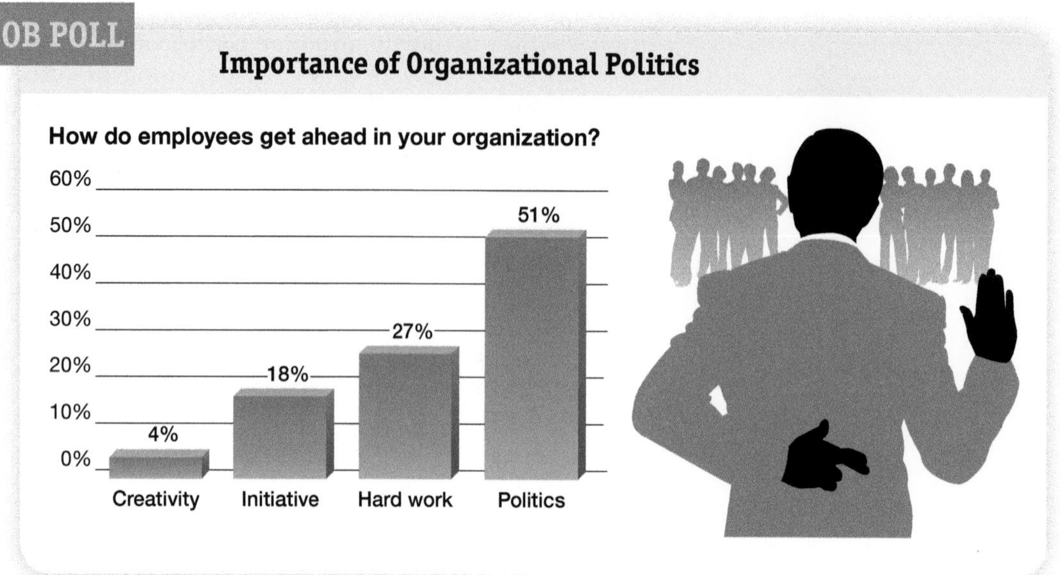

Source: D. Crampton, "Is How Americans Feel about Their Jobs Changing?" (September 28, 2012), http://corevalues.com/employee-motivation/is-how-americans-feel-about-their-jobs-changing.

others for mutual benefit, and lobbying on behalf of or against a particular individual or decision alternative. In this way, political behavior is often negative, but not always.

The Reality of Politics

Interviews with experienced managers show most believe political behavior is a major part of organizational life.[50] Many managers report some use of political behavior is ethical, as long as it doesn't directly harm anyone else.

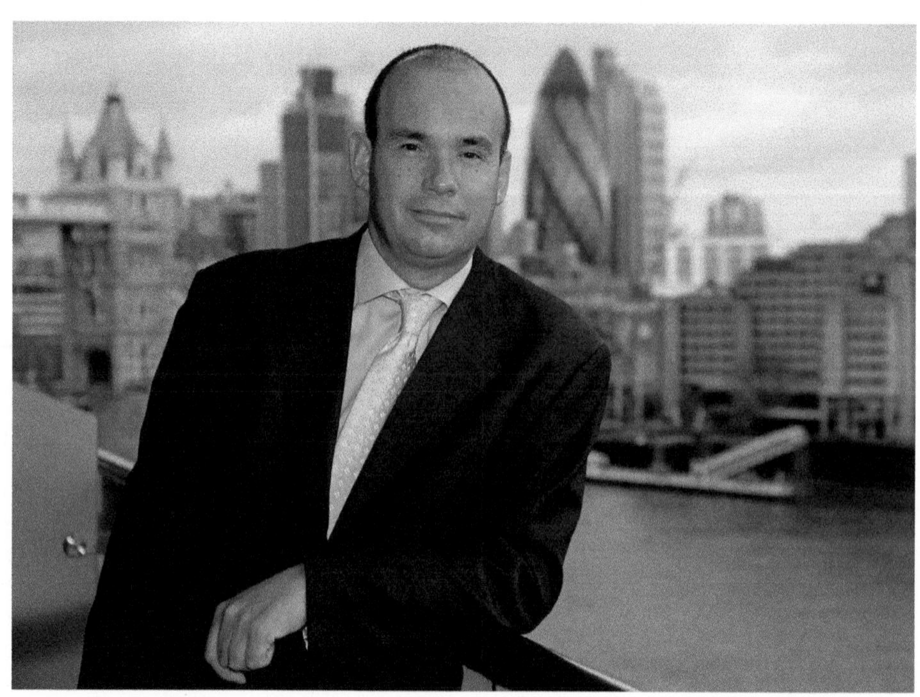

Whistle-blower Michael Woodford was fired from his position as CEO of Japanese camera-maker Olympus after informing company officials about accounting irregularities. Although not part of his job, Woodford uncovered a 13-year accounting fraud by some company executives.
Source: Luke McGregor/Reuters

They describe politics as necessary and believe someone who never uses political behavior will have a hard time getting things done. Most also indicate they have never been trained to use political behavior effectively. But why, you may wonder, must politics exist? Isn't it possible for an organization to be politics-free? It's *possible*—but unlikely.

Organizations have individuals and groups with different values, goals, and interests.[51] This sets up the potential for conflict over the allocation of limited resources, such as budgets, work space, and salary and bonus pools. If resources were abundant, all constituencies within an organization could satisfy their goals. But because they are limited, not everyone's interests can be satisfied. Furthermore, gains by one individual or group are often *perceived* as coming at the expense of others within the organization (whether they are or not). These forces create competition among members for the organization's limited resources.

Maybe the most important factor leading to politics within organizations is the realization that most of the "facts" used to allocate limited resources are open to interpretation. When allocating pay based on performance, for instance, what is *good* performance? What's an *adequate* improvement? What constitutes an *unsatisfactory* job? The manager of any major league baseball team knows a .400 hitter is a high performer and a .125 hitter is a poor performer. You don't need to be a baseball genius to know you should play your .400 hitter and send the .125 hitter back to the minors. But what if you have to choose between players who hit .280 and .290? Then less objective factors come into play: fielding expertise, attitude, potential, ability to perform in a clutch, loyalty to the team, and so on. More managerial decisions resemble the choice between a .280 and a .290 hitter than between a .125 hitter and a .400 hitter. It is in this large and ambiguous middle ground of organizational life—where the facts don't speak for themselves—that politics flourish.

Finally, because most decisions have to be made in a climate of ambiguity—where facts are rarely objective and thus open to interpretation—people within organizations will use whatever influence they can support their goals and interests. That, of course, creates the activities we call *politicking*. One person's "selfless effort to benefit the organization" is seen by another as a "blatant attempt to further his or her interest." [52]

Therefore, to answer the question of whether it is possible for an organization to be politics-free, we can say "yes"—if all members of that organization hold the same goals and interests, if organizational resources are not scarce, and if performance outcomes are completely clear and objective. But that doesn't describe the organizational world in which most of us live.

Causes and Consequences of Political Behavior

13-7 Identify the causes, consequences, and ethics of political behavior.

Now that we've discussed the constant presence of politicking in organizations, let's discuss the causes and consequences of these behaviors.

Factors Contributing to Political Behavior

Not all groups or organizations are equally political. In some organizations, politicking is overt and rampant, while in others politics plays a small role in influencing outcomes. Why this variation? Research and observation have identified a number of factors that appear to encourage political behavior. Some are individual characteristics, derived from the qualities of the people

Exhibit 13-3 Factors That Influence Political Behavior

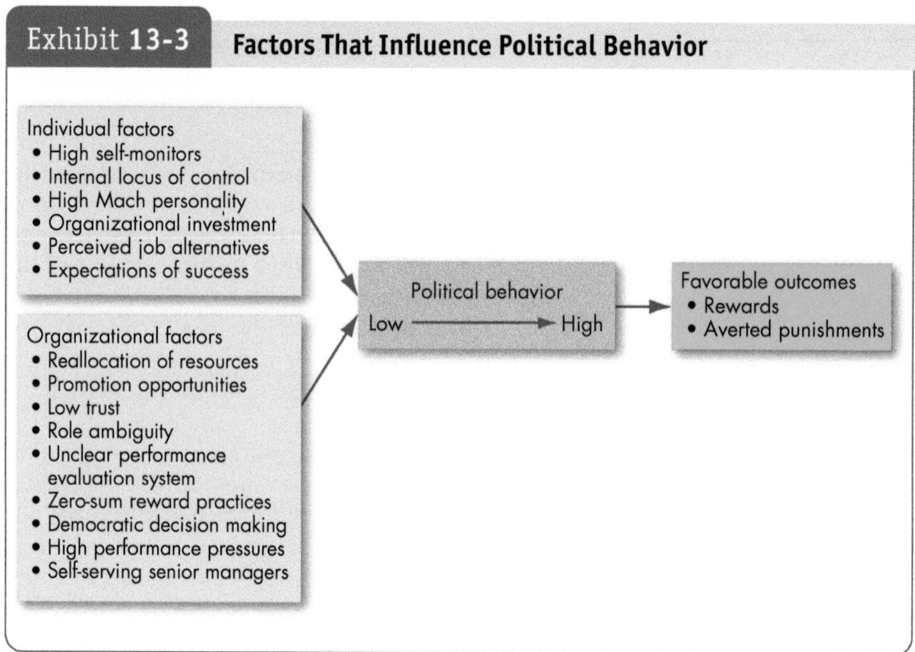

the organization employs; others are a result of the organization's culture or internal environment. Exhibit 13-3 illustrates how both individual and organizational factors can increase political behavior and provide favorable outcomes (increased rewards and averted punishments) for individuals and groups in the organization.

Individual Factors At the individual level, researchers have identified certain personality traits, needs, and other factors likely to be related to political behavior. In terms of traits, we find that employees who are high self-monitors, possess an internal locus of control, and have a high need for power are more likely to engage in political behavior. The high self-monitor is more sensitive to social cues, exhibits higher levels of social conformity, and is more likely to be skilled in political behavior than the low self-monitor. Because they believe they can control their environment, individuals with an internal locus of control are more prone to take a proactive stance and attempt to manipulate situations in their favor. Not surprisingly, the Machiavellian personality—characterized by the will to manipulate and the desire for power—is consistent with using politics as a means to further personal interests.

An individual's investment in the organization and perceived alternatives influence the degree to which he or she will pursue illegitimate means of political action.[53] The more a person expects increased future benefits from the organization, and the more that person has to lose if forced out, the less likely he or she is to use illegitimate means. Conversely, the more alternate job opportunities an individual has—due to a favorable job market, possession of scarce skills or knowledge, prominent reputation, or influential contacts outside the organization—the more likely the person is to employ politics.

An individual with low expectations of success from political means is unlikely to use them. High expectations from such measures are most likely to be the province of both experienced and powerful individuals with polished political skills, and inexperienced and naïve employees who misjudge their chances.

Finally, some individuals engage in more political behavior because they simply are better at it. Such individuals read interpersonal interactions well, fit their behavior to situational needs, and excel at networking.[54] These people are often indirectly rewarded for their political efforts. For example, a study of a construction firm in southern China found that politically skilled subordinates were more likely to receive recommendations for rewards from their supervisors, and that politically oriented supervisors were especially likely to respond positively to politically skilled subordinates.[55] Other studies from countries around the world have similarly shown that higher levels of political skill are associated with higher levels of perceived job performance.[56]

Organizational Factors Although we acknowledge the role individual differences can play, the evidence more strongly suggests that certain situations and cultures promote politics. Specifically, when an organization's resources are declining, when the existing pattern of resources is changing, and when there

Career OBjectives

Should I become political?

My office is so political! Everyone is just looking for ways to get ahead by plotting and scheming rather than doing the job. Should I just go along with it and develop my own political strategy?

— Julia

Dear Julia:

There's definitely a temptation to join in when other people are behaving politically. If you want to advance your career, you need to think about social relationships and how to work with other people in a smart and diplomatic way. But that doesn't mean you have to give in to pressure to engage in organizational politics.

Of course, in many workplaces, hard work and achievement aren't recognized, which heightens politicking and lowers performance. But politics aren't just potentially bad for the company. People who are seen as political can be gradually excluded from social networks and informal communication. Coworkers can sabotage a person with a reputation for dishonesty or manipulation so they don't have to deal with him or her. It's also likely that a political person will be the direct target of revenge from those who feel they've been wronged.

If you want to provide a positive alternative to political behavior in your workplace, there are a few steps you can take:

- *Document your work efforts, and find data to back up your accomplishments.* Political behavior thrives in an ambiguous environment where standards for success are subjective and open to manipulation. The best way to shortcut politics is to move the focus toward clear, objective markers of work performance.
- *Call out political behavior when you see it.* Political behavior is, by its very nature, secretive and underhanded. By bringing politics to light, you limit this capacity to manipulate people against one another.
- *Try to develop a network with only those individuals who are interested in performing well together.* This makes it hard for a very political person to get a lot done. On the other hand, trustworthy and cooperative people will be able to find many allies who are genuinely supportive. These support networks will result in performance levels that a lone political person simply cannot match.

Remember, in the long run a good reputation can be your greatest asset!

Based on: A. Lavoie "How to Get Rid of Toxic Office Politics," *Fast Company*, April 10, 2014, http://www.fastcompany.com/3028856/work-smart/how-to-make-office-politicking-a-lame-duck; C. Conner, "Office Politics: Must You Play?" *Forbes*, April 14, 2013, http://www.forbes.com/sites/cherylsnappconner/2013/04/14/office-politics-must-you-play-a-handbook-for-survivalsuccess/; and J. A. Colquitt and J. B. Rodell "Justice, Trust, and Trustworthiness: A Longitudinal Analysis Integrating Three Theoretical Perspectives," *Academy of Management Journal* 54 (2011): 1183–206.

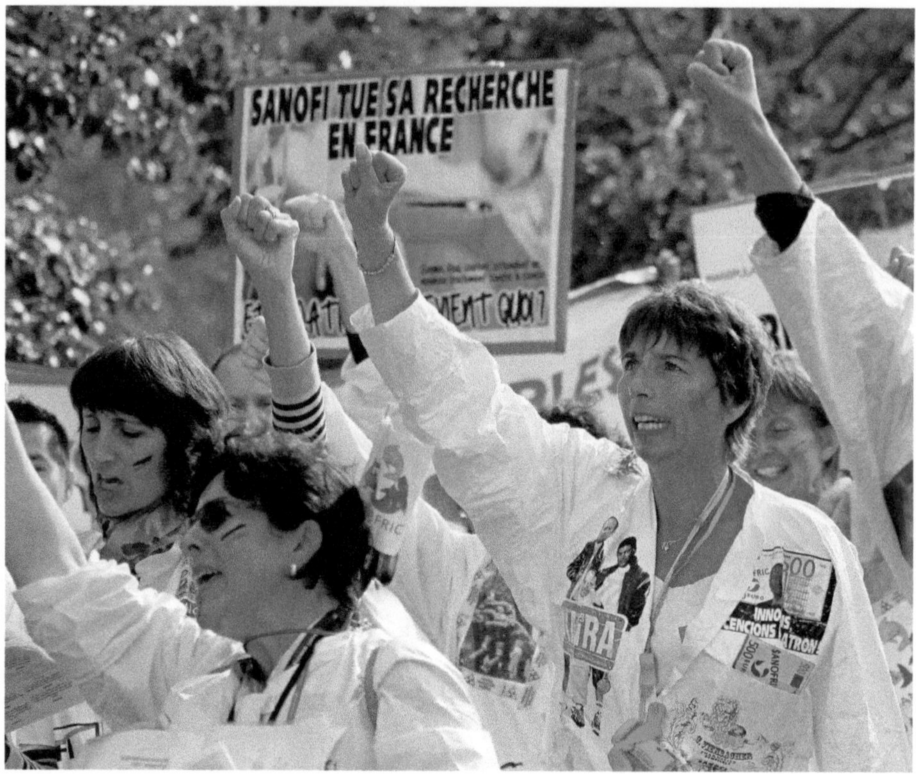

Organizations foster politicking when they reduce resources. By announcing plans to downsize its global workforce of 100,000 employees to increase its competitiveness, French pharmaceutical firm Sanofi stimulated political activity among employees who organized protests against the job cuts.
Source: Robert Pratta/Reuters

is opportunity for promotions, politicking is more likely to surface.[57] When resources are reduced, people may engage in political actions to safeguard what they have. Also, *any* changes, especially those implying significant reallocation of resources within the organization, are likely to stimulate conflict and increase politicking.

Cultures characterized by low trust, role ambiguity, unclear performance evaluation systems, zero-sum (win-lose) reward allocation practices, democratic decision making, high pressure for performance, and self-serving senior managers will also create breeding grounds for politicking.[58] Because political activities are not required as part of the employee's formal role, the greater the role ambiguity, the more employees can engage in unnoticed political activity. Role ambiguity means the prescribed employee behaviors are not clear. There are, therefore, fewer limits to the scope and functions of the employee's political actions.

The more an organizational culture emphasizes the zero-sum or win–lose approach to reward allocations, the more employees will be motivated to engage in politicking. The **zero-sum approach** treats the reward "pie" as fixed, so any gain one person or group achieves comes at the expense of another person or group. For example, if $15,000 is distributed among five employees for raises, any employee who gets more than $3,000 takes money away from one or more of the others. Such a practice encourages making others look bad and increasing the visibility of what you do.

zero-sum approach An approach that treats the reward "pie" as fixed, such that any gains by one individual are at the expense of another.

There are also political forces at work in the relationships *between* organizations, where politics work differently depending on the organizational cultures.[59] One study showed when two organizations with very political environments interacted with one another, the political interactions between them hurt performance in collaborative projects. On the other hand, when companies with less internal political behavior interacted with one another, even political disputes

Myth or Science?

Powerful Leaders Keep Their (Fr)Enemies Close

This statement appears to be true. We all have heard the term "frenemies" to describe friends who are also rivals or people who act like friends but secretly dislike each other. Some observers have argued that frenemies are increasing at work due to the "abundance of very close, intertwined relationships that bridge people's professional and personal lives."

Keeping enemies close may be one reason Barack Obama appointed Hillary Clinton secretary of state after their bitter battle for the U.S. presidency. Or, in the business world, why one entrepreneur decided not to sue a former college classmate who, after working for her startup as a consultant, took that knowledge and started his own, competing company.

Is it really wise to keep your enemies close? And, if so, why?

New research suggests answers to these questions. Three experimental studies found individuals chose to work in the same room as their rival even when informed they would probably perform better apart; sit closer to rivals when working together; and express an explicit preference to be closer to the rival. The researchers further found the primary reason for the "being closer" effect was the desire to monitor the rival's behavior and performance.

The researchers also found the "keeping enemies closer" effect was strong under certain conditions—when the individual was socially dominant, when the individual felt more competition from the team member, and when rewards and the ability to serve as leader were dependent on performance.

These results suggest the concept of frenemies is very real and that we choose to keep our rivals close so we can keep an eye on the competition they bring.

Sources: M. Thompson, "How to Work with Your Startup Frenemies," *VentureBeat*, December 22, 2012, http://venturebeat.com/2012/12/22/frenemies/; and N. L. Mead and J. K. Maner, "On Keeping Your Enemies Close: Powerful Leaders Seek Proximity to Ingroup Power Threats," *Journal of Personality and Social Psychology* 102 (2012): 576–91.

between them did not lead to lower performance in collaborative projects. This study shows companies should be wary of forming alliances with companies that have high levels of internal political behavior.

How Do People Respond to Organizational Politics?

Trish loves her job as a writer on a weekly U.S. television comedy series but hates the internal politics. "A couple of the writers here spend more time kissing up to the executive producer than doing any work. And our head writer clearly has his favorites. While they pay me a lot and I get to really use my creativity, I'm sick of having to be on alert for backstabbers and constantly having to self-promote my contributions. I'm tired of doing most of the work and getting little of the credit." We all know friends or relatives like Trish who regularly complain about the politics at their jobs. But how do people in general react to organizational politics? Let's look at the evidence.

For most people who have modest political skills or are unwilling to play the politics game, outcomes tend to be predominantly negative. See Exhibit 13-4 for a diagram of this. However, very strong evidence indicates perceptions of organizational politics are negatively related to job satisfaction.[60] Politics may lead to self-reported declines in employee performance, perhaps because employees perceive political environments to be unfair, which demotivates them.[61] Not surprisingly, when politicking becomes too much to handle, it can lead employees to quit.[62] When employees of two agencies in a study in Nigeria viewed their work environments as political, they reported higher levels of job distress and were less likely to help their coworkers. Thus, although developing countries such as Nigeria present perhaps more ambiguous and therefore more political environments in which to work, the negative consequences of politics appear to be the same as in the United States.[63]

There are some qualifiers. First, the politics–performance relationship appears to be moderated by an individual's understanding of the "hows" and "whys" of organizational politics. Researchers noted, "An individual who has a clear understanding of who is responsible for making decisions and why they were selected to be the decision makers would have a better understanding of how and why things happen the way they do than someone who does not understand the decision-making process in the organization."[64] When both politics and understanding are high, performance is likely to increase because these individuals see political activity as an opportunity. This is consistent with what you might expect for individuals with well-honed political skills. But when understanding is low, individuals are more likely to see politics as a threat, which can have a negative effect on job performance.[65]

Second, political behavior at work moderates the effects of ethical leadership.[66] One study found male employees were more responsive to ethical leadership and showed the most citizenship behavior when levels of both politics and ethical leadership were high. Women, on the other hand, appeared most likely to engage in citizenship behavior when the environment was consistently ethical and *apolitical.*

defensive behaviors Reactive and protective behaviors to avoid action, blame, or change.

Third, when employees see politics as a threat, they often respond with **defensive behaviors**—reactive and protective behaviors to avoid action, blame, or change.[67] (Exhibit 13-5 provides some examples.) In the short run, employees may find that defensiveness protects their self-interest, but in the long run it wears them down. People who consistently rely on defensiveness find that eventually it is the only way they know how to behave. At that point, they lose the trust and support of their peers, bosses, employees, and clients.

Impression Management

We know people have an ongoing interest in how others perceive and evaluate them. For example, North Americans spend billions of dollars on diets, health club memberships, cosmetics, and plastic surgery—all intended to make them more attractive to others. Being perceived positively by others has benefits in an organizational setting. It might, for instance, help us initially to get the jobs we

Exhibit 13-5 Defensive Behaviors

Avoiding Action

Overconforming. Strictly interpreting your responsibility by saying things like "The rules clearly state..."or "This is the way we've always done it."

Buck passing. Transferring responsibility for the execution of a task or decision to someone else.

Playing dumb. Avoiding an unwanted task by falsely pleading ignorance or inability

Stretching. Prolonging a task so that one person appears to be occupied—for example, turning a two-week task into a 4-month job.

Stalling. Appearing to be more or less supportive publicly while doing little or nothing privately.

Avoiding Blame

Bluffing. Rigorously documenting activity to project an image of competence and thoroughness, known as "covering your rear."

Playing safe. Evading situations that may reflect unfavorably. It includes taking on only projects with a high probability of success, having risky decisions approved by superiors, qualifying expressions of judgment, and taking neutral positions in conflicts.

Justifying. Developing explanations that lessen one's responsibility for a negative outcome and/or apologizing to demonstrate remorse, or both.

Scapegoating. Placing the blame for a negative outcome on external factors that are not entirely blameworthy.

Misrepresenting. Manipulation of information by distortion, embellishment, deception, selective presentation, or obfuscation.

Avoiding Change

Prevention. Trying to prevent a threatening change from occurring.

Self-protection. Acting in ways to protect one's self-interest during change by guarding information or other resources.

impression management (IM) The process by which individuals attempt to control the impression others form of them.

want in an organization and, once hired, to get favorable evaluations, superior salary increases, and more rapid promotions. The process by which individuals attempt to control the impression others form of them is called **impression management (IM)**.[68]

Who might we predict will engage in IM? No surprise here. It's our old friend, the high self-monitor.[69] Low self-monitors tend to present images of themselves that are consistent with their personalities, regardless of the beneficial or detrimental effects for them. In contrast, high self-monitors are good at reading situations and molding their appearances and behavior to fit each situation. If you want to control the impression others form of you, what IM techniques can you use? Exhibit 13-6 summarizes some of the most popular with examples.

Keep in mind when people engage in IM, they are sending a false message that might be true under other circumstances.[70] Excuses, for instance, may be offered with sincerity. Referring to the example in Exhibit 13-6, you can *actually* believe that ads contribute little to sales in your region. But misrepresentation can have a high cost. If you "cry wolf" once too often, no one is likely to believe you when the wolf really comes. So the impression manager must be cautious not to be perceived as insincere or manipulative.[71]

One study found that when managers attributed an employee's citizenship behaviors to impression management, they actually felt angry (probably because they felt manipulated) and gave subordinates lower performance ratings. When managers attributed the same behaviors to prosocial values and concern about the organization, they felt happy and gave higher performance ratings.[72] In sum,

Exhibit 13-6 Impression Management (IM) Techniques

Conformity

Agreeing with someone else's opinion to gain his or her approval is a *form of ingratiation.*

Example: A manager tells his boss, "You're absolutely right on your reorganization plan for the western regional office. I couldn' t agree with you more.

Favors

Doing something nice for someone to gain that person' s approval is a *form of ingratiation.*

Example: A salesperson says to a prospective client, "I've got two tickets to the theater tonight that I can't use. Take them. Consider it a thank-you for taking the time to talk with me."

Excuses

Explaining a predicament-creating event aimed at minimizing the apparent severity of the predicament is a *defensive IM technique.*

Example: A sales manager says to her boss, "We failed to get the ad in the paper on time, but no one responds to those ads anyway."

Apologies

Admitting responsibility for an undesirable event and simultaneously seeking to get a pardon for the action is a *defensive IM technique.*

Example: An employee says to his boss, "I'm sorry I made a mistake on the report. Please forgive me."

Self-Promotion

Highlighting your best qualities, downplaying your deficits, and calling attention to your achievements is a *self-focused IM technique.*

Example: A salesperson tells his boss, "Matt worked unsuccessfully for three years to try to get that account. I sewed it up in six weeks. I'm the best closer this company has."

Enhancement

Claiming that something you did is more valuable than most other members of the organizations would think is a *self-focused IM technique.*

Example: A journalist tells his editor, "My work on this celebrity divorce story was really a major boost to our sales" (even though the story only made it to page 3 in the entertainment section).

Flattery

Complimenting others about their virtues in an effort to make yourself appear perceptive and likeable is an *assertive IM technique.*

Example: A new sales trainee says to her peer, "You handled that client's complaint so tactfully! I could never have handled that as well as you did."

Exemplification

Doing more than you need to in an effort to show how dedicated and hard working you are is an *assertive IM technique.*

Example: An employee sends e-mails from his work computer when he works late so that his supervisor will know how long he's been working.

Sources: M. C. Bolino, K. M. Kacmar, W. H. Turnley, and J. B. Gilstrap, "A Multi-Level Review of Impression Management Motives and Behaviors," *Journal of Management* 34, no. 6 (2008): 1080–109.

people don't like to feel others are manipulating them through impression management, so such tactics should be employed with caution. Not all impression management consists of talking yourself up, either. Recent research suggests modesty, in the form of generously providing credit to others and understating your own contributions to success, may create a more positive impression on others.[73]

An Ethical Choice

How Much Should You Manage Interviewer Impressions?

Almost everyone agrees that dressing professionally, highlighting previous accomplishments, and expressing interest in the job are reasonable impression management tactics to improve your presentation in an interview. Strategies like flattering the interviewer and using positive nonverbal cues like smiling and nodding are also often advised.

Is there an upside to such impression management? Research generally shows there is. The more effort applicants put into highlighting their skills, motivation, and admiration for the organization, the more likely they are to be hired. A recent study in Taiwan examined this relationship, finding that interviewers saw applicants who talked confidently about their qualifications as a better fit for the job, and applicants who said positive things about the organization as a better fit for the organization. Positive nonverbal cues improved interviewer moods, which also improved the applicant's ratings.

Despite evidence that making an effort to impress an interviewer can pay off, you can go too far. Evidence that a person misrepresented qualifications in the hiring process is usually grounds for immediate termination. Even "white lies" are a problem if they create unfounded expectations. For example, if you noted you managed budgets in the past when all you were doing was tracking expenditures, you lack skills your boss will expect you to have. When you fail to deliver, it will look very bad for you. However, if you describe your experience more accurately but note your desire to learn, the company will know you need additional training and that you'll need a bit of extra time.

So what does an ethical, effective interview strategy entail? The key is to find a positive but truthful way to manage impressions. Don't be afraid to let an employer know about your skills and accomplishments, and be sure to show your enthusiasm for the job. At the same time, keep your statements as accurate as possible, and be careful not to overstate your abilities. In the long run, you're much more likely to be happy and successful in a job where both you and the interviewer can assess fit honestly.

Sources: C. Chen and M. Lin, "The Effect of Applicant Impression Management Tactics on Hiring Recommendations: Cognitive and Affective Processes," *Applied Psychology: An International Review* 63, no. 4, (2014): 698–724; J. Levashina, C. J. Hartwell, F. P. Morgeson, and M. A. Campion "The Structured Employment Interview: Narrative and Quantitative Review of the Research Literature," *Personnel Psychology,* Spring 2014, 241–93; and M. Nemko, "The Effective, Ethical, and Less Stressful Job Interview," *Psychology Today,* March 25, 2014, https://www.psychologytoday.com/blog/how-do-life/201503/the-effective-ethical-and-less-stressful-job-interview.

Most of the studies to test the effectiveness of IM techniques have related IM to two criteria: interview success and performance evaluations. Let's consider each of these.

Interviews and IM The evidence indicates most job applicants use IM techniques in interviews and that it works.[74] To develop a sense of how effective different IM techniques are in interviews, one study grouped data from thousands of recruiting and selection interviews into appearance-oriented efforts (like looking professional), explicit tactics (like flattering the interviewer or talking up your own accomplishments), and verbal cues (like using positive terms and showing general enthusiasm).[75] Across all the dimensions, it was quite clear that IM was a powerful predictor of how well people did. However, there was a twist. When interviews were highly structured, meaning the interviewer's questions were written out in advance and focused on applicant qualifications, the effects of IM were substantially weaker. Manipulative behaviors like IM are more likely to have an effect in ambiguous and unstructured interviews.

Performance Evaluations and IM In terms of performance evaluations, the picture is quite different. Ingratiation is positively related to performance ratings, meaning those who ingratiate with their supervisors get higher performance evaluations. However, self-promotion appears to backfire: Those who self-promote actually may receive *lower* performance ratings.[76] There is an important qualifier to these general findings. It appears that individuals high in political skill are able to translate IM into higher performance appraisals, whereas those lower in political skill are more likely to be hurt by their IM attempts.[77] Another study of 760 boards of directors found that individuals who ingratiated themselves to current board members (expressed agreement with the director, pointed out shared attitudes and opinions, complimented the director) increased their chances of landing on a board.[78] Finally, interns who attempted to use ingratiation with their supervisors in one study were usually disliked—unless they had high levels of political skill. For those who had this ability, ingratiation led to higher levels of liking from supervisors, and higher performance ratings.[79]

What explains these consistent results across multiple studies and contexts? If you think about them, they make sense. Ingratiating always works because everyone—both interviewers and supervisors—likes to be treated nicely. However, self-promotion may work only in interviews and backfire on the job because, whereas the interviewer has little idea whether you're blowing smoke about your accomplishments, the supervisor knows because it's his or her job to observe you.

Are our conclusions about responses to politics globally valid? Should we expect employees in Israel, for instance, to respond the same way to workplace politics that employees in the United States do? Almost all our conclusions on employee reactions to organizational politics are based on studies conducted in North America. The few studies that have included other countries suggest some minor modifications.[80] One study of managers in U.S. culture and three Chinese cultures (People's Republic of China, Hong Kong, and Taiwan) found U.S. managers evaluated "gentle persuasion" tactics such as consultation and inspirational appeal as more effective than did their Chinese counterparts.[81] Other research suggests effective U.S. leaders achieve influence by focusing on the personal goals of group members and the tasks at hand (an analytical approach), whereas influential East Asian leaders focus on relationships among group members and meeting the demands of people around them (a holistic approach).[82]

The Ethics of Behaving Politically

Although there are no clear-cut ways to differentiate ethical from unethical politicking, there are some questions you should consider. For example, what is the utility of engaging in politicking? Sometimes we do it for little good reason. Major League Baseball player Al Martin claimed he played football at USC when in fact he never did. As a baseball player, he had little to gain by pretending to have played football! Outright lies like this may be a rather rare and extreme example of impression management, but many of us have at least distorted information to make a favorable impression. One thing to keep in mind is whether it's worth the risk. Another question is this: How does the utility of engaging in the political behavior balance out harm (or potential harm) it will do to others? Complimenting a supervisor on her appearance in order to curry favor is probably much less harmful than grabbing credit for a project that others deserve.

Finally, does the political activity conform to standards of equity and justice? Sometimes it is difficult to weigh the costs and benefits of a political action, but its ethicality is clear. The department head who inflates the performance evaluation of a favored employee and deflates the evaluation of a disfavored employee—and then uses these evaluations to justify giving the former a big raise and the latter nothing—has treated the disfavored employee unfairly.

Unfortunately, powerful people can become very good at explaining self-serving behaviors in terms of the organization's best interests. They can persuasively argue that unfair actions are really fair and just. Those who are powerful, articulate, and persuasive are most vulnerable to ethical lapses because they are more likely to get away with them. When faced with an ethical dilemma regarding organizational politics, try to consider whether playing politics is worth the risk and whether others might be harmed in the process. If you have a strong power base, recognize the ability of power to corrupt. Remember it's a lot easier for the powerless to act ethically, if for no other reason than they typically have very little political discretion to exploit.

PERSONAL INVENTORY ASSESSMENTS

Gaining Power and Influence

Do you like power and influence? Take this PIA to learn more about gaining both.

Mapping Your Political Career

As we have seen, politics is not just for politicians. You can use the concepts presented in this chapter in some very tangible ways we have outlined in your organization. However, they also have another application: You.

One of the most useful ways to think about power and politics is in terms of your own career. What are your ambitions? Who has the power to help you achieve them? What is your relationship to these people? The best way to answer these questions is with a political map, which can help you sketch out your relationships with the people upon whom your career depends. Exhibit 13-7 contains such a political map.[83] Let's walk through it.

Assume your future promotion depends on five people, including Jamie, your immediate supervisor. As you can see in the exhibit, you have a close relationship with Jamie (you would be in real trouble otherwise). You also have a close relationship with Zack in finance. However, with the others you have either a loose relationship (Lane) or none at all (Jia, Marty). One obvious implication of this map is the need to formulate a plan to gain more influence over, and a closer relationship with, these people. How might you do that?

The map also provides for a useful way to think about the power network. Assume the five individuals all have their own networks. In this case, though, assume these aren't so much power networks like yours as they are influence networks of the people who influence the individuals in power positions.

One of the best ways to influence people is indirectly. What if you played in a tennis league with Mark, Jamie's former coworker who you know remains friends with Jamie? To influence Mark, in many cases, may also be to influence Marty. Why not post an entry on CJ's blog? You can complete a similar analysis for the other four decision-makers and their networks.

Of course, this map doesn't show you everything you need to know—no map does. For example, rarely would all five people have the same amount of power. Moreover, maps are harder to construct in the era of large social networks. Try to keep this basic, limited to the people who *really* matter to your career.

All of this may seem a bit Machiavellian to you. However, remember, only one person gets the promotion, and your competition may have a map of his or her own. As we noted in the early part of the chapter, power and politics are a part of organizational life. To decide not to play is deciding not to be effective. Better to be explicit with a political map than to proceed as if power and politics didn't matter.

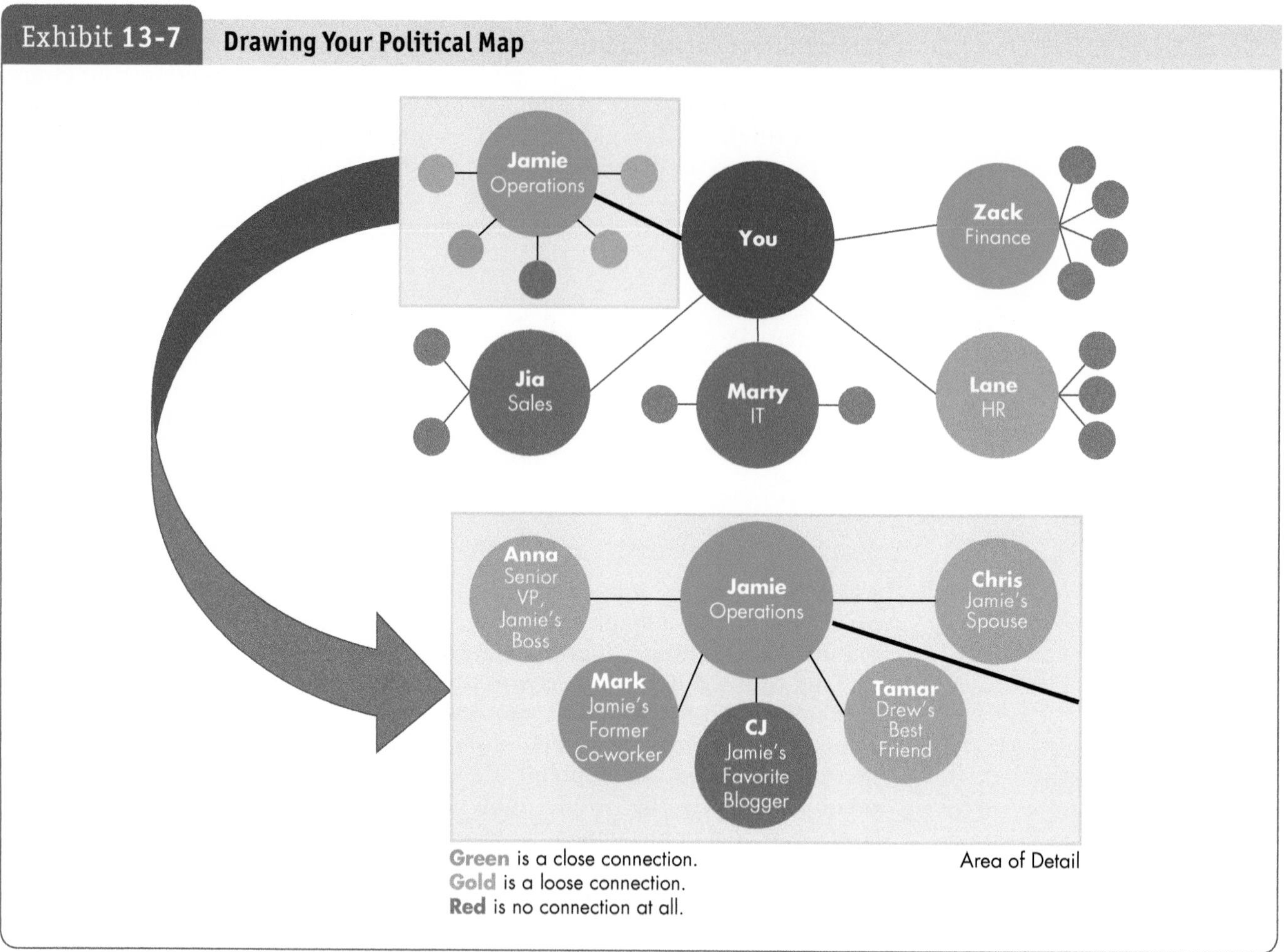

Exhibit 13-7 Drawing Your Political Map

Source: Based on Clark, "A Campaign Strategy for Your Career," *Harvard Business Review*, November 2012, 131–34.

Summary

Few employees relish being powerless in their jobs and organizations. People respond differently to the various power bases. Expert and referent power are derived from an individual's personal qualities. In contrast, coercion, reward, and legitimate power are essentially organizationally granted. Competence especially appears to offer wide appeal, and its use as a power base results in high performance by group members.

An effective manager accepts the political nature of organizations. Some people are more politically astute than others, meaning they are aware of the underlying politics and can manage impressions. Those who are good at playing politics can be expected to get higher performance evaluations and, hence, larger salary increases and more promotions than the politically naïve or inept. The politically astute are also likely to exhibit higher job satisfaction and be better able to neutralize job stressors.

Implications for Managers

- To maximize your power, increase others' dependence on you. For instance, increase your power in relation to your boss by developing a needed knowledge or skill for which there is no ready substitute.
- You will not be alone in attempting to build your power bases. Others, particularly employees and peers, will be seeking to increase your dependence on them, while you are trying to minimize it and increase their dependence on you.
- Try to avoid putting others in a position where they feel they have no power.
- By assessing behavior in a political framework, you can better predict the actions of others and use that information to formulate political strategies that will gain advantages for you and your work unit.
- Consider that employees who have poor political skills or are unwilling to play the politics game generally relate perceived organizational politics to lower job satisfaction and self-reported performance, increased anxiety, and higher turnover. Therefore, if you are adept at organizational politics, help others understand the importance of becoming politically savvy.

Everyone Wants Power

POINT

We don't admit to everything we want. For instance, one psychologist found people would seldom admit to wanting money, but they thought everyone else wanted it. They were half right—everyone wants money. And everyone wants power.

Harvard psychologist David McClelland was justifiably famous for his study of underlying motives. McClelland measured people's motivation for power based on how they described pictures (this method is called the Thematic Apperception Test, or TAT). Why didn't he simply ask people how much they wanted power? Because he believed that many more people really wanted power than would admit or even consciously realize. And that's exactly what he found.

Why do we want power? Because it is good for us. It gives us more control over our own lives. It gives us more freedom to do as we wish. There are few things worse in life than feeling helpless, and few better than feeling in charge of your destiny. Research shows people with power and status command more respect from others, have higher self-esteem (no surprise there), and enjoy better health than those of less stature.

Take Steve Cohen, founder of SAC Capital Advisors and one of the most powerful men on Wall Street. Worth $11.1 billion, Cohen buys Picassos, lives in a mansion, has white-gloved butlers, and travels the world first class. People will do almost anything to please him—or to even get near him. One writer notes, "Inside his offices, vast fortunes are won and lost. Careers are made and unmade. Type-A egos are inflated and crushed, sometimes in the space of hours." All this is bad for Steve Cohen how?

Usually, people who tell you power doesn't matter are those who have no hope of getting it. Wanting power, like being jealous, can be one of those secrets people just won't admit to.

COUNTERPOINT

Of course it's true that some people desire power—and often behave ruthlessly to get it. For most of us, however, power is not high in priority, and for some, it's actually undesirable.

Research shows most individuals feel uncomfortable when placed in powerful positions. One study asked individuals, before they began work in a four-person team, to "rank, from 1 [highest] to 4 [lowest], in terms of status and influence within the group, what rank you would like to achieve." Only about one-third (34 percent) of participants chose the highest rank. In a second study, researchers focused on employees participating in Amazon's Mechanical Turk online service. They found that the main reason people wanted power was to earn respect. If they could get respect without gaining power, that was preferred. In a third study, researchers found individuals desired power only when they had high ability—in other words, when their influence helped their groups.

These studies suggest that we often confuse the desire for power with other things—like the desire to be respected and to help our groups and organizations succeed. In these cases, power is something most of us seek for more benevolent ends—and only when we think it does good.

Another study confirmed that most people want respect from their peers, not power. Cameron Anderson, the author of this research, sums it up nicely: "You don't have to be rich to be happy, but instead be a valuable contributing member to your groups. What makes a person high in status in a group is being engaged, generous with others, and making self sacrifices for the greater good."

Oh, and about Steve Cohen...you realize he pleaded guilty and paid a $1.2 billion fine for failing to prevent insider trading and then had to shut down SAC, right?

Sources: B. Burrough and B. McLean, "The Hunt for Steve Cohen," *Vanity Fair,* June 2013, http://www.vanityfair.com/news/business/2013/06/steve-cohen-insider-trading-case; C. Anderson, R. Willer, G. J. Kilduff, and C. E. Brown, "The Origins of Deference: When Do People Prefer Lower Status?" *Journal of Personality and Social Psychology* 102 (2012): 1077–88; C. Anderson, M. W Kraus, A. D. Galinsky, and D. Keltner, "The Local-Ladder Effect: Social Status and Subjective Well-Being," *Psychological Science 23*(7) (2012): 764–71; S. Kennelly, "Happiness Is about Respect, Not Riches," *Greater Good,* July 13, 2012, http://greatergood.berkeley.edu/article/item/happiness_is_about_respect_not_riches; and P. Lattman and B. Protess, "$1.2 Billion Fine for Hedge Fund SAC Capital in Insider Case," *The New York Times Dealbook,* November 4, 2013, http://dealbook.nytimes.com/2013/11/04/sac-capital-agrees-to-plead-guilty-to-insider-trading/?_r=0.

CHAPTER REVIEW

MyManagementLab

Go to **mymanagementlab.com** to complete the problems marked with this icon.

QUESTIONS FOR REVIEW

13-1 How is leadership different from power?

13-2 What are the similarities and differences among the five bases of power?

13-3 What is the role of dependence in power relationships?

13-4 What are the most often identified power or influence tactics and their contingencies?

13-5 What are the causes and consequences of abuse of power?

13-6 How do politics work in organizations?

13-7 What are the causes, consequences, and ethics of political behavior?

EXPERIENTIAL EXERCISE Comparing Influence Tactics

Students working in groups of three are each assigned to a role. One person is the influencer, one will be influenced, and one is the observer. These roles can be randomly determined.

To begin, students create a deck of cards for the seven *tactics* to be used in the exercise. These are legitimacy, rational persuasion, inspirational appeals, consultation, exchange, ingratiation, and pressure (defined in the chapter). Only the influencer draws cards from the set, and no one else may see what has been drawn.

The influencer draws a card and quickly formulates and acts out a strategy to use this tactic on the party being influenced. The person being influenced reacts realistically in a back-and-forth exchange over a brief period and states whether or not the tactic was effective. The observer attempts to determine which tactic is being used and which power base (coercive, reward, legitimate, expert, or referent) would reinforce this tactic. The influencer confirms or denies the approach used.

Change the roles and cards throughout the rounds. Afterward, the class discusses:

13-8. Based on your observations, which influence situation would probably have resulted in the best outcome for the person doing the influencing?

13-9. Was there a good match between the tactics drawn and the specific role each person took? In other words, was the tactic useful for the influencer given his or her base of power relative to the person being influenced?

13-10. What lessons about power and influence does this exercise teach us?

ETHICAL DILEMMA How Much Should You Defer to Those in Power?

Though it is not always easy to admit to ourselves, often we adapt our behavior to suit those in power. To some degree, it is important for organizational success that we do so. After all, people are in positions of authority for a reason, and if no one paid attention to the rules these people put in place, chaos would rule. But is it always ethical for us to defer to the powerful?

More often than we acknowledge, powerful individuals in organizations push our actions into ethical gray areas, or worse. For example, managers of restaurants and stores (including McDonald's, Applebee's, Taco Bell, Winn Dixie, and others) were persuaded to strip-search customers or employees when an individual impersonating a police officer phoned in and instructed them to do so.

What would you do if you thought a police officer, definitely a symbol of power, ordered you to do something you'd never choose to do as manager?

Outright abuses aside, power is wielded over us in more prosaic ways. For example, many stock analysts report pressure from their bosses to promote funds from which the organization profits most (a fact that is not disclosed to their clients). These might be good funds that the analysts would promote anyway. But maybe they're not. Should the analyst ever promote the funds without discussing the conflict of interest with the client?

Few of us might think we would perform strip-searches. But examples of power taken to the limit highlight the disturbing tendency of many of us to conform to the wishes of those in power. For all of us, knowing that blindly deferring to those in power might cause us to cross ethical lines is enough to keep us thinking.

Questions

13-11. Do you think people tailor their behavior to suit those in power more than they admit? Is that something you do?

13-12. One writer commented that bending behavior to suit those in power reminds "anyone who is under pressure to carry out orders from 'above' to constantly question the validity and prudence of what they're being asked to do." Why don't we question this more often?

13-13. What factors influence how we respond to those with power?

Sources: J. Sancton, "Milgram at McDonald's," *Bloomberg Businessweek,* September 2, 2012, 74–75; and A. Wolfson, "Compliance' Re-Creates McDonald's Strip-Search Ordeal," *USA Today,* September 1, 2012, http://usatoday30.usatoday.com/news/nation/story/2012-09-01/Compliance-strip-search-hoax/57509182/1).

CASE INCIDENT 1 Reshaping the Dubai Model

In early 2013, analysts were warning that Dubai was suffering from the global downturn. Managers and employees across all sectors were worrying about their jobs. Property owners were seeing spectacular falls in the value of their investments. Dubai had been renowned for its extravagant projects and schemes. What had been seen as a glowing example of growth and prosperity was now being cited as an example of a country in crisis management. Dubai's debt burden had reached US $100 billion.

Dubai has always been a magnet for investors. It went tax-free at the beginning of the twentieth century, but by the 1960s, oil revenue funded huge infrastructure projects. Dubai does not have significant oil reserves, so the focus has been on commerce, tourism, and aviation. To some extent it has embraced western lifestyles and courted multi-nationals. While the UAE as a whole, with its rich reserves of oil, had the capacity to ride out the global downturn, Dubai itself would need a radical rethink.

The rethink would come in the shape of new leadership. Out went the ambition to be the regional hub for 2 billion people. Just nine years before, Dubai had been able to confidently state that investors in Dubai would see greater returns on their capital (then around 18 per cent) than leaving their funds in the bank. Dubai could boast that no one who had invested in the city had ever gone bankrupt.

Key decision makers like Sultan bin Sulayem, Chairman of Dubai World; Mohammed al-Gergawi, Chairman of Dubai Holdings; and Mohammed Alabbar, Chairman of Emaar Properties, all lost influence. New, more conservative decision-makers were on the rise, such as Mohammed al-Shaibani, Ahmed al-Tayer, and Abdulrahman al-Saleh. The new decision-makers already had a reputation for careful mergers and acquisitions, cost-cutting exercises and dealing with financial problems.

The "new" men are a combination of close advisers to the ruler, Sheikh Mohammed bin Rashid al-Maktoum, members of old merchant families and, above all, more conservative in their financial approach.

Questions

13-14. How would you prioritize and delegate the tasks of the new key decisions-makers in Dubai?

13-15. Control of decision-making and financial expenditure was the root cause of the debt situation in Dubai. Sheikh Mohammed bin Rashid Al Maktoum has delegated to people who can make decisions on his behalf. Would a more "hands on" approach be more effective, or would this hinder progress?

13-16. Abu Dhabi provides much of the funding for the UAE central bank. They have bankrolled Dubai at cost in terms of political and economic freedom. To what extent do you think Dubai is losing its ability to make its own decisions?

Sources: Roula Khalaf, Simeon Kerr, and Andrew England, "Reinventing Dubai," *Business Spectator,* http://www.businessspectator.com.au/article/2013/2/22/global-financial-crisis/reinventing-dubai, accessed January 23, 2014.

CASE INCIDENT 2 Barry's Peer Becomes His Boss

As Barry looked out the window of his office in Toronto, the gloomy October skies obscured his usual view of CN Tower. "That figures," Barry thought to himself—his mood was just as gloomy.

Five months earlier, Barry's company, CTM, a relatively small but growing technology firm, reorganized itself. Although such reorganizations often imperil careers, Barry felt the change only improved his position. His coworker, Raphael, was promoted out of the department, which made sense because Raphael had been with the company for a few more years and had worked with the CEO on a successful project. Because Raphael was promoted and their past work roles were similar, Barry thought his own promotion was soon to come.

However, 6 weeks ago, Barry's boss left. Raphael was transferred back to the department and became Barry's boss. Although Barry felt a bit overlooked, he knew he was still relatively junior in the company and felt his good past relationship with Raphael would bode well for his future prospects.

The new arrangement, however, brought nothing but disappointment. Although Raphael often told Barry he was doing a great job, Barry felt that opinion was not being shared with the higher-ups. Worse, a couple of Barry's friends in the company showed Barry e-mails in which Raphael had failed to make Berry look good.

"Raphael is not the person I thought he was," thought Barry.

What was his future in the company if no one understood his contributions? He thought about looking for another job, but that prospect only darkened his mood further. He liked the company. He felt he did good work there.

As Barry looked out his window again, a light rain began to fall. The CN Tower was no more visible than before. He just didn't know what to do.

Questions

13-17. Should Barry complain about his treatment? To whom? If he does complain, what power tactics should Barry use?

13-18. Studies have shown those prone to complaining or "whining" tend to have less power in an organization. Do you think whining leads to diminished power and influence, or the other way around? How can Barry avoid appearing to be a "whiner"?

13-19. Do you think Barry should look for another job? Why or why not?

Sources: Based on M. G. McIntyre, "Disgruntlement Won't Advance Your Career," *Pittsburgh Post-Gazette,* September 23, 2012, http://www.post-gazette.com/business/employment/2012/09/23/Office-Coach-Disgruntlement-won-t-advance-career/stories/201209230192); and S. Shellenbarger, "What to Do with a Workplace Whiner," *The Wall Street Journal,* September 12, 2012, D1, D3.

MyManagementLab

Go to **mymanagementlab.com** for the following Assisted-graded writing questions:

13-20. In Case Incident 1, how would you expect employees who have to sign over their rights to their creative projects react in the short term? In the long term?

13-21. After reading the chapter and Case Incident 2, what impression management techniques would you say Raphael is using?

13-22. **MyManagementLab Only** – comprehensive writing assignment for this chapter.

ENDNOTES

[1]D. A. Buchanan, "You Stab My Back, I'll Stab Yours: Management Experience and Perceptions of Organization Political Behavior," *British Journal of Management* 19, no. 1 (2008): 49–64.

[2]B. Oc, M. R. Bashshur, and C. Moore, "Speaking Truth to Power: The Effect of Candid Feedback on How Individuals with Power Allocate Resources," *Journal of Applied Psychology* 100, no. 2 (2015): 450–63.

[3]M. Gongloff, "Steve Cohen, Super-Rich and Secretive Trader, Faces Possible SEC Investigation," *Huffington Post,* November 28, 2012, http://www.huffingtonpost.com/2012/11/28/steven-cohen-sac-capital_n_2205544.html.

[4]E. Landells and S. L. Albrecht, "Organizational Political Climate: Shared Perceptions about the Building and Use of Power Bases," *Human Resource Management Review* 23, no. 4 (2013): 357–65; P. Rylander, "Coaches' Bases of Power: Developing Some Initial Knowledge of Athletes' Compliance with Coaches in Team Sports," *Journal of Applied Sport Psychology* 27, no. 1 (2015): 110–21; and G. Yukl, "Use Power Effectively," in E. A. Locke (ed.), *Handbook of Principles of Organizational Behavior* (Malden, MA: Blackwell, 2004): 242–47.

[5]E. A. Ward, "Social Power Bases of Managers: Emergence of a New Factor," *Journal of Social Psychology,* February 2001, 144–47.

[6]S. R. Giessner and T. W. Schubert, "High in the Hierarchy: How Vertical Location and Judgments of Leaders' Power Are Interrelated," *Organizational Behavior and Human Decision Processes* 104, no. 1 (2007): 30–44.

[7]S. Perman, "Translation Advertising: Where Shop Meets Hip Hop," *Time,* August 30, 2010, http://content.time.com/time/magazine/article/0,9171,2011574,00.html.

[8]R. E. Sturm and J. Antonakis, "Interpersonal Power: A Review, Critique, and Research Agenda," *Journal of Management* 41, no. 1 (2015): 136–63.

[9]M. C. J. Caniels and A. Roeleveld, "Power and Dependence Perpsectives on Outsourcing Decisions," *European Management Journal* 27, no. 6 (2009): 402–17; and R.-J. Bryan, D. Kim, and R. S. Sinkovics, "Drivers and Performance Outcomes of Supplier Innovation Generation in Customer-Supplier Relationships: The Role of Power-Dependence," *Decision Sciences,* 2012, 1003–38.

[10]N. Foulkes, "Tractor Boy," *High Life,* October 2002, 90.

[11]R.S. Burt, M. Kilduff, and S. Tasselli, "Social Network Analysis: Foundations and Frontiers on Advantage," *Annual Review of Psychology* 64 (2013): 527–47; M. A. Carpenter, M. Li, and H. Jiang, "Social Network Research in Organizational Contexts: A Systematic Review of Methodological Issues and Choices," *Journal of Management,* July 1, 2012, 1328–61; and M. Kilduff and D. J. Brass, "Organizational Social Network Research: Core Ideas and Key Debates." *Academy of Management Annals,* January 1, 2010, 317–57.

[12]J. Gehman, L. K. Treviño, and R. Garud, "Values Work: A Process Study of the Emergence and Performance of Organizational Values Practices," *Academy of Management Journal,* February 1, 2013, 84–112.

[13]J. Battilana and T. Casciaro, "Change Agents, Networks, and Institutions: A Contingency Theory of Organizational Change," *Academy of Management Journal,* April 1, 2012, 381–98.

[14]S. M. Soltis, F. Agneessens, Z. Sasovova, and G. Labianca, "A Social Network Perspective on Turnover Intentions: The Role of Distributive Justice and Social Support," *Human Resource Management,* July 1, 2013, 561–84.

[15]R. Kaše, Z. King, and D. Minbaeva, "Using Social Network Research in HRM: Scratching the Surface of a Fundamental Basis of HRM," *Human Resource Management,* July 1, 2013, 473–83; R. Cross and L. Prusak, "The People Who Make Organizations Go—Or Stop," *Harvard Business Review,* June 2002, https://hbr.org/2002/06/the-people-who-make-organizations-go-or-stop.

[16]See, for example, D. M. Cable and T. A. Judge, "Managers' Upward Influence Tactic Strategies: The Roll of Manager Personality and Supervisor Leadership Style," *Journal of Organizational Behavior* 24, no. 2 (2003): 197–214; M. P. M. Chong, "Influence Behaviors and Organizational Commitment: A Comparative Study," *Leadership and Organization Development Journal* 35, no. 1 (2014): 54–78; and G. Blickle, "Influence Tactics Used by Subordinates: An Empirical Analysis of the Kipnis and Schmidt Subscales," *Psychological Reports,* February 2000, 143–54.

[17]G. R. Ferris, W. A. Hochwarter, C. Douglas, F. R. Blass, R. W. Kolodinksy, and D. C. Treadway, "Social Influence Processes in Organizations and Human Resource Systems," in G. R. Ferris and J. J. Martocchio (eds.), *Research in Personnel and Human Resources Management,* vol. 21 (Oxford, UK: JAI Press/Elsevier, 2003), 65–127; C. A. Higgins, T. A. Judge, and G. R. Ferris, "Influence Tactics and Work Outcomes: A Meta-Analysis," *Journal of Organizational Behavior,* March 2003, 89–106; and M. Uhl-Bien, R. E. Riggio, K. B. Lowe, and M. K. Carsten. "Followership Theory: A Review and Research Agenda," *The Leadership Quarterly,* February 2014, 83–104.

[18]M. P. M. Chong, "Influence Behaviors and Organizational Commitment: A Comparative Study."

[19]R. E. Petty and P. Briñol, "Persuasion: From Single to Multiple to Metacognitive Processes," *Perspectives on Psychological Science* 3, no. 2 (2008): 137–47.

[20]J. Badal, "Getting a Raise from the Boss," *The Wall Street Journal,* July 8, 2006, B1, B5.

[21]M. P. M. Chong, "Influence Behaviors and Organizational Commitment: A Comparative Study."

[22]Ibid.

[23]O. Epitropaki and R. Martin, "Transformational-Transactional Leadership and Upward Influence: The Role of Relative Leader-Member Exchanges (RLMX) and Perceived Organizational Support (POS), *Leadership Quarterly* 24, no. 2 (2013): 299–315.

[24]A. W. Kruglanski, A. Pierro, and E. T. Higgins, "Regulatory Mode and Preferred Leadership Styles: How Fit Increases Job Satisfaction," *Basic and Applied Social Psychology* 29, no. 2 (2007): 137–49; and A. Pierro, L. Cicero, and B. H. Raven, "Motivated Compliance with Bases of Social Power," *Journal of Applied Social Psychology* 38, no. 7 (2008): 1921–44.

[25]P. P. Fu and G. Yukl, "Perceived Effectiveness of Influence Tactics in the United States and China," *Leadership Quarterly,* Summer 2000, 251–66; O. Branzei, "Cultural Explanations of Individual Preferences for Influence Tactics in Cross-Cultural Encounters," *International Journal of Cross Cultural Management,* August 2002, 203–18; G. Yukl, P. P. Fu, and R. McDonald, "Cross-Cultural Differences in Perceived Effectiveness of Influence Tactics for Initiating or Resisting Change," *Applied Psychology: An International Review,* January 2003, 66–82; and P. P. Fu, T. K. Peng, J. C. Kennedy, and G. Yukl, "Examining the Preferences of Influence Tactics in Chinese Societies: A Comparison of Chinese Managers in Hong Kong, Taiwan, and Mainland China," *Organizational Dynamics* 33, no. 1 (2004): 32–46.

[26]C. J. Torelli and S. Shavitt, "Culture and Concepts of Power," *Journal of Personality and Social Psychology* 99, no. 4 (2010): 703–23.
[27]Fu and Yukl, "Perceived Effectiveness of Influence Tactics in the United States and China."
[28]G. R. Ferris, D. C. Treadway, P. L. Perrewé, R. L. Brouer, C. Douglas, and S. Lux, "Political Skill in Organizations," *Journal of Management,* June 2007, 290–320; K. J. Harris, K. M. Kacmar, S. Zivnuska, and J. D. Shaw, "The Impact of Political Skill on Impression Management Effectiveness," *Journal of Applied Psychology* 92, no. 1 (2007): 278–85; W. A. Hochwarter, G. R. Ferris, M. B. Gavin, P. L. Perrewé, A. T. Hall, and D. D. Frink, "Political Skill as Neutralizer of Felt Accountability–Job Tension Effects on Job Performance Ratings: A Longitudinal Investigation," *Organizational Behavior and Human Decision Processes* 102 (2007): 226–39; and D. C. Treadway, G. R. Ferris, A. B. Duke, G. L. Adams, and J. B. Tatcher, "The Moderating Role of Subordinate Political Skill on Supervisors' Impressions of Subordinate Ingratiation and Ratings of Subordinate Interpersonal Facilitation," *Journal of Applied Psychology* 92, no. 3 (2007): 848–55.
[29]M. C. Andrews, K. M. Kacmar, and K. J. Harris, "Got Political Skill? The Impact of Justice on the Importance of Political Skills for Job Performance," *Journal of Applied Psychology* 94, no. 6 (2009): 1427–37.
[30]C. Anderson, S. E. Spataro, and F. J. Flynn, "Personality and Organizational Culture as Determinants of Influence," *Journal of Applied Psychology* 93, no. 3 (2008): 702–10.
[31]Y. Cho and N. J. Fast, "Power, Defensive Denigration, and the Assuaging Effect of Gratitude Expression," *Journal of Experimental Social Psychology* 48 (2012): 778–82.
[32]M. Pitesa and S. Thau, "Masters of the Universe: How Power and Accountability Influence Self-Serving Decisions under Moral Hazard," *Journal of Applied Psychology* 98 (2013): 550–58; N. J. Fast, N. Sivanathan, D. D. Mayer, and A. D. Galinsky, "Power and Overconfident Decision-Making," *Organizational Behavior and Human Decision Processes* 117 (2012): 249–60; M. J. Williams, "Serving the Self from the Seat of Power: Goals and Threats Predict Leaders' Self-Interested Behavior," *Journal of Management* 40 (2014): 1365–95.
[33]A. Grant, "Yes, Power Corrupts, but Power Also Reveals," *Government Executive,* May 23, 2013, http://www.huffingtonpost.com/adam-grant/yes-power-corrupts-but-po_b_3085291.html.
[34]J. K. Maner, M. T. Gaillot, A. J. Menzel, and J. W. Kunstman, "Dispositional Anxiety Blocks the Psychological Effects of Power," *Personality and Social Psychology Bulletin* 38 (2012): 1383–95.
[35]N. J. Fast, N. Halevy, and A. D. Galinsky, "The Destructive Nature of Power without Status," *Journal of Experimental Social Psychology* 48 (2012): 391–94.
[36]T. Seppälä, J. Lipponen, A. Bardi, and A. Pirttilä-Backman, Change-Oriented Organizational Citizenship Behaviour: An Interactive Product of Openness to Change Values, Work Unit Identification, and Sense of Power," *Journal of Occupational and Organizational Psychology* 85 (2012): 136–55.
[37]K. A. DeCelles, D. S. DeRue, J. D. Margolis, and T. L. Ceranic, "Does Power Corrupt or Enable? When and Why Power Facilitates Self-Interested Behavior," *Journal of Applied Psychology* 97 (2012): 681–89.
[38]"Facts about Sexual Harassment," The U.S. Equal Employment Opportunity Commission, www.eeoc.gov/facts/fs-sex.html, accessed June 19, 2015.
[39]F. Ali and R. Kramar, "An Exploratory Study of Sexual Harassment in Pakistani Organizations," *Asia Pacific Journal of Management* 32, no. 1 (2014): 229–49.
[40]Ibid.
[41]Workplace Sexual Harassment Statistics, Association of Women for Action and Research, 2015, http://www.aware.org.sg/ati/wsh-site/14-statistics/.
[42]R. Ilies, N. Hauserman, S. Schwochau, and J. Stibal, "Reported Incidence Rates of Work-Related Sexual Harassment in the United States: Using Meta-Analysis to Explain Reported Rate Disparities," *Personnel Psychology,* Fall 2003, 607–31; and G. Langer, "One in Four U.S. Women Reports Workplace Harassment," *ABC News,* November 16, 2011, http://abcnews.go.com/blogs/politics/2011/11/one-in-four-u-s-women-reports-workplace-harassment/.
[43]"Sexual Harassment Charges," Equal Employment Opportunity Commission, from www.eeoc.gov/eeoc/statistics/, accessed August 20, 2015.
[44]B. Popken, "Report: 80% of Waitresses Report Being Sexually Harassed," *USA Today,* October 7, 2014, http://www.today.com/money/report-80-waitresses-report-being-sexually-harassed-2D80199724.
[45]L. M. Cortina and S. A. Wasti, "Profiles in Coping: Responses to Sexual Harassment across Persons, Organizations, and Cultures," *Journal of Applied Psychology,* February 2005, 182–92; K. Jiang, Y. Hong, P. F. McKay, D. R. Avery, D. C. Wilson, and S. D. Volpone, "Retaining Employees through Anti-Sexual Harassment Practices: Exploring the Mediating Role of Psychological Distress and Employee Engagement," *Human Resource Management* 54, no. 1 (2015): 1–21; and J. W. Kunstman, "Sexual Overperception: Power, Mating Motives, and Biases in Social Judgment," *Journal of Personality and Social Psychology* 100, no. 2 (2011): 282–94.
[46]F. Krings and S. Facchin, "Organizational Justice and Men's Likelihood to Sexually Harass: The Moderating Role of Sexism and Personality," *Journal of Applied Psychology* 94, no. 2 (2009): 501–10.
[47]G. R. Ferris, D. C. Treadway, R. W. Kolokinsky, W. A. Hochwarter, C. J. Kacmar, and D. D. Frink, "Development and Validation of the Political Skill Inventory," *Journal of Management,* February 2005, 126–52.
[48]A. Pullen and C. Rhodes, "Corporeal Ethics and the Politics of Resistance in Organizations," *Organization* 21, no. 6 (2014): 782–96.
[49]G. R. Ferris and W. A. Hochwarter, "Organizational Politics," in S. Zedeck (ed.), *APA Handbook of Industrial and Organizational Psychology,* vol. 3 (Washington, DC: American Psychological Association, 2011), 435–59.
[50]D. A. Buchanan, "You Stab My Back, I'll Stab Yours: Management Experience and Perceptions of Organization Political Behavior," *British Journal of Management* 19, no. 1 (2008): 49–64.
[51]J. Pfeffer, *Power: Why Some People Have It—And Others Don't* (New York: Harper Collins, 2010).
[52]S. M. Rioux and L. A. Penner, "The Causes of Organizational Citizenship Behavior: A Motivational Analysis," *Journal of Applied Psychology,* December 2001, 1306–14; M. A. Finkelstein and L. A. Penner, "Predicting Organizational Citizenship Behavior: Integrating the Functional and Role Identity Approaches," *Social Behavior & Personality* 32, no. 4 (2004): 383–98; and J. Schwarzwald, M. Koslowsky, and M. Allouf, "Group Membership, Status, and Social Power Preference," *Journal of Applied Social Psychology* 35, no. 3 (2005): 644–65.
[53]See, for example, J. Walter, F. W. Kellermans, and C. Lechner, "Decision Making within and between Organizations: Rationality, Politics, and Alliance Performance," *Journal of Management* 38, no. 5 (2012): 1582–610.

[54]G. R. Ferris, D. C. Treadway, P. L. Perrewe, R. L. Grouer, C. Douglas, and S. Lux, "Political Skill in Organizations," *Journal of Management* 33 (2007): 290–320.
[55]J. Shi, R. E. Johnson, Y. Liu, and M. Wang, "Linking Subordinate Political Skill to Supervisor Dependence and Reward Recommendations: A Moderated Mediation Model," *Journal of Applied Psychology* 98 (2013): 374–84.
[56]W. A. Gentry, D. C. Gimore, M. L. Shuffler, and J. B. Leslie, "Political Skill as an Indicator of Promotability among Multiple Rater Sources," *Journal of Organizational Behavior* 33 (2012): 89–104; I. Kapoutsis, A. Paplexandris, A. Nikolopoulous, W. A. Hochwarter, and G. R. Ferris, "Politics Perceptions as a Moderator of the Political Skill-Job Performance Relationship: A Two-Study, Cross-National, Constructive Replication," *Journal of Vocational Behavior* 78 (2011): 123–35.
[57]M. Abbas, U. Raja, W. Darr, and D. Bouckenooghe, "Combined Effects of Perceived Politics and Psychological Capital on Job Satisfaction, Turnover Intentions, and Performance," *Journal of Management* 40, no. 7 (2014): 1813–30; and C. C. Rosen, D. L. Ferris, D. J. Brown, and W.-W. Yen, "Relationships among Perceptions of Organizational Politics (POPs), Work Motivation, and Salesperson Performance," *Journal of Management and Organization* 21, no. 2 (2015): 203–16.
[58]See, for example, M. D. Laird, P. Harvey, and J. Lancaster, "Accountability, Entitlement, Tenure, and Satisfaction in Generation Y," *Journal of Managerial Psychology* 30, no. 1 (2015): 87–100; J. M. L. Poon, "Situational Antecedents and Outcomes of Organizational Politics Perceptions," *Journal of Managerial Psychology* 18, no. 2 (2003): 138–55; and K. L. Zellars, W. A. Hochwarter, S. E. Lanivich, P. L. Perrewe, and G. R. Ferris, "Accountability for Others, Perceived Resources, and Well Being: Convergent Restricted Non-Linear Results in Two Samples," *Journal of Occupational and Organizational Psychology* 84, no. 1 (2011): 95–115.
[59]J. Walter, F. W. Kellermanns, and C. Lechner, "Decision Making within and between Organizations: Rationality, Politics, and Alliance Performance," *Journal of Management* 38 (2012): 1582–610.
[60]W. A. Hochwarter, C. Kiewitz, S. L. Castro, P. L. Perrewe, and G. R. Ferris, "Positive Affectivity and Collective Efficacy as Moderators of the Relationship between Perceived Politics and Job Satisfaction," *Journal of Applied Social Psychology*, May 2003, 1009–35; and C. C. Rosen, P. E. Levy, and R. J. Hall, "Placing Perceptions of Politics in the Context of Feedback Environment, Employee Attitudes, and Job Performance," *Journal of Applied Psychology* 91, no. 1 (2006): 211–30.
[61]S. Aryee, Z. Chen, and P. S. Budhwar, "Exchange Fairness and Employee Performance: An Examination of the Relationship between Organizational Politics and Procedural Justice," *Organizational Behavior & Human Decision Processes*, May 2004, 1–14.
[62]C. Kiewitz, W. A. Hochwarter, G. R. Ferris, and S. L. Castro, "The Role of Psychological Climate in Neutralizing the Effects of Organizational Politics on Work Outcomes," *Journal of Applied Social Psychology*, June 2002, 1189–207; and M. C. Andrews, L. A. Witt, and K. M. Kacmar, "The Interactive Effects of Organizational Politics and Exchange Ideology on Manager Ratings of Retention," *Journal of Vocational Behavior*, April 2003, 357–69.
[63]O. J. Labedo, "Perceptions of Organisational Politics: Examination of the Situational Antecedent and Consequences among Nigeria's Extension Personnel," *Applied Psychology: An International Review* 55, no. 2 (2006): 255–81.
[64]K. M. Kacmar, M. C. Andrews, K. J. Harris, and B. Tepper, "Ethical Leadership and Subordinate Outcomes: The Mediating Role of Organizational Politics and the Moderating Role of Political Skill," *Journal of Business Ethics* 115, no. 1 (2013): 33–44.
[65]Ibid.
[66]K. M. Kacmar, D. G. Bachrach, K. J. Harris, and S. Zivnuska, "Fostering Good Citizenship through Ethical Leadership: Exploring the Moderating Role of Gender and Organizational Politics," *Journal of Applied Psychology* 96 (2011): 633–42.
[67]C. Homburg and A. Fuerst, "See No Evil, Hear No Evil, Speak No Evil: A Study of Defensive Organizational Behavior towards Customer Complaints," *Journal of the Academy of Marketing Science* 35, no. 4 (2007): 523–36.
[68]See, for instance, M. C. Bolino and W. H. Turnley, "More Than One Way to Make an Impression: Exploring Profiles of Impression Management," *Journal of Management* 29, no. 2 (2003): 141–60; S. Zivnuska, K. M. Kacmar, L. A. Witt, D. S. Carlson, and V. K. Bratton, "Interactive Effects of Impression Management and Organizational Politics on Job Performance," *Journal of Organizational Behavior*, August 2004, 627–40; and M. C. Bolino, K. M. Kacmar, W. H. Turnley, and J. B. Gilstrap, "A Multi-Level Review of Impression Management Motives and Behaviors," *Journal of Management* 34, no. 6 (2008): 1080–109.
[69]D. J. Howard and R. A. Kerin, "Individual Differences in the Name Similarity Effect: The Role of Self-Monitoring," *Journal of Individual Differences* 35, no. 2 (2014): 111–18.
[70]D. H. M. Chng, M. S. Rodgers, E. Shih, and X.-B. Song, "Leaders' Impression Management During Organizational Decline: The Roles of Publicity, Image Concerns, and Incentive Compensation," *The Leadership Quarterly* 26, no. 2 (2015): 270–85; and L. Uziel, "Life Seems Different with You around: Differential Shifts in Cognitive Appraisal in the Mere Presence of Others for Neuroticism and Impression Management," *Personality and Individual Differences* 73 (2015): 39–43.
[71]J. Ham and R. Vonk, "Impressions of Impression Management: Evidence of Spontaneous Suspicion of Ulterior Motivation," *Journal of Experimental Social Psychology* 47, no. 2 (2011): 466–71; and W. M. Bowler, J. R. B. Halbesleben, and J. R. B. Paul, "If You're Close with the Leader, You Must Be a Brownnose: The Role of Leader–Member Relationships in Follower, Leader, and Coworker Attributions of Organizational Citizenship Behavior Motives," *Human Resource Management Review* 20, no. 4 (2010): 309–16.
[72]J. R. B. Halbesleben, W. M. Bowler, M. C. Bolino, and W. H Turnley, "Organizational Concern, Prosocial Values, or Impression Management? How Supervisors Attribute Motives to Organizational Citizenship Behavior," *Journal of Applied Social Psychology* 40, no. 6 (2010): 1450–89.
[73]G. Blickle, C. Diekmann, P. B. Schneider, Y. Kalthöfer, and J. K. Summers, "When Modesty Wins: Impression Management through Modesty, Political Skill, and Career Success—A Two-Study Investigation," European Journal of Work and Organizational Psychology, December 1, 2012, 899–922.
[74]L. A. McFarland, A. M. Ryan, and S. D. Kriska, "Impression Management Use and Effectiveness across Assessment Methods," *Journal of Management* 29, no. 5 (2003): 641–61; C. A. Higgins and T. A. Judge, "The Effect of Applicant Influence Tactics on Recruiter Perceptions of Fit and Hiring Recommendations: A Field Study," *Journal of Applied Psychology* 89, no. 4 (2004): 622–32; and W. C. Tsai, C.-C. Chen, and S. F. Chiu, "Exploring Boundaries of the Effects of Applicant Impression Management Tactics in Job Interviews," *Journal of Management*, February 2005, 108–25.
[75]M. R. Barrick, J. A. Shaffer, and S. W. DeGrassi. "What You See May Not Be What You Get: Relationships among Self-Presentation

Tactics and Ratings of Interview and Job Performance," *Journal of Applied Psychology,* 94, no. 6 (2009): 1394–411.

[76]E. Molleman, B. Emans, and N. Turusbekova, "How to Control Self-Promotion among Performance-Oriented Employees: The Roles of Task Clarity and Personalized Responsibility," *Personnel Review* 41 (2012): 88–105.

[77]K. J. Harris, K. M. Kacmar, S. Zivnuska, and J. D. Shaw, "The Impact of Political Skill on Impression Management Effectiveness," *Journal of Applied Psychology* 92, no. 1 (2007): 278–85; and D. C. Treadway, G. R. Ferris, A. B. Duke, G. L. Adams, and J. B. Thatcher, "The Moderating Role of Subordinate Political Skill on Supervisors' Impressions of Subordinate Ingratiation and Ratings of Subordinate Interpersonal Facilitation," *Journal of Applied Psychology* 92, no. 3 (2007): 848–55.

[78]J. D. Westphal and I. Stern, "Flattery Will Get You Everywhere (Especially if You Are a Male Caucasian): How Ingratiation, Boardroom Behavior, and Demographic Minority Status Affect Additional Board Appointments of U.S. Companies," *Academy of Management Journal* 50, no. 2 (2007): 267–88.

[79]Y. Liu, G. R. Ferris, J. Xu, B. A. Weitz, and P. L. Perrewé, "When Ingratiation Backfires: The Role of Political Skill in the Ingratiation-Internship Performance Relationship," *Academy of Management Learning and Education* 13 (2014): 569–86.

[80]See, for example, E. Vigoda, "Reactions to Organizational Politics: A Cross-Cultural Examination in Israel and Britain," Human Relations, November 2001, 1483–1518; and Y. Zhu and D. Li, "Negative Spillover Impact of Perceptions of Organizational Politics on Work-Family Conflict in China," Social Behavior and Personality 43, no. 5 (2015): 705–14.

[81]J. L. T. Leong, M. H. Bond, and P. P. Fu, "Perceived Effectiveness of Influence Strategies in the United States and Three Chinese Societies," *International Journal of Cross Cultural Management,* May 2006, 101–20.

[82]Y. Miyamoto and B. Wilken, "Culturally Contingent Situated Cognition: Influencing Other People Fosters Analytic Perception in the United States but Not in Japan," *Psychological Science* 21, no. 11 (2010): 1616–22.

[83]D. Clark, "A Campaign Strategy for Your Career," *Harvard Business Review,* November 2012, 131–34.